Regulating Land-Based Casinos

Policies, Procedures, and Economics

Anthony Cabot and Ngai Pindell, editors

UNLV Gaming Press

UNLV GAMING PRESS
4505 Maryland Parkway, Box 457010
Las Vegas, Nevada 89154-7010

Regulating Land-Based Casinos:
Policies, Procedures, and Economics

Paperback edition ISBN 978-1-939546-07-4

Layout by David G. Schwartz

Set in Minion Pro.

To the late Bob Faiss, a master of his craft, mentor to many, and a true gentleman, whose contribution to gaming law will be missed but whose wisdom will never be forgotten.

Contents

Editors' Note

Once restricted to exotic locations like Las Vegas, Macau, and Monte Carlo, casinos are now operating in many cities nationally and internationally—from the Maryland waterfront to Ho Chi Minh City. This expansion of the gaming industry, both geographically and economically, raises new and important policy questions about the role of government in gaming regulation, the obligations and opportunities for casinos, and public support for gambling and gaming tax revenue. The contributors to this book have decades of experience in gaming regulation and business and are optimistic about the future of gaming and casinos. Each author critically engages the subject and offers his or her insight into what works—and what does not—in the gaming business and gaming regulation.

Whether a jurisdiction is considering legalizing gaming or deciding how to regulate an existing gaming industry, it should engage in a careful cost-benefit analysis informed by available data and the jurisdiction's particular public policy goals. Each chapter in this book considers a key component of this process. The chapters collect and analyze gaming research from a wide variety of disciplines, including law, business, social sciences, economics, and tax to explain the many approaches a jurisdiction might take to identify and address important policy goals and to suggest emerging issues that require additional research and data. The chapters also incorporate extensive industry experience and examples to investigate the effects of different regulatory practices on the gaming industry, industry stakeholders, and the public.

The seventeen chapters in this book can be divided into four, integrated parts. Chapters 1-6 explore the structural components of a successful gaming regulatory regime. A jurisdiction must identify its specific public policy goals and the appropriate policies and procedures to implement them. It can determine the appropriate configuration of agencies and practices to achieve these goals through identifying specific economic, fiscal, and social policy choices and measuring the economic benefits and costs of gaming. A jurisdiction should also be mindful of the costs to the public and to the gaming industry from creating too much, too little, or misdirected regulation.

Chapters 7-9 focus on how a successful gaming regulatory regime must continually reassess risks and respond appropriately to changing values, evolving technology, and new industry developments. These chapters address issues including ethics and possible criminal behavior, industry compliance programs, and the potential for money laundering. The authors consider how the gaming industry can ensure that industry business practices and adopted regulatory regimes are consistent with federal and state public policy goals. At the same time, the authors address the nexus between these public policy goals and the gaming industry. The global growth of gaming depends on public confidence that the industry is free from criminal participation and influence. But statutes and regulations aimed at promoting broad policy goals—like preventing bribery, corruption, and similar crimes or preventing criminals from using the financial system to launder the proceeds from illegal activities—can sometimes conflict with more focused gaming norms and business practices.

Chapters 10-13 describe particular issues of importance to a regulatory regime in the gaming industry. Players who cannot moderate their gambling activity require protection and treatment. Rapid advancements in gaming technology require government regulators to be technically proficient to ensure that games are honest and fair. Effective audit and accounting procedures must ensure the proper taxes are collected, prevent unlicensed people from sharing in casino profits, protect against fraud, ensure the integrity of games, and protect the financial stability of casinos. And identifying the right tax policy for a jurisdiction requires careful consideration of the effects of the tax on the gaming industry itself, complementary industries, and external factors like increased law enforcement needs.

Chapters 14-17 reinforce the ethics and integrity themes in earlier chapters by focusing more directly on the interrelationship between regulatory regimes and individual stakeholders. The contract relationship between a casino and a player is tested when either party uses information or techniques to gain a playing advantage that the other party regards as unfair, unexpected, or even criminal. The applicant for a valuable casino license undergoes a rigorous investigative process that, while necessary to safeguard the integrity of the gaming industry, can also lead to unanticipated and unnecessary consequences for both the regulator and the regulated. Finally, some individuals are subject to exclusion from casinos due to criminal activity, cheating, advantage play, or self-exclusion. These chapters consider how regulations can best respond to these tensions among public policy goals, industry practice, and the players' gaming experience.

We are grateful to the many people who worked to put this book together. UNLV Boyd School of Law students Brittany Cermak, Chandler Pohl, Neethy Eapen, Geneviève Generaux, Lee Gorlin, Evan Simonsen, Kevin Schweitzer, and Elijah Tredup edited the individual chapters and worked with the authors. Thank you to Catherine Bacos, Vaneh Movsessian, Annette Mann, and Kerry Martinez for their editorial and administrative support. Ingrid Mattson provided excellent copy editing work. David G. Schwartz, Director of the UNLV Center for Gaming Research and Publisher of the UNLV Gaming Press, directed the design and publication process. Finally, thank you to UNLV deans Daniel Hamilton (Law), Patricia Iannuzzi (Library), and to the law firm of Lewis Roca Rothgerber for their continuing support of this important research.

Anthony Cabot and Ngai Pindell, editors
July 2014

1

The Debate Over Legal Casino Gambling

Douglas M. Walker

INTRODUCTION

Legalized gambling has expanded dramatically in the United States over the past two decades. Almost all states now have lotteries, and nearly 40 states have some type of legal casino gambling—tribal, commercial, or "racino." Although casinos have proliferated throughout the country, they are still often hotly debated as new states legalize or others expand their casino industries. The same debate occurs in countries around the world.

This chapter discusses the ongoing debate over the key economic and social impacts of casinos. Among the topics to be discussed are the economic benefits from casinos (including tax revenues, employment, wage effects, and economic growth); economic and social costs (including those attributable to pathological gamblers, crime effects, and other social problems); and future issues of interest. All of these issues have been addressed, to some degree, by social science researchers. However, the effects of casinos are still not fully understood.

It is perhaps no surprise why casino gambling is so politically popular in the United States. Casinos began to spread outside of Nevada and Atlantic City, NJ, only after a landmark legal ruling (*California v. Cabazon*[1]) and a subsequent act by the federal government (Indian Gaming Regulatory Act[2]). These events, in 1987 and 1988, set the stage for tribal casinos in a variety of states and for the legalization of commercial casinos by state governments.

By the end of 2012, there were around 920 tribal and commercial US casinos of various sizes.[3] Most Americans live within rather short driving

---

[1] California v. Cabazon Band of Indians, 480 U.S. 202 (1987).

[2] 25 U.S.C. §§ 2701–2721 (1988).

[3] AM. GAMING ASS'N, STATE OF THE STATES: THE AGA SURVEY OF CASINO ENTERTAINMENT (2013), http://www.americangaming.org/sites/default/files/aga_sos2013_rev042014.pdf; Douglas M. Walker & John D. Jackson, *Casinos and Economic Growth: An Update*, 7 J. GAMBLING BUS. & ECON. 80, 81 (2013).

distance to a casino; clearly access to casinos in the United States has increased dramatically in the last 25 years. Why have tribes and state governments found casinos so attractive? Prior to the examination of various benefits and costs from casinos, I address the politics of casino adoption and expansion.[4]

POLITICS OF CASINO GAMBLING

When commercial casinos are introduced to a region, they represent a new source of tax revenues and jobs and perhaps cause upward pressure on wage rates. In addition, they may contribute to increased economic growth. As the influential economist Joseph Schumpeter explained, a new industry is a primary source of economic development,[5] and as such, it can be a catalyst for increased employment and tax revenues. Since state government holds the power to legalize casinos, this is one policy that it has at its disposal to positively impact the regional economy.

However, there are also social and economic costs attributable to commercial casinos. The types and magnitudes of economic and social benefits and costs of casinos continue to be hotly debated in the literature. (They are discussed later in this chapter.) Nevertheless, the motivation for introducing casinos is not always obvious. A 2010 study addressed this question by examining US data from 1985 through 2000.[6] The findings indicate that "casino legalization is due to state fiscal stress, to efforts to keep gambling revenues (and the concomitant gambling taxes) within the state, and to attract tourism or 'export taxes.'"[7] This explanation is a straightforward economic argument for casinos. It is also consistent with the anecdotal observation that state governments have shown increased interest in legalizing or expanding casinos during recessions. In particular, there was a great deal of interest in casinos toward the end of the 1990–1991 recession, with eight states legalizing casinos between 1989 and 1993,[8] as well as during the so-called "Great Recession" of 2007–2009, with Kansas, Maryland, Ohio, and Massachusetts all legalizing casinos around this time.[9]

---

[4] Hereafter the discussion refers to commercial casinos only. This chapter does not discuss the expansion of tribal casinos, as much of the controversy surrounding tribal casinos has to do specifically with the IGRA (e.g., tribal compacts, reservation status with the Bureau of Indian Affairs). Since there is typically much more and heated public debate surrounding state-level proposals to adopt commercial casinos, the discussion focuses on this subject.

[5] JOSEPH A. SCHUMPETER, THE THEORY OF ECONOMIC DEVELOPMENT 66 (1934).

[6] Peter T. Calcagno et al., *Determinants of the Probability and Timing of Commercial Casino Legalization in the United States*, 142 PUB. CHOICE 69 (2010).

[7] *Id.* at 69.

[8] It could be argued that the interest in casinos during the 1990–91 recession was instead due to the fact that the IGRA had recently been passed, and the states were, for the first time, able to legalize commercial casinos.

[9] AM. GAMING ASS'N, *supra* note 3.

Regardless of the magnitude of the various economic effects of casinos, there may also be political motivations for introducing casinos. Voters are particularly unsympathetic to tax increases. Casinos, which are generally taxed at a much higher rate than other purchases (as represented by states' sales taxes), represent an alternative to raising other types of taxes. Casinos may enable politicians to avoid raising other taxes in order to finance spending.

Similar to the above motivation, casinos and the tax revenues they provide can enable politicians to avoid cutting government spending as much as they might have to otherwise. Thus, by legalizing casinos, political pressure for increasing taxes or cutting spending is reduced.

Finally, politicians can easily argue that the introduction of casinos will create new jobs. These apparent benefits of casinos become visible to voters as soon as casino proposals are introduced in a state. A casino company may propose a certain size casino that will employ a particular number of workers. To voters, this represents a clear improvement in the local economy. As a more aggregate example, the American Gaming Association reports the number of people directly employed by the casino industry in each state.[10] However, it is not obvious that the new casino jobs will represent a net increase in regional employment. To the extent that the casino industry creates a "substitution effect" with other industries, job gains in the casino industry may be offset by losses in other industries. (This issue is discussed in more detail later in the chapter.[11]) Nevertheless, from a political perspective, the prospect of new jobs is clearly a political motivation for legalizing casinos or expanding the casino industry.

Given the recent unpopularity of the federal government and its apparent inability to use monetary and fiscal policy to revive the economy, voters are perhaps particularly sensitive to high unemployment rates, new taxes, and cuts to government programs. The legalization of casinos represents one act by state government that appears likely to create jobs, increase tax revenues, and finance greater government spending. This is because state governments literally hold the power to "create" a new industry that did not exist before. The anecdotal evidence provided by the casino industry suggests that it clearly has a positive impact on the local economy, and this translates into a political motivation for introducing casinos, whatever the actual economic impacts are. The next section addresses the economic benefits from legalized casinos.

ECONOMIC BENEFITS

Among the purported economic benefits from casinos, the most commonly cited relate to tax revenues, employment, wages, and economic growth. In addition, there are potentially significant benefits from casinos that accrue to the casinos' customers. This section is a review of the academic literature on these benefits from casinos.

---

[10] *Id.*

[11] In the literature this effect is sometimes referred to as "industry cannibalization."

For each of the casino impacts discussed in this section, understanding the effects is more complicated than it might first seem. This is because the relevant comparison for isolating the changes in the local economy caused by the casino industry is not just between the situations before and after gambling is introduced. Rather, the relevant comparison is between the situation with casinos and what would have otherwise happened—called the counterfactual.[12] Consider, for example, a plot of vacant land in a city. The land's owner is deciding whether to build a casino or a shopping mall. Suppose a casino is built. The casino will create new jobs and pay taxes to state and local government, and it may have an effect on local wage rates. A journalist might report the net employment impact of the casino simply as the number of people working at the casino; this would be a comparison of jobs before and after the casino. But this comparison assumes that if the casino had not been built, nothing else would have been. In the scenario described, however, a shopping mall would have otherwise been built. To determine the net effect of the casino on employment, the journalist would need to compare the jobs created at the casino with the number of jobs that would have existed at the shopping mall. Thus, the net employment effect of the casino could be small, nil, or even negative. The same analysis would be necessary to determine the net impact on tax receipts. It would also apply to social and other economic costs attributed to casinos, discussed later in the chapter.

Casinos are relatively labor-intensive businesses, and taxes on casino revenues tend to be relatively high. For these reasons, intuition suggests that, even comparing casino outcomes with a counterfactual, the casino likely has a net positive impact on employment and tax revenues. But this net effect is not as likely as many observers probably believe.

Tax Revenues

Casinos can have a significant impact on state government budgets. However, this effect may not be as large as the industry may suggest. In its *State of the States* annual publication, the American Gaming Association lists the taxes paid by the casino industry to each state government. The 2013 report lists gaming tax revenue to Colorado for 2012 at $104 million.[13] Pennsylvania raises the most tax revenue of all states, with 2012 casino tax revenues of $1.49 billion.[14] One might imagine that such figures represent large contributions to state coffers, but in 2004, casinos contributed less than 2 percent of state revenues in most states. In Nevada, casino taxes represented only about 10.4 percent of state tax revenues.[15]

---

[12] This point is argued by economists on different sides of the casino debate. *See e.g.*, EARL L. GRINOLS, GAMBLING IN AMERICA: COSTS AND BENEFITS ch. 4 (2004); DOUGLAS M. WALKER, CASINONOMICS: THE SOCIOECONOMIC IMPACTS OF THE CASINO INDUSTRY 11 (2013).

[13] AM. GAMING ASS'N, *supra* note 3, at 11.

[14] *Id.* at 21.

[15] WALKER, *supra* note 12, at 68–69.

Although casinos are usually taxed at relatively high rates, this does not necessarily mean that the casino industry will provide a net increase of state tax receipts. For example, spending at casinos may result in a large "substitution effect" away from other consumption and the resulting taxes. It is conceivable that casinos could actually reduce state government tax revenues, although this result is unlikely in most jurisdictions.

Several published studies have examined the impact of casinos on state tax revenues. For example, a study of riverboat casinos' impact on Missouri county sales taxes found that a 10 percent increase in gambling tax revenue leads to a 4 percent decrease in taxes on other amusement and recreation sources.[16] The authors studied 1994–1996 data.[17] The most comprehensive study of casino taxes in the United States suggests that casinos might actually have a mildly negative impact on state tax receipts.[18] However, when positive impacts related to casinos are accounted for, in terms of increased per capita income and hotel employees (a proxy for tourism), the net tax effects from casinos are likely positive.[19]

As noted in the previous section, whether or not casinos actually result in a net increase to state tax revenues, they may still reduce political pressure to raise other forms of taxes or to reduce state government expenditures. Therefore, there is almost certainly a net positive impact from casinos with respect to a state's fiscal status. In the following subsections, I review some of the academic literature on the various positive economic impacts from casinos.

Employment[20]

Next to tax revenues, "jobs" are the next most common selling point for legalizing casinos at the state level. As noted above, the casino industry makes an effort to publicize the number of people employed by the industry in each state. These data are published annually in the AGA's *State of the States*; the data suggest that the industry can have a significant impact on a state's or at least a city's local employment picture.

The employment debate over casinos hinges on the extent to which the casino industry "cannibalizes" other industries. That is, to the extent that casinos cause other firms or industries to contract through direct competition with the casinos, the positive employment effect attributable to casinos will be diminished. Several studies have been published that analyze these effects.

---

[16] Donald Siegel & Gary C. Anders, *Public Policy and the Displacement Effects of Casinos: A Case Study of Riverboat Gambling in Missouri*, 15 J. GAMBLING STUD. 105 (1999).

[17] *Id.*

[18] WALKER, *supra* note 12, at ch. 7.

[19] *Id.* at 84.

[20] *See* SPECTRUM GAMING GROUP, GAMBLING IMPACT STUDY: STATISTICAL RELATIONSHIPS BETWEEN GAMING AND ECONOMIC VARIABLES FOR COMMUNITIES (2013). The discussion in this section is based on the author's contribution to that work.

A study of Mississippi counties found that the introduction of casinos led to an increase in employment, the number of establishments, and annual payroll, raising questions about the substitution effect of casinos in that state.[21] The results do not include the restaurants offered on casino properties, which suggests that casinos have a clearly positive impact on local employment. One might argue, however, that Mississippi is a special case because, prior to the casinos' arrivals, the Mississippi economy was somewhat stagnant.

A study of selected casino counties in four states (Mississippi, Illinois, Iowa, and Missouri) tracked total employment before and after casino introduction and forecast what employment would have been had casinos not been introduced.[22] The findings indicate that casinos had a positive employment and payroll effect in three of the four rural counties studied.[23]

The most comprehensive study to date on the employment effects of casinos (authored by Chad Cotti) estimated county-level impacts for all industries, as well as for the entertainment/hospitality sector, to give a general picture of the employment effect of casinos in the United States.[24] Overall, the findings are that "casino introduction increases aggregate employment in host communities relative to counties without a casino."[25] Most of the benefits accrue to the entertainment sector, with the strongest impacts found in low-population counties.[26] Large population counties see little impact from the introduction of casinos.[27] The following material is largely based on a detailed review[28] of this employment-effects study.

Cotti's analysis is the most in-depth to date because it analyzes all US counties. He uses an econometric analysis of county employment data to determine the effect of the existence of a casino in the county. One limitation of the analysis, however, is that the data do not account for number or sizes of casinos. So a small single casino is treated the same in the analysis as a cluster of large casinos; the analysis is only for the existence of a casino in the county during a particular quarter. Cotti's general results are summarized in the figure below. Figure 1.1 shows the employment effect and the earnings effect at the county level. The labor market is presented in aggregate (all industries), as well as showing the entertainment and hospitality sectors only.

---

[21] Kathryn Hashimoto & George G. French, *Does Casino Development Destroy Local Food and Beverage Operations?: Development of Casinos in Mississippi*, 7 GAMING L. REV. 101 (2003).

[22] Thomas A. Garrett, *Casino Gaming and Local Employment Trends*, 86 FED. RES. BANK ST. LOUIS REV. 9 (2004).

[23] *Id.*

[24] Chad D. Cotti, *The Effect of Casinos on Local Labor Markets: A County Level Analysis*, 2 J. GAMBLING BUS. & ECON. 17 (2008).

[25] *Id.* at 18.

[26] *Id.*

[27] *Id.*

[28] SPECTRUM GAMING GROUP, *supra* note 20.

Figure 1.1

Sector	Employment Effect	Earnings Effect
All industries	+8.2%	+0.79%
Entertainment (NAICS 71)	+50.5%	+19.1%
Hospitality (NAICS 72)	-1.55%	+3.47%
Weighted average of entertainment and hospitality sectors	+7.52%	+6.16%

As shown in Figure 1.1,[29] there is a modest 8.2 percent employment effect when considering all industries in casino counties relative to non-casino counties. The entertainment industry sees a large positive employment effect, as a casino will often represent a large proportion of the entertainment sector for the average county.

Figure 1.2

Sector	Employment Effect	Earnings Effect
All industries	+0.28%	-0.12%
Entertainment (NAICS 71)	+17.6%	+7.89%
Hospitality (NAICS 72)	+0.65%	+1.1%
Weighted average of entertainment and hospitality sectors	+3.61%	+2.28%

Figure 1.3

Sector	Employment Effect	Earnings Effect
All industries	+10.5%	+1.84%
Entertainment (NAICS 71)	+28.7%	+6.74%
Hospitality (NAICS 72)	+3.1%	+4.59%
Weighted average of entertainment and hospitality sectors	+7.56%	+4.96%

Cotti provides several other results, some of which I reproduce here. When Cotti partitions counties by population count, the results are very different. Figures 1.2[30] and 1.3[31] show the results in the top third and bottom third most populated US counties.

As shown in the figues above, the estimated impact of casinos on employment and earnings are much greater in smaller (i.e., less populated) counties. This is consistent with common sense. A particular casino will represent a larger component of the local labor market in a small county relative to a

---

[29] *Id.* at 653.
[30] *Id.* at 657
[31] *Id.*

larger county. The implication of this finding is that casinos in urban markets are likely to have an insignificant impact on employment, but casinos in more rural areas are more likely to impact the local labor market.

Cotti's analysis provides strong evidence that casinos have at least a modestly positive impact on the local labor market, and it raises doubt about the validity of the "substitution effect" argument against casinos, at least with respect to employment impacts.

Economic growth[32]

Most of the political debate on commercial casinos focuses on employment (and substitution) and industry "cannibalization." The more general question is whether casinos can help promote the general economic welfare, as measured by economic growth (or increasing personal incomes). We might expect that any negative casino labor substitution effects or industry cannibalization effects would ultimately negatively affect a regional economy's rate of growth. Yet, few studies have addressed this issue directly. Indeed, despite commercial and tribal casinos expanding to almost every state in the United States over the past two decades, few studies have actually attempted to analyze whether casinos have any net impact on the regional or state economy.

Two authors addressed the economic growth issue in a series of papers.[33] The authors tested the statistical relationship between casino revenues and economic growth; the analysis and conclusions are summarized here, while omitting technical details. The analysis relies on a statistical test called "Granger causality." The test examines how two data series move together to determine whether one series can help to predict future values of the other variable. If past values of casino revenue, for example, help to predict future values of economic growth, then casino revenue "Granger causes" economic growth. Although this does not mean literally that the one variable causes the other in the normal sense of the word, it is as close as we can come in statistical analysis to say that one variable causes another.

In their most recent paper, the authors used state-level data from 1990 to 2010.[34] There are 12 states included in the analysis—those states that had riverboat or land-based commercial casinos during the sample period (Colorado, Illinois, Indiana, Iowa, Louisiana, Michigan, Mississippi, Missouri, Nevada, New Jersey, Pennsylvania, and South Dakota).[35] Thus, the

---

[32] For background on the information in this section, *see* Walker & Jackson, *supra* note 3.
[33] *See* Douglas M. Walker & John D. Jackson, *New Goods and Economic Growth: Evidence from Legalized Gambling*, 28 Rev. Regional Stud. 47 (1998); Douglas M. Walker & John D. Jackson, *Do Casinos Cause Economic Growth?*, 66 Am. J. Econ. & Soc. 593 (2007); Walker & Jackson, *supra* note 3. For an expanded analysis and discussion, *see* Walker, *supra* note 12.
[34] Walker & Jackson (2013), *supra* note 3.
[35] *Id.*

study includes 252 observations (i.e., 21 years, 12 states).[36] The data used include inflation-adjusted annual data on each of the above-listed casino states' per capita incomes and net casino revenues.[37]

The findings of the analysis are that casino revenues Granger cause per capita income, but not that per capita income Granger causes casino revenues.[38] We can conclude that casinos do have a positive impact on state-level economic growth, at least for the states tested and during our sample period. What the analysis does not allow one to do is determine exactly the magnitude of the positive impact of casinos on state-level economic growth. Nevertheless, these results are consistent with a related study by the same authors on the economic growth effects of the casino industry in the wake of Hurricane Katrina in 2005.[39] In a 2008 paper the same researchers found that casino activity led to a higher growth in per capita income for casino states than non-casino states affected by the hurricane.[40]

As noted earlier in the chapter, politicians may have their own reasons to push for casino legalization. It is likely that measurable impacts—such as employment and tax effects—are more likely than the more aggregate and abstract "economic growth" to be touted by politicians pushing for casino expansion. Nevertheless, the economic growth effect is an important piece of the puzzle.

Consumer Benefits

Among all the benefits and costs typically attributed to legal casino gambling, the most commonly downplayed or ignored are the benefits that accrue to casino patrons. In this section the benefits to casino patrons are discussed. Often these benefits are difficult to measure, but this does not mean that the benefits are any less important or relevant than employment or tax (or other) benefits from casinos.

It is first worth noting that economists see each purchase or expenditure of money by a consumer to be voluntary and mutually beneficial. That is, the casino patron would not choose to place a bet if they did not expect to benefit from the transaction. Note that this is true even though the player realizes that the expected value of the bet is negative. It suggests that the player gains enjoyment from gambling. If this was not the case, then they would not play casino games.[41] Although policymakers and voters often

---

[36] *Id.*

[37] *Id.*

[38] *Id.*

[39] Douglas M. Walker & John D. Jackson, *Market-Based "Disaster Relief": Katrina and the Casino Industry*, 35 Int'l J. Soc. Econ. 521 (2008).

[40] *Id.*

[41] Some critics of this idea have suggested that a person could not possibly receive $100 worth of benefit, for example, from losing a hand of blackjack on which a $100 bet was placed. But this argument assumes an incorrect (overstated) value for the "price" of gambling. The price of gambling is better conceived as the bet placed times the expected value of the bet. For an analysis of this issue, *see* Ricardo C.S. Siu, *A Conceptual Reconsideration*

think of casinos only as a public policy tool for creating jobs and tax revenues, in fact, many people simply enjoy gambling at casinos. These are real benefits that emanate from the casino industry.

An additional consumer-related benefit from the casino industry relates to the economic concept of "consumer surplus." This concept is similar to profit for the producers in an industry. Profit simply represents the difference between selling price and cost of production. It is the reason firms exist. Firms that produce goods or services that are valued by consumers will tend to earn high levels of profit. Consumer surplus is the analogous variable for consumers in a market. For many or perhaps most goods and services, the price a consumer pays for something is actually lower than the value of the product to the consumer. This difference is "consumer surplus." Although people may not explicitly think in terms of "consumer surplus," it is still a benefit to them. It can simply be thought of as the good feeling one gets when one gets a "good deal" on the purchase of a car or something at the mall. Casinos can create a consumer surplus if the value of the experience to the consumer is less than the price the consumer must pay to have it.[42]

A related benefit comes from the fact that the introduction of a new casino to an entertainment market increases competition. Increased competition usually causes prices to fall and the quality of goods and services to increase. These also represent (difficult to measure) benefits to consumers that result from the expansion of the casino industry.

Lastly, consumers benefit from increased options or variety. Consider living in a small town that only has one restaurant. Additional restaurants, representing additional variety, will generally benefit consumers because they will have more choices. A casino does something similar with respect to a consumer's entertainment options: more choices are better than fewer.

Although many of the benefits to consumers discussed here are difficult to measure, they are nevertheless important potential benefits from the introduction or expansion of casinos that deserve attention in the debate over casinos.

Summary of Economic Benefits

The typical public debate over introducing or expanding casinos in a state focuses on the economic benefits most commonly attributed to casinos: jobs and tax revenues. Evidence from the literature suggests that casinos probably do, on net, lead to increases in employment and tax revenues. However, the increases in these variables are likely to be rather modest.

Two less commonly discussed benefits from casinos are economic

---

of Price Issues with Casino Gambling, 15 GAMING L. REV. & ECON. 264 (2011).
[42] For an empirical analysis of the consumer surplus related to casinos, *see* Yuliya Crane, New Casinos in the United Kingdom: Costs, Benefits and Other Considerations (2006) (Ph.D. dissertation, Salford (U.K.) Business School).

growth and consumer benefits. The available empirical evidence suggests that casinos do have a positive impact on state-level economic growth in the United States. Although there has been scant empirical evidence in the literature, it is also likely that casinos are responsible for significant benefits that accrue to their customers, despite the negative expected value of the casino games.

Based on the evidence in the academic literature, it is likely that casinos create substantial benefits to their host communities. However, these benefits are not always easily measured. In any case, there may also be significant economic and social costs created by casinos. Those issues are addressed next.

ECONOMIC AND SOCIAL COSTS

No casino expansion proposal passes without controversy. The most common argument against casinos is based on the social costs of gambling. In this section the most commonly cited social costs from casino gambling are examined. Most of these costs are attributed to "disordered gamblers," discussed in the first subsection below.

Disordered gamblers

Psychologists have intensively studied problematic gambling behaviors for at least the past two decades. During this time, gambling problem terminology has evolved. Past terms include addictive gambling, compulsive gambling, problem gambling, and pathological gambling. The current terminology is "disordered gambling."[43] This refers to gambling to such an extent that the behavior has a problematic negative impact on a person's finances, family, friends, career, or other important aspect of life. Simply put, if gambling is disrupting a person's life, the person may have a gambling disorder.

Social scientists estimate that the prevalence rate of disordered gambling is somewhere between 0.4 percent and 2.0 percent of the general population. This rate does not seem to change dramatically, regardless of the jurisdiction studied or the size of the local gambling market.[44] Because individuals with a gambling disorder often find themselves in a financial crisis, many of the problematic behaviors associated with disordered gambling relate to finances. The following is a list of items that are commonly

---

[43] The different terms also have referred to different severities of problems. A detailed analysis of the changing terminology and diagnosis is beyond the scope of this chapter.

[44] *See* Nancy M. Petry et al., *Comorbidity of DSM-IV Pathological Gambling and Other Psychiatric Disorders: Results from the National Epidemiological Surveys on Alcohol and Related Conditions*, 66 J. CLINICAL PSYCHIATRY 564 (2005). More research is needed on the degree to which gambling expansion affects the prevalence of disordered gambling (*see, e.g.*, Renée A. St-Pierre et al., *How Availability and Accessibility of Gambling Venues Influence Problem Gambling: A Review of the Literature*, 18 GAMING L. REV. & ECON. 150 (2014)). For simplicity, hereafter the prevalence rate is assumed to be 1 percent.

listed in studies on the social costs of gambling:[45]
- Income lost from missed work
- Decreased productivity on the job
- Crime
- Depression and physical illness related to stress
- Increased suicide attempts
- Bailout costs
- Unrecovered loans to pathological gamblers
- Unpaid debts and bankruptcies
- Higher insurance premiums resulting from pathological gambler-caused fraud
- Corruption of public officials
- Strain on public services
- Industry cannibalization
- Divorces caused by gambling

The most commonly cited impact of casinos is crime; this is discussed in the next subsection.

There is little debate that individuals who develop a gambling problem will engage in some antisocial behaviors. A large share of the academic literature on gambling focuses on the prevention, diagnosis, and treatment of gambling disorders. As a result, psychologists have quite a good understanding of the different types of problems often experienced by disordered gamblers and other individuals they affect.

Casinos and Crime

Among the social ills attributed to casinos, crime has perhaps been analyzed the most in the literature. There are several different theories that suggest that there may be a link between casinos and crime. One was alluded to above: disordered gamblers must turn to crime because of the financial bind to which their gambling has contributed. Casinos may also create crime simply because casinos attract a large number of patrons, most of whom carry cash. Thus, a casino may be an ideal place for thieves to go. Economist Gary Becker's theory of crime—that the decision to commit a crime is a rational decision—also applies.[46]

One study of casinos and crime suggested casinos could reduce crime through a wage effect (if casinos increase local wages, the incentive to commit crimes falls) or a development effect (if casinos contribute to economic growth, streets are safer and there may be less crime).[47] The study listed five channels through which casinos might increase crime:[48]

---

[45] Walker, *supra* note 12, at 155.

[46] Gary S. Becker, *Crime and Punishment: An Economic Approach*, 76 J. Pol. Econ. 169 (1968).

[47] Earl L. Grinols & David B. Mustard, *Casinos, Crime, and Community Costs*, 88 Rev. Econ. & Stat. 28 (2006).

[48] *Id.*

- Development (casinos could have a negative development effect and attract criminals, thus draining the local economy)
- Higher incentive to commit crime (casinos attract patrons with cash)
- Pathological gambling
- Visitor criminality (casinos may attract patrons who are more prone to commit and be victims of crime)
- Changes in population composition (casinos increase proportion of unskilled workers, who may be more likely to engage in crime)

In the criminology literature there are also several theories of crime that would seem to apply to casinos. These include the "routine activities" and "hot spot" theories of crime. Both theories can be applied to casinos since casinos may be places that attract both potential victims and thieves.[49]

Since the mid-1980s there have been numerous empirical analyses of the relationship between casinos and crime. Most of the early studies focused on Las Vegas and Atlantic City as they were the only US jurisdictions that hosted casinos until the late 1980s.[50] The aforementioned study, perhaps the most influential study of casinos and crime to date, examined county-level crime statistics from 1977–1996.[51] The study concluded that about 8 percent of crime in casino counties can be attributed to the casinos.[52] This is a statistically significant effect and reflects the fear that many communities have as they contemplate whether the benefits of casinos outweigh the costs.

Among other studies that analyze the link between casinos and crime, about half find a link, while the other half does not. Interestingly, almost all of the studies that find a link between casinos and crime define the "crime rate" one way, while almost all of the studies that do not find a link define the rate differently.[53]

A "crime rate" indicates how likely a person is to be victimized by crime in a particular city or county. Since crime rates can be compared across jurisdictions and through time, they can be valuable for studying how different approaches to crime prevention are working, for example. They are also used to test how different demographic variables affect the amount of crime. If C represents the number of crimes committed, and P represents the population at risk (say, the population of a particular county), then the

---

[49] See, e.g., Lawrence E. Cohen & Marcus Felson, *Social Change and Crime Rate Trends: A Routine Activity Approach*, 44 AM. SOC. REV. 588 (1979), Emmanuel Barthe & B. Grant Stitt, *Casinos as "Hot Spots" and the Generation of Crime*, 30 J. CRIME & JUST. 115 (2007).

[50] For a review a casino crime studies, *see* Douglas M. Walker, *Casinos and crime in the U.S.A.*, *in* HANDBOOK ON THE ECONOMICS OF CRIME 488 (Bruce L. Benson & Paul R. Zimmerman eds., 2010).

[51] Grinols & Mustard, *supra* note 47. The authors examined the FBI's *Uniform Crime Reports* data on Index I crimes.

[52] *Id.*

[53] For a deeper discussion of this issue, *see* Douglas M. Walker, *Evaluating Crime Attributable to Casinos in the U.S.: A Closer Look at Grinols and Mustard's "Casinos, Crime, and Community Costs,"* 2 J. GAMBLING BUS. & ECON. 23 (2008).

crime rate would be represented as *C/P*. The crime rate is usually stated in per capita terms, e.g., crimes per 100,000 people.

Analyses of the link between casinos and crimes are usually done at a local (city) or county level. Without exception, crime studies count all of the crimes committed (*C*) in the relevant jurisdiction during the sample period. However, studies vary in how they treat the population at risk (*P*). Those studies that find that casinos cause crime usually omit visitors (i.e., tourists) from *P*, while those studies that do not find a link usually include tourist count into the measure of *P*. This is the critical issue on which crime study results have seemed to hinge.

Consider a small community prior to the opening of a casino. If the community has a population of 1,000, and 10 crimes are committed on average per year, then the crime rate, *C/P* would be 10/1,000, or 1/100. This means that a person has a 1-in-100 chance of being the victim of a crime during a particular year. This figure can easily be compared to other jurisdictions or across time to have a basis on which to judge whether crime is getting better or worse in the community. Now suppose a casino opens, which attracts 100,000 tourists per year. Suppose the number of crimes committed in the community increases by 1,000 (1/100 of 100,000). Now *C*=1,010.

If we ignore the tourists when we calculate the population at risk, then *P*=1,000. But if we include the tourists in *P*, then it becomes 101,000. The crime rate in the first case would be 1,010/1,000, or 101/100. This means a person has an average chance of slightly over 100 percent of being victimized. Note that this method of calculating the crime rate assumes that all of the crimes are committed against the community's residents, and none are committed against the tourists. This conception of the crime rate is not realistic, and the calculation almost certainly would overstate the risk of being victimized to the person in the community (resident or tourist).

If we include the tourists in the measure of *P*, then the crime rate is calculated as 1,010/101,000, or 1/100. Under this conception of the crime rate, it remains unchanged because the number of crimes committed changed in the same proportion as the total number of people in the community during the year. This measure more accurately reflects the risk of a particular person (tourist or resident) being victimized by crime.

This analysis suggests that studies that find a link between casinos and crime do so because they omit the tourists from the population at risk. There are, however, some studies that find mixed results. For example, one of the best casino-crime analyses suggests that the effect of casinos on crime is likely a community-specific phenomenon.[54] The study analyzed six new casino communities with six control communities. The researchers analyzed both the resident population and population at risk. Crime rates in some communities increased, while in others it decreased.[55]

---

[54] B. Grant Stitt et al., *Does the Presence of Casinos Increase Crime? An Examination of Casino and Control Communities*, 49 Crime & Delinquency 253 (2003).
[55] *Id.*

Another study[56] corrects some of the analytical problems in the influential Grinols and Mustard study, although it only examines the market in Indiana. This study controls for several factors that Grinols and Mustard were unable to—including the number of visitors to the casinos in Indiana—through turnstile counts. It also controlled for the number of hotel rooms in each county, which served in the analysis as a measure of the volume of tourism. The findings suggest that new casinos increase burglaries, but reduce car theft and aggravated assaults. The study finds that increased turnstile counts are associated with lower rates of larceny, car theft, aggravated assault, and robbery.[57] The results are not all consistent, however. Some crimes may increase, but overall the amount of crime falls.

Considering all literature on casinos and crime, the best we can say is that the jury is still out: there is not enough evidence to conclude either that casinos are linked to crime or they are not. It appears that the relationship may be community/market specific.

Other Social Problems

Among the other potential social problems that are rooted in the expansion of casinos, infrastructure costs are often important to local politicians. Casinos can attract a large number of customers, and can create traffic problems, even in large cities with existing tourist attractions. Typically, however, casinos are responsible for making improvements to infrastructure either directly or indirectly through taxes and fees paid to local governments. This issue has not been studied in detail in the literature.

A related problem is the potential for casino expansion to affect drunk driving and related fatalities. Since many casinos offer patrons free alcohol, one might expect that casinos would be linked to drunk driving. One recent study confirmed this, finding that casinos in rural areas increase drunk-driving fatalities by about 10 percent; casinos modestly *reduce* urban drunk driving fatalities, however.[58]

Lastly, there are a variety of "moral" arguments against the expansion of casino gambling. Some people simply believe that government should not encourage, or even allow, gambling. Such arguments seem to be a lost cause, at least in the United States, since lotteries and casinos are now widespread. At the local level, however, voters have quite a bit of control and can successfully prevent a casino being opened in their community. Such opposition is sometimes due to moral concerns, and sometimes it is due to a more general NIMBY (not in my back yard) concern.

---

[56] William S. Reece, *Casinos, Hotels, and Crime*, 28 CONTEMP. ECON. POL. 145 (2010).
[57] *Id.* at 157.
[58] Cotti, *supra* note 24; Walker, *supra* note 50.

Social Cost Estimates

When it comes to the political debates over casino expansion, journalists, voters, and policymakers alike seek simple monetary measures of the impacts of casinos. This explains why sometimes completely baseless estimates of the costs and benefits of casinos are so often repeated. One of the major problems in the academic literature has been how to measure the magnitude of the social costs of gambling. Despite a variety of monetary estimates of social costs that appeared in the literature during the 1990s, researchers still have little understanding of the monetary value of the social costs of gambling. The research methodology for defining and measuring social costs is simply not developed nearly as well as the methodology on the benefits side of the equation.[59] As a result, social-cost estimates of the above-listed negative impacts commonly attributed to casinos range anywhere from $2,000 to $50,000 per disordered gambler, per year. Obviously, such a large range is indicative of something wrong in how the costs are being measured. It is a problem that is not likely to be clarified anytime soon.[60] Criticisms of the social cost literature date back to the 1990s, and are still valid today. For example, the National Research Council writes:[61]

> Most reported economic analysis in the literature is methodologically weak. In their most rudimentary form, such studies are little more than a crude accounting, bringing together readily available numbers from a variety of disparate sources. . . . The consequence has been a plethora of studies with implicit but untested assumptions underlying the analysis that often are either unacknowledged by those performing the analysis, or likely to be misunderstood by those relying on the results. Not surprisingly, the findings of rudimentary economic impact analyses can be misused by those who are not aware of their limitations.

Nevertheless, despite the disagreement amongst researchers about the monetary values, everyone agrees that there are social costs attributable to disordered gamblers. Research that focuses on understanding these costly behaviors is worthwhile. Psychologists have a fairly good understating of the different types of problems that may befall disordered gamblers. Research aimed at producing monetary estimates of the social costs of gambling is not likely to be fruitful.[62]

---

[59] Douglas M. Walker & A.H. Barnett, *The Social Costs of Gambling: An Economic Perspective*, 15 J. Gambling Stud. 181 (1999)

[60] This is despite some attempts at comprehensive analysis; see e.g. Anielski Management Inc., The Socio-Economic Impact of Gambling (SEIG) Framework: An Assessment Framework for Canada: In Search of the Gold Standard (2008), http://www.anielski.com/Documents/SEIG%20Framework.pdf, Brad R. Humphreys et al., Final Report to the Alberta Gaming Research Institute on the Socio-Economic Impact of Gambling in Alberta (2011).

[61] National Research Council, Pathological Gambling (1999).

[62] For a detailed discussion, *see* Walker, *supra* note 12, at chs. 13 and 14. The actual social costs of gambling are likely to be at the lower end of the range mentioned above.

Even if researchers could agree on what types of effects qualify as gambling's social costs and how to measure them, there is still one fundamental problem that precludes the accurate measure of the social costs attributable to gambling: "comorbidity" or co-existing disorders. Without exception, the published social cost studies fail to consider the fact that most disordered gamblers likely have other behavioral disorders, such as alcohol or drug use disorders.[63] Then, if the socially costly behavior of a disordered gambler is estimated at $10,000, it would be inappropriate to attribute all of that cost to problem gambling along. Unfortunately, there is no analytically valid way to partition social costs among a person's various behavioral disorders. Yet it is clear that researchers have overestimated the social costs that should be attributed to disordered gambling, as few researchers who estimate social costs have even acknowledged the problem or attempted to adjust their estimates accordingly. The result is that the literature provides only arbitrary overestimates of the social costs of gambling.[64]

Summary of Economic and Social Costs

As the discussion above suggests, there is much less understanding among researchers of the cost side of the casino question. While there are certainly costs to society that accompany the expansion of legal gambling and casinos in the United States, the monetary measurement of these costs has been a hurdle that no one has successfully cleared. It is currently impossible to develop a reasonably accurate monetary measure of the social costs of casino gambling. This is because the methodology for such research is lacking, and there are inherent problems that simply cannot be ignored—comorbidity in particular. Nevertheless, researchers, politicians, and voters should be aware of the potential harms that accompany the expansion of casino gambling. Even though they do not have good monetary measures of these costs, these costs are still important.

FUTURE ISSUES OF DEBATE

The casino industry is always changing. Nowhere has this been more visible than in Las Vegas. The city was one of the fastest growing in the country during the early and mid-2000s. The casino industry has expanded dramatically in Las Vegas. As the industry has expanded, it has also changed its focus. In the early 1990s, the city began appealing more to fam-

---

[63] Researchers estimate that more than 70 percent of pathological gamblers have other disorders. *See* Petry, *supra* note 44; James R. Westphal & Lera Joyce Johnson, *Mulitple Co-Occurring Behaviours Among Gamblers in Treatment: Implications and Assessment*, 7 INT'L GAMBLING STUD. 73 (2007).

[64] A good example of this is the social-cost estimate of $10,330, which is simply the average of a variety of other, mostly unpublished, social cost estimates. *See* GRINOLS, *supra* note 12. The author also suggests that the costs of casinos outweigh their benefits by a factor of about 4:1. *Id.* at 175. This figure, too, is simply speculation.

ilies, as evidenced by the opening of hotels like the Excalibur. Years later, shows such as Cirque du Soleil became much more popular. Now (non-casino) amenities raise more revenue than casino games at most Las Vegas resorts. In the late 2000s, the city began to move back toward its "sin city" identity. The city seems to be very dynamic, always changing to appeal to a wider audience.

Many other casino markets in the United States have much simpler casinos without the shows, restaurants, or themes. The casino games are the main attraction in these markets. Whether we consider casinos in well-developed markets like Las Vegas, or in younger jurisdictions such as Ohio, there are a variety of issues that deserve additional attention from researchers. This section previews some of the key issues that are likely to be debated in the near future.

Economic and Social Issues

The issues that are addressed earlier in the chapter will continue to be important for researchers to examine. As the casino industry continues to develop, it is quite likely that its employment, tax, and economic growth effects will change. An understanding of these changing effects will be important for guiding future policy with respect to gambling expansion. The same should be said about the social costs and other potentially negative impacts of casino gambling.

Online Gambling

All casinos are likely to be affected by recent developments in online gambling. People have been gambling online for as long as technology would allow it. Online poker has been particularly popular in the United States. Amidst the increasing popularity and availability of online gambling, in 2006 the federal government passed the Unlawful Internet Gambling Enforcement Act (UIGEA). The law aimed to stop banking transactions related to online gambling. Effectively, the law simply forced online gambling service providers out of the country. It is unclear the extent to which online gambling decreased; instead, the main effect likely just made online gambling more of a hassle to players because clever methods had to be created to move money.

In December 2011 the Justice Department released an opinion on the Wire Act that indicated that the Act applies only to sports gambling.[65] This opinion has created a shift in online gambling, and now several states (as of this writing, Nevada, New Jersey, Delaware) have adopted regulations for online gambling; many more states will follow. Little is known how

---

[65] VIRGINIA A. SEITZ, U.S. DEP'T OF JUSTICE, OFFICE OF LEGAL COUNSEL, OPINION: WHETHER PROPOSALS BY ILLINOIS AND NEW YORK TO USE THE INTERNET AND OUT-OF-STATE TRANSACTION PROCESSORS TO SELL LOTTERY TICKETS TO IN-STATE ADULTS VIOLATE THE WIRE ACT (2011).

online gambling will affect bricks-and-mortar casinos. On the one hand, if people see online gambling as a suitable substitute for casino gambling, the expansion of online and social media gambling might harm casinos. However, we might reasonably conceive of online gambling as a different product than gambling at a casino. Casino gambling is more of a social activity; online gambling is done in the privacy of one's home. Perhaps the two forms of gambling are complements to rather than substitutes for each other.[66]

In any case, as online gambling becomes more common in the United States, it will be interesting to see how the traditional casino industry is impacted. This issue will likely be studied in each state that currently has casinos, as the relationship among the forms of gambling is largely unknown.

Since the 2011 Justice Department opinion was issued, lobbying related to online gambling has been interesting to watch. The casino industry, through the American Gaming Association, has argued for federal regulations of online gambling, with only poker allowed online.[67] This appears to be an effort by the industry to restrict competition on the games from which it derives much of its profit, while allowing poker, a game on which the casinos earn little revenue. The industry lobbying for federal regulation (as opposed to state regulation) has explained this as a simple-to-understand, simple-to-enforce strategy. Other voices have argued that state-level regulations would be best.[68]

Casino mogul Sheldon Adelson has taken the position that all online gambling should be banned by the federal government.[69] One reason for his opposition to online gambling appears to be his concern that in the long run it would compete with land-based gaming.

Inter-Industry Relationships

In addition to understanding the potential impact of online gambling on traditional forms of gambling, more research is needed on the inter-industry relationships between casino gambling and other industries. Al-

---

[66] For an examination of the effect of online gambling and online poker on the "offline" gambling market, see Kahlil S. Philander, *The Effect of Online Gaming Revenue on Commercial Casino Revenue*, 15 UNLV GAMING RES. & REV. J. 23 (2011); Kahlil S. Philander & Ingo Fielder, *Online Poker in North America: Empirical Evidence on its Complementary Effect on the Offline Gambling Market*, 16 GAMING L. REV. & ECON. 415 (2012).

[67] Frank J. Fahrenkopf, Jr., *Federal Online Gambling Legislation Needed Now More Than Ever*, AM. GAMING ASS'N, http://www.americangaming.org/newsroom/op-eds/federal-online-gambling-legislation-needed-now-more-than-ever.

[68] Michelle Minton, *Let States Regulate Internet Gambling*, WASH. EXAM'R, March 18, 2012, http://washingtonexaminer.com/article/384241.

[69] Nathan Vardi, *Sheldon Adelson Says He Is 'Willing to Spend Whatever It Takes' to Stop Online Gambling*, FORBES, Nov. 22, 2013, http://www.forbes.com/sites/nathan-vardi/2013/11/22/sheldon-adelson-says-he-is-willing-to-spend-whatever-it-takes-to-stop-online-gambling/.

though concerns that the casino industry "cannibalizes" other industries are commonly heard in casino debates, there is surprisingly little research on this issue. The most comprehensive study finds inconsistent relationships across industries: some forms of gambling complement others while some forms compete with each other. A better understanding of these relationships, especially as legal gambling continues to expand, will help inform gambling policy in the future.

Industry Saturation Point

Casino critics and even some leaders in the casino industry have expressed some concern that the industry may be reaching a "saturation point." That is, there is concern that the industry may over-build in some markets, resulting simply in increased competition for a fixed amount of expenditures by casino patrons, with no other economic benefits.

To date, researchers have not developed any test of a "saturation point." This is likely to be a key issue in the near future as more and more states continue to legalize casinos and expand their existing industries.

CONCLUSION

In this chapter I have examined some of the most contentious issues that are raised when casino gambling introduction and expansion are being considered. To be sure, there are both costs and benefits associated with casino gambling. Many of these effects have been examined by economists, sociologists, and other social scientists. Yet, research has not provided all the answers. There is still much uncertainty about the net impacts of casino gambling.

The debate is likely to continue, despite the fact that the casino industry is already widespread in the United States. Is it worth it for states to legalize casinos when they are already so common? Are we approaching a saturation point? Is online gambling going to make brick-and-mortar casinos obsolete? Are the social costs of gambling more than anticipated by policymakers? These are questions over which the casino debate will continue for the foreseeable future and which should keep researchers very busy.

2

Public Policy and Policy Goals

Anthony Cabot

INTRODUCTION

The seminal gambling-related question any government faces is whether to allow or prohibit it. In non-secular nations or those with a dominant religion that disfavors gambling, this question is easily answered. Several religions condemn gambling, so, not surprisingly, non-secular governments with religious prohibitions against gambling tend to adopt public policies against legal casinos. The religious doctrines of Islam, Hinduism, Buddhism, and Shintoism have affected the gambling laws of most Middle Eastern and Asian countries. This is both understandable and often not retractable.

Once we take religion out of the decision making, the sciences play a major role. Here, gaming industry opponents range from the Right to the Left. For example, Green Party presidential candidate Ralph Nader is alleged to have stated: "No presidential candidate should visit Las Vegas without condemning organized gambling." While gambling debates can have a nonreligious moral underpinning,[1] they more often run to pragmatic amoral pluralist assessments of whether an activity should be legal based on an objective evaluation that considers many principles and effects.[2] Once we debate principles and effects, as Professor Walker ably did in Chapter 1, we have an empirical basis for determining gaming policy on both a macro and micro level. On a macro level, Professor William Eadington suggests that governments considering legal gambling should first weigh benefits—such as taxes, jobs, economic stimulation, and fulfill-

---

[1] See, e.g., William R. Eadington, "The Political Economy of the Legal Casino Gaming Industry in the United States," Paper 84-1, 18 (1984) (describing the moralist claim that gambling influences the general public's values and priorities). See also, infra, text surrounding notes 14-17.

[2] Id.

ing consumer demands—against costs—such as economic displacement, effects on crime, and dysfunctional gambling. Governments should next consider reasonable cost-effective methods to minimize the costs. Then, according to Eadington, "If, at that point, aggregate benefits do not exceed aggregate costs, or the proposed gambling industry is not economically viable, then creation of a new gambling industry would not be wise."[3]

Hope, however misplaced, is that the debate over casino legalization centers on reasoned consideration of such costs and benefits rather than hyperbole, which is so common in these campaigns on both sides. But the cost–benefit analysis should not end with the decision to permit legal casinos because it also should shape public policy toward regulating casinos.

Yet most discussions concerning how a jurisdiction considering casinos should regulate that industry start with a question like "Should we adopt the Nevada, New Jersey, or Singapore regulatory model?" This approach is incorrect. It is, however, understandable. Regulators or politicians often talk about the regulation in their jurisdiction as the "gold standard." Defining something assumes only one correct way to do something, and the regulatory method used by one's own government will inevitably seem the best. Confusion on this topic is amplified because most gaming regulatory systems have similar functions—licensing, enforcement, and auditing. These functions, however, have much different utilities depending on public policy.

When a government adopts another government's model, it is likely to be a failure at some level. The most legendary are "implementation failures." As an example, when one small island nation legalized casino gambling, it hired New Jersey gaming counsel to draft its laws and regulation based on the "New Jersey Model." The ensuing laws and regulations closely tracked the New Jersey regulation. The regulatory system imposed, however, made any prospective casino on the island infeasible for several reasons. As one example, New Jersey required full licensing for gaming chip manufacturers. This may have worked for a multi-billion dollar industry in New Jersey, but no chip manufacturer would pay the licensing expense to service a single small casino market. At the time, it was impossible to run a casino without chips. This and many other implementation problems expose governments' different expertise, resources, and circumstances.

The island nation may have felt that the New Jersey system was the "gold standard" because New Jersey's was the strictest regulatory system in the world at the time. Strict regulation for perception purposes may serve the immediate purposes of politicians seeking to assure voters that supposed harms will not result from legalizing gambling. If it means the difference between legal casinos and no casinos, the industry may even embrace it.

---

[3] William Eadington, *Problem Gambling and Public Policy: Alternatives in Dealing with Problem Gamblers and Commercial Gambling*, in COMPULSIVE GAMBLING THEORY, RESEARCH AND PRACTICE 175 (Howard Shaffer, Sharon Stein, Blase Gammon, & Thomas Cummings eds., 1989).

However, strict regulation that does not further policy goals is bad regulation as it limits competition, creates unnecessary regulatory costs, and increases pricing. Sometimes this goes unnoticed—particularly where there are regional monopolies—because extraordinary profits mask regulatory impacts on pricing. But once the regional monopoly fades because of new regional competition, the industry can quickly become non-competitive. Whether the "strict" casino regulations from New Jersey's initial launch contributed to its decline as a gaming market has not been fully explored,[4] but some have suggested that "liberalizing" the regulations rendering them more efficient could help keep the market more competitive with new competing markets.[5]

A more fundamental problem than implementation failure exists. Policy failure occurs when the regulations or the implementations of those regulations are inconsistent with the policy goals of the jurisdiction, or the policy goals are unclear, conflicting, or ignored. This may seem simple, but public policy should drive how a government regulates gambling from the adoption of regulations, the organization of a regulatory system, and interaction with the gaming industry in applying the regulations. If the public policy of Nevada is different from the public policy of a new jurisdiction, then—implementation issues aside—why would you consider adopting the "Nevada Model?"[6]

Public policy decisions start with the simple and often unexplored question of why a government regulates casinos. At its heart, gambling is a voluntary contract between parties where money exchanges hands based at least partially on a chance outcome, with one party (usually the casino) typically having a mathematical advantage over the other party (usually the player).[7] The first step in creating public policy toward gambling should start with identifying issues or concerns. In other words, what is it about this gambling contract that causes concerns justifying government inter-

---

[4] One study of New Jersey deregulation in 1991 found that removing restrictions on operating hours and limitations on floor space devoted to slot machines had a significant positive impact on casino win. *See* Mark W. Nichols, *The Impact of Deregulation on Casino Win in Atlantic City*, 13 REV. INDUS. ORG. 713 (1998); *see also* Richard Thalheimer & Mukhtar M. Ali, *Table Games, Slot Machines and Casino Revenue*, 40 APPLIED ECON. 2395 (2008); Mark W. Nichols, *Deregulation and Cross-Border Substitution in Iowa's Riverboat Gambling Industry*, 14 J. GAMBLING STUD. 151 (1998); Jeffrey A. Lowenhar, C.J. Lonoff, & Rita Smith, *Regulatory Requirements and Legalized Casino Gaming in New Jersey: The Case for Change, in* GAMBLING AND PUBLIC POLICY: INTERNATIONAL PERSPECTIVES 261 (William R. Eadington & Judy A. Cornelius eds., 1991); Philip Satre, *A Report on the Impact of the New Jersey Casino Control Act and Related Regulations on Harrah's Marina Hotel Casino*, 8 GAMBLING PAPERS: PROC. FIFTH NAT'L CONF. ON GAMBLING & RISK TAKING 144 (1981).

[5] Lori Tripoli, *Wasn't the Gaming Law Business Supposed to Be Recession-Proof?*, 13 GAMING L. REV. & ECON. 23 (2009).

[6] This does not mean that certain aspects of the way Nevada regulates gambling may not be useful as proven practices.

[7] ROBERT C. HANNUM & ANTHONY N. CABOT, PRACTICAL CASINO MATH (2D ED. 2005).

vention? Only valid concerns should propel governments to treat casino gambling proprietors differently from most other vocations such as flower shop owners or car salesmen. These concerns should be the cornerstones of the course of action governments take in addressing gambling.[8] Overwhelmingly, jurisdictions worldwide have concluded that casino gaming presents unique concerns mandating regulation. Chapter 1 discussed what might make gambling different.

The second step requires that governments select among several possible goals in responding to these concerns. This chapter addresses broader policy goals (e.g., protecting players against unfair or dishonest operators or games) in contrast to specific issues (e.g., assuring the veracity of random number generators in gaming devices). Once determined, these goals should guide the final steps of the process—step three, creation of the regulations[9] and the regulatory framework as covered in Chapter 3; step four, the implementation process as covered in Chapter 3; and step five, the enforcement process as covered in part in Chapters 6, 8 and 14.. The remaining chapters deal with specific areas of regulation that merit special consideration.

The government can enforce regulations against the gaming industry because it has the exclusive power to compel conformity to rules by force.[10] Offering casino gaming without a license in most jurisdictions is a crime that could lead to incarceration. Even after obtaining a license, the regulated casinos are subject to civil and criminal laws.[11] Because the

---

[8] This is the essence of public policy, which is the "intentional course of action followed by a government institution or official for resolving an issue of public concern." CLARKE E. COCHRAN ET AL., AMERICAN PUBLIC POLICY: AN INTRODUCTION 1 (8th ed. 2006).

[9] Regulation is an integral subset of the government's public policy.

"The main textbooks on regulation identify three definitions. In the first, regulation is the promulgation of rules by government accompanied by mechanisms for monitoring and enforcement, usually assumed to be performed through a specialist public agency. In the second, it is any form of direct state intervention in the economy, whatever form that intervention might take. In the third, regulation is all mechanisms of social control or influence affecting all aspects of [behavior] from whatever source, whether they are intentional or not." Julia Black, *Critical Reflections on Regulation*, 27 AUSTRALIAN J. LEGAL PHIL. 1, 11 (2002). Gaming regulation tracks the first more centralized definition as the industry regulated is relatively new and focused on a narrow segment of society.

[10] According to German social theorist, Max Weber, "state is a human community that (successfully) claims the monopoly of the legitimate use of physical force within a given territory." MAX WEBER, *Politics as a Vocation, in* FROM MAX WEBER: ESSAYS IN SOCIOLOGY 77 (H. H. Gerth & C. Wright Mills eds. & trans., Oxford Univ. Press 1967).

[11] Gaming regulators most often enforce the rules against licensees through civil sanctions including the threat or imposition of fines or license revocation. Violations by non-licensee are often dealt with by criminal sanctions. Criminal law "should be reserved to prohibiting conduct that society believes lacks any social utility, while civil penalties should be used to deter (or "price") many forms of misbehavior (for example, negligence) where the regulated activity has positive social utility but is imposing externalities on others." John C. Coffee, Jr., *Paradigms Lost: The Blurring of the Criminal and Civil Law Models -- and What Can Be Done About It*, 101 YALE L.J. 1875, 1876 (1992).

government backs regulation by the state's exclusive power to use force, the success of a government's public policy can greatly impact a society. What can go wrong? As one scholar noted regarding centralized regulation:

> Its failings are variously identified as including the following: that the instruments used (laws backed by sanctions) are inappropriate and unsophisticated (instrument failure), that government has insufficient knowledge to be able to identify the causes of problems, to design solutions that are appropriate, and to identify non-compliance (information and knowledge failure), that implementation of the regulation is inadequate (implementation failure), and that those being regulated are insufficiently inclined to comply, and those doing the regulating are insufficiently motivated to regulated [*sic*] in the public interest (motivation failure and capture theory).[12]

In casino regulation, failure can be as simple as having licensing standards so high you have few if any qualified applicants.[13]

This chapter concentrates on the design of the public policy goals concerning gambling underlying the regulatory solutions that address identified concerns associated with gambling or the gaming industry. Absent understanding what policy goals the government wants to accomplish, regulators have no context for developing regulations (or making decisions that advance these goals). Implementation failure can occur when, instead of considering a government's policy goals, regulators substitute their own beliefs or assumptions, or those of their perceived constituency, about the policy goals that are supposed to guide their actions both in adopting and applying regulations.

Understanding a government's policy goals is essential to develop an effective regulatory framework. While policy goals that prohibit gambling are self-evident (the prohibition of gambling), goals that permit gambling may take many forms. This chapter details the most common approaches to achieving those goals: market model, player protection, government protection, industry capture, and hybrid model.

Public Policies Prohibiting Gambling and a Gambling Industry

Eradication

Eradication is the most restrictive public policy concerning gambling. A government may have several reasons for wanting to eradicate gambling. While government opposition to gambling may be founded on economic or social thought, the religious orientation of a society is often paramount.[14] Moralists claim that gambling influences the general public's values and

---

[12] Black, *supra* note 9, at 3.
[13] As identified in Chapter 15, these barriers to entry can have a substantial impact on the market.
[14] Anthony N. Cabot, Casino Gaming: Policy, Economics, and Regulation (1996).

priorities. In essence, people may interact with others differently in a community with gambling as opposed to a community without it. Gambling's emphasis on hedonism, luck, and wealth may affect the nature of these interactions. Undesirable values in the community at large may emerge, including a belief that persons are better off being lucky than working hard and that wealth is the most important attribute, therefore, everyone must have a price. Moralists believe that underlying some negative attitudes toward gambling is the fear of any activities that are hedonistic and the idea that pleasure for pleasure's sake is wrong or shows deviant behavior.[15] In contrast to the moralist,[16] the pragmatic amoral pluralist assesses whether an activity should be legal based on an objective evaluation that considers many principles and effects.[17]

For whatever reason a government decides that legal gambling is unacceptable, a policy of eradication requires intense regulation of an illegal gaming industry and seeks zero quantity outputs. Here, the legislature adopts comprehensive criminal laws that the criminal justice system must strictly enforce prohibiting all forms of gambling. The policy goals to prohibit all gambling opportunities are not achievable unless a framework exists to detect and prohibit gambling activities. It involves law enforcement mechanisms and court systems that enforce laws severe enough to deter a potential violator from engaging in the activity—usually through incarceration.

To be effective, laws must also be sufficiently precise to identify the prohibited gambling activity, and police and prosecutors must have sufficient resources and motivation to enforce such laws. While seemingly simple, activities that resemble gambling like fantasy sports[18] and pachinko[19] can become major industries by working around imprecise laws. Defining gambling is not simple, and missteps can lead to the creation of an unregulated gaming industry, like the pachinko and slot machine industries in Japan.

Non-enforcement

Non-enforcement occurs when a government's official public policy is to eradicate gambling, but it fails, intentionally or not, to deter the illegal activity. While laws prohibit gambling, police or prosecutors do not enforce

---

[15] *See* Vicky Abt, James F. Smith & Eugene M. Christiansen, The Business of Risk: Commercial Gambling in Mainstream America 115 (1985).

[16] Moralists can be either absolute or conservative; the latter allowing for change only within the narrow confines of the body setting the moral code, such as the Church. Jerome H. Skolnick, *Coercion to Virtue: The Enforcement of Morals*, 41 S. Cal. L. Rev. 588, 617–618 (1967).

[17] *See id.* at 618.

[18] Anthony N. Cabot & Louis V. Csoka, *Fantasy Sports: One Form of Mainstream Wagering in the United States*, 40 J. Marshall L. Rev. 1195 (2007).

[19] Erick C. Sibbitt, *Regulating Gambling in the Shadow of the Law: Form and Substance in the Regulation of Japan's Pachinko Industry*, 38 Harv. Int'l. L.J. 568 (1997).

those laws. As one U.S. study concluded: "[t]he meaning of gambling laws and the resulting constraints on gambling behavior are determined less by what legislators write than by how local police and prosecutors carry out their responsibilities."[20]

Non-enforcement occurs most frequently when the attitudes of the state and society, as a whole, differ. Government sets the attitude of the state through the adoption of laws. Popular sentiments define society's conscience as to the propriety of the activity. Usually, the attitudes of the state and society will be in harmony. For example, most people in society believe that a person who robs other people by force should be punished. If the laws and their enforcement attempt to prohibit and punish armed robbery, then the attitudes of the state and society are harmonious.

Perhaps, the greatest difference between the state (laws) and the public conscience in the United States occurred during Prohibition when the government unsuccessfully outlawed the sale of alcohol. Prohibition was a failure. According to one researcher:

Although consumption of alcohol fell at the beginning of Prohibition, it subsequently increased. Alcohol became more dangerous to consume; crime increased and became "organized"; the court and prison systems were stretched to the breaking point; and corruption of public officials was rampant. No measurable gains were made in productivity or reduced absenteeism. Prohibition removed a significant source of tax revenue and greatly increased government spending. It led many drinkers to switch to opium, marijuana, patent medicines, cocaine, and other dangerous substances that they would have been unlikely to encounter in the absence of Prohibition.[21]

Prohibition carried damaging effects far after its demise. It created a national network of organized crime well-financed by enormous alcohol profits.[22]

A more modern and germane example of non-enforcement is sports wagering in the United States. Determining how much is wagered on non-horse sporting events is difficult because virtually all is done illegally, and criminals do not keep open books or pay taxes. When the National Gambling Impact Study Commission (NGISC) issued its Final Report in 1998, its estimate of illegal sports gambling ranged as high as $380 billion annually.[23] More recent estimates for American football placed the Na-

---

[20] Nat'l Inst. Law Enforcement & Criminal Justice, D.O.J., NCJ 046259, Gambling Law Enforcement in Major American Cities (1978) [hereinafter, Nat'l Inst.].

[21] Mark Thornton, *Policy Analysis No. 157: Alcohol Prohibition Was a Failure*, Cato Inst., Jul. 17, 1991, http://www.cato.org/publications/policy-analysis/alcohol-prohibition-was-failure.

[22] *Id.*

[23] Nat'l Gambling Impact Study Comm'n, National Gambling Impact Study Commission Final Report 2-14 (1999), *available at* http://govinfo.library.unt.edu/ngisc/reports/fullrpt.html [hereinafter NGISC].

tional Football League at $80–100 billion annually[24] and college football at $60–70 billion.[25] Probably less than 1 percent of all sports wagering on human athletic events is done legally. Nevada's sports books, which are the only ones legal in the nation, saw $3.45 billion wagered in 2012,[26] up from $2.27 billion in 1998,[27] and realized net revenues of $170.1 million, excluding wagering on horseracing.[28]

Despite the staggering amount wagered illegally, the United States has lapsed into a general approach of non-enforcement of sports wagering laws, both at state and federal levels. Law enforcement efforts to deal with illegal sports wagering have declined dramatically in past decades.[29] In 1960, almost 123,000 arrests were made for gambling offenses.[30] By 2012, gambling arrests dipped to less than 8,000.[31] In contrast, the amount of illegally wagered dollars increased dramatically. In 1983, only about $8 billion were wagered on sports in the United States.[32] That amount increased by a multiple of over 25 in the ensuing 30 years.

Many reasons may contribute to this non-enforcement. First, law enforcement has reallocated its limited resources to more serious crimes.[33] Second, federal laws and prosecutorial policies have become increasingly confusing and contradictory.[34] Therefore, prosecutors may be less eager to test the laws for fear of creating bad precedent. Third, the penalties assessed against those who violate sports betting laws are often low and rarely justify the time or expense of law enforcement. Fourth, improvements in

---

[24] *Top Sports for Illegal Wagering: NFL Football*, CNBC.COM, http://www.cnbc.com/id/34312813/page/2.

[25] *Top Sports for Illegal Wagering: College Football*, CNBC.COM, http://www.cnbc.com/id/34312813/page/4.

[26] NEV. GAMING CONTROL BD., GAMING REVENUE REPORT (Dec. 2012), http://gaming.nv.gov/modules/showdocument.aspx?documentid=7618.

[27] NEV. GAMING CONTROL BD., GAMING REVENUE REPORT (Dec. 1998), http://gaming.nv.gov/modules/showdocument.aspx?documentid=3745.

[28] NEV. GAMING CONTROL BD., *supra* note 26.

[29] Robert Dorr, *With Police Mostly Sidelined, Sports Bettors Run Up the Score*, Omaha World-Herald, Jan. 31, 1999, at 1a, http://infoweb.newsbank.com.ezproxy.library.unlv.edu/iw-search/we/InfoWeb?p_product=AWNB&p_theme=aggregated5&p_action=doc&p_docid=12DD5BB31D96E3E0&p_docnum=2&p_queryname=1.

[30] Dan McGraw, *The National Bet*, U.S. NEWS & WORLD REP., APR. 7, 1997, at 50.

[31] Fed. Bureau of Investigation, *Crime in the U.S. 2012: Table 29*, FBI.GOV http://www.fbi.gov/about-us/cjis/ucr/crime-in-the-u.s/2012/crime-in-the-u.s.-2012/tables/29tabledatadecpdf. In 2012, the FBI estimated that these were 7,868 gambling arrests in the United States. *Id.* The actual figure for 1994 was 18,500 gambling arrests; it reached 21,000 in 1996, but it has decreased to 9,900 by 2010. In contrast, there were about 1.6 million arrests for drug violations in 2010. C. Puzzanchera & W. Kang, *Easy Access To FBI Arrest Statistics: 1994-2010*, http://www.ojjdp.gov/ojstatbb/ezaucr/ (select "Arrest Statistics" then choose option in "select a time period").

[32] McGraw, *supra* note 30.

[33] NAT'L INST., *supra* note 20 at 262. Gambling crimes 25 years ago were considered by police to be less serious than prostitution and about on par with after-hours liquor violations.

[34] NAT'L INST., *supra* note 20; Anthony N. Cabot & Louis V. Csoka, *The Games People Play: Is It Time for a New Legal Approach to Prize Games?*, 4 NEV. L.J. 197 (2004).

technology, such as the rise of the Internet, have made it more difficult to detect and prosecute offenders. Attempting to apprehend and prosecute gambling operators in foreign countries is a challenge.

Fifth, the public does not perceive sports gambling as a serious crime or even a crime at all. In the United States, wagering on fantasy sports is widespread. Office pools on sporting events, such as the NCAA basketball tournament and the NFL Super Bowl, flourish.[35] Governors frequently mark amateur championship games by "friendly" bets between themselves.[36] The media has contributed to the public perception that gambling on sports is an enjoyable and legal pastime. That newspapers post point spreads is just one additional indication that the public enjoys wagering on sporting events. The National Gambling Impact Study Commission in the United States claimed, albeit somewhat incredibly, that because point spreads are available in almost every major US newspaper, many people do not know that sports wagering is illegal.[37] Because most states have laws against sports wagering, law enforcement is placed in the uncomfortable position of enforcing laws unpopular with the public. This is not unique to the United States; gray market casinos openly operate in Tokyo and Taiwan,[38] and unlicensed after-hours mahjong parlors are common in Hong Kong.[39]

This should be a disturbing state of affairs. Citizens can lose respect for government if laws are not popular or enforced,[40] which may create an attitude that not all laws must be taken seriously.[41] Moreover, non-enforcement

---

[35] *March Madness: How to Win Your Office Pool*, Fiscal Times, Mar. 14, 2013, http://www.thefiscaltimes.com/Articles/2013/03/14/March-Madness-How-to-Win-Your-Office-Pool.

[36] Victoria Advocate, *Jindal Sends Saints Flag to Indiana Governor*, VictoriaAdvocate.com, Feb. 11, 2010, 4:01 AM, http://www.victoriaadvocate.com/news/2010/feb/11/bc-la-super-bowl-governors-bet/?sports&nfl.

[37] NGISC, *supra* note 23.

[38] *See, e.g., Gambling in Taiwan*, Islandside chronicle, Apr. 15, 2013, http://islandside-chronicles.wordpress.com/2013/04/15/gambling-in-taiwan/.

[39] Paul v. Kiatani et al., Presentation at The Second Asia Pac. Conference on Gambling & Commercial Gaming Research: The Third Place: A Sociological Investigation of Quasi-Legitimate Gambling Houses in Hong Kong (2013).

[40] Patricia Helsing, *Gambling—The Issues and Policy Decisions Involved in the Trend Toward Legalization, in* Gambling in America: Final Report of the Comm'n on the Review of the Nat'l Policy Toward Gambling 780 (1976).

[41] Once government adopts restrictive laws, repeal often is difficult with a divergence from the public conscience. Often, because of apathy, certain definable groups are under-represented at the polls. Proponents of a position vote and motivate others to vote for that position. Together, they have sufficient political power to convince legislators to adopt a prohibition. After adoption, however, the public may not support the prohibition. This creates disharmony between the attitudes of the state (laws) and the public conscience, which puts the politician in a difficult position. Any movement toward the repeal of the prohibition may incur opposition from the original proponents. Attempting to enforce the prohibition, however, accrues no political benefit as it alienates the politician from the public. This alienation may be beyond any corrupting influence exerted by those conducting illegal activities. The result is an illegal activity readily engaged in by the public without substantial police interference.

may lead the public to believe the police have become corrupt.[42] Although prohibited in its pure form in every state but Nevada, sports wagering is a public preoccupation resulting in mass illegal markets. Criminal operators capitalize by occupying a market forsaken by legitimate operators because of the sports prohibition while simultaneously using unethical means to maintain their businesses. Because of gambling's appeal to a broad sector of the community, protection requires police conspiracy through a system that prevents non-participatory police officers from exposing the conspiracy, thereby stopping the payoffs. Protection also may extend to corruption of politicians to facilitate police cooperation.[43]

PUBLIC POLICIES PERMITTING A GAMBLING INDUSTRY

The reasons for permitting gambling vary, and distinct public policy categories concerning gambling have emerged that reflect concerns with each reason. The categories are market model, player protection, government protection, industry capture, and hybrid model. Industry capture describes circumstances where industry interests prevail over public policy such that the industry itself controls—at least in part—how it is regulated. The final category, the hybrid model, acknowledges that more than one concern may exist to justify regulating legal gambling and recognizes that competing and complementary policies account for how some jurisdictions regulate the industry.

Market Model Approach

A market model approach envisions a gambling industry with no substantial barriers to entering or leaving the industry, with an abundance of potential competitors, and where both operators and players have perfect information about the pricing of homogeneous gambling offerings. This model should result in perfect competition where pricing results in no profit remaining after subtracting costs, including normal interest on capital, excesses required to cover risk, and managerial salary.[44] This assures a fair price to players in terms of odds and minimum bets. Government intervention into the market is often predicated to address market failure or redistribute wealth.

In many ways, gambling lends itself to a market model. The industry has few natural barriers to entry, such as a natural monopoly, with only some disruptions to a perfect market caused by imperfect information and externalities (negative impacts).

---

[42] NAT'L INST., *supra* note 20.

[43] Peter Reuter, *Police Regulation of Illegal Gambling: Frustrations of Symbolic Enforcement*, 474 ANNALS AM. ACAD. POL. & SOC. SCI. 36 (1984).

[44] *See, e.g.*, Avinash K. Dixit & Joseph E. Stiglitz, *Monopolistic Competition and Optimum Product Diversity*, 67 AM. ECON. REV. 297 (1977).

Absence of natural monopoly

First, many casino games are homogeneous public domain games, such as blackjack, baccarat, craps, and roulette. With little cash, a person can operate a gambling game. A pair of dice is all that is needed to offer craps. These games are identical if played in Macau or Las Vegas with rule modifications to change the odds and differing table limits to adjust pricing to the players. The homogenous nature of the gambling product results in minimal barriers to entry.

Two major interventions into the game industry can disrupt the market model: intellectual property rights and regulation. Gambling suppliers can differentiate products—ranging from proprietary table games like Three Card Poker to slot machines—to create artificial demand. While other games or slot machines exist, they are or are perceived to be imperfect substitutes for the new game. When the game's supplier has the right to exclude others from providing the game (perhaps due to trademark or patent protection), the game's provider obtains a monopoly whereby it can influence the market price by altering the rate of production. Because the differentiated product creates a demand over the homogeneous product, the monopoly provider realizes a profit above competitive prices by selling the product above the lowest possible average total cost and producing it at an inefficient output level. For a discussion of the economic impact regulation has on the market model, please refer to Chapter 5.

While artificial monopolies may pose a threat to the market model approach, gambling does not lend itself to one of the more important causes of market failure, a natural monopoly. This occurs when the average cost to a single company continues declining as production increases, such that one company can most efficiently produce the entire demand for the product. Natural monopolies can occur in industries with large fixed costs or where the existence of several large firms would entail the wasteful duplication of a product.[45] Evidence exists that casino gaming is subject to economies of scale in highly competitive gaming markets.[46] This is also consistent with the consolidation of casino properties into a handful of gaming companies in several markets like Las Vegas or Atlantic City. In these markets, the larger casino companies have a price advantage because they can distribute fixed costs such as licensing, legal, accounting, marketing compliance, and some salaries and wages for executives over multiple properties. Some fixed costs may be attributed to general and administra-

---

[45] George Stigler, *Monopoly*, THE CONCISE ENCYCLOPEDIA OF ECONOMICS (David R. Henderson ed., 2d ed. 2007). Some forms of gambling, like online poker, may be natural monopolies because of the desirability of liquidity (large number of players) and the scales of economy that may come from spreading the fixed costs of the poker infrastructure over a large number of players.

[46] *See, e.g.,* Zheng Gu, *Economies of Scale in the Gaming Industry: An Analysis of Casino Operations on the Las Vegas Strip and in Atlantic City*, 9 J. HOSPITALITY & FIN. MGMT. 1 (2001).

tive cost such as government requirements for non-gaming amenities (e.g., integrated resorts requirements) and regulation (e.g., surveillance, accounting, compliance, and licensing) as opposed to natural market forces (e.g., sales, marketing, purchasing, and training).[47]

Imperfect information

Information also affects whether a market is competitive. Without perfect information, consumers might buy the same goods or services from one supplier at a higher price than they could from another supplier. Information allows consumers to buy identical products at the lowest price and set the competitive price levels. Even when the products are not identical, perfect information allows consumers to make better decisions. Although products in a market are rarely homogeneous, they can be close substitutes. Therefore, consumers must know all facts about the product to make informed choices. Regulation might aid market efficiencies by increasing the supply of information, reducing uncertainties, and better matching supply and demand.

Availability of information in the gaming industry is uneven. Most games are homogeneous products. The fundamentals of craps, blackjack, or any other table game at one casino are usually identical to every other casino. Differences in odds and table limits reflect differences in the price that players must pay to play the game. A game's odds are pricing information. With table games, the odds and table limits are usually known to or ascertainable by the players. Most blackjack players know that using multiple decks increases the house advantage[48] and, therefore, all other rules being equal, a single-deck game is preferable. Literally hundreds of available sources provide detailed statistical breakdowns as to the odds of every casino game based on individual casino rules. If players do not like the game that the casino offers, they can either go elsewhere or not play.

Casinos set prices on games by setting the odds and table limits. Odds variations may be accomplished (i) through rule variations that are more or less favorable to the player or (ii) by altering the payoffs on certain wagers.[49] Regardless of the method, the resulting change in house advantage determines how much it costs a player to play a game. Examples of games in which rule variations can affect the odds are blackjack and craps. In blackjack, a rule requiring the dealer to hit a soft seventeen increases the house advantage 0.2 percent from a table where the dealer must stand on soft seventeen.[50]

---

[47] *Id.*

[48] Based on mathematical algorithms applicable to a particular casino game, "[f]rom the caisno's perspective, the house advantage represents how much, in terms of percentage of the money wagered, the casino can expect to retain in the long run." Hannum & Cabot, *supra* note 7, at 19 (2d ed. 2005).

[49] *See generally id.*

[50] The number of decks used, no soft doubling, and no re-splitting of pairs are other ex-

Once the odds on a game are set, the casinos also can impact price by the level of the minimum bet. For example, a minimum wager in Macau may be as high as the equivalent of US$35, while in Las Vegas the same table may have a US$10 minimum bet. All other things being equal such as the number of hands dealt per hour, the pricing would be three-and-a-half times higher in Macau than Las Vegas.

Notable exceptions to the availability of information on pricing in the gaming industry are reel-type and video gaming devices. Players are incapable of figuring out the odds on the device and minimum bet.[51] They must rely on other sources. One source of information is gaming industry advertising (e.g., casinos that advertise the payback on their gaming devices).[52] This could theoretically induce players to patronize the casino with the best odds. Other casino advertising is less helpful, such as claiming their gaming devices are "loose." This implies a high percentage of all coins played are paid back to players. While players may infer the product is offered at a lower price, the advertisement does not provide a means of comparison. It is mere "puffing."

Externalities

Negative externalities—the costs an activity imposes on third parties—is another relevant source of market failure. Externalities often concern the public health or safety. An example of a regulatory agency assigned to mitigate externalities is the Environmental Protection Agency. The perceived externalities of gambling will often shape a jurisdiction's public policy toward gaming. These externalities include lost productivity from

---

amples of rule variations in blackjack that affect the overall price of the game to the player. Likewise, the "free odds" bet in craps can vary the price of the game product by the odds that can be taken. A player who bets the pass line and takes single odds is at a 0.85 percent disadvantage, but only a 0.61 percent with double odds, and 0.47 percent with triple odds. This means for every $100 wagered on the pass line with single odds ($50 pass line and $50 odds), on the average, the player will pay a price of about $0.85 while $100 bet on the pass line with triple odds ($25 pass line and $75 odds) will cost about $0.47. A casino allowing triple odds offers a better priced craps game than one that permits only single odds. Some casinos have offered as high as 100X odds; a player taking full 100X odds will face only a 0.02 percent house advantage on the combined pass line (or come) and odds wagers. *See generally id.*

[51] Kurt Eggert, *Truth in Gaming: Toward Consumer Protection in the Gambling Industry*, 63 MD. L. REV. 217 (2004). Unlike most table games, slot machines possess elements that influence the odds of a particular device that a player would not be able to properly calculate in determining those odds for himself, including random number generators, the casino's ability to alter the probability of certain events occurring, and the likelihood that a particular symbol will stop in a particular spot based on these and other factors. *See id.*

[52] To address the unique nature of gaming devices, minimum regulatory standards for gaming devices are the most common form of price setting in the gaming industry. These are discussed in Chapter 11. The concept of advertising may itself be inconsistent with policy goals espoused by the player protection goals that discourage stimulation of gaming activities.

problem gambling, financial consequences to the player's family, reducing community resources, and stress on community infrastructure (e.g., traffic congestion and police services).[53] Opponents of legalized gambling argue these externalities should lead to a policy of eradication. They claim the availability of convenient gambling increases the incidence of dysfunctional gamblers whose costs to the players or third parties (e.g., family members) are not compensated by the gaming industry.[54] They argue that not all externalities can be attenuated by regulation, and the cost will exceed the benefits that can be derived from legal gaming.

If negative externalities are present and are not internalized by casinos (as part of their costs) or players, the industry will oversupply their specific product (casino games). If the government imposed taxes on casinos to reflect these externality-related costs, the market equilibrium would be a lower quantity (less gambling) at a higher price.[55]

Correcting market failures

Typically, under a market model approach government will intervene into a legal gaming industry where necessary to correct market imperfections. This approach does not reflect a moral or social bias against gambling, nor does it recognize that government has any special obligations to protect the industry.

In a perfectly competitive economy, market forces would determine pricing because the players would have access to all the information necessary to determine the costs of playing and could choose the best price among multiple competitors. Most gaming markets, however, are not perfect and regulators may attempt to ensure fairness by either requiring disclosure of game odds, setting the maximum price a casino can charge players for the gambling experience, or prohibiting games with a high house advantage. Regulations requiring minimum paybacks alone may protect uninformed participants against unexpected outcomes resulting from not having the proper information to judge risk, but these regulations are a poor substitute for actual pricing as the competitive market is more efficient at setting a fair price than regulators.

The market solution to negative externalities is to tax an activity consis-

---

[53] *See* Douglas M. Walker & A. H. Barnett, *The Social Costs of Gambling: An Economic Perspective*, 15 J. GAMBLING STUD. 181 (1999).

[54] *See supra* Chapter 1.

[55] In the gaming industry, the pricing of the gaming experience is not as simple as other businesses where the price of the product goes up if the cost of producing the product increases. Casinos provide games for players to play. Casinos make money by winning it from players. The amount won results from the slight advantage the casino has in the odds of the game, which can be as little as about 1 percent in craps and blackjack. To raise prices, the casino must adjust the odds of the games so that it wins more often or more on a given hand. *See generally infra* Chapter 14. As the costs rise, however, demand for the product decreases if demand is price elastic. The higher the regulatory costs, the smaller the casino product market will become.

tent with the cost of the externality and redistribute the taxes to address the costs imposed on third parties or society. As one economist noted:

> A pigovian tax[56] that is equal in size to the negative externalities caused by gambling is found to improve economic welfare. That is, by forcing the market to internalize the harm caused by the industry—typically called the social costs of gambling—both producers and consumers will be forced to pay the full costs of consumption, including those costs borne on the rest of society. Due to the perceived relationship between problem gamblers and external social costs, gambling industries that tend to have higher rates of problem gambling should be taxed at a higher relative rate. However, many casinos are designed to draw patrons from foreign jurisdictions, and therefore would warrant lower pigovian tax rates since the externalities are not incurred by the local economy.[57]

This alone may not reduce problem gambling as government may not redistribute the tax revenue to gambling treatment/prevention programs but may use it for other public goods or services deemed more beneficial. If the tax is variable according to the magnitude of the financial impact of problem gambling, however, the industry may have a financial incentive to reduce problem gambling by adapting internal harm minimization programs to identify and assist problem gamblers through outreach or exclusion.

A pure market model approach to gambling regulation is rare. While some major jurisdictions have been criticized as under-regulated, almost all have some non-market driven regulation such as licensing or technical approvals of gaming devices. A market model approach is more commonly applied to low stakes or charitable gaming. Governments often impose greater restrictions on business activities based not on the activity but on the monetary amounts involved. Government may decide small-stakes gambling is harmless but that players need protection from high-stakes gambling. These governments may apply a market model approach to some forms of low-stakes gambling and a government protection approach to high-stakes gambling, or even ban high-stakes gambling altogether.[58]

---

[56] Named after economist Arthur Pigou, a pigovian tax is applied to a market activity that creates externalities that equal the amount of the social cost of the activity. *See generally* A. C. Pigou, The Economics Of Welfare (4th ed. 1960).

[57] Kahlil S. Philander, *A Normative Analysis of Gambling Tax Policy*, 17 UNLV Gaming Res. & Rev. J. 17, 23 (2013).

[58] Charitable gaming is common in many American states and in foreign countries where commercial casino gaming is prohibited. While government may approach licensing of charitable gaming with no more intensity than licensing other businesses; the revenues generated by charitable gaming are often significant. In Minnesota, about $1.1 billion is wagered on pull-tabs each year. Shannon Prather, *Pulltabs, Other Charitable Gambling Up 8.6 Percent Across Minnesota*, Star Tribune, Dec. 9, 2013, 9:16 PM, http://www.star-tribune.com/local/north/235166491.html. In Mississippi, licenses to conduct low-stakes bingo games are routinely granted with little regulatory scrutiny, while applicants wishing to operate high-stakes games must undergo more rigorous licensing and follow more stringent regulations. *Compare* Charitable Gaming Div., Miss. Gaming Comm'n, §4.1.1,

Figure 2.1

Player Protection Goals
Games are honest
- Verified RNG or random event   - Preventing third party intervention
Games are fair
- Lowest price possible (no special taxation of gambling, low table limits, best odds)
- Reasonable opportunity of winning
Players are secure in their deposits, payments, transfers, and account balances.
No demand stimulation
- No advertising   - No entertainment
- Waiting periods   - No comps
Protected groups
- Age
- Poor
Problem gambling deterrents
- Prohibition against the use of credit   - No 24/7 gambling
- Operator or player set daily loss limits   - Maximum or player set playing times
- Display of time at play   - Advertising restrictions

Player Protection Goals

A player protection approach engineers a legal gambling industry around social and public health issues.[59] The social engineering involves designing a gaming industry that is legal but only meets the unstimulated demand for gambling in a society. The public health concerns dictate that policy goals should include providing maximum protection for players (and those associated with the player) against the negative impact of an activity inherently designed to the economic disadvantage of the player.

Social engineering

The late Reverend Gordon Moody, former Secretary, Churches' Council on Gambling (UK), describes a gaming industry "legalized and arranged for gamblers."[60] Inherent in this approach is that between unlawful gambling and regulated gambling, the latter is preferable as it better ensures player protections. Proponents believe that stimulating the demand for casino gaming is undesirable because it increases social burdens. For example, if encouraged to gamble, the poor may use non-discretionary dollars for gambling instead of for essentials. Either the standard of living goes down, or the government must provide additional services. Policies behind these theories include that casinos should not engage in exploiting players

---

License Application to Conduct Charitable Bingo (2010), http://www.msgamingcommission.com/images/uploads/cgd_app_charbingolic.pdf. (the Mississippi application for low stakes bingo) and Casino Gaming Miss. Gaming Comm'n, http://www.msgamingcommission.com/index.php/forms_procedures/casino_gaming/ (providing the applications for casino licensure).

[59] David Korn, Roger Gibbins & Jason Azmier, *Framing Public Policy Towards a Public Health Paradigm for Gaming*, 19 J. GAMBLING. STUD. 235 (2003).

[60] Gordon Moody, *Legalized Gambling: For or Against Gamblers*, 9 GAMBLING PAPERS: PROC. FIFTH NAT'L CONF. ON GAMBLING & RISK TAKING 12 (1981).

by promoting gambling, nor should they encourage players to wager more than they can afford to lose or more than they would if not stimulated to do so. Moody also argued that the government should not take taxes from gambling except as levied on any other transaction and should not permit gambling products that provide the highest return for the operators.[61]

Implementation of these goals often involves prohibitions against the casinos from advertising, offering entertainment, sponsoring junkets, conducting any other activities which might stimulate interest in casino gaming, or having mandatory exclusion of problem gamblers. To assure unstimulated demand, government intentionally adopts gaming regulations that hinder industry growth and strictly enforces those regulations even if it decreases industry revenues.

In Great Britain, where the purest form of this approach was *once* found, an applicant for a casino license had to prove that a substantial unstimulated demand existed for a casino to obtain a license. Unlike other businesses, a successful license applicant could not advertise, offer complimentary services, provide entertainment, or use any other methods to promote the casino or gambling.

Social engineering has among its goals to ensure that the games are honest and fair and that player transactions (deposits, payments, and transfers) and account balances are secure. Honesty refers to whether the casino operator offers games whose determinative outcomes are random. Randomness in gaming is the observed unpredictability and absence of pattern in a set of elements or events that have definite probabilities of occurrence.[62] This could be the shuffle of the cards in blackjack, the roll of the dice in craps, or the random number generator in a slot machine. A slot machine is honest if the outcome of each play is not predetermined or influenced beyond the established house advantage (or player's skill) in the gaming operator's or another player's favor.

A second aspect of honesty is whether forces outside of the established rules of the game influence the outcome. Take, as an example, community poker. The method of shuffling/distributing cards must meet prescribed standards of randomness. But, beyond this, the game must be free of col-

---

[61] *Id.*

[62] The concept of random is elusive and its precise meaning has long been debated among experts in the fields of probability, statistics, and the philosophical sciences. Some dictionaries might define random in a more general sense while others will provide a meaning in a more specific statistical sense. *Compare* THE AMERICAN HERITAGE DICTIONARY 1025 (2d college ed. 1991) (defining random as "[h]aving no specific pattern or objective; haphazard"), *and* THE CONCISE OXFORD DICTIONARY 1185 (10th ed. 1999) (defining random as "made, done, or happening without . . . conscious decision"), *with* WEBSTER'S II NEW COLLEGE DICTIONARY 916 (2001) (defining random as "an event having a relative frequency of occurrence that approaches a stable limit as the number of observations of the event increases to infinity"), *and* THE AMERICAN HERITAGE DICTIONARY OF THE ENGLISH LANGUAGE (5th ed. 2013), http://ahdictionary.com/word/search.html?q=random&submit.x=52&submit.y=13 (defining random as "[o]f or relating to an event in which all outcomes are equally likely").

lusion between players and have controls to prevent players from gaining an advantage by having access to other players' hole cards or unexposed cards in the deck.

Fairness deals with whether the operators offer games that give the players a reasonable opportunity of winning. This relates to price setting because game odds and table limits determine the cost to play house banked casino games and rake requirements determine the cost of playing community pooled games like poker.[63]

While a player protection approach focuses on the concerns above, this broad public policy can seek to protect the player (and related parties) from other potential harms. Notable examples include protecting players from risks to player data and privacy and ensuring casino operators timely pay winnings and protect and return player funds on deposit with the casino.

Public health

Public health issues dictate additional goals designed to minimize the impact of problem gambling. These goals have been described as follows:

- Prevent gambling-related problems in individuals and groups at risk of gambling addiction;
- Promote informed and balanced attitudes, behaviors and policies towards gambling and gamblers both by individuals and by communities; and
- Protect vulnerable groups from gambling-related harm.[64]

A more detailed analysis of the impact policy goals have on public health can be found in Chapter 1.

Like all reasoned public polices, a policy statement is a foundational tool. Korea provides an example of a public policy statement centered on player protection. The Korea National Gambling Control Commission (NGCC) adopted the following goal statement to regulate gambling in Korea:

Without appropriate integration, control and supervision, the gaming industry will prevail in the entire society and cause various social pathologies such as gambling addiction, broken families, laxity at work, reckless pursuit of fortune and crimes. The National Gambling Control Commission is taking all possible measures to promote appropriate policies with an aim to prevent such side effects and establish a 'safe and reliable gambling' culture.[65]

Because the state's policy—player protection—is clear, the commission can establish policy goals consistent with this policy.[66]

---

[63] *See generally* HANNUM & CABOT, *supra* note 7.

[64] Korn, *supra* note 59, at 246.

[65] *Goals of NGCC: Safe & Responsible Gambling*, NAT'L GAMBLING CONTROL COMM'N, http://ngcc.go.kr/eng/ngcc03.html.

[66] *See Duties of NGCC: Establishing a Healthy Leisure Industry*, NAT'L GAMBLING CONTROL COMM'N,http://ngcc.go.kr/eng/ngcc04_1.html.

Figure 2.2

Player Protection – Goals, Options, and Implementation		
Policy Goals	Examples of Regulatory Options	Implementation
Fairness	Minimum payback Testing of equipment Low taxes	Testing Licensing Auditing
Honesty	Equipment testing Oversight of game play	Testing Enforcement
Assuring Payment of Winnings	Minimum reserves/ segregated funds	Auditing
Protected Classes	Prohibiting minors: identification checks Problem gambling exclusion lists Mandated casino training and intervention regarding problem gambling Implementation of tools to identify problem gamblers	Enforcement
Public Education	Problem gambling warnings, responsible gambling awareness	Outreach/Enforcement
Preventing Demand Stimulation	No Advertising No comps No entertainment	Enforcement
Social Impact	Prohibitions against the use of credit Operator or player set daily loss limits Maximum or player set playing times Display of time at play Advertising restrictions	Enforcement
Other protection	Protection of player data and privacy	Enforcement

Government Protection Goals

Like player protection goals, government protection goals can be met through strict regulation of a legal gaming industry. While a player protection approach provides regulation to safeguard the player, a government protection approach supports the government's economic and political interests such as generating new taxes, creating new jobs, revitalizing urban areas or stimulating employment. For example, the public policy toward gambling in Ohio is government protection oriented. Ohio memorialized its interests in the state constitution:

Casino gaming shall be authorized at four casino facilities (a single casino at a designated location within each of the cities of Cincinnati, Cleveland, and Toledo, and within Franklin County) *to create new funding for cities, counties, public school districts, law enforcement, the horse racing industry and job training for Ohio's workforce.*[67] (Emphasis added.)

---

[67] OHIO CONST. art. XV, § 6 (2014).

Figure 2.3

Tax Rate Examples		
Jurisdiction	Tax Rate	How Derived
Pennsylvania	55%	State Tax (34%), Local Share Assessment (4%), Economic Development and Tourism Fund (5%), Pennsylvania Race Horse Development Fund (approx. 12%)
Macau	38–39%	Gross Gaming Revenue tax (35%), Contribution to the Macao Foundation (1.6%), and contribution to the Infrastructure/Tourism/Social Security Fund (1.4% for one licensee or 2.4% for all others)
Ohio	33%	Gross Gaming Revenues.
South Korea	20%	Gaming Revenues.
Singapore	12–22%	Gross Gaming Revenue generated from premium players tax (5%), Gross Gaming Revenue from other players tax (15%), and Goods and Services Tax on all Gaming Revenue (7%)
Mississippi	12%	State tax (8%), plus up to 4% local tax
New Jersey	9.25%	Gross Revenue tax (8%) and Casino Redevelopment fee (1.25%)
Nevada	7.75%	Gross Revenue tax (6.75%) and miscellaneous tax (1%)

Here, Ohio has not only stated the purpose of casinos is to raise tax revenue and create jobs, but also that it will only allow casinos as an oligopoly. This may be for many reasons, such as limiting the proliferation of gambling or overcoming political opposition to neighborhood gambling. Given the explicit government protection goals listed in the statute, however, a likely reason for this provision is that the state may maximize its gain through collecting some economic rents described later in this chapter.

To some, it is confusing when a government proclaims gambling is a moral and acceptable activity and simultaneously has an extraordinary regulatory apparatus. The regulation required to achieve government protection goals is analogous to the number of restrictions that a bank may put on a business to which it lends money. Although the bank wants to see a business succeed and will help a borrower when it can, its main obligation is protecting its assets consistent with risk. A bank may only require a simple one-page promissory note for a $100 loan. In contrast, loan papers for a $100 million loan will likely be voluminous. The larger the loan, the more concerned the bank will be to protect its interests. Government protection goals and corresponding regulations are more sophisticated where the government relies heavily on the gaming industry to meet tax expectations, provide employment, or stimulate economic growth. Like a bank, one government role is to ensure the government receives its fair monetary return from tax revenues. (Chapter 13 delves into greater detail on the subject of taxes.) Unlike a bank, the government's interest in regulating the gaming industry goes beyond proper accounting controls.

Whether gambling is immoral or produces undesirable social effects is not a direct policy behind a government protection approach. These goals do not seek to minimize negative externalities unless their costs exceed their benefits to the government or are necessary to protect broader governmental or political interests. For example, if voters are inclined to revoke legal gambling (or not reelect a politician) because gambling is impacting the quality of community life, then the government may act to improve community services. Likewise, government will look to curb negative externalities when their costs exceed the benefits of the regulated activity. For example, not preventing a casino from cheating a player may create a short-term benefit (e.g., increased profits resulting in increased tax revenue), but over time the industry will suffer if the public perceives the industry as dishonest. The gaming industry is willing to pay for these regulatory costs because they provide a tangible benefit. When the regulation is more than what the industry requires to capture benefits, however, that willingness vanishes. Likewise, when the cost of treatment related to problem gambling becomes a significant burden to government, it may implement measures to reduce its impact. Under these goals, however, jurisdictions with a predominately tourist base are unlikely to give significant attention to problem gambling because the impact is exported.[68] A more detailed analysis addressing problem gambling can be found in Chapter 10.

Under a government protection approach, a government realizes it has significant economic power because gambling is an industry that was historically illegal. By legalizing gambling, the government has the rare opportunity to seize a large portion of the economic rents by issuing regional monopoly or oligopoly licenses. These artificial quotas allow the government to manipulate prices (or set equilibrium quantities) above (or below) what would be achieved in a competitive market. The licensed operator may capture some of the economic rents while the government may realize others in higher taxes. Some of these economic rents can also be directed toward the development of non-gaming related amenities in integrated resorts, discussed below, that the casino operator might not otherwise provide in a competitive market.

Government protection goals can have a direct economic basis. As Dr. Skolnick noted, Australia was among the first to popularize the Zoning Merit Selection System[69] for the selection of casino operators based on the creation of integrated resorts. The government can use the Zoning Merit Selection System for both social planning and to minimize opposition by setting criteria for size, costs, amenities, and location of the casino. After that, the government could ask for a request for proposals.[70] After receiving proposals, the government can then choose between candidates based on

---

[68] Philander, *supra* note 57, at 21.
[69] Jerome H. Skolnick, *A Zoning Merit Model for Casino Gambling*, 474 ANNALS AM. ACAD. POL. & SOC. SCI. 48 (1984).
[70] *Id.*

experience, project specifications, and other qualifications.[71] The government is effectively a partner to the enterprise and needs to protect both its real and political capital in the success of the project.

The integrated resort model poses two major economic challenges. First, creation of a monopoly or oligopoly to justify the investment and its accompanying higher pricing supports the extraordinary cost of the resort model. This is the antithesis of a player protection model that Reverend Moody described as "legalized and arranged for gamblers" because the economic rents are passed on to the players in higher prices (i.e., worse odds).[72] Second, governments need to be adept in calculating the division of economic rents between it and the selected operators. A government could create a regional monopoly by granting only one or a few licenses with the intent of capturing economic rents associated with monopoly pricing (by way of high taxes) (discussed in Chapter 5). This absolute barrier to entry can create extraordinary profits for the licensee if the government fails to properly assess the market in granting the regional monopoly.

Government protection goals need not have genesis based on acquisition of economic rents where a state has significant reliance on an industry for employment and growth. This can be markedly different from placing quotas on casinos and may be more consistent with market goals. Nevada provides an interesting historical perspective. Nevada has a relatively low gaming tax rate (a maximum of 6.75 percent of gross revenues)[73] and modest government-imposed barriers to entry, so the capture of economic rents based on limiting competition was not its major focus. Between 1931 and 1978, Nevada was the only state with legal casino gaming. Nevada regulated gaming in the late 1950s to keep criminals out of the gaming industry. It feared that the federal government would outlaw casino gaming if organized crime used Nevada-based operations to finance or conceal profits from other illegal activities.[74] Once the threat of direct intervention was minimized, reasons for keeping criminals out of the industry were broadened to help develop the industry.[75] Principally, this concerned broadening the player base and opening financial markets. Increased regulation helped create the perception that criminals were not involved in casino operations and that the games were honest.[76] Keeping the criminal element out

---

[71] *Id.*

[72] *See generally* Moody, *supra* note 60.

[73] Nev. Rev. Stat. § 463.370(1) (2013).

[74] Eugene M. Christiansen, *The Role of Government in Commercial Gaming*, 1 Gambling Stud.: Proc. Sixth Nat'l Conf. On Gambling & Risk Taking 128 (1984).

[75] For example, when New Jersey allowed casinos, its purposes for licensing extended beyond those of Nevada. Richard Lehne, Casino Policy 45–46 (1984). Likewise, the public policy of Nevada toward gaming has evolved since 1931, as shown by the additions to its policy statement to include, as example, that casinos do not "unduly impact the quality of life enjoyed by residents of the surrounding neighborhoods," and "that the rights of the creditors of licensees are protected." Nev. Rev. Stat. § 463.0129(1)(b) (1999).

[76] Alfred N. King, *Public Gaming and Public Trust*, 12 Conn. L. Rev. 740 (1980).

Figure 2.4

Government Protection Goals	
Direct Harm	Indirect Harm
Tax and tax evasion	Federal or legislative intervention
Employment	Player rejection of protections
Economic development	Conduct consistent with other government goals
	Money laundering

also helped the government ensure proper accounting for tax revenues.[77] As Nevada showed, the gaming industry faces eradication if the gambling public perceives the industry as dishonest or associated with organized crime. As a growth industry, gaming needs the support of capital markets, such as banks and stock exchanges. Access to these markets is often contingent on favorable perceptions of the gaming industry by these institutions.[78] Under a government protection approach, government attempts to create the characteristics that will encourage the financial market to invest in the gaming industry.

Nevada is brutally honest as to its policy goals, including the statement that "[t]he continued growth and success of gaming is dependent *upon public confidence and trust* that licensed gaming and the manufacture, sale and distribution of gaming devices and associated equipment are conducted honestly and competitively . . . and that gaming is free from criminal and corruptive elements" (emphasis added).[79] While subtle, the statement focuses on public confidence and trust as opposed to assuring the honesty of the games for strict player protection purposes. The best way to assure that the public perceives the games as honest is through regulation mandating the games actually function as such.

But, what happens if things go wrong? Government has several roles in protecting its own interests. The first is as a vehicle for the industry to gain and uphold credibility in order to maintain a vibrant industry that has access to capital, helps fund government and creates jobs.[80] Its existence in many places is tenuous. Governments respond to these external challenges by providing a mechanism to assure a national government, the voting public, actual and potential players, and the financial community that the industry is honest and free of criminals. This mechanism involves licensing and detection and strict discipline of casino operators who tarnish the perception of honesty and freedom from criminal elements. Most casino operators realize this protection is effective only if

---

[77] Richard I. Aaron, *Maintaining Financial Integrity of the Casino Through Licensing Regulation*, 9 Gambling Papers: Proc. Fifth Nat'l Conf. On Gambling & Risk Taking 127 (1982).

[78] William R. Eadington, *The Casino Gaming Industry: A Study of Political Economy*, 474 Annals Am. Acad. Pol. & Soc. Sci. 23, 25 (1984).

[79] Nev. Rev. Stat. § 463.0129(1)(b) (2013).

[80] Another goal that often accompanies the protection of the industry is the protection of the state's principal interest in tax revenues. Stringent accounting, auditing, and reporting requirements accomplish this.

provided by government. Convincing others that the industry is honest and free of criminals by self-regulation is difficult, if not impossible. Therefore, most operators are willing to subject themselves to losses of freedoms, risk, and expense as the price of maintaining the desired public perception. Often, this price is high. To achieve the desired results, governments create a burdensome licensing process, costly accounting and reporting systems, and disciplinary procedures that could cause severe fines or license revocation.

Government's second role is to protect its own financial interests. Because the primary gambling benefit is often tax revenues, a government must provide such accounting controls and audit functions as it deems reasonable to ensure it receives its fixed share. This requires a much greater focus on accounting regulations, including internal controls and audit functions, than given under the player protection approach. Where the benefits are ancillary (such as employment), government checks ensure that casinos comply with all legislative mandates for protecting jobs through regulatory actions such as imposing a receivership rather than closing a non-compliant casino.

A third role is to promote and defend the gaming industry. This requires the government to take an active interest in convincing the outside world the regulatory system has successfully excluded organized crime and is protecting the honesty of the games. When attacked, the government typically defends the industry against its critics.

Government's fourth role is to provide a vehicle for solving the industry's problems. For example, no single casino may be capable of testing equipment or games sold by distributors to assure they cannot be manipulated or cheated to the casino's detriment. Equipping and maintaining a lab and employing trained personnel would be too costly for one casino. Therefore, government, through collective funding from casino taxes, may finance and operate a games laboratory to provide this function.[81] Expert law enforcement also may be available to detect and apprehend criminals who cheat the casinos. This requires employing agents trained in cheating detection and special laws to address the peculiarities of the gaming industry.

Another role for government involvement is to keep the gaming industry from interfering with paramount government goals. For example, the government may be more interested in preventing the gaming industry from becoming a conduit for money laundering because its cost to society may be higher than any benefit the gaming industry may realize from not having to police cash transactions.

---

[81] As an alternative, the private sector could provide these same functions. In fact, several private gaming laboratories will review and certify gaming equipment. Government roles in these circumstances are to assure that the laboratories are competent and perform the certifications to government standards.

Industry Capture/Influence

The quote "what is good for Ford is good for America" was attributed to American industrialist Henry Ford, the founder of Ford Motors.[82] What is advantageous regulation for casino owners, however, is not necessarily good regulation. Corporations control most casinos and have a principal responsibility to derive profit for their shareholders. While many casino companies undertake actions that contribute to a competitive economy, are fair to the players, and are socially responsible, including the minimization of problem gambling, governments should not expect this to be the norm.

Government should create regulation designed to direct casino behavior in a way that is consistent with public policy. This does not mean, however, that the industry cannot benefit from player or government protection goals. When considering some government protection goals, such as maximizing employment, the interests of government and the industry are often congruent. Even when the goals are different, the regulatory solution could be the same, benefiting the government, the players, and the industry. For example, government may police and arrest people who cheat in the casino. Arresting cheaters benefits players by preventing theft, benefits the industry by protecting casino revenues, and benefits the government by ensuring revenues are collected and taxes are maximized.

Other times, however, the regulated industry influences the regulatory process solely for its own profit maximizing goals. Regulatory capture is often associated with the teachings of George Stigler. He postulated that "as a [general] rule . . . regulation is acquired by the industry and is designed and operated primarily for its benefit."[83] This acquisition, argues Stigler, comes about because the industry can use the regulatory machinery to (1) acquire cash subsidies, (2) limit entry, (3) gain control over complements and substitutes, and (4) help in price-fixing schemes.[84]

---

[82] *Quotes By and About Henry Ford*, Abelard.org, Feb. 14, 2014, http://www.abelard.org/ford/ford4_quotes.php.

[83] George J. Stigler, *The Theory of Economic Regulation*, 2 Bell J. Econ. & Mgmt. Sci. 3, 3 (1971). Others liken regulatory agencies to stages of life. Gestation is when the agency is born of sincere belief that issues of public importance exist that can be managed by regulation. In its youth, the agency is exuberant but vulnerable and inexperienced and can be manipulated by the regulated. As support for the agency fades from the public conscience, it enters the maturing stage where "[r]egulation becomes more expert and settled, but as the agency moves out of the ...mainstream it begins to pay increasing attention to the needs of industry." Robert Baldwin, Martin Cave & Martin Lodge, Understanding Regulation: Theory, Strategy, And Practice 47 (2d ed. 2012); In its mature stage, a regulatory agency becomes "more concerned with the general health of the industry and tries to prevent changes which adversely affect it. Cut off from the mainstream of political life, the commission's standards...are determined in...light of the desires of the industry affected." Marver H. Bernstein, Regulating Business By Independent Commission 87 (1955).

[84] George J. Stigler, The Citizen and the State: Essays on Regulation, 116 (1975). The acquisition of cash subsidies, Stigler's first reason for industry to demand regulation,

Economist Sam Peltzman, expounding on the works of Stigler, theorized that while the regulated will attempt to influence the regulatory process, no single economic interest could capture a regulatory body.[85] Peltzman proposed that a regulatory equilibrium exists where politicians act to maximize political returns. In other words, elected politicians follow a course of action that most likely ensures their reelection. When faced with regulating an industry, politicians will balance the benefits and costs to the regulated, the public, and other interest groups to maximize chance of reelection.[86]

Interest analysis assumes that interest groups or their members influence the course of regulation to their economic favor. [87] A major determinate of whether an interest group's influence affects regulation is the extent of the influence that can be exercised and is exercised by each interested party. The intensity and strength of an interest group determine the balance of political power on a subject.[88] Professor Louis Jaffe noted that "[t]he elements of this political process are common to all potential lawmaking activity—the intensity of a given problem, the degree to which it is felt throughout an organized and stable constituency, and the representation (or lack thereof) of varying interests within and without the lawmaking body."[89] An interest group tends not to have intense feelings about a subject where it is only marginally, or not at all, affected by the outcome. This is because the transaction cost of influencing the outcome exceeds the benefit from the result.[90]

---

is tenuous because it would tend to excite entry by new firms. Cash subsidies would only be sought by an industry having control over entry or if the subsidies could be earmarked for existing firms. Although Stigler appears to come to this realization in *The Citizen and the State*, his same general argument holds for his contention that an industry demands regulation to control complements and substitutes, and to assist in price-fixing schemes.

[85] *See* Sam Peltzman, *The Economic Theory of Regulation After a Decade of Deregulation*, 1989 BROOKINGS PAPERS ON ECON. ACTIVITY (SPECIAL ISSUE) 1 (1989).

[86] For an excellent discussion on the government role in a political-economic decision game, see Grossman's and Helpman's work related to free-trade agreements which can be extended to other areas, such as regulations. Gene M. Grossman & Elhanan Helpman, *The Politics of Free-Trade Agreements*, 85 AM. ECON. REV. 667 (1995).

[87] During the constitutional debate, the anti-federalists adopted Madisonian or republican concepts. They urged decentralized government where citizen participation could involve the concepts of public virtues necessary to overcome faction politics. Interest group theory is grounded in the pluralist concept. Here, the discrete factions dictate political outcomes through promoting their self-interest. Cass R. Sunstein, *Interest Groups in American Public Law*, 38 STAN L. REV. 29, 32–33 (1985). Federalists, however, did not espouse the pluralist concept. They, like the anti-federalists, did not accept that interest group politics would result in compromise that would promote the public good. Instead, they envisioned a large republic with checks and balances to control the self-interested representation. *Id.* at 39, 43–44.

[88] Henry H. Perritt, Jr., *Negotiated Rulemaking Before Federal Agencies: Evaluation of Recommendations by the Administrative Conference of the United States*, 74 GEO. L.J. 1625, 1640 (1986).

[89] Louis L. Jaffe, *The Illusion of the Ideal Administration*, 86 HARV. L. REV. 1183, 1188 (1973).

[90] ROBERT A. DAHL, A PREFACE TO DEMOCRATIC THEORY, 48–50 (1956).

If the public, as the consumer, lacks sophistication or information, they are unlikely to be organized or have collective abilities to assert political power. Consumers tend to be unsophisticated unless an issue becomes salient in their lives. Where the public is not the consumer, its interest is not the cost of the product but rather receiving a share of the wealth through taxing the industry.

Interest groups have greater interest in issues that affect their well-being. Peltzman's research into congressional behavior suggests that the higher the economic stakes, the more likely legislators will do the bidding of constituents. In typical situations, this explanation is better for legislative or regulatory behavior. Ideology prevails over constituency preference only in areas of morality not involving economic stakes, such as abortion and school prayer[91]

Several primary factors determine the power of an interested party to assert influence over the regulatory process. First is the strength of the regulated occupation. In jurisdictions where gaming affects the economy, the industry has greater ability to hold political power. Beyond influencing voters by political contributions or direct appeal, members and groups in a large gaming industry have the resources to hire lobbyists, create and fund cohesive trade associations, and mobilize.

Second is the strength of competing interested parties. This competition may occur in two ways. One competition is between groups attempting to use regulation to transfer wealth and groups wanting regulation for social gains. Interest groups will attempt to increase their power on given issues by forming alliances with other interest groups. This is often a battle between consumers who want regulation only to cure market imperfections and other interested parties who want to create inefficiencies to acquire wealth from the consumer. Competition may also exist between groups attempting to use regulation to transfer wealth for their own benefits. Here, the fight is to gain the largest benefit from the inefficiencies and the transfer of excess wealth from the consumer.

The third determinant factor is whether the jurisdiction has a competitive political party system. Jurisdictions not dominated by a sole political party tend to be less influenced by a single interest group. While reviews of congressional voting behavior show direct influence of interest groups, this influence is less important than party membership and political ideology.[92]

---

[91] Sam Peltzman, *Constituent Interest and Congressional Voting*, 27 J.L. & Econ. 181, 184, 210 (1984).

[92] However, there is evidence that other patterns of voting behavior can be observed. The spread of gambling across the country is likely to create a large constituency (more employees, etc.) which can change voting patterns in Congress. It is analogous to the protection of the textile industry compared to the leather industry. For example, one commentator notes that "a geographically dispersed industry can obtain the support of a larger number of elected representatives than a regionally centralized one." Robert E. Baldwin, *The Political Economy of Trade Policy*, J. Econ. Persp., Fall 1989, at 119, 122.

Because the gaming industry has such a large stake in regulation, it often devotes significant resources toward influencing the regulatory process. Therefore, besides a consistent focus on policy goals, a regulatory system should have safeguards to prevent interest-group influences (as discussed in Chapter 7). Such safeguards range from the obvious (prohibiting regulators from being compensated by the regulated) to the subtle (ensuring input from all interest groups on regulatory changes). Moreover, in jurisdictions where casino tax revenues from the gaming industry are important, stronger methods to ensure against "capture" are often necessary.[93]

Hybrid Goals

Sometimes intentionally but often haphazardly, a hybrid goals approach borrows elements of the market model, and player and government protection goals. Colorado's declaration of public policy incorporates a unique blend of government protection and player protection approaches with a vague reference to providing for the concerns of a market model approach. Specifically, the Colorado General Assembly has declared the following:

> The success of limited gaming is dependent upon public confidence and trust that licensed limited gaming is conducted honestly and competitively; that the rights of the creditors of licensees are protected; and that gaming is free from criminal and corruptive elements; . . . All [gaming] establishments . . . must therefore be licensed, controlled, and assisted to protect the public health, safety, good order, and the general welfare of the inhabitants of the state to foster the stability and success of limited gaming and to preserve the economy and policies of free competition of the state of Colorado.[94]

Government protection goals are implied in Colorado's desire "to preserve the economy" of the state and ensure the "success of limited gaming" through promoting public perception.[95] Player protection goals can be seen in the Assembly's directive that establishments be controlled to protect public health and welfare. The desire that gaming be free of criminal and corruptive elements could support either type of goal. Finally, un-

---

[93] That is not to say, however, that capture is inevitable simply because a particular jurisdiction heavily relies on tax revenue from a particular industry. When the National Commission of the Study of Gambling reviewed the Nevada regulatory system, it did so with a critical eye. Because tax revenues from gambling made up about half of the State budget, the Commission was influenced by the perception that the State regulators might concede to every request of the industry. The Commission found otherwise. "Serious questions arise as to whether a State that relies so heavily on a single industry for its revenue needs is truly capable of regulating that industry properly." The Commission concluded, "The Nevada control structures have stood the tests of time and, often, bitter experience. . . ." Robert D. Faiss & Gregory R. Gemignani, *Nevada Gaming Licensing: Qualifications, Standards, and Procedures, in* FRONTIERS IN CHANCE: GAMING RESEARCH ACROSS THE DISCIPLINES 126, 131 (David G. Schwartz ed., 2013), http://gamingpress.unlv.edu/pdfs/chap9.pdf.

[94] COLO. REV. STAT. §12-47.1-102 (2014).

[95] *See id.*

dertones of a market model approach are contained in the references to gaming being conducted competitively and the preservation of the state's free competition policy.

Unfortunately, the vagueness and ambiguity in this example show just why defining public policy is so important. In Colorado, is government protection supposed to yield to player protection? Should public confidence be valued higher than free competition? It is unclear.

In comparison, the Pennsylvania General Assembly provided this guidance when establishing its hybrid goals: "[t]he primary objective of this part to which all other objectives and purposes are secondary is to protect the public through the regulation and policing of all activities involving gaming and practices that continue to be unlawful."[96] Pennsylvania makes apparent that its leading goal is protecting players and the community, but to realize just how absurd this goal is, consider that Pennsylvania taxes gaming at 55 percent for gross slot machine revenue and 16 percent for table games revenue. By doing so, Pennsylvania garnered gaming tax revenues of $1.456 billion in 2011.[97] It also created regional monopolies for licensees. Where exactly does Pennsylvania think these revenues come from? Would a government, for example, pronounce a policy to permit only two stores in a country to sell televisions and then do a Request for Proposals to award these exclusive rights? If it did, what would a retailer pay to have monopoly rights to sell televisions in Philadelphia, and what would that do to the price of televisions? But Pennsylvania does this with gambling and at the expense of the players who have a much worse chance of actually emerging from the casino as winners. Why? Because in large part the government can reap the economic rents that come from granting regional monopolies so they can charge extremely high tax rates. Pennsylvania public policy is not and never was based on protecting the public but rather on exploiting the public through the state's monopoly powers to permit gambling, access an enormous tax, and grant exclusive franchises.

New Jersey provides an example of contradictory polices played out to their natural conclusion. New Jersey wanted gaming to regenerate an urban area, Atlantic City, by increasing tourism, stimulating construction, providing new jobs, and generating additional tax revenues.[98] These common policy goals are typical of government protection goals. Had this been the government's only set of goals, casino gaming might have had a different history in New Jersey. At the time of legalization, however, another set of policy considerations were adopted. In particular, New Jersey decided that the government had a duty to protect players from exploitation by prevent-

---

[96] 4 Pa. Cons. Stat. § 1102 (2014).

[97] Melissa Daniels, *PA Gambling Tax Revenue Highest in the Country*, Pennsylvania Indep., June 1, 2012, http://Paindependent.Com/2012/06/Pa-Gambling-Tax-Revenue-Highest-In-The-Country/.

[98] R. Benjamin Cohen, *The New Jersey Casino Control Act: Creation of a Regulatory System*, 6 Seton Hall Legis. J. 1, 3 (1982).

ing casinos from stimulating demand for the casino product. The unison of these two policies was based on the idea that gambling is not an end, but a means, to fulfill worthwhile goals.[99] The reality of the New Jersey gaming experiment was that the government was uneasy and hostile to the gaming industry, but it accepted the industry with the view it could achieve the worthwhile goals, minimize social and governmental costs, and be strictly controlled.

New Jersey officials were trying to serve two masters with contradictory policy goals. What emerged through the political process was a compromise on virtually every aspect of casino operations. Instead of a defined public policy and quantifiable policy goals, vague ambitions resulted in laws not designed to meet either goal. Instead of either allowing credit or not, the government allowed unlimited credit but required casinos to deposit the instrument promptly. This frustrated player protection goals because players could play on credit, and it frustrated government protection goals because the credit terms in Atlantic City were less favorable to the players than its competition, resulting in lost business. Similarly, instead of banning or permitting advertising, New Jersey came up with rules allowing casinos to advertise the casinos themselves, but not their odds, while requiring the slogan "Bet with your head, not over it."[100] The message was confusing.

Not all hybrid goals are blatantly contradictory. Some can attempt to apply different policies to distinct persons based on geography. Puerto Rico, for example, allows casinos to stimulate demand through advertising outside Puerto Rico but not within the Commonwealth.[101] Other jurisdictions allow casinos to pursue nonresidents, but prohibit their own population from engaging in gaming. These countries might adopt a market model or government protection goals as applied to nonresidents and a policy of eradication or player protection as it concerns its own residents.

Nevada also has an interesting blend of policies. In 1977, Nevada adopted a public policy that while clearly based on government protection policies also introduced the goals of maintaining a competitive economy. This policy reads "All establishments where gaming is conducted and where gaming devices are operated . . . must therefore be licensed, controlled and assisted . . . to preserve the competitive economy and policies of free competition of the State of Nevada."[102] This was less problematic than Pennsylvania as Nevada then had no contradictory policies limiting the number or physical requirements for casinos, limited licensing expense

---

[99] Bruce Ransom, *Public Policy and Gambling in New Jersey*, in GAMBLING AND PUBLIC POLICY: INTERNATIONAL PERSPECTIVES 155, 159 (William R. Eadington & Judy A. Cornelius eds., 1991).

[100] Davis & Gilbert LLP, *Gambling with New Jersey's Casino Advertising Rules: A Bad Bet*, Mar. 2014, http://www.dglaw.com/images_user/newsalerts/Advertising_Gambling_With_New_Jersey_Casino_Advertising_Rules.pdf.

[101] *See Posades de Puerto Rico Assocs. v. Tourism Co. of Puerto Rico*, 478 U.S. 328 (1986).

[102] NEV. REV. STAT. § 463.0129(1)(d) (2013).

and had a very low tax rate (5.5 percent). As the Nevada industry matured, however, the barriers to entry increased, including integrated resort requirements for new casinos and costly and lengthy licensing investigations. This historical evolution makes consistent adherence to different policy goals problematic.

Another more nuanced approach is to apply different goals to distinct behavior. This occurs where the government wants the benefits of casino gambling but feels that gambling may have negative consequences to certain classes of its citizens. If, for example, Pennsylvania acknowledged that the costs of problem gambling were unacceptably high to a small segment of the players, it could declare that the major purpose of legalized gambling, as in Ohio, is to create tax revenues but with a narrower exception to protect a vulnerable subset of the population. A theoretical approach defines the costs and benefits of various types of activities, such as credit, advertising, and alcohol consumption. It is best to look for less burdensome alternatives when the costs associated with the creation of externalities exceed the benefits. If alternatives are available that produce greater benefits than costs, choose one that maximizes the benefits to cost ratio. If none exist, then the activity can be prohibited.

A hybrid approach can attempt to reconcile any number of individual public policies. Careful consideration must be given as to whether the policies conflict or complement one another. If the policy goals conflict and are not prioritized, then regulators have no guidance in implementation of the regulations or laws. As New Jersey discovered, a hybrid approach that seeks to appease too many interests or concerns may fail to resolve any at all.

SUMMARY

Public policy guides, or should guide, a government's regulatory decisions. Critically important to effective regulation is that a government's public policy toward gambling be clearly communicated. Without such statement, a government's intention to achieve government protection goals such as maximizing tax revenues may be subsumed by regulators' preference for player protection. Even worse, ambiguity in public policy could provide the gaming industry with an avenue for regulatory capture by allowing the industry to persuade regulators that their interests are the interests of the government. And even where the public policy is explicitly stated but encapsulates a hybrid approach, the statement must be clear enough to provide regulators with priorities when policies conflict.

What is a reasoned approach for government to undertake? First, the government needs to study the gaming industry, and if it decides to permit it, to understand its benefits and problems. Government needs to be as smart as the industry it intends to regulate (avoiding information and knowledge failure). Second, government needs to define policy goals that are appropriate to what it hopes to accomplish through regulation (avoiding instrument failure). Third, it needs to design regulations and regulatory systems that are sophisticated given the unique expertise, structure and capabilities of the government (avoiding implementation failure). Fourth, government must have the expertise, training and motivation to properly regulate (avoiding motivation failure and regulatory capture). Many factors threaten to derail a jurisdiction's creation of an effective gaming regulatory structure. Sadly, most governments get caught in these pitfalls, with their failures masked by an enormously profitable industry.

APPENDIX[103]

Figure 2.5

Public Policy Statements

	Government Protection	Player Protection	Hybrid
Colorado			X
Indiana	X		
Iowa		X (but a tax rate over 20%)	
Louisiana			X
Maryland	X		
Massachusetts			X
Michigan			X
Nevada	X (strong market leanings)		
New Jersey			X
Ohio	X		
Pennsylvania			X
South Dakota			X
Washington		X	
Tribal Lands	X		
Australia		X (but only one integrated resort in each state)	
Singapore		X (but only two integrated resorts)	
Korea		X (but a 20% tax rate)	
Macao			X (limited licenses but many sublicenses and stronger market leanings)
Malta		X	
South Africa			X

[103] Not all jurisdictions have explicit policy statements. Of those that do, not all are contained in legislative declarations. The categorizations collected in this table represent statements found in state constitutions, legislative declarations, and regulatory mission statements/goal statements. Where policy statements were available from more than one source in a given jurisdiction, only the statement form the highest authority was considered. Moreover, while this book focuses on casino-related issues, it is uncommon for policy statements to be similarly narrow in scope. Accordingly, these categorizations should be viewed as describing a jurisdiction's policy toward gaming generally. This list categorizes only a small sample of jurisdictions permitting gambling and is not meant to be exhaustive. Finally, while various Native American tribes may establish independent public policies towards gambling, this categorization reflects the policy goals established in the Indian Gaming Regulatory Act, the mission statement of the National Indian Gaming Commission.

3

Public Policy Implementation and Regulatory Practice

Kevin Mullally & Stephen Martino

INTRODUCTION

This chapter continues the discussion regarding public policy by delving into the process of implementing broader public policy goals as part of regulatory practice—what is frequently referred to as the "practice of risk control." Chapter 2 discussed the inherent challenges with developing clearly-communicated, appropriate public policy goals in order to guide the regulation of the gaming marketplace and the enforcement policies needed to prohibit gaming activity in a jurisdiction. This chapter explores the implementation of those policy goals and the creation of more specific policies and procedures that establish the parameters of organizational and individual behavior within the gaming industry.

Regulations are authoritative rules issued by executive agencies or law enforcement that control behavior and have the force of law. However, this definition lacks the complexity and dimension a thorough understanding of regulatory practice demands. Academics continue to argue over the appropriate definition(s) for regulation, but one that expresses much of the modern thought on the subject comes from London School of Economics and Political Science Professor Julia Black:

> Regulation is the sustained and focused attempt to alter the behavior of others according to defined standards or purposes with the intention of producing a broadly identified outcome or outcomes, which may involve mechanisms of standard setting, information-gathering and behavior-modification."[1]

This definition encompasses the idea that regulatory activities can have an expanding scope depending on how one defines "regulation." A good

---

[1] Julia Black, *Enrolling Actors in Regulatory Systems: Examples from UK Financial Services Regulation*, 63 Pub. L. 65 (2003).

example of how the scope of what is considered "regulation" expands depending on your perspective is illustrated by the following types of regulatory practices:

- *A Specific Set of Commands* - This is the most commonly understood form of regulatory practice whereby an administrative agency issues rules (which have the force of law) governing a specific area of conduct, such as the regulation of prescription drugs or the environment.[2]

- *A Deliberative State of Influence* - This encompasses a broad range of government activities designed to affect or influence behavior. This category also encompasses command-based regulation, but it includes other factors that influence behavior such as tax rates, economic incentives, use of government resources, contractual powers, and licensing authority.[3]

- *All Forms of Social or Economic Influence* - This form of regulation occurs when our sphere of influence is expanded to all activities that affect behavior to include not only government activities but also markets, trade organizations, labor organizations, special interest groups, and others. This theory does not require the regulatory influence to be deliberate or designed, but merely recognizes it exists.[4]

These same authors state a difference exists between "red light" regulation designed to restrict behavior and control certain activities and "green light" regulation, which "enables or facilitates" a certain activity. Gaming regulation includes both theories in that gaming has historically been a proscribed activity requiring authorization by popular mandate or legislative action.

These practices are exhibited in most gaming regulatory environments. On the surface, regulators are primarily command-based. They take the general regulatory framework set forth in a constitutional provision, statute, or decree and promulgate rules to enact those public policy goals.

However, a more thorough examination of the interactions between regulators and licensees reveals a complex web of relationships. Regulators engage in many activities beyond formal rulemaking that affect behavior. Despite the exclusive jurisdiction granted to most regulators over gaming, other interested parties can and do influence the regulatory environment. The following interested parties are examples:

- legislators in an oversight role;
- special interest groups, such as labor unions, problem gambling advocacy groups, advocates for minority groups, and trade associations (e.g., restaurants, construction interests, and gray-market gaming providers);

---

[2] Robert Baldwin, Martin Cave & Martin Lodge, Understanding Regulation: Theory, Strategy, and Practice 3 (2nd ed. Oxford University Press 2012).
[3] *Id.*
[4] *Id.*

- gaming operators and suppliers;
- employees of the gaming facilities;
- local government officials;
- local law enforcement; and
- other executive branch agencies.

The nature of risk also changes over time, affecting the regulatory effort's focus. This requires regulators to constantly reevaluate every aspect of risk control to ensure the regulatory strategies being deployed are still relevant and effective. In the United States, the legislative processes that created nearly every gaming regulatory agency originally focused on the need for robust tools to combat the influence of organized crime. The threat, while minimal, does remain. However, it is no longer the principle purpose for why gaming regulation is needed. The threat diminished in part because today's gaming operators include large publicly-traded companies that are regulated on many levels. Further, the nature of their structure makes them highly resistant to influence from organized crime. Even most privately-held casino companies have financial structures that make them resistant to organized crime's influence.

Thus, regulatory focus has shifted a great deal in the past 20 years. Now, regulators are more interested in deterring white collar criminal activity. Furthermore, the rapid expansion of gaming from a few destination resort communities to markets focused on local and regional communities requires more consumer-focused regulations to ensure the games' fairness. Additionally, because many casino markets are characterized by government-controlled monopolies or oligopolies, there is greater regulatory emphasis on oversight of the processes for collecting public revenue in order to justify the limited or exclusive markets enjoyed by gaming operators.

This chapter discusses the components necessary to implement a successful regulatory policy that controls risk and encourages positive social behavior within the context of legalized gaming. It focuses on the regulator's role as a problem solver and the jurisdiction's responsibility to establish regulations that have clearly-communicated public policy objectives. It emphasizes the need to involve a variety of perspectives in the problem-solving process and the importance communicating expectations and responsibilities to achieve the overall goal of compliance. Finally, in order to identify shortfalls of some gaming regulatory efforts, it analyzes instances where a lack of adequate processes exists. Often, these shortfalls result from an allegiance to past policies or a reticence to adapt regulatory focus to address new risks. It also explains the importance of regular policy reviews and the development of performance metrics to gauge the effectiveness and relevance of each regulatory strategy.

THE POLICY IMPLEMENTATION ENVIRONMENT: THINGS TO CONSIDER BEFORE ENGAGING IN RULEMAKING

Chapter 2 discussed problems associated with seeking to draft "gold standard" model legislation without regard to the political, economic, and social environment of the jurisdiction (i.e., those elements that should ultimately drive public policy goals). This same problem can occur when implementing public policy goals established by legislators. Regulators frequently seek a "model rule" on subjects ranging from surveillance to money laundering. While regulatory cooperation and uniformity should be sought wherever appropriate, it is equally true that every policy should be analyzed with respect to the environment in which it is applied. No single magic formula can adequately address the many problems regulatory agencies encounter. Thus, a principle issue to consider when addressing public policy implementation is whether the nature of the policy objective, the environment, or the culture demands that a jurisdictionally-specific strategy be employed. If a subject matter involves issues of international commerce, for example, the most effective strategy may be to harmonize regulations with another jurisdiction.

Before discussing how to identify areas for rulemaking and things to consider in the rulemaking process, consider the ideal regulatory environment. While no panacea "model rule" will fit every jurisdiction in every situation, imagine an environment that most stakeholders and interest groups—regulators, operators, manufacturers, gaming employees, legislators, executive branch officials, attorneys general, players, and citizens—would agree ideal. A gaming regulatory *Camelot* looks something like this:

- Every rule, policy, and procedure implemented by regulators has a clear public policy objective.
- Each public policy objective identifies the specific risk being mitigated or the public benefit being advanced and serves as a constant compass to guide the rulemaking and policy implementation process to ensure the focus of the regulatory intervention stays on course over time and through changes in leadership and administration.
- Development of the policy, at an early stage, includes all parties directly affected. As the draft policy becomes clearer, those peripherally involved are also given a chance to add their perspectives so the most appropriate solution to the problem the policy seeks to address is reached.
- During this process all parties have an opportunity to help refine the public policy objective or to propose other, less intrusive ways to achieve the objective (e.g., technology solutions, innovative industry initiatives that might mitigate the risk without regulation, third-party solutions, more flexible process-based approaches as opposed to rigid procedural requirements).

- Regulators and interested parties consider how other regulatory agencies have addressed the same or similar problems; look for opportunities to standardize or harmonize processes and requirements to create efficiencies in the global gaming marketplace, while still satisfying the policy objective; and use international regulator groups to facilitate the standardization process and develop ways to monitor its effectiveness.
- As a result of this ideal process, the policy will be accompanied by specific expectations and responsibilities the regulation target must meet to achieve compliance. When appropriate, the regulator will design a plan to educate stakeholders about their responsibilities under the policy, and stakeholders will have a forum to seek answers to any questions they may have.
- Because the process has allowed for full stakeholder involvement, which resulted in general agreement on the benefits of the public policy objective and a clear understanding of the specific expectations and responsibilities required for compliance, all parties are invested in the compliance process.
- The policy objective and communicated expectations and responsibilities provide the regulator and those who oversee the regulator with the building blocks to create specific metrics with which to measure the effectiveness of the regulation.
- The end result is a system where everyone's goal is compliance and regulators enjoy the added benefit of a performance measurement that assists in the identification of policy objectives that failed or need revision to make them more relevant or effective. Sometimes policies fail because the thinking behind the objective was flawed or, more likely, the nature of the risk has changed or was not adequately understood when the policy was created. The ability to measure regulatory performance allows regulators to continue managing risk in the most efficient and effective ways possible. It also reduces cross-jurisdictional inefficiencies and frees up wasted resources that can be devoted to improved regulatory compliance.

This type of regulatory system can best serve the public interest, ensure gaming integrity, maximize the gaming industry's economic benefits, and minimize its economic and social harms. Therefore, this chapter is designed to serve as an effective guide to assist a new jurisdiction in implementing this type of system. Undoubtedly challenges await. For example, not all parties will agree on every public policy objective or the methods prescribed for achieving them. In the end, the regulator has the final say. Being a part of the implementation process, however, is an extremely effective method for understanding what will be expected of the regulated community even if one of the parties disagrees with the underlying policy objective.

If a jurisdiction has a different vision of the "ideal" regulatory system, some of the techniques and examples used in this chapter hopefully will spur further innovation in gaming regulation so that an understanding of the most appropriate direction for implementing gaming policy, controlling risk, and managing the gaming industry is advanced.

THE EXTRAORDINARY POWER AND DISCRETION OF GAMING REGULATORS

Before any rulemaking commences, enabling laws are passed, which generally grant gaming regulators extraordinary power. Unlike most regulatory and law enforcement agencies, gaming regulators usually enjoy a monopoly over the implementation of public policy relating to gaming within their jurisdiction. Furthermore, standard statutory provisions often grant gaming regulators plenary authority to investigate individuals and companies doing business in their jurisdiction as well as worldwide affiliates and personnel of those individuals and companies. This puts gaming regulators in the relatively unique position of having total, unfettered control over the industry they regulate. Therefore, prior to engaging in the rulemaking process, it is imperative to understand that when gaming regulators promulgate a rule, they are usually limiting their own discretion. Nearly all regulatory and enforcement agencies enjoy significant discretion that greatly impacts public policy implementation. The authority and discretion enjoyed by gaming regulators can be an effective tool to ensure industry integrity, consumer fairness, and positive economic impact, or it can be misused with less positive results. Regulatory authority that is misused can cause oppressive, amorphous rulings and policies that unnecessarily constrict the industry and fail to achieve the result the legislative body and the people desired when gaming was authorized. Misuse can also cause uneven application of policies, depending on how broadly or deeply within the regulatory agency the discretionary powers are dispersed.

Gaming regulators' extraordinary power is best demonstrated by comparing the environment a typical gaming regulator operates in versus that of most other regulatory and law enforcement agencies. For instance, a police officer enjoys extensive powers similar to those of a gaming regulator. He has the power to arrest, wide-ranging investigatory authority and resources, the power to intercept communications, limited powers of search and seizure, and the authority to use force. However, law enforcement agencies must work within a patchwork of overlapping jurisdictions where their powers can be overridden. For example, they may be required to chase criminals into areas where they have no power at all. In contrast to gaming regulators, who maintain jurisdiction over their licensees even when they engage in conduct outside the jurisdiction, policing agencies are often hindered by jurisdictional boundaries.

A report for the Congressional Research Service observed that "[i]ndividual criminals as well as broad criminal networks exploit geographic borders, criminal turf, cyberspace, and law enforcement juris-diction to dodge law enforcement countermeasures. Further, the in-terplay of these realities can encumber policing measures."[5] This issue is apparent with cybercrimes, which are commonly transnational and thus hamper law enforcement's ability to follow the criminal activity. The report also notes the difficulty encountered when what is con-sidered a crime in one country is not recognized as such in another.[6] Gaming regulators are able to avoid such problems because they main-tain jurisdiction over their licensees no matter where they are located. The plenary regulatory authority mentioned before that is granted by most enabling laws applies to the conduct of licensees both inside and outside the jurisdiction. Consequently, in a very real way, the reach of gaming regulators is global.

Financial market regulators provide another example of overlapping jurisdictional authority. One problem identified as the result of the global financial collapse in 2007–08 was the myriad regulatory agencies involved and the lack of a clear indication of which agency was responsible for mit-igating each specific risk. Paul Joskow provides a vivid description of this problem in an article he wrote on deregulation:

> The one thing that we can be sure of is that we have no shortage of reg-ulatory agencies with overlapping responsibilities for investor protection, financial market behavior and performance, and systemic risk mitigation (prudential regulation) that collectively were supposed to work to keep this kind of financial market mess, as well as scams that were allegedly em-ployed by Madoff and others, from occurring. These regulatory agencies have overlapping jurisdictions, opaque goals, arbitrarily limited authori-ties, and histories that can often be traced back to Great Depression era financial markets and economic conditions. These regulatory institutions have evolved over the last seventy-five years in a haphazard fashion that has not responded effectively to the evolution of financial institutions, prod-ucts, and markets but more as a series of fingers in the dike to try to keep new leaks from damaging the integrity of the entire dam.[7]

This analysis of overlapping financial markets regulation illustrates some of what could happen to gaming regulation as the industry con-tinues to converge, as markets becomes more global, and where there is insufficient progress towards cooperation in understanding and mit-igating cross-border risks. As already established, gaming regulators possess powers that are rare in the law enforcement and regulatory world. Granting such powers requires special attention in the imple-mentation process to ensure that proper controls are in place to achieve

---

[5] Kristin M. Finklea, Cong. Research Serv., R41927, The Interplay of Borders, Turf, Cyberspace, and Jurisdiction 2 (2013), http://www.fas.org/sgp/crs/misc/R41927.pdf.
[6] Id. at 5.
[7] Paul L. Joskow, Sloan Foundation & MIT, Deregulation, MIT Economics, Feb. 28, 2009, http://economics.mit.edu/files/3875.

evenly applied policy goals and to establish the oversight necessary to ensure the regulators' extraordinary power is used as intended in the legislation.

Gaming regulators also differ from those regulating banking, insurance, and public utilities. While it is not a common practice, gaming regulators can compel licensees to waive attorney–client privilege.[8]

Gaming regulators are able to do this because although the applicant or licensee has every right to assert the privilege, they also have the right to waive it. If the privilege is not waived, regulators often accuse an applicant or licensee of being "uncooperative" or failing to provide information necessary to prove suitability. Sometimes they threaten to deny license renewals or other requests by gaming licensees unless attorney–client privilege is waived. While there have been instances of nongaming regulators pressuring corporations to waive attorney–client privilege, those attempts have generally been short-lived and severely limited after receiving heavy criticism from the legal community, lawmakers, and the judiciary.[9]

For instance, the controversial "Thompson Memorandum" issued by Deputy Attorney General Larry Thompson on January 20, 2003, encouraged prosecutors to increase pressure on companies wishing to show the "authenticity" of their cooperation with the government by encouraging them to waive attorney–client privilege, among other rights.[10] The Security and Exchange Commission soon followed with a similar policy of its own.[11] Under pressure from the American Bar Association, US Congress, and the judiciary, this policy has been greatly constrained, and while pros-

---

[8] Nevada Gaming Control Board, Form 18, http://gaming.nv.gov/index.aspx?page=49. The form contains the following language:

> I/We hereby authorize and request all persons to whom this request is presented having information relating to or concerning me/us to furnish such information to a duly appointed agent of the State Gaming Control Board of the State of Nevada, whether or not such information would otherwise be protected from disclosure by any constitutional, statutory, or common law privilege.

> I/We hereby authorize and request all persons to whom this request is presented having documents relating to or concerning me/us to permit a duly appointed agent of the State Gaming Control Board of the State of Nevada to review and copy any such documents, whether or not such documents would otherwise be protected from disclosure by any constitutional, statutory, or common law privilege.

In addition, there have been several instances in Missouri where regulators have successfully compelled licensees or applicants to waive attorney–client privilege or face a recommendation of unsuitability based on a failure to cooperate in the licensing investigation.

[9] Alan I. Raylesberg, *DOJ Revises Guidelines to Limit Demands that Corporations Waive Attorney-Client Privilege or Not Advance Employees' Legal Fees as a Condition of 'Cooperating' with a Government Investigation*, CHADBOURNE & PARK LLP, Sept. 8, 2008, http://www.chadbourne.com/clientalerts/2008/dojrevises/.

[10] *Id.*

[11] *Id.*

ecutors may still seek privilege waivers, their ability to do so remains constrained and under continued pressure for further reform.[12]

The most powerful tool furthering gaming regulators' exceptional discretion is the rare evidentiary standard employed in many jurisdictions to prove suitability for licensure. Most regulatory agencies that issue licenses for commercial activity, such as day care facilities, nursing homes, and banks, require that suitability be proven by a "preponderance of the evidence" or "competent substantial evidence."[13] Moreover, in most professional licensing instances, the regulator often has the burden of proof in any action to revoke or restrict a license once it has been granted.[14] In contrast, most gaming laws require licensees to prove their suitability for licensure by "clear and convincing evidence," which means the burden is on the license applicant to prove it is substantially more likely than not that they meet the criteria for licensure.[15]

Consider this excerpt from a New Jersey appeal regarding a regulator's finding that two shareholders were not suitable for licensure and therefore must divest themselves of their interest in the Caesar's World gaming operation in order for the company to be licensed. The New Jersey Gaming Commission found the applicant failed to establish its licensure suitability by clear and convincing evidence. The shareholders appealed, and the court upheld the commission's decision:

> The statutory burden to demonstrate affirmatively the qualifying attributes, whatever they might be, has been expressly and clearly placed on the applicant by the Legislature and is subject to the canon of clear and convincing evidence. It is not necessary to disqualification that the applicant or any personnel required to be qualified be of demonstrably bad character. Disqualification is justified by their failure to prove themselves qualified by clear and convincing evidence.[16]

In addition, rather than shifting the burden of proof to the regulator when a license is being proposed for revocation or restriction, gaming licensees in many US jurisdictions maintain a continuing burden to demonstrate their suitability by clear and convincing evidence.[17]

The point of this rather lengthy discussion regarding the unusual power most gaming regulators possess is the imperative of understanding the

---

[12] See Julie R. O'Sullivan, *Does DOJ's Privilege Waiver Policy Threaten the Rationales Underlying the Attorney-Client Privilege and Work Product Doctrine? A Preliminary "No"*, 45 Am. Crim. L. Rev. 1237, 1296 (2008) (discussing why this prosecutorial tool should remain in place).

[13] *Ass'n of Data Processing Serv. Orgs., Inc. v. Bd. of Governors of the Fed. Reserve Sys.*, 745 F.2d 677 (1984); *See also Eng'g Mgt. Servs., Inc. v. Md. State Highway Admin.*, 375 Md. 211 (2003).

[14] *Jones v. Conn. Med. Examining Bd.*, 309 Conn. 727 (2013).

[15] *See, e.g.*, Mass. Gen. Laws ch. 23K, §§ 9(a)(5), 13(a).

[16] *In re the Application of Boardwalk Regency Corp. for a Casino License*, 434 A.2d 1111 (N.J. Super. Ct. App. Div. 1981), *modified*, 447 A.2d 1335 (N.J. 1982).

[17] *See, e.g.*, Mo. Rev. Stat. § 313.812.14(9).

value of the discretion and the need to implement necessary controls in order to ensure its proper use. When used wisely, discretion can be a valuable tool for dealing with unique, esoteric problems that require regulatory intervention but that are not addressed by applicable regulations because a reoccurrence of the specific situation is so unlikely that promulgating a rule or policy to address it would be imprudent. Given the extensive authority granted to most gaming regulators, proper oversight is a key component of regulatory policy. There is a reason that the phrase *Quis custodiet ipsos custodes?* is inscribed on so many government buildings.[18]

As Chapter 16 demonstrates, nearly every regulator has been tasked with reviewing or conducting background investigations for potential corporate and individual licensees. Some state statutes set out automatic disqualification for holding a gaming license, especially for individuals. In many states, any felony or gambling-related conviction is a bar to holding a gaming license.[19] Although it is no longer the case, initially, in Maryland, a conviction at any time in a person's life for a crime of moral turpitude merited a lifetime ban from holding a gaming license.[20]

Apart from the requirements of automatic disqualification, regulators possess enormous discretionary power to assess the previous anti-social, bad acts of gaming license applicants. Somewhere between inappropriate-but-not-disqualifying conduct and past acts that would reflect poorly on the industry (thus justifying a license denial), lies the near-complete discretion of gaming regulators. Rarely are such discretionary thought processes reduced to written regulation. Rather, it is gaming regulators' ongoing responsibility to exercise considered and consistent decision-making when reviewing background investigations, especially given how inherently personal and individually-impactful such decisions are.

When reviewing a person's criminal, civil, and financial history, no single event may be legally disqualifying, but the totality and weight of the individual's record may make them a poor candidate for working in a highly regulated industry like gaming. If this is the case, the regulator has a dual responsibility: (1) to articulate his or her concerns and the standard of review, even if they are not explicitly written in regulation; and (2) to ensure that internal processes are refined and strong enough to withstand turnover in staff so that applicants with similar backgrounds receive consistent suitability judgments.

If the goal of regulatory policy is to achieve high levels of compliance with carefully selected public policy objectives, then it is necessary for reg-

---

[18] A Latin phrase typically attributed to the Roman poet Juvenal, it is literally translated as "Who will guard the guards themselves?"

[19] *See, e.g.,* 230 Ill. Comp. Stat.10 / 7(a)(1); 230 Ill. Comp. Stat. 40 / 45(d)(1); La. Rev. Stat. Ann. § 27:28; Mo. Rev. Stat. § 313.812.8; S.D. Codified Laws § 4207B-33(3).

[20] *See* Michael Dresser, *Assembly passes bill to open casino jobs to some ex-offenders,* Balt. Sun, April 3, 2013, http://www.baltimoresun.com/news/maryland/politics/bs-md-casino-hiring-20130403,0,1783383.story. The law was revised in 2013 to focus on more recent offenses.

ulators to develop an effective system for communicating informal decision making to licensees. This provides the licensee with the necessary guidance to create better compliance methods. While the formal rulemaking process provides an essential structure to guide licensees, regulators often make informal decisions regarding casino operating procedures, liquor service, marketing issues, player disputes, public safety concerns, and other matters that refine those broader requirements. These decisions must be tracked and communicated to applicants and licensees—not only to achieve higher levels of compliance, but also to allow regulatory management to obtain a clear vision of how regulatory policy is being implemented in the field.

Tracking informal decision-making is also important because when discretion is dispersed too widely, lacks proper oversight, or is used to create on-the-fly rules and policies, it can cause unfair results and inconsistent application of regulatory authority. This has the potential to unnecessarily harm the industry and/or its employees. It can also result in damage to the regulator's standing and spark a reaction by lawmakers to reduce or constrain regulatory authority.

CASINO LICENSE SELECTION PROCESSES

States conclude that casino gaming is appropriate public policy for a variety of reasons, but all seek some benefit from introducing the industry. For many, this benefit is an additional, ongoing source of tax revenue that is too enticing to pass up. In the United States, several waves of new gambling authorizations in began with the expansion of lotteries in the early 1970s, which lasted into the mid-1990s when tribal gaming and regional, primarily riverboat gaming began. Most recently, when state and local budgets were constricted due to the Great Recession in 2008, another wave of expansion was sparked.

During tough fiscal times, states need new forms of revenue, and they need them fast. However, as unemployment soars and corporate earnings shrink, raising taxes is an increasingly politically unpalatable solution. Therefore, many states with existing lotteries and other forms of gaming, including charitable and pari-mutuel betting, believe that commercial casino gambling expansion provides a voluntary solution to immediate budget needs. This desire for expansion is furthered when nongaming states find themselves bordered by states with commercial casinos and realize they are losing profits to those states. Additionally, states and their elected officials are always called on to boost employment rates. Casinos create jobs immediately through construction employment and then as the result of ongoing operating positions that can number in the thousands, especially for destination resorts.

When commercial casino gambling is authorized, in some jurisdictions regulators are tasked with determining which gaming facilities will be the most economically beneficial to the state. By placing this power in the hands of the gaming commission, lottery commission, or some other appointed body that is responsible for granting gaming licenses, regulators have the discretion to determine the complexion of the industry itself—a power that effects the entire gaming market.

To illustrate the work gaming regulators or pseudo-gaming regulatory bodies have conducted along these lines, consider Kansas and Maryland— two states that ventured into casino gaming at virtually the same time. To compete with neighboring states and claw back their fair share of gaming revenues, Kansas and Maryland authorized a number of casino licenses and charged specially-created panels to grant licenses on application. While neither of the deciding panels was the assigned gaming regulator in the state, the standards for how each approached their responsibilities and their resulting long-term impact on gaming regulatory policy are important. The lessons from these impacts are not only applicable to competitive bid selection processes but can be applied to general rulemaking procedures and efforts to ensure comity within the regulated community.

Articulated Objective Standards for Evaluation

Applicants must know what standards they will be graded on, how the evaluators will process information, and what policy requirements they need to work toward to be selected. Both states set those out in statute, although with distinctly different specificity. In Kansas, the review panel was charged to "determine which contract best maximizes revenue, encourages tourism and otherwise serves the interests of the people of Kansas."[21] In Maryland, the General Assembly was far more specific:

> (k) Factors considered for award of license:
> (1) In awarding a video lottery operation license [casino], the VLFLC [license granting authority] shall evaluate the factors under this subsection in the manner specified:
> (2) 70% - business and market factors:
> the highest potential benefit and highest prospective total revenues to be derived by the State; the potential revenues from a proposed location based on a market analysis; the extent to which the proposed location encourages Maryland gaming participants to remain in the State; the extent to which the proposed location demonstrates that the facility will be a substantial regional and national tourist destination; the proposed facility capital construction plans and competitiveness of the proposed facility; the amount of gross revenues to be allocated to the video lottery operator over the term of the license; the percent of ownership by entities meeting the definition of minority business enterprise under Title 14, Subtitle 3 of the State Finance and Procurement Article; the extent to which the proposed location will preserve existing Maryland jobs and the number of net new jobs to be created; and the contents of the licensee's plan to achieve minority business participation goals in accordance

---

[21] Kan. Stat. Ann. § 74-8736(b).

with the requirements described under § 9-1A-10(a)(1) and (2) of this subtitle.

(3) 15% - economic development factors:
the anticipated wages and benefits for new jobs to be created; any additional economic development planned in the area of the proposed facility.

(4) 15% - location siting factors:
the existing transportation infrastructure surrounding the proposed facility location; the negative impact, if any, of a proposed facility location on the surrounding residential community; the need for additional public infrastructure expenditures at the proposed facility.[22]

Despite the obvious differences between the two states' articulation of the standards for evaluation, they existed and were reinforced consistently throughout the evaluations process. Each applicant knew the license requirements, how to tailor their proposals and presentations, and the factors the evaluators would consider when granting a license.

Other jurisdictions have used a less rigid approach, either because the legislative body could not agree on specific criteria or deemed the legislative process insufficiently scientific to create the criteria needed to weigh casino proposals varying vastly in size, scope, cost, mission, geographic location, and ever-changing market conditions. The least scientific of these processes occurs when the legislation predetermines the number and location of casinos. Legislative bodies are not well suited to conducting market studies and possess little knowledge of the gaming industry. The legislature is similarly ill-suited to obtain and analyze expert testimony that might provide it with this knowledge. Thus, these jurisdictions often fail to initially create an efficient marketplace, which results in years of legislative and regulatory tinkering to correct market flaws.

A more recent trend is for the legislative body to establish zones within the state and establish general policy objectives for the consideration of a gaming facility in each zone. The process for adopting specific evaluation criteria and awarding licenses is then delegated to an administrative agency. The agency is either the gaming commission or an entity specifically created to evaluate proposals for gaming facilities. While this approach can be slow and deliberate, it is better suited to conduct a thorough factual evaluation of all selection criteria.

Transparent Process

With articulated standards determined by the state, the gaming regulator or entity awarding the license must carefully craft a licensing process that makes as much information public as possible and prevents obscure or closed-door decision-making. During the casino selection process in Kansas between 2008 and 2010, a transparent process was one of two

---

[22] MD. CODE ANN. 9 § 1A-36k(1)–(4).

driving forces (the other to be discussed below) behind how the licensing group conducted its business.[23] All discussions regarding applicants or the process were done in open meetings. All submissions from the public, applicants, and any state-retained consultants were provided to the public and all other applicants. Similarly, in Maryland during the fall of 2013, in order to grant the state's sixth and final authorized casino license, which is in Prince George's County in suburban Washington, D.C., the commission charged with making the decision made a deliberate choice to err on the side of transparency and full public disclosure. Like in Kansas, all meetings were held in public, no executive sessions occurred behind closed doors, and all consultant reports, which were used to weigh the relative strength of three proposals against the statutory criteria for selection articulated above, were provided for all to examine.

Transparency in granting casino licenses, just as it does in other regulatory functions, has its advantages—one of which is decreased litigation. In granting three casino licenses in Kansas and the final one in Prince George's County, Maryland, no lawsuits were filed by the losing bidders to challenge either the outcome or the process.

Ethical Conduct of Decision-Makers

Finally, the basis for reliable, fact-based decision-making rests with independent decision-makers. Removing any ethical encumbrances is a good place to start for all regulatory bodies regardless of the industry. It is especially important in the gaming industry where past reputations for entanglements with organized crime and fixed political systems continue to be part of the perception, if not the reality, of present-day gaming. Regulators are well-advised to adopt codes of conduct to govern their behavior. A code of conduct was not adopted in Maryland by those granting casino licenses; however, all members were asked by the chairman to publicly note any relationships with applicants that could create the appearance of a conflict of interest.

In Kansas, the license-granting body approved a wide-ranging code of conduct to ensure its work held up to scrutiny. Included in the terms were prohibitions on gift acceptance from applicants, gambling at any property owned by the applicant or an affiliate, direct stock ownership of applicants' businesses, and ex parte communications with anyone having an interest in or pending matter before the body.

SCOPE AND PROCESS FOR RULEMAKING

For a regulating body to implement a regulatory structure initiated by legislators, it must first understand the scope of its mandate and the extent

---

[23] *See generally* Stephen Martino & William R. Eadington, *Allocation of Gaming Licenses and Establishment of Bid Processes: The Case of Kansas, 2008 and 2009*, 14 UNLV GAMING RES. & REV. J. 1 (2010).

of its powers. When a gaming regulatory agency is established by statute or decree, it is provided with a basic management structure, which typically consists of a "Gaming Control Board" or "Gaming Commission," a broad grant of powers that enable it to carry out its responsibility to create and manage the gaming industry within its jurisdiction, and a specific list of duties.[24]

The rules for managing the industry come with varying levels of specificity as discussed in Chapter 2. Most gaming regulatory practice involves social regulation that concerns itself with admittedly vague issues such as integrity, public health, public safety, public welfare, and consumer fairness. However, several regulators may be charged with economic regulatory responsibilities giving them an important role in developing and managing gaming markets within the confines of their jurisdiction. This can also have important implications within their region.[25] Similarly, some gaming regulators are forced by law to be business partners with the facilities they regulate, primarily by being required to own and maintain the slot machines and other electronic gaming devices the facility utilizes in order to achieve one of the jurisdiction's core missions: to generate taxable gaming revenue. In many states the lottery, which also serves as the regulatory authority, provides slot machines to casinos.[26] Often, this is a legal requirement facilitated through an ongoing process that adds complexity to the regulator-regulatee relationship. Some regulatory agencies are also charged with adjudicating matters they themselves initiated. This concept is rarely seen in other regulated industries and will be examined more thoroughly in Chapters 14 and 15, which address enforcement issues and licensing.

Many jurisdictions confine regulatory activities to licensing and operational control of gaming facilities. These jurisdictions are primarily interested in creating rules governing three general areas: (1) corporate and individual suitability, which involves ensuring the integrity of the people involved in financing, managing, and operating the facility; (2) gaming integrity, which involves the formulation of rules to ensure the games are conducted fairly, operators are transparent with consumers, the house advantage is understood, and all players are entitled to fair play; and (3) protection of government interests, which involves charging the regulator with implementing policies and procedures that ensure the proper collection of public funds—e.g., taxes, license fees, regulatory expenses—ensuring gaming facilities are safe and secure and preventing criminal activity or social behavior that is deemed detrimental to society, such as money

---

[24] *See, e.g.,* Mo. Rev. Stat. §§ 313.004, 313.805.

[25] Malcolm K. Sparrow, The Regulatory Craft: Controlling Risks, Solving Problems, and Managing Compliance 7 (2000) (suggesting that the distinction between social and economic regulation is "somewhat fuzzy").

[26] This is the case in Delaware, Maryland, New York, Oregon, Rhode Island, and West Virginia.

laundering, cheating, underage gambling, problem gambling, intoxicated patrons, and participation by persons affiliated with organized crime.

Identifying Areas for Rulemaking

The first step in any rulemaking process should be to define the regulatory objective. In other words, what risk is being mitigated or what public benefit is to be advanced by the rule? Without a clear regulatory purpose and an expected benefit from it either by reducing potential for harm or inducing some public benefit, then it will be difficult for the regulation's targets to develop compliance strategies or for the regulator to create performance metrics demonstrating results.

Often, rules are created to provide necessary detail to provisions in the enabling law, which should serve as the outline for a regulator's initial rulemaking efforts. Enabling laws typically consist of a section granting powers followed by enumerated criteria for regulatory oversight. The best enabling laws provide general policy guidance to the regulator and only provide specific instructions for how to the implement the policy in areas of particular importance to the jurisdiction. For example, an enabling law might require interagency cooperation or include instructions delineating how taxes are to be collected and distributed.

As in most states, Pennsylvania law requires licensees to prohibit persons under 21 years of age from operating or using slot machines or playing table games.[27] The Pennsylvania Gaming Control Board felt the best way to ensure compliance with this provision was to stop underage patrons from entering the gaming area. Therefore, the rulemaking process added the following details to ensure compliance with the general statutory provision articulating the state's policy that underage gambling should not be allowed:

(a) An individual under 21 years of age may not enter or be on the gaming floor of a licensed facility except that an individual 18 years of age or older who is employed by a slot machine licensee, a gaming service provider, the Board or other regulatory or emergency response agency may enter and remain in that area while engaged in the performance of the individual's employment duties.

(b) An individual under 21 years of age, whether personally or through an agent, may not operate, use, play or place a wager on, a slot machine in a licensed facility.

(c) An individual under 21 years of age may not receive check cashing privileges, be rated as a player, or receive any complimentary service, item or discount as a result of, or in anticipation of, gaming activity.

(d) An individual under 21 years of age may not collect in any manner or in any proceeding, whether personally or through an agent, winnings or recover losses arising as a result of any gaming activity.

(e) Winnings incurred by an individual under 21 years of age shall be re-

---

[27] 4 Pa. Cons. Stat. Ann. § 1207(8).

mitted to the Board to support compulsive and problem gambling programs of the Board.

(f)   For the purposes of this section, winnings issued to, found on or
about or redeemed by an individual under 21 years of age shall be presumed to constitute winnings and be subject to remittance to the Board.[28]

In this instance, the statute's public policy goal was to prevent underage gambling. Pennsylvania regulators believed the most appropriate way
to ensure the rule met this policy objective was to prohibit access to the
gaming area unless the underage person was licensed by the Commission
in which case they could only access the gaming floor to do their job. Furthermore, persons under 21 cannot be involved in any part of a gaming
transaction.

In contrast, Missouri has a similar statute prohibiting underage wagering, but it provides greater detail than the Pennsylvania statute. The Missouri law states

> A person under twenty-one years of age shall not make a wager on an ex-
> cursion gambling boat and shall not be allowed in the area of the excursion
> boat where gambling is being conducted; provided that employees of the
> licensed operator of the excursion gambling boat who have attained eigh-
> teen years of age shall be permitted in the area in which gambling is being
> conducted when performing employment-related duties, except that no
> one under twenty-one years of age may be employed as a dealer or accept a
> wager on an excursion gambling boat. The governing body of a home dock
> city or county may restrict the age of entrance onto an excursion gambling
> boat by passage of a local ordinance.[29]

Because of the statute's specificity, Missouri regulators did not feel the
need to provide much additional guidance in its regulations, which only
state that a patron must be 21 years or older to gamble, and those under 21
are not eligible to claim gambling winnings.[30] Missouri includes additional
detail in its Minimum Internal Control Standards (MICS) that have the
force and effect of law.[31]

Likewise, in Maryland, legislators deployed an even stricter standard
than Missouri or Pennsylvania: no one under age 21 is allowed on the
gaming floor for any purpose or reason, even employment. "[Those u]nder

---

[28] 4 Pa. Code § 513a.2.

[29] Mo. Rev. Stat. § 313.817.4.

[30] Mo. Code Regs. Ann. tit. 11, § 45-5.053(6)(B)(stating that wagers may only be made
"b]y persons twenty-one (21) years of age or older"); Mo. Code Regs. Ann. tit. 11, § 45-
5.065(2) (stating that "[p]atrons that are excluded from excursion gambling boats pursuant to 11 CSR 45-10.115, 11 CSR 45-15 et seq., 11 CSR 45-17 et seq., and patrons who are
under twenty-one (21) years of age are not eligible to claim gambling game payouts").

[31] Mo. Code Regs. Ann. tit. 11, § 45-9.114,

https://www.mgc.dps.mo.gov/MICS/MICS%20Chapter%20N%20effective%20Novem-
ber%2030,%202012.pdf (asserting at § 4.01 in that persons under 21 years of age shall not
be permitted access to the casino floor or be allowed to place a wager, and at § 4.04, stating
that the enforcement of admission and gambling restrictions for persons under 21 years of
age shall include, at a minimum, checking their government-issued photo identification).

the age of 21 years . . . are not allowed in areas of the video lottery facility where video lottery terminals or table games are located."[32] Again, it was determined that no further regulation was necessary to enhance an already-clear legislative mandate on this area of policy.

Nevada provides one more illustration of how a statutory provision can guide the rulemaking process. Nevada's statute contains provisions similar to Missouri's except that it requires all gaming employees to be 21 unless they work in a count room.[33]

The foregoing example illustrates how four states addressed the identical issue differently. Nevada is a jurisdiction where tourism is king and where its most significant gaming venues are destination resorts that attract a variety of guests including families. Destination resorts constantly innovate to create a more unique, attractive environment for their guests. As a result any blanket policy on how to best deter minors from gambling would be difficult to apply evenly throughout the industry and may deter future innovation. Thus, Nevada felt it best to let the statute speak for itself, allowing the Gaming Control Board to use its discretionary enforcement powers to require licensees to develop individual plans specifically designed for their facility to comply with the statutory requirement.

The Missouri statute took it upon itself to provide detailed requirements rather than leaving it up to the gaming commission to develop rules to implement a broader policy. Since the statute already provided significant detail, additional clarification in its gambling rules was deemed unnecessary. Missouri regulators provided licensees with additional guidance in the MICS most likely because each property has the ability to request a variance from MICS requirements, thus allowing flexibility for a facility with unique physical requirements.

The Pennsylvania solution represents a traditional example of the legislative body providing general guidance in the law and leaving it to the regulator to provide specific methodology for implementing the policy goals in its rules. The advantage of Missouri and Maryland's approach is that regulations are easier to change over time as risk shifts, compared to statutes, which are subject to the legislative process. While the issue of minors in a casino presents little potential for a shift in risk, other policy areas, particularly those that might involve a technological solution, are best addressed through regulatory implementation rather than providing rigid mandates regarding the issue in the enabling legislation.

Finally and conversely, the Maryland General Assembly removed all possible discretion from its gaming regulators by pronouncing statutorily that individuals under the age of 21 could not legally gain entrance to

---

[32] MD. CODE ANN. 9 § 1A-24(c).

[33] NEV. REV. STAT. § 463.350 (2013). It should be noted that Nevada's definition of "gaming employee" differs significantly from that of Missouri and many other states, so the difference here is not as much as one might expect.

the casino gaming floor. In so doing, the legislature complicated the ability of its facilities to achieve their dual missions of generating revenue for the state and creating economic development and empowerment. Casinos cannot fill high turnover, nongaming positions such as cocktail servers, facility maintenance, housekeeping, and food service positions, with the readily available under-the-age-of-21 labor pool. This has resulted in positions necessary to create a positive guest experience going unfilled for long periods of time, making it more challenging for casinos to operate at the standards they desire. The legislature also removed its gaming regulators' ability to craft a regulatory solution that could have protected the state's interest in ensuring that those under age 21 were not gambling, while also allowing its facilities to operate with maximum efficiency.

The Working Group

Once the public policy objective is identified, an internal group of subject-matter experts should create the regulations' building blocks, which regulations can be drafted by the legal department. This group should not be limited to the specific practice area within the agency that will administer the regulation, but it should instead include people with a sufficiently broad area of expertise in order to provide a variety of perspectives. A theme throughout this description of the rulemaking process is collaboration: including a variety of perspectives in the problem-solving process is an invaluable tool. For example, when writing regulations about tax collections, the working group should not be restricted to tax auditors but also should include those who audit internal controls (often a separate section within the agency), someone from information technology (IT) who might implement software in conjunction with the rule change, and technical staff that understand the capabilities of the casinos' slot and table games accounting systems. Staff from the legal department should always be included in the working groups.

The working group's first task is to refine the public policy objective and outline the critical scope of the rule. It is not necessary to immediately write rule language, but the group should initially focus on the risk to be mitigated or the public benefit to be advanced as well as what will constitute "compliance." Then, the working group should assemble a list of those who will be directly impacted by the rule. They should develop their own estimate of the resources the regulated community will need to expend to comply.

The group should ultimately produce a general outline of the requirements and expectations for resource expenditures that can be provided to the regulated community for comment. Regulators should ask the regulated community what they are already doing to address the public policy objective of the rule. Once this response is received, the working group should determine to what extent those activities can be monitored by the regulator.

An important aspect of regulatory rulemaking is that it does not always demand its licensees engage in some activity or conduct that it would not otherwise perform if there were no rule. Instead, it often sets requirements that licensees are generally already performing but that need a regulator's independent verification to ensure they are performed properly and regularly. Some jurisdictions establish minimum standards for these routine activities.

As the influence of technology grows and the operational nature of casinos becomes more complex and diverse, this practice can become cumbersome and difficult to maintain. Typically, there is a process for considering variances from the minimum standards. If regulators employ this level of oversight, sufficient resources must be dedicated to updating the standards and reviewing whether the original objective is still relevant. Furthermore, there should be periodic review to determine whether there are better, more efficient ways to achieve the same objective.

Once the initial conceptual design process is complete, and assuming there is still agreement that the public policy concern is valid, it is time to write the rule. The most important aspect of good rule writing is to ensure the end product clearly communicates expectations and responsibilities to be met in order to comply. Thus, a purpose statement is necessary. Not all jurisdictions require purpose statements, and a few even prohibit them. A purpose statement is the first sentence or paragraph of the rule that announces the public policy objective that is the goal of the regulation.

As an example, consider a rule originally drafted for the Missouri Gaming Commission in 1995–96 by one of the authors that established the first self-exclusion program in the United States. This is not a perfect example of rulemaking, rather it can be used as a case study in how a policy that was ultimately successful could have been improved through better rulemaking techniques. Fortunately, Missouri's rulemaking process requires a "purpose statement." This provides an ideal opportunity to establish the public policy objective that can serve as a fixed guide to ensure the primary goals of the policy stay on course. Unfortunately, it is rarely used that way. Often, instead, purpose statements are cursory and merely describe the broad subject matter of the rule.

The self-exclusion concept the Missouri Gaming Commission envisioned in 1995 was the creation of a platform for problem gamblers to step forward, admit they have a gambling problem, and agree to take personal responsibility for the problem. The concept was designed to inform gamblers of the various treatment and self-help resources available to them and also to shield them from the direct marketing efforts of casinos so that they could pursue their recovery without the constant personalized enticements to return to the casinos. While self-excluders assumed responsibility for refraining from gambling, casinos also had to take reasonable steps to identify those who violated their agreement. When discovered in a casino, self-excluders were arrested for trespassing, and any winnings were denied since they were ineligible to gamble, rendering all their wagers illegal. The program ultimately achieved high levels of success, serving over 15,000 problem gamblers.[34] It remains the largest of its kind in the world. However, the process for creating it was inefficient, lacked adequate stakeholder involvement, and suffered unnecessary growing pains to fully develop. As a result, it serves as an excellent example of how to improve a rulemaking process.

Involving Industry Stakeholders

This vision of the self-exclusion program did not emerge immediately. The initial program was based on a citizen's request to be placed on the commission's List of Excluded Persons. Placement on this list was historically involuntary and intended to prohibit known criminals, persons affiliated with organized crime, and gambling cheats from being allowed in casinos. The gaming commission did not believe the exclusion list was the appropriate mechanism for the citizen but felt that a voluntary exclusion would be appropriate. Therefore, the first draft of the rule allowed gamblers to petition the commission for placement on the List of Disassociated Persons.[35] The remaining provisions of the proposed rule modeled itself after the requirements of the List of Excluded Persons, tasking casino operators with the principle responsibility for preventing people on the list from entering the casino.

Casino operators opposed this approach. They believed they were being unreasonably assigned with the impossible task of preventing a very small proportion of their customers from entering the casino. Surprisingly however, the problem gambling treatment community also opposed the approach. Many problem gambling organizations and treatment professionals emerged to comment that while the commission's intentions were laudable, the proposed rule would do more harm than good. Their primary concern was that the rule created a formal process to allow the gambler to place the responsibility for controlling their gambling behavior on a third party rather than encouraging them to take personal responsibility for it.

The importance of stakeholder input during the initial rule drafting process cannot be overstated. Even the most experienced regulators may not be able to spot every possible issue. It is not a question of intellect, ability, judgment, or wisdom; rather, it involves the inherent limitations of a single or narrow perspective. Involving known industry stakeholders

---

[34] *2011 Annual Report*, Missouri Gaming Comm'n 19, https://www.mgc.dps.mo.gov/annual%20reports/2011_ar/00_FullReport.pdf.

[35] To distinguish participants in the program from criminals and gambling cheats on the Exclusion List, the Commission decided to name the program the List of Disassociated Persons. The intent was to make it clear that these gamblers were, of their own accord, disassociating themselves from casino gambling. As mentioned, the term is regrettable and likely has perplexed more people than it has informed.

in the policy implementation process gives the regulator the broadest possible vision of the operational aspects and consequences of the rule being considered. It also helps the regulator avoid being put in a defensive position when a serious, but previously unknown operational risk or consequence emerges after the rule has been formally offered for adoption.

Once a rule is proposed, there is a natural tendency toward defending the proposed concept. Involving stakeholders early in the process allows all relevant issues to be given visibility before a final decision is made as to the most appropriate policy objective and how to implement it. There may continue to be disputes regarding the best and most efficient way to achieve the objective, but at least all the issues and impediments have been aired and identified. This exercise is so valuable that in certain appropriate circumstances it may be advisable to expand the net even beyond identified industry and stakeholder groups to include consumers.

Using the Missouri self-exclusion program as an example, let us examine the rule-writing process. The original purpose statement for the rule establishing the self-exclusion program (regrettably named the "List of Disassociated Persons") read as follows:

> PURPOSE: This rule establishes a List of Disassociated Persons which consists of those persons who have voluntarily declared that they will no longer visit excursion gambling boats in Missouri because they are problem gamblers.

This purpose statement falls far short of what is needed to ensure proper understanding of the public policy goals of the program. It merely acts as a guide to ensure fidelity to the principle necessary for proper implementation over the long term with the understanding that the rule must survive changes in leadership within the regulatory agency and within the legislative, judicial, and executive branches of government. It also fails to properly inform the intended users of the program and, instead, may confuse and frustrate them. Based on the general description of the program previously provided, consider this purpose statement:

> PURPOSE: This rule creates the framework for a self-exclusion program for problem gamblers, providing them with a formal process for acknowledging that they have, or believe they may soon have, a gambling problem and agreeing to take personal responsibility for it. It is intended as a therapeutic means for the problem gambler to voluntarily agree to accept the sole responsibility to stop gambling at or visiting Missouri casinos. While casino operators are not responsible for preventing self-excluders from entering a casino, they must refrain from enticing them to a casino with marketing material directed at self-excluders and shall not allow them to join players clubs or cash checks. Related rules will explain other features of the self-exclusion program that are designed to encourage treatment, promote prevention and/or harm minimization measures, and assist in the recovery process.

This purpose statement informs the public, the gaming industry, and the regulatory staff responsible for implementing the rule of its objective. It articulates that the obligation of staying out of the casinos lies firmly in the hands of the self-excluder. A critical aspect of self-exclusion is that it requires the gambler to accept responsibility for their behavior.[36] It does not allow them to point fingers or blame their gambling problem on others. [37] It is also based on sound research, which is comforting to any rule maker.

A phenomenon that has negatively affected many self-exclusion programs is the tendency for them to become "enforcement centric." Many regulatory agency activities are focused on enforcing rules. Thus, over time they might look at self-exclusion as something that needs to be "enforced." Since most enforcement activity is directed at casino operators, it is natural for regulators to want to look for ways to "enforce" a self-exclusion policy. By carefully articulating that the primary policy purpose of the self-exclusion program is for gamblers to take personal responsibility for their actions and that it is up to them to stay out of casinos, the rule helps provide a compass that can keep the focus of policy implementation on track over time.

Implementing the Policy Objective

Once the public policy objective has been clarified, the next step is to identify implementation issues and communicate to the industry the specific responsibilities necessary for compliance. Often, the best way to do this is to enumerate requirements in an outline format, confining each requirement to a single, citable paragraph. This allows the target of the regulation to formulate a "checklist" of compliance requirements and develop a strategy for meeting those requirements. It also allows regulators to create an audit profile used to verify compliance and develop performance metrics that can track the effectiveness of the rule over time. The audit profile should be shared with the licensee since the licensee has presumably been part of the rule-making process and thus has agreed on the validity of the public policy objective, resulting in a mutually-agreed-upon goal of compliance.

The Missouri rule effectively communicates the specific compliance requirements for the self-exclusion program. If I revisited the rulemaking process, the principle change would be to set out each specific requirement separately rather than combining several requirements into a single section. This makes understanding and creating a compliance strategy much easier. Consider, for instance, the following provision that combines several specific requirements into a section of the rule with one subsection:

---

[36] Robert Ladouceur, *Self-Exclusion Program: A Longitudinal Evaluation Study*, 23 J. GAMBLING STUD. 85, (2003).
[37] Tobias Hayer & Gerhard Meyer, *Self-Exclusion as a Harm Minimization Strategy: Evidence for the Casino Sector from Selected European Countries*. 27 J. GAMBLING STUD. 685, (2011).

(2) Any Class A licensee or its agent or employee that identifies a person present on an excursion gambling boat and has knowledge that such person is included on the List of Disassociated Persons shall immediately notify or cause to notify the commission and the Class A licensee's senior security officer on duty. Once it is confirmed that the person is on the List, the Class A licensee shall—

(A) Notify the commission agent on duty of the presence of a Disassociated Person on the excursion gambling boat. The licensee shall remove the Disassociated Person from the excursion gambling boat. After the Disassociated Person has been removed from the excursion gambling boat, the licensee shall cooperate with the commission agent in reporting the incident to the proper prosecuting authority and request charges be filed under section 569.140, RSMo for criminal trespassing, a class B misdemeanor.

Substantively, the rule is fine. It gives appropriate guidance and leaves little for interpretation. However, consider how some simple formatting changes might make the rule easier to understand and implement:

(2) Any Class A licensee or its agent or employee that identifies a person present on an excursion gambling boat and has knowledge that such person is included on the List of Disassociated Persons shall:

(A) Immediately notify or cause to notify:

1. the commission; and

2. the Class A licensee's senior security officer on duty.

(B) Once it is confirmed that the person is on the List, the Class A licensee shall:

1. Notify the commission agent on duty of the presence of a Disassociated Person on the excursion gambling boat;

2. Remove the Disassociated Person from the excursion gambling boat; and

3. Cooperate with the commission agent in reporting the incident to the proper prosecuting authority and request charges be filed under section 569.140, RSMo for criminal trespassing, a class B misdemeanor.

Breaking down each requirement into a separate section allows the reader to follow each step of the process and facilitates a cite-based compliance checklist for the licensee. Not only will this improve process management, but it also will allow regulators to focus on each requirement and identify those that are not working or that may need further clarification.

This exercise emphasizes the importance of creating a clear record for those who will be expected to comply with the rule, as well as future generations of regulators who will not have been involved in the rulemaking process. Most regulators do an excellent job of rule writing. However, where there is a failure to carefully articulate the public policy objective and provide step-by-step requirements for compliance, it creates confusion that results in compliance problems. In these instances, attempts at compliance turn into a "guessing game." It also opens the door for an amorphous interpretation of the rule over time as the regulatory staff changes. Paying close attention to the drafting of policy statements and the enumeration of each specific requirement necessary for compliance ensures the regulation's intent is recognized and provides a better compliance environment.

The Continuously Evolving Nature of Risk Control

An inescapable, yet too-often-ignored aspect of regulatory practice is that risk changes over time. As with any other area of regulatory focus, the gaming industry is constantly changing. There are changes in operational business practices, the technology used to deliver products and services, market focus and marketing efforts, the way the industry interacts with consumers and, in turn, the way consumers interact with gaming products. Consequently, over time, areas of risk change, requiring the regulator to refocus efforts, change allocation of resources, abandon unnecessary procedures, and identify new ways of managing the new risk environment.

Consider the gaming floor of the 1990s. Nearly all slot machines included self-contained payment systems primarily implemented through the use of metal "tokens" used in lieu of currency. Patrons inserted cash into a bill acceptor that would then place credits on the slot machine.[38] When a player cashed out, tokens from the machine's "hopper" would dispense into a tray, and patrons would use small buckets to carry their tokens to another machine for further play or to a cage cashier to convert the tokens into currency. If the player won a jackpot over a certain amount, the machine would lock up and trigger a "hand pay" to reduce the throughput from the hopper. This practice was regulated in some states and left for the casino to manage in others. All jackpots requiring a form W-2G required a hand pay.

While some communication existed between slot devices for player tracking purposes and early generation progressive jackpot features, the network configuration of the machines was crude by today's standards. All of the money handling was isolated in the machine, and none of it was handled by the network.

Slot machines of this generation presented a variety of "street crime" issues for regulators. Criminals developed "shaved tokens" that would reg-

---

[38] Some states required that all currency be converted chips or tokens. For instance in Missouri, prior to 2000, all currency inserted into a slot machine had to be converted to tokens which emptied into the tray of the slot machine and then had to be reinserted in order to place credits on the machine for play. This practice was reformed by SB 902 in 2001, which read in relevant part

> Section 313.817.3. Wagering shall not be conducted with money or other negotiable currency. The licensee shall exchange the money of each wagerer for electronic or physical tokens, chips, or other forms of credit to be wagered on the gambling games. The licensee shall exchange the [gambling] tokens, chips, or other forms of wagering credit for money at the request of the wagerer.

Missouri Session Laws, 90th General Assembly, SB 902 (2000).

ister a credit when inserted into the machine but would drop though to the tray. The skillful gambling cheat could easily stack large numbers of tokens, quickly feed them into the machine with one hand, and catch them coming out of the coin return with the other hand. The cheaters would develop techniques to disguise this activity to avoid detection.

Perhaps one of the most infamous gambling cheats of this period was created by Tommy Glenn Carmichael, the originator of the "monkey paw." Carmichael's first generation device was constructed from spring steel and guitar wire. He inserted it into the chute where tokens (or coins) were dispensed and snaked it through the machine until he tripped the payout switch, thus emptying the hopper. A few years later, the industry developed a new technology that utilized a light beam to count coins or tokens as they exited the payout chute. Undeterred, Carmichael invented a second-generation device that used a strong light wand to blind the sensor, once again tricking the machine into emptying its hopper. Carmichael was eventually caught and sent to prison. He described his methods for defeating slot machines as simple: "Figure out how a machine counts money and then work your way into the machine."[39]

These types of cheating scams were identified and discovered using typical street crime policing techniques. Regulators used surveillance and cooperative policing to track Carmichael and his gang of cheats. He was arrested in 1999 by a joint task force using informants, wiretaps, and ongoing surveillance to build a case against him.

Let us fast forward to today's slot floor. Slot machines no longer sit on an island. They are part of an elaborate computer network that monitors every aspect of the machines' behavior. The banking system no longer uses hoppers in each device but is centralized through an encrypted network ticketing system that produces carefully controlled tickets, which can be used in other casino devices or cashed out at the cage or an electronic kiosk. The security system now consists of many layers of complex technology. The nature of risk has changed. On one hand, today's system is far more advanced and difficult to defeat than the slot machines compromised by Carmichael and others. Yet, risk is concentrated into a much smaller area that requires increasing levels of sophistication to understand and administer. While security is more robust, if a criminal can find a weakness in the system, the entire bank is exposed rather than a lone hopper in a machine.

This evolution of gaming technology has changed the way regulators handle risk. Regulations once focused intensely on the manual process of moving tokens around the floor. Now regulators must develop a deeper understanding of the inner workings of the technology that manages the casino's banking system, devise ways to properly "follow the money," and audit the technology to ensure its controls are working. For most regulato-

---

[39] David Crenshaw, *Slot Machine Cheat Bilked Casinos with Ingenious Gadgets*, USA To-
DAY, Aug. 11, 2003.

ry agencies, this has resulted in changes in staffing levels, job descriptions, training, the drafting of new rules and procedures, and the elimination of outdated rules and procedures.

The ability to identify and manage evolution in the gaming industry requires constant vigilance. It requires formal monitoring and review processes to identify changes before they fully take shape and to review existing policies to determine if they continue to adequately and efficiently address a valid public policy objective. Some methods to accomplish this are discussed in the section on performance measurement. First, this chapter examines less formal ways in which regulators can address problems of risk control.

REGULATORY COOPERATION

The value of harmonizing regulatory practices when there is agreement between jurisdictions on the specific policy objective of a regulatory requirement is mentioned several times during this chapter. This is important for several reasons. First, it provides greater clarity regarding the regulatory objective, which helps regulators cooperate efforts to measure compliance rates. Second, harmonized industry standards should cause higher levels of industry compliance. Given the global nature of the gaming industry, non-compliance sometimes occurs because of a lack of understanding of an unusual or "one-off" requirement in a jurisdiction. This is understandable if the jurisdiction has a specific policy issue it finds important, but when the policy objective is nearly universal, compliance rates will inevitably improve if regulators can agree on common requirements for achieving compliance. Finally, given the global nature of the gaming marketplace, harmonized standards provide efficiencies that benefit the market and free resources that can be devoted to increasing compliance rates.

Despite the nearly constant call for regulation harmonization, little progress has been made. The most significant progress has been had through the work of the International Association of Gaming Regulators (IAGR), which developed the multi-jurisdictional licensing form. While this has been a helpful tool for many jurisdictions seeking to increase the efficiency of their background investigations and leveraging the work of other regulatory agencies, the benefits have not expanded the scope of cooperation to other areas of regulation.

One reason for the lack of progress in this area has been the gaming industry's inability to present a case for why certain areas of harmonization would benefit regulators. Instead, industry focus has been on how the current system burdens them. Inevitably, it comes across as whining. In 2011, the American Gaming Association published a white paper entitled, "Improving Gaming Regulation: 10 Recommendations for Streamlining Processes While Maintaining Integrity."[40] While the paper illustrated that certain practices were a

---

[40] DAVID O. STEWART, IMPROVING GAMING REGULATION: 10 RECOMMENDATIONS FOR

burden to the industry, little attention was paid to how the regulator would benefit from the suggested reform measures. As a result, the response to the paper has been a collective "Meh!" from gaming industry regulators.

Harmonization efforts have also stagnated because of the process that typically accompanies these efforts. In the rare instances a formal group of regulators gathers to consider harmonization issues, the process typically consists of an agenda or outline of issues to be considered. In preparation for the meeting, participants typically arm themselves with volumes of regulations and policies they have created relating to the subject along with the underlying reasons for why their approach is superior. They support their views with a collection of anecdotal "war stories" highlighting their success in dealing with issue. The end result is a long meeting that involves sharing stories that suggest each jurisdiction's approach is sound and reasonable. Rarely does the effort even reach the point of drafting a harmonized regulation for consideration.

Two strategies should be considered to resolve these problems. First, the industry should concentrate on trying to understand the current requirements from the regulator's perspective. While regulators should consider a variety of perspectives when creating policy, equally important is for the industry to consider the regulator's role as the protector of the consumer, public trust, and public assets (including granting the right to operate a gaming facility or to work in the industry).

Second, current harmonization methods are backwards. They start with what is already occurring and try to cobble together a solution. Because of loyalty to internal processes and pride-of-authorship issues, these efforts inevitably fail. The first step in any harmonization process should be the same as the first step in any rulemaking process—to first establish the regulatory objective. This helps start the effort organically without reliance on what is already in place mechanically. If regulators can first agree on a precise statement defining the regulatory objective, then the group can begin to discuss the best mechanics for establishing the requirements to meet the objective. If the group disagrees on the underlying policy, then there is no need to harmonize the requirements.

Only through mindful focus on the underlying objective and a commitment to the best, most efficient way to achieve it will harmonization efforts succeed. It will require the industry to shift its focus towards public policy issues and regulators to appreciate the value of efficiency.

REGULATORS AS PROBLEM SOLVERS

An important, often overlooked aspect of regulatory practice is the activity of the agency that goes on outside the formal rulemaking and administration process. Frequently, regulators must address issues that

STREAMLINING PROCESSES WHILE MAINTAINING INTEGRITY, WHITE PAPER (2011).

emerge "between the lines" of formal regulation. These issues require a blend of skills and tools. Professor Malcolm Sparrow argues what regulators really do is "pick important problems and solve them."[41] Regulatory problem-solving involves the things regulators do when risks are identified that do not fit within any existing rule or policy and require immediate attention. It often requires them to step outside their enforcement powers comfort zone to rely on a blend of tools and strategies to fully expose the problem and craft a solution to it. Consider this passage from Sparrow's book, *The Regulatory Craft*, in which he summarizes the regulatory activities of the winners of the Ford Foundation's annual Innovations in American Government competition:[42]

> These innovative programs seem utterly focused on their regulatory task and on the agency's ability to break it down into manageable pieces and then tackle each one. Those pieces invariably take the form of specific, well-articulated problems, risks, or risk concentrations. Where these agencies have focused on patterns of noncompliance, they have chosen forms of noncompliance perceived as particularly troubling or dangerous (such as aggressive running of red lights in New York City).
>
> The vast majority of these programs avoid any a priori preferences for particular means, using enforcement without hesitation if necessary, and using alternatives without hesitation when they might work better. These agencies seem willing to cooperate with regulated industry whenever the problem gets fixed quicker that way – and provided the manner and terms of cooperation do no damage to their enforcement capacity, nor to broader deterrence. They proactively select whom to work with on the basis of analysis, picking the partners they need *for the job*.[43]

The skills regulators use in creating these risk control measures often involve cooperating with other government agencies and leveraging available resources. This is a good environment in which to create performance metrics that can measure the effectiveness of the effort or its failings.[44]

---

[41] Sparrow, *supra* note 25, at 132.

[42] *See Innovations in American Government Award Finalists Announced*, HARVARD, JOHN F. KENNEDY SCHOOL OF GOVERNMENT, http://www.hks.harvard.edu/news-events/news/press-releases/innovations-in-american-government-award:

> Funded by the Ford Foundation, the Innovations in American Government Award Program identifies and promotes excellence in the public sector. Winners are chosen based on novelty, effectiveness, significance, and the degree to which their innovations can inspire replication in other government entities. Past winners offer unique solutions to a range of issues including economic opportunity, public health, education, juvenile justice, and environmental management. Many programs act as harbingers for reform, and often inform research and academic study around key policy areas both at Harvard Kennedy School and academic institutions worldwide.

[43] Sparrow, *supra* note 25, at 97.

[44] *Id.* at 98.

A great example of this type of problem-solving activity is the way the controversy over the proximity of ATMs to the casino floor played out following the release of the National Gambling Impact Study Commission's (NGISC) report in 1999.[45] The NGISC report issued the following recommendation regarding ATM machines:

> Because of the easy availability of automated teller machines (ATM's) and credit machines encourages some gamblers to wager more than they intended, the Commission recommends that states, tribal governments, and pari-mutuel facilities ban credit card cash advance machines and other devices activated by debit or credit cards from the immediate area where gambling takes place.[46]

The recommendation resulted in a wave of state and federal legislation to ban ATMs from the casino floor. In 1999, Congressman John LaFalce (D-NY) introduced the Gambling ATM and Credit/Debit Reform Act, which amended the Electronic Fund Transfer Act and the Truth in Lending Act to prohibit placing an electronic terminal for initiating a consumer credit transaction (including an automated teller machine or a point -of-sale terminal) in an area where any form of gambling is occurring.[47] Scores of states including Florida, Illinois, Iowa, Maine, Missouri, Michigan, and Washington either considered similar state legislation or regulatory policy to ban or restrict the location of ATM machines at casinos.[48]

While these policy discussions identified some risks associated with placing ATM machines on casino floors, the proposed legislative response to the risk also created problems. The prospect of an ATM ban left gaming regulators with the difficult problem of having to manage the risk of patrons carrying large sums of cash from parking lots to the casino floor and the criminal activity that naturally emanates from this practice.

Gaming regulators responded with policies offering strategies more precise than a blanket ban on ATMs that eventually gained lawmakers' confidence. As a result, efforts to ban ATMs through legislation have for the most part faded away. The success of these policies provides a great example of how regulators can work with the industry, technology providers, other regulatory agencies, and special interest groups to develop policies that target identified areas of risk and can be evaluated for effectiveness.

---

[45] *See* John Wilen, *Nevadans Talk about Banning ATMs from Casino Floors,* Las Vegas Sun, Aug.14, 1998, http://www.lasvegassun.com/news/1998/aug/14/nevadans-talk-about-banning-atms-from-casino-floor/.

[46] Nat'l Gambling Impact Study Comm'n, National Gambling Impact Study Commission Final Report 7-30 (1999), http://govinfo.library.unt.edu/ngisc/reports/fullrpt.html

[47] Gambling ATM and Credit/Debit Card Reform Act, H.R. 2811, 106th Cong. (1999), http://www.govtrack.us/congress/bills/106/hr2811.

[48] *See, e.g.,* 16-633 Me. Code R. Ch. 8 § 1(F) ("No ATM or cash advance machine shall be located on the gaming floor. For the purposes of this rule, the gaming floor shall include that area from which people under 21 can be excluded and perimeters of which shall be shown on the Uniform Location Agreement.").

One of the more interesting responses to the attempted ATM ban was an effort by various regulatory agencies to engage in discussions with technology providers to develop an ATM functionality that would allow gamblers to restrict usage of debit or credit cards at ATMs located in or near casinos. The concept originated with Global Cash Access (GCA) through its Self Transaction Exclusion Program (STeP), which allowed gamblers to ban the usage of their debit or credit card across GCA's entire network of ATMs, cash access kiosks, and booth services around the world. The technology also allowed regulators to verify that casino operators had stopped patrons enrolled in state self-exclusion programs from being able to access GCA's cash machines. Many other companies have developed related technologies to help gamblers manage their usage of credit and debit cards in casinos. For instance, some providers allow gamblers to set daily, weekly, or monthly limits on the amount of cash that can be withdrawn from ATM machines at casinos. In Australia, many states require ATMs to be limited to $400 withdraws during a 24-hour period.[49]

Apart from technology controls, regulators recognized the opportunity to use ATMs to communicate important responsible gaming information. For example, it is now a common regulatory practice to require ATMs to display problem gambling helpline numbers on the physical device, on introductory screens prior to initiating a transaction and on the ATM receipt itself.[50] Any caller to the GCA consumer helpline is given a "Think. Be Responsible" Greeting, and the caller simply needs to say the word "help" to be connected to the local NCPG hotline.

Some regulators also require responsible-gaming brochures to be placed near ATMs. These materials describe available treatment programs, provide information to patrons regarding the odds of the games and chances of winning, and also communicate helpline numbers and information about self-exclusion programs.

Regulators have also used their problem-solving skills to manage legislative or policy mandates that ATMs be located off the casino floor. If the ATMs are too remote, the risk of theft and assault increases. Thus, many regulators have defined the parameters of the casino floor in a way that will accommodate safe usage of ATMs while still complying with the legislative mandate.[51] The effectiveness of removing ATMs from the casino floor remains questionable. A report to the Ontario Problem Gambling Research Centre found that while removing ATMs from the gaming floor resulted in an initial drop in ATM use for gambling purposes, patrons quickly adapted

---

[49] *Information Sheet: Responsible Gambling in Australian Casinos*, AUSTRALIAN CASINO ASSOCIATION 6, http://www.auscasinos.com/assets/files/pdf/RG%20Initiatives%20 Aust%20Casinos.pdf (March 2009).

[50] 16-633 ME. CODE R. § 18

[51] *See, e.g.*, IOWA CODE ANN. § 99F.7(10)(b)(enabling Iowa regulators to define the casino floor, thereby allowing them to very strategically and specifically place ATMs off the casino floor but keep them in an area that is safe and reasonably convenient so that they can still adhere to the public policy objective of the statutory provision).

to the new ATM locations, and the resulting impact on their long-term behavior was insignificant.[52]

CHALLENGES TO THE PROBLEM SOLVING APPROACH AND THE IMPORTANCE OF MEASUREMENTS AND OVERSIGHT

The problem-solving approach to risk control presents many challenges for regulators. This technique is not the easy way out. It requires diligent analysis, the consideration of a variety of perspectives, the ability to identify a specific result expected from the policy, and often the willingness to cooperate with other agencies and/or the regulated industry. Moreover, even the most carefully designed risk control strategy can have adverse side-effects that must be studied as part of the continuing evaluation of a policy's effectiveness.

For instance, recent emphasis on the importance of sunscreen to prevent skin cancer has produced excellent results. However, it has also been accompanied by a rise in Vitamin D deficiency, and some studies have raised concerns about oxybenzone.[53] The common installation of airbags in automobiles has been an important tool for reducing fatal auto injuries, yet it has been accompanied by an increase in injuries to faces, arms, and shoulders.[54] A more extreme example is found in the early 1970s mandate to use the chemical TRIS as a fire retardant in children's pajamas. It was not until years later that it was discovered the chemical presented significant cancer risks.[55] Thus, just as doctors are advised to "first, do no harm," regulators must be cautious to ensure their policies do not produce a worse result than would the underlying risk.

To be fair, it is unlikely that any gaming regulatory intervention will cause cancer. However, the industry is not without a history of policy failures that resulted in harm to consumers. Consider Australia's experiment with placing time limits on slot machines as a strategy to reduce problem gambling. One of the unintended consequences of this policy was that many problem gamblers would increase bet levels and play faster as the limit on their time grew nearer.[56]

---

[52] Kevin Harrigan, Vance MacLaren & Mike Dixon, *Effectiveness of a Brief Educational Intervention and ATM-removal in Reducing Erroneous Cognitions and Over-Expenditure during Slot Machine Play in Problem and Non-Problem Gamblers* 13 (May 2010), www.gamblingresearch.org/download.php?docid=11411.

[53] *The Trouble with Sunscreen Chemicals*, ENVIRONMENTAL WORKING GROUP, http://www.ewg.org/2013sunscreen/the-trouble-with-sunscreen-chemicals/.

[54] L A Wallis & I Greaves, *Injuries Associated with Airbag Deployment*, 19 EMERG. MED. J 490–493 (2002).

[55] Chris Whipple, *Redistributing Risk*, AEI J. ON GOV'T & SOC'Y 37, 38 (1985), http://object.cato.org/sites/cato.org/files/serials/files/regulation/1985/5/v9n3-6.pdf.

[56] A. BLASCZYZYNSKI, ET. AL., FINAL REPORT: THE ASSESSMENT OF THE IMPACT OF THE RECONFIGURATION OF ELECTRONIC GAME MACHINES AS HARM MINIMISATION STRATEGIES FOR PROBLEM GAMBLING, UNIVERSITY OF SYDNEY GAMBLING RESEARCH UNIT

The potential for policies to fail to achieve their intended objective, or worse, to result in harm, emphasizes the need for regulators to include evaluation and performance metrics in each of their risk-control strategies. This can be much more challenging for gaming regulators than many other forms of regulatory practice because so much of what regulators do involves mitigating the risk of harm from an activity that if conducted without a license is illegal. How do you measure the number of gaming cheaters deterred because of regulation? How do you measure how many would-be hackers are prevented from compromising the security of a casino's network because of regulation? How do you measure how much tax revenue would have been skimmed if casinos were regulated like movie theatres?

The available data regarding resulting harms if gambling was left unregulated is limited, consisting primarily of historical anecdotes. Instinctively, regulators might conclude that unregulated gambling results in an increased potential for cheating, unfair consumer practices, equipment malfunctions, loss of tax revenue, and lack of protections for people with gambling problems. While illegal gambling occurs even in jurisdictions where gambling is regulated, there is little data available regarding to what extent it would thrive absent regulation. It is certainly not as easy as comparing pollution rates before and after scrubbers are installed in a coal plant or comparing the rate of disease after a new vaccine is introduced.

Still, regulation without measurement leaves regulators unable to demonstrate the worthiness of the resources and authority that have been granted to them. Legislators and agencies responsible for regulatory oversight are without tools to conduct a proper evaluation. The Organisation for Economic Co-Operation and Development (OECD) consists of 34 member countries working together to address the economic, social, and environmental challenges of globalization. In 2012, OECD published a remarkably helpful guide on Measuring Regulatory Performance.[57] The OECD guide identifies two areas that require evaluation when measuring regulatory policy: (i) the substantive outcomes of the regulations developed under the regulatory policy; and (ii) any relevant process outcomes based on administrative, democratic, or technocratic values.[58]

While the OECD evaluation structure provides valuable guidance, gaming regulation requires some additional metrics. Professor Sparrow argues for a broader perspective proposing a four-tiered classification scheme for regulatory results to include (1) effects, impacts, and outcomes; (2) behavioral outcomes; (3) agency activities and outputs; and (4) resource efficiency.[59]

(2001), http://www.psych.usyd.edu.au/gambling/GIO_report.pdf.

[57] Cary Coglianese, *Measuring Regulatory Performance: Evaluating the Impact of Regulation and Regulatory Policy*, http://www.oecd.org/gov/regulatory-policy/1_coglianese%20web.pdf (Aug. 2012).

[58] *Id.* at 7.

[59] Sparrow, *supra* note 25 at 119.

Professor Sparrow's classification system is well suited to a gaming regulatory environment because it allows for a tabulation of prevention activities that are inherently difficult to measure, such as outreach, education, partnership programs, and customer service.[60] Furthermore, it is not irreconcilable with OECD's approach, which emphasizes that not only do regulators need indicators to "measure relevant outcomes of concern", but they also need "research designs to support inferences about the extent to which a regulation or regulatory policy under evaluation has actually *caused any change* in the measured outcomes."[61]

Table 1 from the OECD study provides a helpful perspective on the enormous scope of regulatory impact and the need to measure not only the outcome of the specific regulatory strategy but also to identify its possible side effects and analyze whether each effect results from the regulation, or policy, or something else. For instance, for many years Missouri imposed a $500 loss limit at its casinos. The public policy objective of the loss limit was to reduce the incidence of problem gambling. A principle outcome of the policy was that Missouri had significantly lower rates of gaming loss per patron than adjoining states with no loss limits. This might suggest the policy was working. However, also consider the limit was easy to circumvent, and that a survey of player data showed that less than 2 percent of the patrons reached the $500 limit during a gaming session.[62] Missouri later rescinded the loss limit, and while per player spending increased, there has been no discernable impact on problem gambling rates.

Thus, in designing performance measures, regulators should be careful to examine the causal chain of each regulation, not only within the boundaries of its jurisdiction, but also in neighboring markets. Furthermore, it is important to measure the resources used to implement the policy in order to determine the efficiency of the effort. As Sparrow writes to support his fourth tier, regulators have an obligation "to make efficient use of public resources; to minimize the burden on the regulated community; and to be sparing with the use of that precious commodity, the coercive power of the state."[63]

---

[60] *Id.* at 120.

[61] *Coglianese, supra* note 56, at 7 (emphasis added).

[62] The Missouri loss limit was controlled through a buy-in limit that restricted gamblers from buying in for more than $500 per two hour "gambling excursion." It was enforced by requiring every patron to use a player's card for buy-in purposes. The player would insert the card into a slot machine or hand it to a dealer to be swiped into the central system monitoring the buy-in of each card holder. It would not allow a patron to buy-in for more than $500 in any one gambling session. However, there was no requirement to show identification during the buy-in process. Thus, players could borrow cards from friends or pick up abandoned cards on the gaming floor, bathrooms or parking lots allowing them to buy in on other accounts.

[63] *Sparrow, supra* note 25, at 119.

CONCLUSION

There is near universal agreement that commercial gaming requires a thorough, structured regulatory scheme to assure consumer confidence, prevent social harms, and maximize the economic benefits the industry presents.[64] The main issue for stakeholders involved in the industry is whether the pace of regulatory risk control practices are keeping up with changes in the gaming environment, many of which are being driven by technology and global economic factors. This chapter was intended to provide ideas for improving regulatory processes so that regulators can become more nimble, focused, efficient, and effective. A goal was to highlight the importance of gaining a thorough understanding of the public policy objective of each regulatory requirement before embarking on the procedural requirements to implement it. The chapter also stresses the value of establishing performance metrics that measure the effectiveness of each risk control strategy. This must be accompanied by periodic evaluations of how new strategies are affecting those strategies established previously.

This chapter tries to present a holistic view of regulatory practices and techniques that can achieve good results, adapt to changing risk patterns, include measurable results, and do so with optimum efficiency of public and private resources and government authority. These efforts require meticulous attention to the creation of the regulatory framework and the way it is administered. For the industry to achieve high compliance rates, participants must have a clear vision of what is expected of them and why it is important.

Even the most carefully crafted framework, however, will need adjustment from time to time; just as the most meticulously designed engineering plans require change orders. It is important to be mindful that risk is not static, nor is the gaming industry under regulation. New technology is continually changing the casinos' fundamental operations, and new ideas, such as introducing alternative currencies or the mobilization and socialization of gaming content, result in significant, often unpredictable changes in the gaming business. Thus, regulatory systems must include processes for monitoring risk and providing the ability to quickly organize teams of specialized staff that are able to unravel complex issues and create solutions to address new risks.

The ultimate goal is to achieve a highly responsive, well-focused, accountable, effective risk management system that ensures the integrity of the gaming industry and optimizes its economic and social impact on the communities it serves.

---

[64] *Stewart, supra* note 40, at 1 (illustrating that even the largest US casino trade association, the American Gaming Association, embraces effective regulation).

4

Structuring a Casino Industry

Eugene Martin Christiansen and Alex Hua

INTRODUCTION

The editor defines public policy as "an intentional course of action followed by a government institution or official for resolving an issue of public concern." Casinos raise important issues of public policy. These include *fiscal policy*, in that gaming licensees typically pay gaming privilege taxes as a condition of conducting gaming operations; *economic policy*, in that casinos create jobs and require capital investment; and *social policy*, in that casinos stimulate obsessive or compulsive gambling behavior and have implications for the quality of life in the communities that host them. Casinos may be intended to serve other public policy purposes: for example, casinos may be engines of tourism development or urban re-development. The ability of a casino industry to realize any or all of these public policies depends in large measure on the form the industry takes, i.e., on its structure.

The structure of a casino industry should be established *prior* to the enactment of gaming law. Government's ability to structure a casino industry is greatest *before* gaming law is enacted and gaming licenses are awarded. Once gaming licenses are issued and capital is invested in casino facilities, gaming industry structures are difficult to change.[1]

---

[1] A case in point is Macau's gaming industry, the world's largest measured by gross gaming revenue, or consumer spending on casino games. William R. Eadington & Ricardo C.S. Siu, Between Law and Custom—Examining the Interaction between Legislative Change and the Evolution of Macau's Casino Industry, INT'L GAMBLING STUD., April 2007, at 1. The abstract of this paper is as follows: This paper examines the evolution of regulatory and business structures of the casino industry in Macau in the context of its current rapidly changing legal and economic environment. This analysis discusses the interaction between legislative change and the evolution of Macau's casino industry from the middle of the nineteenth century to the present. The role of institutions, the process of institutional change and their interrelationships with the industry's performance in both the short and the long run are examined. Models are developed to explain the relaxation of formal constraints that permit the main stakeholders to maximize economic rents within the historic and current context of Macau casinos. The paper also discusses some of the business

Gaming regulations should flow from policy goals, not the other way around.

The structural aspects of a casino industry are thus a public policy concern. Depending on the jurisdiction, the relevant agency or entity deciding the public policy issues casinos raise may be the legislature, the executive, or a commission appointed for this purpose. In choosing an appropriate structure for a casino industry government should consider the threshold issues outlined below.

FISCAL VS. ECONOMIC POLICY: GAMING PRIVILEGE TAX RATES

Determining appropriate rates of gaming privilege tax is fundamental to structuring a casino industry. Gaming privilege tax rates imply a policy choice between the *fiscal* as opposed to the *economic* contributions casinos make. High rates of gaming privilege tax maximize gaming tax receipts, which serve government fiscal needs. Low rates of gaming privilege tax encourage capital investment, jobs, tourism and so forth, which contribute to economic development.

To some extent, the choice between high and low rates of gaming privilege tax is a mutually exclusive choice: it may be impossible to establish a rate of gaming privilege tax that maximizes *both* the economic and the fiscal contributions of casinos.[2] High rates of gaming privilege tax maximize the contribution casinos make to government finances, but discourage capital investment and employment and thus the contribution casinos make to the general economy.

The best modern example of gaming law intended to serve economic policy is Nevada's Gaming Act of 1931. Nevada began its history as a state of the United States in 1864 with an economy primarily dependent on mining.[3] By the 1920s Nevada's mines were exhausted. The onset of the Great Depression in 1930 made Nevada's economic needs acute. In an atmosphere of worsening economic crisis the Nevada legislature decided to legalize all forms of gambling (other than lotteries, which were prohibited by Federal law, and pari-mutuel betting), giving Nevada a monopoly on legal casino gaming in the United States. The legislature hoped this monopoly would provide Nevada with a new engine of economic development to replace its exhausted mining sector—with raising revenue for government through gaming taxation an important secondary purpose.[4] Nevada's hopes were

---

practices and regulatory challenges that will confront Macau's casino industry in the years ahead.

[2] CHRISTIANSEN CAPITAL ADVISORS, LLC, THE IMPACTS OF GAMING TAXATION IN THE UNITED STATES, (June 2005), http://www.americangaming.org/industry-resources/research/white-papers (follow "download" hyperlink under synopsis of this white paper for full text).

[3] Cattle ranching and farming were secondary economic activities.

[4] NEV. REV. STAT. § 463.0129(1)(a) (2013) (stating that the gaming industry is vitally important to the economy of the State and the general welfare of the inhabitants.).

abundantly realized. In the decades following the Second World War Nevada's Gaming Act stimulated the development of the world's largest casino industry. Las Vegas, little more than a desert railroad crossing when the Act was passed, developed into a global destination for tourists attracted to the Strip's elaborate casino resorts, a leisure innovation Las Vegas invented. Mindful of gaming's importance to Nevada's economy, the State resisted the temptation to increase gaming privilege tax rates: Nevada's gaming privilege taxes remain the lowest in the United States, effectively 8 percent of gross gaming revenue in 2013.[5] Gaming is the State's largest employer, and even with its low tax rate, revenues generated from taxes paid by gaming licensees constitute Nevada's largest single source of government revenue.[6]

Pennsylvania provides an example of casino legalization as fiscal as opposed to economic policy. In 2004 the Commonwealth of Pennsylvania authorized slot machines ("limited gaming") at seven racetracks and seven stand-alone casinos for the primary purpose of providing ". . . a significant source of new revenue to the Commonwealth to support property tax relief, wage tax reduction, economic development opportunities and other similar initiatives."[7] Pursuant to this purpose (and in sharp contrast to Nevada, which does not levy high fees for its gaming licenses) the Commonwealth imposed a license fee of $50 million and gaming privilege tax rates of 55 percent for slot machines and 16 percent for table games.[8] Casino gaming proved highly successful in Pennsylvania, principally because casinos in neighboring jurisdictions—New Jersey (Atlantic City), West Virginia, Delaware, and Connecticut—had created an experienced consumer base for casino gaming. Through 2013 license fees and gaming tax receipts generated $7.96 billion in tax revenue for the Commonwealth, public funds that enabled Pennsylvania's governor and legislature to make good on their promise of property tax relief.

It is also important to recognize that regardless of what constitutes an appropriate rate of gaming privilege tax (and license fees if any), the public policies or purposes for which casinos are authorized cannot be accomplished unless the casino industry has access to investment capital. Casinos

---

1. The Legislature hereby finds, and declares to be the public policy of this state, that:

(a)   The gaming industry is vitally important to the economy of the State and the general welfare of the inhabitants.

[5] A summary of gaming privilege tax rates for US States for 2013 can be found at the American Gaming Association's 2013 State of the States report, http://www.americangaming.org/sites/default/files/uploads/docs/aga_sos2013_fnl.pdf.

[6] The historical evolution of Nevada gambling law is reviewed in William R. Eadington and James S. Hattori, *A Legislative History of Gambling in Nevada*, 2 NEV. REV. BUS. & ECON. 13 (1978) and William R. Eadington, *The Evolution of Corporate Gambling in Nevada*, 6 NEVADA REVIEW OF BUSINESS AND ECONOMICS 13 (1982).

[7] 4 PA. CON. STAT. § 1102(3) (2010).

[8] Multi-million-dollar license fees are practically speaking capital items, and are typically financed (i.e., companies typically borrow money to pay multi-million dollar license fees, which adds to the debt service burden of the license holder.

are capital-intensive. If a casino industry does not have access to capital, whether because gaming privilege tax rates are too high or for any other reason, the industry will be unable to accomplish whatever public policy purpose it is intended to serve.

Nevada's success in attracting investment capital for its casino industry was a function of its US monopoly on legal gaming: there were no other legal casino investment opportunities in the United States until New Jersey authorized casinos in 1976. The enormous success of Atlantic City's first casino precipitated a second wave of investor interest in gaming. Macau's 2001 decision to issue gaming licenses to foreign companies stimulated a third round of large-scale gaming investment. The unprecedented success of Macau's *de facto* opening of the Chinese market to foreign casino companies prompted Singapore to emulate Macau by issuing two licenses in 2006, attracting capital investment that through 2010 totaled approximately $10.2 billion.[9]

The effectiveness of casinos as engines of economic development and their ability to pay gaming privilege taxes are directly proportional to demand for gaming. The grossly under-supplied market conditions that underlay the success of casinos in Nevada, Pennsylvania, Macau and Singapore have vanished in much of the world today. As the global gaming map fills up, untapped pools of unsatisfied demand for gaming are becoming harder to find. Some older casino industries, notably Atlantic City's, are undergoing long-term contraction; their contributions to government revenues and the local economy are steadily diminishing.

There is a lesson in this experience. The decision to set rates of gaming privilege tax (and license fees large enough to be capital items) has long-term consequences. Casinos, especially elaborate casino resorts that depend on long-distance travelers, are the most capital-intensive leisure products ever brought to market. They are costly to build and even more costly to maintain in competitive condition. Casino properties that are not periodically refreshed with capital spending will fall behind the curve of ever-rising, constantly evolving consumer expectations. The problem is not immediately apparent. New casinos are, by definition, new; if their design is a fit with their target market demographics they will almost certainly succeed—initially. Atlantic City casinos posted annual year-over-year double-digit gross gaming revenue gains for nearly two decades following the opening of the Chalfonte-Haddon Hall, Atlantic City's first casino. But while Atlantic City's gaming privilege tax rate was low, 8 percent, its capital structure was so highly leveraged most of the free cash Atlantic City casinos generated went to debt service, leaving Atlantic City's casino hotels essentially without funds available for further investment. When casinos opened in the neighboring markets of Delaware and Pennsylvania, Atlantic City

---

[9] Sonia Kolesnikov-Jessop, *Operators Pin High Hopes on Singapore Casinos*, N.Y. Times, Feb. 3, 2010, http://www.nytimes.com/2010/02/04/business/global/04casino.html.

was helpless. Its market contracted, and, in the last quarter of 2013, the first of its aging, obsolete casinos closed.[10]

NUMBER OF GAMING LICENSES

A related policy choice is the number of licenses a jurisdiction chooses to create. Like the decision to set rates of gaming privilege taxes and the amount of license fees, the number of gaming licenses is fundamental to a casino industry's structure. By exercising its power to create gaming licenses, government is able to control the supply of gaming. The number of licenses determines the market economics casinos operate in (assuming the jurisdiction is coterminous with the casinos' market, which may or may not be the case).

The licensing jurisdiction may decide to allow market economics to determine the number of casinos, as Nevada and Mississippi do (in which case the supply and demand for gaming will tend toward balance, and the market will be fully supplied), or conversely it may limit the number of licenses, as Macau and Singapore do (thereby preserving under-supplied market conditions and a quasi-monopoly for casino licensees).

This decision has far-reaching implications.

The casino industry as we know it today is the product of highly unusual relationships between supply and demand. The industry's above-average returns on invested capital (ROIC) that make multi-billion-dollar integrated casino resorts feasible in large markets; the ability of integrated casino resorts to attract long-distance travelers and their effectiveness as a driver of tourism;[11] the industry's ability to put large amounts of capital to productive use; its tendency to rely on highly leveraged capital structures; its power as an engine of economic development; its ability to create jobs; its ability to pay taxes over and above normal business taxes for the privilege of conducting gaming—all of these things are consequences of the fact that until quite recently demand for gaming in most parts of the world greatly exceeded supply.

Industry Structure and the Marketplace

In free economies (as distinct from controlled economies like the former Soviet Union) demand and supply tend towards balance. Consumers have as

[10] On December 20, 2013, the Atlantic Club Casino Hotel announced that it would close its doors on January 13, 2014. *See* Victoria Bekiempis, *Atlantic City's Last "Low-Roller" Casino Busts*, NEWSWEEK, Jan. 16, 2014, http://www.newsweek.com/atlantic-citys-last-low-roller-casino-busts-226283.

[11] William R. Eadington & Eugene Martin Christiansen, *Tourist Destination Resorts, Market Structures, and Tax Environments for Casino Industries: An Examination of the Global Experience of Casino Resort Development, in* INSTITUTE FOR THE STUDY OF GAMBLING & COMMERCIAL GAMING, UNIVERSITY OF NEVADA-RENO, RENO: NEVADA, INTEGRATED RESORT CASINOS: IMPLICATIONS FOR ECONOMIC GROWTH AND SOCIAL IMPACTS 3 (William R. Eadington & Meighan R. Doyle eds., 2009) (examining large-scale integrated casino resorts).

many shoes, ships, sealing wax, and widgets as they want (or can afford). An economist would say this is because consumer demand calls supply into being. Casinos are an exception, because without a license demand for gaming cannot legally be supplied. The result is under-supplied casino market economics: an imbalance between the supply of casino machine and table games and the demand for these activities. This was true in most of the world as recently as the closing decade of the twentieth century. It is no longer true in much of the world today. The under-supplied market economics that allowed the gaming industry to grow to its present dimensions are, outside Pacific Asia, increasingly a thing of the past. As the world's map fills up with casinos gaming market economics increasingly resemble the market economics for everything else.

Supplying unsatisfied demand for gaming is not the only basis for a successful casino industry. Casinos can stimulate new demand for gaming and new demand for leisure consumption of other kinds as well. Perhaps the best example is The Mirage, which opened in 1989 on the Las Vegas Strip, a market that had appeared to be fully supplied and unable to productively absorb additional capital investment.

The Mirage was a new species of leisure product, a diversified casino resort, designed to satisfy multiple consumer appetites in addition to the appetite for casino games. It did this so successfully that it stimulated demand for new kinds of leisure consumption while generating unprecedented gross gaming revenue.

The Mirage's success instigated a process of capital-intensive diversified gaming resort development along the Las Vegas Strip that continues today. Prior to The Mirage, Las Vegas resorts derived nearly all of their revenue from their casinos' gaming operations, with hotel rooms, food and alcoholic beverages, and outdoor recreations—golf, swimming pools and so forth—provided essentially as loss leaders for casino games. In the decades following The Mirage's opening the percentage of Las Vegas Strip resort facility revenue generated from casino floors has steadily fallen (to less than 50 percent for some large Strip properties), with the balance derived from night clubs, hotel rooms, spas, restaurants, retail and other non-gaming leisure activities. Diversified resorts attracted a new kind of visitor to Las Vegas: visitors who do not spend money on gaming.[12]

FINANCIAL STABILITY AND LICENSEE CAPITAL STRUCTURES

Appropriate rates of gaming privilege tax, the amount of license fees if any, and the number of gaming licenses are issues any jurisdiction contemplating casino gaming is obliged to decide. The question of whether casino financial stability should be a regulatory concern is less easy to answer. Should definitions of financial stability be incorporated in gaming law or

---

[12] In 2012, 28 percent of visitors to Las Vegas did not gamble. *See* Las Vegas Convention and Visitors Authority, Visitors Statistics, http://www.lvcva.com/stats-and-facts/visitor-statistics/ (follow "2012 Las Vegas Visitor Profile Study" hyperlink, at 61).

regulations? Should the financial stability of casinos be a regulatory concern? If so, should regulators have a degree of oversight regarding licensee capital structures?

These questions do not have simple answers. The financial stability of private-sector gaming license holders is not obviously a governmental concern, at least for casinos operating in free as opposed to planned economies. Moreover, casino financial stability is intrinsically related to casino capital structures. The capital structure of casinos and casino industries is a technical matter, one which government regulatory agencies may not be competent to evaluate or oversee. Large issues of public policy are at stake. Financially unstable casino industries shed jobs, pay diminishing gaming privilege taxes, discourage capital investment and in general frustrate the purposes for which casinos were authorized in the first place. While categorical, one-size-fits-all answers to the questions financial stability raises may be impossible to formulate, a review of the experience with casino financial stability to date provides a context for evaluating these complicated issues.

There have been two major financial stability crises in the casino industry: one in Atlantic City in the late 1980s and early 1990s; and one following the global fiscal crisis of 2007 and the ensuing recession, which affected casinos around the world. Both were characterized by an abrupt slackening in demand and a sharp contraction of the availability of credit. Both made leveraged casino capital structures suddenly unstable. And both precipitated waves of bankruptcies and restructurings.

These two episodes differ in their causes and consequently in their implications.

Atlantic City 1989–1991

The construction of Atlantic City's casinos in the late 1970s and 1980s was largely financed with debt, including high yield ("junk") bonds. Drexel Burnham Lambert Inc., which pioneered the use of this form of debt, was a prominent source of this financing: between 1978 and 1987 Drexel raised $851.2 million for the Atlantic City casino industry.[13] The resulting industry capital structure was highly leveraged. A substantial portion of the cash generated by Atlantic City casino operations was consequently needed to service the industry's debt, which was high yield—i.e., expensive for the borrower. Drexel's worsening problems with federal authorities[14] and the unexpected collapse of the junk bond market in 1989 precipitated a financial crisis in the Atlantic City casino industry. Suddenly, the debt in the

---

[13] Rick Gladstone, *Drexel Required to Obtain License by New Jersey Gambling Authority*, Assoc. Press, Aug. 14, 1987, *available at* http://www.apnewsarchive.com/1987/Drexel-Required-To-Obtain-License-by-New-Jersey-Gambling-Authority/id-2e70436b220260 290b53074058b4b716.

[14] For a detailed history of Drexel Burnham Lambert *see* http://en.wikipedia.org/wiki/Drexel_Burnham_Lambert.

industry's capital structure could not be re-financed, destabilizing the industry's financial foundation.

This change in the industry's financial environment coincided with an unanticipated maturing of the Atlantic City gaming market. Atlantic City gaming's early years had been characterized by rapid growth. From 1978 through 1985, Atlantic City casinos' average growth rate (in gross gaming revenue) was 55.07 percent. In 1985, however, year-over-year growth in Atlantic City gross gaming revenue dropped below 10 percent; in 1989 the year-over-year percentage growth in this crucial indicator fell to 2.64 percent.[15] The conjunction of constricted credit and falling demand resulted in a wave of casino restructurings and bankruptcies. To its embarrassment New Jersey's gaming regulatory agency, the New Jersey Casino Control Commission, discovered that it did not have a definition of casino financial stability to rely on in dealing with this crisis. In 1991 the Commission engaged consultants to supply it with a definition of financial stability.[16]

---

[15] UNLV CENTER FOR GAMING RESEARCH, Atlantic City Gaming Revenue: Statistics for Casino, Slot, and Table Win, 1978–2013 at 2, (Jan. 2014), http://gaming.unlv.edu/reports. html (follow "Atlantic City Gaming Revenue: Statistics for Casino, Slot, and Table Win, 1978–2013" hyperlink); STATE OF NEW JERSEY CASINO CONTROL COMMISSION, Historical Statistics, 1978–2004, http://www.nj.gov/casinos/financia/histori/ (follow "1978–2004" hyperlink).

[16] Christiansen/Charterhouse was engaged by the State of New Jersey in September 1991. The definition Christiansen/Charterhouse supplied is codified at N.J. ADMIN. CODE § 19:43-4.2 (2014):

19:43-4.2 Financial stability

   (a) Each casino licensee or applicant shall establish its financial stability by clear and convincing evidence in accordance with section 84(a) of the Act and this subchapter.

   (b) The Commission may consider any relevant evidence of financial stability; provided, however, that a casino licensee or applicant shall be considered to be financially stable if it establishes by clear and convincing evidence that it meets each of the following standards:

      1.   The ability to assure the financial integrity of casino operations by the maintenance of a casino bankroll or equivalent provisions adequate to pay winning wagers to casino patrons when due. A casino licensee or applicant shall be found to have established this standard if it maintains, on a daily basis, a casino bankroll, or a casino bankroll and equivalent provisions, in an amount which is at least equal to the average daily minimum casino bankroll or equivalent provisions, calculated on a monthly basis, for the corresponding month in the previous year. For any casino licensee or applicant which has been in operation for less than a year, such amount shall be determined by the Commission based upon levels maintained by a comparable casino licensee;

      2.   The ability to meet ongoing operating expenses which are essential to the maintenance of continuous and stable casino operations. A casino licensee or applicant shall be found to have established this standard if it demonstrates the ability to achieve positive gross operating profit, measured on an annual basis;

      3.   The ability to pay, as and when due, all local, State and Federal taxes,

The Las Vegas Strip 2007–2010

The combination of leveraged industry capital structures, a sudden contraction in the availability of credit, and falling consumer demand recurred on the Las Vegas Strip in late 2007.[17]

The decade following 1998 saw an unprecedented increase in the indebtedness of large Strip casinos. This increase in indebtedness was a product of an era of easy credit that extended into the early years of the twenty-first century. Las Vegas Strip casinos entered the twenty-first century with a dominant position in the global market for destination resort gaming. The highly favorable market economics large Strip properties enjoyed translated into high and reliable cash flows, which made them ideal clients for financial institutions with money to lend. The temptation to increase the leverage (the ratio of debt to equity) of casino capital structures was hard for Strip resort management to resist. As long as Strip resorts continued to generate high cash flows and credit remained readily available high leverage appeared to be risk-free, an efficient use of equity.

The increase in gaming industry indebtedness was singularly ill-timed. While the industry was leveraging up its balance sheet the Las Vegas Strip's global monopoly of destination resort gaming was eroding. Macau opened its market to foreign investment in 2001, stimulating capital investment in gaming resorts that equaled and then surpassed the Strip—generating gross gaming revenue that by 2008 made Macau the largest gaming market in the

---

including the tax on gross revenues imposed by subsection 144(a) of the Act, the investment alternative tax obligations imposed by subsection 144(b) and section 144.1 of the Act, and any fees imposed by the Act and Commission rules;

4.   The ability to make necessary capital and maintenance expenditures in a timely manner which are adequate to ensure maintenance of a superior first class facility of exceptional quality pursuant to subsection 83(i) of the Act. A casino licensee or applicant shall be found to have established this standard if it demonstrates that its capital and maintenance expenditures, over the five-year period which includes the three most recent calendar years and the upcoming two calendar years, average at least five percent of net revenue per annum, except that any casino licensee or applicant which has been in operation for less than three years shall be required to otherwise establish compliance with this standard; and

5.   The ability to pay, exchange, refinance or extend debts, including long-term and short-term principal and interest and capital lease obligations, which will mature or otherwise come due and payable during the license term, or to otherwise manage such debts and any default with respect to such debts. The Commission also may require that a casino licensee or applicant advise the Commission and Division as to its plans to meet this standard with respect to any material debts coming due and payable within 12 months after the end of the license term.

[17] For further analysis of the financial crisis that impacted large Las Vegas Strip casino resorts following the onset of the global financial crisis in the latter half of 2007, *see* David G. Schwartz & Eugene Martin Christiansen, *Financial Stability and Casino Debt*, 16 GAMING LAW REV. & ECON. 193 (2012).

world. In 2010 two mega-destination gaming resorts opened in Singapore, further diluting the Strip's share of the global market for destination resort gaming. Then, unexpectedly, in August 2007 global credit markets abruptly froze, precipitating the most serious financial crisis of modern times and triggering the worst economic contraction since the Great Depression.[18]

For gaming the timing could not have been worse. Casino companies entered the financial crisis with capital structures that were more highly leveraged than at any time since Nevada's Corporate Gaming Acts of 1967 and 1969 removed the barriers to the direct involvement of publicly traded corporations in the industry.[19] In 2008 alone, Las Vegas Strip casinos with revenues greater than $72 million added almost $7 billion of debt.[20] The collapse of global credit markets made casino industry debt impossible to re-finance. At the same time, the ensuing recession reduced consumer spending on gaming in Las Vegas and throughout the United States. It was a perfect storm. The conjunction of these events precipitated a wave of cancelled projects, collapsing casino equity values, restructurings, and bankruptcies.

Conclusions

The financial crises that impacted Atlantic City casinos in the late 1980s and early 1990s and casinos on the Las Vegas Strip in 2007–2010 had similar consequences but dissimilar causes.

The Atlantic City financial crisis of the late 1980s was precipitated by a single event: the implosion of Drexel Burnham Lambert and the consequent collapse of the junk bond market, with the coinciding maturation of the Atlantic City gaming market an important contributing factor. To a considerable degree, the events precipitating the crisis were under the control of New Jersey gaming regulators. In August 1987 Drexel Burnham was required by the New Jersey Casino Control Commission and the New Jersey Division of Gaming Enforcement (DGE) to apply for a supplier's license, bringing the bank under the regulatory control of the Commission.[21] Subsequently, in February 1989, the Commission voted unanimously to bar Drexel from further dealings with Atlantic City casinos because it

---

[18] The National Bureau of Economic Research (NBER) announced on December 1, 2008, that the US economy entered a recession in December 2007 which ended in June/July 2009. *See* THE NATIONAL BUREAU OF ECONOMIC RESEARCH, http://www.nber.org/dec2008.html.

[19] WILLIAM R. EADINGTON, THE EVOLUTION OF CORPORATE GAMBLING IN NEVADA (1980); Eadington & Hattori, *supra* note 6.

[20] Schwartz & Christiansen, *supra* note 17.

[21] Gladstone, *supra* note 13. New Jersey's Division of Gaming Enforcement (DGE) recommended that Drexel should be required to apply for a non-gaming service industry license because of the huge revenues it had received for financing much of the Atlantic City casino business; under New Jersey's gaming regulations, a company that is paid $50,000 a year or more by a casino is required to be licensed.

planned to plead guilty to six federal felony charges.[22] To an extent, therefore, the Atlantic City financial crisis had its origins in the activities of a New Jersey gaming license holder.

In sharp contrast, the financial crisis that engulfed casino resorts along the Las Vegas Strip in 2007–2010 was precipitated by an event wholly outside the control of the gaming industry: the sudden freezing of global credit markets, which was triggered by the US subprime mortgage crisis.[23] As had been the case in Atlantic City in the late 1980s, the impact of the financial crisis of 2007 on Las Vegas Strip casino resorts was exacerbated by falling demand. Long-term erosion of the Strip's quasi-monopoly on destination resort gaming and the onset of recession in late 2007/early 2008 severely depleted the amount of out-of-town business on the Strip.

Some conclusions with implications for casino industry structures may be drawn from these experiences.

First, demand for casino gaming does not increase indefinitely. Nothing grows to the sky. Given sufficient supply, demand for gaming will cease to increase at rates above the average for the general economy. Gaming markets, like markets for goods and services of other kinds, eventually mature. Supply and demand for casino games will eventually tend toward balance, and in their market economics casinos will come to resemble other forms of leisure consumption.

Second, the problems in Atlantic City in the early 1980s and Las Vegas in 2007 proved that the casino industry's tendency to use leveraged capital to build and operate its facilities is dangerous. Historically the gaming industry was able to exploit quasi-monopoly market conditions for something—casino machine and table games—for which there was massive unsatisfied consumer demand. Monopoly market conditions made it possible for casinos to generate highly reliable above-average cash flows and returns on invested capital. These above-average cash flows made highly leveraged

---

[22] David Johnston, *No More A.C. Work For Drexel. Brokerage Barred From Casino Deals*, PHILADELPHIA INQUIRER, Feb. 23, 1989, *available at* http://articles.philly.com/1989-02-23/business/26151224_1_drexel-burnham-lambert-casino-deals-casino-commission.

[23] *See, Subprime Mortgage Crisis*, WIKIPEDIA, http://en.wikipedia.org/wiki/Subprime_mortgage_crisis (summarizing the U.S. subprime mortgage crisis and its relation to the global financial crisis). *Compare*, Alan Greenspan, *Never Saw it Coming, in* FOREIGN AFFAIRS 88 (Nov./Dec. 2013) (explaining why economists, and by implication the Federal Reserve, failed to anticipate the financial crisis.); *with* Richard Katz, *Blind Oracle: A Response to 'Never Saw it Coming,' in* FOREIGN AFFAIRS 179 (Jan./Feb. 2014) (explaining the linkage between the crash in U.S. housing prices and the global financial crisis by stating that the packaging and re-packaging by investment banks of home mortgages, in ever more esoteric derivative securities, produced a package of derivatives with a face value of $35 trillion, or 14 times the value of the underlying mortgages, thus magnifying the impact of the collapse of U.S. housing prices throughout the global financial system.). *See also*, Harold L. Vogel, FINANCIAL MARKET BUBBLES AND CRASHES (2010) (Analyzing the framework for the U.S. housing bubble and the global financial crisis); and *The origins of the financial crisis*, THE ECONOMIST, Sept. 7, 2013 (providing an easy-to-understand, accessible discussion of the causes and consequences of the financial crisis).

capital structures apparently stable: there was sufficient cash generated from gaming operations to service above-average debt service burdens.

As the world's markets fill up with casinos, however, the industry's historic monopoly market economics necessarily erode. Gaming market conditions become more competitive. More competitive market conditions inevitably reduce casino free cash flows; decreasing cash flows make leveraged casino capital structures harder to sustain in a normal business environment and vulnerable to a contraction of credit, such as the financial crises that destabilized leveraged casino capital structures in Atlantic City in the late 1980s and Las Vegas Strip casino resorts in late 2007–2010.

If market forces determine the number of licenses and hence the supply of gaming, returns on capital invested in casinos will approach returns on capital in non-gaming bricks-and-mortar investments, reducing the ability of casinos to pay high rates of gaming privilege tax and impairing their ability to make refreshment capital investments. The above-average cash flows characteristic of casinos operating in quasi-monopoly market conditions will decline into more usual ranges. Decreasing cash flows can make highly leveraged casino capital structures increasingly risky. Casino designs that do not satisfy consumer expectations are riskier. Penalties for subpar management performance increase. The risk of failed casino investments rises, as the bankruptcy of the Aladdin, the foreclosure and restructuring of Cosmopolitan (both on the Las Vegas Strip), and the bankruptcy of Revel (in Atlantic City), multi-billion-dollar investments in fully supplied markets, demonstrate.[24] In fully supplied markets casinos will compete for debt and equity with other bricks-and-mortar investments on more or less equal terms. It will be harder to finance casinos ten years from now than it was ten years ago—unless those casinos are in under-supplied markets, like Macau today or Japan, perhaps, tomorrow.

Third, while decisions concerning casino capital structures are in the first instance the prerogative of casino management, there is precedent in New Jersey for making the financial stability of casino license holders a regulatory concern. In light of the experience with highly leveraged casino capital structures that became unstable in Atlantic City in the late 1980s and in Las Vegas in 2008–2010, this implies a degree of regulatory attention to the use of leverage in casino licensee capital structures.

GENERAL LICENSEE REQUIREMENTS AND CONDITIONS

Government can stipulate specific license requirements or conditions in addition to the ones discussed above. For example, licensees can be required to build certain kinds of casino, designed to serve particular public policies in addition to the usual fiscal and economic development purposes.

---

[24] For a detailed summary of the history of the Cosmopolitan and the Aladdin, see http://en.wikipedia.org/wiki/Cosmopolitan_of_Las_Vegas and http://en.wikipedia.org/wiki/Planet_Hollywood_Resort_%26_Casino#The_Aladdin.

The Singapore Model

Singapore legalized casinos in 2006.[25] Two licenses, each for a multi-billion-dollar integrated resort, were also granted in 2006. Gaming was permitted for the specific purpose of attracting substantial capital investment in destination resorts designed for long-distance tourists. The terms of the licenses limit the casino area and stipulate that the casino can be only one component of a diversified resort incorporating elaborate and capital-intensive non-gaming leisure attractions, including hotels, restaurants, retail shopping, convention centers, museums, spas, recreational facilities and theme parks. Effectively the license terms limit the percentage of property revenue contributed by gaming.

To illustrate the specific license terms and conditions Singapore sought to impose, the following is a summary of key specifications of the Request for Proposals for one of the two Singapore licenses, for an integrated resort on Sentosa Island.[26]

Summary of Key RFP Specifications for the Integrated Resort on Sentosa Island

By granting only two licenses, Singapore tried to ensure that licensees would enjoy quasi-monopolies in a very large gaming market. The Singapore government sought to use the above-average ROIC and profits generated from this lucrative quasi-monopoly "as an engine for strengthening Singapore as a long-distance tourist destination, not a day-trip or locals' casino market. [27]

Singapore imposed a two-tiered gaming privilege tax rate: 5 percent of gross gaming revenue (GGR) derived from premium players, and 15 percent of gross gaming revenue derived from other players.[28] The purpose of this tax rate was two-fold: to create an incentive for licensees to market to high-income premium players; and, since the combined or effective tax rate is about 12 percent, to create a consumer price advantage for Singapore casinos with respect to casinos in Macau, where the effective gaming privilege tax rate is nearly 40 percent.[29]

While as a general rule casinos that operate in quasi-monopoly market conditions can afford to pay high rates of gaming privilege tax, Singapore was willing to forego a portion of fiscal benefits of casino gaming (i.e.,

---

[25] Singapore Casino Control Act (CHAPTER 33A) (Original Enactment: Act 10 of 2006).

[26] See also http://archivesonline.nas.sg/speeches/view-html?filename=20051104981.htm (showing the Request for Proposal for an Integrated Resort at Marina Bay).

[27] Eadington & Christiansen, *supra* note 11.

[28] Singapore Casino Control Act, *supra* note 21, at Part IX, § 146(2).

[29] Guihai Huang, Ph.D., Macau Polytechnic Institute, Casino Taxation in Macau, Singapore and Las Vegas, 8th European Conference on Gambling Studies and Policy Issues (Sept. 15, 2010) (Presentation materials *available at* http://www.easg.org/website/conference.cfm?id=13&cid=13&section=AGENDA&day=2 follow "Casino Taxation in Macau, Singapore and Las Vegas" hyperlink).

Figure 4.1

	Key Specification	Description
1.	Achieving a Large-scale Iconic Development	The IR on Sentosa is envisaged to be a large-scale iconic development and a "must-visit" attraction for tourists to the region. It shall be a world-class tropical integrated resort that offers the whole family a fun and memorable leisure experience. It shall also play an important part in Singapore's overall tourism strategy that will broaden Singapore's tourism and entertainment options, complement existing tourist attractions as well as catalyse new tourism investments.
2.	Site Parameters	The site area is approximately 49ha with a maximum Gross Floor Area of 343,000sqm. The land tenure is for 60 years. The design and layout of the IR should reflect and respect the local context of the site, specifically its tropical island nature with its lush natural greenery and marine / coastal frontage. This translates to low-rise structures along the waterfront, open spaces, extensive landscaping, preservation of selected trees and attractive shade structures. In addition, the IR shall provide good physical connectivity and integration with the rest of Sentosa.
3.	Public Facilities	A visitor arrival centre, public promenades along the waterfront, and adequate car parking facilities will be required. The Sentosa Express (to be completed by end 2006) will also provide direct public access to the IR. Examples of key attractions include thematic attractions, theatre shows, edutainment facilities and programmes, and shows / performances with international appeal. In view of the local equatorial climate, special consideration should be given to the design and planning of the key attractions in order to enhance the visitors' experience at the IR. An additional 60,000sqm of GFA for shelters that are only used for weather protection purposes over outdoor attractions and their circulation spaces, outdoor queuing areas and landscaped areas will be allowed. However, no commercial activity will be allowed within these spaces.
4.	Casino Concession and Casino Licence	The IR operator will have the concession to operate a casino for 30 years. Apart from this concession, the IR operator has to apply to the Casino Regulatory Authority for a Casino Licence to operate the casino. During the period of 10 years from the date of the signing of the Sentosa Agreement, only two Casino Licences will be issued – one for the IR on Sentosa and the other for the IR at Marina Bay.

5.	Law and Order Requirements	The IR Operator must comply with the Regulator's requirements and standards in areas such as surveillance systems, security personnel and anti-money laundering program.
6.	Restrictions on Gaming Area and Machines	• The maximum gaming area allowed is 15,000 sqm. • The maximum number of gaming machines allowed is 2,500.
7.	Social Safeguards	The IR Operator must comply with the following: • Prohibit entry to the casino for those below 21 years. • Collection of a casino entry levy of $100 per day or $2,000 per year for Singapore residents. • Provision of self and third party exclusion schemes. • Display information on problem gambling, help services, rules of games and odds of winning. • Restrictions on advertising of casino and casino gambling. • Restrictions on extension of gaming credit to Singapore Residents, with the exception of premium players. • No ATMs allowed within the casino. • Provision of a system to allow loss limits to be set voluntarily.
8.	Casino Tax	The IR Operator shall pay a casino tax of: • 15% on monthly gross gaming revenue from regular players • 5% on monthly gross gaming revenue from premium players The Government is committed not to raise this casino tax for at least 15 years. The prevailing GST will also be applicable to gross gaming revenue.
9.	Cross Shareholding Restrictions	The Controlling Shareholder of one IR will not be permitted to hold an interest or a management contract for operating the casino in the other IR. The Controlling Shareholder is defined as the entity that owns the largest direct and indirect interest of at least 20% of the voting shares in the Successful Proposer.
10.	Commencement Requirements	The IR Operator can apply for the Casino Licence only when at least half of the Proposed Gross Floor Area has been completed, at least half of the committed investment has been expended, and at least half of the Proposed Development Area (land area) has been completed. The IR operator is required to expend 100% of its committed development investment three years after the casino licence has been issued.
11.	Evaluation Criteria	The evaluation criteria are: • Tourism appeal and contribution (45%) • Architectural, design, and concept excellence (25%) • Level of development investment committed (20%) • Strength of consortium and partners (10%) Weights indicated are approximate.

Source: Singapore Tourism Board

gaming privilege tax receipts) in the interests of creating long-term economic benefits in the form of long-distance tourism. Singapore's two integrated casino resorts represent a combined capital investment of approximately $7.1 billion (exclusive of land acquisition and other costs, which when added to the sunk costs of the two resort properties raise the two licensees' aggregate investment to more than $10 billion).

SOCIAL CONCERNS

For the most part, the social concerns casinos raise do not affect decisions regarding the structure of casino industries *per se*. The ubiquitous nature of some of these social concerns, however, has prompted responses by governments that permit casinos to operate that, in some instances, have implications for casino industry structures. The most important of these social concerns is compulsive gambling.

Compulsive Gambling

Compulsive gambling is an unavoidable consequence of allowing casinos to operate, regardless of how the casino industry is structured. This policy concern is discussed in greater detail in Chapter 10 of this book.

Very generally, governments that permit casino gaming have evolved three responses to the compulsive gambling behavior that casinos (and other forms of gambling, legal or otherwise) stimulate: (i) funding research by qualified independent professionals to ascertain, and monitor on a continuing basis, the incidence of compulsive gambling behavior (i.e., the dimensions of the problem); (ii) requiring licensees to institute management policies and practices designed to make casino personnel sensitive to compulsive gambling; and (iii) measures, which may have the force of law, intended to reduce compulsive gambling by residents of the jurisdiction authorizing casinos. The two most common measures of this kind are self-exclusion by compulsive gamblers, and restricting access to casinos by local residents or, as is currently the case in Singapore, requiring local residents to document minimum levels of financial wherewithal as a prerequisite for entry.

The first two of these responses do not have implications for casino industry structures.[30] The third response, restricting access to casinos wheth-

---

[30] Massachusetts, which legalized casino gaming in 2011 after years of contentious public debate, provides a recent example of allocating funds for compulsive gambling research. MASS. GEN. LAWS ch. 23K, §58 (2012) (establishing a Public Health Trust Fund to received revenue generated from Massachusetts casinos earmarked for public health). Pursuant to this provision of its gaming law, in 2013 the Massachusetts Gaming Commission selected a University of Massachusetts team of researchers headed by Dr. Rachel Volberg to "study the economic and social impacts of introducing casino gambling to Massachusetts, as well as problem gambling". Lori Stabile, *UMass research team chosen to conduct $3.64 million research project on casino gambling*, THE REPUBLICAN, May 9, 2013, http://

er by self-exclusion of compulsive gamblers, barring local residents from casino premises, or attempting to limit entry to persons with minimum levels of personal wealth affects the market environment casinos do business in and thus have implications for casino industry structures.

Singapore provides an example of this latter category. Singapore's Casino Control Act requires citizens and permanent residents to purchase a valid entry levy (admissions tax) in order to enter a Singapore casino.[31] The following shows the detail of the requirement and illustrates a typical hotel's policy:

Entry Levy Required For Entry By Singapore Citizens And Permanent Residents

a. Singapore Citizens and Permanent Residents are required to purchase a valid Entry Levy before entering the casino:
   i. Entry Levy of S$100 for every consecutive period of 24 hours; or
   ii. Entry Levy of S$2,000 for a consecutive period of 12 months.
b. It is an OFFENCE for any Singapore Citizen or Permanent Resident to enter the Casino premises without purchasing a valid Entry Levy.
c. If you are convicted, you may be liable for a fine of up to S$1,000 and the amount of Entry Levy due for the period of entry.

Entry and Exit Only Through Designated Lanes

a. Singapore Citizens and Permanent Residents are to enter and exit the casino premises solely through the lanes designated "Singapore/PR".
b. Persons who are not Singapore Citizens or Permanent Residents are to enter and exit the casino premises solely through the lanes designated "Foreigners."

Over-Stay Without A Valid Entry Levy

a. If your entry levy has expired, it is an OFFENCE if you:
   i. remain in the Casino i.e., over-stay; and
   ii. fail to pay the entry levy/levies for the over-stay period before leaving the casino.
b. If you are convicted, you may be liable for a fine up to S$1,000 and the amount of entry levy/levies due for the over-stay period.

---

www.masslive.com/news/index.ssf/2013/05/umass_research_team_chosen_to.html.
[31] *See* Singapore Casino Control Act (CHAPTER 33A); Singapore Casino Control (Entry Levy) Regulations 2010 (amended 2013). *See also* MBS Entry Levy for Singapore Citizens and PR, mbs-casino.blogspot.com/2013/01/mbs-entry-levy-for-singapore-citizend.html (providing the Entry Levy Rules for the Marina Bay Sands).

See also Casino Visit Limit on Financially Vulnerable Singaporeans and PRS Takes Effect from 1 June, http://www.news.gov.sg/public/sgpc/en/media_releases/agencies/msf/press_release/P-20130528-1:
How to Purchase Entry Levy:
Entry Levy can be purchased at the following locations:
   1.   Entry Levy Kiosks and Cashier Counters located at the entrances to the casino
   2.   From AXS Machines
Identity Documents will be required for verification when purchasing Entry Levy.

c. Please CHECK that your entry levy is valid before exiting the Casino premises by swiping your identification document at the kiosks located near the casino exits.

d. If your entry levy has expired, please proceed to the cashier's cage to purchase the entry levy/levies due for the over-stay period before exiting the casino.

Additional Information on Entry Levy

a. Entry Levy payments may be made by cash, Nets/Direct Debit or credit card only.

b. Entry Levies paid are neither refundable nor transferable.

Identification Documents for Verification Checks

Patrons must upon request produce valid identification documents for verification checks of their age, identity and entry levy payment status (if applicable).

a. Singapore Citizens and Permanent Residents may provide the following identification documents:

　i. Residents National Registration Identification Cards (the "NRICs");

　ii. Driving licences issued by the Singapore Traffic Police ("Singapore Driving Licences");

　iii. Singapore Armed Forces ("SAF") identification cards;

　iv. Singapore Civil Defence Force National Services ("SCDF NS") identification cards;

　v. Singapore Police Force National Service ("SPF NS")'

　vi. Re-entry permits with passports issued to Singapore Permanent Residents ("SPRs");

　vii. Passports issued by the Singapore Government; or

　viii. NRIC collection slips issued by the Immigration and Checkpoints Authority ("ICA"), together with an original identification document issued by the Singapore Government which contains both a photo identification and date birth

b. Patrons who are not Singapore Citizens or Permanent Residents, may provide the following identification documents:

　i. Foreign passport with short-term immigration pass (Note: This includes group passports with the particulars and photograph of each member in the group);

　ii. Long-term visit pass with photograph identification

　iii. Long-term visit pass without photograph identification together with foreign passport;

　iv. Student pass with photograph identification

　v. Student pass without photograph identification together with foreign passport;

　vi. Work pass;

　vii. Ministry of Foreign Affairs Identification Cards Issued to Diplomats in Foreign Embassies and Professional Staff in International Organisations;

　viii. Special pass with photograph identification issued by the Ministry of Manpower or the Immigration and Checkpoints Authority; or

　ix. Dependent's pass issued by the Ministry of Manpower.

In addition to imposing an entry levy, effective June 1, 2013, Singapore (acting through its Ministry of Social and Family Development pursuant to November 2012 amendments to its Casino Control Act) established three types or kinds of monthly casino visit limits for citizens and permanent residents. These casino visit limits are intended to serve as "an additional safeguard for financially vulnerable locals who visit the casinos frequently."[32]

Policies that limit local resident access to casinos are consistent with casinos predicated on patronage by long-distance travelers; nineteenth century European spa casinos and Singapore's integrated casino resorts are examples. Such limitations, if they are enforced, require casinos to rely on long-distance travelers (as did nineteenth century European spa casinos). In Singapore's case, efforts to limit the local population's access to casinos is consistent with Singapore's primary purpose in legalizing gaming, which was to use the enormous regional demand for this activity as an engine of tourism. Essentially, by forcing its casinos to rely on foreign visitors, Singapore seeks to attract consumer spending to Singapore that, absent casinos, would not be spent in Singapore or contribute to its economy. Singapore is using casinos to mine the personal incomes of regional Pacific Asian economies.

Conversely, policies that limit local resident access to casinos are inconsistent with casinos predicated on local patronage.

Quality of Life

Other social concerns include the implications of introducing casinos into the community for quality of life.

---

[32] The Singapore Ministry of Social and Family Development details casino visit limits:

1. The Casino Visit Limit will come into effect from 1 June 2013, as part of a new set of social safeguards introduced following amendments to the Casino Control Act in November 2012.

2. To be administered by the National Council on Problem Gambling (NCPG), the Casino Visit Limit serves as an additional safeguard for financially vulnerable locals who visit the casinos frequently. The Visit Limit, if imposed on an individual, will set a cap on the number of times that individual may visit the casinos at the Integrated Resorts each month.

3. Three types of Casino Visit Limits are available to Singapore Citizens and Permanent Residents:

    a) Voluntary Visit Limit - Individuals may apply to the NCPG to limit their visits;

    b) Family Visit Limit - Family members may apply to the NCPG to limit a family member's visits; and

    c) Third-Party Visit Limit - Persons found to have poor credit records or are vulnerable to financial harm due to gambling could be imposed with a Third-Party Visit Limit by a Committee of Assessors appointed by the NCPG.

As noted, by setting maximum percentages of gaming resort facilities for areas devoted to gaming and requiring substantial capital investment in various non-gaming amenities Singapore sought to ensure that its two casinos satisfy a broad range of consumer appetites in addition to the appetite for casino games.

This concern (i.e., that casinos satisfy a broad range of consumer appetites, not simply the appetite for gaming) likewise figured prominently in the public discussion of gaming leading up to its authorization in Massachusetts. A related public policy concern that was intensively debated in Massachusetts was local community impacts (increased burdens on public sector infrastructure, roads, bridges, tunnels, water, education and so forth) including quality of life (noise pollution) resulting from introducing casinos in the densely populated Commonwealth. The Massachusetts legislature attempted to ameliorate these impacts by allocating revenues generated from gaming to a Community Mitigation Fund, which

> shall expend monies in the fund to assist the host community and surrounding communities in offsetting costs related to the construction and operation of a gaming establishment including, but not limited to, communities and water and sewer districts in the vicinity of a gaming establishment, local and regional education, transportation, infrastructure, housing, environmental issues and public safety, including the office of the county district attorney, police, fire and emergency services.[33]

INTEGRITY

Like the social concerns discussed above, integrity concerns do not affect casino industry structures as such. Licensee integrity is a paramount concern of all jurisdictions that authorize casinos, regardless of the industry structure the jurisdiction decides on. This policy concern is discussed in greater detail in Chapter 7 of this book.

---

[33] Mass. Gen. Laws ch. 23K, §61 (b) (2012).

5

The Economics of Gambling Regulation

Richard Schuetz

Years ago, I noticed one thing about economics, and that is that economists didn't get anything right.
Nassim Nicholas Taleb[1]

The basis of economics is the study of the manner in which rational actors manage scarce resources—often money, time, and labor—with the rational goal of maximizing return or utility. And when one thinks of the gambling industry, one thinks of probabilities and efforts to maximize returns. As the chapters in this book illustrate, the gambling industry and its regulators face significant challenges identifying and measuring the right gambling policies, outcomes, and procedures. This makes the measure of gambling economics more difficult and the measure of gambling regulation economics more difficult. This chapter analyzes the economics of gambling regulation to better understand the limitations of this economic approach.

CURRENT ERA OF LEGAL GAMBLING REGULATION IN THE UNITED STATES

While the modern era of gambling in the United States is popularly considered to have started in 1931 when Nevada passed the "wide open" gambling act, it is a little-known fact that California has the longest continuously-operating legal gambling industry in the United States, permitting social games for over 100 years.[2] In 1931, Nevada had little interest in regulating this newly legalized industry, and the initial legislation had only one stipulation: the applicant had to be an American citizen.[3] From this modest start, gambling regulation has grown; Nevada now has over 400 employees engaged in gaming regulation within the state, and regulatory

---

[1] Outspoken, *Interview with Nassim Nicholas Taleb*, WASH. POST, Mar. 15, 2009.
[2] CAL. GAMBLING CONTROL ACT §19801(b).
[3] Robert D. Faiss & Gregory R. Gemignani, *Nevada Gaming Statutes: Their Evolution and History*, 10 OCCASIONAL PAPER SERIES, CT. GAMING RES. 1 (2011).

agencies span the United States from coast to coast to accommodate the widespread presence of commercial and tribal casinos in over one-half of the United States.

The proliferation of casino gambling would not have happened without the efforts of many within the regulatory community working arduously to make the industry acceptable. A most unanticipated effect of Nevada's regulatory efforts is that by creating a conventional industry, it made casino gambling suitable for export. Discussing the worldwide spread of gambling, Bo Bernhard, Executive Director the International Gaming Institute, noted, "But *one* clear reason why the industry was able to take off was because it effectively 'cleaned up' via government regulation."[4] This theme of legitimization is probably the most significant economic implication of gambling regulation in the United States, if not the world. This theme is best reflected by the sentiments of Steven Perskie, who was the Chairman of the Casino Control Commission in New Jersey from 1990–1994, when he stated, "We legitimized an entire industry. We legitimized casino gambling to Wall Street—legitimized it to Main Street."[5]

Dating back to the Nevada roots established in 1931, the industry now spans the globe. The gambling industry's entrepreneurs and operators occupy prominent spots on the lists of the world's richest individuals. Gaming facilities are noted architectural wonders, generating significant tourism, tax revenues, investment, and employment. And the regulatory actions surrounding this industry have generated a history of interest and intrigue, be it the murder of the Flamingo Casino visionary Benjamin "Bugsy" Siegel in Beverly Hills in 1947; Frank Sinatra being forced to "surrender" his gaming license to Nevada in 1963 for hosting crime boss Sam Giancana at the Club Cal-Neva in Stateline, Nevada;[6] the decision by MGM Mirage to exit Atlantic City rather than sever its relationship with Pansy Ho, who New Jersey regulators determined to be an "unsuitable partner;"[7] or the regulatory drama Caesars Entertainment experienced in Massachusetts.[8]

Throughout this history, the basic US regulatory model has evolved to offer five primary features:

- The games offered should be fair, honest, and operate with a high level of security and integrity.
- The owners, vendors, managers, and sources of finance should be free from inappropriate past or present associations or behaviors, and uphold high ethical standards.

---

[4] Bo Bernhard, *The Battered Gaming Industry: A Case Study for our Times?*, 13 UNLV GAMING RES. & REV. J. 55, 57 (2009).

[5] Bill Kent, *What Has Gambling Wrought? Ask the Man Who Wrote the Rule Book*, N.Y. TIMES, Dec. 15, 1996.

[6] DAVID G. SCHWARTZ, ROLL THE BONES 362 (2006).

[7] Beth Jinks, *MGM Partner Ho is 'Unsuitable,' Gambling Agency Says*, BLOOMBERG, Mar. 18, 2010.

[8] *See* Dimitri Kassenides, *Caesars Sues Massachusetts Gaming Commissioner over Licensing Practices*, BLOOMBERG BUS. WEEK, Dec. 12, 2013.

- The operations should possess sound operational and financial controls.
- All fees, taxes, and related payments should be appropriately accounted for and paid.
- Appropriate controls should be in place to protect the vulnerable.[9]

A PROBLEM WITH PERCEPTION

A story of old tells of six blind men asked to describe an elephant. The sightless men each touched the elephant, and as the story develops each describes a different reality depending upon which part of the elephant the individual touched.[10] Such is the case with gambling regulation. Ask a variety of people why casino gambling should be regulated and what such regulation should accomplish, and many different answers emerge, depending on where one grabs it.[11]

---

[9] Tiffany Conklin & Richard Schuetz, *A Discussion of the Strategic Approaches to Securing Legal Internet Wagering in the US*, EUROPEAN GAMING LAW., at 10–11, 2013.

[10] All indications are this story originated in India and has been told from a great many different perspectives, including Buddhism, Islam, and Hinduism. It was apparently introduced into English by John Godfrey Saxe who published the story as a poem in the nineteenth century. One of the interesting attributes of this story is that different authors see it as saying different things, which seems to indicate that the story has universal relevance.

[11] Before embarking on the topic proper, a slight digression will hopefully dispel a larger myth surrounding the gambling regulation discussion: that the casino industry is rigorously regulated. Ask any casino executive or a gambling regulator about the rigor applied towards regulating this industry and they will almost uniformly suggest it is one of the most tightly regulated industries in the United States. Yet a most convincing story can be told that casino industry regulation is one of the most lax of any industry in operation in the United States. How can this be? It depends on where you grab it.

Licensing the individuals and institutions that want to participate is the aspect of the industry that primarily generates its reputation for rigor. These licensing investigations are very rigorous for two primary reasons. First, the background of the individuals and institutions that participate in controlled gambling can shape the industry's image. Because the industry often exists at the will of the people and the governing process, a bad image can cause pressures to make the business illegal or curtail its growth. Second, the industry has lax internal controls in central components of its operations and, therefore, to maintain business integrity, only individuals of exemplary background should participate. In short, background investigations help ensure the industry participants are honest, which is important because there exist many opportunities for financial mischief.

Gaming is a cash business—and cash transactions move quickly. A substantial number of transactions within the casino business have no receipts or other types of documentation to chronicle a transaction. If a player wins a hand of blackjack for $100, the dealer will quickly give the player a $100 chip. There will be no receipt. The chip will probably be indistinguishable from thousands of identical chips both inside and outside the property. The casino does not have a precise count or know the locations of those chips. It will know how many it purchased, that some are in the vault, some are in cage drawers, some are on the games, and some are with players, but any reconciliation of these chips will involve uncertainty. On the next hand the player might lose, and the chip just given to that player will go back into game inventory, once again, with no written record. And that table is next to another table, which is next to another table, and all of these tables have several

When discussing industry regulation one might be tempted to seek the input of an economist, a profession gifted at making blind observations. This approach is not without risk. Dr. Joel Waldfogel, a Ph.D. economist who held esteemed academic positions across the United States, once wrote an article regarding the Christmas holiday for the prestigious American Economic Review. His conclusion was that Christmas is essentially a waste of time and resources, having potentially enormous, theoretical deadweight losses and subjecting people to unreasonable transaction costs, primarily in commodity searches. Waldfogel's position was that social welfare would be maximized if people simply bought what they wanted, when they wanted it.[12] Applying this type of economic analysis to gambling regulation, therefore, risks diminishing the pure wonder and pleasure of "risking it all on black."

CHALLENGES IN APPLYING ECONOMICS TO GAMBLING REGULATION

A real challenge in introducing economics into the gambling regulation discussion is that economic studies concerning gambling are in their infancy, and the cupboards of institutional knowledge are sparse. Existing studies often point in opposite directions. Knowledge about the economics of gambling and its regulation are sparser still, contradictory, and shallow. Studies in gambling present a long list of challenges.

Data Can Be Deceptive

The first challenge is data source reliability and the ability to interpret this data accurately. In 1960, there were 123,000 arrests for illegal gambling whereas in 2008, there were fewer than 10,000. This suggests a marked decrease in unlawful wagering in the United States. Yet the Federal Bureau of Investigation estimates that illegal gambling grew substantially during this period,[13] and recent estimates place illegal sports betting on major league baseball at $30–40

---

players on them, in a noisy room full of people, many of whom have been drinking and are distracted by the whole variety of things that make a casino such a fascinating place.

Simply put, the casino floor is organized chaos, especially those aspects of the operation not mechanized, electrified, or digitalized; and not everyone fully understands the nature of this chaos. What needs to be appreciated about live gaming is that it is an activity that involves a constant stream of transactions, and the tools to audit this stream of transaction are weak *vis-à-vis* other businesses. Thus, when someone suggests the casino business is tightly regulated, they are not talking about the live gaming environment. The myth that the casino industry is rigorously regulated obscures a thorough understanding of the gambling industry and its regulation.

[12] *See* Joel Waldfogel, *The Deadweight Loss of Christmas*, 83 Am. Econ. Rev. 1328 (1993).
[13] *See* Nat'l Gambling Impact Study Comm'n, Nat'l Gambling Impact Study Comm'n Final Report 2-14 (1999), http://govinfo.library.unt.edu/ngisc/reports/fullrpt.html.

billion a year and college football at $60–70 billion.[14] In reality, the decrease in arrests for illegal and non-regulated gambling had little to do with the presence of unlawful gambling and much more to do with a fundamental shift in enforcement activities. For a variety of reasons, law enforcement agencies directed their attentions elsewhere, and the data captures this enforcement trend rather than the underlying reality of the presence of illegal gaming.

Data Can Be Biased

Data can be biased when the data source has an interest in the research. Publicly-funded law enforcement entities regularly generate data concerning illegal gambling. Access to public funds can increase if a perception exists that substantial unlawful activity exists. Funding sources are often driven by a desire to right a perceived wrong, so the reporting agency may stand to benefit if the magnitude of the perceived wrong is inflated. In short, law enforcement might be tempted to be imaginative about the scope of illegal activity if that position could enhance their budgets, avoid layoffs, and benefit their departments.

Conversely, the gambling business generates a fair share of advocacy research. Impact studies that show the economic importance of the gambling industry without mentioning or estimating the social costs related to the activity can mislead the public and policymakers. Insights can be gained from advocacy research, but one must be cautious when sifting through this data.[15]

Not only can one find advocacy research provided by those who want to support the industry but also by those who oppose it. The Judeo-Christian ethic of the western world, and particularly of the United States, leaves many feeling that gambling is contrary to the spiritual guidance of their religions. Gambling can excite strong emotional reactions in people, and the possibility always exists that these beliefs can spill over into their research efforts.

Data May Not Be Comparable

Another data issue concerns comparability. Across jurisdictions, notable metrics may be called the same thing but are calculated differently. For example, a fundamental measure such as gaming revenue, defined most

---

[14] Gillian Spear, *Think Sports Gambling Isn't Big Money? Wanna Bet?*, NBC News, July 15, 2013.

[15] On a related note, some research is not undertaken or provided to the public. If an industry group undertakes or sponsors a research effort they are not obligated to make it public, especially if it reveals something unfavorable about their industry. Industry-friendly groups will not address some topics, such as the health risks to guests, employees, and regulators of smoking in casinos following the 2006 report by Surgeon General Richard Carmona, which ended the debate by conclusively demonstrating the scientific community had established that second-hand (or passive) smoke was a serious health hazard. Any effort by the industry or its lobbying groups to shape-shift around this hard science is probably best avoided completely, and one is secure in predicting that future industry-sponsored research will not address this topic hoping that out–of-sight is out-of-mind.

basically as the amount wagered minus winnings returned to players, can be presented differently across jurisdictions. Yet-to-be-collected credit instruments, including boarding fees, credit write-offs (depending on whether the credit documents were properly or improperly executed), the treatment of wide-area progressives, payments on participation machines, and promotional allowances combine to yield different meanings to things assigned to the gaming revenue bucket.

Using historical data and trying to compare slots to table games are also especially tricky data issues. Slot drop means something different than table game drop, and the two terms are not comparable from an analytic standpoint. Even today, slot win-percent in the Nevada Gaming Revenue Reports is a different concept from table game win-percent. The variables isolated for the calculation are different, and missing the point is easy if one does not understand the origins of the numbers.

Ceteris Paribus

Ceteris paribus, meaning "all other things equal," can be another challenge. When one's car breaks a mechanic will typically fiddle with one thing at a time to isolate the problem. A *ceteris paribus* methodology isolates a response by looking at the change in only one variable at a time. This is the cornerstone of economic analysis. However, research in the real world of gambling challenges the notion of keeping all other things equal. There are an endless number of variables changing at the same time: a state can raise the tax rate, a neighboring state can legalize casinos, the region can drift into a recession or depression, a new competitor may enter the industry, or something can alter the environment for the consumption of substitutes[16] and complements.[17] While research can try to suppress and control for these effects, it is no simple task. The result is that it is sometimes very difficult to determine just why the car will not start.[18]

Behavior Can Impact Data

Executives' behavior can distort the numbers within a casino, thus preventing one from ascertaining what is really going on. For example, many

---

[16] Substitute. "A product or service that satisfies the need of a consumer that another product or service fulfills. A substitute can be perfect or imperfect depending on whether the substitute completely or partially satisfies the consumer." INVESTOPEDIA.COM, http://www.investopedia.com/terms/s/substitute.asp.

[17] Complement. "A good or service that is used in conjunction with another good or service. Usually, the complementary good has little to no value when consumed alone but, when combined with another good or service, it adds to the overall value of the offering." INVESTOPEDIA.COM, http://www.investopedia.com/terms/c/complement.asp.

[18] The notion of *ceteris paribus* deals with just one thing changing. One can then ask the question as to what happens when nothing or everything changes? What is suggested here is the challenge presented with counterfactual or virtual history, i.e., the world of "what if," which, while entertaining, most certainly crosses over into areas of non-science and speculation.

years ago, a casino reconfiguration resulted in an unoccupied section of the interior space, resulting in a furious scramble for footage by department heads. The slot guy had the first shot. With no budget for machines, he secured machines on trial from one of the property's suppliers. The machines were of little interest to the public. The slot guy knew he could not justify keeping the space with these low-performing machines, so he grabbed the highest-producing machines from throughout the gaming floor, moved them into this space, and distributed the borrowed machines in their place. Not surprisingly, this space then became some of the highest producing real estate in the building, and the slot guy felt he was now entitled to place his brand on this area. In the end, however, the building's overall slot win did not change, and the slot guy simply walked people from all over the building into this one section.[19] The numbers do not always represent what they seem to represent, and those inside the casinos know this and can use the numbers to their advantage.

Assumptions Can Skew Conclusions

Aspiring economists are required to learn the joke about assumptions. The standard setting for the assumption joke involves three hungry people stranded on a deserted island confronted with a can of something edible. The two non-economists develop a variety of suggestions to open the can, but all of their solutions seem to jeopardize the contents. All is saved when the economist assures them the solution is simple: they merely need to assume they have a can opener. Economists rely on assumptions, and they rely on them a lot. They use them to frame studies, instill some sense of *ceteris paribus,* and make up for data lapses or uncertainties. The result is often that the project is more about the assumptions than the area supposedly under review.

Measuring Regulation Presents Challenges

Defining a concept as simple as how to measure regulation is a significant challenge for an economist. What is growth in a regulatory context? Is it an increase in the number of regulations on the books? Is it the number of regulators working for the agency? Is it an increase in expenditures for the regulatory agency? If it is the increase in agency expenditure, it can be hard to accurately capture the level of expenditures. Often the charge for the regulatory effort is passed on to the license applicant in fees, so

---

[19] Slot departments are not alone in trying to distort the internal accounting of casinos. Food departments charge gaming revenue departments extravagantly for casino special events for invited guests, greatly improving the food margins. Similarly, hotel department managers are known for taking rooms out of order to secure occupancy targets and upgrading comp customers to higher-rated rooms that are charged against the gaming department generating the comp. In short, there are many internal accounting distortions within casinos that can skew research conclusions.

these cost components may escape capture when looking at agency expenditures. Furthermore, a third-party may provide a certification in the regulatory process such as in technical standards testing, investigations, forensic accounting, or audit reports. These expenditures are often unknown to individual researchers, and they escape capture in any effort to "measure" regulation.

Is the notion of regulation then to be captured by the *number of individuals* assigned to the agency? Once again, third-party regulatory assets can escape calculation if one looks at the number of human resources employed in the effort. Can regulation then be measured by the *number of regulations* or the pages dedicated to their codification? In California, the Gambling Control Act is hundreds of pages, yet some aspects of the regulations are of enormous consequence while others are essentially irrelevant. For example, Regulation 19858.5,[20] which prohibits licensing anyone with a greater than 1 percent interest in a gambling business outside of the state, has significant regulatory implications for the operation of the industry within the state, yet it occupies but a few lines of the regulation. These few words have kept many industry participants out of the state and have protected the market for a few California operators. The point is, something as simple as measuring or defining regulation from a quantitative standpoint can present enormous obstacles from a research perspective, and if it cannot be quantified it does not fit well into the analytic approach of modern economics.

These data issues, taken with other challenges,[21] illustrate that the body of analyses that exists within economics concerning gambling is young, contradictory, and susceptible to a wide variety of methodological challenges. We do not seem to know a lot, and what we think we know is subject to challenge. Having said that, exploring people's beliefs about gambling, especially when those people can effectuate legislative change regarding gambling, is important. If one picked up the debate in the mid-1970s as New Jersey was contemplating introducing gambling to Atlantic City and fast-forwarded to the present day, the following beliefs would follow the legislative history of gambling:

- Gambling attracts bad actors, so the government must regulate the entry of participants;

---

[20] CAL. DEP'T OF JUST., CALIFORNIA GAMBLING LAW, REGULATIONS AND RESOURCE INFORMATION 27 (2013).

[21] Economic studies are also challenged because they tend toward linearly continuous solutions and are not well suited to handle discontinuities, quantum leaps, tipping points, asymmetries, and other real-world occurrences. Economic studies of gambling often appear to be more exact and impressive than they are. Economics depends on sophisticated mathematical tools and analyses. These tools often give the impression of incredible precision and sophistication, but looks can be deceiving. A massive array of equations, graphs, and charts can lead many to believe that something important is taking place when it is not. Moreover, economic analysis generally assumes robust market competition. The quasi- and full-monopoly casino markets make this analysis more difficult.

- The cash nature of gambling presents substantial opportunities for leakage and theft, so gambling operations need strong regulatory controls;
- Games can be manipulated, so the government must provide consumer protections to prevent this activity;
- Gambling can become a destructive influence in some people's lives;
- Gambling can increase the availability of tax revenues to a jurisdiction;
- Legal gambling can be a tool to increase tourism in a jurisdiction;
- Gambling can lead to increased services provided by the local government;
- Legal gambling can stop the flow of gaming tax revenues and tourism to other jurisdictions;
- Legal gambling can increase investment in a community; and
- Legal gambling can have a positive influence on employment in a jurisdiction.

Again, while always subject to challenge, these conclusions are of significance when the people who decide whether to permit legal gambling or not believe them to be true.

GAMBLING REGULATION IS NOT ALL ECONOMICS

Legislation aimed at controlling business activities and using regulatory agencies to affect these legislative goals is a topic that can be examined from a variety of disciplines' perspectives. It has been examined as a topic of law, economics, political science, sociology, history, business, and many other disciplines. Examining gambling legislation through the economics discipline focuses on activity assumed to be designed to bring about economic change, or in the activity's implementation, economic change is experienced. It is seen as a consciously orchestrated action designed to alter the economic landscape of a jurisdiction and targets economic variables it desires to influence. The regulatory agency is the primary entity assigned to ensure the economic change desired by the legislation is executed, and the agency's actions must be understood as market disturbances. This section discusses how these regulatory-induced market disturbances can radiate throughout the gambling ecosystem. This chapter views gambling legislation and its regulation as being primarily driven by economic forces or possessing economic effects and will address regulation in this context.[22]

The idea that gaming legislation is an activity designed to bring about economic change is subject to challenge. Many argue a variety of goals may be met through gambling legislation, and many have to do with the "public

---

[22] This chapter uses an institutional economics frame rather than relying on mathematical analyses. Institutional economics looks at how institutions are driven by evolutionary forces in shaping the behavior of the participants in the economic system.

interest" and social theories of regulation. Most economists would agree, however, that every activity can be reduced to its economic essence. For instance, Queen Anne, who reigned over England from 1701–1714, is well-known in gambling law as having helped to establish gambling debts as legally unenforceable instruments. While some may argue this demonstrated a commitment to protect the public from the deleterious impacts of gambling, an economist might argue that what the good queen was responding to was a tendency of those people in her class spending significant time in gambling houses operated by people not in her class. While perhaps under the influence of too much alcohol or testosterone and in the euphoria of the thrill of the game, these nobles often signed away a portion of their, or their family's, estate. The queen, to protect her power base, interrupted this redistribution of wealth and so mandated that credit decisions made in gambling houses were nonbinding.[23]

If one believes that addressing a topic within the science of economics then subjects that topic to a disciplined and unambiguous treatment, one has little, if any, understanding of economics. George Bernard Shaw argued that if all economists were laid end to end, they would never reach a conclusion. There are Marxist economists, behavioral economists, institutional economists, economic historians, econometricians, neoclassical economists, political economists, and so on; even among economists within the same groupings there are vastly divergent opinions and conclusions.

While most economists believe that essentially everything touches their discipline, events have transpired within the casino regulatory environment that have nothing to do with economics. In the 1950s and early 1960s, the Las Vegas Strip was called the Mississippi of the West because the casinos had a policy of not allowing people of color to enter. If they were entertainers, they could perform but not stay at the casino. Organizations and people began to challenge this policy and to pressure the Las Vegas casino owners to change their racially segregated business practices. Two people interested in affecting this change were Ed Olsen, Chairman of the Nevada Gaming Control Board (NGCB), and Grant Sawyer, Governor of Nevada from 1958–1966. Driven by the need of the gaming agents to inspect and monitor (often undercover) the operation of the games, a regulation required that all gambling areas of the casinos had to be open to the public. Chairman Olsen appointed an African-American schoolteacher as a deputy of the NGCB and had him enter a casino on the Las Vegas Strip. When the casino's security officers walked the deputy off of the property, Chairman Olsen informed the casino operator it was placing its licenses in jeopardy by restricting casino access to the agent. News spread among the executive offices along the Strip that their profiling efforts could now be met with the loss of their gaming licenses, and the ugly edifice of segregation began to be removed. One then sees that actions within the sphere of regulation were not motivated by economics.[24]

---

[23] *See generally* DAVID MEIRS, REGULATING COMMERCIAL GAMBLING 27–29 (2004).

[24] Richard Schuetz, *Ed Olsen's Gift*, 13 GLOBAL GAM'G BUS. (2013), http://ggbmagazine.

To discuss the full-range of economic consequences that can result from the array of actions a regulatory entity can undertake is well beyond the scope of this chapter. Rather, the intent is to discuss a few examples to demonstrate how regulations and the actions of a regulatory agency introduce both intended and unintended economic changes into the gambling ecosystem. Understanding a regulated gambling activity is impossible without understanding the industry, the regulatory agency, and the interaction between them.

Regulatory decisions are tough. To ensure games are fair in this age of advanced technology, regulatory agencies have developed strong standards concerning how this technology gets approved. Navigating through this maze is expensive and time consuming, but it adds a layer of protection that the games offered within the jurisdiction will not cheat the public or, arguably more importantly, the jurisdiction's tax collectors. So too, however, these standards impede innovation by restricting experimentation. They provide a barrier to entry for those desiring to offer new, innovative products to the industry, and hence they slow time-to-market. These are all real costs, and as is often the case in regulation, there is no perfect solution.

GAMBLING AND ECONOMIC RENTS

Two sacred topics require homage when discussing gambling and its regulation: economic rent and the goal of the regulatory entity. An economic rent is a value accruing to the owner of a resource over and above that which the resource would command in the fictional world of free competition. A labor union is an example of an economic rent generator. A union can restrict the availability of labor within the production process, causing labor costs to artificially rise over a level in which would exist in a theoretically purely competitive labor market. The resulting premium generated by this induced scarcity is known as economic rent. The laborer and the union, by moving the economic system away from something approaching a purely competitive solution, can capture and split this rent.

Economic rent exists in the gambling industry in part due to the many gaming jurisdictions' common practice to create barriers for new entrants into the market. By legislating and limiting the supply of gaming activities, both by type and number, prices artificially increase creating a profit larger than would exist had there been a free market and an absence of the supply restriction.

Other regulations can also affect supply causing economic rent. This occurs, for example, when legislation allows only a few geographic locations or sites to be suitable for a casino or when the government requires substantial investment to qualify for a license. While it may make investment attractive for the first market entrant who can make monopoly profits and, perhaps, other early entrants, later competitors may not be willing to enter the market because the potential profits do not justify the capital costs.

com/issue/vol-13-no-5-may-2014/article/ed-olsens-gift.

Finally, the licensing system employed by a state influences the number of competitors. In a perfectly competitive system, competitors will enter the market if the existing entrants are making extraordinary profits. The relative speed or ease with which they can enter the market is greatly influenced by licensing. The higher the barrier to entry, the more of an advantage existing competitors will have.

A primary motivation for legalizing gambling is to create this rent, and once it is produced, the discussion is then focused on determining who has the ability to claim or share in the rent.

Moving from an illegal gambling environment to a legal gambling environment is typically a conscious decision to change the beneficiaries of the economic rent premium. An illegal gambling market does not operate as an example of a freely competitive market. Numerous barriers to entry exist in illegal gambling including the risk of prosecution, bribery costs, influence payments, protection costs, and societal taboos. Much of the conflict portrayed in motion picture and television accounts of unlawful gambling dramatizes how different individuals and organizations fight for control of this rent premium. When a jurisdiction legalizes a previously illegal activity, such as gambling, it is doing so to capture this rent and to eliminate the negative externalities of the illegally-operated industry such as bribing politicians and enforcement officials and murdering and hurting of citizens.

Identifying the primary claimants to economic rent is reasonably simple. William Eadington and Ricardo Sui, in discussing the evolution of the Macanese gaming market suggest that much of Macau's gambling history can be explained by rent-seeking behavior by the three beneficiaries of this rent: the Macau-Portuguese government; the casino monopolist; and the Macanese population through charitable and social overhead contributions to the local community by the casino operator.[25] In Atlantic City, the recipients are the casino operators; the state government through imposing an 8 percent tax; and the city of Atlantic City through increased employment, investment, and a 1.5 percent tax on gaming revenues directed to redevelopment efforts for the city. With tribal gaming in the United States, the distribution of the economic rent is often dictated by the Indian Gaming Regulatory Act of 1988 (IGRA). In Oklahoma, Arizona, California, and other states, tribal governments have exclusive rights to operate casinos, and this exclusivity generates substantial rents. IGRA primarily controls distribution of these rents "to promote tribal economic development, tribal self-sufficiency, and strong tribal governments."[26]

Economic rents can also be captured by suppliers of gambling equipment. Regulation can cause biased equipment standards. If a manufacturer has

---

[25] William R. Eadington & Richard C.S. Sui, *Between Law and Custom - Examining the Interaction between Legislative Change and the Evolution of Macau's Casino Industry*, 7 INT'L GAMBLING STUD. (2007).

[26] Indian Gaming Regulatory Act, 25 U.S.C. § 2701.

patented a method of account wagering on gaming devices, and regulators adopt standards mandating use of that method, that manufacturer will have a significant competitive advantage both in the account wagering market and, potentially, in the sale of slot machines with integrated account wagering technology.

Public Interest Versus Capture?

A critical area of discourse surrounds the goals of the regulatory agency. The initial evolutionary path of the study of regulation headed in two distinct directions: those who suggested agencies work to ensure the public interest, and those who suggested regulation was "supplied in response to the demands of interest groups struggling among themselves to maximize the incomes of their members."[27] The first group is the public interest school, and the second group is the capture theorists.

Thomas McCraw articulates the essence of the public-interest argument:

> Although the reasons for regulation varied according to the industry involved, the notion of the 'public interest' continued to dominate the rhetoric of reformers, the utterances of presidents, and the decisions of the commissions. It served as ideological glue binding together the quasi-legislative, quasi-executive, and quasi-judicial duties of the regulators. In the 1930s, the doctrine reached its rhetorical zenith, a paradoxical result in view of the New Deal's frequent recognition and assistance to private interest groups. Legislative draftsmen inserted the phrase repeatedly into the flood of regulatory laws that created the Federal Communication Commission, the Securities and Exchange Commission, and the Civil Aeronautics Authority (now Board). The 'public interest' occurs a dozen times in the Communications Act, and dozen and a half in the Securities Act, and more than two dozen in the Civil Aeronautics Act, as a guide for regulators and as a justification of the immense discretionary powers these statutes bestowed. [28]

As mentioned, regulatory agencies affect legislation's desired economic goals and are often legitimized by being portrayed as working to secure the *public good*. The notion of capture turns this noble end on its head and, in its most simplistic description, a capture theory asserts that a regulatory agency becomes a tool whereby certain participants use (or create) the agency to assist the industry to acquire cash subsidies, limit entry, gain control over complements and substitutes, and assist in price-fixing schemes.[29] In this sense, the "public" that benefits from the agency's actions

---

[27] Richard Posner, *Theories of Economic Regulation*, 5 Bell J. Econ. & Mgmt. Sci. 358 (1974).

[28] Thomas K. McCraw, *Regulation in America: A Review Article*, Bus. Hist. Rev. XLIX 161–162 n. 2 (1975).

[29] *See* Anthony Cabot & Richard Schuetz, *An Economic View of the Nevada Gaming Licensing Process*, in Gambling and Public Policy: International Perspectives 123 (Wil-

are those who can reap the financial benefits of the economic rents generated by market disturbances induced by regulators; the "public" in this case has nothing to do with the "general public" or its best interest.

Adam Smith, the father of economics, led the discipline towards an understanding of capture when he wrote

> People of the same trade seldom meet together, even for merriment and diversion, but the conversation ends in a conspiracy against the public, or in some contrivance to raise prices. . . . But though the law cannot hinder people of the same trade from sometimes assembling together, it ought to do nothing to facilitate such assemblies, much less to render them necessary.[30]

Regulatory institutions can also change over time, reflecting the public interest theory at one point in time and the capture theory at other points. John Kenneth Galbrath who developed the following in his discussion of the Securities and Exchange Commission during the Great Depression, offered an example of a more interesting dynamic capture notion:

> [R]egulatory bodies, like the people who comprise them, have a marked life cycle. In youth they are vigorous, aggressive, evangelistic, and even intolerant. Later they mellow, and in old age—after a matter of ten or fifteen years—they become, with some exceptions, either an arm of the industry they are regulating, or senile.[31]

The political scientist Marver Bernstein, writing in 1955, also offered up a notion of capture as a process. Bernstein's regulatory stages are gestation, youth, maturity, and decline, and he articulates the decline period as "marked by the Commission's surrender to the regulated. Politically isolated, lacking a firm basis of public support, lethargic in attitude and approach, bowed down by precedent and backlogs, unsupported in its demands for more staff and money, the Commission finally becomes a captive of the regulated group."[32]

Fear of gambling regulatory agency capture goes beyond normal capture concerns in other industries, most likely because of the industry's colorful past and its media portrayal. A significant effect of this fear of capture is that most regulatory agencies are staffed by people who have no first-hand experience in the industry they are empowered to regulate. In California, the Gaming Act states, "A person is ineligible for appointment to the commission if, within two years prior to the appointment, the person, or any partnership or corporation in which the person is a principal, was employed by, retained by, or derived substantial income from any gambling establishment." [33]

This California law adopts the view that anyone who has worked in the industry in the past two years is unqualified to regulate it.[34] And while this

---

liam Eadington & Judy Cornelius, eds. 1991)

[30] ADAM SMITH, THE WEALTH OF NATIONS 145 (1776).

[31] JOHN KENNETH GALBRAITH, THE GREAT CRASH 172 (1954).

[32] MARVER BERNSTEIN, REGULATING BUSINESS BY INDEPENDENT COMMISSION 90 (1955).

[33] CAL. GAMBLING CONTROL ACT §19812(d).

[34] An interesting implication of this law is that a large portion of tribal people within the

California requirement is somewhat unique, gaming regulators in other jurisdictions, especially those regulators assigned policy and adjudicatory roles, rarely have gambling experience. A portion of this is related to the salary disparity between the industry and government service, making it difficult to recruit knowledgeable people from the industry to assist in regulating it. But it also indicates a certain distrust of the motives or goals of people associated with the industry. Further restrictions driven by fear of capture include cooling-off periods during which the regulator cannot enter the industry within the jurisdiction for a defined period of time (e.g., one year in Nevada and three years in California). Whether these cooling off periods actually prevent capture is subject to debate.[35] Other controls driven by the fear of capture are restrictions on political contributions (illustrated in New Jersey where it is illegal for a casino or a key employee to contribute to a political party or candidate) and on having investments or family members affiliated with the industry.

Risk of capture may increase as the firms within the industry become larger and more important to local and state economies. In May 2009, New Jersey released a "Special Report"[36] addressing MGM's relationship with Ms. Pansy Ho in Macau, SAR China. The report detailed how certain MGM executives inadequately discussed their findings with the company's compliance committee concerning both Ms. Ho and her father, famed Macanese casino owner, Stanley Ho. The report concluded that MGM was interested in partnering with Mr. Ho until they concluded he was unlikely to be licensed. At that point, MGM substituted his daughter in the partnership for Mr. Ho, while Mr. Ho funded her participation. The report also claimed Mr. Ho had long associated with organized criminals and had other suitability issues. As a result, New Jersey regulators said MGM either needed to end its relationship with Ms. Ho or surrender its New Jersey license. The company opted to end its association with New Jersey.

When an entity is found unsuitable in one jurisdiction, the finding is normally relevant to other jurisdictions, especially when the finding entity is as well respected as the New Jersey regulators. Based on this dramatic action in New Jersey, one would anticipate it attracting the attention of the Nevada regulatory authorities. During New Jersey's actions, however, MGM controlled over 38,000 hotel rooms on the Las Vegas Strip and over 1.1 million square feet of casino space with its ownership of 10 casino

---

state are precluded from serving the state as commissioners because they have either worked for a gambling facility or received a portion of their income from a one. In this sense, this law creates a *de facto* restriction on tribal citizens in California, certainly not the intent of the law.

[35] Brett Pulley, *The Spinning Door: A Special Report; Regulators Find Easy Path to Gambling Industry Jobs*, N.Y. TIMES, Oct. 28, 1998.

[36] Anne Milgram & Josh Lichblau, *Special Report of the Division of Gaming Enforcement to the Casino Control Commission on its Investigation of MGM Mirage's Joint Venture with Pansy Ho in Macau, Special Administration Region, People's Republic of China*, STATE OF NEW JERSEY DEPARTMENT OF LAW AND SAFETY (May 18, 2009).

properties in Las Vegas.[37] MGM also appeared on the brink of bankruptcy, having filed a "going concern" notice in the company's 2008 10-K. Besides that, the early 2000s "Great Recession" ravaged the Nevada economy, leaving it with the highest unemployment rate of any state in the nation. Moreover, no real market existed for casino assets in Las Vegas. Just about any action Nevada would have taken against the MGM would have further impacted a dismal economic situation in Nevada, imperiling the survival of the firm and jeopardizing employment, tax revenues, and the general well-being of the state. Responding to the actions of New Jersey, the Chairman of the Nevada Gaming Control Board, Dennis Neilander, stated that the New Jersey Report included no information that it did not already know,[38] and therefore Nevada regulators took no action against MGM.

THE COSTS OF AGENCY REGULATION
Monopoly Pricing

A brick-and-mortar casino enterprise is subject to many federal, state, and local regulatory regimes including building codes, employment and workplace safety laws, access for the disabled, alcohol service and food safety standards, financial document preservation, fire codes, and many others. A critically important agency to the casino enterprise within this maze of agencies is the gaming regulatory authority, and an American operator has no choice as to who the responsible regulatory authority will be; it will be the gaming authority of the state in which the operation exists and/or operates.

In other parts of the world, especially where Internet gambling is ubiquitous, this is not necessarily the case. Throughout much of Europe, Internet operators have something of a choice among jurisdictions and agencies. At the International Casino Exposition (ICE) in London, the largest gaming show in the world, numerous regulators staff booths selling their competing products differentiated by tax rates, band width and data handling infrastructures, and the proximity of a good pub. This latitude, however, does not exist in the United States. In the United States there are but three options: 1) deal with the defined regulatory entity; 2) do not enter the market; or 3) enter the market without regulatory approval and face the criminal consequences.

Here, the regulatory agency is a monopolistic supplier of regulation, and the gambling operator is forced to buy from this monopoly. This has many ramifications. Regulatory monopolies possess the power to charge higher prices than those in more competitive markets because there is no possibility the operator will move to a substitute supplier of regulatory ser-

---

[37] David G. Schwartz, *Concentration on the Las Vegas Strip: An Exploration of the Impacts*, 17 GAMING L. REV. & ECON., (2013).

[38] Alexandra Berzon, *MGM Mirage Knew of Pansy Ho's Links to Triads 14K and Sun Yee On through Stanley Ho*, WALL ST. J., Mar. 18, 2010.

vices. Monopolies, however, are typically slow to innovate and need not worry about staying up with the competition. Monopolies may also offer poor service without fear of competitive pressures.

Regulatory agencies can charge higher prices in several ways. Most regulatory agencies charge the applicant for the licensing background investigation. The agency has a high degree of discretion to determine the scope of the investigation, its urgency, the human resources to be assigned, and the travel needs of the investigators. In this context, monopoly power can be abused by the agency to maintain high levels of employment and internal growth. William Niskanen, a respected author on the behavior of bureaucracies, argues that regulatory agencies often exhibit a maximizing behavior desiring larger salaries, office space, and perceived importance.[39] This process is particularly facilitated when the agency can direct-charge the applicant rather than rely on appropriations from a higher government entity. An agency costs money to run, and these costs are often charged directly to industry participants through earmarked fee and tax structures and upfront charges to enter, or even apply for entry into, a market. Again, the applicant or participant's "choice" is pay to play, leave the market, or suffer the consequences. The regulatory agency can also fine the licensee, and in Nevada these fines are often in the millions of dollars. These fines are important enforcement tools to ensure compliance, but they could also become used as important revenue tools for a jurisdiction or an agency, especially during fiscally tough times.

A monopoly supplier of regulation may also be slower to innovate. Regulatory agencies are not subject to the compelling pressures of the free-market to continually reinvent themselves, offer new and better processes, reduce costs, enhance efficiency, and stay alive. Slower regulatory innovation imposes costs on gambling operators. For example, in the California card room industry, many transactions performed by the third-party proposition players must be recorded on a playing book form. The playing book form must be paper, all entries must be recorded in ink, and all playing books for the operation must be physically stored in one location within California.[40] Most third-party providers in California long ago computerized digital tracking of these forms, but to comply with the state regulation they must run redundant copies with the paper and ink system. This imposes an additional labor storage and environmental cost on the company without any obvious regulatory benefit. An all-paper system does not contain internal checks and controls, and the regulatory entity has no ability to develop a meaningful database of this incredibly important stream of transactions. To become more arcane, California would have to regress to clay tablets.

An extension of the slow-to-innovate situation is the slow-to-revise situation. Gaming regulatory agencies rarely sunset their regulations, leading

[39] WILLIAM A. NISKANEN, JR., BUREAUCRACY AND REPRESENTATIVE GOVERNMENT (1971).
[40] CAL. CODE REGS. tit. 4, §12200.13.

to regulatory atrophy and increased red tape. Companies find it difficult to track a growing body of regulations, many of them no longer relevant. A White Paper prepared for the American Gaming Association captures the consequences of these issues below:

> ...regulatory practices that made good sense when adopted can become outdated. A regulation that no longer serves its initial purpose, or has become duplicative, has sharply negative effects. By sharply increasing costs, it diverts industry resources away from investment and innovations that create jobs and economic opportunity. It saps the creative spirit of employees. It wastes taxpayer dollars and industry resources on misguided enforcement. And it reduces the morale of regulators, who recognize that they are imposing standards that are losing their relevance.[41]

Monopolies also are not pressured by the threat of competition to offer and maintain high levels of client and customer service, especially if a particular regulator has no interest in later joining the industry. This dynamic can result in slow response times, poorly thought-out communications, indifference to helping the industry understand what the regulator wants, lack of concern for the cost conditions imposed upon the firm by the regulation, and lack of motivation to streamline processes and regulations. Many of these consequences hurt the firm directly, but more often they make it more difficult for a firm to stay current in the market as approval times extend, costs grow, and the critically important notion of speed-to-market is hampered by the regulatory agency.

Cost of Regulating

Public administrative costs, i.e., the cost of management and maintenance of regulatory authorities, are also an issue. Gaming regulation is only one of a myriad of government services. Because gaming generates more in taxes does not necessarily mean it should have a correspondingly higher share of the government budget, but too often money is thrown at gaming regulation with significantly reduced returns. For example, Nevada spends $13 million less in regulation than New Jersey but manages over three times as much gross gaming revenue.[42] Neither Nevada nor New Jersey would likely argue their industries are poorly regulated nor their agency budgets excessive.

---

[41] David O. Stewart, *Improving Gaming Regulation: 10 Recommendations for the Streamlining Processes While Maintaining Integrity,* AMERICAN GAMING ASSOCIATION WHITE PAPER (2011).

[42] Econsult Solutions, Inc., *The Current Condition and Future Viability of Casino Gaming in Pennsylvania* 120 (2014). http://www.econsultsolutions.com/wp-content/uploads/PA-Gaming-Report-from-ESI_May-6.pdf (prepared for the Pennsylvania Legislative Budget and Finance Committee).

Cost of Compliance

Every new regulation can alter the cost conditions of the operator. As such, new regulations should be considered an additional tax. This tax is not fee-based on revenues and may not even be collected by the jurisdiction, but instead the tax is the operator's internal cost of compliance imposed by the regulation. These taxes can lead to unexpectedly large financial consequences for the operator.

The costs that can accompany a regulatory change often reverberate throughout the organization. A regulatory change typically needs to be codified into policies and procedures, and these policies and procedures must be inspected by a compliance committee and the legal staff. They then must be prepared for dissemination to the current employees, and documentation and audit trails need to be established to make sure employees are aware of the changes. Training manuals must be amended, and media presentations utilized in the training environment will need to be altered to accommodate the new practices. Tracking systems, accounting systems, security systems, and the whole system of software and system interfaces must be viewed to see how the change resonates throughout these systems, and alterations will need to be made. Reports may need to be altered, and adjustments must be incorporated into all analytic routines to maintain comparability with past data trails.

While all of the regulatory compliance apparatus is being adjusted, none of the corporate employees involved with these processes are thinking about new and better marketing programs, better ways to enhance the employee experience, ways to enhance efficiency and productivity, or anything else that improves the revenue of the business. That is, the opportunity costs of developing a culture of compliance with a new regulation can be substantial and are extraordinarily difficult to measure.

Impact on Innovation

Regulation can severely impact innovation and the industry's ability to adapt to customer preferences and technology. For example, New Jersey casinos were initially forced to deal every blackjack game according to the exact same rules. While relatively easy to administer, it is difficult to innovate or offer different blackjack games.

Likewise, gaming manufacturers accept few third-party titles each year partially because of the high costs for both time and money of getting regulatory approval for each new game. While the regulator will be concerned about the validity of a game on the casino floor within its jurisdiction, the costs and speed-to-market obstacles dissuade local innovation. Local innovators know that foreign manufacturers without these restrictions can alpha- and beta-test their devices on the casino floors of other jurisdictions and perfect them before experiencing an expedited approval process in other jurisdictions.

Agency Failures
Information and knowledge failure - the experience of regulators

Gaming legislation often requires appointments be divided between the two major political parties and that appointed individuals should possess specific background requirements, such as one being from the law profession, one being from an accounting or finance background, one representing the general public, and one representing law enforcement. As previously discussed, gambling regulators' biographies across the United States rarely reveal any casino industry experience. This is dissimilar to other industries where the people assigned to these regulatory agencies have a lot of experience working in the industry they are empowered to regulate. Not surprisingly, people that regulate medicine typically have medical or related backgrounds. This is also true for construction, nuclear energy, architecture, and pharmaceuticals fields. One would be surprised to find a state that would not allow lawyers to later become judges or to discover that most judges had no prior legal experience. In gambling, however, the regulators typically have little, if any, experience in the gambling industry.

After his 2011 appointment as chairman of the Massachusetts Gaming Commission, Stephen Crosby acknowledged he had never before gambled in a casino, and his stepson gave him the book "Casinos for Dummies" as a humorous appointment gift.[43] That Mr. Crosby felt safe making such a statement to the press shows the public's level of comfort with having individuals with no gaming experience regulating the industry. Chairman Crosby had an extensive background in high profile positions in "policy making, entrepreneurship, non-profits, and academics."[44] Nonetheless, the public would certainly have had a different reaction if they learned the person overseeing the medical profession in Massachusetts had never been in a hospital, and a family member gave them a book called "Medicine for Dummies."

In a perfect economic model, regulators would have complete knowledge of the industry that would allow them to make decisions that maximized the public policy goals for the industry (whether reflecting the public interest school or capture theorists). In other words, there would be no cost for ignorance or inexperience. By staffing regulatory commissions with individuals who have little or no knowledge of the industry, politicians demonstrate their fear of industry capture, which often outweighs their concerns about industry inexperience and ignorance. The question, then, is what are the potential costs of industry inexperience?

Expertise in the gaming industry is not the most critical in accessing the suitability of applicants for licensing. Although an industry veteran

---

[43] Phil Primack, *Casino Czar Steve Crosby's Impossible Mission*, Bost. Globe Mag., April 22, 2012, http://www.bostonglobe.com/magazine/2012/04/21/casino-czar-steve-crosby-impossible-mission/tA75P1WAZy9Ud1AYzNND7K/story.html.
[44] Mass. Gaming Comm'n, Meet the Commissioners, http://massgaming.com/the-commission/meet-the-commissioners/stephen-crosby.

may be better positioned to select the *better* person for a particular license (because of the industry veteran's greater appreciation for the cash nature of the business, the ease with which transactions can be misdirected, and the weaknesses of the surveillance and other internal control procedures), even an inexperienced regulator can identify instances of an applicant's past behavior or image concerns that reflect poorly on the applicant's suitability or the reputation of the industry as a whole.

The areas that likely incur the highest costs from inexperience and ignorance are making regulatory compliance judgments and in creating new regulations.

Some compliance issues are so dramatic and serious in nature that even those with no gaming experience can understand them. In Nevada in the early 1980s, state regulators encountered inappropriate activities at the Stardust Hotel and Casino that resulted in Al Sachs and Herb Tobman being asked to vacate the premises and pay a $3.5 million fine. In 1989, Nevada fined casino owner Ralph Engelstad $1.5 million for damaging the image of the state and the industry by holding parties at his casino resort that celebrated Adolph Hitler's birthday. For an 84-week period beginning in May 2001, Las Vegas' MGM Mirage failed to file 14,905 Currency Transaction Reports, the tool designed to make money laundering more difficult.[45] As result of this lapse, the company paid a $5 million fine to Nevada.[46] In 2013, Caesars Entertainment was fined $225,000 by the New Jersey Bureau of Gaming Enforcement for how the company handled employee sexual harassment claims and for the widely-publicized drug-use by one of its high-rollers (what the Wall Street Journal described as a "gambling spree, by former toy entrepreneur Terrance Watanabe, to be the single largest continuous binge in Las Vegas history" that resulted in an alleged loss of over $100 million).[47]

Inexperienced regulators' problem lies in addressing more mundane and nuanced violations. Inexperience carries the risk of imposing a regulator-ignorance tax on the industry. Casino floors, especially those offering live games, may be best characterized as organized chaos. A fundamental reality of the casino business is that revenues are generated through turns on the money, and much thought and effort go into maximizing the speed at which these gambling transactions take place. As the speed of these transactions increases, so too do the risks associated with errors and control lapses. Anyone who has ever spent any appreciable time in a live

---

[45] State of Massachusetts redacted report *Investigative Report for the Massachusetts Gaming Commission,* for applicant Blue Tarp reDevelopment, LLC, Nov. 27, 2013, http://massgaming.com/wp-content/uploads/MGM-Report-REDACTED.pdf.

[46] Ken Ritter, *MGM Mirage to Pay $5 Million State Fine,* AP News Archive, Mar. 24, 2003.

[47] Alexandra Berzon, *Caesars Fined for Role in 2007 Gambling Spree,* Wall St. J., Mar. 19, 2013. *See also* State of Massachusetts redacted report *Investigative Report for the Massachusetts Gaming Commission,* Applicant: Sterling Suffolk Racecourse, LLC, Oct. 18, 2013, http://massgaming.com/wp-content/uploads/SSR-Report-REDACTED.pdf.

gaming environment understands that fill slips contain errors, get dropped on the wrong games, get signed on the wrong line, and can have a variety of other administrative or regulatory failures. An employee can miss a cash transaction or assign it to the wrong person. Hands can be miscounted or set incorrectly; a losing bet can be paid, and a whole variety of events can take place that may sound incredible in the daylight of a hearing room but are an integral part of the culture and industrial reality of a gambling floor.

While management tries to minimize errors and control lapses, setting a goal to eliminate these events would have a deleterious impact on game-speed. A regulatory agency with no insight into this industrial reality will have difficulty weighing the seriousness of violations brought to their attention. If the regulatory agency punishes an operator or the industry for honest mistakes that are a natural result of the casino-processes, operator or industry economics can be severely adversely impacted.

A regulatory agency may potentially use mistake-catching as a revenue source for the agency or the state. Sometimes referred to within the industry as "gotcha regulation," this process shifts the goals of regulatory enforcement away from ensuring compliance to generating revenue. To justify their existence, enforcement agents often feel obligated to find violations during an inspection. As any automobile driver knows, if his driving were continuously monitored, police would inevitably find traffic violations. So too with the operation of a casino, and if the regulatory agency wants to find violations, it is only a matter of patience. Therefore the response to compliance issues by a regulatory authority can dramatically impact the financial performance of the firm or industry. It can result in the firm finding it necessary to slow the game speed, which can dramatically impact revenues. It can also force the firm to exercise greater energies on supervision, training, hiring standards, and discipline, and discharge—all actions that can impact the cost side of the operator or the industry. This is one example where a regulatory agency can tax, and the tax can be an excessive reaction to simple and understandable mistakes. But they are only simple if one understands the business he or she is regulating. Individuals who have been in any business for an appreciable amount of time understand the culture, challenges, and rhythms of that business. They understand how to distinguish honest mistakes from serious violations of the firm's internal controls. When regulators have only a slight understanding of the business they are regulating, this insight is lost.

One would anticipate these ignorance taxes to be highest with relatively new agencies because the regulatory actors are at the beginning of the learning curve. They possess little understanding of the industry they are regulating, and they carry with them a strong desire not to be wrong and to appear important. This presents the perfect scenario for over-regulation. When Atlantic City first allowed legal casino gaming, the industry was subjected to incredibly strong regulatory controls, which ultimately damaged the industry through additional costs and lost revenues. Examples include requirements that casinos (i) close daily in Atlantic City to protect players from becoming captured by the gambling moment, and (ii) be staffed full-time with regulatory agents always accessible to the public. The regulations also established limits on reel strips and denomination mix requirements and even specified the machine mix requirements by manufacturing source. In short, the Atlantic City experience offered a dramatically more rigorous regulatory environment than in Nevada because of the lack of experience held by the initial regulators as well as a strong desire to avoid risk or make a mistake. In other words, it was heavily influenced by ignorance and fear.[48] The evolution of the New Jersey experience in the years since opening has been a movement away from these rigorous regulations and towards a much more business friendly regulatory environment.[49]

WHERE REGULATORS CAN IMPROVE THE CASINO INDUSTRY

Regulators must ensure they are operating efficiently, coordinating their efforts with other jurisdictions, and operating from a position of knowledge and intelligence rather than fear and ignorance. States with established regulatory systems should regularly solicit comments from the industry about how regulation can work better and be more efficient. Old regulations must be examined regularly from a cost–benefit analysis standpoint, and jurisdictions can accomplish this by having sunset laws on regulations.

States implementing gaming and regulations should not blindly adopt laws of other states without examining their costs and benefits in light of their own unique circumstances, capabilities, and goals. The states should look to best practices, and adjust them accordingly. This will significantly increase the efficiency of laws and reduce unnecessary burdens on operators to conform to regulations that are not relevant to the goals of the jurisdiction. This will reduce both regulatory and operator costs and in the latter circumstance, increase taxable profits, thereby benefitting the operator and the jurisdiction.

States should also work with each other to ensure conformity among jurisdictions. The states should help fund regulators' travel to events that allow them to network and interact. It would also be in the industry's best interest to help them lobby for this because the fewer the regulatory differences among states, the easier it is to conduct business across states lines

---

[48] We can make a similar observation about the gaming equipment manufacturing industry. Three-hundred-and-sixty-five gaming jurisdictions in North America have unique regulations on the shipping of machines. Each of these jurisdictions has essentially the exact same goal: to ensure the integrity of the game, yet there is little effort to coordinate among the many jurisdictions. *See* David O. Stewart, *Streamlining Shipping Recommendations for Regulatory Reform*, AMERICAN GAMING ASSOCIATION WHITE PAPER (2013).

[49] *See, e.g.,* N.J. CASINO CONTROL COMM'N, CASINO GAMBLING IN NEW JERSEY 16 (1998), http://www.nj.gov/casinos/reports/docs/njccc.pdf (noting the repeal of some regulations and the adoption of a "Common Sense" regulatory approach).

and, again, the more efficient the outcome. This can also be accomplished by states working more closely with regulatory associations and providing and funding staff.

Effective regulation has legitimized the gaming industry, made gaming an enjoyable experience for patrons, and made it a profitable business for operators. As the industry becomes more regulated and more accepted by Main Street, it is increasingly important for the industry and regulators to communicate. This is especially true of those agencies that require non-industry experienced regulators. While there is sometimes the fear that too much communication can lead to government capture by the industry, the Las Vegas experience demonstrates that this need not be the outcome. Regulators and the industry work together benefiting both the public and the casino industry.

6

Regulatory Agency Organization

Toni Cowan

INTRODUCTION

Developing an effective, efficient gaming regulatory structure requires an understanding of the different functions and responsibilities inherent in gaming regulation. Successful regulation results from careful planning that considers (1) the policy goals of the gaming industry as a whole (i.e., retaining public confidence and industry integrity while allowing the global industry to flourish); (2) the components of a robust system of regulation in light of a jurisdiction's[1] cultural and legal environment (i.e., particular concerns of the jurisdiction's population and government, budgetary and expertise limitations); and (3) national and international best practices in the gaming industry. This last category is an invaluable asset in any jurisdiction because it is an extensive library of policy and practice information available through global industry and regulatory cooperation.

We are experiencing rapid technological development. The best regulatory systems can respond to this development because they include efficient change mechanisms, enabling them to meet the new technology's inevitable updates and challenges while achieving the policy goals that accompany the technology. Regulatory systems must be living structures that can evolve while providing uninterrupted benefits to the jurisdiction and the industry. This chapter discusses the functions inherent in gaming regulation that determine the structure of such a regulatory agency.

---

[1]   [J]urisdiction sometimes refers to a particular geographic area containing a defined legal authority. . . . [T]he federal government is a jurisdiction unto itself. Its power spans the entire United States. Each state is also a jurisdiction unto itself, with the power to pass its own laws. Smaller geographic areas, such as counties and cities, are separate jurisdictions to the extent that they have powers that are independent of the federal and state governments.

The Free Legal Dictionary, http://legal-dictionary.thefreedictionary.com/jurisdiction.

SEPARATION OF POWERS

The separation of powers model has been adopted in varying forms by most democratic governments worldwide and by regulatory agencies structured with two or more branches to provide the balance of powers necessary for effective regulation.

While the doctrine was originally intended for sovereign governments, its application has expanded to include gaming regulations. The enabling gaming statute should include a balanced distribution of power among the regulatory agencies, the units of a single agency, or other government units in the regulatory system.[2]

Gaming regulation involves executive, legislative, and judicial powers. Such checks and balances in a gaming regulatory structure assure the public that the gaming regulatory process is fair and trustworthy.[3] "The impression that a jurisdiction could have a "gaming czar," who single-handedly would direct an investigation and then make the definitive licensing decision, is not appropriate."[4] Too much power in a single leader of a regulatory agency is frequently avoided by parceling out functions. For example, the investigation and prosecution functions of regulatory power are often separated from the judicial function into distinct agencies; this often occurs with the review and assessment function as well. This separation is a delicate balance between avoiding a single concentration of power and building a cumbersome multi-agency regulatory system where territorial battles and uncertainty burden the effectiveness and duplicate the efforts of regulators.

Three critical executive gaming regulatory functions are (1) enforcing laws and regulations, (2) investigating applicants and incidents, and (3) accounting for revenues. These functions can be done either by internal personnel within an agency or by other divisions of the government which may have extensive experience in that area already. They also involve much of the administrative functions that are critical to providing the infrastructure for the system to work properly.

Legislative functions are also critical because gaming control relies on laws and rules that define the expected conduct of licensed casinos. In traditional forms of government, it is the legislature that adopts these laws. The legislature, however, can delegate some or all of its legislative authority to an agency. Where this occurs, the agency must have rule-making procedures. Adoption of regulations involves establishing the rules that govern the conduct of the casino industry.

Regulators have two methods to create these rules. The first and primary method is through rulemaking. This is a process by which the regulators

---

[2] Sean McGuiness, *Gaming Policy Models, Pt. II: Regulatory Organization*, CASINO ENTERPRISE MGMT., Aug. 2010, http://www.casinoenterprisemanagement.com/articles/gaming-policy-models-pt-ii-regulatory-organization.
[3] *Id.*
[4] *Id.*

consider and adopt rules that define such areas as the expected conduct of licensees, the criteria for approval of applicants, and others things, such as gaming equipment. The secondary method is through case adjudication. Regulators determine applications or disciplinary actions that may provide some level of precedent, though not the binding precedent that may exist in the civil and criminal context typical in common law jurisdictions.

Quasi-judicial functions are a vital part of regulatory control. This decision-making is commonly exercised in the issuance, denial, and revocation of gaming authorizations. Regulators or other government officials must decide who should be granted licenses, work cards, or other types of approval; they must decide if a licensee should be punished and, if so, the nature of the punishment. Often, regulators or courts interpret the laws or regulations. Finally, they can be called upon to resolve disputes, such as whether a patron is entitled to a jackpot or whether a casino owes some amount of gaming taxes.

EXAMPLES OF THE STATUTORY FOUNDATION

There are as many interpretations of the ideal regulatory structure as there are gaming jurisdictions. New York amended its gaming law effective February 1, 2013, to create the New York State Gaming Commission, which

> regulates all aspects of gaming and gambling activity in the state, including horse racing and pari-mutuel wagering, Class III Indian Gaming, the state lottery (including video lottery terminals) and charitable gaming. . . .[It] merged the New York State Racing and Wagering Board with the New York State Division of Lottery into a single state agency. The law also consolidated the administration of the New York Thoroughbred Breeding & Development Fund and The Agriculture & New York State Horse Breeding Development Fund into the Office of Racing Promotion and Development under the umbrella of the Gaming Commission. . . . By consolidating various regulatory functions into one oversight body with broad powers, the Commission seeks to ensure fair and strict regulation of all gaming activity while reducing costs and regulatory burdens to the gaming industry.[5]

New Jersey did not consolidate all gaming regulation under one agency. Instead, it reduced the staff and size of the New Jersey Casino Control Commission[6] by giving the Division of Gaming Enforcement all authority to make and enforce regulations[7] and "the authority to initiate and decide any actions against licensees or registrants, and impose sanctions on them

---

[5] N.Y. State Gaming Comm'n, http://www.gaming.ny.gov/about/.
[6] Duane Morris LLP Alerts and Updates, *New Jersey's Bill S-12 Redesigns the Regulatory System for the Gaming Industry*, Feb. 11, 2011, http://www.duanemorris.com/alerts/NJ_bill_S12_regulation_gaming_gambling_Atlantic_City_3946.html.
[7] This is so though the Commission retains the ability to make regulations regarding the governing of hearings before it. *Id.*

for violation of the Act."[8] This illustrates how New Jersey's experience led it to realize there needs to be a balance between separation of powers, cost, and efficiency. Having a fully-staffed commission may not be efficient if it is duplicating what any other agency is doing. Duplication is not a check and balance.

Administrative agencies allow governments to deal with the kind of specialized knowledge and oversight necessary in certain areas of regulation. Legislatures often turn to administrative agencies as an effective method of resolving legislative disagreements. Legislators may be politically hesitant to take any position on a policy dispute because it will likely alienate some potential voters. Therefore, it is easier to delegate decision-making to a specialized agency.

A single administrative agency regulating the industry, as opposed to multiple branches of government, may also have other advantages. An administrative agency can specialize in a subject, and with that increased expertise can come an increased likelihood of more pertinent and consistent policies and priorities. Moreover, industry-savvy persons with control over the agency should better understand and coordinate regulatory policy. Advantages of agency adjudications include not only cost savings but also more accurate and consistent results and the relief of an overburdened court system. Finally, a single administrative agency may be subject to greater accountability because it is responsible for all aspects of carrying out regulatory policy.

THE AGENCY ARCHITECTURE

The organizational "structure and size of a regulatory agency is influenced by many factors."[9] No one structure is universally appropriate. The extent and nature of the facilities and activities that must be regulated should determine the size of the agency and structure of the regulatory body.[10] The structure should ensure that the organization has adequate resources to discharge its responsibilities[11] as those jurisdictions initially open and evolve into a mature operational development.

In many areas the functions of a gaming regulatory agency include many of the more general governmental functions, such as tax collection or industry policing. Furthermore, a gaming regulatory organization cannot function completely independently from other parts of the government within the same jurisdiction but must operate within that governmental framework, just as other branches of the government, including private

---

[8] *Id.*

[9] Int'l Atomic Energy Agency, Vienna, *Organization and Staffing of the Regulatory Body for Nuclear Facilities*, IAEA SAFETY STANDARDS SERIES No. GS-G-1.1, at 6, (2002), http://wwwpub.iaea.org/MTCD/publications/PDF/Pub1129_scr.pdf.

[10] *Id.*

[11] *Id.*

and public entities, must. A gaming regulatory agency needs sufficient independence from the promoters of the industry, both inside and outside the jurisdictional government, to remain credible and effective.[12] This neutrality is established in the enabling legislation.[13] Independence ensure regulators can make judgments and enforcements without undue influence from the proponents of the industry it regulates.

Working Agencies in Other Governmental Structures

Nothing requires all critical functions be done only by administrative agencies or only by pre-existing government structures. For example, pre-existing state or local police may conduct gaming investigations for the gaming regulators. Likewise, legal gaming advice may be provided by independent legal counsel.

Some advantages may exist to using other pre-existing government branches. As the functions are divided among agencies or different units within agencies, another way to interject safeguards against a single central power (besides creating formal checks and balances) is to provide in the enabling statute that the role of the agency's legal counsel will be served by the state attorney general's office. Using an external agency to fulfill the legal responsibilities of the regulatory agency provides a check on the power of the head of the agency, whether that power rests in a single individual or a multi-person board or commission.

Single Agency Head Versus a Multiple Member Agency

Frequently, multi-member boards or commissions head a regulatory agency. Other agencies may have a single individual to head the agency.[14] Mississippi has a single executive director and a multi-member commission, as opposed to Nevada which has a multilevel board and commission.

Multi-member boards can have shared responsibility, wherein each board member has equal authority on all matters with all other members, or segregated responsibility, wherein each board member primarily has segregated responsibility for different aspects of the agency's responsibilities.

Commonly, when a multi-member board has segregated responsibility, segregation is by agency function, e.g., investigations, enforcement, and accounting. For example, the agency member with the accounting back-

---

[12] *Id.* at Section 2.3, p.3 (describing the importance of independence in the nuclear regulatory industry).

[13] *See, e.g.,* Fed. Comm. Comm'n, Regulatory Challenges and Opportunities: Establishing And Maintaining Regulatory Independence, http://transition.fcc.gov/connectglobe/sec1.html.

[14] The New Jersey Division of Gaming Enforcement has a single director, David L. Rebuck. *See* Dep't of Law & Pub. Safety, Office of the Att'y Gen., http://www.nj.gov/oag/ge/index.html.

ground may have primary responsibility for the agency's audit function. Under the segregated responsibility model, board members often jointly decide issues, but deference is given to the board member in whose area the issue arises or to the member with chief administrative responsibility.

The main advantage of a segregated responsibility agency is that the agency benefits from the specialization of its various board members. For example, the board member in charge of accounting may be, or can even statutorily be required to be, a certified public accountant. Similarly, enforcement functions could fall under the supervision of a board member with extensive law enforcement experience. This greatly increases the probability that actions taken in these areas are more in line with industry norms and make more sense to those who must implement the policies.

Multi-member boards are also advantageous when the agency's primary function is decision-making rather than applicant investigation, regulation enforcement, or accounting. Its function can be accomplished by having the agency members meet to consider the positions of all interested parties and only then making a decision. No one board member has responsibility separate from another to coordinate the agency's activity or that of any employees. Instead, much like a jury, their responsibility is only to hear evidence and make a decision.

Another advantage of multi-member boards is their value in checking arbitrary decisions or those that contravene policy goals. The other board members create a check on each other's powers. Where a director of an agency may decide a matter based on emotion, friendship, or politics, with a multi-member board if that decision is counter to the public interest, the other members should override his vote.

Multi-member boards also may provide an escape valve for dealing with intergovernmental pressures. Laws may require that the agency have members that represent all major political parties. Therefore, if a partisan issue arises, one political party may have greater difficulty asserting effective influence over the agency decision. It may allow board members to retain political support despite political opposition to a proper agency decision. Suppose an influential politician is pressing for the licensure of a person who is "unsuitable." The politician may affect a board member that needs his support for proper agency funding. If the other board members will vote against the license, one board member can vote for it knowing the application will be denied, saving face, and potentially maintaining the political support.

Single directorships do have advantages. First, having a single person with administrative control can help reduce debilitating interagency politics. Shared responsibility can split loyalties, causing some employees to support one board member while others support another, with standard office politics ensuing. Brought to extremes, these divisions can immobilize the agency if coordination of functions ceases. Even without agency politics, multi-member boards may be less coordinated when different agency members control different functions. This can result from differences in management styles, poor communication within and across functions, and philosophical and priority differences. As the number of agency members increases, so does the potential for poor coordination.

Agencies with a single director can react quicker to problems and issues that arise. A single director can give definitive directions to all agency divisions, enforcement, accounting, and investigations that are needed to accomplish a goal. When doing so, the director can also set the priorities. Another advantage is the budget. An agency with a single head may have lower administrative and salary costs than an agency with many members.

No matter which organizational approach to gaming regulation is chosen, there are fundamental, unavoidable, and critical functions that must be implemented in all gaming regulatory systems. For example, as gaming has become more technology-centered, focused on communication and information processing, valuable lessons can be learned by looking at telecommunications regulation and other technology-advanced industries. Traditional vertically structured (i.e., "top down") regulation silos organized from the larger, more general structure down to smaller more detailed units within the larger structure has been a familiar regulatory model.[15] These structures assume clear, unwavering distinctions and static characteristics of gaming when regulating both delivery and content. They do not account for converging markets and new types of technology. Internet gaming and other technological gaming do not fit easily, if at all, into these legacy regulation models.

A newly emerging regulatory model, more horizontal in structure, acknowledges that services and the technology platforms that deliver those services can be treated differently by different regulators.[16] The Internet has horizontal network layers. The lowest layers include services, networks, hardware, functional layers, and physical and logical networks.[17] The upper levels include user applications and content. The Internet Protocol resides in the middle of the layered stack.[18] Regulatory systems in gaming and other industries must learn to adapt and amend operations and regulations to the type of regulatory structure that best integrates new technology.

An example of poor legacy regulation is the National Indian Gaming Act (NIGA),[19] which has not been amended since it was passed in 1988. The Indian gaming industry suffers from a regulatory apparatus meant for firehouse cardboard bingo, not the electronic-based bingo gaming ma-

---

[15] Rob Frieden, *Adjusting the Horizontal and Vertical in Telecommunications Regulation: A Comparison of the Traditional and a New Layered Approach*, 55 FED. COMMS L.J. 207, 209 (2003), http://www.repository.law.indiana.edu/fclj/vol55/iss2/3,_

[16] Richard S. Whitt, *A Horizontal Leap Forward: Formulating a New Public Policy Framework Based on the Network Layers Model*, MCI PUBLIC POLICY PAPER, at iii (March 2004), *available at* http://efile.mpsc.state.mi.us/efile/docs/14073/0019.pdf.

[17] *Id.* at iv.

[18] *Id.* at ii.

[19] 25 U.S.C. § 2701.

chines that are now on the floor of most Indian casinos. These machines and Indian gaming regulation in general are stuck with the gaming classification types devised in 1988 in order to protect commercial gaming and, at the same time, allow some gaming on Indian lands, i.e., class I, class 2, and class 3 levels of gaming operations. In some states, tribes without the tribal state compact required to operate class 3 gaming—the broadest category of games and technologically advanced games—nonetheless operate such games in contravention of NIGA. Neither state nor federal gaming regulators have found a way to restructure such gaming to conform to the law.

No matter which regulatory structure is initially introduced for gaming, upon the implementation of the enabling statute, it is possible that the agency form originally conceived may well change as the industry evolves. The regulatory body structure can always shift to meet new challenges whether it be vertical or horizontal, new or mature, part-time[20] or full-time.[21]

THE FOUNDATION: THE STATUTE THAT ALLOWS LEGAL GAMING
Fundamental Statutory Provisions

An enabling statute that allows for legal gaming should provide the following:[22]

- Framework
  - Creating a fundamental framework for each agency, its powers, duties and responsibilities, the head(s) of the agency, the qualifications to serve as head of the agency, and compensation.
- Protecting the System
  - Establishing measures to avoid conflicts of interest,[23] such as pre-determined restrictions from industry employment, for heads of agencies and management.[24]
- Delegating Agency Powers

---

[20] NEV. REV. STAT. § 463.021 (2013). The Nevada Gaming Policy Committee is an eleven-member body appointed by the governor which serves in a part-time capacity. The Nevada Gaming Commission, though not designated as part-time, meets once a month for two days. Its members may and do hold other employment. NEV. REV. STAT. §463.022–029 (2013). *See also* NEV. GAMING CONTROL BD., http://gaming.nv.gov/index.aspx?page=53 (last visited June 24, 2014).

[21] NEV. REV. STAT. § 463.030 (2013). The Nevada Gaming Control Board consists of three members who work on a full time basis.

[22] *See generally* NEV. REV. STAT. § 463.010 *et seq.* and N.J. STAT. ANN. § 5:12-233.

[23] "Conflict of interest is a conflict between the private interests and the official responsibilities of a person in a position of trust." MERRIAM-WEBSTER, http://www.merriam-webster.com/dictionary/conflict%20of%20interest (last visited June 24, 2014). A conflict occurs if a person has multiple obligations that may be opposing such as employment, family or other personal beliefs or commitments that may influence his or her motivation.

[24] *See, e.g.,* NEV. REV. STAT. § 463.022–110 (2013).

- o Vesting specific powers and discretionary powers[25] to provide the authority to accomplish any duties assigned by the legislation.
- o Quasi-Executive Powers
  - Establishing whether agencies have police powers;
  - The degree and scope of such powers; and
  - Creating rights to audit and inspect.
- o Quasi-Legislative Powers
  - Regulating persons involved in gaming, including those with a certain percentage of beneficial ownership, senior management, workers on the casino floor, and manufacturers, and sellers and distributors of gaming equipment and technology. A minority of jurisdictions require some regulation of every casino resort employee, including kitchen and housekeeping staff, though best practices should prevail;
  - Establishing specific topics for which the agency must adopt regulations, such as financial practices for operators of casinos and excluding undesirable patrons;
  - Establishing procedures for disciplinary actions;
  - Establishing procedures for appeals from agency actions, though those appeals may be limited in nature by the statute itself. Establishing methods for assessing and collecting state, county, city, and municipal fees;
  - Establishing regulations over certain types of business entities;
  - Establishing procedures and reporting for transportation of gaming devices; and
  - Adopting specific regulation for specific types of gaming, e.g. horse racing, sports betting, lottery, table games, slot machines, Internet gaming, mobile gaming, and gaming in other jurisdictions by holders of gaming authorizations within the jurisdiction (sometimes called foreign gaming).
- o Quasi-Judicial Powers
  - Granting licenses and approvals;
  - Deciding disciplinary acts/assessing fines;

---

[25] *See* Charles H. Koch Jr., *Judicial Review of Administrative Discretion*, 54 GEO. WASH. L. REV. 469 (1986).

> Discretion . . . refers to the discretionary decision-maker's authority to adjust applicable rules... in order to improve a program's ability to do individual justice. That is, even where the general rule mandates a result, the implementing decision-maker has some power to modify that result in a specific application if doing so will better carry out the general spirit of the program."

Id. at 472.

- Deciding patron disputes; and
- Settling tax audit disputes between the licensee.
- Creating the Status of Licensee
  - Establishing the "privilege" status as opposed to the "right" status of any authorization or credential (a term meaning any type of authorization issued by a regulatory agency). That credential may solely be a privilege that can be revoked with basic due process, not a property right.[26] This is the majority practice in the United States, though other jurisdictions wherein gaming is viewed as less deleterious may take a different position.
- Creating a responsible gambling[27] program that addresses the potential social costs[28] associated with gaming and describes operator

---

[26] Shannon S. Bybee, *The Legal Status of Gaming and Its Impact on Licensing*, 2 UNLV Gaming Res. & Rev. J. 61 (1995). *See also* Thomas v. Bible, 694 F.Supp. 750, 759 (D. Nev.1988) (stating "Licensed gaming is a privilege conferred by the state and does not carry with it the rights inherent in useful trades and occupations."

[27] Responsible gambling means the practice of gambling in a way that minimizes any harm to the gambler or others. The American Gaming Association (AGA) Code of Conduct reflects this principle:

> The Code of Conduct is a pledge to employees, patrons and the public to promote responsible gaming in every aspect of the casino business, including employee training, customer education, the prevention of underage gambling, responsible alcohol service, and responsible marketing and advertising. All AGA member companies adhere to the provisions of the Code, and its reach has extended well beyond AGA membership. The Code has become a model for responsible gaming programs in international jurisdictions and non-member casinos across the country as well.

AGA Code of Conduct for Responsible Gaming, http://www.americangaming.org/.

[28] Christine Reilly & Nathan Smith, *The Evolving Definition of Pathological Gambling in the DSM-5*, National Center for Responsible Gaming White Paper (2013).

DSM-IV DIAGNOSTIC CRITERIA FOR GAMBLING DISORDERS:

1. A preoccupation with gambling (e.g., preoccupation with reliving past gambling experiences, handicapping or thinking of ways to get money with which to gamble)

2. A need to gamble with increasing amounts of money in order to achieve the desired level of excitement

3. Repeated, unsuccessful efforts to control, cut back or stop gambling

4. Feels restless or irritable when attempting to cut down or stop gambling (withdrawal symptoms)

5. Uses gambling as a way of escaping from problems or of relieving a dysphoric mood (e.g., feelings of hopelessness, guilt, anxiety and depression)

6. After losing money gambling, often returns another day to get even ("chasing" one's losses)

7. Lies to family members, therapist or others to conceal the extent of one's involvement with gambling

8. Has committed illegal acts such as forgery, fraud, theft or embezzlement to

responsibility to address such concerns as problem gaming, underage gambling, self-exclusion, and betting limits. The greater the local understanding of the jurisdiction's culture, the more effective this will be.

THE FRAMEWORK: FORM FOLLOWS FUNCTION

Besides basic regulatory functions (i.e., authorization, review and assessment, inspection, collection, and enforcement),[29] the notion of regulatory structure encompasses four less obvious, but equally important, concepts:

- Separation of regulatory and operational functions;
- Freedom from direct political pressure;
- Fair and transparent procedures; and
- Delegation of broad authority to an agency dedicated to a specific expertise to establish rules, to adjudicate disputes, and to regulate in the public interest. [30]

THE SUPPORT
Quasi-Legislative - Comprehensive Regulations

As a regulatory agency exercises its quasi-legislative authority within the jurisdiction's administrative law structure, it is afforded certain powers. These may include drafting regulations, publishing proposed regulations, collecting recommendations from the industry and the public, republishing the final draft, and adopting regulations in a fair and transparent manner that establishes all regulatory actions. It also has the power to adopt less prescribed rulemaking, which is decided on a more case-by-case basis. To be truly fair and transparent, this process requires full consultation within and without the regulatory organization, including the industry and the public. It makes sense those with the most knowledge and experience, both regulatory and industrial, should produce prescribed regulations.[31]

Three principal types of rule-making procedures exist: notice and comment, negotiated, and formal rulemaking.

Notice and comment is a more abbreviated, albeit less desirable, procedure. The agency provides notice that it is considering a new regulation

---

finance gambling

9. Has jeopardized or lost a significant relationship, job or educational or career opportunity because of gambling

10. Relies on others to provide money to relieve a desperate financial situation caused by gambling.

Id. at 2.

[29] Int'l Atomic Energy Agency, *supra* note 9, at Section 3.4.

[30] *See* FED. COMMS. COMM'N., *supra* note 13.

[31] Int'l Atomic Energy Agency, *supra* note 9, at Section 3.11.

and asks interested parties to provide written comments on the proposals. After a set time, the agency will convene, consider the comments, and either issue or decide not to issue a new regulation. In gaming, this formal and more rigid process has been tried and in most jurisdictions, abandoned for the less formal negotiated rulemaking. In perhaps the most notable circumstance, the NIGA published for potential adoption what was called an effort to establish a bright line difference between class II and class III gaming. The Indian gaming industry was consulted in this effort, but opposition to the rules became so complete across the gaming industry that the rules were abandoned by the agency and never adopted.

Negotiated rulemaking involves bringing broad groups of interested parties and the agency representative together for informal meetings. There, they can work together to come to an accord on a proposed rule consistent with policy and law and which can be practically observed or executed by the industry.

The fundamental basis of administrative law is notice provided by established rules. Rules must be sufficiently specific to allow the licensee to operate without doubt or confusion as to what is permissible and what is not. The availability of regulators for consultation with the industry whenever the approved action may not be clear is essential.

Formal rulemaking is a superior method of adopting codes of conduct.[32] Beyond the obvious argument that it helps to know what the rules are before playing the game, unlike adjudication, formal rulemaking also allows for broad participation by all groups interested in the process.[33] Broad participation in the process is desirable because it provides regulators with many perspectives valuable to deriving appropriate rules, especially the practicalities of their implementation. Broad-based participation also contributes to accountability of agency actions.[34]

Formalized prescribed agency rules are more effective for communicating regulatory expectations, laying out the rules of the game. These rules are published and available for licensees to review.[35] Published rules also contribute to agency accountability because the executive and legislative branches of government can review and decide if the agency is following legislative intent.[36]

Another advantage of prescribed rulemaking is that regulators can make changes with no case or controversy to come before it.[37] This could result from the creation of new innovations not permitted under existing law or regulation. It also does not place innovators in the position of having either

---

[32] KENNETH CULP DAVIS & RICHARD J. PIERCE, JR., ADMINISTRATIVE LAW § 6.7 (3rd ed. 1994).

[33] *Id.*

[34] *Id.*

[35] *See* Arthur Earl Bonfield, *State Law in the Teaching of Administrative Law: A Critical Analysis of the Status Quo*, 61 TEX. L. REV. 95, 125–131 (1982).

[36] DAVIS & PIERCE, *supra* note 32, at § 6.7.

[37] *See* Bonfield, *supra* note 35, at 127.

to potentially violate the law or challenge regulators to create a case that would allow the regulators to create new law by the decision. Prescribed rulemaking also helps insure uniform treatment between licensees.[38]

Technology Sensitive Regulations

As previously discussed, rapidly developing technology impacts the gaming industry and regularly requires new or revised regulations if the government hopes to continue pursuing policy goals. Therefore, government should establish a permanent organizational unit dedicated to technology issues, and if it cannot afford an exclusive unit, at least redirect staff assigned to other duties to familiarize themselves with the technological landscape to draft these new regulations.

Minimum internal controls

Minimum internal control standards (MICS) are the standards set by a regulatory agency, then implemented by gaming operators as tailored to the operators' particular organizations. Regulators create MICS; then operators must create their own controls incorporating at least the regulators' minimum standards. These personalized MICS are reviewed and approved by regulators. The controls created by the operators must be comprehensive and include, though are not limited to, accounting systems, player-related systems (like player accounts and methods for identification protection), anti-money laundering protection, jackpot reservations, and recording play.

Quasi-Judicial Power - Issuance, Denial, or Revocation of Authorizations

The head of the agency, which may be a single individual, a board, a commission, or a surrogate hearing examiner, acts in a quasi-judicial capacity when he or she determines which individuals, business entities, devices, gaming related products, and technology satisfy a suitability determination and can participate in the gaming industry within that jurisdiction. While other functions of the regulatory structure may be assigned to related agencies or take place at a management level, this decision-making "is the principal mechanism connecting the laws and regulations which form the legal framework of the regulatory system"[39] and is the one most protected from judicial action because of the presumption of agency expertise. Review, assessment, and authorization rest in the person or persons who form the judicial or decision-making unit of the agency, the head of the agency with the assistance of the staff or consultant specialists, and the Office of General Counsel.

---

[38] *Id.* at 129.
[39] Int'l Atomic Energy Agency, *supra* note 9, at 3.16.

One of the three important hearing systems in a gaming regulatory structure is one that begins with the application that starts a regulatory investigation, a formal investigation on the application, and ultimately leads to a determination as to suitability. Gaming patron complaints against operators and regulator complaints against holders of gaming credentials are also part of the quasi-judicial function of the regulatory system.

The head of the agency (i.e., the decision-maker) requires teams of specialists in law enforcement, accounting, finance, and law to provide facts, analysis, and recommendations on actions to be taken in all these hearings. These specialists may be organized into permanent units of the regulatory agencies, ad hoc or as-needed units of the agencies, or outside consultants. If outside consultants are employed, then careful instruction on the potential conflicts of interest must be given to the outside consultant subject to the same restrictions as agency employees.

This core function requires effective communication and interaction among the different units and disciplines. An in-house agency senior supervisor or staff manager should be appointed to coordinate the work that needs to be accomplished to prepare the decision-maker. Authorizing a business entity to operate or supply gaming equipment or technology, the regulatory agency could condition the license on safeguards that may include a board-level compliance committee, a compliance officer with a compliance plan, and an expectation that the holder of the gaming authorization will exercise due diligence[40] in all its dealings. While regulators have a duty to conduct investigations, the applicant and operator's equivalent duty to investigate is called "due diligence."

The results of the review, any assessment, and action(s) taken should be recorded in a written decision structured as findings of fact and conclusions of law and regulation and maintained by administrative staff as public information. This decision does not record the decision-making process, but it records the ultimate decision on the facts and the law.

This review and assessment action by the head of the agency results in a decision that may not be subject to appeal to a higher court or other

---

[40] Due Diligence means

1. General: Measure of prudence, responsibility, and diligence that is expected from, and ordinarily exercised by, a reasonable and prudent person under the circumstances.

2. Business: Duty of a firm's directors and officers to act prudently in evaluating associated risks in all transactions.

3. Investing: Duty of the investor to gather necessary information on actual or potential risks involved in an investment.

4. Negotiating: Duty of each party to confirm each other's expectations and understandings, and to independently verify the abilities of the other to fulfill the conditions and requirements of the agreement."

BusinessDictionary.com, http://www.businessdictionary.com/definition/due-diligence.html.

authority, depending on the enabling statute's authorization. The Nevada statute NRS 463.318 provides that judicial review is not available for actions, decisions, and orders of the Commission relating to the denial of a license or to limited or conditional licenses. Other jurisdictions allow limited judicial review, usually grounded in a high tolerance and respect for the exercise of discretion given to the administrative agency.

In granting gaming credentials, planned periodic review of any authorization is typically necessary. Traditionally, authorizations had a designated valid period and expiration date, and while this is still the circumstance in many jurisdictions, there is a growing trend to use the Nevada model[41] (i.e., no expiration date but an annual fee assessment). The length of validity of gaming credentials varies widely from jurisdiction to jurisdiction from one-to-five, though some jurisdictions give an open-ended authorization that is valid until the person or entity fails to pay fees, changes employers, or circumstances reveal the original finding of suitability is no longer appropriate. If regulators are in some doubt about suitability, credentials can always be shortened or put in a probationary status.

A minority view in some US jurisdictions, including Michigan and Pennsylvania, is that non-gaming employees of casinos must qualify for a low level credential, sometimes called a registration. This practice was used in New Jersey until 2009 when it abandoned the practice because such a low level regulation of employees absorbed important regulatory time and did not contribute to the enabling legislation's policy goals.[42] Most US jurisdictions now minimize the licensing requirement of non-gaming employee registrations or licenses as the investigation of every staff-member who cannot influence the conduct of gaming would put casino resorts at a disadvantage compared to nongaming resorts, which may hire food, beverage, and housekeeping employees without such regulatory restrictions.

Quasi-Executive Powers
Enforcement for non-compliance with regulations

Enforcement ensures compliance through the legitimate threat of imposing sanctions. Ideally, gaming operators would readily and voluntarily comply with all the laws and regulatory standards out of respect for the industry and their credentials. However, when faced with non-compliant operators, regulatory agencies respond in many ways including written

---

[41] NEV. REV. STAT. § 463.160 (2013). Nevada credentials are issued for a specific employer. Changes in employment require new credential applications.

[42] "Casino service employees are people whose job requires them to have access to the casino floor, but the work they do is not directly gaming related. . . . bartenders, bar porters, cocktail servers and maintenance workers need casino service employee registrations." Press Release, *N.J. Casino Control Comm'n, Inactive Casino Employee Registrations Set to Expire* (July 2, 2009), http://www.state.nj.us/casinos/news/archive/pdf/2009/cse_expiration_release.pdf

warnings, civil financial penalties,[43] suspensions, and ultimately, to withdrawal of credentials.

In all cases, the gaming operator must remedy the non-compliance through performing a thorough in-house investigation on an agreed time schedule, taking all necessary remedial measures to prevent recurrence and providing proof of these actions with the assurance they will achieve the desired results. Usually, the head of the agency has some discretion as to the sanction imposed. Standardized procedures that provide some level of minimal due process and notice, even in the instance of a revocable privilege, are needed for any revocation action. Enforcement actions should be proportionate to the violation, consistent, and recorded for future reference when subsequent decisions on sanctions are made.

Tax or fee collection for the sovereign

Collection of the jurisdiction's sovereign's share of gaming revenue, along with other fees, is usually billed, collected, and paid to the government through a separate unit within the regulatory agency. Some enabling statutes avoid using the word "tax," though the practicality of the procedures would suggest that they are in fact taxes. Some fees are quid pro quo for the privilege of operating gaming. Proof of such payments should be recorded in this or the administration unit.

Laboratory certification systems for gaming technology

The agency's technology function includes being in charge of performing tests independent from the manufacturer or promoter of the technology either within the agency or through outside specialists. Before the agency head approves a gaming site, all of the hardware, software, and any delivery technology, must be tested and approved. The testing process contributes to the integrity of gaming and reassures the public all games are operated fairly, accounting systems are accurate, no hidden software exists in the program or device, a complete audit-trail[44] is operational with security in place to prevent hacking, and the random number generator functions properly. Whether this testing must be done on every line of code or whether a sample size is large enough to be valid must be determined. As technology is constantly updated and new versions are introduced, each version requires an additional regulatory approval.

---

[43] "Civil penalties are fines or surcharges imposed by a governmental agency to enforce regulations such as late payment of taxes, failure to obtain a permit, etc." THE FREE LEGAL DICTIONARY, http://legal-dictionary.thefreedictionary.com/Civil+penalty.

[44] An audit is the "Systematic examination and verification of a firm's books of account, transaction records, other relevant documents, and physical inspection of inventory by qualified accountants (called auditors)." BUSINESSDICTIONARY.COM, http://www.business-dictionary.com/definition/audit.html.

Having the agency perform this function in-house is expensive, even though the cost may be passed on to the person or entity whose system is being evaluated. Staff in this discipline demand high salaries. Many jurisdictions have outsourced this function to third-party laboratories, the cost of which is then directly billed to the gaming operator. If a regulatory organization or its dedicated support organization, does not have adequate qualified personnel and equipment to complete a technical review within a reasonable period of time or their workload does not justify the recruitment of a full-time staff, consultants may complete the technical reviews.[45] The regulatory organization may also occasionally use consultants to assist in performing tasks requiring an additional level or area of expertise or to provide a second opinion on important issues. Since the regulatory organization must evaluate and use the consultants' work, the agency must define the scope of the work to be performed. The consultants must provide a detailed written report, which includes the basis and method of evaluation, conclusions, and recommendations that will assist the regulatory organization complete its evaluation. The regulatory organization may give formal structure to the processes by which expert opinion and advice are provided, with advisory committees derived from other government departments, international regulatory bodies, and technology organizations. Such advisory committees can bring broad valuable perspectives to bear on the formulation of regulatory policy and regulations.[46]

Audit and inspection

Auditing is comprised of several major functions including budgeting (i.e., ensuring there are resources necessary to accomplish the duties assigned by the legislature in the gaming enabling statute), conducting audits and inspections, and monitoring gaming industry operations. The functions are usually assigned to separate units within the agency. The regulatory agency must have a sufficient number of professional and experienced staff working to manage these duties.

Within the regulatory agency, the audit unit is responsible for the entire agency's budgeting and procurement. Outside the agency, the audit unit has the very serious responsibility of auditing the industry, setting the aforementioned minimum internal control standards (MICS) for the industry, and inspecting and monitoring measures needed to maintain the trust and the integrity the regulatory body seeks to foster.

Verification methods include audits, examinations, and monitoring to ensure that each regulatory requirement has been satisfactorily performed. However, the basic responsibility for meeting regulatory standards remains with the holder of the authorization, not the regulator.

---

[45] *See, e.g.,* Howard Stutz, *Pair of Independent Testing Labs for Gaming Equipment OK'd By State,* L.V. Rev. J. (June 22, 2012) ("The Gaming Control Board Thursday approved Gaming Laboratories International and BMM International as the state's first independent testing laboratories to certify gaming equipment for use in Nevada casinos.").

[46] Int'l Atomic Energy Agency, *supra* note 9, at 3.6.

Operators and other organizations engaged in gaming activities, must establish policies that make the trust and integrity of gaming their highest priority. The gaming staff charged with these compliance responsibilities within the operators' management structure need clear reporting lines indicating who is responsible for the ultimate implementation.

The head of the regulatory agency should have statutory and regulatory authority to take any action necessary to ensure the integrity of the gaming operation, including monitoring certain transactions and recouping reasonable costs associated with such a monitoring program.

Administration

The regulator's administrative functions are extremely important in the overall effectiveness of the organization and should not be overlooked. These functions include staffing the regulatory agency or engaging outside consultants, legal professionals, accounting, and law enforcement; overseeing gaming technology, office management, human resources, data administration (including document retention, storage and retrieval, and maintaining the confidentiality of proprietary information), general administration (such as internal planning, maintenance of buildings and equipment, operation of communication systems and security); and publication of agendas and notices to the industry. The size of the unit will typically depend on the size of the regulatory organization and the budget.

The human resources department should ensure the proper training of regulatory employees on potential conflicts of interest, pre-employment, employment, and post-employment restrictions. Post-employment restrictions may include the inability to work within the local casino industry due to the perception of influence that the individuals may have on the regulators with whom the individual used to work.

Public information

The public information office of a gaming regulatory organization must communicate with and provide information to other governmental entities, international organizations, and the public. A regulatory organization must provide public information on its activities, both regularly and in response to special events. Information provided to the public should be objective, reflecting the regulatory organization's independence. The regulatory organization should be transparent while complying with the jurisdiction's legislation and regulation on confidentiality. Articulate individual or individuals experienced in public information should present information that is both clear and understandable. Depending on the size of the regulatory organization, a specialized public information unit may be required.

RECOMMENDATIONS FOR REGULATORY REFORM

In 2011, industry lobbying group the American Gaming Association published recommendations[47] for improvement to the gaming regulatory system in the United States. While some of those recommendations have not been readily accepted by US regulators, others could be adopted with little controversy.

More than a decade ago, the International Association of Gaming Regulators (IAGR), in coordination with the International Association of Gaming Advisors (IAGA), developed a personal history disclosure called the "Multi-Jurisdictional Personal History Disclosure Form" for individuals seeking responsible positions in gaming operations. The form's purpose is to facilitate a thorough regulatory investigation in multiple jurisdictions and a finding of suitability, or the lack therof, by using only one document that would ask all the questions necessary for multiple jurisdictions. While using this standard form has had some success, most jurisdictions that employ the form also require a supplemental form, justified by including some pieces of information the jurisdiction feels are not addressed or not addressed adequately by the standard form. One AGA recommendation is that the standard form should be widely used and unique jurisdictional forms should be kept to a minimum.[48] For the sake of uniformity in the questions asked, in the way they are asked, and the ease of answering questions, the standard form should be the only initial form used, remembering follow-up questions can always be used to clear up any confusion or ambiguity. This could also mean an expansion of the current multi-jurisdiction form to include all of the information requested in all of the current supplements.

Another recommendation concerns credit inquiries. In the United States,[49] each credit inquiry has a negative effect on that person's credit rating, thereby affecting the person's ability to borrow in the future. This negative consequence is magnified for those who must be found suitable in multiple jurisdictions, as the credit test is done multiple times, each time lowering the person's credit score. When investigating a person's application, care should be taken to ensure the inquiry is characterized as "employment-related" and not "credit-related." Ideally, credit reporting agencies would have a special category to more precisely fit the circumstances.

The AGA paper also recommended that the admittedly awkward process of submitting fingerprints to regulatory agencies, some of which insist that fingerprints be taken upon every renewal despite the fundamental unchanging nature of fingerprints, should be streamlined. Regulators could accept certified electronic images of an applicant's fingerprints that were

---

[47] David O. Stewart, *Improving Gaming Regulation: 10 Recommendations for Streamlining Processes, While Maintaining Integrity*, American Gaming Association white paper (2011).

[48] *Id.*, Recommendation 2.

[49] *Id.*, Recommendation 9.

previously scanned by a legitimate law enforcement agency without requiring that new fingerprints be taken every time.[50]

Regulatory bodies could better use improvements in technology to reduce unnecessary waste of time and financial expense. Such improvements could include allowing regulatory interviews of applicants for gaming credentials to be done using video-conferencing technology. Regulators should also accept electronic submissions by persons and entities that hold gaming credentials within the jurisdiction, as is done in many global regulatory environments.

---

[50] *Id.*, Recommendation 7.

7

Politics of Gaming Regulation and Protecting the Process

Anthony Cabot

Even the best-designed regulatory systems can fail if structures, checks, and balances do not prevent improper influence over decisions. This chapter focuses on controls to prevent such corruption. Ideally, these controls enable regulators and their staffs to dedicate their efforts independent of outside influences to pursue legislatively-mandated public policy goals for legal casinos.

CORRUPTION

Protecting the decision-making process is critical in gaming regulation because of the broad discretionary authority often given to regulators. As Professor Charles Koch noted

> The term discretion has at least five different uses in administrative law. The authority to make individualizing decisions in the application of general rules can be characterized as "individualizing discretion." Freedom to fill in gaps in delegated authority in order to execute assigned administrative functions may be called "executing discretion." The power to take action to further societal goals is "policymaking discretion." If no review is permitted, the agency is exercising "unbridled discretion." Finally, if the decision cannot by its very nature be review, the agency is exercising "numinous discretion."[1]

Investigative agents may have the discretion to pursue one course of inquiry into an applicant's background and abandon another. An audit agent may determine whether an accounting violation justifies an informal warning or a more formal complaint. Most gaming agents exercise some level of discretion every day. Regardless of context, regulators should garner facts and weigh factors without unethical influences before exer-

---

[1] Charles H. Koch, Jr., *Judicial Review of Administrative Discretion*, 54, GEO. WASH L. REV 469 (1986).

cising discretion.[2] Human fallibility, however, suggests that the regulatory system needs safeguards against dishonesty, self-dealing, and other faults. The most insidious of improper influences is corruption, which can either be external or internal.

External Corruption

External corruption occurs when persons offer incentives to a public official who accepts the incentives to perform, omit, or delay an official act.[3] Bribes can come in many forms, including cash, gifts, accommodations, or comps for favorable regulatory action. Bribes are simple to understand as both illegal and unethical. They are not a theoretical concern. One study found legalized casinos have a higher–than-normal instance of corruption convictions of public officials.[4] This could be expected because "commercial casinos are large cash businesses that operate in a highly regulated environment. . . ." This breeds corruption among the regulated, causing regulators to create new or interpret existing regulations, resulting in the transference of economic rents from the government to the casinos.[5] Bribing a government official or employee is, with rare exception, a crime.

Unlike illegal bribes, corruption of authority occurs when a regulator receives a material benefit without violating the law. More nuanced corruption involves contributions to political campaigns for favorable consideration in regulatory matters now or in the future. This rarely involves a direct "quid pro quo" where a donor asks the candidate for a result on a regulatory matter for a contribution. Instead, political corruption more often occurs when a single person or a group acquires such pervasive strength regulators will do their bidding despite contrary obligations. This may not be a criminal offense. For example, a major political supporter of or person belonging to the same political party as a state governor may receive preferential treatment in licensing and other regulatory decisions. That supporter may not have asked for special favor, but an unspoken understanding may exist. This is not overt corruption, such as pay-offs, but it involves deciding matters other than on the merits consistent with public

---

[2] *See, id.* at 475.

[3] One commentator noted that corruption occurs

when an official receives or is promised significant advantage or reward (personal, group or organisational) for doing something that he is under a duty to do anyway, that he is under a duty not to do, for exercising a legitimate discretion for improper reasons, and for employing illegal means to achieve approved goals.

M. Punch. *Rotten Barrels: Systemic Origins of Corruption, in* Strategies for Controlling Police Corruption (E.W. Kolthoff, ed. 1994).

[4] Douglas M. Walker and Peter T. Calcagno, *Casinos and Political Corruption in the United States: A Granger Causality Analysis*, 45 APPLIED ECON 4781 (2013).

[5] *Id.* The authors note, however, that "if the casino market becomes more competitive and casino regulations are relaxed, the potential for economic rents and the corruption will decrease. *Id.* at 28.

policies and goals. In some jurisdictions, licensing attorneys often blatantly differentiate their services not based on knowledge, experience, or advocacy skills, but rather on their close relationships to the governor, the chief government executive, or their role as campaign bundler.

Internal Corruption

Internal corruption occurs when a public officer uses his or her position to perform, omit, or delay an official act for immediate or long term personal gain or to benefit someone else, such as a family member or friend. Direct personal gain could be as simple as a regulator or a family member owning stock in a regulated company, where a decision could negatively impact earnings or where a new casino, if licensed and constructed, could increase the value of neighboring real estate owned by the regulator or an affiliate.

Internal corruption can take many other forms as well. Industry "capture" can be a type of corruption, where regulators favor the position of the regulated to improve their chances to secure future employment. No one is attempting to corrupt a regulator, but decisions are not being made free from improper influence.

Opportunistic thefts are those in which an agent steals from an applicant or licensee, usually based on his position of trust or authority. For example, an agent may divert or use moneys in an investigative fund for personal use. This could include taking unnecessary "investigative trips" for personal enjoyment.

Corruption Versus Legitimate Influences

Gaming regulators should be free from corruption but not all external influences. Policy considerations and political value judgments are legitimate influences; raw political goals or pure partisan politics are not.[6] Regulators are expected to use their knowledge or experience to make political value judgments, consider public opinion, and balance competing public goals. Regulatory bodies are often made up of multiple members with varied backgrounds and skills precisely because collective discretion involving competing perspectives can lead to better decisions. For the proceeding to be fair, however, the regulator should not be influenced by a "direct, personal, substantial, [or] pecuniary interest" that may influence a decision.[7]

This chapter addresses those things a jurisdiction can do to protect the integrity of the gaming regulatory process.[8] It covers five areas. The

---

[6] *Kathryn Watts, Proposing a Place for Politics in Arbitrary and Capricious Review,* 119 Yale L.J. 2, 55-56 (2009).

[7] *See* Tumey v. Ohio, 273 U.S. 510, 523 (1927)

[8] This chapter does not discuss how law enforcement efforts can detect and prosecute corruption. Broader government structure, such as separation of powers between federal

first is supporting the agency with the proper resources to ensure integrity. Second is ensuring the agency has internal policies and codes of conduct that protect the agency from corruption. Third is ensuring the agency has internal structure and procedures to hold its employees accountable for ethical compliance. Fourth is creating anti-corruption laws applicable to gaming regulators and public officials. Fifth is creating the method by which public officials, regulators, or agents must justify the performance of their duties. This system includes three different types of accountability: political, program, and judicial.

SUPPORTING THE MECHANISM

Factors that play a role in police corruption have a direct correlation to gaming regulatory agencies, which have law enforcement responsibilities. The Wood Commission reviewing police corruption in Australia concluded:

> a service which is seen to do what it can to maintain high morale, to encourage personal and career development, to avoid boredom, frustration, stress and cynicism, to develop meaningful understanding and practical guidance in relation to ethical and integrity issues, and to emphasize its role of service, is far less likely to have a serious corruption problem than a service which ignores these factors.[9]

A gaming regulatory agency functions best when that agency (1) has clear and realistic goals; (2) has the financial resources to hire qualified employees and provide them with proper training and tools; (3) provides opportunity to advance the agents' education and career paths; (4) involves regular training and education on ethical and anti-corruption requirements; (5) has merit-based promotions; (6) provides job security for its employees; and (7) creates an internal structure that segregates responsibilities and provides accountability. Some of these considerations deserve separate comment.

Realistic Goals

Both under- and over-utilization of regulators can create morale issues. If regulation is merely a façade, regulators may feel they serve no public

---

and state authorities can impede corruption. In the United States, where a state or local government is corrupt, the federal government has concurrent jurisdiction to investigate and prosecute bribery as a crime. This has resulted in several high profile convictions for corruption, such as former Louisiana Governor Edwin W. Edwards, who, with others, was convicted of racketeering conspiracy to extort money from businesses seeking Louisiana riverboat casino licenses. Many countries do not have dual system, making detection and prosecutions more difficult. In either case, however, laws, policies, procedures, and structures to deter corruption are critical.

[9] JRT Wood, FINAL REPORT OF THE ROYAL COMMISSION INTO THE NEW SOUTH WALES POLICE SERVICE, VOLUME 1: CORRUPTION 32 (1997).

purpose other than to present a public face that the industry is regulated. Left adrift with little guidance or purpose, regulators can be subject to industry influence.

Professor Cass Sunstein suggests a different regulatory paradox where over-regulation results in under-regulation. This occurs when the legislature sets such stringent nondiscretionary controls the administrative agency does not issue regulations or enforce the law because not acting at all may be better than enforcing too strict a regulation.[10] A similar paradox may occur with gaming regulation. Suppose the legislature mandates stringent licensing of almost every casino employee but places this burden on a regulatory agency with a small staff. The result will be that the agency will either do a poor job trying to investigate everyone or ignore the legislative mandate and adopt a system that allows regulators to set priorities for processing applications based on sensitivity.

To illustrate, imagine an emerging casino jurisdiction looking to the gaming acts and regulations in Nevada or New Jersey as "models" and adopting them as their own almost verbatim. The emerging jurisdiction ignored that these acts require specialized employees and significant capital investment to become functional and efficient. The new jurisdiction forged ahead without either. Many gaming agencies in the jurisdiction began with a small budget and a few inexperienced agents. The regulators had neither the resources nor the expertise to properly investigate and grant approvals or licenses according to the adopted laws and regulations. After receiving hundreds of applications for licenses for ownership, operations, manufacturing, and employment, the regulators either reach a standstill or totally ignore the laws and regulations and process the applications under an ad hoc system that allows the regulators to realize the creation of a viable competitive casino industry. Ignoring the dictates of the laws and regulations leaves regulators operating under "voodoo" rules.

Under these far-from-ideal circumstances, agency dynamics may cause the informal adoption of a "witch doctor." Perhaps, it is a person with a strong personality or who had prior regulatory experience in another jurisdiction. Often, the witch doctor is not one of the appointed regulators. The gaming law in these jurisdictions is not based on the written regulation or law. The rules become whatever the witch doctor says the rules are. To outsiders, the rules often appear arbitrary and unreasoned, and often reality matches perception.

More problematic to agency morale is when the legislature acts according to unstated policy goals that contradict the stated policy goals. An example of this is if the legislature originally legalized casinos under gambler protection goals, but later changed its policy to favor government protection goals. If the stated legislative policy is to protect the patron, the agency may feel abandoned when politicians consistently criticize the regulators for being unfriendly to business because it believes it is trying to achieve antithetical goals.

---

[10] Cass R. Sunstein, *Paradoxes of the Regulatory State*, 57 U. CHI. L. REV. 407, 416 (1990).

Political support requires the government to create an environment that allows regulators to make the best decisions for the industry as a whole, despite the ramifications. Agencies also need support in the political process to obtain legislation that helps them in achieving these goals. Without this support, the agency may feel isolated and become demoralized.

Financial Support

The need for financial support is obvious. Government must provide resources to hire and train qualified staff and fund ongoing operations. Gaming regulation requires technical expertise that involves proper staffing with skilled personnel. An agency making decisions also needs adequate organizational resources to understand the issues, collect and process information, consider alternatives, and understand the consequences of agency action—in terms of economic impacts, social costs, and compliance costs. If the agency is underfunded, it may lack the resources to meet these challenges, which may lower morale.

Underpaid employees with limited opportunities for advancement may be more subject to seeking favor (if not outright bribes) from an industry with greater resources. Competitive salaries are a major factor in retaining qualified employees. Salaries paid to government employees in the United States tend to be less than their counterparts in the private sector. This is also true in the casino industry. This discrepancy may motivate government employees to leave government services after acquiring skills that are marketable to the private sector. Former government background investigators and enforcement agents can easily join casino security departments. Government auditors can move to a casino's internal audit sections or cage operations. The expectation that government work is a stepping stone to the industry may create an atmosphere where government employees are currying industry favor to ease the transition. Moreover, a consistent loss of talent to the casino private sector can burden an agency with staff that is inexperienced or who do not have either the talent or the motivation to succeed in the private sector. To retain qualified persons, regulatory agencies need to either provide competitive salaries or compensate for lower salaries with additional benefits. The latter can include a sense of job security often lacking in the casino industry, retirement benefits, opportunities for continuing education and training, realistic prospects of promotion, and a congenial work environment. Where possible, job experience should qualify for certain professional accreditation, such as certified public accounting experience.

Lack of quality and quantity of technical staff also can cause problems. The poorer the quality of technological advice, the more likely the results will be of lesser quality. Sometimes, technical advice may not be available at all.[11] Where the regulatory agency has limited or poor-quality staff, an

---

[11] Arthur Earl Bonfield, *State Law in the Teaching of Administrative Law: A Critical*

easy solution is to rely on the casinos for information that may be incorrect, biased or incomplete. Proper funding can reduce an agency's need for the private sector's assistance, because it allows for hiring specialist regulators who can independently analyze and monitor industry issues. The greater the agency's skill, the more likely it will resist interest-group pressures.

Merit-Based Promotions and Selections

A gaming agency filled by political appointments will likely be less qualified than those filled by a merit-based selection process. For example, rather than the governor merely appointing regulators, a committee may vet applications under a fixed set of criteria, including education, experience, and job-related factors. By making the criteria for appointment clear in advance, sudden questionable appointments of those who would not otherwise qualify can be eliminated. Effective criteria might include a certain level and type of education or a certain number of years of relevant employment.

Job Security

Whether regulators should have fixed terms or be removable at the chief executive's will goes to the heart of political accountability. Proponents of fixed terms argue they protect the regulatory process from undue influence from the chief executive (e.g., the state governor). Without fixed terms, the governor could use the threat of removal to dictate the decisions of the agency, which would be contrary to the legislature's policy goals. The governor could unduly influence regulators to grant a license to a major campaign contributor who is otherwise unsuitable. Fixed terms provide regulators with the security that if they make correct decisions, they need not fear job loss if their decisions are contrary to the wishes of the chief executive.

Proponents of at-will appointments feel they provide accountability to the process. Without the ability to remove persons, voters have no one to hold accountable for agency decisions. They cannot vote the regulators out of office or remove them because the regulators are not elected.

Others argue for the chief executive, who is responsible for a coordinated government policy, to have a restricted right of removal. For example, removing an agency member for failing to comply with the chief executive's policy decisions would be valid.[12] An agency member would not be subject to removal for a decision to license or not license an applicant, absent misfeasance, such as bribery or failure to reveal a conflict of interest. Where the chief executive has the power to remove a regulator "for cause,"

Analysis of the Status Quo, 61 Tex. L. Rev. 95, 129 (1982).
[12] Kenneth Culp Davis & Richard J. Pierce, Jr., Administrative Law Treatise 54 (3rd ed. 1994).

he should be required to state the reasons for the removal, even if the reasons diverge from policy preferences.[13] This ensures that the chief executive remains accountable for the removal of regulators.

PROTECTING THE MECHANISM
Personnel Protection
Appointment criteria

> Political influence over regulatory decision-making is more likely if the regulators who sit on a multi-member board are all from the same political party. Agency actions may reflect a partisan bias. Requiring a multi-member regulatory agency membership to reflect at least some representation from different political parties may further the independence of the agency. California provides an example of such a provision: "No more than three of the five members of the commission shall be members of the same political party."[14]

Such requirements, however, may cause a less-qualified person to be appointed to the agency because the more-qualified person is prohibited due to his political party affiliation.

Background checks

A background check of regulatory candidates may reduce the risks involved in appointments to sensitive positions of public trust. Such background checks are common for appointments to a judicial office. They are similar to the background investigation conducted on applicants for casino licenses, and they may involve the same criteria, such as honesty, criminal history, associations with unsuitable persons, and management abilities. The investigation also may include reviews of financial and familial information to ensure no conflicts of interest exist.

Code of conduct and anti-corruption policy

Agencies should have a defined code of conduct and an anti-corruption policy. Major topics for inclusion are covered below. Besides a code of conduct, the agency should have an ongoing training program on the requirements of the code of conduct and ethics in general. This program should be created for gaming regulation and reflect the particular circumstances of the jurisdiction. It should use real and hypothetical situations to emphasize particular vulnerabilities. Training should include protected internal reporting and procedures for agents wishing to discuss and resolve potential conflicts with an agency ethics officer. It should also emphasize consequences for non-compliance.

---

[13] *Id.*

[14] CAL. BUS. & PROF. CODE § 19812(c) (2013).

Conflict of interest

Prohibiting a regulator or agent from having an interest in a licensed-casino operation is a common feature of most regulatory systems.[15] This prohibition usually extends to any financial interest, including ownership or employment. Nevada's law, as an example provides, "A member shall not be pecuniarily interested in any business or organization holding a gaming license under this chapter or doing business with any person or organization licensed under this chapter."[16] Some jurisdictions, like California, prohibit some former employees of casinos from being appointed to a regulatory position. California law provides, "A person is ineligible for appointment to the commission if, within two years prior to appointment, the person, or any partnership or corporation in which the person is a principal, was employed by, retained by, or derived substantial income from, any gambling establishment."[17]

Casino employment prior to public appointment should not be a ground for disqualification. Regulators with prior experience and knowledge may provide a substantial agency benefit. Appointing only persons with no prior gaming experience to the regulatory agency would be the equivalent of appointing only persons to judgeships who have never practiced law. By appointing former agents to leadership roles, government may narrow the perception of the agency.

Conflict of interest rules should go beyond the appointed regulators and extend to agents. The rules should be applied before the agent is hired, and the code of conduct should contain a continuing obligation to report conflicts.

Items to consider in a code of conduct include standards related to
- Ownership or acquisition, directly or through a third party including a family member, of any financial interest in an applicant or licensed entity, an affiliate, intermediary, subsidiary, or holding com-

---

[15] *See* Mich. Comp. Laws § 432.204 Sec. 4(10); Miss. Code Ann. § 75-76-15 (7) (2013).

[16] Nev. Rev. Stat. § 463.060(3) (2013). Nevada's Gaming Commission structure poses several challenges. First, the Commission is a part-time agency. Trying to find qualified regulators that have no conflicts may be a greater challenge where regulators are only part-time government employees. Second, the Nevada Gaming Commission has no staff so that it must rely on the same legal counsel as the Gaming Control Board. This can be an inherent conflict where the interests of the parties to a matter before the Commission have a position different from the Gaming Control Board. Third, the Commission both adopts the regulations (quasi-legislative) and then determines the application of the regulations in adverse settings such as the imposition of a fine. They would not be inclined, as example, to find that the regulation that they adopted was ambiguous and should be read favorable to a licensee as opposed to the government. Fourth, as part time, the positions are not seen as career oriented, but political appointments. This may not provide adequate distance from the political process, including securing the tenure of regulators against termination based on exercising independent decisions. *See generally* Thomas A. James, *Protecting the Administrative Judiciary from External Pressures, a Call for Vigilance*, Drake L. Rev. 827 (2012).

[17] Cal. Bus. & Prof. Code § 19812.

pany thereof during their employment, and for one year thereafter;

- Having interests that may reasonably bring into question regulators' ability to carry out the obligations of their position in a fair, impartial, and objective manner;
- Undertaking any outside employment by any entity that maintains a license or is subject to regulation by the agency; and
- Avoiding any situation where regulator independence can be questioned, including involvement in any matter involving family or friends.

Conflict of interest rules that may disqualify a regulator from hearing a case will often extend beyond those that would disqualify a person from becoming a regulator. Suppose the regulator is an accountant, and his firm had done work for a person appearing before the agency. This might be a conflict of interest requiring regulator disqualification from the matter, but it would not require he resign from his post.

Comps and other material benefits

Comps have always been an important part of the casino industry. They include everything from free drinks to private jet travel. Casinos allow virtually every employee who has contact with the public to offer some level of comps to players, from cocktail waitresses who offer drinks to casino presidents who can offer expensive gifts to casino guests. As part of the fabric of the industry, comps naturally bleed over to how the regulated treat regulators. Like any other guest or visitor of importance, offering visiting regulators some typical minor comps, such as a soda or even a meal, is a natural inclination. Because of this nuance, a concrete policy on comps is more important in gaming than in most other industries.

Preventing casinos from giving material gifts or comps to regulators and staff is without serious debate. What is questioned, however, is the threshold for prohibiting gifts. On one extreme, the law can prohibit the regulator from accepting any comps. The problem with an absolute prohibition is the nature of general hospitality. If a regulator or an agent is working at a licensed casino, should she be prohibited from accepting even a soft drink or a cup of coffee? Should a regulator be prohibited from attending a cocktail reception for an academic conference because it is hosted by a casino licensee or from attending a grand opening party for a new casino? If a regulator has had a lifelong friendship with or is family of a licensee, on appointment does she have to cease accepting dinner invitations to the person's home? With an absolute prohibition, the answer to these questions is "yes."

Some jurisdictions provide more flexible and fewer definitive standards. An example would be to prohibit the acceptance of any comps or gifts over a certain monetary value or of a subjective value such that it is likely to influence the person in the conduct of his responsibilities as a regulator. These standards attempt to apply a materiality standard to the gift or comps. These jurisdictions recognize a distinction between an absolute prohibition against all comps and a reasonable restriction on gratuities. Some distinguish between bribes and gratuities, the former suggesting corrupt purposes and the latter offered as a symbolic gesture of hospitality, appreciation, or custom without corrupt intent. Minor comps, such as lunch or coffee, can show reasonable appreciation to public servants. It would be against societal norms to refuse. These insignificant comps can benefit the regulatory process by fostering the exchange of information helpful to understanding the industry and sharing common goals and concerns. In other cases, the item offered is done so in an official capacity where a university, regulator, or other government official offers some symbolic gift, such as an inscribed pen. Moreover, the nature of gaming regulation places great trust and discretion in the regulators, while an absolute prohibition calls into question whether the regulators can be trusted to do what is ethical and moral.

Comps, however, often raise more issues due to their subjectivity. Is accepting free tickets to a college football game material? What about Super Bowl tickets that have a face value of $500 and a street value of $5,000? Former New York City Police Commissioner Patrick V. Murphy once said "except for your paycheck, there is no such thing as a clean buck."[18]

Murphy's sentiment is based on several arguments. It removes the temptation to accept items that may be more material or become regular. Regular, small gifts, can create a sense of obligation over time. This can create a situation where certain licensees receive disproportionate considerations or access. A risk also exists that some comps will lead to a 'slippery slope' with temptations becoming imperceptibly greater and refusal increasingly difficult. An absolute prohibition removes all temptations and takes away discretionary decisions regarding the propriety of a comp.

Items to consider in a code of conduct include standards related to regulators such as the following:

- Using, or attempting to use, their position to obtain unwarranted comps, privileges, or advantages for themselves or others;
- Accepting any fee for any service connected with their office or employment other than the salary and expenses provided by law; and
- Accepting or soliciting any discount, gift, gratuity, compensation, travel, lodging, favor, entertainment, or any other thing of value, directly or indirectly, from an applicant or licensee.

Cooling off

The industry may attempt to influence or "capture" regulators through the promise of private employment after government service. A 2005 study

---

[18] HERMAN GOLDSTEIN, POLICE CORRUPTION: A PERSPECTIVE ON ITS NATURE AND CONTROL, 29 (1975).

by a University of Nevada, Las Vegas student showed that 78 percent of former members of the Nevada Gaming Control Board (the Board) entered the private sector of the gaming industry after leaving the Board.[19] One way to prevent this is to require "cooling off" periods. This prevents regulators from leaving their positions to take gaming-industry jobs in the jurisdiction in which they practiced, and it avoids the appearance that the casino industry can influence a regulator by holding out the possibility of post-public sector employment.

In many jurisdictions, casinos may not employ a former regulator for a defined period, such as a year, following the last day of that person's service with the agency.[20] This prohibition may apply generally or selectively to certain employees. An example of selective prohibition would be that a company involved in the casino industry may not employ a former non-clerical employee of the regulatory agency for a period following the last day of that person's employment with the agency if that person (1) had principal duties that included formulating gaming regulation policy; (2) conducted an audit or investigation of the person's prospective employer within the last year; or (3) had knowledge of the trade secrets of a direct competitor because of his government service.

An example of a cooling off statute is New Jersey Statute § 5:12-60, which provides

a. No member of the commission shall hold any direct or indirect interest in, or be employed by, any applicant or by any person licensed by or registered with the commission for a period of 4 years commencing on the date his membership on the commission terminates.

b. (1) No employee of the commission or employee or agent of the division may acquire any direct or indirect interest in, or accept employment with, any applicant or any person licensed by or registered with the commission, for a period of 2 years commencing at the termination of employment with the commission or division, except that a secretarial or clerical employee of the commission or the division may accept such employment at any time after the termination of employment with the commission or division. At the end of 2 years and for a period of 2 years thereafter, a former employee or agent who held a policy-making management position at any time during the five years prior to termination of employment may acquire an interest in, or accept employment with, any applicant or person licensed by or registered with the commission upon application to and the approval of the commission upon a finding that the interest to be acquired or the employment will not create

---

[19] Jason Woywod, *The Professional Career Paths of Members of the Nevada State Gaming Control Board* (2005), UNLV theses/dissertations/professional papers/capstones.Paper 406.

[20] Nev. Rev. Stat. § 281.236(2).

the appearance of a conflict of interest and does not evidence a conflict of interest in fact. . . .

c. No commission member or person employed by the commission or division shall represent any person or party other than the State before or against the commission for a period of 2 years from the termination of his office or employment with the commission or division.

Two problems occur with a cooling off period. First, knowing one cannot use skills in the private sector obtained while working for the government makes the public job less appealing, resulting fewer quality applicants for regulatory employment. A second problem is scope. The cooling off period rarely prevents professionals, such as accountants or lawyers, immediately after leaving government employment, from representing casinos before their former agency employer, while all other professions are prohibited.

These issues can be addressed. Due to the proliferation of gaming across the country, former gaming agents from one jurisdiction can often find lucrative jobs with companies in other jurisdictions that do not hold a license in the area in which the agent worked. The impact of a cooling off period may be significantly diminished if government salaries and benefits for the gaming agents and regulators are competitive with the private sector. Regarding scope, a cooling off period may be extended to prevent representation of gaming clients by former regulators, their employees, and attorneys. This would prevent a departed regulator who is an attorney from representing applicants shortly after resigning.

Thus, items to consider in a code of conduct include standards related to soliciting, or recommending to any applicant or licensed entity, the appointment or employment of any individual in any capacity by the applicant, licensed entity, or an affiliate, intermediary, subsidiary, or holding company.

Prohibiting play in regulated casinos

Regulators and agents should not gamble in the casinos they regulate for two reasons. The first is public perception that regulators should be independent of casinos, which includes no contractual relationships even if they are limited to being a customer. Second, potential issues are substantial. A regulator or agent that falls into debt to a casino may seek solutions inconsistent with his duty. A casino wishing to disguise bribes can do so in the form of winnings. Indiana law provides an example of a restriction on gaming by regulators: Except as provided in section 3 of this rule, no member, member's spouse, employee, or agent may participate in any game conducted on any riverboat licensed by the commission.[21] Exemptions should be rare and limited to agents en-

---

[21] 68 IND. ADMIN. CODE § 9-4-2 and § 9-4-3

gaged in playing as part of their official duties such as surveillance, enforcement, or auditing.

Public perception

While reality and public perception can differ, the success of the gaming industry is often based on the public's perception that the games are fair and honest, and players are paid if they win. This perception can be negatively impacted if the public perceives that the regulators entrusted to ensure fairness and honesty of the games are corrupt. Therefore, a focus on public perception in the code of conduct is warranted.

Items to consider in a code of conduct include standards related to regulators or agents

- Conveying or permitting other persons to convey the impression that any persons are in a position to influence them;
- Acting in any way that would reasonably be expected to create an impression among the public that they are engaged in conduct that violates the public's trust; and
- Expressing views, outside of public session, on the merits of a pending matter relating to proceedings of a quasi-judicial nature before a review board.

Internal managerial and program accountability

Accountability means, in its simplest terms, the method by which public officials or public employees must justify the performance of their duties to another person or body. While accountability can be used to assess job performance, as in the private sector, this chapter focuses is on misfeasance, specifically corruption. In this context, accountability can either require inward responsibility or be subject to external direction. External accountability is covered later and focuses on how forces outside the agency can control agency behavior. Inward responsibility looks to the agency to ensure that regulators, supervisors, and others can properly manage public employees so they meet all ethical standards according to law, agency policy, and applicable professional standards. The laws include general case law, statutes that govern corrupt practices, or specific laws and/or regulations that apply to the gaming industry. Equally important is compliance with the agency's code of conduct.

Internal agency controls are required to ensure agents pursue policy goals rather than other agendas.

There is no doubt that there has to be close supervision, formal prohibitions, and strong sanctions in an organisation with such a sensitive task as police have and with a mandate that is defined by the criminal law. If a policeman is corrupt then he is a criminal and must expect tough sanctions. But it is doubtful if a tough 'regime' is the best remedy for the corruption issue. Probably the two most important elements are clarity of guidelines and seriousness of resources. . . . Everyone in the organisation must know what is not acceptable and that infringements will be pursued professionally and with vigour.[22]

Regulatory agencies must have well-considered procedures to create internal accountability. These procedures start with risk assessment. Different gaming agents have distinct responsibilities. These roles have greater risk of corruption based on many factors. Audit agents with access to proprietary financial information could be approached by competitors for competitive advantage. Background agents may have access to investigative funds that could be diverted for personal uses. Technical agents may have access to computer programs that operate casino games that could be abused to cheat a casino. Some of these roles have greater discretion in the exercise of their authority. Investigative agents, as an example, often may follow leads and information to explore the suitability of an applicant. While a legitimate exercise of authority, it increases the possibility for abuse of discretion for personal gain. Therefore, a strong internal program would involve

- appraising corruption risks in the agency and the casino industries;
- identifying regulatory agents involved in vulnerable positions;
- reviewing work practices for corruption vulnerabilities;
- reviewing codes of conduct to ensure they addresses vulnerabilities;
- ensuring internal controls address these vulnerabilities including
  - personnel controls (e.g., whether supervisors adequately oversee their employees);
  - access controls (e.g., whether sensitive information is protected from unauthorized access); and
  - documentation controls (e.g., whether agent field expenditures are audited or the agency reviews agent's field work reports related to their use of time, such as appointments and contacts);
- assuring the internal controls are properly enforced;
- requiring periodic work reviews;
- providing procedures for reporting ethical violations (i.e., whistle blowers); and
- having enforcement procedures with consequences for violations.[23]

Program accountability should ensure proper delegation within the agency. A regulatory program should be designed to minimize the unsupervised discretionary power of lower-level agency employees. Sub-delegation means transferring authority over an issue or area from the appointed regulators to their employees, called agents. Sub-delegation becomes vital when the workload requires the appointed regulators to concentrate on important issues, policy, and administration. The appointed regulators often rely on employees to deal with lesser issues and details.

---

[22] Punch, *supra* note 3.

[23] INDEPENDENT COMMISSION AGAINST CORRUPTION (AUSTRALIA), STRATEGIES FOR PREVENTING CORRUPTION IN GOVERNMENT REGULATORY FUNCTIONS (1999)

A program's design may unexpectedly transfer discretion to lower-level employees. For example, a highly-regulated program may provide more than one statute to cover a problem. Consequently, a lower-level employee could choose which statute to apply. This choice could be motivated by improper considerations beyond public policy.[24] Therefore, a greater risk exists that their discretionary decisions will be based on personal preferences rather than on what is best for the parties involved.

Even without a hierarchical structure to inhibit ethical breaches, an agency can inhibit ethics violations through a supervisor who is not responsible for the work on assigned cases, using different combinations of agents on assignments, and undertaking periodic and unscheduled reviews of assignments.

Internal affairs

An agency should have internal procedures for receiving and considering potential ethical violations whether notice of the violations comes from the public, the regulated, or whistle blowers within the agency. These procedures should involve agents independent of those being investigated, with full powers to review documents and conduct interviews to determine the credibility of the allegations. Conclusions and recommendations should flow to the highest level of the agency to both determine disciplinary action and to help assess vulnerabilities that can be addressed through changes to the code and procedures. As one commentator noted:

> A strong proactive internal affairs initiative provides 'an excuse for being honest' that may be acceptable to many of the rank and file. . . . Under intense supervision, reluctance to engage in unethical conduct may be viewed not only as acceptable but also prudent. As a result, many officers who are seeking ethical guidance may secretly welcome such efforts if policies are realistic and fair.[25]

External accountability

External accountability refers to a review by a person or agency outside the regulatory agency. It implies that the reviewing party (1) has access to the information needed to assess whether the public official is meeting all his ethical responsibilities; (2) can question and require justification for certain actions; and (3) can cause sanctions to be imposed. This oversight can either be an internal or external governmental function. If it is intergovernmental, regulators are held responsible by the authority who appointed them (e.g., a governor), to another agency (e.g., an anti-corruption body or government auditing agency), or to a different branch of government (e.g.,

---

[24] Davis & Pierce, *supra* note 12, at § 17.1.
[25] Robert McCormack, *An Update, in* MANAGING POLICE CORRUPTION: INTERNATIONAL PERSPECTIVES 155 (Richard Ward et. al., eds. 1987).

a prosecutor). If the oversight is extra-governmental, an outside organization such as the press can investigate the regulators. If corruption is uncovered, a free press can cause public condemnation triggering replacement of the corrupt official by the person who appointed him or by election.

Most democratic governments have an elaborate system of checks and balances that aid accountability. For example, judges may be appointed by a chief executive only after legislative confirmation. Legislative enactments can be vetoed by the executive branch or declared unconstitutional or invalid by the judiciary. Funding for programs carried out by the executive branch may come from the legislative budget, and so on.

Administrative agencies, particularly in gaming regulation, may have legislative, executive, and judicial powers, but they may lack the checks and balances that confine the uncontrolled actions of the three branches of government. Critical to success is giving the agency discretion to decide what best achieves policy goals while still ensuring that the checks and balances provide accountability and remedies for agency transgressions from appointed tasks.

The nature and extent of the checks and balances on agency powers are subjects of substantial debate. Many center on the role of the executive, legislative, and judicial branches in overseeing the administrative agencies. One position regarding chief executive review is that it should be "unitary;" in other words, the chief executive should have absolute control over all agencies. Under this theory, accountability for major decisions should be placed with the executive branch that appoints regulators. The chief executive can step in to prevent agency capture and can ensure the makeup or influence of legislatures does not result in "regional" or factional favoritism.[26]

The reasoning behind the unitary position is that the executive branch is carefully scrutinized by the press, which directly informs the public. While the chief executive may be influenced by certain interest groups, he is accountable to the voting public through elections. Press exposure provides a meaningful check and balance. Three principles of a "unitary" executive branch are (1) the power to remove "at will," (2) the power to affirmatively direct a subordinate, and (3) veto power.

Under a unitary system, checks and balances on the agency's promulgation of regulations should fall on the legislature to ensure that the regulations are furthering policy goals. Finally, checks on the agency's quasi-judicial powers should done be through forms of judicial review. Others argue that a regulatory agency should be free from any political accountability.

In contrast, Dean James Landis, in 1938, espoused the concept of an independent agency being granted broad administrative powers to carry out the public interest. He asserted that regulatory agencies should have "an assemblage of rights normally exercisable by government as a whole" to

---

[26] See, e.g., Steven G. Calabresi, *Some Normative Arguments for the Unitary Executive*, 48 ARK. L. REV. 23, 81-86 (1995).

decide as problems arise.[27] The policy goals of the agency should be loosely defined by the legislature, while the responsibility for implementing these policy goals should be delegated to the agency which has the expertise. Accordingly, "the assumed predicates were a body of technology relevant to the solution of problems in the field and a consequent self-sufficiency or autonomy, implying immunity from the political process."[28]

Yet, "independent agency" is an oxymoron. It implies that no branch of government can control its actions.[29] The operation of any regulatory agency, however, requires *someone* to appoint its members, assure proper conduct, and decide a budget. Some methods can reduce the degree of control but can never create an entirely independent agency. For example, an agency's budget may be created independent of the legislative appropriation process, such as being funded directly from gaming taxes. Another example of indirect control occurs when the chief executive has power over appointment and removal of agency members. Independence, in the sense of no executive control, may be promoted where the executive branch's power of removal of an agency member is limited to misfeasance or malfeasance.

Moreover, the notion of the truly "independent" agency has critics. Making the agency truly independent of the other three branches of government may increase the influence of outside interest groups. In other scenarios, the legislature may make agencies independent of the executive branch to increase the influence of the legislature or a legislative committee. They attempt to assure political accountability through "keeping agencies attentive to multiple voices" that are likely to "maximize the dialogue, openness, and responsiveness that define accountability in the most important sense."[30] With this, a variety of checks create accountability: elections, appointments, removal, judicial review, and grass roots political pressure.[31]

But, does achieving independence from government influence even result in the agency making independent decisions? Professor Cass Sunstein postulates a regulatory paradox that independent agencies are not truly independent. He suggests that when the Executive Branch does not have direct authority over the regulatory agency, the agency then be-

---

[27] James Landis, The Administrative Process (1938).

[28] Louis L. Jaffe, *The Illusion of the Ideal Administration*, 86 Harv. L. Rev. 1183, 1187 (1973).Despite significant criticism, many modern-day writers still implicitly adhere to it by writing from the vantage point of the "public-spirited" regulator, or concerned modern citizen. Rarely do works in economics, especially at the textbook level, give insight and advice to the firm or industry on how to thwart, capture or screw-up regulations. A notable exception is Chapter one of Bruce Owen & Ronald Braeutigam, The Regulation Game (1978).

[29] Davis & Pierce, *supra* note 12, at § 2.5.

[30] Peter Shane, *Political Accountability in a System of Checks and Balances: The Case of Presidential Review of Rulemaking*, 48 Ark. L Rev. 161, 213-214 (1995)

[31] *Id.* at 210.

comes more susceptible to legislative influence and well-organized interest groups. He attributes this paradox to the inability of the chief executive to buffer the agency from the legislature's attempt to do the bidding of interest groups.[32]

Attempting to bring accountability to gaming regulation is often difficult because gaming agencies, perhaps more often than other agencies, are built around the concept of independence because of the fear of corruption. Wide discretion is often given to gaming agencies to conduct applicant and licensee investigations free of the power of the chief executive. Agencies also will use the fact that licensing is a privilege, not a right, as the rationale to conduct far-ranging activities that other government agencies would not consider. This could include flying across the world on the expense account of an applicant or making unexpected visits to an applicant's house to go through private files and emails on her home computer.

Independence with broad discretion and unrestrained budgets can create serious accountability issues. Without necessary checks and balances, investigative agents can treat an applicant's accounts as the opportunity to vacation in foreign countries. Overzealous agents may go off on tangential investigations involving new applicants that are not germane to the pending application. Moreover, there may practically be no limits to investigatory techniques. Is it acceptable to go through private text messages, conduct random body searches, or water-board? In many jurisdictions, gaming regulatory agencies do not have the same restraints as police agencies, the latter of which must comply with constitutional or other protections afforded citizens line protection against unwarranted search and seizures or violation of privacy acts.

Implementation of a regulatory program may involve three levels of accountability: political, program, and judicial. Political accountability means that if the voting public disagrees with the actions of its government, it can express its dissatisfaction at the voting booth. It is meaningful in democratic societies wherein the government is elected by, and answerable to, the voting public for its actions. But what if the public disagrees with the actions of an agency? Who stands accountable? If an elected official or body has review power over the agency, then that elected officer can have political accountability.

While political accountability usually involves issues of important policy sufficient to draw the attention of the voting public, program accountability often concerns the efficiency of implementation. Some programs become so inefficient and waste sufficiently large funds that voters take heed, but this is a rare situation. On a broad scale, program accountability means a method to test whether the program is meeting public policy goals in the most efficient way.

Judicial accountability results when the judiciary can review the action taken by the agency and assures it is within the agency's power, follows

---

[32] Sunstein, *supra* note 10, at 426.

Figure 7.1

Function	Nature of Accountability	Possible Checks/Balances
Licensing Investigations	Program	Government budget reviews
Licensing decisions	Political or Judicial	Governor review of decisions Judicial review of decisions
Audits	Program	Multiple agency involvement Government budget reviews
Tax assessments	Judicial	Multiple agency involvement Judicial review
Disciplinary investigations	Program or Political	Chief law enforcement office involvement
Disciplinary decisions	Judicial	Judicial review of decisions
Enforcement	Program or Political	Chief law enforcement review of complaints
Patron disputes	Judicial	Judicial review
Rulemaking	Political or Judicial	Executive review Legislative review Judicial review

the law, and is constitutional. Occasionally, the judiciary is given broader power of review, even to the extent of substituting its judgment for that of the agency. Other times, its power to review certain regulatory decisions, such as licensing, can be minimal or nonexistent.

POLITICAL ACCOUNTABILITY

Political accountability involves a direct relationship between politicians and voters. This relationship balances on the effect that politicians' decisions have on their political future. This accountability can come from voters who disapprove of a politician's decision and vote against the elected official in the next election. It also can come from "affected" interest groups that are persuaded not to contribute to the official's campaign or to support an opponent or are motivated to remove the elected official.

Transparency
Open government

Few debate that open government is a prerequisite for political accountability, particularly regarding those arenas where government considers and adopts public policy. Open government includes public access to information about decisions, policy dialogue, and an opportunity for the dialogue to be well-informed and salient to actual decision-making.[33]

The benefits of open government are substantial. The most meaningful is the ability to hold decision-makers accountable for their actions. The public, however, cannot make informed choices unless it knows the agency's decisions, how they were made, and why they were made.

---

[33] Shane, supra note 30, at 210

Louis Brandeis wrote, "Publicity is justly commended as a remedy for social and industrial diseases. Sunlight is said to be the best disinfectant; electric light the most efficient policeman."[34]

A major player in this form of accountability is the mass media. Experienced television, radio, newspaper, and other media with proper access to the decision-making process are the gatekeepers to the informed voters. Three critical components to open government are open meetings, open access to agency records, and public participation.

Public access

Public access to certain types of agency records is without controversy. This includes final opinions and decisions, agendas, record of votes, orders, public statements, official interpretations, transcripts/minutes of meetings, regulations, rules, and licenses granted. This provides the public with adequate information to review and understand the decisions of the agency. It provides those regulated by the industry sufficient access to information concerning the behavior the legislature and regulators expect of them. Agencies offer a public service by providing an organized and relatively simple method for accessing these records.

Two recognized types of records that should not be subject to disclosure are confidential financial information and trade secrets. The former is information the applicant or licensee does not disclose to the public because it could create economic harm. In the casino industry, this may include disclosures regarding sources and expenditures of revenues that reveal much about the casino's marketing strategy. Likewise, information about profits and reserves can give competitors critical information about the casino's strengths and weaknesses.

Trade secrets are those methods of compiling information or carrying out business that can give the casino a competitive advantage and are unknown to competitors. This could include something as mundane as the method by which the casino compares lists of potential patrons to target for a direct-mail campaign or as important as future expansion plans into other markets.

Another reasonable exemption from disclosure is agency memoranda, which are writings sent between agency employees conducting investigations, audits, or other agency business. Exempting these memoranda allows the agency to share ideas and information that may be useful to the agency's proper function. Without such exemption, the exchange of information within agencies may be inhibited because staff and regulators know they can be subject to public scrutiny and criticism.

Public access to personal information about a licensee or applicant for licensing is a difficult issue. Does government have the right to reveal

---

[34] LOUIS BRANDEIS, OTHER PEOPLE'S MONEY, 67 (1933), quoted in Buckley v. Valeo, 424 U.S. 1, 7 (1976).

embarrassing things about an applicant for license? The answer involves weighing the applicant's right to privacy against the public's right to know the bases on which government makes decisions. Three options are available. First, the applicant can waive all privacy rights relevant to its investigation. This would allow anyone access to the information provided by the applicant or uncovered by the regulators not otherwise exempted from disclosure. This position may be justified because licenses are a privilege not a right. By pursing a license, the applicant is requesting regulators to determine his suitability. Because this involves review of matters that may be embarrassing, the applicant must accept tpublic disclosure as a consequence of seeking a license. If he does not want to risk exposure, then he should not apply for the license.

This approach may be unfair and cause qualified persons to decide not to apply for a license. Suppose the application requests information on the criminal history of family members. This is a reasonable request because if a family member is associated with organized crime, regulators will closely scrutinize the relationship between the applicant and that family member to make certain that the family member has no influence over the applicant. Suppose further that the applicant's deceased father-in-law, whom he never met, was a convicted sex offender. This is wholly irrelevant to the applicant's suitability, but it may be very embarrassing to the applicant and his family. If the jurisdiction provides access to all such information, then the person may decide not to seek a license.

The second option is less intrusive and keeps confidential all private information provided by the applicant except the information regulators consider relevant to decision-making. This provides the public access to all non-private information, such as an applicant's address, former employees, and education, but not to personal information, such as criminal history and financial information. The system, however, relies on the regulators to identify and disclose private information on which they rely when assessing applicant suitability.

A third approach protects all private information relevant to an applicant from public disclosure. This prohibits regulators from disclosing any personal information, except in open hearings when the regulators question the applicant to test his credibility. While this approach protects the privacy rights of the individual, the public may not know or understand the bases for the agency's decisions.

Another area frequently exempted from disclosure is information and records recovered during a law enforcement investigation. Information relevant to an applicant's background may come from other police agencies. This information may be confidential, particularly if the information is part of an ongoing police investigation. In other instances, the investigators will obtain information from a source that wishes to remain confidential.

In these circumstances, should the regulators be able to consider the information without disclosing it to either the applicant or the public?

This appears unfair to the applicant. If his suitability is being decided, the best way to derive the truth is for him to confront negative allegations because often he may adequately refute them. Without this opportunity, regulators may make decisions based on false evidence, especially information from third parties. While police conducting a continuing investigation may have legitimate reasons for requesting confidentiality, a third-party informant may demand confidentiality only because he knows the information is false and that a request of confidentiality prevents the applicant from challenging the allegations. Moreover, an investigative agent may routinely characterize most of his interviews or evidence as coming from confidential sources, knowing the information gleaned may cause the applicant's denial. The agent also may submit it as confidential to prevent the applicant from challenging his findings because the investigator is unsure of his own competency or because of personal animosity toward the applicant.

The opposing view is that the licensing process is not punitive against the applicant but is intended to protect the state's interest. Failing to license an applicant should not indicate the applicant is a bad person but rather that regulators do not have sufficient evidence to ensure he meets the highest standards. Regulators should be able to consider evidence from every source, even if it is confidential. If this evidence is credible and creates enough doubt as to the applicant's suitability, the application should not be granted, even if no opportunity exists to refute the evidence. Because the gaming license is a privilege, the applicant must appreciate and accept this risk.

Again, risks create barriers that even suitable applicants may not wish to challenge. Despite the intentions of the licensing process, most people interpret the denial of a license application as indicative of bad reputation. While a person may risk negative publicity to defend his reputation from all allegations, he may not be willing to risk ruining his reputation based on false allegations about which he is not privy.

Open meetings

Open meetings are most often associated with open government. This connotes a forum unclosed to public observation.[35] Open meetings may provide opportunities for interest groups, including the public, to express their positions to decision-makers.[36] Decision-makers gather to hear, review, and consider all the evidence and then publicly deliberate. A resulting decision results only from the evidence and arguments presented in the open forum. It is free from backroom negotiations or other influences.

---

[35] A prerequisite to open meetings is public notice of the meeting reasonably calculated to give interested persons notice of the time, place and subject matter of the hearing *See, e.g.,* The Government in the Sunshine Act, 5 U.S.C. § 552b(e).

[36] Jerry Markham, *Sunshine on the Administrative Process: Wherein Lies the Shade?* 28 ADMIN. L. REV. 463, 465 (1976).

As one commentator noted, "Transparency allows concerned parties—both public and political—to understand governmental decisions, to detect improper motives, and to assign blame. In this way, transparency promotes accountability (in the majoritarian sense) and prevents arbitrary administrative action."[37]

Even if the public does not attend the hearings, open meetings still provide an opportunity for more accurate reporting of what occurred in the media.[38] Otherwise, media reports must rely on leaks and hearsay.[39]

Merely knowing the deliberation process is transparent may inhibit regulators from making decisions that are extreme or abusing their authority.[40] Finally, requiring open meetings may inspire regulators to attend the deliberations, be better prepared, and be more organized.[41]

Yet open meetings may inhibit meaningful dialogue because regulators may feel they will be embarrassed in public if they ask questions or make comments that show ignorance or inexperience, however justified.

As Professors Davis and Pierce noted, "[Commissioners in open meetings] attempt to disguise their uncertainty with stilted and contrived discussions that greatly impede the frank exchange of views that is essential to high quality decision making by a collegial body."[42]

Deliberations involve decision-makers evaluating evidence, exchanging views, narrowing issues, and discarding alternatives. A regulator, however, may fear engaging in free dialogue because the public might believe he supports a position rather than merely exploring options. A regulator may not even consider unpopular ideas for fear of possible consequences.

Ex parte communications

The antithesis of an open meeting is an ex parte communication. This occurs when one party to a matter communicates with the decision-maker outside of a public forum or the presence of the other parties to the same matter. An ex parte communication may occur when an applicant pleads his case for approval to the regulators in a private meeting prior to a public hearing. With a gaming license application, an applicant or his attorney calling the decision-maker and plead his (client's) case would constitute ex parte communication.

---

[37] *Id.*

[38] Note, *Facilitating Government Decision-Making: Distinguishing Between Meetings and Non-Meetings Under the Federal Sunshine Act*, 66 Tex. L Rev. 1195 (1988).

[39] Note, *Open Meeting Statutes, The Press Fights for the "Right to Know*," 75 Harv. L. Rev. 1199, 1201 (1962).

[40] *Id* at 465.

[41] Note, *Facilitating Government Decision-Making: Distinguishing Between Meeting and Non-Meeting Under the Federal Sunshine Act*, 66 Tex. L. Rev. 1195, 1197 (1988).

[42] Davis and Pierce, *supra* note 12, § 5.18, at 221.

Whether ex parte communications should be allowed depends on the type of proceeding. Ex parte communications are improper in an adjudicatory proceeding, such as a patron dispute, where the decision-maker is deciding conflicting rights of two private parties. In this situation, both parties have the right to know and rebut the evidence on which the decision will be made.

Whether ex parte communications should be allowed in licensing decisions involves other considerations. Unlike a patron dispute, the rights of only the applicant are being decided. But two other reasons exist to prohibit ex parte communications in licensing situations. First, prohibition avoids the perception that "deals" are made in the back room. Such perception erodes public confidence in the regulatory system. Second, political accountability requires that the public has the salient information on which the agency makes decisions. Without this information, voters cannot assess whether agency decisions justify their votes for the person who appointed the regulators.

> A counter argument for allowing some ex parte communications in licensing applications pertains to handling sensitive information. For example, a licensee must provide substantial amounts of financial information to the regulators to support an application. As one court noted, "The public's right to know and to participate in the decision-making process frequently comes into sharp conflict with the need for confidentiality in certain areas."[43]

The application may require disclosing the personal arrest records of the applicant's father, which do not affect the applicant's suitability as his father may have died when he was young. This information, however, might cause embarrassment or discomfort to the applicant and his family if made public. The applicant's arrest at a young age may also be embarrassing, though it is relevant to the applicant's suitability.

Another problem with open government and the licensing process occurs when the investigator is also the decision-maker. Having all conversations between the investigator and the applicant held only in public is impractical and probably unworkable. Scheduling a hearing to ask an applicant to provide the identity of a check payee is ridiculous. Where the decision-maker is not the investigator, allowing the conversations between the investigator and the applicant to remain private poses few issues. In this situation, the information collected by the investigator can be complied and presented to the decision-maker in an open forum.

Whether agencies should receive and consider ex parte communications in rulemaking is controversial. One reason to permit such communications is that regulators need input on the political acceptability of a proposed rule from legislators and interest groups. This type of frank discussion cannot occur if it must be on the record. This might involve a level

---

[43] Hokanson v. High Sch. Dist. No. Eight, 589 P.2d 907, 910, (Ariz. Ct. App. 1978).

of political compromise needed to fashion an acceptable resolution. It also may avoid the need for, and cost of, formal legislative intervention.

At the same time, allowing ex parte communications may create certain problems. If the agency uses the opportunity to receive ex parte communications to make decisions in private, it defeats the purpose of open government. Moreover, information received through ex parte communications is not subject to adversarial comment. This is unfair and may contribute to an agency's incorrect decision. Information received through ex parte communications is also not available to a court that reviews the agency's decision.

Public participation

Regulatory agencies often must rely on input from interested parties, including the regulated person, for access to information, understanding potential impacts, assessing risk, and determining the most appropriate solutions to regulatory problems.[44]

Wide participation in administrative decision-making has many benefits, including bringing multiple viewpoints and information, making the process more transparent, decreasing the influence of the regulated, and increasing the public confidence in the regulatory process.[45] Concerted political action for decision-making also may decrease the power of private interest groups.[46]

Requiring gaming regulators to systematically collect all relevant information before making a decision also has the benefit of mediating any bias based in the regulator's limited knowledge or experience.[47]

Public participation in rulemaking should be encouraged. Rulemaking is most effective when the agency understands the holistic impact on all interested groups and parties. Open participation allows these groups to voice the positive and negative aspects of a proposed action and to respond to the comments of other parties. The probability that an agency will make the proper decision increases as it acquires more credible information on an issue. This could involve many active steps undertaken by regulators, including informing, consulting, and collaborating with all interested groups, including the public.

To inform the public it is considering regulations, the administrative agency must provide reasonable notice, a degree of specificity, and balance to allow each interest group to understand the potential impact. At a minimum, this may require the agency to provide public notice of future actions.

---

[44] Kenneth A. Bamberger, *Regulation as Delegation: Private Firms, Decision-making, and Accountability in the Administrative State*, 56 Duke L.J. 377, 380-381 (2006)

[45] Cheryl Simrell King et.al.,, *The Question of Participation: Toward Authentic Public Participation in Public Administration*, 58 Pub. Admin. Rev. 317 (1998).

[46] Lisa Schultz Bressman, *Beyond Accountability: Arbitrariness and Legitimacy in the Administrative State*, 78 N.Y.U. L. Rev., 461, 500 (2003).

[47] Bamberger, *supra* note 44, at 441.

Consulting should occur where a prospective action impacts specific interests. Regulators may actively want to consult those groups. This is often more difficult in the gaming context wherein the decision impacts the customer, but the customers are predominately tourists or otherwise disengaged. Involvement means ensuring a process wherein all interested parties can express their concerns or aspirations in a forum where their information will be considered in light of policy goals.

Collaboration requires the administrative agency to take all the positions of the various interest groups into consideration to "clarify issues, develop alternative, and identify the preferred solution" consistent with achieving public policy goals with the least negative impact. As one commentator noted:

> The view that government regulation tends to give inadequate weight to the general public interest, as distinct from the special interests which participate so effectively in regulatory processes, does not rest on simplistic notions that regulators are incompetent, narrow-minded, or corrupt. Nothing could be further from the truth; our regulators and government servants are generally persons of ability who are trying to do the best job they can under difficult circumstances. But their perspectives are limited by the information that is available to them, and their attitudes are shaped by the rewards and feedback that our system provides to them.[48]

Rulemaking often has a direct impact on the public. For example, Nevada debated the conditions under which gaming devices could be placed in businesses that served alcohol. It was a protracted debate between "tavern" owners and large casino interests. Notably absent from the debate where those who would likely be most impacted by the decision, the public, either from the perspective of the customer who may have preferences for the local taverns or the residents who lived in the neighborhoods housing the taverns.

Some regulatory proceedings lend themselves to open participation, while others do not. No good reason exists to allow persons to participate in licensing decisions other than to provide information to the regulators during an investigation. Likewise, unless a disciplinary action involves questions of regulatory interpretation, an agency should not allow open participation. In both cases, the primary purpose of the proceeding is to assess the behavior of the applicant or licensee. Additional parties to these proceedings can be intrusive, time-consuming, and unproductive.

Situations justifying open participation are more common in tax and patron disputes. By their nature, the parties to these actions have a difference in either the interpretation of the facts or applying the law to those facts. In the latter case, the decision involves interpretation of laws or regulations that can affect other licensees in similar situations, in which case open participation is appropriate.

---

[48] Roger C. Crampton, *The Why, Where and How of Broadened Public Participation in the Administrative Process*, 60 GEORGETOWN L.J. (1972).

Participation should be structured to avoid abuses, even when a right to do so exists. For example, a regulatory agency gains no additional useful information from repetitive presentations by members of the same interest group. While the group has the right to be repetitive, it is a waste of valuable time and effort.

Judicial accountability

Careful consideration must be given to the role of the judiciary in gaming regulation. The legislature may grant regulators broad discretion to accomplish some policy goals. For example, a licensing statute may give the regulatory agency the power to deny a license to a person whose character may threaten the integrity of the casino industry. This is a discretionary statute because it does not define which character attributes justify a denial. Here, the legislature probably intends the regulatory agency to resolve the ambiguity by defining disqualifying attributes. In such circumstances, the judiciary's involvement may be counterproductive. In other situations, the judiciary may be ill-suited to review the agency decision. For example, the judiciary may not have the mechanical expertise to decide the reasonableness of regulations covering the operation of a random number generator in a gaming device.

Judicial accountability, however, may ensure the agency does not transcend the powers the legislature intended. Suppose the regulators impose the condition on a casino that it must maintain a cash reserve to pay its vendors. If the legislature did not intend the agency to protect creditors' rights, this action may be beyond the power of the agency. In this role, courts are not part of the primary implementation mechanism but serve in a supervisory role.[49]

What powers the judiciary may have in reviewing the actions of a regulatory agency may be, in some circumstances, set by law or constitution. For example, a licensee involved in a tax dispute with the regulators may have the right to have an independent judiciary resolve any issues of law that may arise.

In other circumstances, however, no rights to judicial review may exist, such as review of licensing decisions. This allows the legislature to craft the law to provide no, minimal, or absolute judicial accountability for certain agency actions. In structuring a gaming regulatory system to achieve accountability, policy-makers may consider a hybrid system in which certain actions are subject only to limited accountability, while others are fully reviewed.

In some adjudicatory decisions, such as granting a gaming license, independence from the executive branch is an advantage.[50] In these circum-

---

[49] Edward L. Rubin, *Law and Legislation in the Administrative State*, 89 Colum. L. Rev. 369, 374 (1989).
[50] Davis & Pierce, *supra* note 12, at § 2.5.

stances, isolating the agency from political influences eliminates the potential that a regulator will award a license based on friendship, contributions to, or party affiliations with the chief executive. Buffers from the legislature also may reduce the ability of those elected officials to influence licensing decisions or elected judges from reversing a licensing decision based on improper considerations. For these reasons, external review of licensing decisions is either prohibited or subject to limited review (such as whether any evidence exists to support the decision or whether it was made in bad faith).

Bad faith or improper behavior by agency decision-makers is one of the more common reasons used to justify expanding the scope of review[51]. Showing bad faith rebuts the presumption of regularity to which an agency and its administrative record is entitled.[52] Another exception to the 'record rule,' agency inaction, also has much in common with bad faith.

The United States Supreme Court counseled "where there are administrative findings that were made at the same time as the decision . . . there must be a strong showing of bad faith or improper behavior before such inquiry can be made."[53] Clearly, there is a sense that expanding the scope of discovery beyond the record and probing into the mental processes of the administrative decision-makers is undesirable.

In contrast, greater accountability for spending where the regulated pay the bills (e.g., in the licensing investigation) is warranted. Applicants are unlikely to complain for fear that it could impact their licensing while other licensees may support high investigation fees because they serve as another barrier to entry. But, left unrestricted, the excessive costs translate into reduced competition and higher pricing that negatively affects players, could impact policy goals, and hurts industry viability. Expense auditing could be subject to legislative rather than judicial oversight, perhaps through the creation of a government auditing department.

Other decisions are less sensitive, such as a contested tax assessments based on a regulatory audit, so more traditional forms of judicial review are more appropriate. In these cases, the decisions are generally less sensitive and more frequently based on statutory interpretation that is more often effectively administered by the judiciary.

Political Protections
Campaign contributions

One method to corrupt the regulatory process is to gain influence over the politician who appoints the regulators, then have that politician influence the decisions of the regulators. If politicians act in a manner to maximize re-election, then influence over the politician may be achieved by either

---

[51] Hoffman, 132 F.3d at 14.
[52] San Luis Obispo Mothers for Peace v. NRC, 751 F.2d 1287, 1329 (D.C. CIR. 1984).
[53] Citizens to Preserve Overton Park, Inc. v. Volpe, 401 U.S. 402, 420 (1971).

controlling a large block of voters or by controlling election funds that the politician can later use to influence voters. Banning any political contributions by casino operators and employees is one method to protect the regulatory process. If the legislators or governor do not receive contributions from casino interests, then they are less likely to promote casino interests either directly (through legislation) or indirectly by attempting to influence the electoral process. New Jersey has a policy preventing casinos, their owners, and their key employees, from contributing to political campaigns, parties, or groups,[54] and even further isolates the industry. This greatly reduces the casino industry's ability to influence the political process.

A total ban against contributions, however, may disenfranchise the casino industry by denying it a reasonable opportunity to support a preferred candidate. It also may allow other groups, such as labor unions, suppliers, or others, to obtain economic benefits at the expense of the casino industry. For example, a strong teachers union may convince the legislature to overtax the casino industry to support pay raises for teachers. This may occur despite the fact that taxing the industry may harm the state economy by making the industry less competitive in its quest to attract tourists and to retain local businesses. Carrying out a regulatory program involves balancing the need to protect the process from these faults, on one hand, and seeking to encourage needed political participation, on the other. The latter may involve ensuring that the interests of all parties affected by a decision are represented or, at least, expressed in the process. A jurisdiction also may consider whether general limits on the campaign contributions, applicable to all businesses, unions, and groups may adequately address the issue without discrimination. This is seen in Victoria, Australia, wherein holders of casino and gaming licenses can only donate up to AU$50,000 to each political party.[55]

A second method used to isolate the casino industry is to prevent anyone who is associated with the casino from running for office. This prevents the regulated from becoming principals over the regulators. New Jersey also prohibits casino employees from running for or holding political office. However, it may seem discriminatory to deny a person the right to participate in government because of his or her chosen profession, and it may even violate the legal rights of casino employees. A less extreme approach may be to require the person to resign from the casino industry's private sector once elected.

Certain jurisdictions have even found unconstitutional the prohibition of political contributions by a spouse, parent, child or spouse of a child of a casino or supplier licensee because it restricts political expression too broadly, in violation of the US Constitution's First Amendment.[56]

---

[54] *See, e.g.,* Annmarie Timmins, *Latest Casino Bill Bans Political Contributions and Sets Other Limits*, Concord Monitor, http://www.concordmonitor.com/home/5378179-95/ latest-casino-bill-bans-political-contributions-and-sets-other-limits.

[55] *Electoral Act* 2002, Vict. Acts, § 216(1).

[56] *See, e.g.,* Campaign Contributions, Michigan Gaming Control Board,

Fundraising

Another way to insulate regulators from unwanted outside influences is to prohibit gaming licensees and persons who appear before regulators from serving in any capacity, either as a director, advisor, or fundraiser, for the campaigns of persons seeking public offices that regulate gaming or appoint the regulators. This would prohibit an attorney who was the chief executive's chief fundraiser from representing an applicant for a gaming license. This would avoid the appearance that a person close to the government official regulates the industry or that one who appoints or advises regulators can influence their decisions.

Sources of funding

Usually the legislature determines the jurisdiction's budget and allocates funding to each of the government agencies based on what it believes is the best use of the government's limited resources. Under this system, the legislature is accountable to the voting public for spending public funds. Because this system results in the legislature deciding the regulatory agency's budget, it allows the legislature to assert some influence over the agency.

To many, this is not problematic because the agency is under directive to achieve the policy goals established by the legislature. If the legislature as a whole uses the funding process to indicate the agency is not meeting its expectations, then this may serve as a valuable check on the power and direction of the agency.

More problematic, however, is when the legislature is fragmented and a single member of the legislature controls the agency's funding. This may occur when the controlling legislator is the influential chair of an appropriations committee. Unlike a chief executive, who is elected by and accountable to all the voters, the powerful legislator needs only to answer to his or her constituency. This leaves the possibility the legislator can influence agency actions or policy for her own personal benefit or the benefit of the region she represents. This problem, however, is not unique to regulatory agencies and can affect all agencies and legislation. It must be addressed the way the jurisdiction establish its budgets.

To avoid influence from both the legislature and specific legislators, New Jersey attempted to protect its Casino Control Commission by having its financial backing come from a casino control fund derived from gaming taxes.[57] This funding method, however, still poses two problems. First, it may create a built-in inefficiency because the Commission may feel it must use all the funds available, even if they exceed what is reasonably needed to regulate

---

http://www.michigan.gov/mgcb/0,4620,7-120-57144_57145-245363--,00.html.

[57] Robert P. Culleton, *The Implementation of the Credit Controls of the 1977 New Jersey Casino Control Act, in* GAMBLING AND PUBLIC POLICY 203 (William R. Eadington & Judy Cornelius, eds. 1991).

the industry.[58] Second, no political accountability exists for the spending of government funds. No one reviews whether the funds spent to achieve a goal were excessive or could have been used more wisely elsewhere.

Reliance on revenues

Undue reliance by the government on gaming tax revenues may provide abnormal political power to the private sector of the casino industry. When the casinos contribute little to the government's budget, and the public sector employs few workers, the casinos' political influence is no stronger than the private sector in most other industries. In designing a regulatory system, governments should consider greater protections against industry influence, especially when the industry is likely to be significant to the economy. If the government does not want the industry to grow beyond a certain size, it should address those issues in the enabling legislation.

Dedication of gaming revenues, called "earmarking," to fund social programs, can pose practical and political problems. Gaming revenues offer no guarantee that dollars will remain constant or increase.[59] If gaming revenue decreases, the government may encounter pressure from a new interest group—the beneficiaries of the tax revenues—to expand gaming or relax regulation.

---

[58] Jeffrey Lowenhar, *et al., Regulatory Requirements and Legalized Casino Gaming in New Jersey: The Case for Change, in* GAMBLING AND PUBLIC POLICY 266, 269 (William R. Eadington & Judy Cornelius, eds. 1991).

[59] *See generally,* NEW JERSEY, GOVERNOR'S ADVISORY COMMISSION ON GAMBLING, REPORT AND RECOMMENDATIONS OF THE GOVERNOR'S ADVISORY COMMISSION ON GAMBLING 11–12 (1988). *See also,* Bruce Ransom, *Public Policy and Gambling in New Jersey,* GAMBLING AND PUBLIC POLICY 155, 163 (William R. Eadington & Judy Cornelius, eds. 1991).

8

Compliance

Anthony Cabot

INTRODUCTION

The notion that regulators can maintain casino licensees' full compliance through enforcement is impractical. A day in a casino involves thousands of transactions—many undocumented—with players, vendors, tenants, and others. Almost any of these transactions can cause regulatory violations. Regulators have the expertise to define compliance goals and expectations of the companies through regulation; however, they do not have the resources or the institutional knowledge of the internal workings or structure of each gaming company to ensure compliance with all regulations. A government-mandated compliance program attempts to bridge this gap. Ideally, a gaming company can use its resources to fashion a plan that creates a compliant environment by detecting and preventing regulatory issues.

Mandated compliance plans have a long history. An old proverb, ascribed to Plato, is that necessity is the mother of invention. So is the case with compliance plans. In 1987, Nevada regulators faced a problem. Ginji Yasuda, a Japanese national, purchased the Aladdin Hotel out of bankruptcy for $54 million and set forth to become the first foreigner to obtain a casino license in Nevada. This presented many challenges, including determining how to ensure that a first-time casino owner from a different culture would comply with all gaming laws and regulations. The solution, fashioned by then Nevada Gaming Control Board Chairman Mike Rumboltz, required the Aladdin to implement a compliance plan as a condition of its license. The condition required one member to be independent of the company. The concept was good, but implementation ultimately failed and the regulators revoked the license two years later.[1]

---

[1] Assoc. Press, *Casino Owner Loses License in Wake of Loan Allegations*, N.Y. TIMES, Aug. 26, 1999, http://www.nytimes.com/1989/08/26/us/casino-owner-loses-license-in-wake-of-loan-allegations.html.

The experiment did, however, establish a framework for designated compliance plans. In 1991, the Nevada Gaming Commission adopted a regulation providing guidelines for future compliance plans. This regulation was still focused on imposing such plans only in special circumstances that "require additional management review by a licensee or registrant."[2] Although the regulation has never changed or been codified in a statute, in 1999, the Gaming Commission decided that compliance plans would be required for all public companies.[3] New Jersey statutorily mandated the first comprehensive compliance plans shortly thereafter.

PURPOSES OF MANDATED COMPLIANCE PLANS

Compliance plans are intended to prevent possible regulatory violations, monitor activities impacting the licensee's or registrant's continuing-qualifications as a licensee, and report those activities to senior management and the gaming regulators. In other words, the inquiry is whether the licensee is engaging in any activities regulators may have found objectionable when the person or company was first licensed. Mandated plans address various potential activities, the most common of which are (1) detection of unsuitable prospective employees or associations,[4] (2) preventing unacceptable situations including unethical or unlawful business practices, and (3) specific compliance with license conditions.[5] With casino companies, the obvious emphasis is on gaming laws and regulations, but the scope can extend to related areas such as drug and liquor laws and anti-money laundering and campaign laws.

Mandatory compliance programs can prevent certain issues, as illustrated by their use in timely identifying and excluding unsuitable persons

---

[2] Nevada Gaming Regulation 5.045 still reads:

   1. Whenever the commission is acting upon any application of a licensee or registrant, or pursuant to its powers provided in NRS 463.310, and if the commission determines that special circumstances exist which require additional management review by a licensee or registrant, the commission may impose a condition upon any license or order of registration to require implementation of a compliance review and reporting system by the licensee or registrant.

   2. The terms of the condition may include, but shall not be limited to:

       (a)   That the condition shall expire on a certain date or after a designated period of time without commission action;

       (b)   That the condition may be administratively removed by the board should a specified activity cease or a specified event occur; or

       (c)   That a periodic review shall be conducted by the board and upon such review the board may recommend and the commission may remove or continue to require the condition.

[3] Jeff Rodefer, *Creating and Implementing An Effective Gaming Compliance Plan*, NEV. GAMING LAW., Sept. 2011.

[4] More sophisticated compliance plans may create methodologies to use the compliance process to help ensure regulatory compliance with laws other than gaming laws.

[5] NEV. GAMING REG. 5.045(6).

from gaming activities. Most jurisdictions have regulations that prohibit associating with unsuitable persons. In Nevada, this includes "associations with persons denied licensing or other related approvals by the commission or who may be deemed unsuitable for association with a licensee or registrant."[6] Without a compliance requirement, casino licensees could take varied approaches. Some might voluntarily do due diligence on vendors. Management may review these due diligence reports but no one independent of the company is likely to review the reports and advise the company. Other companies may commit no resources to background due diligence before commencing a business relationship. Still other companies may do due diligence in an ad hoc fashion. In total, this may create an overall regulatory environment where licensees may inadvertently enter a business association with an inappropriate person.

Mandated compliance plans create a minimum level of consistency among licensees by defining who is subject to background checks, the nature of the checks, and procedures to review those checks. These procedures should produce information and awareness that could cause a licensee to avoid an unsuitable association. If this information is communicated to management and the casino's board of directors, then the expectation is that with due deliberation, the licensee will make a reasoned decision to avoid business relationships with unacceptable persons. Likewise, a licensee with knowledge that a prospective association is unsuitable but still decides to enter the relationship may not be worthy of maintaining a privileged license.

AREAS COVERED BY COMPLIANCE PLANS
Unsuitable Associations
Definition

The substance of each company's compliance program may differ based on the size of the company, the nature of its operations, special circumstances, and past regulatory issues. Certain due diligence procedures, however, are customary within most mandated compliance programs. One common safeguard ensures that the licensee does not associate with unsuitable persons.

The definition of an unsuitable person is helpful for focusing policies to meet company objectives. An unsuitable person typically is someone who gaming authorities or company officials determine is unfit to be associated with a gaming licensee. This assessment may be subjective such as determining whether an individual is so notorious or has engaged in such unsavory personal conduct or affairs as to justify barring them from the casino or being a vendor. In other circumstances, suitability may be determined more objectively based on a prior denial of a gaming license, other

---

[6] NEV. GAMING REG. 5.045(6).

regulatory approvals, or on felony convictions involving moral turpitude, gaming law, narcotics law, or any criminal activities.

The concept of unsuitability may vary depending on position. For example, when reviewing a prospective casino executive, emphasis may be placed on regulatory transgressions, past violations of corporate compliance plans, and any misleading or false information of application.

Compliance plans relating to unsuitable persons focus on obtaining information and making recommendations that management can use to avoid such persons. Several methods that may be incorporated into a compliance plan are available to obtain the information.

Typical Compliance Plan Provision Dealing with
Vetting Officers, Directors and Key Employees

The Parent Company and its Subsidiaries shall exercise care to ensure that prospective Directors, Executive Officers and Key Gaming Employees of any Gaming Subsidiary, and Directors and Executive Officers of the Company are not Unsuitable Persons. The suitability of prospective Directors, Executive Officers and Key Gaming Employees shall be investigated and the results reviewed at the direction of the Compliance Officer. The results of such investigation, should any derogatory information be revealed, shall be reported to the Compliance Committee for review and appropriate action.

Methods of detection

Information about an unsuitable association can come from myriad sources including news reports, a whistleblower, law enforcement, and industry associates. The most common source is required background investigations.

Background investigations

The primary information source concerning associations is the background investigation. This may include due diligence reviews of

- Certain consultants, lobbyists, suppliers, vendors, distributors, advisors, lessees, and tenants;
- Prospective officers, directors, and key employees;
- All material financings, such as significant debt or equity;,
- Material transactions, such as joint ventures and partnerships;
- Major acquisitions or other strategic alliances; and
- Any material litigation against the company or its employees.

Collected information is typically limited to material or major matters. For example, suppliers receiving more than $100,000 annually could be required to complete preprinted background forms and undergo a background investigation.[7] Investigation of parties to a transaction may not

---

[7] The plan should then specify what happens to the information once submitted. The compliance officer may have the responsibility to review the forms for completeness and

be required where the party under review is regulated by a governmental agency. A compliance plan may permit a company to forgo an independent investigation of a publicly-held company regulated by the Securities and Exchange Commission. This permission may extend to a financial institution regulated by federal banking authorities, a company or individual regulated or licensed by one of the gaming authorities, or a foreign jurisdictions' gaming regulatory authority, other than to determine the other party's standing with such governmental agency. Even compliance plans permitting a company to forgo an independent investigation usually contain a caveat that if any reason exists to believe that the company may be unsuitable, then an independent investigation still may be warranted.

For material transactions and major acquisitions, the nature of the information collected and reported varies depending on the transaction. In material financing, this information typically includes

- The source of the funds,
- Disclosure of any relationships between the company, any subsidiary, and any other parties to the proposed financing, and
- Identifying any finder, broker, or other person to receive compensation in connection with securing, arranging, negotiating or otherwise dealing with the proposed material financing

Where the funds are not from institutional lenders, due diligence may be conducted on the lender.

Material transactions are typically defined by reference to thresholds appropriate to the size of the gaming business. Here the reports typically include the following information on the other party to the transaction:

- Name and address;
- Legal form, such as corporation, partnership, or joint venture;
- Nature of business conducted;
- Geographical area where business is conducted;
- Names, addresses, and a due diligence investigation of all directors, principal officers, shareholders holding over 5 percent interest, general partners and any limited partners holding over 5 percent interest;
- Brief statement as to the company's reasons for the proposed transaction;
- Specific laws under which the business operation is permitted, if relevant; and
- Identification of any person such as a broker or finder to receive any form of compensation for suggesting, proposing or arranging the transaction, including the arrangement for such compensation.

Where financing is involved and the funds are not from institutional lenders, due diligence may be conducted on the lender.

---

to conduct other investigations to complete the information required for the compliance committee's review.

Typical Compliance Plan Provision Defining a Material Transaction

Material Transaction means a transaction whereby the compliance officer or a member of the compliance committee has knowledge that pertains to

a. *A commercial transaction involving an unsuitable person or an entity that reasonably may be regarded as an unsuitable person*

b. *The acquisition or disposition of assets or equity interests where the value given or received by the company or a subsidiary exceeds three million dollars ($3,000,000) or five hundred thousand dollars ($500,000) if solely related to the company, except for such transactions involving temporary investments in securities as included on the company's consolidated balance sheets or the purchase or disposition of less than 20 percent interest in a non-gaming entity or facility.*

Unacceptable Situations
Definitions

The second common purpose of most compliance programs is to detect and prevent unacceptable situations including unethical or unlawful business practices. An unacceptable situation is typically any event or circumstance that may adversely affect public perceptions of the games' honesty and the industry's integrity. Unlawful business practices are defined as any activity that contravenes any local, state, or federal laws. Casinos must be more vigilant regarding certain laws. These laws may include or be related to (1) securities laws, including those related to insider trading and false or misleading disclosure; (2) the Bank Secrecy Act and anti-money laundering laws; (3) campaign contribution laws; (4) the Foreign Corrupt Practices Act; (5) antitrust laws; (6) advertising and marketing policies; (7) conflicts of interests; and (8) the USA PATRIOT Act. Violating laws can both impact the company's continuing qualifications as a licensee and result in significant fines. For example, a Las Vegas casino company paid $47.4 million in fines to avoid criminal charges stemming from a money laundering investigation.[8]

Unethical business practices are more difficult to define. Some argue the entire notion of gambling where the house has an advantage is unethical. In a compliance plan, however, unethical business practices are those that involve practices that if exposed would jeopardize any specific government policy goal adopted in a jurisdiction, as generally discussed in Chapter 2. Unethical practices are numerous. They can involve deceptive trade practices as when the casino resorts to dishonesty or trickery to win or gain money from patrons; paying or accepting bribes, even if not illegal;

---

[8] David Knowles, *Sheldon Adelson's Sands Casino to Pay $47 Million Fine for Failing to Report Deposits from Alleged Drug Trafficker*, N.Y. DAILY NEWS, Aug. 28, 2013, http://www.nydailynews.com/news/national/sheldon-adelson-sands-casino-pay-47-million-fine-article-1.1439489#ixzz2slePSFCe.

altering or forging documents to avoid taxes or regulatory violations; or, simply, a lack of candor in dealing with regulators or otherwise obstructing a regulatory investigation.

While the unacceptable situations a casino licensee may encounter are nearly endless, certain activities are more common in the gaming industry and provide examples of the functionality of compliance plans.

Advertising

Compliance plans and advertising seem like strange bedfellows. Which advertisements could cause gaming regulatory compliance issues? One Las Vegas casino attracted the unwanted attention of gaming regulators when it embarked on a risqué series of billboards. One showed cards, poker chips, and a couple in a suggestive pose with the tag line, "There's always a temptation to cheat." Another declared the casino supported "your Monday night rights: large quantities of prescription stimulants [and] having wives in two states. . . . Tell your wives you are going; if they are hot, bring them along." Nevada's gaming regulators decided that illicit sex, illegal drugs, and casino cheating were unacceptable and brought a complaint alleging a violation of Nevada Gaming Regulation 5.011(4), sanctioning the casino for a "[f]ailure to conduct advertising and public relations activities in accordance with decency, dignity, good taste, honesty and inoffensiveness. . . ." The casino ultimately agreed to pay a fine of $300,000 and implement new compliance procedures to review future advertisements. While the Nevada Gaming Commission eventually rejected two of the three counts in the final decision on First Amendment grounds,[9] such conflicts can strain relationships with the regulators and the community.

Other advertising issues do not invoke constitutional considerations. Even the ardent civil rights lawyer will acknowledge that the Constitution offers no protection against false or misleading advertisements. Both gaming regulatory laws and general consumer protection laws provide civil and criminal sanctions for such advertisements. The same Nevada regulation cited above prohibits "advertising that is false or materially misleading."[10] California has a statute that criminalizes advertising that concerns "any circumstance or matter of fact connected with the proposed performance or disposition thereof, which is untrue or misleading, and which is known, or which by the exercise of reasonable care should be known, to be untrue or misleading."[11] Regulators are frequently interested in quantifiable claims that are untrue. For example, a casino cannot ethically advertise it has the loosest slot machines in town, unless they can show by some reasonable standard their slot machines have the highest average return.

---

[9] For a description of this 2004 incident involving the Hard Rock Hotel, *see* http://www.8newsnow.com/story/2347193/hard-rock-wins-racy-billboard-decision.

[10] *See* NEV. GAMING REG. 5.011(4).

[11] CAL. BUS. & PROF. CODE §17500.

A casino can also get into trouble not by what it says in advertisements, but what it does not say. Some states, like New Jersey, require all casino advertisements provide information regarding compulsive gambling programs, including providing an 800 number.[12]

Finally, a casino can violate gaming regulations and other laws by sending casino advertisements to prohibited groups. Michigan gaming attorney Robert Stocker issued this warning to the Michigan gaming industry:

> On August 10, 2006, the Michigan Attorney General filed criminal and civil charges against two senders of unsolicited messages to minors whose e-mail addresses were registered under the Michigan Child Protection Registry Act. The Michigan Act declares it is the Legislature's intent 'to provide safeguards to prevent certain messages regarding ... *gambling* ... from reaching minor children of this state.' In reality, the Michigan Act places at risk of criminal and civil prosecution a wide variety of lawful commercial business activity within the gaming industry."[13] Minors are not the only group protected from casino advertisements. In New Jersey, for example, problem gamblers can request to be placed on the list of self-excluded persons.[14] Once on these lists, casinos should not send these individuals any forms of casino advertising or offer them any related benefits.

Advertising is not the only form of communications that can lead to regulatory problems. Gaming companies have faced stiff fines for public relations attempts that have gone astray. In one recent case, the Nevada Gaming Commission fined a manufacturer for issuing a press release that claimed it entered into a contract with another party when it had only entered into a letter of intent that was never consummated.[15]

Reviewing every press release or advertisement for proper content or scrutinizing mailing lists for such advertisements is not necessarily an efficient use of compliance personnel if the company has not had a history of compliance issues. The compliance plan, however, can recognize the potential problems that can occur with both advertisements and public relations. The plan can inform company employees of their obligations regarding appropriate advertising, describing and warning personnel of the dangers of false or misleading advertisements or press releases. The plan may provide systematic policies for review of all advertisements and press releases by the respective company personnel and outside advisers. Policies can be implemented to require that email lists be regularly compared to the rolls of states with Child Protection Registry laws to ensure that advertisements

---

[12] N.J. Rev. Stat. § 5:12-70(o)(3).

[13] Robert W. Stocker II & Peter J. Kulick, *Child Protection Registry Acts: A Constitutional Gamble for the Gaming Industry*, ABA Sect. Bus. L. eNewsletter (2007), http://apps. americanbar.org/buslaw/committees/CL430000pub/newsletter/200711/home.shtml#78639C03-BF0A-16A1-2A75C7B9C213C20A.

[14] *See, e.g.,* N.J. Rev. Stat. § 19:48-2.1 (defining self-excluded person).

[15] *See* Cy Ryan, *Gaming board: No more 'tolerance' with Vegas company*, L.V. Sun, June 5, 2009, http://www.lasvegassun.com/news/2009/jun/05/gaming-board-no-more-tolerance-vegas-company/.

do not inadvertently reach minors on the list. Likewise, all advertisement lists can be checked against any state lists of excluded persons and purged appropriately to avoid regulatory violations.

Conflicts of interest

In the wake of the Enron scandal that rocked the public company sector, Rod Smith, a reporter for *Casino City Times*, questioned why the gaming industry had not experienced similar problems. The late Terry Lanni, then MGM Mirage Chairman and Chief Executive Officer, had a simple explanation: "We're a highly regulated business. Therefore, any partnerships (involving conflicts of interest) would be impossible to occur in this business. Any such event such as those in Enron would have been impossible (in the gaming industry)." Likewise, Steve Crown, compliance committee chairman at Park Place Entertainment Corporation, noted: "From a compliance perspective, we've become our own watchdogs." Mr. Crown continued, "What saved the gaming industry from the financial turmoil that enveloped other industries was stringent adherence to compliance policies that prevent 'conflicts of interest.'"[16]

A conflict of interest arises when a person has two duties that conflict. More specifically, *Black's Law Dictionary* defines it as "a real or seeming incompatibility between one's private interests and one's public or fiduciary duties."[17] In the corporate context, for example, a conflict of interest exists if an employee has a direct or indirect pecuniary or personal interest in a decision being made that needs to be made objectively and in the best interests of only the company. The occurrence of conflicts of interest, however, does not necessarily signify impropriety, especially considering that conflicts can arise in everyday life.

Although all conflicts may not be unethical or improper, the heightened state of today's corporate regulatory environment demands companies implement and enforce industry-specific compliance plans designed to safeguard against conflicts of interest at all levels of the corporate structure.[18]

---

[16] *See* GLENN LIGHT & KARL RUTLEDGE, GAMING MANAGEMENT: CONFLICTS OF INTEREST (2008), http://www.lrrlaw.com/gaming-management-conflicts-of-interest-12-01-2008/#. U6H-TF6ZqCs.

[17] BLACK'S LAW DICTIONARY 295 (7th ed. 2009).

[18] States have passed or enacted conflict of interest statutes and regulations recognizing a need for conflicts of interest oversight. Regarding the gaming industry, states have adopted conflict of interest laws regulating how state employees may interact with gaming licensees. For example, the Nevada Revised Statutes state, "[A] person who holds a license issued pursuant to chapter 463 or 464 of NRS or who is required to register with the Nevada Gaming Commission pursuant to chapter 463 of NRS shall not employ a former member of the State Gaming Control Board or the Nevada Gaming Commission for 1 year after the termination of the member's service on the Board or Commission." In both New Jersey and Colorado gaming licensees must comply with multiple government-imposed mandates.

New Jersey Conflicts of Interest Law controls licensee conduct in numerous situations, including prohibiting a licensee from employing state employees responsible for

Many conflicts of interest can be avoided through appropriately designed compliance controls. In a highly regulated industry like gaming, perhaps the foremost concern is to avoid all conflicts of interest that would reflect poorly on a gaming organization's standing with regulators and could jeopardize its gaming license. This includes ensuring all employees know of acts and situations that i) are improper; ii) might give an appearance of impropriety; or iii) might impair their good judgment when acting for the company.

Potential situations that would establish conflicts of interest should be detailed in a compliance plan. These situations include

- Having a significant interest in a firm that does business with the company;
- Borrowing or accepting money or gifts or other favors from a person or firm doing business with the company;
- Engaging in a private business relationship with a person or firm doing business with the company, particularly if the company's employee supervises the relationship with that person or firm;
- Engaging in a private business relationship with a supervisor or another team member whom the team member supervises;
- Engaging in a competing business or owning stock or other securities of a competitor other than insignificant interests in public companies;
- Engaging in a private business venture with an officer or other employee of a firm that competes with the company;
- Using company resources for personal benefit, such as the extension of complimentary items or services, to further personal rather than a company business purpose;
- Use of company staff or assets for personal business;
- Having an interest in or speculating in products or real estate whose value may be affected by the company's business;

casino matters within two years of termination from state employment. Additionally, the New Jersey Casino Control Act regulates political conflicts of interest originating from licensees, one example of which prohibits licensees and their agents from making political donations.

Colorado's Limited Gaming Act and Gaming Regulations control similar conflicts of interest situations. For instance, licensees and their agents are prohibited from giving anything of value to Colorado Limited Gaming Control Commission members and their close relatives or from allowing Commission members and their close relatives from having interests in their casino license. Furthermore, licensees and their agents are prohibited from allowing Commission employees to participate in any gaming authorized by the state and operated by the licensee.

The rationale for these policies is compelling: control employee behavior to both bolster regulatory compliance and limit possible violations that could otherwise result in severe financial penalties and subject the company to critical licensing issues, while assuring corporate resources are not squandered through employee self-dealing. Therefore, to adequately educate and yield beneficial results, these written policies should not only set forth the objectives of the policy but also the reasons for it.

- Improperly divulging or using confidential information such as plans, operating or financial data, or computer programs; and
- Indirect conflicts of interest such as transactions involving a spouse, children, other close relatives (dependent or independent), or a business associate.

Because conflicts of interest arise as a matter of course, a company should adopt a compliance plan with internal controls to identify and report conflicts. This should include procedures enabling employees to report these conflicts and a subsequent review process to determine whether the conflict requires intervention or can exist without detriment to the company. Adherence to such a plan enables a company to ensure regulatory compliance while providing employees with knowledge their relationships do not conflict with their duties to the company.

Special circumstances

Compliance plans can also address recurring issues or special circumstances that impact a particular property or a particular market. For example, illegal drug sales in casino entertainment venues have made significant news in Las Vegas beginning in 2009. Las Vegas as a whole has seen a revenue shift from casino gaming to nongaming sources, where almost two-thirds of visitor spending is on rooms, entertainment, food, drinks, and retail sales.[19] Significant revenue is derived from nightclubs. A trade magazine reported that seven of the ten top-earning nightlife venues in the United States were located in Las Vegas.[20] Venues, like nightclubs featuring electronic music can also attract illegal drug use.[21] When the clubs are on casinos' premises, gaming regulators may have concerns over the public's perception of the ability to properly regulate the casino environment to meet policy goals.

In a letter dated April 9, 2009, the Gaming Control Board noted "it is the Nevada gaming licensees' responsibility to ensure operations conducted within the boundaries of their property are run in accordance with all laws and regulations and in a manner that does not reflect badly on the State of Nevada or its gaming industry."[22] By July 2009, the message was brought home when Planet Hollywood, a Nevada casino was fined $500,000 for failing to prevent illegal activities, principally the sale and use

---

[19] Cy Ryan, *Strip Casinos Continue to See Revenue Shift Toward Nongaming Sources*, L.V. SUN, Nov. 10, 2012, http://www.lasvegassun.com/news/2012/nov/10/gaming-trend-continues/; Charles Higgins, *Sixty-two Percent of Vegas Strip Casino Revenues Come from Nongaming Sources*, L. V. EXAMINER, Nov. 17, 2012, http://www.examiner.com/article/sixty-two-percent-of-vegas-strip-casino-revenues-come-from-nongaming-sources.

[20] Andrea Domanick, *Party Capital: Seven of 10 Top-Grossing U.S. Nightclubs are in Las Vegas*, L.V. SUN, Feb. 21, 2013, http://www.lasvegassun.com/vegasdeluxe/2013/feb/21/las-vegas-strip-nightclubs-top-revenue-list-top-10/.

[21] Brenda A. Miller et al., *Assessment of Club Patrons' Alcohol and Drug Use: The Use of Biological Markers*, 45 AM. J. PREVENTIVE MED. 637 (2013).

[22] Industry Letter, Gaming Control Board, April 9, 2009.

of illegal drugs, at a nightclub leased to a third party.[23] Other fines followed including $500,000 for the Hard Rock Hotel & Casino's Body English and Vanity nightclubs, where casino hosts and security guards offered drugs to undercover law enforcement, and a $1 million fine for the Palms where undercover agents allegedly bought drugs from nightclub employees.

Casinos can police nightclubs operated within their casinos by installing surveillance cameras in and around the club, using casino security in the clubs, and creating and enforcing contractual provisions against the nightclub owners requiring training and implementation of a strict anti-drug policy.

The casino's compliance plan can also help police the venues. This can be accomplished through several means. The compliance committee can collect data from many sources. All reported or observed issues at the club may be reported to the compliance committee. Procedures can be implemented for club employees or guests to report illegal drug sales or use. The compliance committee can retain private investigators to periodically visit the clubs and assess compliance through undercover operations. After collecting this information, the compliance committee can determine if a problem exists and whether to recommend any corrective action to management. If management has contractual language that requires corrective action or permits termination of a club lease based on violations of laws or regulations, then it can act on the committee's recommendations.

Methods of detections
Internal reports

Besides investigations, the company may automatically collect information on transactions or situations (such as incidents in suspicious activity reports) and internal audit reports on regulatory violations (such as the number of internal control or cash transaction reporting violations). Significant or persistent errors may present the need for additional training or other corrective measures.

Self-reporting

Due diligence on vendors and suppliers may be effective to deter many unethical or unlawful business practices because it can prevent transactions with some unethical persons. Other methods may be more effective in revealing such practices. A common method is self-reporting by corporate officers and upper management of any defined events. Effectively, the compliance plan may require these individuals have a clear and defined affirmative obligation to report unsuitable situations, whether they are personal (such as arrests) or involve business operations (such as attempted bribes). The system is designed to detect any criminal conduct by the company's employees or other agents.

---

[23] Liz Bentson, *Is the Party over for Prive?*, L.V. SUN, July 29, 2009, http://www.lasvegassun.com/news/2009/jul/29/party-over-prive/.

Whistleblower programs

Besides investigations and self-reporting, another method to collect information relevant to compliance is through whistleblower programs. These programs allow anonymous reporting of unsuitable situations observed or suspected by company employees or others. Whistleblowers may be found inside and outside the company. Insiders include employees and directors. Outsiders may be vendors, regulators, and investors. Whistleblower programs may also meet other legal mandates such as the federal sentencing guidelines that recommend companies have in place and publicize a system whereby employees and agents can report criminal conduct by others within the organization without fear of retribution.

Reported violations or outside investigations

Information received from gaming regulators or other law enforcement entities regarding operational issues or relationships may also be a source for identifying compliance risks. This could include a written notice from gaming authorities concerning alleged wrongdoing that could contravene policy goals, specific laws or regulations, or violate compliance policies.

Specific compliance with license conditions

During the licensing process, regulators may be faced with a variety of unique circumstances. In some instances, the applicant may be thinly capitalized. In those cases, regulators may place a special condition that the licensee monitor and ensure certain financial thresholds be maintained. A compliance plan can help monitor the company's financial status to ensure that these minimum thresholds are met.

GOVERNMENT APPROACHES

Two major approaches exist to implementing mandatory compliance systems for licensees. Nevada adopted a discretionary model through which the Gaming Commission mandates the adoption of a compliance committee as a condition of licensing but grants the Gaming Control Board the discretion to require what should be in the compliance plan. While the regulation provides some suggested areas the plan may cover, ultimately Board staff determines "the activities to be monitored . . . determined by the circumstances applicable to the licensee or registrant."[24] Under Nevada law, few structural requirements exist for the compliance plan other than (a) a compliance officer must be designated, (b) one member of the committee must be independent, and (c) periodic reports must be provided to the licensee's senior management.[25] Gaming companies must draft and submit their compliance plans for approval to the Corporate Securities

---

[24] NEV. GAMING REG. 5.045(6)(a).
[25] Id.

Section of the Nevada Gaming Control Board. In practice, this creates internal agency guidelines for what staff expects in a compliance plan and more flexibility in structuring the plans. This allowed MGM, as an example, to create its own compliance structure. As noted in a report prepared for the Massachusetts Gaming Commission, Nevada permits different compliance structures between casino licensees:

> MGM's compliance process has evolved, chiefly in response to weaknesses identified in practice. Before 2007, the Compliance Committee was comprised of MGM executives and a single independent member; the Company's General Counsel was a Committee member while also being charged with development responsibilities. In 2007, after the formation of the MGM Resorts International/Pansy Ho joint venture, the Plan underwent substantial revisions, chief among them a transformation of the Compliance Committee to a completely independent body consisting only of three outside members. The 2007 revisions substantially limited the ability of MGM to proceed with a proposed material relationship or transaction if the Corporate Security Department or the Compliance Officer either objected or indicated caution and the need for more information in pursuing such relationship or transaction. In such cases, the unanimous approval of the Committee is now required. If unanimous approval is not obtained, then approval of MGM's Board of Directors is required. Following the Terry Christensen matter, the Plan was again revised to include the insertion of a defined reporting and review process addressing association with individuals charged with felonies, both post-indictment and post-conviction. MGM considers the Plan to be an evolving document that is subject to review and revision as deemed necessary.

* * *

> The Plan recites that it has established a Compliance Committee to oversee procedures to enhance the likelihood that no activities of the Company or any Affiliate would impugn the reputation and integrity of the Company, any of the specific jurisdictions in which the Company maintains gaming operations or the gaming industry in general.[26]

In contrast, the New Jersey statute has greater specificity regarding the obligations of the licensee including the establishment, membership, and direct responsibilities of the compliance officer and the compliance committee.[27]

Leaving regulators discretion as to plan requirements has the advantage that the size, scope, and structure of the compliance plan can be based on the nature, size, geographic coverage, and unique issues and circumstance of each licensee. For example, casino operators and gaming device manufacturers face much different regulatory challenges. A gaming device manufacturer rarely has to concentrate on anti-money laundering but is more concerned about legal compliance in selling and shipping devices to potentially hundreds of jurisdictions.

---

[26] INVESTIGATIVE REPORT FOR THE MASSACHUSETTS GAMING COMMISSION, BLUE TARP REDEVELOPMENT, LLC, November 27, 2013 at 68-9, http://massgaming.com/wp-content/uploads/MGM-Report-REDACTED.pdf
[27] N.J.A.C. 13:69C-8.8

BASIC ASPECTS OF COMPLIANCE PLANS

Compliance requirements are not unique to the gaming industry. Sarbanes Oxley compliance has five key requirements: (1) assign responsibility for overseeing compliance to a high-level employee; (2) communicate the compliance plan standards and procedures to all employees through training or any other means; (3) institute monitoring and reporting systems to detect unauthorized conduct, enable employees to report unauthorized conduct, and report such conduct to the high-level employees overseeing compliance; (4) enforce the compliance plan; and (5) ensure internal corporate disciplinary and remedial actions for employee violations. These same basic elements should be found in gaming compliance plans.

Written Program

Where required, compliance programs must be in a written format and explain how the company will implement the plan. Most plans begin with a general statement of the corporate policy and then detail the general goals common to all plans, such as due diligence and any special circumstance to be addresses. Companies can either do the minimum required by law or use the compliance plan as a broader tool to avoid potential problems. A company commitment to compliance starts with the minimum required by law and then prioritizes further company objectives. The company may survey its current business activities and past compliance history to detect potential problem areas. Past compliance issues may require special assessment of needs to be considered in the investigation, monitoring, or reporting of company activities. For example, if the casino has a history of errors when completing credit and fill slips, a special audit and reporting system showing the percentage of errors may assist the compliance committee in recommending further actions, if necessary, to solve the problem. Often a good place to begin a needs-assessment is past regulatory audits, disciplinary proceedings, or issues that may have arisen during the course of the licensing investigation. Once the needs are identified, the company should assess its infrastructure and organization to understand current capabilities to implement a response procedure for the problem activities.

The Compliance Structure

The plan must delineate responsibilities and the operational aspects of the plan including due diligence, self-reporting, whistleblowing, and other methods of acquiring information. Ultimately, all officers, directors, and employees of a company and the regulators must be involved in the compliance process. That said, compliance typically falls on a compliance committee, a compliance officer, management, and the board of directors. The compliance plan must create and delegate authority to each group. To avoid confusion and possible duplication of efforts, the compliance plan must provide a description of duties, responsibilities, authority, and lines of reporting for the compliance officer, the compliance committee, senior management, company employees, and the board of directors. Checks and balances are preferred. For example, the compliance officer may report to management, but the compliance committee reports to the board of directors. If designed correctly, the compliance plan is a management tool with each key player serving a distinct and appropriate role. However, compliance plans may fail by not properly defining these functions and responsibilities.

Compliance Officer

Legislation may require the company to designate a compliance officer. For example, New Jersey requires

(e) The casino licensee or holding company, as applicable, shall designate an individual to serve as a compliance officer in accordance with this subchapter. The compliance officer shall be an individual who has been found qualified by the Commission under the Act.

1. The compliance officer shall report directly to the Compliance committee on matters related to this subchapter. All reports prepared by the compliance officer relating to the compliance review and reporting system shall be filed with the compliance committee.

2. The compliance officer shall have no functions which are incompatible with his or her duties and responsibilities as a compliance officer as set forth in this subchapter. Such incompatible functions shall include, without limitation, market development activities.

3. The compliance officer shall:

   i. Notify the compliance committee in writing of the following:

   (1) All efforts by the casino licensee, its holding companies, affiliates or employees in connection with the development of gaming activities in any jurisdiction not having a distinct system which regulates such activity, and the names of all individuals and business entities including, but not limited to, consultants, having any material association or proposed association with such efforts; and

   (2) All outstanding material litigation involving the casino licensee, its holding companies or affiliates or any executive employee, which is not routine business litigation such as, without limitation, negligence, workers compensation and employment claims; and

   ii. Provide the Division with notice of the information in (e)3i above at least semi-annually on or before January 1st and July 1st of each year.[28]

Usually, the compliance officer is chosen by the company president and is part of the management team. Other methods for selecting the compliance officer are available. The description of the MGM plan presented to the Massachusetts Gaming Commission provides

---

[28] N.J.A.C. 13:69C-8.8

To accomplish the goals of the plan, a Compliance Officer is selected by the Compliance Committee, a position currently occupied by Thomas A. Peterman, who holds the title of Senior Vice President and Chief Compliance Officer. Peterman is a natural person qualifier in this application. Responsibility for day-to-day administration of the Plan rests with the Compliance Officer. According to the Plan, the Compliance Committee is to be comprised of no fewer than three individuals independent of the Company, who, by virtue of their familiarity with law enforcement, regulated businesses, ethics, or gaming compliance, are sensitive to the concerns of gaming authorities and capable of determining the existence or likelihood of an unsuitable situation. One of the three members must be a person who is knowledgeable about the Nevada gaming regulatory process; alternatively, independent legal counsel may be retained. Members serve terms no longer than three years, and successive terms are permitted. The Chair is rotated annually. The Plan requires that the Audit Committee shall select one of its members to serve as an ex officio member of the Compliance Committee.[29]

In the MGM case, the compliance officer has greater independence because he is chosen by the independent members of the compliance committee. This may present issues where the independent members of the committee are independent contractors without the ability to oversee and evaluate the performance of the compliance officer. Equally problematic, given independent authority the compliance officer may modify his or her role from advising management to dictating decisions regarding transactions or reporting directly to the regulators. A compliance officer that believes he or she has the obligation to collect, judge, and report situations to regulators outside the compliance process will soon lose the faith of the company and the compliance committee. Regulators also could receive raw information without the informed review by the compliance committee whose input is vital.

Typical Compliance Plan Provision Dealing with Reporting Detail by Compliance Officer

Reports to the compliance committee and the minutes of meetings of the compliance committee shall contain that detail necessary and appropriate to permit a well-reasoned decision by the compliance committee member on each subject considered by the compliance committee. Except in circumstances indicating that reliance is unreasonable or unwarranted, independent investigation is not required with respect to information that is widely disseminated or otherwise a matter of public knowledge, and such information may be excluded as the subject of a compliance committee report unless the information relates directly to an issue to be considered by the compliance committee.

The compliance officer may also be selected by and report directly to the board of directors. This allows the officer to be both independent from management and directly accountable to the group chosen by the equity holders to lead the company.

---

[29] INVESTIGATIVE REPORT, *supra* note 26, at 69.

After selecting the compliance officer, regulators may require administrative or formal approval of the compliance officer. Some jurisdictions require the compliance officer obtain a gaming license. Here, the experience of the compliance officer may be a factor in granting the approval or license. The expectation is that compliance officer's background includes knowledge and application of the laws that govern gaming operations and an understanding of the expectation of the gaming regulators regarding the proper conduct of a gaming licensee. To be effective, the compliance officer also must be familiar with the company's corporate structure (including the functions of parent, affiliate, and subsidiary companies) and possess the administrative skills to coordinate compliance across the company departments. The compliance officer typically implements and administers the company's compliance programs and internal reporting system. The compliance officer may have multiple responsibilities, including the following:

- Conducting and coordinating mandatory background investigations, including prospective management and key employee hiring, review of suppliers and vendors, and material litigation;
- In-taking and coordinating review and investigations of business practices that may be an unsuitable method of operation, employee reported violations, criminal investigations of or involving the company or management;
- Interacting with the corporate divisions to determine situations requiring reporting under the internal reporting system and review by the compliance committee; and
- Providing the necessary reports to the compliance committee that establishes the information upon which the committee makes recommendations.

The compliance officer coordinates monitoring, testing, and reporting company compliance efforts. He collects information the compliance committee needs to make informed decisions. The compliance officer should have the ability to conduct employee training, document all compliance activities and functions, and coordinate internal investigations. Documenting all activities and preparing all reports for the compliance committee as required by the compliance plan or by law is important. He should be provided with the resources to conduct his job and to ensure interdepartmental and management cooperation exists regarding the compliance program.

Compliance Committee

Historically, compliance committees had at least three members in addition to the chief executive officer or the president, the chief financial officer, and an independent member. Laws or regulations can mandate the qualifications of compliance committee members or require regulators to approve appointments of members. Regulations typically require one member to be independent and not employed by the licensed company who can exercise independent judgment. Members should be individuals who, through their familiarity with the law and the business activities of the company, are sensitive to gaming authority concerns and can determine the existence or likelihood of an unsuitable situation that could adversely affect the reputation of the gaming company. Members are expected to be sensitive to the concerns of gaming authorities and capable of determining compliance with gaming statutes and company compliance policies. Committee members should have the cognitive ability to assess situations and proffer recommendations that meet regulatory objectives and have the least adverse impact on business operations.

Some companies, like the MGM, have broken with this model by having all independent committee members. This promotes decision-making less influenced by business considerations. While some compliance committees have gravitated toward more or all outside members for greater independence, inside members—such as corporate officers— have a better understanding of corporate structure, dynamics, and culture invaluable to the committee's work. Completely independent committees, however, may not appreciate the intricacies and institutional capabilities of the company sufficient to make recommendations that have the least adverse impact on business operations. For example, if reports indicate a property or casino group produces many errors when completing cash transaction reports, the committee may not understand the severity of the problem or the most appropriate response. Where the committee involves both the chief financial officer and an independent member, the likelihood of an effective solution is enhanced. An additional benefit to having certain management sit on the committee is it gives management a continuing stake and awareness of compliance obligations and specific issues facing the company.

Typical Compliance Plan Provision Dealing with Composition of Compliance Committee

The compliance committee shall be comprised of at least three (3) members and not more than five (5) members. The membership of the compliance committee shall include the Chief Financial Officer and the President of the company. The membership of the compliance committee also shall include at least one person experienced in the gaming regulatory process who is familiar with the laws governing gaming activities in the jurisdictions where the company conducts business and who is a person independent of the company. The members of the compliance committee should be individuals who, by virtue of their familiarity with law enforcement, regulated businesses, the business activities of the company or gaming control, are sensitive to the concerns of the gaming authorities and capable of determining the existence or likelihood of an unsuitable situation.

To function well, a gaming compliance plan requires structure and a clear delegation of authority to the compliance committee. Structure and delegation can be statutorily mandated, as in New Jersey:

(f) The casino licensee or holding company, as applicable, shall establish a compliance committee consisting of at least three members, each qualified by the Commission under the Act. At least one member thereof shall not hold any employee, officer, executive or operational position with the casino licensee, its holding companies or affiliates, and one or more members of the committee shall be familiar with the New Jersey gaming regulatory process.

1.   The compliance committee shall meet at least once a calendar quarter.

2.   The compliance committee shall not report to any employee, officer, executive or operational person or entity within the casino licensee, its holding companies or affiliates, and shall file its reports and recommendations with the company's board of directors and the general counsel.

3.   The written agenda for each meeting of the compliance committee shall be promptly filed with the Division, and the minutes for each such meeting, whether or not ratified or adopted, shall be filed with the Division in accordance with N.J.A.C. 13:69C-8.1.

4.   Any casino licensee or holding company thereof which has a compliance committee constituted in accordance with gaming laws shall be entitled to utilize that committee for purposes of this subchapter, provided that the charter for such committee expressly imposes responsibility for compliance with this subchapter and the committee and its members meet the requirements of this subchapter.[30]

The compliance plan should delineate how compliance committee members are appointed and how changes may be made. In many jurisdictions, the company may be required to report or obtain approval for changes in compliance committee membership. If so, this should be reflected in the compliance plan. Compliance committee members are usually appointed by and serve at the will and pleasure of the company's board of directors, subject to any required gaming authority approvals. Compliance committee composition, including the number of members, qualifications, and division of duties between internal staff members (officers and employees) and outside members, should, consistent with the law, be described within the compliance plan.

Typical Compliance Plan Provision Dealing with Minutes
of the Compliance Committee

The compliance committee shall prepare and maintain minutes recording the business considered and decisions rendered by the compliance committee at each meeting. Copies of the minutes of the committee meetings shall be provided within ten (10) days after ratification by the compliance committee to the Regulatory Committee, all compliance committee members, and concurrently to the Chairman of the Gaming Control Board, along with copies of all documents, reports and exhibits submitted to the compliance committee by

---

[30] N.J.A.C. 13:69C-8.8

the compliance officer. The minutes shall identify all matters considered by the compliance committee and shall contain the amount of detail appropriate to permit a well-reasoned decision by the compliance committee members. In those matters in which the compliance committee takes no action, the minutes shall reflect the reasons why no action was deemed appropriate.

The compliance committee, acting through and with the assistance of the compliance officer, should be empowered to investigate, evaluate, report facts, and recommend possible responses or initiatives for senior management's consideration, including disciplinary action related to misconduct by company employees or agents.

Compliance committee efforts should be focused on reviewing information and reports developed by the compliance officer and determining a proper course of action. They should be afforded the cooperation of company personnel, including security, surveillance, and internal audit to accomplish company compliance objectives. The compliance committee should also have the authority and financial resources to hire outside expertise if necessary to conduct a complete and comprehensive investigation.

The committee must meet periodically as required by law or its plan to review reports and other information provided by the compliance officer. The committee is expected to review and act on source materials such as original complaints; police reports; employment applications; background investigations; detailed minutes of past committee hearings, including compliance-related decisions like why an investigation was terminated; and the report of the compliance officer. The committee should make specific, clear recommendations to management concerning how to handle particular issues—from hiring and firing decisions to the acceptability of entering certain gaming markets. The committee will prepare and submit to the board of directors, or an equivalent body designed by the compliance plan, a periodic report summarizing its activities and decisions.

Once the compliance committee has all the information it believes is necessary, it must act on the information. With the MGM plan, this was described as follows:

> The Compliance Plan requires the Committee to review information brought to the Committee's attention or discovered by the Compliance Officer, and to formulate recommendations to management regarding a course of action to appropriately address the specific event, transaction, circumstance or situation. Per language in the Plan, "The Committee is not intended to displace the Board or the Company's Executive Officers with decision-making authority but is intended to serve as an advisory body to better ensure that the Company's goals of avoiding Unsuitable Situations and relationships with Unsuitable Persons remains satisfied."[31]

All compliance committee activities, except for certain investigative actions, should be transparent to company directors, top management, and

---

[31] INVESTIGATIVE REPORT, *supra* note 26, at 70.

gaming regulators. This can be accomplished by disciplined record keeping and reporting. The compliance plan should prescribe record production, maintenance, and retention requirements. This should include original complaints, police reports, employment applications, and records of investigations and other materials. Finally, the compliance committee should maintain detailed minutes of meetings and decisions.

Board of Directors

The board of directors is typically responsible for appointing the compliance officer and supervising the compliance committee. All reports generated by the committee through the compliance officer should be submitted to the board of directors for approval by the chairman of the board. The board should have discretion to change, modify, or update the plan as it deems necessary. The board bears primary responsibility for the compliance plans and the actions taken by management. The compliance plan will remain in effect until the compliance plan is rescinded by the board.

Senior Management

Senior management bears the overall responsibility to oversee compliance functions. The program should create and delegate clear authority for each group within the compliance structure, including the compliance officer, the compliance committee, employees, and the board of directors. Senior management should have the primary responsibility to implement the compliance plan. Senior management must properly fund the program, provide leadership to implement and integrate the compliance plan, and be willing to evenly enforce the plan across all levels of the company.

Company Employees

This reporting system's success also depends on coordination and cooperation between company departments, such as corporate planning, development, acquisition, human resources, procurement, finance, legal, internal audit, and sales, whose business functions may establish compliance review issues. Employees should be reminded to remain vigilant and report violations. Gaming businesses should therefore include compliance behavior as an element of employee evaluation for promotion, bonus, and salary decisions. Conversely, bad compliance behavior should result, when warranted, in disciplinary action.

Specific Goals

Once a gaming company knows what it wants to accomplish, it must determine how to accomplish it. In most circumstances, implementation can be tailored to the unique circumstance of each corporation. For example, the challenges facing a company with casinos in multiple jurisdictions, particularly in under-regulated jurisdictions, differs from a single casino company in an established, highly regulated market. Likewise, some companies may already have sophisticated compliance structures for other purposes, such as to prevent foreign corrupt practices that can be leveraged for gaming compliance purposes.

Communicating

Compliance should be implemented through employee training, program monitoring, and enforcement. Communication methods may differ depending on the size of the company. Compliance should not be seen as a "one size fits all" concept. Smaller companies may communicate requirements informally, while larger companies may need to formalize the method of communication. Methods of communication may include new employee orientation, employee newsletters, pay stubs, messages, posters, public recognition for ethical behavior, and ethical review in performance evaluations and promotion considerations. Companies should also provide employees with publications that explain practically what is required for compliance; the publications should include the name and contact information for the compliance officer.

Compliance training should be tailored to each employment role within the company and the separate duties and responsibilities those roles entail. For instance, cashiers need instruction on certain subjects, casino hosts on others, while accounting reviewers need a different type of training. Compliance should not be seen as a onetime event. A constant review of industry practices may assist in augmenting an existing compliance plan. Training courses should occur on a periodic basis to refresh the understanding of compliance fundamentals, introduce changes in gaming laws and regulations, and address the compliance plan's impact and any emerging issues resulting from it.

Recordkeeping and Reporting

The plan must establish record keeping and reporting obligations.

Discipline for Non-Compliance

The plan should mandate adherence and detail consequences for non-compliance. Violation penalties may include prosecution, demotion, and summary termination of employment. Communication, education, and training are a key component of success. As with any critical company objective, gaming management and officials should lead by example by fully complying with the policies to set the proper tone at the top.

ROLE OF GAMING AUTHORITIES

Gaming authorities play a key role in a compliance program's success. The compliance officer, compliance committee, board of directors, and senior management should establish a working relationship with gaming authorities, which those authorities should promote. In Nevada, for example, gaming regulators set minimum standards for, review, and approve the program (after endorsement by the board of directors). They then assist the company with the program's implementation. All copies of minutes, reports, exhibits, and documents relating to items considered by the compliance committee must be provided to gaming regulators for review and recommendation.

Gaming regulators should periodically audit their licensed companies' compliance programs. This periodic review should ensure the compliance program continues to remain effective after implementation. The review will consider several questions, including the following: Are the compliance controls working? Do the compliance controls adequately detect the regulatory violations and crimes to which the company is vulnerable? Has the compliance program been modified or adapted to consider any known criminal or regulatory violations? Should the compliance program be reviewed or updated to reflect any new company or industry threats or to reflect best practices within the industry?

Gaming regulators may ask to review (1) the compliance committee's proceedings and recommendations, (2) the compliance officer's due diligence when collecting and presenting information, (3) the sufficiency of the company's consideration of compliance issues and response to committee recommendations, and (4) the accurate reporting of situations to the authorities. This inquiry is conducted within the confines of the delegated authority in the compliance plan.

Compliance audits should occur periodically. However, a company's conduct may subject it to an audit. For example, if a company commits an egregious compliance violation, regulators will direct their attention to that company's compliance plan and its adherence to it.

The review will consider several regulatory objectives, evaluating whether

- the compliance controls are working;
- the compliance controls adequately detect the regulatory violations and crimes to which the company is vulnerable;
- the compliance program has been modified or adapted to consider any known criminal or regulatory violations; and
- the compliance program should be reviewed or updated to reflect any new company or industry threats or to reflect best practices within the industry.

For the company, the audit often begins with the receipt of a document request letter detailing an initial list of documents the regulators want to review. Typically, this letter includes a request to access the compliance plan and procedures, compliance committee minutes and due diligence checks. This is only the first request for the production of documentation, as additional requests are likely throughout the audit. These requests can be broad and directed at documents in any area of the gaming company's operations. Compliance plans customarily have policies that all personnel must respond to requests by the gaming authorities for access to books, documents, records, and papers relating to the company's business activities. Willful failure to comply with the directive is usually grounds for summary termination of employment.

An audit includes crosschecks to assure that procedurally all aspects of the plan are being adhered to. This can include crosschecking the company's compliance plan with written records and reports to ensure the company is conducting appropriate safeguards and vetting. For example, each plan typically mandates activities requiring due diligence reviews of those vendors, suppliers, lobbyists, key employees, and consultants whose compensation or other payments are material because they exceed designated financial thresholds. A crucial question in the audit, therefore, becomes whether the activities that trigger these requirements are being caught and the company has conducted the appropriate due diligence in response.

The audit also evaluates compliance committee minutes to assess the adequacy and effectiveness of compliance controls and to determine if the committee is following the company's instituted policies and procedures. Regulators should consider whether the committee is being notified of the issues and whether, when notified, it diligently and knowledgeably discusses the presented issues. As important as recognizing what activities trigger due diligence requirements is the commitment of the company to actively engage in meaningful discussions about those activities.

Common shortcomings include the following:

- Not undertaking proper and complete due diligence of individuals, vendors, and suppliers as required by their compliance plans.
- Exceeding a monetary thresholds without reporting or due diligence because of a failure of the segregated divisions to inform each other of the requirements or the company's internal failure to demonstrate to the divisions the importance of such compliance
- Failure to keep adequate records (e.g., records do not go far enough back, cannot be located, or do not exist).
- Failure of segregated company divisions to understand when compliance actions should be taken and then failure to forward compliance issues to the compliance officer or compliance committee.
- Failure to provide the compliance committee with all information necessary to properly perform compliance duties.

While these shortfalls are not minor, compliance staff typically can remedy many through awareness and education. Serious violations may result in disciplinary action. Less serious violations may warrant plan modification, retraining, or renewed commitments.

9

Bank Secrecy Act Requirements

Leonard C. Senia

INTRODUCTION

The casino industry does not exist in a vacuum. Instead, casinos exist within a broader economic and social environment. Governments may regulate this broader environment to achieve specific policy goals only peripherally related to the casino industry that may significantly impact casino regulation. One example of this is Federal programs aimed at achieving the policy goals of preventing criminals from using the financial system to launder the proceeds from illegal activities. Money laundering is the process by which criminals disguise the illegal source of their funds to make it appear as if they were derived from legitimate sources. While exact numbers are impossible, according to an October 25, 2011United Nations Office on Drugs and Crime (UNODC) report, "[t]he resulting best estimate of the amounts available for money-laundering would be within the IMF's original 'consensus range,' equivalent to some 2.7% of global GDP (2.1-4 percent) or US$1.6 trillion in 2009."[1] On a broader policy basis, anti-money laundering laws and regulations assist law enforcement in controlling criminal activities by requiring financial institutions and other regulated entities to prevent, detect, and report money laundering activities.

"Established as the informational center of mass for [Bank Secrecy Act (BSA)] data, the Financial Crimes Enforcement Network (FinCEN) is where the financial industry, law enforcement, and regulators meet with a common purpose to protect the integrity of the financial system."[2] FinCEN provides educational and technical support to the law enforcement, intelli-

[1] *See* UNITED NATIONS OFFICE ON DRUGS AND CRIME, ESTIMATING ILLICIT FINANCIAL FLOWS RESULTING FROM DRUG TRAFFICKING AND OTHER TRANSNATIONAL ORGANIZED CRIMES, 5 (October 2011), http://www.unodc.org/documents/data-and-analysis/Studies/Illicit_financial_flows_2011_web.pdf.

[2] FINANCIAL CRIMES ENFORCEMENT NETWORK, ANNUAL REPORT i. (2010), http://www.fincen.gov/news_room/rp/files/annual_report_fy2010.pdf.

gence, and regulatory examination communities to enhance their existing knowledge of financial industry operations and systems.

Casinos and card clubs, like other various sectors of the financial industry, are subject to BSA reporting, recordkeeping, and anti-money laundering (AML) compliance program requirements. They are required to maintain or file certain reports or records determined to be highly useful in criminal, tax, or regulatory investigations or proceedings or in the conduct of intelligence or counter-intelligence activities (including analysis), to protect against terrorism, and to prevent, deter, and detect money laundering. Casinos and card clubs also collect and retain other types of information pursuant to their own best practices and risk management processes.[3]

Casino and card club operations and services are ever-changing and fluid, based on steady enhancements to gaming operations and computerized systems. Over the years, financial services provided by casinos and card clubs have proven to be similar to services provided by depository institutions and certain non-bank financial institutions. Such services include providing customer deposit or credit accounts, transmitting and receiving funds transfers directly from other financial institutions, check cashing, currency exchanging, and certain prepaid services. Although these financial services are necessary for casino and card club operations to function efficiently and effectively, criminals have misused them to move and launder illicit proceeds.

From a functional perspective, a casino is a gambling establishment that offers customers the opportunity to bet or wager on a series of house-banked games[4] and electronic gaming devices. A casino earns revenues by banking games of chance[5] (e.g., baccarat, bingo, craps, roulette, keno, and slot machines[6] in which customers bet against the casino) as well as non-banked card games (e.g., poker), although this varies based on the types of governmental licenses. Additionally, casinos offer games of chance and skill such as blackjack and sometimes off-track pari-mutuel race betting. Although all casinos offer gambling, the types of specific gambling

---

[3] Language expanding the scope of the Bank Secrecy Act to intelligence or counter-intelligence activities to protect against international terrorism was added by section 358 of the Uniting and Strengthening America by Providing Appropriate Tools Required to Intercept and Obstruct Terrorism ("USA PATRIOT") Act of 2001, Pub. L. 107-56 (October 26, 2001).

[4] There is no IRS-imposed income tax for certain gambling winnings on the proceeds from a wager placed by nonresident alien individuals in any of the following games: blackjack, baccarat, craps, roulette, or big-6 wheel. *See* 26 U.S.C. § 871(j).

[5] A game of chance is one in which bets are accepted on the outcome of various games or contests.

[6] Slot machines and video lottery terminals are the most popular type of gambling offered by casinos in the United States. Industry sources indicate these electronic gaming devices constitute an estimated range of 65–75 percent of an average casino's annual income. For casinos that do not offer table games, electronic gaming devices can be even a higher percentage of an average casino's annual income. *See* Marc Cooper, *Sit and Spin: How Slot Machines Give Gamblers the Business*, ATLANTIC, Dec. 1, 2005, http://www.theatlantic.com/doc/200512/slot-machines.

offered vary by establishment (e.g., table games, card games,[7] slot machines or video lottery terminals, and pari-mutuel wagering—horse and/or greyhound). Larger casinos offer VIP rooms (also known as salons), which are private gambling rooms designed for "high rollers"[8] and "whales"[9] who want to gamble away from a casino's public gambling areas. Also, in Nevada, a casino is permitted to offer sports betting.

Typically, a casino is more than just a place where people go to gamble. Casinos vary in size and complexity, from a one-room riverboat[10] that offers a limited number of table games and services to a large, corporate-owned mega-facility with hundreds of table games, thousands of slot machines, and a wide variety of services. It addition to the gambling casino itself, larger casino properties also include hotel rooms, restaurants, lounges, bars, theaters, luxurious showrooms, exclusive retail stores, health clubs, and convention facilities.

In contrast, a card club (also known as a card room) is a gaming establishment that offers non-house banked card games to customers. It earns revenue by receiving a fee from customers (e.g., when they deal each hand, rent a seat at a table, and/or take a fixed percentage of each "pot"). It operates like a traditional casino except that it does not offer house-banked games such as baccarat, craps, roulette, and slot machines. Instead, it provides tables, dealers, chips, and other services to customers who gamble against one another in non-house banked games such as poker and games commonly referred to as "California Games."

Casinos and card clubs are regulated in differing degrees by various State, local, and tribal governmental agencies, and Federally for compliance with anti-money laundering and terrorist financing requirements. United States casinos are subject to a decentralized regulatory structure and are primarily regulated by the States and by tribal regulatory authorities. Card clubs are subject to a decentralized regulatory structure and primarily are regulated by the States and, in some cases, by local governments or tribal regulatory authorities.

---

[7] Many casinos have a separate room that offers card games where players compete against each other rather than the house. This room is typically called a "poker room" or sometimes a "cardroom."

[8] A high roller is a customer who consistently makes wagers of $100–$500 or more per bet (depending on the relative size of the casino). A casino considers such a rated individual a high limit/high stakes player or a premium player. Such a customer qualifies for a casino's premium complimentary services, including a hotel room. High rollers are also known as "Big Spenders," though some mid-size casinos also use the term "VIP" (i.e., Very Important Player).

[9] A "whale" is a casino customer who makes very large wagers. Unlike a high roller (i.e., a big spender) who wagers consistently $100.00–$500 or more per bet, depending on the relative size of a casino, a whale will consistently wager thousands, if not tens of thousands of dollars per bet. Whales are also known as VIPs.

[10] While six states have authorized this type of casino to limit the areas where casinos can be constructed, in general, a riverboat casino operates in a similar manner as a land-based casino.

FinCEN is responsible for measuring and enforcing compliance with the BSA, but it does not examine financial institutions for compliance. The Internal Revenue Service (IRS) examines duly-licensed or authorized casinos and card clubs to determine compliance with the BSA's suspicious activity and currency transaction reporting, identification, recordkeeping, record retention, and compliance program requirements. The IRS's Small Business/Self Employed (SB/SE) Division conducts BSA compliance examinations during which an audit team will examine recordkeeping and suspicious activity and currency transaction reporting procedures, compliance program policies, internal controls, internal or external audit reports, training, management supervision, and use of computer systems and programs to aid in assuring compliance with the BSA. The IRS's Criminal Investigation Division (IRS-CI) covers legal and illegal source tax crimes and narcotics-related financial crimes. In addition to its core mission of investigating criminal violations of the Internal Revenue Code and the BSA, IRS-CI lends its financial investigative expertise to money laundering, narcotics, and counterterrorism investigations conducted in conjunction with other law enforcement agencies at the Federal, State, and local levels.

This chapter is divided into 23 sections: (I) Introduction, (II) Historical Perspective, (III) Casinos and Card Clubs Financial Services, (IV) Casino-Specific BSA Requirements Summary, (V) Casino Anti-Money Laundering Compliance Programs, (VI) File Currency Transaction Reports, (VII) File Suspicious Activity Reports, (VIII) Suspicious Activity Report (SAR) - Supporting Documentation, (IX) SAR - Non-Disclosure Provisions, (X) File Report of International Transportation of Currency and Monetary Instruments, (XI) File Report of Foreign Bank and Financial Accounts, (XII) Casino-Specific Recordkeeping Requirements, (XIII) Other BSA Filing Requirements, (XIV) Other BSA Recordkeeping Requirements, (XV) Geographic Targeting Order Provisions, (XVI) USA PATRIOT Act of 2001 - Information Sharing - Sections 314(a) and (b), (XVII) FinCEN Casino Guidance and Administrative Rulings, (XVIII) IRS Casino Civil Examinations, (XIX) Areas Of Concern With Casino Recordkeeping, (XX) Chip, Token, and Ticket Redemptions by Unknown Customers, (XXI) Federal Civil and Criminal Penalties, (XXII) Other Currency Transaction Form, and (XXIII) Conclusion.

The first three sections provide an introduction, a historical perspective, and a summary of financial services; the next 13 sections pertain to current BSA requirements applicable to casinos, followed by seven sections covering FinCEN casino regulatory guidance and rulings, IRS casino examinations, concerns with casino recordkeeping, chip, token, and ticket redemptions by unknown customers, civil and criminal penalties, other currency transaction form, and a conclusion. Additionally, these sections summarize 53 specific BSA requirements, along with providing their citations, to which casinos and card clubs are subject. Also, this chapter provides 41 references/Web links to specific documents or Web sites so that readers can do further research if they wish.

HISTORICAL PERSPECTIVE

During the last three decades, the belief that casinos were vulnerable to money laundering was not confined to officials within the US Department of the Treasury. In 1984, two days of Congressional hearings before the Subcommittee on Crime concerning casinos included testimony ". . . that drug traffickers and other criminals have been utilizing gambling casinos in Nevada and in New Jersey with increased frequency to conceal their cash operations."[11]

In October 1984, the President's Commission on Organized Crime, comprised of distinguished individuals from academia, the judiciary, law enforcement, and Congress, recommended to then-President Ronald Reagan that casinos be included as financial institutions subject to the reporting and recordkeeping requirements of the BSA. A reason for their recommendations included "[t]o discourage the use of casinos by criminals as conduits for money laundering. . . ."[12] The Commission's report provided a casino example to help support its case. During 1983, a drug trafficker in Baltimore, Maryland, was convicted of Federal narcotics violations after using an Atlantic City, New Jersey, casino to launder his drug profits. Specifically, the report stated

> [a]ccording to Congressional testimony . . . , the trafficker and his associates took $118,000 in drug profits to the casino, opened an account, and stayed several days but did not gamble. They left the casino with checks, made payable to third parties, which they deposited in a securities firm. The money was later withdrawn and used to refurbish a number of legitimate businesses owned by the trafficker and his associates. On still other occasions, the trafficker deposited cash in the casino in small denominations, gambled, and left with most of the cash in $100 bills. . . . [During] search warrants . . . executed . . . , $300,000 in $100 bills were found with the casino's wrappers still on the money. Law enforcement authorities have estimated that the trafficker and his group laundered approximately $500,000 in heroin proceeds through the casino in question.[13]

In May 1985, after the Congressional hearings and President's Commission Report, the Treasury Department made casinos subject to the BSA noting

> [i]n recent years Treasury has found that an increasing number of persons are using gambling casinos for money laundering and tax evasion purpos-

---

[11] *See* U.S. HOUSE OF REPRESENTATIVES, HEARINGS BEFORE THE SUBCOMMITTEE ON CRIME OF THE COMMITTEE ON THE JUDICIARY, 98TH CONGRESS, 2ND SESSION ON USE OF CASINOS TO LAUNDER PROCEEDS OF DRUG TRAFFICKING AND ORGANIZED CRIME 53 (1984), http://babel.hathitrust.org/cgi/pt?id=pst.000014761539;view=1up;seq=57.

[12] *See* PRESIDENT'S COMM'N ON ORGANIZED CRIME, INTERIM REPORT TO THE PRESIDENT AND THE ATTORNEY GENERAL, THE CASH CONNECTION: ORGANIZED CRIME, FINANCIAL INSTITUTIONS, AND MONEY LAUNDERING 58 (1984), https://www.ncjrs.gov/pdffiles1/Digitization/166517NCJRS.pdf.

[13] *Id.* at 11.

es. In a number of instances, narcotics traffickers have used gambling casinos as substitutes for other financial institutions in order to avoid the reporting and recordkeeping requirements of the Bank Secrecy Act.[14]

The 1985 casino rulemaking was based on the authority of the Secretary of the Treasury to designate as financial institutions for BSA purposes: (i) businesses that engage in activities that are "similar to, related to, or a substitute for" the activities of covered businesses listed in the BSA; as well as (ii) other businesses "whose cash transactions have a high degree of usefulness in criminal, tax, or regulatory matters."[15]

In 1987, Treasury issued broad based regulations which, among other things, clarified that financial institutions including casinos, must report multiple, same day currency transactions of which they are aware that total more than $10,000.[16] In 1989, Treasury issued a specially tailored rule for casinos that required the retention of player rating records and certain computer information.[17]

The Annunzio-Wylie Anti-Money Laundering Act of 1992 made many changes to the BSA.[18] One change authorized the Treasury Department to develop rules requiring financial institutions, including casinos, to develop and implement anti-money laundering compliance programs.

In March 1993, the Treasury Department issued a final rule that required casinos to develop and implement AML compliance programs containing the following elements: (i) a system of internal controls; (ii) internal and/or external independent testing; (iii) training of casino personnel; (iv) an individual or individuals designated to assure compliance; (v) procedures for using all available information to determine and verify, when required, the name, address, social security number or taxpayer identification number, and other identifying information for a person; and (vi) use of automated systems and programs to assure compliance.[19] Casinos were the first nonbank financial institutions required to develop an anti-money laundering program.

In recognition of the importance of the application of the BSA to the gaming industry, the Money Laundering Suppression Act of 1994 added casinos and other gaming establishments to the list of financial institutions specified in the BSA. Specifically, the definition of casino includes a casino, gambling casino, or gaming establishment that is duly licensed or

---

[14] *See* Financial Crimes Enforcement Network; Proposed Amendments to the Bank Secrecy Act Regulations Regarding Tribal Gaming, 50 Fed. Reg. 5065, 5065 (Feb. 6, 1985) (to be codified at 31 C.F.R. pt. 103).

[15] *See* 31 U.S.C. § 5312(a)(2)(Y) and (Z).

[16] *See* 52 Fed. Reg. 11443 (Apr. 8, 1987).

[17] *See* 54 Fed. Reg. 1165 - 1167 (Jan. 12, 1989).

[18] *See* Annunzio-Wylie Anti-Money Laundering Act of 1992, Pub. L. No. 102-550, 106 Stat. 3672 (1992).

[19] *See* Amendments to the Bank Secrecy Act; Regulations Regarding Reporting and Recordkeeping Requirements by Casinos, 58 Fed. Reg. 13538, 13550 (Mar. 12, 1993) (to be codified at 31 C.F.R. pt. 103).

authorized to do business as such, and has gross annual gaming revenue in excess of $1 million, or that is an Indian gaming operations conducted under or pursuant to the Indian Gaming Regulatory Act other than a Class I gaming operation.[20]

In December 1994, FinCEN put into effect the original casino AML provisions adopted in March 1993 stating

> [t]he casino industry is vulnerable . . . because casinos engage in a fast-paced cash intensive business and can provide their customers with financial services nearly identical to those generally provided by depository institutions. Federal law enforcement organizations have documented the use of casinos as surrogate "banks" for individuals.[21]

Few can dispute, casinos are "fast-paced, cash intensive business[es]"[22] and provide many of the same financial services offered by depository institutions. Because of this, casinos were the first non-bank financial institutions required to develop and implement AML compliance programs.

In December 1994, FinCEN made other significant amendments to its casino regulations, which (i) clarified the knowledge requirement for filing a currency transaction report on multiple transactions to include when employees obtain such knowledge through examining manual or automated records; (ii) required obtaining and verifying customer identification when depositing funds or opening an account or establishing a line of credit; and (iii) required records of customer transactions of more than $3,000 involving traveler's checks or other negotiable instruments.[23]

---

[20] *See* Section 409 of the Money Laundering Suppression Act of 1994, Title IV of the Riegle Community Development and Regulatory Improvement Act of 1994, Pub. L. 103-325 (Sept. 23, 1994). The current statutory specification reads as follows:

(2) financial institution means . . . (X) a casino, gambling casino, or gaming establishment with an annual gaming revenue of more than $1,000,000 which--

    i.   is licensed as a casino, gambling casino, or gaming establishment under the laws of any State or any political subdivision of any State; or

    ii.   is an Indian gaming operation conducted under or pursuant to the Indian Gaming Regulatory Act other than an operation which is limited to class I gaming (as defined in section 4(6) of such Act). . . .

31 U.S.C. § 5312(a)(2)(X).

[21] *See* Amendments to the Bank Secrecy Act Regulations Regarding Reporting and Recordkeeping Requirements by Casinos, 59 Fed. Reg. 61660 (Dec. 1, 1994) (to be codified at 31 C.F.R. pt. 103) http://www.fincen.gov/statutes_regs/frn/pdf/frn19941201.pdf (modifying and putting into final effect the rule originally published at 58 Fed. Reg. 13538 (March 12, 1993)).

[22] *See* FINANCIAL CRIMES ENFORCEMENT NETWORK, SUSPICIOUS ACTIVITY REPORTING IN THE GAMING INDUSTRY: BASED ON FILINGS OF SUSPICIOUS ACTIVITY REPORTS BY CASINOS AND CARD CLUBS FROM JANUARY 1, 2004, THROUGH JUNE 30, 2011 at 2 (March 2012).

2 (2012), http://www.fincen.gov/news_room/rp/files/GamingIndustry508March2012.pdf.

[23] *See* Amendments to the Bank Secrecy Act Regulations Regarding Reporting and Recordkeeping Requirements by Casinos, *supra* note 18.

In a January 1996 report, which supported the Treasury Department's position regarding casinos' vulnerability to money laundering, the US General Accounting Office (GAO) stated "[t]he proliferation of casinos, together with the rapid growth of the amounts wagered, may make these operations highly vulnerable to money laundering."[24] The GAO report continued by stating "[w]ith this much cash changing hands, casinos may be particularly vulnerable to money laundering in the form of money from illegal activities being placed into legal gaming transactions."[25]

In February 1996, FinCEN expanded its AML programs when it issued BSA regulations applicable to gambling casinos authorized to do business under the Indian Gaming Regulatory Act (IGRA),[26] effective as of August 1, 1996.[27] FinCEN's final rule provided the justification when it stated that stated

> [t]he potential risk of money laundering in casinos on Indian lands is not any less than the risk of money laundering in state-licensed casinos. Thus, this final rule makes casinos operating on Indian lands subject to the full set of reporting and recordkeeping provisions, and anti-money laundering safeguards, of the Bank Secrecy Act to which other casinos in the United States are subject.[28]

In January 1998, FinCEN issued BSA regulations that expanded its jurisdiction again to include the class of gaming establishments known as "card clubs." Typically, card clubs offer facilities for gaming by customers who bet against one another, rather than against the establishment. FinCEN's final rule provided the rationale for including card clubs within the BSA. FinCEN's final rule provided the justification when it stated that

> . . . card clubs are at least as vulnerable as other gaming establishments to use by money launderers and those seeking to commit tax evasion or other financial crimes, both because of their size and because those institutions lack many of the controls found at casinos. Given their growth, their prevalence in the nation's most populous state [i.e., California], and their potential for expansion, there is no basis for distinguishing card clubs from casinos for purposes of the Bank Secrecy Act.[29]

As the BSA regulations imposed on depository institutions became stricter, on May 18, 1998, FinCEN proposed amending BSA regulations

---

[24] *See* U.S. Gen. Accounting Office, Report to the Ranking Minority Member, Permanent Subcommittee on Investigations, Committee on Governmental Affairs, U.S. Senate: Money Laundering: Rapid Growth of Casinos Makes Them Vulnerable, 2 (1996), *available at* http://www.gao.gov/assets/230/222140.pdf.

[25] *Id.* at 29.

[26] *See* 25 U.S.C. §§ 2701–2721.

[27] *See* Amendments to the Bank Secrecy Act; Regulations Regarding Tribal Gaming, 61 Fed. Reg. 7054 (Feb. 23, 1996) (to be codified at 31 C.F.R. pt. 103), http://www.fincen.gov/statutes_regs/frn/pdf/frn19960223.pdf.

[28] *Id.*

[29] *See* Amendments to the Bank Secrecy Act Regulations Regarding Reporting and Recordkeeping by Card Clubs, 63 Fed. Reg. 1919, 1921 (Jan. 13, 1998) (to be codified at 103 C.F.R. pt. 103), http://www.fincen.gov/statutes_regs/frn/pdf/frn19980113.pdf.

to require casinos report suspicious transactions. As justification for this proposal, FinCEN stated

> [a]s government and industry programs have made it more difficult for customers to launder money at banks . . . , the interest of money launderers in moving funds into the financial system through non-bank financial services providers has increased. Gaming establishments have not been spared from this trend.[30]

The successes of depository institutions' AML efforts forced criminals to find other avenues to introduce their ill-gotten gains into the US economy.

In September 2002, FinCEN issued a final rule that required casinos and card clubs to report suspicious transactions relevant to a possible violation of law or regulation involving or aggregating $5,000. FinCEN stated

> [w]ith this rule, the Department of the Treasury extends to casinos . . . the suspicious transaction reporting regime to which the nation's banks . . . are already subject. . . . These actions reflect the continuing determination not only that casinos are vulnerable to manipulation by money launderers and tax evaders but, more generally, that gaming establishments provide their customers with a financial product—gaming—and as a corollary offer a broad array of financial services, such as customer deposit or credit accounts, facilities for transmitting and receiving funds transfers directly from other institutions, and check cashing and currency exchange services, that are similar to those offered by depository institutions. . . .[31]

These casino final rules clarified that the Federal government has concluded casinos in many ways are similar to depository institutions (especially regarding casino cage operations).[32] The 2002 casino final rule amended one AML requirement and added other compliance program requirements, namely (i) enhanced internal and/or external independent testing by centering it on the scope and frequency that is commensurate with money laundering and terrorist financing risks, and products and

---

[30] *See* Proposed Amendment to the Bank Secrecy Act Regulations; Requirement That Casinos and Card Clubs Report Suspicious Transactions, 63 Fed. Reg. 27230, 27333 (May 18, 1998) (to be codified at 31 C.F.R. pt. 103), http://www.gpo.gov/fdsys/pkg/FR-1998-05-18/html/98-13053.htm.

[31] *See* Amendment to the Bank Secrecy Act Regulations - Requirement That Casinos and Card Clubs Report Suspicious Transactions; Final Rule and Notice, 67 Fed. Reg. 60722, 60723 (Sept. 26, 2002) (to be codified at 31 C.F.R. pt. 103.), http://www.gpo.gov/fdsys/pkg/FR-2002-09-26/html/02-24147.htm. Please note this casino final rule put into effect another key Annunzio-Wylie provision, which was to require any financial institution or any financial institution employee to report suspicious transactions relevant to any possible violation of law or regulation.

[32] The casino cage is a secure work area within a casino that houses cashiers, a storage area for the gaming facility's bankroll (i.e., the inventory of cash, chips, tokens, and credit), and a place where banking services are provided to customers and other casino banks. In this capacity, it is the casino's in-house bank where customers can open deposit and credit accounts, deposit and withdraw funds, receive and pay off credit instruments (e.g., markers), purchase and cash checks, wire transfer funds, purchase and redeem (or exchange) gaming chips, tokens and tickets, and exchange currency.

services provided, and (ii) requiring procedures for using all available information to determine the occurrence of any transactions or patterns of transactions required to be reported as suspicious.

In 2007, likely because of heightened scrutiny on terrorists and how their operations are financed, FinCEN expanded its interpretation in another casino final rule by stating ". . . casinos offer services similar to and may serve as substitutes for services ordinarily provided by depository institutions and certain non-bank financial institutions. As such, casinos are vulnerable to abuse by money launderers, terrorist financiers, and tax evaders."[33]

Unquestionably, many understood the Federal government believed casinos to be vulnerable to money launderers and tax evaders, but in 2007, everyone was put on notice that the government considered casinos to be vulnerable now to "terrorist financiers" as well.

Finally, in March 2012, FinCEN published a report entitled "Suspicious Activity Reporting in the Gaming Industry" stating once again that

> [c]asinos and card clubs are vulnerable to money laundering and other financial crimes because of the nature of their operations. These gaming institutions are fast-paced, cash-intensive businesses that often provide a broad array of financial products and services, some of which are similar to those provided by depository institutions. . . . Moreover, gaming institutions serve a diverse and transient customer base about which they may have relatively little knowledge.[34]

Thus for almost thirty years, and as recently as two years ago, the Treasury Department and FinCEN espoused that casinos and card clubs are vulnerable to money laundering and are similar in the type of financial services that depository institutions provide when compared to casinos and card clubs. Apparently questioning the alleged similarity between banks and casinos, a January 25, 2013, report in *The Wall Street Journal* quotes a senior Las Vegas casino executive as stating "[i]f someone goes into a department store and buys a $20,000 purse, does anybody ask where [the money] comes from?"[35] Given the cash-intensive nature of the casino business and the many financial services that casinos provide, perhaps a casino is more like a bank than a department store. Reasonable minds can differ on this point.

---

[33] *See* Amendments to Bank Secrecy Regarding Casino Recordkeeping and Reporting Requirements, 72 Fed. Reg. 35008, 35009 (June 26, 2007) (to be codified at 31 C.F.R. pt. 103), http://www.gpo.gov/fdsys/pkg/FR-2007-06-26/html/E7-12332.htm.

[34] *See* FINANCIAL CRIMES ENFORCEMENT NETWORK, SUSPICIOUS ACTIVITY REPORTING IN THE GAMING INDUSTRY: BASED ON FILINGS OF SUSPICIOUS ACTIVITY REPORTS BY CASINOS AND CARD CLUBS FROM JANUARY 1, 2004, THROUGH JUNE 30, 2011 at 2 (March 2012). http://www.fincen.gov/news_room/rp/files/GamingIndustry508March2012.pdf.

[35] *See* Kate O'Keeffe & Alexandra Berzon, *Sands Bolsters Safeguards Against Money-Laundering*, WALL ST. J., Jan. 24, 2013, http://online.wsj.com/news/articles/SB100014241278873 23854904578261363501815322.

Casinos and Card Clubs Financial Services

In the United States, casinos and card clubs with gross annual gaming revenue over $1 million are considered financial institutions under the BSA. Casinos and card clubs are subject to the BSA because they are cash-intensive businesses that also offer a broad array of financial services. These services include providing customer deposit[36] or credit accounts, transmitting and receiving funds, transfers directly from other financial institutions, check cashing, currency exchanging,[37] account access cards, and certain stored value services. Consequently, casinos offer services that are similar to and may serve as substitutes for services ordinarily provided by depository institutions and certain non-bank financial institutions. As such, casinos are vulnerable to abuse by money launderers, terrorist financiers, and tax evaders. Additionally, criminals that gamble at casinos can blend in with legitimate customers so that when illegal proceeds are bet and the bets are won, such funds have an appearance of legitimacy because they are gambling winnings.[38]

Casinos also organize and facilitate various types of gambling activities, table game, and slot club rewards programs for customers, and host entertainment events. Also, casinos offer financial services that have no counterpart in the traditional financial services industry. Perhaps the most unique commodities casinos provide to customers are the sale of chips and slot machine or video lottery terminal tokens (a casino chip is a bearer gaming instrument and title (i.e., ownership) thereto passes upon delivery). These services are provided to enable the customer to engage in ongoing wagering activities on the casino floor. Ultimately, the casino's primary business after selling or exchanging these chips and tokens is to win them back from their customers. Casinos do this by offering customers a series of games of chance and skill where bets are accepted on the outcome of various games or contests. Also, some casinos sell wagering tickets to customers for race and sports book events, which are bearer gaming instruments that are converted to wagering credits.

---

[36] Please note that for card clubs, deposit accounts are known as "player's accounts."

[37] *See Statement of William J. Fox, Director, Financial Crimes Enforcement Network, United States Department of The Treasury, Before the Senate Committee on Banking, Housing, and Urban Affairs,* Fin. Crimes Enforcement Network (Sept. 28, 2004), http://www.fincen. gov/news_room/testimony/html/20040928a.html.

[38] Casinos are considered by their nature to be cash intensive businesses as the majority of their transactions are cash-based. In March 2009, the Asia Pacific Group (APG) and Financial Action Task Force (FATF) published a report titled "Vulnerabilities of the Casino and Gaming Sector" that showed that there is significant global casino activity that is cash intensive, competitive in its growth, and vulnerable to criminal exploitation. In fact, the APG/FATF report states on page 20 that "[c]riminal influence and exploitation of casinos appears to be both for possible money laundering, but also for recreation and in some cases enhancing their criminal endeavours outside the casino. Casinos have been noted as a place where criminals and organised crime figures like to socialise and particularly like to spend and launder their criminal proceeds." Financial Action Task Force, Vulnerabilities of Casinos and Gaming Sector (2009),

Mostly, casinos earn revenue offering house-banked games and electronic gaming devices. Card clubs offer non-house banked card games to customers and earn revenue by receiving a fee from customers (e.g., when they deal each hand, rent a seat at a table, and/or take a fixed percentage of each "pot").

Card clubs offer the same types of financial services to their customers as do traditional casinos (e.g., deposit accounts, credit accounts, check cashing accounts, money transfers, and currency exchange services). As with casinos, card clubs maintain cages where cashiers conduct financial transactions using a drawer that operates on an imprest basis or inventory. While the differences between casinos and card room cages are notable, the operational differences at the gaming floor are numerous and significant. Since these differences fall outside the purpose of this chapter, they will not be discussed further.

Additionally, many casinos know a great deal about their customers from information routinely obtained through deposit, credit, check cashing, and player rating accounts. These accounts generally require casinos to obtain basic identification information about accountholders and to inquire into the kinds of wagering activities in which the customer is likely to engage. For example, deposit and credit accounts track customer deposits and casino credit extensions. Casino customers can draw down[39] on either account to fund their gaming, purchase chips, and conduct other activities on casino properties. The "player rating" account tracks gaming activity and is designed to award complimentary perquisites to higher volume players and serve as a marketing tool to identify frequent customers and encourage continued patronage. Thus, casinos are interested in knowing their customers both to market to them for future visits and to provide complimentary items[40] commensurate with their policies based on the level of customer play. Also, in certain instances, casinos use credit bureaus to verify information obtained from customers. All of these sources of information can help a casino better understand its customer base.

---

http://www.fatfgafi.org/media/fatf/documents/reports/Vulnerabilities%20of%20Casinos%20and%20Gaming%20Sector.pdf.

[39] This is a withdrawal of previously deposited funds. Typically, the term "draw down" is used to reflect a customer's withdrawal of funds in the form of chips while at a gaming table (i.e., a front money withdrawal).

[40] Complimentary items (so-called "comps") typically are goods or services that a casino gives to a customer at reduced or no cost based on significant play and can include beverages, coupons or other representations of money for use in wagering including free casino play, beverage, food, entertainment, merchandise, lodging, show ticket and ticket to special events, transportation (e.g., airplane tickets, car rentals), or cash back on points earned. Some casinos allow customers to apply their complimentary points to outstanding casino markers.

CASINO-SPECIFIC BSA REQUIREMENTS SUMMARY

Casinos and card clubs must meet the following specific BSA casino requirements: (i) a written compliance program;[41] (ii) reporting each transaction in currency, involving either "cash in" or "cash out," of more than $10,000 in a gaming day of which a casino has obtained knowledge;[42] (iii) reporting suspicious activity when a casino knows, suspects, or has reason to suspect that the transaction or pattern of transactions is both suspicious and involve $5,000 or more;[43] and (iv) detailed recordkeeping on casinos.[44] Generally, card clubs are subject to the same rules as casinos, unless a different treatment is explicitly stated in 31 C.F.R. Parts 1010–1029.[45] The types of gaming establishments covered by FinCEN requirements are

- State/territory-licensed casinos (both land-based and riverboat),
- Tribally regulated casinos,
- State/local-licensed card clubs, and
- Tribal card clubs.

Casinos and card clubs must comply with other BSA obligations required of all financial institutions. What follows are the specific BSA casino requirements and other general BSA obligations required of all financial institutions, including casinos and card clubs.

CASINO ANTI-MONEY LAUNDERING (AML) COMPLIANCE PROGRAMS

Section 352 of the USA PATRIOT Act of 2001[46] requires financial institutions to establish AML programs.[47] Specific compliance program requirements are found in 31 C.F.R. § 1021.210(b). These requirements apply to both casinos and card clubs. Each program must be commensurate with the risks posed by the products and financial services provided by the casino and card club. An effective program is developed, implemented, maintained, and reasonably designed to prevent the casino and card club from being used to facilitate money laundering or terrorist financing. Therefore, the BSA regulations that apply to casinos are to a degree risk-based.

At a minimum, each AML compliance program must be in writing and must have the following:

- System of internal controls (e.g., policies, procedures, and internal

---

[41] *See* 31 C.F.R. § 1021.210(a)–(b).
[42] *See* 31 C.F.R. §§ 1021.311(a)–(c) and 1021.313.
[43] *See* 31 C.F.R. § 1021.320.
[44] *See* 31 C.F.R. § 1021.410.
[45] *See* 31 C.F.R. § 1021.410(b)(11).
[46] The USA PATRIOT Act stands for Uniting and Strengthening America by Providing Appropriate Tools Required to Intercept and Obstruct Terrorism Act of 2001.
[47] *See* 31 U.S.C. § 5318(h).

controls) reasonably designed to assure ongoing compliance with the BSA;[48]

- Internal and/or external independent testing for compliance with a scope and frequency commensurate with the risks of
  ◦ money laundering and terrorist financing and,
  ◦ products and services provided;[49]
- Training personnel in BSA requirements (e.g., providing education and/or training for appropriate personnel);[50]
- Designation of an individual or individuals (e.g., a compliance officer) responsible for day-to-day compliance with the BSA and the compliance program;[51]
- Procedures for using all available information to determine and verify, when required, the name, address, social security number or taxpayer identification number, and other identifying information for a person;[52]
- Procedures for using all available information to determine the occurrence of any transactions or patterns of transactions required to be reported as suspicious;[53]
- Procedures for using all available information to determine whether a record required under the BSA must be made and retained,[54] and
- For casinos and card clubs with automated data processing systems, use of the programs to aid in assuring compliance.[55]

FILE CURRENCY TRANSACTION REPORTS

A casino or card club must file a report of each currency transaction involving "cash in" or "cash out" of more than $10,000 conducted by, through, or to the casino or card club on any one gaming day by or for the same customer. Therefore, a FinCEN Form 112, Currency Transaction Report (CTR),[56] must be filed when a transaction meets all of the following conditions:

- In currency,
- Greater than $10,000 in either "cash in" or "cash out,"
- By, or for, the same customer, and
- Occurs on one gaming day.[57]

---

[48] *See* 31 C.F.R. § 1021.210(b)(2)(i).
[49] *See* 31 C.F.R. § 1021.210(b)(2)(ii).
[50] *See* 31 C.F.R. § 1021.210(b)(2)(iii).
[51] *See* 31 C.F.R. § 1021.210(b)(2)(iv).
[52] *See* 31 C.F.R. § 1021.210(b)(2)(v)(A).
[53] *See* 31 C.F.R. § 1021.210(b)(2)(v)(B).
[54] *See* 31 C.F.R. § 1021.210(b)(2)(v)(C).
[55] *See* 31 C.F.R. § 1021.210(b)(2)(vi).
[56] *See* FinCEN Form 112, available at: http://sdtmut.fincen.treas.gov/news/Currency-TransactionReport.pdf.
[57] The BSA definition of "gaming day" is left to the discretion of a casino or card club and

Also, casinos must aggregate transactions in currency (that is, treat the transactions as a single transaction) if the casino knows the transactions are conducted by or for the same person and result in cash in or cash out of more than $10,000 during any gaming day.[58] The rule requiring casinos to report transactions in currency also lists examples of transactions in currency involving cash in and cash out.[59]

If a currency transaction exceeds $10,000, a casino files a CTR that has three parts.

- Part I, Person Involved in Transaction, is for the identification of the customer (i.e., name, permanent address, and social security number (or other required identification)) and verification of identity.
- Part II, Amount and Type of Transaction(s), is for the identification of the type of transaction(s) and amount(s) and the date of currency transaction(s).[60]
- Part III, Financial Institution Where Transaction(s) Takes Place, is for the identification of a casino or card club and the preparer.

"Cash in" and "cash out" transactions for the same customer in the same gaming day are to be aggregated separately and must not be offset against one another. However, if there are both "cash in" and "cash out" transactions that individually exceed $10,000 for the same customer in a gaming day, a casino should enter the amounts separately on a single FinCEN CTR.

Typically, a casino or card club will stipulate that pit personnel and cage cashiers must prepare an internal CTR worksheet when they know a currency transaction, or a series of currency transactions when aggregated, exceeds the $10,000 threshold in a gaming day in the same directional flow. These employees are instructed to obtain the required identification information from a customer. Typically, these internal worksheets are forwarded daily to accounting to prepare a CTR. A casino or card club also must file a CTR for reportable multiple transactions identified through the aggregation of daily records.

A casino or card club is not required to file a CTR for a transaction between itself and a commercial bank.[61] Also, casinos and card clubs can exempt some transactions from filing a CTR.[62]

---

is defined as its normal business day. If a casino or card club offers 24-hour gaming, the term "gaming day" means that 24-hour period by which a casino or card club keeps its books and records for business, accounting, and tax purposes. A casino or card club must have only one gaming day, which is common to all its gambling operating divisions or departments. *See* 31 C.F.R. § 1021.100(d).

[58] *See* 31 C.F.R. § 1021.313.

[59] *See* 31 C.F.R. § 1021.311(a)–(b). The list is not exhaustive. The terms cash in and cash out refer to direction—currency to the casino in the case of cash in transactions, and currency from the casino in the case of cash out transactions.

[60] The dollar amounts as "cash in" or "cash out" are totaled and if foreign currency is involved it is specified.

[61] *See* 31 C.F.R. § 1010.315.

[62] *See* 31 C.F.R. § 1021.311(c).

FILE SUSPICIOUS ACTIVITY REPORTS

A casino or card club must file a FinCEN Form 111, Suspicious Activity Report (SAR)[63] when it knows, suspects, or has reason to suspect that the transaction or pattern of transactions is *both*

- Suspicious, *and*
- Involves $5,000 or more (in the single event or when aggregated) in funds or other assets.[64]

A transaction or pattern of transactions (conducted or attempted) is suspicious if it

- **Involves funds derived from illegal activity,** or is intended or conducted to hide or disguise funds or assets derived from illegal activity or to disguise the ownership, nature, source, location, or control of the funds;[65]
- **Designed to evade BSA reporting or recordkeeping requirements,** whether through structuring or other means;[66]
- **Has no business or apparent lawful purpose,** or is not the sort in which the customer would normally be expected to engage, and the casino or card club knows of no reasonable explanation for the transaction after examining all available facts, including the background and possible purpose of the transaction;[67] or
- **Involves use of the casino or card club to facilitate criminal activity.**[68] (Emphasis added.)

A casino or card club must file a mandatory SAR no later than 30 calendar days after initial detection of facts that may constitute a basis for filing a SAR. If no suspect is identified on the date of detection, a casino or card club may delay filing a SAR for an additional 30 calendar days to identify a suspect.[69] FinCEN requires casinos and card clubs to e-file FinCEN Form 111 (SAR) through the BSA's E-filing System.

Once a casino or card club files a SAR and a customer's suspicious activity continues over a period of time, it should report continuing suspicious activity with a report being filed at least every 90 days. This will notify law enforcement of the continuing nature of the activity and provide a reminder to the organization that it must continue to review the suspicious activity to determine if other actions may be appropriate.[70]

---

[63] *See* FinCEN Form 111, available at http://sdtmut.fincen.treas.gov/docs/SuspiciousActivityReport.pdf. Please note that this FinCEN reporting form is an electronic format only, and a login and password are required to access the system.

[64] Other casino or card club assets would be chips, tickets, tokens, or other gaming instruments since these are not listed as legal tender of the United States in 31 U.S.C. § 5103.

[65] *See* 31 C.F.R. § 1021.320(a)(2)(i).

[66] *See* 31 C.F.R. § 1021.320(a)(2)(ii).

[67] *See* 31 C.F.R. § 1021.320(a)(2)(iii).

[68] *See* 31 C.F.R. § 1021.320(a)(2)(iv).

[69] *See* 31 C.F.R. § 1021.320(b)(3).

[70] *See* Bank Secrecy Act Advisory Group, *Issues & Guidance*, 1 SAR ACTIVITY REV.: TRENDS, TIPS, & ISSUES 27, 27–28 (Oct. 2000).

A casino or card club is not required to report on a SAR form a robbery or burglary it reports to an appropriate law enforcement authority.[71] However, a casino or card club may voluntarily file SARs for suspicious activity below the reporting threshold if it believes it is relevant to the possible violation of any law or regulation.[72]

In situations requiring immediate attention (i.e., when a transaction is ongoing, like a money laundering scheme, or when a delay would hinder the government's ability to take action), a casino or card club is required to immediately notify by telephone an appropriate law enforcement authority besides filing a SAR with FinCEN. If the casino or card club has reason to suspect a customer's transaction may be linked to terrorist activity against the United States, the casino or card club should immediately call the Financial Institutions Hotline at 1-800-566-3974.[73]

An element of a BSA compliance or anti-money laundering program is to have procedures for using all available information to determine the occurrence of any transactions or patterns of transactions that are required to be reported as suspicious, including for automated systems.[74] Also, the extent and specific parameters under which a casino or card club must monitor customer accounts[75] and transactions for suspicious activity must be commensurate with the risks posed by the type of products and services it offers, the locations it serves, and the nature of its customers.

SAR — SUPPORTING DOCUMENTATION

SAR supporting documentation or business record equivalents must be maintained with a copy of the filed SAR for five years from the filing date. Such supporting documentation "is deemed filed with the SAR." Upon request, the casino or card club must provide all supporting documentation to FinCEN and any other appropriate law enforcement or supervisory agencies (including the IRS in its capacity as BSA examination authority).[76] Such documentation can include canceled checks, confessions, credit bureau reports, credit slips/vouchers, deposit/withdrawal slips, multiple transaction

---

[71] *See* 31 C.F.R. § 1021.320(c).

[72] 31 U.S.C. § 5318(g)(3) provides protection to any financial institution and its directors, officers, employees and agents from civil liability for all reports of suspicious transactions made to appropriate authorities (including supporting documentation) regardless of whether such reports are filed pursuant to this report's instructions or are filed on a voluntary basis to disclose any possible violation of law or regulation.

[73] *See* 31 C.F.R. § 1021.320(b)(3).

[74] *See* 31 C.F.R. § 1021.210(a), (b)(2)(i), (b)(2)(v)(B), (b)(2)(vi).

[75] Types of casino accounts that would be subject to suspicious activity reporting include deposit (i.e., safekeeping, front money, wagering, or access), credit, check cashing, player rating or tracking, and slot club accounts.

[76] *See* 31 C.F.R. § 1021.320(d).

logs, player rating records,[77] slot club player records,[78] identification credentials, spreadsheets, photographs, surveillance audio and/or video recording media, and surveillance logs. For casinos with hotels and absent any information other than a customer's name, other supporting documentation can include credit/debit cards, guest folios, and safety deposit box registrations.[79] All supporting documentation referenced above must be provided to appropriate authorities upon request. Supporting documentation should not be filed with a SAR and is not entered into the FinCEN database.

When requested to provide supporting documentation, a casino or card club should take special care to verify that a requestor of information is a representative of FinCEN or an appropriate law enforcement or casino regulatory agency. A casino or card club should incorporate procedures for such verification into its BSA anti-money laundering compliance program. These procedures may include, for example, independent employment verification with the requestor's field office or face-to-face review of the requestor's credentials.[80]

SAR — Non-Disclosure Provisions

No financial institution or director, officer, employee, or agent of any financial institution who reports a suspicious transaction, may notify any person involved in the transaction that the transaction has been reported, including any person identified in the SAR.[81] A filed SAR and information that would reveal the existence of a SAR (including any document, memorandum, record, log, or work papers that references a SAR) must be treated as confidential.[82]

---

[77] Player rating records reflect all cash activity recorded on them (regardless of the amount) that have occurred on the gaming floor. Examples of cash activity that occurs on the gaming floor that are <u>not</u> recorded follow: (i) cash below a casino's established player rating dollar recording threshold (typically small buys-ins), and (ii) cash activity of a player who asks not to be rated (which a casino may rate still anonymously if buys-ins are high enough in hope that a customer will change his/her mind about being rated). Nonetheless, once rating begins, casinos record on player rating records all cash buy-ins regardless of the dollar amount. A customer's computerized player rating account record typically contains the customer's name, permanent address, date of birth, and sometimes other identification information as well as a player's table gaming activity.

[78] Slot club accounts, like player rating accounts, track gaming activity and are designed to award complimentary perquisites to higher volume players and to serve as marketing tools to identify frequent customers and to encourage continued patronage. Casinos utilize internal controls to help to ensure accountability for customers using slot club account cards. A customer's computerized slot account record typically contains the customer's name, permanent address, date of birth, social security number, and additional identification information, as well as a player's slot gaming activity.

[79] Some casino-hotels offer safety-deposit boxes, which are available to hotel guests.

[80] *See* FIN-2007-G003 *Suspicious Activity Report Supporting Documentation*, (June 13, 2007), http://www.fincen.gov/statutes_regs/guidance/html/Supporting_Documentation_Guidance.html.

[81] *See* 31 C.F.R. § 1021.320(e)(1).

[82] *See* 31 U.S.C. § 5318(g)(2); 31 C.F.R. § 1021.320(e).

FILE REPORT OF INTERNATIONAL TRANSPORTATION OF CURRENCY AND MONETARY INSTRUMENTS

FinCEN Form 105, Report of International Transportation of Currency and Monetary Instruments (CMIR),[83] must be filed by individuals or businesses who transport, mail, or ship, or cause the transportation, mailing, or shipping of $10,000 or more in currency and/or other monetary instruments at one time into or out of the United States or its territorial jurisdiction.[84] The term monetary instrument includes (i) coin or currency of the United States or of any other country; (ii) traveler's checks in any form; (iii) negotiable instruments (including checks, promissory notes, and money orders) in bearer form, endorsed without restriction, made out to a fictitious payee, or otherwise in such form that title thereto passes upon delivery; (iv) incomplete instruments (including checks, promissory notes, and money orders) signed but on which the name of the payee has been omitted; and (v) securities or stock in bearer form or otherwise in such form that title passes upon delivery.[85]

FILE REPORT OF FOREIGN BANK AND FINANCIAL ACCOUNTS

Treasury Form TD F 90-22.1, Report of Foreign Bank and Financial Accounts (FBAR), is required to be filed by each US person who has a financial interest in, signature authority, or other authority over one or more financial accounts (including bank, securities, or other types of financial accounts) in a foreign country, if the aggregate value of these financial accounts exceeds $10,000 during a calendar year.[86] Such financial relationship must be reported each calendar year by June 30 of the succeeding year. When a casino has established financial accounts in a foreign country that exceed $10,000, it would be required to file this form annually. Casinos and card clubs must file Treasury Form TD F 90-22.1 when they conduct such transactions.

CASINO-SPECIFIC RECORDKEEPING REQUIREMENTS[87]

Specifically, the regulations implementing the BSA require a casino or card club to maintain and retain the following source records (either the originals, microfilm versions, or other copies or reproductions of the documents) that relate to its operation:

- Records of each deposit of funds, account opened, or line of credit extended, including a customer's identification and the verification

---

[83] *See FinCEN Form 105: Report of International Transportation of Currency or Monetary Instruments*, http://www.fincen.gov/forms/files/fin105_cmir.pdf.

[84] *See* 31 C.F.R. § 1010.340.

[85] *See* Form 105, *supra* note 83, at 2.

[86] *See* 31 C.F.R. § 1010.350.

[87] *See* FIN-2007-G005, *Frequently Asked Questions – Casino Recordkeeping, Reporting and Compliance Program Requirements Question and Answer*, at 16 (Nov. 14, 2007).

of that identification and similar information for other persons having a financial interest in the account, regardless of residency;[88]

- Records of each receipt showing transactions for or through each customer's deposit or credit account, including a customer's identification and the verification of that identification, regardless of residency;[89]

- Records of each bookkeeping entry comprising a debit or credit to a deposit account or credit account;[90]

- Statements, ledger cards, or other records of each deposit or credit account, showing each transaction in or regarding the deposit or credit account;[91]

- Records of each extension of credit over $2,500, including a customer's identification and the verification of that identification, regardless of residency;[92]

- Records of each advice, request, or instruction regarding a transaction of any monetary value involving persons, accounts, or places outside the United States, including a customer's identification, regardless of residency;[93]

- Records prepared or received in the ordinary course of business that would be needed to reconstruct a customer's deposit or credit account;[94]

- Records required by other governmental agencies, e.g., Federal, State, local, or tribal;[95]

- Records prepared or used to monitor a customer's gaming activity, e.g., player rating records, multiple transaction logs;[96]

- A list of transactions involving various types of instruments, cashed or disbursed, in face amounts of $3,000 or more, regardless of whether currency is involved, including customer's name and address;[97] and

- A copy of the written compliance program required by 31 C.F.R. § 1021.210(b).[98]

Also, card clubs are required to maintain and retain the original or a microfilm copy of records of all currency transactions by customers, in-

---

[88] *See* 31 C.F.R. § 1021.410(a).
[89] *See* 31 C.F.R. § 1021.410(b)(1).
[90] *See* 31 C.F.R. § 1021.410(b)(2).
[91] *See* 31 C.F.R. § 1021.410(b)(3).
[92] *See* 31 C.F.R. § 1021.410(b)(4).
[93] *See* 31 C.F.R. § 1021.410(b)(5).
[94] *See* 31 C.F.R. § 1021.410(b)(6).
[95] *See* 31 C.F.R. § 1021.410(b)(7).
[96] *See* 31 C.F.R. § 1021.410(b)(8).
[97] *See* 31 C.F.R. § 1021.410(b)(9). The negotiable instrument list includes personal checks (excluding markers); business checks (including casino checks); official bank checks; cashier's checks; third-party checks; promissory notes; traveler's checks; or money orders with a face value of $3,000 or more.
[98] *See* 31 C.F.R. § 1021.410(b)(10).

cluding without limitation, records in currency transaction logs and multiple currency transaction logs.[99] BSA regulations stipulate for card clubs a requirement to maintain multiple transaction logs (MTLs).

A casino or card club that inputs, stores, or retains, in whole or in part, for any period of time, any record required to be maintained by 31 C.F.R. §§ 1010.410 or 1021.410(a) and (b) on computer disk, tape, or other machine-readable media must retain the records in such media. Also, a casino or card club must maintain the indexes, books, file descriptions, and programs that would enable a person readily to access and review these computer records.[100] These computerized records, source documentation, and related programs must be retained for five years.[101] However, FinCEN does not require computerized records be stored in online memory and on a computer past their normal business use; either will suffice.[102] Records must in all events be filed or stored to be accessible within a reasonable period of time.[103]

OTHER BSA FILING REQUIREMENTS

Besides rules specific to casinos, reporting, recordkeeping, and other requirements under the BSA apply to all financial institutions, including casinos and card clubs, such as

- Filing of complete currency transaction reports within 15 days;[104]
- Identifying persons involved in currency transactions;[105]
- Prohibiting any person from evading the requirement to report currency transactions or FinCEN recordkeeping requirements, from causing or attempting to cause a casino not to file a currency transaction report, to file filing a currency transaction report with material misstatements or omissions, to maintain FinCEN required records, or to maintain those records in a form that is incomplete or inaccurate;[106]
- Reports of the transportation of currency or monetary instruments into or out of the United States;[107]
- Reports of foreign financial accounts;[108] and

---

[99] *See* 31 C.F.R. § 1021.410(b)(11).

[100] *See* 31 C.F.R. § 1021.410(c).

[101] *See* 31 C.F.R. § 1010.430(d).

[102] For example, for casinos that maintain computerized records, such as daily player rating records, marker issued records, and cage voucher records for each customer deposit, deposit withdrawal, and marker redemption, they may store such information online in computer memory or in off-line storage media, such as magnetic tape, magnetic disk, magnetic diskette, or CD-ROM disk.

[103] *See* 31 C.F.R. § 1010.430(d).

[104] *See* 31 C.F.R. § 1010.306(b)(2).

[105] *See* 31 C.F.R. § 1010.312.

[106] *See* 31 U.S.C. § 5324; 31 C.F.R. § 1010.314.

[107] *See* 31 C.F.R. § 1010.340.

[108] *See* 31 C.F.R. § 1010.350.

- Whenever an amount is stated in dollars in 31 C.F.R. Parts 1010–1029, it is deemed to also mean the equivalent amount in any foreign currency.[109]

The BSA implementing regulations require retention for five years[110] of the source records (either the originals, microfilm versions, or other copies or reproductions of the documents) of all records required to be retained by 31 C.F.R. Parts 1010–1029. These records must be filed or stored to be accessible within a reasonable period of time.

OTHER BSA RECORDKEEPING REQUIREMENTS

Section 31 C.F.R. § 1010.410 lists certain records that must be made and retained by *all* financial institutions including casinos and card clubs. These records include the original, microfilm, or other copy or reproduction of each of the following:

- Records by persons having financial interests in foreign financial accounts; [111]
- A record of each extension of credit of more than $10,000, except for those secured by real property, including the person's name and address;[112]
- A record of each transaction involving the transfer of more than $10,000 in funds to or from a person, account, or place outside the United States;[113]
- A record of each transaction involving more than $10,000 with another financial institution or person inside or outside the United States intended to result in transferring the funds to a person, account, or place outside the United States;[114]
- A record of each funds transmission over $3,000 requiring the identity verification and the recording, retrievability, and reporting of information to other financial institutions in the payment chain, regardless of the method of payment;[115] and
- The nature of records and retention period for records.[116]

Rules implementing the BSA also include certain recordkeeping requirements for casinos or card clubs. These are set forth in 31 C.F.R. § 1021.410. Where the dollar threshold differs between the two provisions, a casino or card club must keep records based on the lower threshold.

31 C.F.R. § 1021.410(b)(4) requires casinos and card clubs to maintain and retain a record of each extension of credit over $2,500, including a cus-

---

[109] *See* 31 C.F.R. § 1010.980.
[110] *See* 31 C.F.R. § 1010.430(d).
[111] *See* 31 C.F.R. § 1010.420.
[112] *See* 31 C.F.R. § 1010.410(a).
[113] *See* 31 C.F.R. § 1010.410(b).
[114] *See* 31 C.F.R. § 1010.410(c).
[115] *See* 31 C.F.R. § 1010.410(e)–(f).
[116] *See* 31 C.F.R. § 1010.430.

tomer's identification and the verification of that identification (regardless of residency),[117] although the requirement regarding extensions of credit in 31 C.F.R. § 1010.410(a) is tied to a threshold of more than $10,000. Therefore, when a casino or card club complies with 31 C.F.R. § 1021.410(b)(4), it has satisfied the requirement for 31 C.F.R. § 1010.410(a) for maintaining records over $10,000.

As a corollary, 31 C.F.R. § 1021.410(b)(5) requires casinos and card clubs to maintain and retain a record of each advice, request, or instruction regarding a transaction involving persons, accounts or places outside the United States, including customer identification (regardless of residency), without a monetary threshold,[118] although the requirement regarding "domestic" and cross-border wire transfers in 31 C.F.R. § 1010.410(f) for non-bank financial institutions is tied to a threshold of $3,000 or more. Therefore, when a casino or card club complies with 31 C.F.R. § 1021.410(b)(5), it has satisfied the requirement for 31 C.F.R. § 1010.410(f) for maintaining records over $3,000 for cross-border wire transfers.

GEOGRAPHIC TARGETING ORDER PROVISIONS

The Secretary of the Treasury can issue a Geographic Targeting Order (GTO) requiring any domestic financial institution subject to the BSA and operating within an US geographic area to report on currency transactions greater than a specified dollar value in the order. GTOs only last for a limited period of time. Originally each order lasted 60 days. However, the USA PATRIOT Act of 2001 lengthened the effective period of such orders from 60 days to 180 days.[119]

A GTO allows the Treasury Department, either on its own initiative or on request from an appropriate Federal or State law enforcement agency, to require a financial institution or group of financial institutions in a geographic area to comply with special reporting or recordkeeping requirements in the order. The special requirements are put in place upon a finding there is a reason to believe that such reporting or recordkeeping is necessary to ensure compliance with, or prevent evasions of, the BSA. Additionally, 31 U.S.C. § 5321(a)(1) authorizes civil financial penalties for willful violations of "orders issued" under the BSA, which includes geographic targeting orders issued under 31 U.S.C. § 5326.

USA PATRIOT ACT OF 2001 - INFORMATION SHARING, SECTIONS 314(A) AND (B)

---

[117] See 31 C.F.R. § 1021.410(b)(4).
[118] See 31 C.F.R. § 1021.410(b)(5).
[119] See 31 U.S.C. § 5326(a) (formerly Title III, Section 353(d) USA PATRIOT Act); 31 C.F.R. § 1010.370. 31 U.S.C. § 5326(d) permits geographical targeting orders to be effective up to 180 days, versus 31 C.F.R. 1010.370(d), which permits only 60 days.

Federal law enforcement may request, via FinCEN, information from financial institutions (under 31 U.S.C. § 5312(a)(2)) to support terrorist and money laundering investigations, which are known as Section "314(a) requests." Casinos and card clubs must comply with 314(a) requests.[120]

Section 314(b) provides a safe harbor from liability for a financial institution or associations of financial institutions that voluntarily share information with other financial institutions to identify and, where appropriate, report money laundering or terrorist financing activity (if required notification, verification, and information security is in place).[121] Section 314(b) promotes voluntary information-sharing among financial institutions. Casinos may share information under 314(b).

FINCEN CASINO GUIDANCE AND ADMINISTRATIVE RULINGS

FinCEN has issued many casino guidance documents and several casino administrative rulings that provide useful insight into FinCEN's view of the application of the BSA and its implementing regulations when the guidance was issued. For example, in December 2003, FinCEN issued "Suspicious Activity Reporting Guidance for Casinos," which should be used as a supplement to the original Suspicious Activity Report by Casino form instructions.[122] Also, FinCEN issued three casino administrative rulings and ten other guidance documents, listed below:

- FIN-2012-G004, *Frequently Asked Questions - Casino Recordkeeping, Reporting and Compliance Program Requirements* (August 13, 2012).[123]

- *Suspicious Activity Reporting in the Gaming Industry: January 1, 2004–June 30, 2011* (March 2012).[124]

- FIN-2010-G002, *Suggested Best Practices - Casino or Card Club Risk-Based Compliance Indicators* (June 30, 2010).[125]

---

[120] *See* 31 C.F.R. § 1010.520.

[121] *See* 31 C.F.R. § 1010.540(b)(5).

[122] *See* FinCEN, Suspicious Activity Reporting Guidance for Casinos (2003), http://www.fincen.gov/news_room/rp/files/sar_guidance_casino.pdf.

[123] *See* FIN-2012-G004, *Frequently Asked Questions: Casino Recordkeeping, Reporting, and Compliance Program Requirements* (Aug. 13, 2012), http://www.fincen.gov/statutes_regs/guidance/html/FIN-2012-G004.html.

[124] *See* FinCEN, Suspicious Activity Reporting in the Gaming Industry: Based on Filings of Suspicious Activity Reports by Casinos and Card Clubs from January 1, 2004, through June 30, 2011 (2012), http://www.fincen.gov/news_room/rp/files/GamingIndustry508March2012.pdf. A two-page press release is also available. Bill Grassano, *FinCEN Analysis Shows How Casino Reporting of Suspicious Activity Has Increased Annually Since 2004*, FinCEN (Mar. 8, 2012), http://www.fincen.gov/news_room/nr/pdf/20120309.pdf.

[125] *See* FIN-2010-G002, Casino or Card Club Risk-Based Compliance Indicators (2010), http://www.fincen.gov/statutes_regs/guidance/pdf/fin-2010-g002.pdf. It was issued initially in "The SAR Activity Review - Trends, Tips & Issues, Issue 17," May 2010. The guidance provides factors to consider and suggested best practices to assist in the development of BSA risk-based approach indicators, procedures, and internal controls

- FIN-2010-G003, *Suggested Best Practices - Casino or Card Club Compliance Assessment* (June 30, 2010).[126]
- *The SAR Activity Review - Trends, Tips & Issues, Issue 17* (May 2010), focused on the casino and gaming industry.[127]
- FIN-2009-G004, *Frequently Asked Questions - Casino Recordkeeping, Reporting and Compliance Program Requirements* (September 30, 2009.[128]
- FIN-2009-A003, *Structuring by Casino Patrons and Personnel* (July 1, 2009.[129]
- *FinCEN Educational Pamphlet on the Currency Transaction Reporting Requirement - Notice to Customers: A CTR Reference Guide* (May 2009).[130]
- FIN-2008-G007, *Recognizing Suspicious Activity - Red Flags for Casinos and Card Clubs* (August 1, 2008).[131]

---

standards for casinos and card clubs to combat money laundering and terrorist financing. Also, it provides a basic framework for casinos and card clubs to reference when developing their own compliance policies, procedures, internal controls and systems that accurately and proportionately reflect their business/customer risk profile.

[126] *See* FIN-2010-G003, Casino or Card Club Compliance Program Assessment (2010), http://www.fincen.gov/statutes_regs/guidance/pdf/fin-2010-g003.pdf. It was issued initially in "The SAR Activity Review Trends, Tips & Issues, Issue 17," May 2010. The guidance provides factors to consider in the development of an effective BSA risk-based compliance self-assessment for casinos and card clubs.

[127] In "The SAR Activity Review: Trends, Tips & Issues, Issue 17," articles include an assessment of SARs filed by casinos and card clubs and an analysis of inquiries from casinos and card clubs regarding suspicious activity reporting requirements. An article by IRS staff describes how examiners use BSA data to scope and plan casino examinations. The issue includes industry viewpoints on how casinos and card clubs can detect suspicious activity and implement effective AML programs. FinCEN also provides guidance on applying a risk-based approach to the development and implementation of a solid BSA compliance program. 17 SAR Activity Rev.: Trends, Tips, & Issues 1 (May 2010), http://www.fincen.gov/news_room/rp/files/sar_tti_17.pdf.

[128] The document interprets the BSA regulation requirements as it applies to the casino and card club industries to help them comply with regulatory responsibilities. The document provides 25 questions and answers which cover the following regulatory areas: (i) what gambling establishments are subject to the regulations, (ii) how to comply with the currency transaction reporting requirement; (iii) how to comply with suspicious activity reporting requirement; (iv) what types of records to make and retain to comply with the recordkeeping requirements; and (v) how to comply with the compliance program requirement. FIN-2007-G005, "Frequently Asked Questions – Casino Recordkeeping, Reporting and Compliance Program Requirements" (November 14, 2007), available at: http:// www.fincen.gov/statutes_regs/guidance/pdf/fin-2009-g004.pdf.

[129] *See* FIN-2009-A003, Structuring By Casino Patrons and Personnel (2009), http://www.fincen.gov/statutes_regs/guidance/pdf/fin-2009-a003.pdf.

[130] This FinCEN CTRC brochure addresses frequently asked questions posed by customers of casinos and card clubs regarding the BSA requirement to report transactions that exceed $10,000 in currency. Financial institutions do not have to use the pamphlet, but they may find it useful when educating their customers. *See* FinCEN, *Notice to Customers: A CTR Reference Guide* (May 2009), http://www.fincen.gov/whatsnew/pdf/CTR-CPamphlet.pdf. *See also* FinCEN Ruling 2005-1, *Currency Transaction Reporting: Aggregation by Casinos at Slot Machines* (February 7, 2005).

[131] *See* FIN-2009-A003, Recognizing Suspicious Activity - Red Flags for Casi-

- FIN-2007-G005, *Frequently Asked Questions - Casino Recordkeeping, Reporting and Compliance Program Requirements* (November 14, 2007).[132]
- FinCEN Ruling FIN-2006-R002 - *A Cash Wager on Table Game Play Represents a "Bet of Currency"* (March 24, 2006).[133]
- FinCEN Ruling 2005-5, *Definition of Money Services Business (Casinos as Money Services Businesses)* (July 6, 2005).[134]
- FinCEN Ruling 2005-1, *Currency Transaction Reporting: Aggregation by Casinos at Slot Machines* (February 7, 2005).[135]

IRS CASINO CIVIL EXAMINATIONS

Casinos in the United States are subject to a decentralized regulatory structure and are primarily regulated by the States and by tribal regulatory authorities. Card clubs are also subject to a decentralized regulatory structure and primarily are regulated by the States and, in some cases, local or tribal regulatory authorities. Under the BSA and its implementing regulations, a gaming operation is defined as a financial institution subject to the requirements of the BSA if it has annual gaming revenue of more than $1 million and is duly licensed or authorized to do business as a casino, gambling casino, or card club under State or local law to do business in the United States, or is an Indian gaming operation conducted under or pursuant to the Indian Gaming Regulatory Act (IGRA).

FinCEN, as administrator of the BSA, is responsible for measuring and enforcing compliance with the BSA, but it does not examine financial insti-

---

NOS AND CARD CLUBS (2008), http://www.fincen.gov/statutes_regs/guidance/pdf/fin-2008-g007.pdf. Note, in July 1998, FinCEN issued initial guidance providing examples of suspicious activities occurring at casinos to assist in detecting and complying with suspicious activity reporting requirements (entitled "Suspicious Activity Reporting & Casinos") which was posted on its Web site until March 2003.

[132] The document interprets the requirements of the BSA regulation as it applies to the casino and card club industries, to help them comply with regulatory responsibilities. The document provides 23 questions and answers which cover the following regulatory areas: (i) what gambling establishments are subject to the regulations, (ii) how to comply with the currency transaction reporting requirement; (iii) how to comply with suspicious activity reporting requirement; (iv) what types of records to make and retain to comply with the recordkeeping requirements; and (v) how to comply with the compliance program requirement. *See* FINCEN, "FIN-2007-G005, FREQUENTLY ASKED QUESTIONS – CASINO RECORDKEEPING, REPORTING AND COMPLIANCE PROGRAM REQUIREMENTS" (NOVEMBER 14, 2007).

[133] See FINCEN, ADMINISTRATIVE RULING FIN-2006-R002, A CASH WAGER ON TABLE GAME PLAY REPRESENTS A "BET OF CURRENCY" (2006), http://www.fincen.gov/news_room/rp/rulings/pdf/fincen_ruling2006-24.pdf.

[134] *See* FINCEN ADMINISTRATIVE RULING 2005-5 - DEFINITION OF MONEY SERVICES BUSINESS (CASINOS AS MONEY SERVICES BUSINESSES) (2005), http://www.fincen.gov/news_room/rp/rulings/pdf/fincen_ruling2005-5.pdf.

[135] *See* FINCEN ADMINISTRATIVE RULING 2005-1 - CURRENCY TRANSACTION REPORTING: AGGREGATION BY CASINOS AT SLOT MACHINES (2005), http://www.fincen.gov/news_room/rp/rulings/pdf/fincen_ruling2005-1.pdf.

tutions for compliance. Instead, FinCEN has delegated authority to the IRS to examine all financial institutions other than banks, Federally-insured credit unions, brokers and dealers in securities, introducing brokers for commodities and futures, and futures commission merchants, for compliance with BSA requirements.[136] This delegation is memorialized in Treasury Directive 15-41, which delegates to the Commissioner of the IRS the authority to conduct BSA examinations of certain non-bank financial institutions to assure compliance. This currently involves the following non-bank financial sectors: all money services businesses (MSBs) (e.g., check cashers, and money transmitters throughout the United States), insurance companies, non-Federally insured banks or credit unions, and credit card operators, all duly licensed or authorized casinos and card clubs having gross annual gaming revenue in excess of $1 million, and dealers in precious metals, stones, and jewels. IRS SB/SE Division examiners conduct these examinations. IRS examinations are funded under a separate budget from the United States Congress.

While SB/SE is charged with examining casinos and card clubs for compliance with the BSA requirements, there is no Federal functioning regulator for these industries, except to some extent the National Indian Gaming Commission, which has some regulatory oversight for tribal casinos. Also, IRS SB/SE has issued some Federal BSA examination techniques for the casino and card club industries for its examiners to follow; these techniques can be found in Internal Revenue Manual (IRM) 4.26.9 from June 2006, which numbers approximately 25 pages.[137]

As part of agency responsibilities, IRS personnel may conduct an informational visit to a gaming establishment to explain the BSA requirements including reporting of suspicious and currency transactions, identification of customers, recordkeeping and record retention obligations, the need to establish a written AML compliance program, and the potential for civil and criminal penalties for violations of the Act. Also, IRS personnel may provide a copy of BSA regulations[138] along with the applicable reporting forms and other informational documents. In addition, IRS personnel may participate in employee training programs at the gaming establishment, upon request and availability.

Furthermore, the IRS SB/SE Division conducts BSA compliance examinations during which audit teams examine duly licensed or authorized ca-

---

[136] *See* 31 C.F.R. § 1010.810(b)(8). IRS SB/SE Division has examination authority for civil compliance with the BSA for all financial institutions that do not have a Federal functional regulator as defined in the BSA. Furthermore, on December 1, 1992, the Department of the Treasury's Directive 15-41 delegates to the Commissioner of the IRS the authority to conduct BSA compliance examinations of certain non-bank financial institutions, http://www.treasury.gov/about/role-of-treasury/orders-directives/Pages/td15-41.aspx.

[137] Specifically, *see* Part 4. Examining Process, Chapter 26, Bank Secrecy Act, Section 9, Examination Techniques For Bank Secrecy Act Industries.4.26.9 Examination Techniques For Bank Secrecy Act Industries, IRM 4.26.9.1 - 4.26.9.2.10.1 (for casinos and card clubs), http://www.irs.gov/irm/part4/irm_04-026-009.html.

[138] *See* 31 C.F.R. §§ 1010–1028.

sinos and card clubs to determine compliance with the BSA's suspicious activity and currency transaction reporting, identification, recordkeeping, record retention, and compliance program requirements. This exam includes an assessment of the adequacy of compliance programs' policies, procedures, and internal controls; internal and/or external testing for compliance; personnel training; personnel designated to assure compliance; whether all available information is used to determine and verify (when required) the name, address, social security number or taxpayer identification number of a person; using all available information to determine the occurrence of any transactions or patterns of transactions required to be reported as suspicious, and use of computer systems and programs to aid in assuring compliance with the BSA.[139] Also, IRS examinations include a three-month testing of (i) related currency and suspicious transactions to ensure forms have been correctly filed, (ii) recording of checks on the $3,000 negotiable instrument log, (iii) recording of $3,000 domestic wire transfers of funds, (iv) recording of international wire transfers, (v) recording of deposit and credit account transactions, (vi) currency exchanges, (vii) establishment of an written and effective BSA anti-money laundering compliance program, and (viii) following of FinCEN regulatory guidance and administrative rulings. In this regard, FinCEN's casino guidance document states IRS

> compliance examinations will look at whether a casino's written program is designed to address the money laundering risks of your particular business, whether the casino and its employees are following the program, whether employees are being properly trained, whether the program is being audited and the results of that audit, and whether the casino responds to red flags and other indicia that the compliance program is deficient.[140]

If, during a civil examination, a non-bank financial institution refuses to provide IRS examiners with any and all books, papers, records, or other data required under the BSA, the IRS can issue a summons to that non-bank financial institution for such documents. Specifically, for any investigation for the purpose of civil enforcement of violations of the BSA, the IRS may issue a summons (which is not predicated upon a court order) to a non-bank institution or an officer or employee of a non-bank financial institution (including a former officer or employee), or any person having possession, custody, or care of any of the records and reports required

---

[139] The scope and depth of an IRS BSA compliance examination will depend on the facts and circumstances in each case. At the beginning of each examination, IRS submits Form 4564, Information Document Request (IDR), to a casino or card club that lists the documents to be made available to it on the date of the first scheduled appointment. *See* http://www.irs.gov/pub/irs-utl/form4564.pdf. The request includes access to all records required to be maintained pursuant to 31 C.F.R. §§ 1010.410 and 1021.410(a)–(b). More than one IDR may be issued to a casino or a card club during an examination. The IDR will specify a time period (i.e., dates) involved for a records request. Also, IRS conducts interviews of executives, AML compliance officer(s), department managers, and frontline employees, as warranted.

[140] *See* Suspicious Activity Reporting Guidance for Casinos at 4 (December 2003).

under the BSA to produce such books, papers, records, or other data as may be relevant or material to such investigation, or to appear at a time and place named in the summons, and to give testimony, under oath, and be examined, and to produce such books, papers, records, or other data as may be relevant or material to such investigation.[141]

The IRS casino examinations are not meant to be checklist examinations but instead are intended to be risk based. Therefore, individual examinations of casino properties will not have the exact same scope and depth from examination to examination. Nonetheless, the broad overall process should be the same. In addition, in 2005 the IRS changed some of its casino examination processes to be more risk-based, top-down, and compliance-process oriented.

Unlike Federal banking and securities regulators, the IRS is not obligated to undertake examinations on any particular cycle. Its program is largely implemented on a risk basis and by the relative size of the institutions for which it is responsible. If the IRS discovers significant alleged BSA violations and deficiencies at the financial institution, the matter is referred to FinCEN for disposition, including consideration of civil money penalties or other sanctions.[142]

Areas of Concern with Casino Recordkeeping

Customers can gamble anonymously at US casinos and card clubs *unless* they (i) open a deposit, credit, check cashing, player rating, or slot club account; (ii) conduct reportable currency transactions, involving either "cash in" or "cash out," in excess of $10,000 in a gaming day, including multiple transactions;[143] or (iii) fall under BSA customer identification requirements for deposit and credit accounts, checks with a face value of $3,000 or more, domestic money transfers in excess of $3,000, and international funds transfers at any value.[144]

Also, there are certain longstanding casino recordkeeping practices that cause concerns in the areas of BSA examination, compliance, and enforcement, although they are fully acceptable for financial and tax accounting purposes:

---

[141] *See* 31 C.F.R. § 1010.911, et al.

[142] The limitations on information gathering during a BSA compliance examination were the subject of a court's holding in the case of United States v. Deak-Perera & Co., 566 F.Supp. 1396 (D.D.C.) (1983). In that case, the court ruled that the government could not use its regulatory authority under the BSA to request or gather information about specific customers during a compliance examination, which was intended actually for use in tax administration purposes, without the knowledge and consent of the financial institution. This does not preclude IRS examiners from preparing an internal examination information report on information discovered within the scope of a BSA examination that may have possible civil and/or criminal income tax consequences.

[143] *See* 31 C.F.R. §§ 1021.311 and 1021.313.

[144] *See* 31 C.F.R. §§ 1010.410(e) and (f), and 1021.410(a), (b)(1), (b)(5), and (b)(9) for all these BSA casino recordkeeping requirements.

- Lack of certain recordkeeping related to some types of common currency transactions, and
- The fungibility of chips/tokens and currency in the casino cage, which when combined with the lack of certain business record-keeping, creates a self-balancing effect on the cashier's imprest drawer which can cause a transaction to go unnoticed and be undetectable as to its nature.[145] This exists because casino chips/tokens and currency are exchangeable or interchangeable with each other.

Additionally, in the ordinary course of business, many casinos and card clubs do not prepare or maintain internal records with reliable customer identification information associated with certain common currency transactions of significant value (except in excess of $10,000 in a gaming day) such as the following: (i) chip and token purchases, (ii) chip, token, and TITO ticket[146] redemptions, (iii) domestic currency exchanges, (iv) foreign currency exchanges, (v) wagering ticket purchases,[147] and (vi) wagering ticket redemptions.[148]

Also, several international organizations, which have made efforts to combat money laundering and terrorist financing in casino gambling, have also noted problems with organized crime groups, customer due diligence (CDD), and knowing a customer's source of funds. The latter of these three tie into gaps with casino recordkeeping. For example, a joint project conducted by the Financial Action Task Force (FATF)[149]–

---

[145] Casinos and card clubs maintain cages where cashiers conduct financial transactions using a drawer that operates on an imprest basis or inventory. An imprest basis is a method of accounting for funds inventories whereby any replenishment or removal of funds is accounted for by an exchange of an exact amount of other funds in the inventory. The imprest drawer opens with a stated amount of currency and/or chips. Any subsequent additions or removal of funds in the drawer are accounted for by either a document or an exchange of an equal amount of funds of another form. Since chips and currency are fungible (i.e., interchangeable with one another), no imprest records of these transactions are prepared or maintained. Therefore, the specific makeup of the funds accounted for in a cashier's drawer does not make a business difference so long as the drawer remains in balance.

[146] A ticket-in/ticket-out (TITO) is a gaming instrument issued by a slot machine/video lottery terminal, to a customer as a record of a payout of accumulated credits on a machine credit meter and/or substitute for currency. Tickets are slot voucher slips printed with the name and the address of the gaming establishment, the stated monetary value of the ticket, date and time printed, machine number (i.e., asset or location), an 18-digit validation number, and a unique bar code. Tickets represent a monetary value only within a casino and are intended for the purposes of gambling. Thus, tickets are a type of casino bearer "IOU" instrument, meaning that they can be cashed out by anybody in a casino. A customer can use a TITO ticket at a machine or terminal that accepts tickets to place a wager, or cash a ticket at a cage, slot booth, or a redemption kiosk.

[147] A betting/wagering ticket is a written record of a wager for a race or sporting event.

[148] Redemptions of winning race book and sports pool wagering tickets require the filing of IRS Form W-2G, Certain Gambling Winnings, only if the amount paid (reduced by the wager) is (i) $600 or more and (ii) at least 300 times the wager. *See* 26 C.F.R. §§ 3402 and 6041; 26 U.S.C. § 3402g.

[149] The FATF is an inter-governmental body whose purpose is the development and pro-

Asia/Pacific Group on Money Laundering (APG)[150] issued the report *Vulnerabilities of Casinos and Gaming Sector*, which considers casinos with a physical presence and discusses related money laundering and terrorist financing methods, vulnerabilities, indicators to aid detection and deterrence, and international information exchange.[151] The Casino Vulnerabilities Report considered vulnerabilities and gaps in domestic implementation of AML/combating the financing of terrorism (CFT) measures.[152] The Casino Vulnerabilities Report pointed out that criminals have an interest in casinos, when it stated

> [c]asinos are attractive venues for criminals. Casinos are consistently targeted by criminals for criminal influence and criminal exploitation. Organised crime groups seek to control or own casinos or aspects of casino operations. Criminals attempt to infiltrate or influence casinos to facilitate theft, fraud, money laundering and other crimes.[153]

Further, the Casino Vulnerabilities Report pointed out that casino deposit accounts are vulnerable to criminals, when it stated that

> [c]asino accounts provide criminals further opportunities to attempt to laundering crime proceeds. Many casinos offer deposit accounts and lines of credit with less scrutiny and CDD requirements than financial institutions. The frequent movement of funds between financial institutions and casinos, or between casino accounts held in different casinos may be vulnerable for money laundering. Many casinos offer private safe deposit boxes, particularly to VIP/'high roller' customers.[154]

Moreover, the Casino Vulnerabilities Report noted that, in general, casinos do not do enough CDD to be able to identify customer source of funds and to recognize customer suspicious activity. Specifically, the report stated

---

motion of policies and standards, both at national and international levels, to combat money laundering and terrorist financing, which include its 40 Recommendations. Currently, FATF has 36 members (34 countries and governments (including the United States) and two international organizations), more than 20 observers, five FATF-style regional bodies, and more than 15 other international organizations or bodies. For further information about FATF's programs, visit the FATF Web site located at http://www.fatf-gafi. org/.

[150] The APG is an international organization (regionally focused) consisting of 41 members and a number of international and regional observers including the United Nations, International Monetary Fund, FATF, Asian Development Bank, and World Bank. The APG is closely affiliated with the FATF. All APG members commit to effectively implement the FATF's international standards for anti-money laundering and combating the financing of terrorism, referred to as the 40 Recommendations. *See* APG Web site located at http://www.apgml.org.

[151] *See* APG/FATF's "Vulnerabilities of Casinos and Gaming Sector," Mar. 2009, http://www.fatf-gafi.org/media/fatf/documents/reports/Vulnerabilities%20of%20Casinos%20and%20Gaming%20Sector.pdf (hereinafter Casino Vulnerabilities Report).

[152] Please note that data in the Casino Vulnerabilities Report was derived from members of the FATF, APG, other FATF-style regional bodies, and open sources.

[153] *Id.* at 26, ¶ 94.

[154] *Id.* At 36, ¶ 119.

[a] key issue is that in general casinos are not doing enough to establish source of funds and failing to recognise suspicious activity by their customers. Casino security and marketing systems tend to pay particular attention to customer's financial transactions and gambling behaviours, but mostly in terms of patterns of winning and opportunities to encourage greater participation. There is a need for greater vigilance of patterns of transactions and play, unusual transactions and possible indicators of suspicious transactions.[155]

Unfortunately, for high roller or whale casino customers, typically US casinos do not determine the source of funds for any gambling transactions, unless they involve casino credit, some type of fraud, or a request from law enforcement. However, limiting casino due diligence checks of high-end customers only to these three categories is insufficient. For example, on June 12, 2014, Jennifer Shasky Calvery, Director of the Financial Crimes Enforcement Network, stated the following at a Bank Secrecy Act Conference in Las Vegas, NV that

[c]asinos are required to be aware of a customer's source of funds under current AML requirements. Specifically, under existing regulations, a casino is required to develop and maintain a robust risk-based anti-money laundering program. In fact, the regulations explicitly state that casinos must implement reasonably-designed procedures for "using all available information to determine... the occurrence of any transactions or patterns of transactions required to be reported as suspicious."

Among the various reporting and recordkeeping obligations imposed on casinos is the obligation to identify and report suspicious activity. Meeting this obligation relies largely upon the casino's ability to understand with whom it is doing business. FinCEN expects that casinos, like other financial institutions, inquire about source of funds as appropriate under a risk-based approach.[156]

Chip, Token, and Ticket Redemptions by Unknown Customers

When a customer launders currency at a casino or card club, he or she physically places illegally obtained money into the establishment's financial system. Then the customer layers the illegally-obtained money through a series of financial transactions and subsequently redeems chips, tokens, TITO tickets, or betting tickets at the cage for large denomination bills, monetary instruments, or funds transfers which makes it difficult to trace the money back to its original source. For example, casinos and card clubs do not always distinguish between chip transactions and currency transac-

---

[155] *Id.* at 59, ¶ 207.

[156] *See* "Remarks Of Jennifer Shasky Calvery, Director , Financial Crimes Enforcement Network, 2014 Bank Secrecy Act Conference, Las Vegas, NV" at 3–4 (June 12, 2014), http://www.fincen.gov/news_room/speech/pdf/20140612.pdf.

tions at the cage because chips and currency transactions are interchangeable with each other; therefore the character of currency transactions at the cage easily can be misidentified as non-reportable chip transactions, whether by accident or intent. This means the most critical vulnerability is when a customer redeems gaming instruments for currency at a cage cashier's window.

While BSA internal records are required to be created for casino monetary instruments of $3,000 or more or funds transfers in excess of $3,000, no specific BSA record is required to be created for chip, token, TITO ticket, or betting ticket redemptions[157] in currency between $3,000–$10,000 inclusive. US casinos and card clubs that maintain multiple transaction logs (MTLs) for currency transactions usually at $2,500–$3,000 (pursuant to State or tribal law or regulation, or in the ordinary course of business) will log these transactions on the MTL if they are greater than the threshold amount, but the customer identifying information recorded on the log is limited. For example, typical casinos record on the MTLs only a customer's name (if known) and do not request any other customer identification information (e.g., permanent address) before concluding a transaction. Although card clubs are required to maintain and retain records of all currency transactions by customers, including without limitation records in the form of currency transaction logs and multiple currency transaction logs,[158] customer identification is limited also for chip redemptions.

FinCEN has addressed identifying betting ticket, chip, token, or TITO ticket redemptions for currency at a cage conducted by "unknown" customers[159] in regards to suspicious activity reporting.[160] A casino must implement procedures reasonably designed to assure the detection and proper reporting of suspicious transactions.[161] Also, the BSA requires that casinos and card clubs have internal controls for customer chip redemption and a cage to monitor customer transactions of less than $10,000 if there is an attempt to avoid reporting requirements by structuring transactions.[162]

Although 31 C.F.R. §§ 1010.311, 1010.313(b), and 1021.311 do not state specifically that a casino or a card club must create a record of transactions

---

[157] FinCEN has not viewed the purchase of a casino chip, token, or "ticket in/ticket out" voucher ("TITO ticket") to involve the use and/or establishment of an account for purposes of § 1021.410(a).

[158] *See* 31 C.F.R. § 1021.410(b)(11).

[159] Unknown customers would include those without a casino deposit (i.e., access, front money, wagering, or safekeeping), credit, check cashing, player rating/player tracking, or slot club account.

[160] *See* FIN-2007-G005, *Frequently Asked Questions - Casino Recordkeeping, Reporting and Compliance Program Requirements, Question and Answer at* 16 (Nov. 14, 2007).

[161] *See* 31 C.F.R. § 1021.210(b)(2)(v)(B).

[162] *See* FIN 2009-G004, *Frequently Asked Questions - Casino Recordkeeping, Reporting and Compliance Program Requirements Question and Answer at* 5 (Sept. 30, 2009). *See* 31 C.F.R. § 103.36(b)(8).

that are less than $10,000,[163] a casino or card club would need an effective internal control for customers (known or unknown),[164] to be able to identify large chip redemptions at a reasonable threshold under $10,000 that were paid with currency and that may have been structured[165] to avoid reporting requirements or otherwise to obscure large cash out transactions. For example, for a customer that has an established casino account number,[166] a casino that (i) is not required by State or tribal regulations to maintain multiple currency transaction logs at the casino cage, or (ii) does not maintain such logs within the ordinary course of its business, nonetheless, would need a method to identify large chip redemptions at a reasonable threshold under $10,000 that were paid with currency from the imprest drawer. If implementing this internal control requirement or any other casino policy or procedure creates a record,[167] this would constitute knowledge as well as a BSA record which would be maintained for five years.[168]

A casino or card club must aggregate customer currency transactions that occur on the floor or the cage, when it has obtained knowledge of such transactions either from examining records or actual knowledge (including of large chip redemptions for currency).[169] For example, as part

---

[163] To the author's knowledge, casinos in only one State do not maintain currency logs for such cage transactions, namely, New Jersey, which currently has 10 operating casinos.

[164] A known customer would include one who has a check cashing, credit, or deposit account, or whose identity (i.e., name, date of birth, address, and government identification number) has been previously verified on a filed CTR or any Federal tax form containing customer information. Also, an effective BSA internal control will include, in many instances, the creation and retention of records, including those not otherwise produced in the ordinary course of business. *See* 31 C.F.R. § 1021.210(b)(2)(i) and 1010.430(b).

[165] Structuring would be any attempt to evade a currency reporting requirement by breaking up transactions into multiple, smaller transactions. *See* 31 C.F.R. §§ 1010.100(xx), 103.22(b)(2) and (c)(3), and 1010.314. Structuring may be indicative of underlying illegal activity. Furthermore, structuring itself is unlawful under the BSA, and could render a person subject to both civil and criminal penalties, including if a casino or a card club fails to file a currency transaction report on structuring activity that it reasonably should have detected. *See* 31 U.S.C. §§ 5321(a)(4) and 5324, and 31 C.F.R. §§ 1021.320(a)(2)(ii), 1010.820(e) and 1010.314.

[166] A "casino account number" means any and all numbers by which a casino identifies a customer." *See* 31 C.F.R. § 1021.100(b). Types of casino accounts that a customer could have include deposit (i.e., safekeeping, front money, or wagering), credit, check cashing, player rating or tracking, and slot club accounts.

[167] Also, a cage log or listing of these types of large currency transactions would assist internal or external auditors and examiners in their assessment of the effectiveness of currency transaction reporting processes by allowing systematic, quick references.

[168] *See* FIN-2007-G005, *Frequently Asked Questions - Casino Recordkeeping, Reporting and Compliance Program Requirements, Question and Answer* at 16 (Nov. 14, 2007).

[169] This includes instances such as when (i) customers provide to cage cashiers their identification credentials and/or casino account numbers for such large redemptions for currency (i e., just before, during or immediately after); or (ii) cashiers know who such customers are i.e., known customers) even in the absence of identification credentials or given account numbers for such redemptions. Also, casino regulations require a casino to use all available information to determine a customer's ". . . name, address, social se-

of a casino's risk-based prevention program and based on common industry business practice, when a customer presents at a cage a large chip redemption (typically in amounts with a face value of $1,000–$5,000 inclusive) and/or a large plaque redemption (in amounts above $5,000), a cage cashier is trained to confirm the associated circumstances by placing a telephone call to a pit boss, floor person, table game room supervisor, card room supervisor, or other casino employee to determine if the chips and/or plaques were (i) put at risk, or won at a table game as "verified winnings," or (ii) purchased at a table (e.g., when a customer is "walking with" chips and/or plaques at the end of table game play).[170] A cage cashier does this to identify (i) any temporary advance of chips and/or plaques to a customer who is well known to a casino until a marker is prepared (i.e., rim credit), (ii) whether a customer is on a State or tribal casino's exclusion list for problem gamblers, (iii) potential counterfeit chips and/or plaques, and (iv) stolen chips and/or plaques. Additionally, a cage cashier will query a casino's credit management system to determine if any funds are owed to a casino and for credit issuance (i.e., marker) and credit payment (i.e., marker redemption) activities for a customer with large chip redemptions. To effectively search its casino management system, a casino would request identification from a customer.[171] For similar reasons, a casino would need a method for identifying large redemptions at a reasonable threshold under $10,000 of a betting ticket, token, or TITO ticket that were paid with currency to a known customer. Thus, when an identification credential is presented, because a customer's name and often his or her address is known (except, in the case of an address, for a passport), a casino would have to consider how to use such information for purposes of aggregation to ascertain potentially reportable currency transactions (e.g., a MTL entry).

Given the above, all casinos and card clubs should consider enhancing the existing cage MTL for two types of currency transactions: (i) chip, TITO ticket, token, or betting ticket (including race book and sports pools in Nevada) for currency, and (ii) exchanges of currency (domestic or foreign). These enhancements should include requiring a customer's name, address, date of birth, and a government identification number *unless* the customer has a check cashing, credit, or deposit account, or is "a known customer" whose identity (i.e., name, date of birth, address, and government identification number) has been previously verified on a filed Currency Transac-

---

curity number, and other information, and verification of the same . . . ." *See* 31 C.F.R. § 1021.210(b)(2)(v)(A).

[170] This is a casino term of art for the amount of chips that a customer leaves a gaming table with at the end of play.

[171] A casino management system is the part of a casino accounting system that contains the data pertaining to the actual gaming operations of a casino. A typical casino management system is usually a hybrid system made up of financial accounting records, banking style deposit and credit records, and non-financial marketing records. It is the collective hardware, software, communications technology and other ancillary equipment used to collect, monitor, interpret, analyze, report and audit data on gaming operations.

tion Report or any Federal income tax form filed. As a corollary, for known customers, the cage MTL for chip, TITO ticket, token, or wagering ticket redemptions for currency, and exchanges of currency (domestic or foreign), should contain a data element field to record the customer's account number. Casinos and card clubs could then identify customers for purposes of aggregating these types of transactions for currency transaction reporting as well as detecting "unknown" customers who are engaged in minimal or no gaming activity for purposes of suspicious activity reporting.

Furthermore, for unknown customers, as a best practice all casinos and card clubs should consider enhancing the existing cage MTLs for chip and token purchases using currency of an equal amount to require a surveillance photograph of each such customer. Similarly, for unknown customers, casinos that offer race book and sports pools should consider enhancing the existing cage MTL for wagering ticket purchases using currency of an equal amount to require a surveillance photograph of each such customer. Casinos and card clubs could then identify customers for purposes of aggregating these types of transactions for currency transaction reporting. Also, it is much easier to compare black-and-white surveillance photographs of "unknown" customers than it is to review many cage MTLs containing physical descriptions of customers (e.g., age, gender (male or female), eye color, hair color, height, weight) and name (if known) to identify customers conducting more than one large purchase transaction at the cage in the same gaming day. Nonetheless, the physical description on the cage MTLs has some value because it contains a customer's eye color and hair color, which cannot be ascertained from a black-and-white surveillance photograph for purpose of suspicious transaction reporting for unknown customers.

FEDERAL CIVIL AND CRIMINAL PENALTIES

Civil and criminal penalties can be imposed for violations of AML laws and regulations. Penalties can result in substantial fines and in prison terms.

Any financial institution faces possible civil penalties for the following willful violations of the BSA:

- Compliance Program: $25,000 per day per violation of any program requirement[172]
- Failure to File Report: $25,000 or amount involved in transaction up to $100,000[173]
- Structuring: Amount of transaction[174]
- Other Recordkeeping: $1,000 per violation[175]

---

[172] *See* 31 U.S.C. § 5321(a)(1).
[173] *See* 31 U.S.C. § 5321(a)(1); 31 C.F.R. § 1010.820(f).
[174] *See* 31 U.S.C. §§ 5321, 5324; 31 C.F.R. §§ 1010.820(e), 1010.314.
[175] *See* 31 U.S.C. § 5321; 31 C.F.R. § 1010.820(c).

Willfulness is not defined in the BSA. Over time, the definition of willfulness has developed from Federal court cases. Evidence to support willfulness demonstrates awareness of but reckless disregard for legal requirements. Therefore, willfulness requires an intentional violation of a known legal duty (e.g., possessing a specific intent to evade BSA requirements). Also, willfulness may include willful blindness. Willful blindness occurs when an individual's suspicions are aroused, but the individual deliberately does not make further inquiry to remain in ignorance.

These civil sanctions are for willful violations of the BSA and may be applied not only to any casino or card club subject to the BSA, but also to any partner, director, officer, or employee of such gaming operations.

Also, any financial institution that fails to comply with BSA reporting, recordkeeping, or AML compliance program requirements faces possible civil penalties of up to $500 for negligent violations or up to $50,000 for a pattern of negligence.[176]

Finally, FinCEN may file an action for injunctive relief in a civil case in the appropriate Federal district court against a financial institution to prevent future BSA violations.[177]

Under certain circumstances, businesses can also be held criminally liable for their employees' acts. Criminal penalties for willfully violating a BSA requirement (except for structuring) are a fine of up $250,000, a term of imprisonment of up to five years, or both.[178] These penalties can be *doubled* (i.e., up to $500,000, imprisonment up to 10 years, or both) upon conviction, if committed while violating another Federal law (e.g., specified unlawful activity) or as part of a pattern of illegal activity exceeding more than $100,000 in a 12-month period.[179] (Emphasis added.)

Also, there are criminal penalties for structuring transactions to evade BSA reporting requirements.[180] These structuring penalties can be

---

[176] See 31 U.S.C. § 5321(a)(6).

[177] See *Rubin v. Brunswick Bank & Trust Co.*, Civ. A. No. 93-3184 (NHP), 1996 WL 571010 (D.N.J. Mar. 28, 1996).

[178] See 31 U.S.C. § 5322(a); 31 C.F.R. § 1010.840.

[179] See 31 U.S.C. § 5322(b); 31 C.F.R. § 1010.840.

[180] See 31 U.S.C. § 5324(d). Structuring is a crime, punishable by a fine and up to five years in prison, for anyone who breaks currency transactions purposely into amounts less than $10,000 to avoid reporting requirements, including casino employees. See 31 U.S.C. § 5324; 31 C.F.R. § 1010.314. As background, in 1988, Waldemar and Loretta Ratzlaf were high rollers and established lines of credit in 15 casinos in Atlantic City and Nevada. On October 20, 1988, High Sierra Casino in Reno increased Waldemar Ratzlaf's credit line from $25,000–$160,000, which he lost playing blackjack. The High Sierra Casino gave them a week to pay the $160,000. On the due date, Waldemar Ratzlaf returned to the Casino with currency of $100,000. A casino official informed Waldemar Ratzlaf that all transactions involving more than $10,000 in currency had to be reported to State and Federal authorities. The official added that the casino could accept a cashier's check for the full amount due without triggering the Nevada CTRC reporting requirement. The High Sierra Casino let the Ratzlafs have a casino limousine and driver so that they could go to banks in the vicinity, purchasing cashier's checks in amounts less than $10,000, each one from a different bank. Waldemar Ratzlaf delivered these checks to the High Sierra Casino. A

doubled upon conviction, if committed while violating another Federal law (e.g., specified unlawful activity) or as part of a pattern of illegal activity exceeding more than $100,000 in a 12-month period.[181] (Emphasis added.)

Criminal penalties for a financial institution or an individual convicted of money laundering or terrorist financing can be a fine of up to $500,000, imprisonment up to 20 years, or both.[182] Any property involved in a transaction or traceable to the proceeds of the criminal activity may be subject to forfeiture.[183] "Proceeds" is defined as "any property derived . . . through some sort of unlawful activity, including the gross receipts of such activity." In 2009, the US Congress added this definition to 18 U.S.C. § 1956(c)(9) to address the US Supreme Court's decision in United States v. Santos, 553 U.S. 507 (2008), which determined that the term "proceeds," as applied to laundering the proceeds of gambling from a lottery, meant "net profits."[184]

Further, the criminal penalty for a BSA recordkeeping violation is payment of an amount not to exceed $1,000 per violation or a term of imprisonment up to one year.[185] The fine increases to $10,000, a term of imprisonment up to five years, or both, if committed in furtherance of another Federal crime.[186]

Any person who knowingly makes any false, fictitious, or fraudulent statement or representation on a BSA report violation may be, upon conviction, fined an amount not to exceed $10,000, imprisoned up to five years in prison, or both.[187]

Besides the above, there are two Federal criminal statutes that focus on money laundering. Money laundering is taking the proceeds from a specified unlawful activity (SUA) and spending, concealing, or moving it

---

Federal court convicted the Ratzlafs of willfully structuring financial transactions to avoid currency reporting requirements. Waldemar was sentenced to 15 months in Federal prison and assessed a $26,300 fine; Loretta received five years probation and a fine of $7,900. On January 11, 1994, however, the US Supreme Court ruled that the Ratzlafs had not "willfully" broken the law because they did not know that what they were doing was illegal. *See* Ratzlaf v. United States, 510 U.S. 135 at 149, 114 S.Ct. 655, 126 L.Ed.2d 615 (January 1994). In response, the Money Laundering Suppression Act of 1994, Pub. L. 103-325 (September 23, 1994) included an amendment to 31 U.S.C. § 5324 to exclude the willfulness requirement for structuring, which addressed the Supreme Court's *Ratzlaf* decision.

[181] *See* 31 U.S.C. § 5324(d)(2).

[182] *See* 18 U.S.C. § 1956.

[183] *See* 18 U.S.C. §§ 981–982.

[184] *See* United States v. Santos, *et al.,* Certiorari to the United States Court of Appeals for the Seventh Circuit, No. 06 -1005 (June 2, 2008), http://supreme.justia.com/cases/federal/us/553/06-1005/.

[185] Title I of the BSA, which is found in 12 U.S.C. §§ 1829b–1953, gives the Secretary of the Treasury authority to issue regulations requiring certain records be maintained by financial institutions subject to that Title. The Director of FinCEN is the delegated administrator of the BSA.

[186] *See* 31 C.F.R. § 1010.840(a).

[187] *See* 18 U.S.C. § 1001; 31 C.F.R. § 1010.840(d).

to make the proceeds appear to have been earned from a legitimate business activity. One statute, 18 U.S.C. § 1956, makes it a crime to knowingly conduct or attempt to conduct, a financial transaction with the proceeds from a SUA with the specific intent to accomplish one of the following purposes:

- To continue to further (i.e., promote) the criminal activity that generated the property (intent);
- To conceal or disguise the nature, source, location, ownership, or control of the property obtained from the criminal activity (knowing);
- To avoid a transaction reporting requirement under Federal (e.g., structuring transactions) or State law (knowing); or
- To evade taxes.

Title 18 U.S.C. § 1956, which lists several Federal crimes, includes among them offenses for:

- 18 U.S.C. § 1956(a)(1) - Domestic money laundering;
- 18 U.S.C. § 1956(a)(2) - International transfers of funds; and
- 18 U.S.C. § 1956(h) - Conspiracy to violate any part of Title 18 U.S.C. § § 1956 or 1957.

The above four purposes apply to both 18 U.S.C. § 1956(a)(1) and 18 U.S.C. § 1956(a)(2). Although Section 1956(a)(1) has a fourth purpose—to evade Federal taxes (intent)—it is rarely charged. 18 U.S.C. § 1956(c)(7) contains the list of 215 violations of Federal criminal statutes, 10 State criminal statutes, and 12 foreign criminal statutes.

The other statute, 18 U.S.C. § 1957, makes it a crime for anyone to knowingly engage or attempt to engage in a "monetary transaction" with proceeds from an illegally-derived property of more than $10,000 by, through, or to a financial institution knowing the property came from an SUA. The prohibition against transactions in criminally-derived property applies to all activities of "United States persons" either domestically or abroad. A "United States person" is defined in 18 U.S.C. § 3077 to include corporations organized in the United States.

Under 18 U.S.C. § 1956, the criminal penalties for each offense are a fine of not more than $500,000 or twice the value of the monetary instrument or funds, whichever is greater, and up to 20 years of imprisonment. Section 1957 criminal penalties for each offense are a fine of not more than twice the amount of the criminally-derived property involved in the transaction and up to 10 years of imprisonment.

Therefore, employees must receive comprehensive, effective training on how to comply with BSA regulations. There must also be a system of policies, procedures, and internal controls in place to ensure employees are following Federal AML laws and regulations.

OTHER CURRENCY TRANSACTION FORM

Before concluding, currency transactions conducted in other operational businesses co-located and owned by a casino or transported into or out of the United States on a casino's behalf may be subject to other reporting requirements. FinCEN/IRS Form 8300, Report of Cash Payments Over $10,000 Received in a Trade or Business, is used for currency received in a trade or business and applies to any businesses that are not casinos.[188] The term "cash" for Form 8300 reporting purposes includes coin and currency of the United States or any other country, as well as cashier's checks, bank drafts, traveler's checks, or money orders received over $10,000 in one transaction (or two or more related transactions) during a 12-month period. Negotiable instruments include those that have a face amount of $10,000 or less. To illustrate, the following gambling establishments or nongaming related businesses normally would be subject to Form 8300 requirements: (i) casinos or card clubs with gross annual gaming revenue of $1 million or less[189]; (ii) tribal bingo halls, off-track betting parlors, greyhound tracks, horse racetracks,[190] or (iii) a casino hotel, gift shop, caterer/banquet service receives, conference/seminar facilities.

CONCLUSION

In conclusion, an effective BSA AML compliance program manages potential money laundering and terrorist financing risks arising from a casino's or card club's products, services, customer base, and geographical location. Once a casino or card club has identified the specific risk factors unique to its operation, it should conduct a detailed analysis of its level of vulnerability. The level and sophistication of the analysis will depend on the comprehensiveness of the casino's or card club's risk assessment process and the risk factors that apply. Also, the results may differ according to its business risk model and governmental gambling regulations. By understanding its risk profile, a casino or card club can apply appropriate risk management processes to its BSA compliance program to identify and mitigate its operational risk. Thus, casinos or card clubs should update their risk indicators to reflect changes in operational risk profiles, as needed (e.g., revised products and services, new products and services, changes with the opening and closing or closer monitoring of specific types of ac-

---

[188] *See* FinCEN/IRS Form 8300, http://www.irs.gov/pub/irs-pdf/f8300.pdf.

[189] *See* 31 C.F.R. § 1021.330(d).

[190] Please note that FinCEN addressed the treatment of bingo under the BSA in FinCEN's Frequently Asked Questions – Casino Recordkeeping, Reporting and Compliance Program Requirements, FIN-2007-G005, Question and Answer 2. (November 14, 2007). FinCEN addressed the treatment of off-track betting in FIN-2007-G005, Question and Answer 5. FinCEN addressed the treatment of greyhound tracks in FIN-2007-G005, Question and Answer 6. FinCEN addressed the treatment of horse racetracks, in FIN-2007-G005, Question and Answer 7.

counts because of the nature of customer relationships, new categories of accounts, or changes resulting from acquisitions or mergers).

It is a sound practice for a casino or card club to periodically review its BSA risk-based indicators or factors to assure sufficiency and effectiveness.[191]

Disclaimer: The opinions in this article are those of the author alone, and do not reflect necessarily the opinion or policies of any governmental agency or business organization. The author has made every reasonable effort to ensure that the data and information contained in this chapter reflect the most accurate and timely information publicly available at the time of publication.

---

[191] For additional guidance *see* FINCEN, CASINO OR CARD CLUB COMPLIANCE ASSESSMENT (2010), http://www.fincen.gov/statutes_regs/guidance/pdf/fin-2010-g003.pdf.

10

Addressing Problem Gambling

Frank Catania and Gary Ehrlich

INTRODUCTION

In a country in which every state except Hawaii and Utah has some form of gaming—i.e., legalized gambling[1]—the issue of problem gambling is significant. On a societal level, problem gambling is viewed as a public health issue,[2] requiring a multi-faceted approach that includes prevention, education, treatment, enforcement, and research.[3]

As observed in an influential article on the subject:

> It is important to clarify and separate the principles of responsible gambling from those approaches to harm minimization and rehabilitation that are directed toward assisting gamblers that already have problems. The treatment of gamblers who already have developed gambling-related harm remains the domain of specialists working in public health programs, including counseling and other health services. . . . From the perspective of the gambling industry, the primary objective of a coordinated responsible gambling strategy is to reduce the incidence of gambling-related harms at the individual, group,

---

[1] Although the terms "gambling" and "gaming" have distinct origins, they have come to be used interchangeably, www.americangaming.org/industry-resources/research/fact-sheets/gaming-vs-gambling (last visited Jan. 9, 2014), and will be so used in this chapter. Nevertheless, a recent study indicates that whether an activity is labeled "gambling" or "gaming" has a distinct effect on how positively or negatively the activity is perceived by consumers. Ashlee Humphries & Katherine LaTour, *Framing the Game: Assessing the Impact of Cultural Representations on Consumer Perceptions of Legitimacy*, 40 J. CONSUMER RES. 773 (2013), http://www.jstor.org/discover/10.1086/672358?uid=3739808&uid=2134&uid=2&uid=70&uid=4&uid=3739256&sid=21103823688601.
[2] Alex Blaszczynski et al., *A Science-Based Framework for Responsible Gambling: The Reno Model*, 20 J. GAMBLING STUD. 301, 301–302 (2004), www.divisiononaddiction.org/html/reprints/ renomodel.pdf.
[3] Marlene Warner, *Problem Gambling Within a Public Health Framework in the Commonwealth of Massachusetts* (Mass. Gaming Comm'n 2013), http://massgaming.com/wp-content/uploads/1-Problem-Gambling-Within-a-Public-Health-Framework.pdf.

community and societal level. Incidence refers to the number of new cases of a disorder or condition (i.e., harm) that occur over a defined period of time. Responsible gambling is about reducing the rate of the development of new cases of harm or disorder that is gambling-related.[4]

This chapter addresses responsible gambling as a player protection mechanism in the context of casino gaming, addressing both prevention and harm minimization.

NATURE AND PREVALENCE OF PROBLEM GAMBLING

Problem gambling encompasses a spectrum of behaviors and symptoms. At the most severe end lies "pathological" or "compulsive" gambling.[5] In the revised version of its widely used encyclopedia of mental illnesses, the American Psychiatric Association relabeled its previous diagnosis of "pathological gambling" as "gambling disorder" to reclassify it from an impulse control to an addiction disorder:

> An important departure from past diagnostic manuals is that the substance-related disorders chapter has been expanded to include gambling disorder. This change reflects the increasing and consistent evidence that some behaviors, such as gambling, activate the brain reward system with effects similar to those of drugs of abuse and that gambling disorder symptoms resemble substance use disorders to a certain extent.[6]

People reporting five or more of the following experiences might meet the criteria for pathological gambling:

1. Preoccupation with gambling;
2. Needing to gamble with increasing amounts of money in order to achieve the desired excitement;
3. Repeated unsuccessful efforts to control, cut back, or stop gambling;
4. Restless or irritable when attempting to cut down or stop gambling;
5. Gambling as a way of escaping from problems;
6. After losing money gambling, often returning another day to get even ("chasing" losses);
7. Lying to family members, a therapist, or others to conceal the extent of involvement with gambling;
8. Committing illegal acts such as forgery, fraud, theft, or embezzlement to finance gambling;
9. Jeopardizing or losing a significant relationship, job, or educational or career opportunity because of gambling; or

---

[4] Blaszczynski et al., *supra* note 2, at 308.
[5] MASS. COUNCIL ON COMPULSIVE GAMBLING, GAMBLING & DISORDERED GAMBLING FACTS 1 (2011).
[6] AMERICAN PSYCHIATRIC ASSOCIATION, HIGHLIGHTS OF CHANGES FROM DSM IV-TR TO DSM-5, at 16 (2013), www.dsm5.org/Documents/changes%20from%20dsm-iv-tr%20 to%20dsm-5.pdf.

10. Relying on others to provide money to relieve a desperate financial situation caused by gambling.[7]

Pathological gambling is associated with a number of negative consequences including family dysfunction and domestic violence including spousal and child abuse; suicide, suicide ideation and suicide attempts; significant financial troubles including bankruptcy, loss of property, and poverty as a direct result of wagering; and criminal behavior ranging from prostitution and theft to drug trafficking and homicide.[8]

Pathological gamblers are also significantly more likely to exhibit co-morbidity, i.e., have additional mental health and/or substance use disorders, as compared to those without gambling problems.[9] Of course, "[i]f pathological gambling is simply a symptom of some more basic disorder, then it is the more basic disorder rather than gambling itself that is the underlying cause of the adverse consequences and social costs of the pathological gambling."[10]

The National Council on Problem Gambling (NCPG) has formulated a useful working definition of "problem gambling" which includes, but is not limited to, pathological or compulsive gambling:

> Problem gambling is gambling behavior which causes disruptions in any major area of life: psychological, physical, social or vocational. The term "Problem Gambling" includes, but is not limited to, the condition known as "Pathological", or "Compulsive" Gambling, a progressive addiction characterized by increasing preoccupation with gambling, a need to bet more money more frequently, restlessness or irritability when attempting to stop, "chasing" losses, and loss of control manifested by continuation of the gambling behavior in spite of mounting, serious, negative consequences.[11]

Problem gambling is also referred to as "sub-clinical pathological gambling," i.e., behavior that does not necessarily meet the criteria for pathological gambling but nevertheless results in harmful effects to a gambler, his or her family, significant others, friends, co-workers, and others.[12] "Disordered gambling" is used to describe the combination of pathological and sub-clinical pathological gambling.[13]

Those who suffer from disordered gambling can be seriously affected. Typical adverse consequences include the following:

- financial difficulties such as being unable to find enough money to pay bills and living expenses (e.g., rent, food, providing for others including children);

---

[7] Massachusetts Council on Compulsive Gambling, Facts about Disordered Gambling 2 (2011).

[8] Id.

[9] Id.

[10] Douglas Walker, MD., Challenges that Confront Researchers on Estimating the Social Costs of Gambling 2 (2007).

[11] What is Problem Gambling?, NCPGambling.org, www.ncpgambling.org/i4a/pages/index.cfm?pageid=1.

[12] Mass. Council on Compulsive Gambling, supra note 5.

[13] Id.

- psychological and emotional problems such as stress, anxiety, depression, anger, loss of self-esteem and being unable to control one's own behaviour;
- loss of time for work or study due to gambling;
- family and relationship difficulties, missing out on family commitments due to gambling activities and causing problems with relationships with others;
- physical health problems through loss of sleep, self neglect, poor diet, smoking and alcohol use/overuse; and
- legal issues and police involvement.[14]

The most widely accepted estimates are that approximately 1 percent of the United States population meets the criteria for pathological gambling in a given year and that another 2–3 percent could be considered problem gamblers, not meeting the full diagnostic criteria for pathological gambling but exhibiting one or more of those criteria and experiencing problems due to their gambling behavior.[15] However, inasmuch as these estimates relate to the population *as a whole*—including those who do not gamble at all—they may underestimate the percentages among *actual gamblers*, as pointed out by the National Gambling Impact Study Commission:

> [A]mong those for whom gambling is a regular activity, the risks appear much higher. A survey of 530 patrons at gambling establishments conducted for this Commission showed that 13 percent of those patrons were classified as lifetime problem or pathological gamblers.[16]

Whatever the actual numbers, two things appear clear: (1) most adults who choose to gamble are able to do so responsibly;[17] but (2) the number of people who are pathological, problem, or the more amorphous category of "at-risk" gamblers, is substantial.[18]

RESPONSIBILITY FOR ADDRESSING PROBLEM GAMBLING

Generally, responsible governments, regulators, and operators across the globe accept that, when a new form of gaming is legalized and made available to the public, those who profit from such gaming must formulate

---

[14] Dep't of Treasury and Fin., Responsible Conduct of Gambling Tasmania 23 (2012), www.treasury.tas.gov.au/domino/dtf/dtf.nsf/LookupFiles/WorkbookV3.PDF/$file/WorkbookV3.PDF.

[15] *How widespread is problem gambling in the U.S.?*, NCPGambling.org, www.ncpgambling.org/i4a/pages/index.cfm?pageid=3390 [hereinafter NCPGambling.org]. *See generally* Howard Shaffer et al., *Estimating the Prevalence of Disordered Gambling Behavior in the United States and Canada: A Research Synthesis*, 89 Am. J. of Public Health 1369 (1999), www.ncbi.nlm.nih.gov/pmc/articles/PMC1508762/pdf/amjph00009-0065.pdf.

[16] Nat'l Gambling Impact Study Comm'n, National Gambling Impact Study Commission Report 7-19 (1999), http://govinfo.library.unt.edu/ngisc/reports/7.pdf. [hereinafter NGISC].

[17] NCPGambling.org, *supra* note 15.

[18] NGISC, *supra* note 16, at 7-20.

and implement policies to minimize any harm resulting from that activity, especially to the most vulnerable members of society.[19] Nevertheless, the ultimate decision to gamble represents a choice that resides with the individual, and "[u]njustified intrusion is likely not the way to promote responsible gambling. . . . Responsible gambling is best achieved at the direction of the player by using all of the information available. The guiding principle of responsible gambling practices is that people have freedom of choice regarding their decision to gamble."[20]

Each party—the government, casino, and individual—has a role to play in advancing the goal of responsible gaming. However, inasmuch as those suffering with gambling disorders are, by definition, unable to gamble responsibly, the focus here will be on what the government and casino can do.

Role of Government

When it comes to accountability for responsible gaming, governments have a conflict of interest because of their dependence on gaming tax revenues. The maximization of tax-generating casino profits may take precedence over other goals.[21]

In the view of one commentator, this conflict has resulted in an identifiable hierarchy of governmental and casino operator approaches to responsible gaming in the United States and elsewhere:

- First Stage: Denial
  - There is no such thing as problem gambling;
  - If there is, it is not my fault;
  - Such people would destroy themselves elsewhere anyway;
  - If I take the high road, I lose ground to my less caring competitors; only the low road will do.
- Second Stage: Lip Service
  - There is problem gambling, and we do acknowledge it as long as it does not cost us any business or any serious resources;
  - We will talk the talk, but we cannot walk the walk;
  - Our primary responsibility is to our shareholders and stakeholders. Too bad about the problem gamblers;
  - We will look at the high road, but we cannot go there unless we are certain there is no down-side;
  - Why don't you get contributions from the other gaming and wagering industries?
- Third Stage: Halfway House
  - There is problem gambling, and we realize it affects both our business and our legitimacy;

---

[19] *See* Garry Smith & Dan Rubenstein, *Socially Responsible and Accountable Gambling in the Public Interest*, 25 J. GAMBLING ISSUES 54, 54–60 (2011), http://jgi.camh.net/doi/pdf/10.4309/jgi.2011.25.5 (last visited Apr. 16, 2014).

[20] Blaszczynski, *supra* note 2, at 312.

[21] *See* Smith & Rubenstein, *supra* note 19, at 54.

- o   We will talk the talk, and will try to walk the walk;
- o   Our responsibility is both to our shareholders <u>and</u> our stake-holders. We want to be "doing the right thing";
- o   We will strive to take the high road, but may be constrained by the demands of the marketplace.
- Fourth Stage: Full Commitment
  - o   There is problem gambling, and it is part of our mission to mit-igate it as much as is possible;
  - o   We are committed to talking the talk, and walking the walk;
  - o   Our responsibility is to "do the right thing," even though it may be expensive. In this way, we best represent both our sharehold-ers and all our stakeholders;
  - o   We will take the high road, and will not be constrained by the demands from other conflicting objectives.[22]

The author's view is that gaming in the United States has moved through the "Lip Service" stage into the "Halfway House" stage, while some other countries (specifically Holland and Canada) are looking beyond the "Half-way House" stage to "Full Commitment."[23]

A vision of what full commitment looks like has been provided by an-other expert in the field, who refers to it as a "culture of social responsibil-ity":

> A culture of social responsibility starts with a respect for the dignity of all citizens and is a prerequisite for a just, ethical, and caring society. In a gambling context, this refers to
> - social responsibility and harm minimization taking precedence over profit-seeking
> - the precautionary principle undergirding all gambling public policy
> - consumers being informed to the extent that sound decisions can be made about gambling formats based on a knowledge of probabilities, how games work, what the house edge is, and the foreseeable conse-quences of participating in the activity
> - definitive jurisprudence that outlines the gambling provider's duty of care to discourage improvident gambling and safeguard against con-tributing to the incidence and prevalence of problem gambling
> - the provision of therapies to assist those at risk for developing or who have already developed gambling problems and to help them stop or curb their reckless gambling behaviour and temper the impact of these behaviours on the problem gamblers, their families, their friends, their employers, and the community at large.[24]

---

[22] William Eadington, *Trends in Gambling and Responsible Gaming in the United States and Elsewhere* 15–18, 888BetsOff (Dec. 1, 2003), http://www.888betsoff.com/links/04_pre-sentations/Eadington.pdf.

[23] *Id.* at 19.

[24] Smith & Rubenstein, *supra* note 19, at 59.

Establishment of legal duty of casinos to problem gamblers

As indicated above, one of the steps governments can take to address problem gambling is to establish "definitive jurisprudence that outlines the gambling provider's duty of care to discourage improvident gambling and safeguard against contributing to the incidence and prevalence of problem gambling."[25] However, legislatures have failed to take such action and, given the legal void, courts within the United States and in most jurisdictions around the world have been unwilling to recognize the existence of a legal duty owed to problem gamblers by casinos.[26] An illustrative decision is *Taveras v. Resorts Int'l Hotels.*[27]

Taveras involves claims by a former attorney that a casino facilitated her gambling addiction and induced her to gamble away money belonging to her and others, causing her money loss, emotional injury, reputational damage, and ultimate disbarment. These alleged actions by the casino were said to violate the casino's common-law duty of care to her, as well as to breach contractual obligations owed to her.[28]

As summarized in the decision:

> On numerous occasions, Plaintiff's behavior during that period consisted of "consecutive days of gambling, without eating or sleeping...."... Plaintiff alleges that certain casino employees "refused to permit [her] family members from taking her home,"... and continued to allow her to gamble in spite of clear indications that she was a compulsive gambler, confirmed by information about her condition provided to casino employees by her brother.... At the height of her addiction, Plaintiff was gambling five days per week and losing an average of $5,000 per hour.... In a weekend of continuous gambling, Plaintiff lost $150,000....
>
> During this period, Plaintiff alleges, she received numerous "enticements" from Defendant-casinos, including casino event promotions, gambling tournament invitations, promotions for free televisions, as well as free limousine rides, hotel rooms, food, entertainment, and gift coupons.[29]

Rejecting Plaintiff's argument that the casino owed her a legal duty, the court stated:

> Plaintiff requests that the Court innovate a new doctrine akin to dram-shop liability in which casinos would have a duty to identify and exclude

---

[25] *Id.*

[26] *See generally* Joe Kelly, *An Operator's Duty of Care*, GamblingCompliance (Apr. 27, 2007). *See also* Hakimoglu v. Trump Taj Mahal Assoc., 70 F.3d 291, 293–94 (3d Cir.1995); Merrill v. Trump Indiana, Inc., 2002 WL 1307304, *5 (N.D. Ind. May 9, 2002); Rahmani v. Resorts Int'l Hotel, Inc., 20 F. Supp. 2d 932, 937 (E.D. Va. 1998); Tose v. Greate Bay Hotel & Casino Inc., 819 F.Supp. 1312, 1319 (D.N.J. 1993).

[27] Taveras v. Resorts Int'l Hotel, Inc., 2008 WL 4372791 (D.N.J. Sept. 19, 2008).

[28] *Id.* at 1.

[29] *Id.* at 2. One highly-publicized allegation was that during her five-day gambling binge, the plaintiff subsisted only on juice and candy bars provided by the casino staff. *See* Deborah Roberts et al., *Gambler Seeks $20 Mil From Casinos For Addiction*, ABCNews, Mar. 10, 2008, http://abcnews.go.com/GMA/MindMoodNews/story?id=4420153.

gamblers exhibiting compulsive tendencies. . . . [T]he Third Circuit declined to expand dram-shop liability to make casinos responsible for the gambling losses of intoxicated patrons. . . . Here, Plaintiff asks the Court to go even further, imposing upon casinos a duty to stop sober casino patrons who are gambling too much. The Court is unwilling to do so. Plaintiff's theory would, in effect, have no limit. For example, if adopted by this Court, her theory would impose a duty on shopping malls and credit-card companies to identify and exclude compulsive shoppers. This Court will not sacrifice common sense and stretch the common-law duty of care as Plaintiff urges.[30]

The court also rejected the theory that gambling constitutes an "abnormally dangerous activity," so as to render casinos strictly liable for resulting harm, finding that "gambling can indeed be a safe activity, gambling is common, and state-regulated casinos are not inappropriate locations for gambling. Playing blackjack, roulette, or the slots bears no likeness to dumping toxic waste into environmentally sensitive areas . . . demolition of buildings in populated areas . . . and transportation of highly flammable substances. . . ."[31]

Clearly, the "personal responsibility" argument figures prominently in the problem gambling debate. This is illustrated—ironically enough—by a question and answer on the website of the Nevada Council on Problem Gambling:

> Do casinos cause problem gambling?
> The cause of a gambling problem is the individual's inability to control the gambling. This may be due in part to a person's genetic tendency to develop addiction, their ability to cope with normal life stress and even their social upbringing and moral attitudes about gambling. The casino merely provides the opportunity for the person to gamble. It does not, in and of itself, create the problem any more than a liquor store would create an alcoholic.[32]

In fairness, it should be observed that many potential actions to address problem gambling may have unintended consequences, and it is not clear that the establishment by statute or court decision of a legal duty owed to problem gamblers by casinos would actually benefit most problem gamblers. A few plaintiffs could conceivably recover losses or other damages in extreme cases in which a casino clearly exploited an identifiable, vulnerable problem gambler. But the very existence of such potential cause of action could actually *stimulate* more problem gambling in casinos. Many problem gamblers, whose judgment concerning gambling is, by definition, already impaired, might decide to gamble more on the theory that if they win, they win, and if they lose, they can recover their losses from the casino.[33]

---

[30] *Id.* at 4-5.

[31] *Id.* at 5.

[32] *Do Casinos Cause Problem Gambling?*, NEVADACOUNCIL.ORG, http://www.nevadacouncil.org/faqs.php?bi=1179269148.

[33] *See* ROBERT WILLIAMS ET AL., PREVENTION OF PROBLEM GAMBLING: A COMPREHENSIVE REVIEW OF THE EVIDENCE AND IDENTIFIED BEST PRACTICES 50 (2012), https://www.uleth.

Given the generally pervasive and strict regulation of casino gaming in the United States and most jurisdictions, as well as the substantive arguments against it, it is unlikely a legal duty owed to problem gamblers by casinos will be recognized widely if at all. Therefore, further analysis in this chapter is restricted to the regulatory means by which problem gambling can be addressed.

Addressing problem gambling through casino regulation

The lack of a recognized legal duty owed to problem gamblers by casinos does not mean that problem gambling must go unaddressed. In fact, most jurisdictions in the United States and worldwide require casinos to implement problem gambling programs.[34] This is generally mandated in broad terms by statute, Massachusetts providing a recent example:

> [A]pplicants for gaming licenses and gaming licensees shall demonstrate their commitment to efforts to combat compulsive gambling and a dedication to community mitigation, and shall recognize that the privilege of licensure bears a responsibility to identify, address and minimize any potential negative consequences of their business operations.[35]

Statutory mandates are implemented by regulations promulgated by the gaming regulatory bodies and requiring more specific actions by casinos. An example of this is the Nevada regulation governing programs to address problem gambling, which provides in part:

* * *

2. Each licensee shall post or provide in conspicuous places in or near gaming and cage areas and cash dispensing machines located in gaming areas written materials concerning the nature and symptoms of problem gambling and the toll-free telephone number of the National Council on Problem Gambling or a similar entity approved by the chairman of the board that provides information and referral services for problem gamblers.

3. Each licensee shall implement procedures and training for all employees who directly interact with gaming patrons in gaming areas. That training shall, at a minimum, consist of information concerning the nature and symptoms of problem gambling behavior and assisting patrons in obtaining information about problem gambling programs. This subsection shall not be construed to require employees of licensees to identify problem gamblers. Each licensee shall designate personnel responsible for maintaining the program and addressing the types and frequency of such training and procedures. Training programs conducted or certified by the Nevada

---

ca/dspace/bitstream/handle/10133/3121/2012-PREVENTION-OPGRC.pdf?sequence=3.

[34] *See generally* Responsible Gaming Statutes and Regulations (Am. Gaming Assoc., 3rd ed. 2008), www.americangaming.org/sites/default/files/uploads/docs/statutes_and_regs_final_091709.pdf; Joe Kelly, *Expert Commentary: Duty Of Care And Self-Exclusion*, GamblingCompliance (Apr. 29, 2009).

[35] Mass. Gen. Laws ch. 23K, § 1(8).

Council on Problem Gambling are presumed to provide adequate training for the period certified by the Nevada Council on Problem Gambling.

4. Each licensee that engages in the issuance of credit, check cashing, or the direct mail marketing of gaming opportunities, shall implement a program containing the elements described below, as appropriate, that allows patrons to self-limit their access to the issuance of credit, check cashing, or direct mail marketing by that licensee. As appropriate, such program shall contain, at a minimum, the following:

    (a) The development of written materials for dissemination to patrons explaining the program;

    (b) The development of written forms allowing patrons to participate in the program;

    (c) Standards and procedures that allow a patron to be prohibited from access to check cashing, the issuance of credit, and the participation in direct mail marketing of gaming opportunities;

    (d) Standards and procedures that allow a patron to be removed from the licensee's direct mailing and other direct marketing regarding gaming opportunities at that licensee's location; and

    (e) Procedures and forms requiring the patron to notify a designated office of the licensee within 10 days of the patron's receipt of any financial gaming privilege, material or promotion covered by the program.[36]

It is the role of gaming regulatory bodies to ascertain, to the extent possible given the current state of knowledge, which actions by casinos are most likely to achieve the desired results.[37] On this point expert advice may prove useful. Nevertheless, regulators must also consider the interests of casinos and other players who do not suffer from disordered gambling.

Two competing approaches to minimizing harm to those with gambling issues are easily identifiable. One is to regulate all gamblers equally by building protections into the games, venues, and conditions of play. The other is to isolate and treat problem gamblers differently.

The former approach risks inconveniencing or otherwise detracting from the gaming experience for the majority of players in order to *prevent* harm to a minority. Under the latter approach, players can choose to identify themselves as having a gambling problem and enroll in self-exclusion and other programs to prevent them from gambling.[38] But these after-the-fact remedies may come too late for the gambling disordered. These approaches need not be mutually exclusive, however, and, in fact, most jurisdictions employ both.[39]

Ironically, the existence of state- or regulatorily-mandated responsible gambling programs has been relied upon by courts as a reason for denying

---

[36] Nev. Gaming Reg. 5.170.

[37] *See, e.g.*, Mass. Forum on Responsible Gaming (Oct. 28, 2013), http://massgaming.com/wp-content/uploads/Transcript-10-28-13.pdf [hereinafter Transcript].

[38] Eadington, *supra* note 22, at 24.

[39] *See* RESPONSIBLE GAMING STATUTES AND REGULATIONS, *supra* note 34.

a direct cause of action by problem gamblers against casinos. This occurred in *Taveras*:

> The strongest argument against the existence of a casino's duty to restrain compulsive gamblers is the State's deliberate decision not to impose such a duty. "[S]tatutory and administrative controls over casino operations . . . are extraordinary[,] pervasive and intensive. . . . [State law regulates] virtually every facet of casino gambling and its potential impact upon the public. The regulatory scheme is both comprehensive and minutely elaborate." . . . Yet, in spite of the "extraordinary[,] pervasive and intensive" regulations over "virtually every facet of casino gambling," . . . the State's policymakers have notably declined to impose the duty upon which Plaintiff relies here. . . . [T]he Court declines Plaintiff's invitation to impose a public policy on the State that the State itself has disclaimed.[40]

As with the legal duty itself, the issue of the problem gambler's personal responsibility appears to take precedence for both the court and the state legislature: "Notably, while patrons may voluntarily place their names on lists of persons to be excluded from casinos, state law expressly absolves casinos from liability for failure to exclude these self-identified persons from gambling."[41]

Role of Casino

As with the government, casinos inevitably face tension between the goals of minimizing problem gambling and maximizing profits, particularly given a business model that rewards players with rebates known as "comps" (short for complimentaries) based on how much and how long they gamble. The following is typical advice from one of the many online sites that instruct prospective players on how to obtain casino comps:

> Comps are usually based on *how much you play*, not how much you lose. You'll still get comps even if you win. The casino knows that $X of wagers is worth $Y of profit to them *on average*, so they just look at the amount you bet and pretty much ignore whether you won or lost.
> One exception is that you can get more comps if you have a *large* loss. . . .
> Another exception is that you can get big comps if you have a large *win*. When you win big the casino will comp the hell out of you to keep you in the casino so they can win their money back from you.[42]

Some studies have even concluded that casinos knowingly rely on problem and pathological gamblers to produce a substantial portion of casino revenues.[43] The casino industry disputes such claims, as made clear by the

---

[40] Taveras, 2008 WL 4372791, at 4.

[41] *Id.*

[42] *How to Get Casino Comps*, VEGAS CLICK., http://vegasclick.com/gambling/comps.html.

[43] *See, e.g.,* NGISC, *supra* note 16, at 4-15 to 4-16; COUNCIL ON CASINOS, WHY CASINOS MATTER: THIRTY-ONE EVIDENCE-BASED PROPOSITIONS FROM THE HEALTH AND SOCIAL SCIENCES 18, 37–55 (Inst. for Am. Values 2013) (citing studies); Caesars Riverboat Casino v. Kephart, 903 N.E.2d 117 (Ind. Ct. App. 2009) (Crone, J., dissenting).

policy statement of the American Gaming Association (AGA) regarding responsible gaming:

> Gaming is, first and foremost, an entertainment industry, and members of the gaming industry want everyone who visits a casino to be there for the right reasons—to simply have fun. The industry doesn't want people who don't gamble responsibly to play at its casinos, period.[44]

Conflicts also arise when determinations are made regarding across-the-board actions that may assist the minority of players who are problem gamblers but negatively impact the majority who are not. For casino operators, these issues create a dilemma.

Of course, casinos are required as a condition of licensure to comply with all applicable statutes and government regulations mandating specific actions with regard to problem gambling. Sometimes those directives are broad, and leave the casinos with flexibility in designing and implementing problem gambling initiatives. Even when regulatory requirements are specific, however, casinos are authorized—perhaps encouraged—to go beyond the baseline requirements and to experiment and innovate.

Such proactivity is the policy of the AGA, as expressed in its responsible gaming statement:

> Responsible gaming is an issue of prime importance to the gaming industry, and the AGA, its member companies and their employees are committed to making responsible gaming a priority. By funding scientific, peer-reviewed research on gambling disorders, following the guidelines of the AGA Code of Conduct for Responsible Gaming and educating the public about the odds of games and making responsible decisions about when and

---

[44] *Responsible Gaming*, AMERICANGAMING.ORG, http://www.americangaming.org/social-responsibility/responsible-gaming (last visited Apr. 16, 2014). An executive of the AGA has reportedly asserted:

> [M]ost of the casino revenues are from "whales" — big gamblers who can afford their spending. . . . [T]he average debt of a pathological gambler isn't enormous: about $5,000.00. The industry focuses its marketing on people who can afford and enjoy the experience.

James M. Odato, *Study: Adding Casinos Bad Bet*, TIMESUNION.COM, Oct. 7, 2013, 6:30 AM, www.timesunion.com/local/article/Study-Adding-casinos-bad-bet-4874319.php. An executive of the National Center for Responsible Gaming (a casino-industry funded group), *see* www.americangaming.org/social-responsibility/responsible-gaming/national-center-responsible-gaming, has also been quoted as saying:

> Problem gamblers make for lousy customers. By their very nature, they will turn into bad debt.

> For them to hit bottom, they have to cause a lot of pain along the way, to themselves, their families and to companies. . . . It serves no purpose in any business to have customers who can't pay their bills.

For Atlantic City Casinos, A Delicate Balance Between Helping Addicts and Turning a Profit, NJ.COM, Feb. 26, 2012, 1:50 PM, www.nj.com/news/index.ssf/2012/02/for_atlantic_city_casinos_a_de.html.

how to gamble, the gaming industry demonstrates that responsible gaming is a fundamental part of how it does business.

Although the vast majority of Americans are able to gamble responsibly, a small percentage of people – approximately 1 percent of the adult population – cannot. The industry recognizes how serious this is and is taking concrete steps to address it. As part of their commitment to responsible gaming, members of the commercial casino industry work with a wide variety of stakeholders – problem gambling researchers, treatment providers, state problem gambling councils and government and community leaders – to make sure that those people who cannot gamble responsibly get the help they need and those who can understand the importance of gambling responsibly.[45]

Toward that end, the AGA promulgated a member Code of Conduct for Responsible Gaming, which addresses such matters as employee assistance and training, alcohol service, the provision of casino games, casino gambling advertising and marketing, financial support for research initiatives, and public awareness surrounding responsible gaming and underage gambling.[46] The AGA also provides resources to assist its members in complying with the code.[47]

MEANS OF ADDRESSING PROBLEM GAMBLING
Means Currently in Use/Potential Means

As indicated earlier, many elements of addressing problem gambling—including both prevention and harm minimization—are beyond the scope of this chapter. Instead, this chapter focuses only on the most significant means currently or potentially available to address problem gambling as a player protection mechanism in the context of responsible casino gaming.

As governments, regulatory agencies, casinos, and other gaming stakeholders consider and decide on means of addressing problem gambling, they need to take note of a few key principles. First, even among experts in the field, very little consensus exists regarding how responsible gambling should be defined or what responsible gambling measures are most effective.[48] Nevertheless, as has been observed:

Policymakers cannot know in advance the precise impact of new gambling policies. Demanding a very high or potentially unachievable standard of

---

[45] *Responsible Gaming*, AMERICANGAMING.ORG, www.americangaming.org/social-responsibility/responsible-gaming.

[46] AM. GAMING ASSOC., CODE OF CONDUCT FOR RESPONSIBLE GAMING (2012), www.americangaming.org/sites/default/files/uploads/docs/aga_code_conduct_2012_revision_final.pdf.

[47] *Code of Conduct*, AMERICANGAMING.ORG, www.americangaming.org/social-responsibility/responsible-gaming/code-conduct.

[48] *See, e.g.*, GERHARD BÜHRINGER ET AL., POLICY BRIEF 2: GAMBLING – TWO SIDES OF THE SAME COIN: RECREATIONAL ACTIVITY AND PUBLIC HEALTH PROBLEM (Alice Rap 2013), www.alicerap.eu/resources/documents/doc_download/128-policy-paper-2-gambling-two-sides-of-the-same-coin.html; WILLIAMS, *supra* note 33.

proof about "what works" would risk policy paralysis in an area where there are demonstrably large costs to society from inaction. Policy needs to take account of both the costs of mistakenly introducing ineffective policies, as well as the costs of failing to act when a policy option may in fact be effective.[49]

Second, different United States and foreign jurisdictions have different responsible gaming requirements, selecting specific tactics to effectuate each jurisdiction's strategies (i.e., policies and goals).[50] While policy makers need not ignore what has been done elsewhere, they should not feel either restricted by, or obligated to exceed, existing responsible gaming programs.

Finally, the "state of the art" in this area remains dynamic. Where hard science is lacking, experimentation and innovation are not only possible but may be required. An interesting side-note is that some of the means of addressing problem gambling discussed herein bear a similarity to best practices employed in the field of Internet gaming.[51]

Prevention
Player information/informed decision-making

Accepting that gambling ultimately represents an individual decision, the goal of the government and casino should be to provide sufficient information to allow the player to make an informed decision regarding his or her gambling or non-gambling. The necessary information falls into the following broad categories:

a. information generally explaining the probabilities of winning or losing at the various gambling games offered by the casino;[52]
b. information dispelling some of the "myths" surrounding gambling, particularly those involving slot machines;[53] and
c. information concerning responsible gambling, and specific ways to avoid gambling problems.[54]

---

[49] AUSTL. GOV'T PRODUCTIVITY COMM'N, *The Policy Framework, in* GAMBLING (2010), www.pc.gov.au/__data/assets/pdf_file/0010/95689/06-chapter3.pdf.

[50] *See, e.g.* EUROPEAN COMMITTEE FOR STANDARDIZATION, RESPONSIBLE REMOTE GAMBLING MEASURES (CEN 2011), ftp://ftp.cen.eu/CEN/AboutUs/Publications/Gambling-Measures.pdf; RESPONSIBLE GAMING STATUTES AND REGULATIONS, *supra* note 34.

[51] *See* REGULATING INTERNET GAMING: CHALLENGES AND OPPORTUNITIES 273–294 (Anthony Cabot & Ngai Pindell eds., 2013).

[52] *See, e.g.,* AGA CODE OF CONDUCT, *supra* note 46.

[53] *See, e.g.,* TAKING THE MYSTERY OUT OF THE MACHINE (Am. Gaming Assoc.), www.americangaming.org/sites/default/files/uploads/docs/taking_the_mystery_out_of_the_machine_brochure_final.pdf.

[54] *See, e.g.,* KEEPING IT FUN: A GUIDE TO RESPONSIBLE GAMBLING (Am. Gaming Assoc. 2003), www.americangaming.org/sites/default/files/uploads/docs/keep_it_fun_prev.pdf.

Technological design features of electronic gaming machines

According to the AGA, "[r]esearch has found no evidence that slot machines lead to greater rates of gambling addiction."[55] Nonetheless, contemporary electronic gaming machines (EGMs) have evolved to employ a wide array of attributes that maximize revenue generation, and they are associated with the highest problem gambling rates in Western countries.[56] For that reason, some have suggested certain modifications which could be made to EGMs that could be of assistance in reducing problem gambling behavior:

> Such features include: eliminating early big wins (perhaps by decreasing maximum win size), slower speed of play, reducing the frequency of near misses, reducing the number of betting lines, eliminating bill acceptors, reducing the interactive nature of EGMs, presenting dynamic pop-up messages, reducing maximum bet size, and perhaps, reducing the availability of seating. There is insufficient evidence to support the utility of: varying payback rates, establishing a maximum win size, requiring mandatory cashouts, introducing on-screen clocks, substituting monetary for credit displays, providing less privacy, and manipulating ambient light and sound.[57]

Pre-commitment

"Pre-commitment" refers to a strategy whereby pre-set limits on time, frequency, or money spent gambling are registered prior to the start of play on an EMG. It is believed to be a useful harm minimization strategy in that it allows players to make rational decisions about gambling involvement prior to actually engaging in gambling and obliges them to retain these limits despite subsequent temptations that arise during play.[58]

As has been observed:

> More flexible pre-commitment systems that give gamblers the capacity to control their gambling, rather than cease it, are relevant to gamblers generally. A "partial" system of pre-commitment with non-binding limits would produce some benefits, and provide lessons for a later, more comprehensive, system but the capacity for gamblers to circumvent the limits they set represents a major deficiency. A "full" pre-commitment system would allow players to set binding limits. This requires: identification of all players (except for occasional gamblers making small bets), but with strict privacy arrangements [and] a system that applies to all machines and venues.[59]

---

[55] Taking the Mystery Out of the Machine, *supra* note 53.

[56] Williams, *supra* note 33, at 30, 52.

[57] *Id.* at 61; *see also* Austl. Gov't Productivity Comm'n, *Game Features and Machine Design, in* Gambling (2010), www.pc.gov.au/__data/assets/pdf_file/0009/95697/14-chapter11.pdf.

[58] Williams, *supra* note 33, at 61. *See generally* Austl. Gov't Productivity Comm'n, *Pre-Commitment Strategies, in* Gambling (2010), www.pc.gov.au/__data/assets/pdf_file/0008/95696/13-chapter10.pdf [hereinafter *Pre-Commitment Strategies*].

[59] *Pre-Commitment Strategies, supra* note 58.

In casinos, pre-commitment would require a "smart card," that is, a plastic card with embedded integrated circuits providing limited memory and/ or microprocessor capabilities when interacting with external card-reading devices. Smart cards are already used as player loyalty/reward cards and/or as debit cards for cashless gambling. Such cards could be programmed to allow pre-commitment, or the pre-commitment card could be a different card altogether.[60]

As one study concluded,

Reward Cards have significant potential to promote responsible gambling if used to *reward responsible play*, rather than amount of play. For example, players could receive points up to a reasonable operator-set daily level of spending, beyond which they receive no points or start losing points. Another strategy would be for players not being able to collect their player points if they have exceeded their pre-commitment levels. Finally, players could receive points for opting to view educational resources.[61]

Still, as one expert recently observed, "Although the notion of mandatory pre-commitment appears very compelling and possibly useful, its implementation appears to be dictated by a political rather than a scientific agenda."[62]

Credit and cash access

In the United States, granting credit and/or check-cashing are common practices in casinos. Automated teller machines (ATMs) are also commonly located in casinos, and there are often no limits on ATM withdrawal amounts. Restrictions or prohibitions on one or more of these things exist in other countries.[63]

Overall,

[t]here is a lack of empirical research examining the effectiveness of monetary restrictions. However, anecdotal and existing survey data indicate that restricting ready access to cash is a potentially effective strategy. First, it is well established that problem gamblers access cash machines more frequently than regular gamblers. . . . Second, problem gamblers in treatment report that the most common reason for terminating a gambling session and leaving a gambling venue is because they have run out of money. . . . Indeed, self-reports of problem gamblers consistently identify easy and immediate access to cash as exacerbating gambling-related harm. . . .[64]

The casino industry opposes policies banning credit, limiting ATM

---

[60] WILLIAMS, *supra* note 33, at 62.

[61] *Id.* at 93.

[62] ROBERT LADOUCEUR, PRE-COMMITMENT: IS THE SMART CARD THAT SMART? (2013), http://massgaming.com/wp-content/uploads/7-Pre-Commitment.pdf (presentation to Mass. Gaming Comm'n).

[63] WILLIAMS, *supra* note 33, at 71.

[64] *Id. See also* AUSTL. GOV'T PRODUCTIVITY COMM'N, *Access to Cash and Credit, in* GAMBLING (2010), www.pc.gov.au/__data/assets/pdf_file/0011/95699/16-chapter13.pdf.

withdrawals, or removing ATMs from or near gaming areas due to the potential inconvenience to non-problem gamblers.[65]

Advertising and marketing practices

Although relatively little research exists on the effects of gambling advertising on gambling behavior,[66] most jurisdictions in the United States and around the world include restrictions on advertising and marketing practices as elements of their responsible gaming policies.[67] The AGA Code of Conduct for advertising represents the most frequently cited points:
Casino gambling advertising and marketing will:

- o   Contain a responsible gaming message and/or a toll-free help line number where practical.
- o   Reflect generally accepted contemporary standards of good taste.
- o   Strictly comply with all state and federal standards to make no false or misleading claims.

Casino gambling advertising and marketing will not:

- o   Contain images, symbols, celebrity/entertainer endorsements and/or language designed to appeal specifically to children and minors.
- o   Feature anyone who is or appears to be below the legal age to participate in gambling activity.
- o   Contain claims or representations that gambling activity will guarantee an individual's social, financial or personal success.
- o   Be placed before any audience where most of the audience is ordinarily expected to be below the legal age to participate in gambling activity.
- o   Imply or suggest any illegal activity of any kind.[68]

Marketing has become something of a double-edged sword. Player tracking, by means of reward cards or otherwise, is a widespread casino industry practice that provides the casino with copious player information to assist marketing efforts.[69] But the existence of such tracking systems raises

---

[65] WILLIAMS, *supra* note 33, at 71.

[66] *Id.* at 75.

[67] *See* RESPONSIBLE GAMING STATUTES AND REGULATIONS, *supra* note 34; AUSTL. GOV'T PRODUCTIVITY COMM'N, *Appendix K - Advertising, in* GAMBLING (2010), www.pc.gov. au/__data/assets/pdf_file/0010/95716/33-appendixk.pdf.

[68] CODE OF CONDUCT FOR RESPONSIBLE GAMING, *supra* note 46.

[69] *See, e.g., Player Tracking,* BALLY TECH, http://ballytech.com/Systems/Player-Tracking which states in part:

> Casino marketers who wish to outpace their competition must have a player-tracking system that allows them to collect real-time player information and translate it to their bottom line. Bally Technologies' player-tracking systems enable you to manage your systems – from accounting to marketing – with powerful, versatile industry leading tools that engage players

the questions whether they could be used as an "early warning system" for problem gambling, and if so, why casinos are not using them for that purpose. Some reports indicate that functioning "addiction algorithms" do exist, but that casinos are reluctant to use them either because they fear "the tool will show that some of their best customers are addicts, and that the casino's bottom line will suffer if management intervenes with troubled high-rollers,"[70] or because the casinos fear being held liable for failing to intervene with a potential problem gambler or violating privacy concerns.[71]

Employee training

Inasmuch as casino staff is usually the first point of contact for gamblers experiencing problems, most jurisdictions have mandatory or voluntary requirements for casino staff training in "responsible gambling":[72]

> Front line employees at casinos typically receive a one-time knowledge and skill development session to understand and recognize problem gambling behaviours in patrons so as to alert their supervisors to these individuals. More extensive training is typically provided for supervisory and management personnel at casinos, whose responsibilities include approaching the identified individual to offer immediate crisis management or treatment referral.[73]

Few employee-training programs have been scientifically evaluated for efficacy.[74]

Employee-training programs do not only enable employees to identify and/or assist problem gamblers who are customers; they also provide information and assistance as needed to employees who may experience a gambling problem.[75]

---

through:

- Patron loyalty programs
- Player extracts and analysis
- Group and promotion tracking
- Single player cards
- Multi-property support
- Hotel integration
- Direct mail

[70] Alan Farnham, *Casinos' Data Could ID, Help Problem Gamblers*, ABC News, Aug. 8, 2013, http://abcnews.go.com/Business/casino-data-identifies-problem-gamblers/story?id=19875823.

[71] *See* transcript, *supra* note 37, at 188–89; Different Regulatory Approaches, http://massgaming.com/wp-content/uploads/4-Models-of-Accountability.pdf.

[72] *See generally* Austl. Gov't Productivity Comm'n, *Venue Activities*, in Gambling (2010), www.pc.gov.au/__data/assets/pdf_file/0010/95698/15-chapter12.pdf [hereinafter *Venue Activities*]; Code of Conduct for Responsible Gaming, *supra* note 46.

[73] Williams, *supra* note 33, at 67.

[74] Debi A. LaPlante, Casino Employee Training (Oct. 28, 2013), http://massgaming.com/wp-content/uploads/8-Casino-Employee-raining.pdf.

[75] *See* Code of Conduct for Responsible Gaming, *supra* note 46.

Alcohol service/underage gambling

Other practices falling under the "prevention" rubric include responsible service of alcohol (i.e., no service to minors or visibly intoxicated persons and no gambling by visibly intoxicated persons), and the preclusion of gambling by underage persons.[76] Here, the only controversial issue is whether *any* customer—visibly intoxicated or not—should be served alcohol while gambling.[77]

Codes of conduct

Codes of conduct for responsible gaming (like the AGA's member code[78]) can address problem gambling if effective means to do so are incorporated, whether required by law or not.

Education
Games

Education concerning casino games has already been discussed above in connection with prevention efforts. Educational information should be readily available on-premises as well.

Problem gambling information

The most basic and productive means of education is having a casino provide responsible gaming awareness information, including a toll-free help-line number, at prominent locations throughout the casino.

Treatment
By government

Problem-gambling treatment by government agencies (whether in a clinical setting or otherwise) serves only as a destination for problem gamblers identified in a casino setting. Though it is a significant element of addressing problem gambling as a public health issue, it is otherwise beyond the scope of this chapter.

By casino/on-site counseling

As noted above, employee-training programs are designed in part to enable employees to assist problem gamblers. However,

> even with . . . a list of problem gambling indicators, there are several major difficulties and drawbacks for venues with problem player behaviour iden-

---

[76] *Id.*

[77] *See* WILLIAMS, *supra* note 33, at 95.

[78] CODE OF CONDUCT FOR RESPONSIBLE GAMING, *supra* note 46.

tification and intervention. Notwithstanding training, staff may find intervention too hard—they may see it as confrontational or fear the reactions of patrons. Even well trained staff will inevitably make a mistake and wrongly identify a person as a problem gambler, risking giving offence. Once approached by venue staff, a gambler might simply leave the venue and go to another. Venues could be exposed to litigation by vexatious or opportunistic gamblers who lose money gambling and then claim that the venue failed to intervene when there were apparent indicators of a problem. Mere regulation is not sufficient for transforming a venue culture from one that is reactive—based on responding to situations where a gambler self-reports and approaches staff for assistance—into one that is proactive. [79]

Despite these issues, casinos could offer some type of on-site counseling to problem gamblers or at least to problem gamblers who seek such assistance. [80]

Enforcement
Self-exclusion

Self-exclusion is an extreme form of pre-commitment, in which gamblers can bar themselves from one or more casinos to prevent themselves from gambling, with legislation empowering casinos to enforce their commitments. [81] Self-exclusion programs have been around since the late 1980s, [82] and they are the most widely-employed problem gambling enforcement measure. [83]

There are actually two types of self-exclusion. The first involves a government-administered program whereby a person voluntarily places him or herself on a list of self-excluded gamblers. The list is made available to all casinos in that jurisdiction, whose duty it is to refrain from knowingly allowing the self-excluded person to gamble. [84]

The other involves a voluntary choice by a casino to allow a person to self-exclude from gambling or other activities. An illustration of this is found in the AGA Responsible Gaming Code of Conduct:

> Each AGA casino company will have a policy in effect for all of its casino properties providing opportunities for patrons to request in writing the revocation of their privileges for specific services such as:
>
> ° Casino-issued markers
> ° Player club/card privileges
> ° On-site check-cashing

---

[79] *Venue Activities, supra* note 72, at 12.43.
[80] Marlene Warner, Onsite "Counseling" Centers and Community Collaborations (Oct. 28, 2013), http://massgaming.com/wp-content/uploads/11-Onsite-Treatment-Centers-and-Community-Collaborations.pdf.
[81] *Pre-Commitment Strategies, supra* note 58, at 10.6.
[82] Williams, *supra* note 33, at 46.
[83] *See* Responsible Gaming Statutes and Regulations, *supra* note 34.
[84] *Id.*

- ○ Complimentaries
- ○ Gambling promotions

In addition, each AGA casino company shall make reasonable efforts on a facility-by-facility basis to honor a written request from any person that it not knowingly grant that person access to gambling activities.[85]

The measured effectiveness of self-exclusion as a means of combating problem gambling is decidedly mixed.[86] Where problem gamblers who have self-excluded do exhibit

> a significant reduction in their gambling and problem gambling symptomatology . . . a good portion of this effect is due to the fact that people taking this step have recognized they have a problem, are highly motivated to do something about it, and have made a public proclamation that they do not intend to reenter casinos.[87]

Although third-party-initiated exclusions have been employed in some jurisdictions,[88] the complex legal and privacy-related issues raised by such procedures effectively preclude their adoption in the United States for the foreseeable future.

Duration of ban

One of the key policy determinations in adopting a self-exclusion program is the most effective duration of the ban, and on this point, the research is inconclusive.[89] The challenge is to make the ban long enough to have a meaningful effect on the problem gambler's behavior, but not so long as to discourage problem gamblers from signing up at all. Many jurisdictions in the United States offer optional lengths, with one year, five years, and lifetime bans being common choices.[90]

A subsidiary issue is how the casino enforces the self-exclusion program. Studies show that where enforcement relies primarily on casino staff's recognition of self-excluded persons, detection rates of those violating a ban are low.[91]

---

[85] Code of Conduct for Responsible Gaming, *supra* note 46.

[86] Williams, *supra* note 33, at 46-49.

[87] *Id.* at 49. Interestingly, legislation is pending in New Jersey which, if enacted, would allow individuals to self-exclude from the state's casinos or Internet gaming without any acknowledgment of problem gambling. *See* New Jersey Assembly Bill A-2444 and New Jersey Senate Bill S-2129 (introduced 2014).

[88] Austl. Gov't Productivity Comm'n, *Appendix E – Self Exclusion Programs and Exclusion on Welfare Grounds, in* Gambling (2010), www.pc.gov.au/__data/assets/pdf_file/0004/95710/27-appendixe.pdf.

[89] *Id.*

[90] Responsible Gaming Statutes and Regulations, *supra* note 34.

[91] Williams, *supra* note 33, at 50. *Id.* at 49.

Violation of ban/remedies

What is the appropriate remedy when, as happens with some frequency, a self-excluded person violates the ban?[92] Possibilities range from arrest and prosecution to mere refusal of service or ejection.[93]

What if a self-excluded person gambles and either wins or loses money? Logic dictates the self-excluded person should neither be able to collect winnings nor recover losses, so as to remove the incentive to violate the ban.[94] Forfeiture to the state provides a neat solution to prevent unjust enrichment by either the self-excluded gambler or the casino that allowed (even unknowingly) him or her to gamble.[95]

Research
Funding

Although funding for problem gambling research is primarily a public health-related government function, many governments require casinos, as beneficiaries of valuable and lucrative gaming licenses, to contribute funding for gambling-related research.[96] Casinos may also do so voluntarily or as part of an industry code of conduct.[97] Other creative gambling-related sources of funding also exist[98] but may not be sufficiently stable.

Evaluation of efforts

While self-regulation by casinos via codes of conduct or otherwise are commendable, scientific experts contend that to truly be effective, such efforts require evaluation by an outside body whether governmental or private.[99]

CONCLUSION

Protecting players by addressing problem gambling involves many policy choices by governments and casinos. To date, policymakers have operated under the unrealistic desire to implement effective prevention policies that do not inconvenience non-problem gamblers or reduce revenues.

---

[92] *Id.* at 47.

[93] RESPONSIBLE GAMING STATUTES AND REGULATIONS, *supra* note 34.

[94] Frank Catania & Gary Ehrlich, *When Crime Pays: A Gaming Regulatory Perspective on What to Do When a Minor or Other Prohibited Person Wins or Loses Money in a Casino*, 3 GAMING L. REV. 129, 142 (1999); WILLIAMS, *supra* note 33, at 50.

[95] *See, e.g.,* N.J.S.A. § 5:12-71.3.

[96] *See, e.g.,* UK GAMBLING COMM'N, LICENSE CONDITIONS AND CODES OF PRACTICE 17 (May 2012), www.gamblingcommission.gov.uk/pdf/LCCP%20consolidated%20version%20-%20May%202012.pdf.

[97] *See* CODE OF CONDUCT FOR RESPONSIBLE GAMING, *supra* note 46.

[98] *See, e.g.,* N.J.S.A. § 5:12-71.3 (providing that some forfeited funds may be used for compulsive gambling treatment and prevention programs).

[99] *See Venue Activities*, *supra* note 72, at 12.15; Transcript, *supra* note 36, at 114–15.

In reality, effectively preventing problem gambling is only likely to occur with some level of inconvenience to non-problem gamblers and a loss of revenue.[100]

As has been observed:

> The effective prevention of harm associated with potentially dangerous products or activities has always required some inconvenience to the general public and loss of revenue. The general public accepts the fact that aggressive government policies restricting tobacco advertising and consumption have resulted in reduced tax revenue. The general public also accepts the legal restrictions on their unfettered right to own firearms (e.g., restricted access to handguns and automatic weapons), to operate motor vehicles (e.g., need a driving license; mandatory seat belt use; speed limits), and to consume alcohol (e.g., not while driving, only in licensed establishments) despite the fact these restrictions are only really needed for a small minority of people with potential to misuse these products. These are the sorts of limitations that citizens routinely and willingly accept to produce a safer and healthier society overall.[101]

Perhaps the same is true with regard to addressing problem gambling.

---

[100] WILLIAMS, *supra* note 33, at 86.
[101] *Id.*

11

Regulating Electronic/Computer Games and Equipment

Patrick Moore

INTRODUCTION

A fundamental policy goal to most gaming regulators is to assure that the games offered to the public are honest. When casino gaming was first introduced in Macau, or Monte Carlo in the 1850s, or even Las Vegas in the 1930s, government monitoring and policing of games focused on having experienced investigators inspect and observe the games on the casino floor. This changed dramatically with the introduction of computer controlled slot machines and table games.

Control and verification of gaming technology are inherent in the regulated nature of the gaming industry itself. The gaming industry is built on the back of technology, and it ebbs and flows in response to technology innovation, or a lack thereof. Technical regulation and controls have struggled to catch up to the continual technological advancements experienced by the industry.

This chapter addresses the increasingly sophisticated methods utilized by gaming regulatory agencies and gaming operations to regulate and manage the gaming technology assets used in the modern-day casino industry. This chapter will also address some of the key technical processes regulatory agencies employ to mitigate risk to meet their primary objective of establishing a well-regulated and monitored operation.

In any form, regulation is built on the simple premise of controlling, monitoring, and/or verifying a particular activity. When technology plays a central role in that activity, as it does in the gaming industry, it is natural for the regulatory process to be equally technical in its approach. These technical processes are fostered through the promulgation of regulation, technical standards, and policy, with these directives based on understanding, controlling, and isolating critical gaming components.

As one would expect in any culturally- and procedurally-diverse business, there are numerous forms of specialized regulation employed by the industry. This chapter explains the general intent and key characteristics of industry standard technological regulations so the reader can make informed decisions regarding an appropriately-measured approach to technology control. The chapter also explains the key subjects commonly voiced by gaming regulators relating to gaming technology regulation and control.

When gaming technology regulation and control is stripped to its core principles, it is best described as regulators' method of confirming, verifying, and monitoring the implementation of technology in the regulated activity of gambling. Regulators are tasked with maintaining the integrity of gambling in that jurisdiction. This obligation spans a broad spectrum of tasks and methods that ensure the technologies, facilities, companies, and persons involved in gaming are addressed in a standard regulated model developed from the cultural and legal precedents of their jurisdiction.

As the gaming industry continues to evolve and technological diversity increases, technology regulation and verification must effectively adapt to these changes. This adaptation is initially accomplished through the enhancement or augmentation of existing technical requirements as well as through the advancement of the applications and utilities available to regulators. Additionally, as the scale and complexity of gaming systems grows, it is increasingly important for regulators to identify the skills and core competencies required within their agencies to effectively regulate these technologies.

THE ROLE OF TECHNICAL STANDARDS IN THE GAMING INDUSTRY

Technical standards are best described as the requirements for addressing technologies used in the gaming industry and that evolve from the basic principles of ensuring that the devices and systems utilized in the industry are fair, safe, secure, auditable, and reliable. These core principles form the basis from which the exacting technical requirements of the industry are created. Technical standards in the gaming industry are a fundamental resource for implementing and regulating a compliant gaming operation, and they have played an essential role in shaping the modern gaming industry. In other industries, technical standards may be *suggested* industry best practices or simply used to set guidelines from which certain products or product features *may* be developed. Technical standards in the gaming industry, however, are more like minimum compulsory technical requirements. Gaming regulators establish these technical standards as a way to standardize or create an operational baseline expectation of the devices and systems that operate under their purview.

The gaming industry's technical standards foundation originated at a time when technology providers first began to insert electromechanical devices controlled by micro-processors within gaming devices. Shortly after, regulatory bodies in Australia, New Zealand, Nevada, New Jersey, South Dakota, Illinois, Missouri, Indiana, Louisiana, Mississippi, Colorado, and Iowa devised technical language with intent to better understand these devices and draw limitations on their use in order to control the technology. Additionally, forward-focused Tribal–State Gaming Compacts included minimum technical considerations for the devices and systems envisioned for those markets. In many cases, the influence of technical requirements initially authored some 30 years ago can still be observed today in contemporary technical standards.

Technology author Andrew S. Tanenbaum is credited with one of the most appropriate quotes relating to technical standards. He quipped "The good thing about standards is that there are so many to choose from." His humor keenly reveals the ambiguity associated with his industry's usage of the term "standard," which by its very definition is meant to describe a common and unifying trend; in reality, a diverse menu of varying "standards" is available for selection.

The next section covers many of the shared concepts and intentions of today's contemporary technical standards in the gaming industry. It describes the general intent of contemporary gaming industry technical standards instead of exhaustively detailing the tens of thousands of unique technical clauses and jargon used in practice. While there are numerous technical standards represented within the industry, they do exhibit many common requirements and were largely authored in the shared-spirit of ensuring the games and systems operating in the industry are fair, safe, secure, auditable, and reliable.

FUNDAMENTAL TECHNICAL REQUIREMENTS OF ELECTRONIC GAMING DEVICES

Physical Security

Industry technical standards addressing electronic gaming devices and systems nearly always address the issue of physical security. Player-facing devices must be manufactured to be sufficiently robust to resist forced entry into the device. Additionally, the devices must be made of material that would leave conspicuous evidence of forced entry. Servers, controllers, and other back-of-the-house gaming components must be housed in a secure area of the gaming facility with controlled access and security monitoring. The intent here is clear: to protect these sensitive devices from a physical attack or manipulation to ensure the continued integrity of the device.

Environmental Effects on Device Integrity

Current industry requirements contemplate a minimum set of tests that may impact the operation of gaming devices and systems. In general, these tests are focused on environmental factors such as electromagnetic interference, electrostatic discharge, and radio-frequency interference. Generally these requirements are formed from the perspective of consumer safety and are confirmed under product safety certification requirements from agencies such as Underwriters Laboratories (UL). However, some environmental testing focuses on game operational integrity with the tests themselves focused on using these environmental factors as attempted manipulation or "cheating" methods to ensure that game outcomes cannot be influenced. Devices today have been designed to withstand significant environmental stressors and may reset or reboot under these conditions, though they are expected to recover to the proper game-state and continue operation.

Device Identification

Most jurisdictions require gaming devices to include a permanent identification badge or tag that provides standard information about the gaming device such as the manufacturer, a unique serial number, model number, and the date of manufacture. This information may be used by casino operations for asset tracking and similar purposes.

Tower Lights

Most jurisdictions require a tower light, which serves as a physical indicator for machine states such as error conditions, open doors, jackpots, and similar events. The light is conspicuously located on the gaming device, so attendants and surveillance can easily spot the tower light conditions and act on those events. As systems continue to evolve, casinos have introduced more sophisticated attendant-notification methods for these game-level events, such as SMS messaging identifying the location of the game alert. Tower lights, however, continue to be relied on in hundreds of markets across the industry.

External Doors

Related to the aforementioned physical security of the gaming device, current technical standards go to great lengths to detail the physical security requirements of the external access points into a gaming device. Doors must be securely locked and utilize sensors that trip when the door is moved from its fully closed and locked position. These sensors cause the gaming device to enter a unique door-open state, illuminate the tower light, and activate an alert that is sent by the gaming device to any host monitoring system.

Logic Area

The logic area of a traditional gaming device is best described as the device's brain. This secure area holds all of the control logic for gaming device operation (i.e., any logic which plays a substantive role in the operation of the device including the random number generator, pay-tables, the primary operating system, and communication logic). The logic area is typically required to be keyed differently than other access points on the gaming device so that access to the logic area can be effectively limited using key controls.

Currency Storage Compartments

Currency storage requirements create a standard level of security in the areas of a gaming device that store items of monetary value including coins, tokens, bills, tickets, or other notes. For obvious reasons, these areas may require different locking mechanisms or in many cases multiple levels of locks to ensure that access to these areas is limited to authorized persons.

Gaming Device Control Program and Critical Memory Authentication

Many people may not realize contemporary electronic gaming devices are one of the most intrinsically secure user-centric products. Current industry requirements significantly emphasize the security and viability of the control programs and operating data used by these devices. Gaming device developers must create advanced internal authentication schemes within their devices that continually monitor and assess the legitimacy of their installed software and critical program data. These methods may include the use of hash-codes, advanced encryption, write-protection mechanisms, unique security certificates, sector level media scans, and similar methods to ensure that only legitimate programs may execute within the device.

Additionally, gaming devices must maintain and authenticate key operating data on an ongoing basis. For example, gaming devices must maintain essential computer memory locations using backup mechanisms. This typically includes the use of a battery or other alternative power source that will maintain these memory locations if primary power to the gaming device is lost. Some jurisdictions require these memory locations be maintained by the device 180-days after primary power to the gaming device is lost. This continually-maintained area of the device's memory is commonly referred to as non-volatile memory.

Additionally, particularly sensitive areas of non-volatile memory are validated at defined events to ensure these memory locations contain expected values and have not been manipulated or corrupted since their last update. These memory locations must be validated as they contain important operational data to the gaming device. For example, they contain the mandatory accounting meters of the device, a record of current player credits, gaming device configuration data, historical recall of last x games, the last known software state of the gaming device, the current paytable data, and similar data. This area of non-volatile memory is most commonly referred to as critical memory as these locations hold the most critical data responsible for device compliance.

Contemporary industry requirements are generally forward-thinking in their approach to control program validation and critical memory validation. The requirements do not prescribe an exact method that must be employed when the gaming device is performing these functions and, instead, set the minimum hashing functions or algorithms that the mechanisms must employ. These regulations typically define the minimum instances at which these checks must occur and generally will allow the developer to expand on those security requirements using more recent security methods and protocols.

The above information regarding control program validation and critical memory validation requirements is an intentionally simplified representation of the extremely complex and variable function of electronic gaming devices. The control program and critical memory validation are the most intricate and least understood of all classes of gaming technical regulation. This complexity is exacerbated by the unique platform infrastructures engineered within the industry that introduce varying computer operating systems, varying computer media, new security methodologies, and other unique considerations that must then be reviewed for minimum equivalency to current industry standards.

Credit Issuance and Redemption Devices

The term "slot machine" is widely accepted as derived from the fact that gaming devices had a slot where patrons would insert their wager(s) in the hopes of winning something of greater value. That slot has evolved over the many decades since its first iteration through advancements in security, accuracy, and counterfeiting countermeasures until eventually the slot was replaced entirely by today's contemporary note acceptance devices.

Modern devices generally forgo the acceptance of coins and tokens as those credit mediums have been largely replaced by newer technologies and mediums. Ticketing is a form of cashless technology that allows the casino to account for patron credits using bar-coded paper script or "tickets." These bearer instruments are also commonly referred to as vouchers. Ticketing has become the primary method of gaming device credit issuance and redemption.

In simplistic terms, casino ticketing works through the use of a ticket validation system interfaced to each gaming device in the gaming operation. Players typically activate a gaming device by inserting cash into the device's note acceptor. The note acceptor's software validates the authenticity of the inserted note and works with the gaming device's software to convert the value of the note into electronic gaming credits. Players then play any number of games on the gaming device, and any remaining credits on the gaming device may be retrieved by the player at their leisure. This is when a ticket validation system initiates the creation of a casino ticket or voucher.

In this communication flow, the gaming device and system collaborate to convert the remaining electronic casino credits on the gaming device into a bar-coded ticket or voucher. Current requirements dictate the minimum information required to be printed on the ticket, which includes the amount of credit, date/time, location, expiry detail, and, most importantly, a validation number the system uses to reference the ticket in a database when a player chooses to later redeem that ticket.

This validation number is tantamount to a complex, unique key that allows the system to properly track the status of the ticket and ensures a ticket cannot be duplicated and perpetually redeemed. When a player chooses to redeem the ticket at another gaming device, redemption kiosk, or cashier, the system looks up this unique validation key in its database and then, if found to be valid, authorizes the chosen redemption device to issue funds to the player.

Note acceptors (or bill acceptors as they are called commonly) also play a critical role in the verification of player funds and the issuance of electronic gaming credits. Note acceptors are sophisticated scanning devices that utilize bi-directional communication protocols to interface with gaming devices to ensure the validity and value of notes inserted into the gaming device. These devices utilize advanced optical recognition sensors, speed and direction measurement mechanisms, and other identification routines to validate the authenticity and value of currency notes.

The exact operation of these devices is a tightly-held secret as one can imagine the significance of knowing the exact criteria and methods these devices use to deduce the validity of a note. In fact, developers of these note acceptor devices commonly work with the United States Department of the Treasury on enhancements to counterfeit countermeasures based on counterfeit notes passed and captured through other industries.

The Player Interface

Current player interface requirements are an essential part of the gaming regulation space because they address the forward-facing characteristics of gaming devices—the characteristics that directly interact with the end user or players. Therefore, significant attention is paid to the exactness of these requirements. Additionally, because these requirements have as their goals player fairness and satisfaction, the human element of these requirements can sometimes make their application subjective.

Game Rules

As one might expect in the gaming industry, the rules of the game are as important as its operation. The developer of the game asks a player to wager hard-earned money on a game offering, and therefore that player deserves the opportunity to understand the proper, expected operation of the game. Players should understand the opportunity or risk offered by the gaming device before making that wager. Game rules are probably best described as a contract with the player, laying out all the possible winning outcomes, bonus features, considerations, and other game elements so a player may make informed decisions about wagering.

The authors of these requirements and those who certify devices have developed a "reasonable player standard" to account for the variety of players interacting with devices. Such a standard falls somewhere between a neophyte and a veteran gaming device player. This is important in the context of game rules because developers must continually strike a balance between too much and not enough information made available to the player. A reasonable player standard helps to focus game rule requirements in an otherwise broad area of regulation.

In the end, the intent of these requirements is apparent. Game rules must accurately portray the design and operation of gaming devices in a clear and concise manner, and those game rules must not be misleading to the player. These requirements are rooted in player fairness and transparency.

Persistent Information

Drivers have expectations about the information that should appear on an automobile dashboard such as the speed and fuel level. Persistent information in the context of the player interface of a gaming device describes the informational elements that must be available to players on a persistent basis during the operation of the gaming device.

These informational elements typically include the following:
1. The player's current credit balance;
2. The current bet amount;
3. All possible winning outcomes;
4. Any amounts won from the last completed game;
5. Available player options (e.g., number of lines in play, credits bet per line); and
6. The currently selected denomination.

Randomness Requirements

If players and gaming industry stakeholders were polled regarding what they thought was the single most significant characteristic of electronic gaming devices, it is likely that randomness (i.e., unpredictability) of the electronic gaming device would be at or near the top of the list. Randomness has been a long-held principle since the earliest iterations of technical regulation. Regulatory intent typically centers on the need for games to be unpredictable and completely independent of prior game outcomes. It is also relatively easy to understand why patrons would care about random outcomes—gambling would not be very entertaining if the result were already known.

The vast majority of random number generators (RNGs) in use are more accurately described as pseudo-random number generators (PRNGs). They are deterministic computational algorithms that do not demonstrate "randomness" in the truest sense of the term but do demonstrate sufficient random traits in their output to pass industry-standard statistical tests and have historically proven acceptable for producing unpredictable outcomes for electronic gaming devices.

Put simply, RNGs produce outcomes. To ensure the outcomes are sufficiently random, the output stream of random numbers is analyzed using a battery of sophisticated statistical tests specifically designed to identify anomalies. Additionally, RNGs are scrutinized by these statistical tests in the context of the application in which the RNG is used; an RNG may be found suitable for a single-deck video poker application but less so for a complex slot-style game. RNGs used in gaming devices must also be cryptographically strong, meaning they must be resistant to attackers attempting to manipulate or detect the random selection process. This is typically done by continually streaming the RNG as a background process so that calls to the RNG happen at varying states. Additionally, the seeding or starting point of the RNG typically varies and may be repositioned at varying times to create additional disorder to the random selection process, thereby making it less susceptible to detection and manipulation.

Requirements related to the randomness of electronic gaming devices extend past the RNG itself and into thoughtful prohibitions of ancillary features and functions that may inhibit or manipulate the operation of the RNG.

These requirements are premised on the game's mandatory use of the RNG-generated outcome rather than a secondary or alternative decision after the RNG outcome is produced.

Payout Percentage

"Theoretical payout percentage," "theoretical payback percentage," or "theoretical return percentage" are all terms that refer to the ratio of "payout" to "bet" that can be expected from an electronic gaming device over its lifetime. Based on the mathematical model of the game (which considers the game's rules, programmatic logic, probabilities of elements/symbols, and implementation of the RNG), it is possible to calculate the lifelong expectations of this return-versus-bet ratio with a great level of precision. There are various mathematical principles that allow for such calculations ranging from Monte Carlo style simulations over programmed models of the games to comprehensive theoretical proofs offering definitive precision. As technology has progressed, games have become increasingly complex and these developments have propelled the industry to devise more sophisticated and advanced methodologies for performing these calculations efficiently. A simple and fictitious game example, *Florida Oranges*, below, illustrates the calculation of theoretical payback percentage:

Game rules

Florida Oranges is a 3-Reel Game that has three different types of outcomes:

Figure 11.1

3 🦃 Pays **63** Credits. In other words, the win-value of this alignment is 63.

3 ⚫⚫ Pays **10** Credits. In other words, the win-value of this alignment is 10.

Any other combination Pays 0 credits. The win-value of these alignments is, of course, zero.

Reel strips

To calculate a theoretical return percentage for this simple slot game, it is necessary to understand the set consisting of all possible game outcomes. Because this game lacks any complex bonus feature (e.g., symbol weight assignments, transforming features), the set, commonly known as game cycle, is calculated by simply multiplying each reel's symbol count (see Figure 11.2, opposite).

Game cycle

10x10x10 = **1000** possible combinations

Probability

We then continue by drilling down to each category of game outcome including all unique winning combinations and losing combinations, and calculate the probability of each of those categories which is ultimately used to determine the contribution, or expected value (EV), of each combination.

Figure 11.2

Reel Strip #1	Reel Strip #2	Reel Strip #3
🍒	🍒	🍒
<blank>	🍒	<blank>
<blank>	<blank>	🍒
🍒	<blank>	🍒
<blank>	🍒	<blank>
🍒	<blank>	🍒
<blank>	🍒	🍒
🍒	<blank>	🍒
<blank>	🍒	🍒
<blank>	<blank>	🍒
Reel 1 = 10 Stops	Reel 2 = 10 Stops	Reel 3 = 10 Stops
3 Cherries	3 Cherries	3 Cherries
1 Orange	2 Oranges	5 Oranges
6 <blanks>	5 <blanks>	2 <blanks>

Figure 11.3

What is the probability of 3 🍒 occurring in a winning alignment?

(3) 🍒 on Reel 1 x (3) 🍒 on Reel 2 x (3) 🍒 on Reel 3 Divided By the Game Cycle (1000) = .027 or 2.7%

What is the probability of 3 🍊 occurring in a winning alignment?

(1) 🍊 on Reel 1 x (2) 🍊 on Reel 2 x (5) 🍊 on Reel 3 Divided By the Game Cycle (1000) = .01 or 1%

What is the probability of a non-winning alignment?

100% - (2.7% + 1%) = 0.963 or 96.3%

Therefore 96.3% of the 1000 possible combinations within the game cycle will result in a non-winning alignment.

Contribution

After determining the probability of both winning and non-winning alignments occurring within the game cycle, we determine the contribution of those alignments to the theoretical payback percentage. These contributions representing each category of game outcome, when summed, equal the overall theoretical return percentage of the game.

Contribution is most clearly represented as follows:

Probability of Alignment during Game Cycle x Win Value of Alignment

Figure 11.4

3 🍊 Contribution: .01 x 63 = .63 or **63%**

3 🍒 Contribution: .027 x 10 = .27 or **27%**

Non-Winning Alignment Contribution:
0.963 x 0 = 0 or 0%

The theoretical payback percentage of Florida Oranges is **90%** (the sum of the three contributions 63% + 27% + 0%).

Again, Florida Oranges is an intentionally elementary illustration of theoretical return percentage. Additionally, an analytical analysis of the theoretical return percentage does not account for the random selection process which, as previously detailed, is an essential characteristic of electronic gaming devices.

Who would enjoy playing an electronic device where for every dollar wagered, the device paid back 90 cents? Such a device would then just be an expensive change machine at the point that also charges you for the transaction. In the end, the entertaining characteristic of an electronic gaming device is that its random attributes afford the player an opportunity to win more than what they wager based on varying degrees of chance and/or skill. Due to the random characteristics of electronic gaming devices, those tasked with controlling and regulating these devices must also consider other mathematical factors like volatility, confidence intervals, and asymptotic behaviors. In the end, gambling is gambling for both the house and the player with no guarantees, only probability.

Metering and Accounting

Electronic gaming devices are essentially transactional devices that input player funds, accept wagering of those funds on events of chance and/or skill, and display a result to the player. Because these are monetary transactions that are heavily regulated and taxed, electronic gaming devices must maintain a record of all transactions. Wagering transactions are recorded to the appropriate accounting meters, which record all funds in and out of the gaming device as well as all wagers and wins. These meter sets also categorize and delineate the source of values in and out of the device, i.e., awards paid by the gaming device itself versus those paid by an attendant.[1] These meter sets make the gaming device fully auditable from a revenue-reporting standpoint and can also recreate play history should players become confused and believe they are entitled to a different outcome than the one presented to them.

As discussed in greater detail later in this chapter, contemporary gaming establishments almost universally employ the use of data collection systems which "poll" these meter sets and record this information in a centralized database. Such a configuration efficiently collects and synthesizes accounting information from all gaming devices on the casino floor.

A Brief View of Technology Control and Verification Methods and Tools

Gaming component control by regulators is as old as the implementation of the first electro-mechanically controlled slot machines. These initial processes evolved from the knowledge that a computer chip or micro-processor would assume a principal role in the operation of a gaming device, the determination of game outcome, and therefore the overall integrity of the gaming device.

As gaming devices continued to incorporate computer-based technologies, gaming regulators began to adopt verification and authentication disciplines from other regulated industries that employed the use of cryptography and security protocols to protect and validate data. Gaming device

---

[1] See, e.g., Nev. Tech. Stand. 2.040 Meters for Conventional Gaming Devices, System Supported and System Based Games.

verification became focused on the use of hash codes, or "message digests," as an effective, feasible way to validate the legitimacy of gaming device data by confirming the approved or expected gaming device data had not been unintentionally corrupted or, worse, intentionally manipulated by an attacker.

While computer-based gaming devices inevitably changed the way regulators approached the verification of gaming devices, they also introduced a reproducible and logical way for regulators to confirm the ongoing operational integrity of gaming devices. With the introduction of computer-based gaming devices, regulators were empowered to use "type" verification.[2] This means that a single type of gaming device control software could be tested, validated, certified, and assigned a hash-code using a hashing program. Software could be continually re-validated and re-verified in every instance and installation simply by verifying its hash-code against a known good hash-code result.

In other words, type verification provided regulators a more consistent, feasible approach to confirm gaming device operations were compliant because the software responsible for various functions could be easily confirmed to be of a specific approved "type" and therefore quickly approved and put into operation on the casino floor. This fundamental change in the ability of regulators to assess the compliance of electronic gaming devices is a perfect example of technology enhancing the efficiency of regulatory tasks while also facilitating the primary regulatory objective of ensuring gaming integrity.

Below are a few simple definitions related to the basic elements of software verification and control:

- A *hash function* is a function that maps a variable-length data block or message into a fixed-length value called a hash code.
- A *hash code* is a fixed-length value created through the use of a hash function. It is also referred to as a message digest.
- *Checksum*[3] is a sum derived from the bits of a segment of computer data that is calculated before and after transmission or storage to ensure the data is free from errors or tampering.
- A *CRC (Cyclic Redundancy Check)*[4] is a hash function designed to detect accidental changes to raw computer data, **and** it is commonly used in digital networks and storage devices such as hard disk drives. It is also known as a polynomial code checksum.
- In cryptography, *MD5 (Message-Digest Algorithm 5)*[5]is a widely used cryptographic hash function with a 128-bit hash value. Spec-

---

[2] In a fully mechanical gaming device, to truly confirm operational integrity, one would likely have to confirm each device or component off the assembly line to ensure that critical functions of each gaming device were operationally equivalent to other like-parts off the same line.

[3] First used around 1940.

[4] First used around 1960.

[5] First used around 1991.

ified in RFC 1321, MD5 has been employed in a wide variety of security applications and is also commonly used to check the integrity of files. An MD5 hash is typically expressed as a 32-digit hexadecimal number.

- The *SHA (Secure Hash Algorithm)*[6] is one of a number of cryptographic functions published by the National Institute of Standards and Technology (NIST) as a US Federal Information Processing Standard.

Put simply, a hash-code, or "hash" as it is commonly called, is one of the single most important elements in the regulation and control of gaming. Like a fingerprint or DNA is used to identify the true identity of a person, program components designed for use in computer systems are comprised of unique binary attributes to allow for the proper identification of authentic or inauthentic components.

Common Hashing Tools
Kobetron Inc.

In 1984, Kobetron, Inc., developed a unique device for reading data from gaming device control program media. Media read into the Kobetron device is assigned a hash code based on a proprietary algorithm developed by Kobetron. This device became the ubiquitous method of gaming device verification. Kobetron remains active in the gaming industry today, offering various methods of gaming device verification across various mediums.

Gaming Laboratories International (GLI) CDCK/SFCK/GLI Verify

In the early 1990s, the independent gaming-testing laboratory GLI developed a program for reading data in blocks from newer media types such as CD, DVD, and Flash Media and injecting that data into various hashing algorithms to produce a message digest. While this program included standard hashing algorithms such as MD5, it also included a proprietary CRC variant algorithm called CDCK. CDCK was then developed to also operate in a Linux computing environment and was designated as SFCK. GLI's CDCK has been continually modified and is today widely known as GLI Verify.

Gaming Standards Association (GSA) Game Authentication Terminal (GAT)

In the late 1990s a gaming industry supplier, Bally Gaming and Systems, developed what was termed Game Authentication Terminal (GAT). The premise of this development was to create a consistent approach to gaming device component verification across many variations of gaming

---

[6] First used around 1993.

devices and interface elements. GAT was a unique concept in that regulatory agencies would require suppliers to design GAT support within their gaming platforms. Gaming regulators could then access a device's GAT features by plugging a computer into a designated communication port of the device to initiate a verification session.

In 2005, GAT protocol development was transitioned from Bally Gaming and Systems to a gaming industry trade association called the Gaming Standard Association or GSA. This was an important step in the development lifecycle of GAT, and GSA's members worked to standardize what had become a fairly patchwork industry implementation of the original GAT protocol. This exercise resulted in the development of GAT3. GAT3 usage in the gaming industry continues to gain momentum, largely due to its common approach to gaming device and system verification.

Although GAT3 alleviates a key burden for regulators by standardizing the verification method, it creates limitations because of its reliance on the gaming device to perform key functions of the verification process. This means the gaming device must be fully operational to complete a GAT3 session, and it restricts the use of this feature in instances when the game has experienced a critical malfunction and therefore is unable to respond to a GAT session request from the regulator's computer.

Due to GAT3's convenience to regulators it will likely become an everyday means of floor-based gaming device audit and verification. Most industry regulations, however, will continue to require a forensic-level independent mechanism of device verification capable of being used for critical gaming device malfunction because these situations often present the most likely source of patron confusion or dispute.

Third-Party Verification Mechanisms

Third-party verification mechanisms are the current standard in the industry. "Third-party," here, refers to a party that is neither the gaming device developer/supplier nor the regulator of that gaming device.

This standard for third-party verification stemmed from the idea of ensuring independence wherever possible in the tools, methods, applications, and mechanisms used in the crucial role of gaming device and system verification. While each jurisdiction defines their own local policy regarding approved verification tools and mechanisms, the requirement for third-party mechanisms has been widely adopted by the industry based on the simple premise that mandating the independence of these critical mechanisms assists in preventing, however rare, device manipulation by those with knowledge and continued exposure to those gaming devices and systems operating within gambling establishments.

PHYSICAL REGULATION AND CONTROL

Today's predominant form of technology regulation and control in the gaming industry involves regulators manually verifying gaming device control components. This typically involves a defined process executed either during routine audits or upon specific events defined within each jurisdiction's internal controls. This process involves regulatory agents understanding the composition of each gaming device or system to be verified and then utilizing reference material to determine the expected and approved hash code results from their audits. Agents utilize various verification methods and tools during this audit, and the audit often includes the removal of computer media such as EPROMs, ROM Discs, Flash Media, and Hard Discs for further evaluation.

Because gaming devices and systems are supplied from many different gaming suppliers, these devices are unique in their design and implementation, and agents must use a diverse toolkit when performing regulatory tasks. Even if a similar media type is encountered, each media type may introduce sub-types, which will impact the hash-code result. Therefore, understanding which tool is needed for which media type is only the beginning. Agents must also understand the numerous configurations and options of each verification tool to consider these sub-types. Sub-types may include the size of the media, its file structure, any security features of the media, and additional data points.

Given each gaming device may be comprised of several different media types, it becomes clear that the complexity and scope of each instance of gaming device verification is significant. This process also includes various levels of physical control and security including multiple locking mechanisms that are keyed differently and must be accessed by agents after conforming to stringent key controls, the use of seal or evidence tape, machine entry information recording, and other procedural requirements to ensure only authorized personnel have been granted access to the sensitive areas of these heavily regulated devices. This is not to suggest that this is the exact process followed in each gaming jurisdiction. However, this represents the predominant method of gaming device and system verification utilized in the industry. Jurisdictions define their individual risk tolerance and employ various verification and control methods based on their risk aversion.

SYSTEM-BASED REGULATION AND CONTROL

System-based regulation and control can come in many forms; however, the most common form has various monikers depending on the jurisdiction: Central Monitoring System (CMS), Central Control System (CCS) or simply the "Central System." The central system regulatory approach was developed out of a basic need for regulatory agencies to have a programmatic, near-omniscient solution to monitor and control gaming devices operating under its purview. These systems provide a centralized network operation model where the regulatory agency or its contractor is tasked with continual monitoring, assessing, and reporting on gaming device operations.

A central control system is a computer-based system under the control of a gaming regulatory body in which the accounting data, security exception reports, and software verification is centralized and controlled by that regulatory agency. This includes the ability to manually or automatically disable gaming devices based on a defined schedule or on the occurrence of defined triggers.

Virtually all of today's regulated games are microprocessor-controlled, and the data from game play is sent almost immediately to an online accounting or control system. Central control systems originated in 1989 in South Dakota as a response to a highly regulated and distributed gaming network.[7] Regulators quickly recognized that some sort of centralized control was needed. Other states with fewer gambling sites and a smaller geography most often opted to utilize an on-demand dial-up data collection mechanism, but this approach can be cumbersome and is prone to sporadic outages and lengthy polling times. Oregon was the first state to go "online," in the sense that every gaming machine is connected to a central computer system and communicates with that system in real-time.

"Lottery" or "Revenue" departments implemented most early central control systems. These organizations required a high-level of machine accountability, but at the same time these departments were focused on reducing overall expenses and manpower requirements. However, these reductions could not compromise the security of the data in any way. Therefore, video lottery systems became the precursor to today's advanced central control system implementations.

Monitoring and collection systems were somewhat slower to take root in the casino gaming sector. This is because casino regulation and gaming device monitoring were historically location-centric. This model began to change as the complexity of the slot floor increased and was driven by overall advancements in gaming device technology. Casino marketing efforts also drove the deployment of systems in casinos as did ticketing and wagering account transfers. Large-scale data collection systems are now in virtually every major casino in North America.

The systems are typically located at each casino site, require on-site administration and auditing, and rely heavily on internal controls. Despite the prevalence of a central control model in the video lottery market, most casino gaming jurisdictions did not adopt the lottery model of a regulator-administered central system. Therefore, most regulators in casino markets still perform on-site software verification (i.e., manual sealing and inspection of each gaming device control program). This, too, is slowly

---

[7] *See generally* SOUTH DAKOTA LOTTERY, lottery.sd.gov/games/video.

changing with the advent of networked gaming systems, which are explained in more detail later in this chapter.

Casino operators quickly realized the benefits of data collection, and local systems were installed in many casinos. As technology further developed and some operators expressed the need for data collection capabilities across several properties, linked systems developed.

Logically, casino operators identified the value of the data collected by such systems and adopted reliable local site systems, some which rival banking systems in terms of accuracy. High system availability is critical because system uptime is paramount due to other developments like the implementation of wagering account transfers and casino ticketing.[8]

That said, today's truest examples of CCS technologies continue to be lottery jurisdictions, examples of which include modern "racinos." These venues incorporate CCS heavily but also continue to rely on local site systems for some functionality. For example, racinos may manage their customer data differently than their revenue and security monitoring data, and therefore they have deployed their own site systems for functionality such as progressives, player bonusing, and player marketing. At the same time, gaming devices have become largely indistinguishable between lottery and gaming jurisdictions as CCS systems move away from the proprietary protocols of the past and implement the same communication protocols as those used in other gaming sectors.

These systems are true to their monikers in that they allow administrators to monitor all activity occurring at a gaming device. This includes information regarding gameplay but also key security events such as doors being opened and loss of communication. Additionally, these systems provide for the centralized control of gaming devices. For example, devices can be remotely verified, enabled, and disabled, among other functions. Overall, gaming operators and their regulators understand the inefficiencies of stand-alone machine regulation and are focused on creating efficiencies through the use of computer networks.

FUTURE TECHNOLOGY ADVANCEMENTS IN THE REGULATION OF GAMING DEVICES AND SYSTEMS

Gaming devices themselves are evolving to support centrally controlled and administered configurations. Gaming devices are being standardized and integrated into networks that introduce a framework for downloading software, issuing control commands or configuration instructions to the gaming device, or any combination of other actions facilitated by a broadband network environment.

---

[8] A "wagering account" is an electronic ledger for a cashless wagering system patron deposit account. NEV. TECH. STAND. 1.010 (33) Definitions.

With the advent of networked gaming technologies, it is no longer necessary to open each machine, manually access its secure components, or manually reconfigure the device. This can be done remotely, over a secure network, and literally broadcast to thousands of machines in relatively short order. Network technologies allow gaming operators to change a gaming device's game program, currency denominations, and bonus payouts and offer advanced incentives through a central computer server rather than requiring an army of slot technicians to perform the work manually. In fact, slot technicians will likely evolve over time into information technology (IT) professionals working to maintain the required network infrastructure.

Reconfiguring a bank of gaming devices, let alone just a single machine, is not straightforward. The machine typically has to be opened in the presence of a regulator, evidence tape broken, the old game program media removed, a memory clear performed, and new program media inserted (or other new program media installed). The machine must be resealed with evidence tape, the machine closed, and all required paperwork completed. Following this procedure on a crowded slot floor for thousands of machines is an arduous task and, when performed, requires significant device down time.

Gaming device and system manufacturers are clearly committed to networked gaming technology, and gaming's future is beginning to be realized through various system-based gaming architectures such as mobile gaming and interactive gaming. This makes it all the more critical that an open network design philosophy be maintained as this technology evolves. The industry must properly learn from past design mistakes that were overly reliant on proprietary technologies, which further complicate the regulation and control mechanisms needed to effectively regulate these systems.

For regulators, this technology will require continual player education to disabuse them of the myth that the casinos change the payback of a machine with the flip of a switch. Networked gaming fuels this misconception as players become more aware of the interrelationship between the server and the gaming devices. Obviously, the regulatory reality is that the process will be tightly controlled to protect player fairness and ensure game integrity.

The regulators' role in the control and verification of these advanced systems will inevitably be impacted. That is not to say it will be impacted negatively. To the contrary, the regulator will have capabilities once thought impossible. Regulators will have increased confidence in game and system integrity due to the availability of network-based security protocols and policies, trusted logs, third-party audit tools, and similar methodologies. Critical gaming device control program installs can be programmatically approved by the regulator before any change or update occurs, and the authenticity of such updates will be tightly secured throughout the entire process.

These systems will also reduce human error by automating once-manual tasks. Additionally, regulatory agencies will find that navigating today's complex landscape of proprietary programs, interfaces, and methods will be replaced by an organized and familiar centralized control of critical programs and key configuration data. Imagine for a moment sitting in front of a single computer terminal and running all necessary verification mechanisms over thousands of games. Further imagine a scenario where those same mechanisms can be scheduled to occur at regulator-defined intervals. These examples portray how gaming regulation will become more effective and efficient, which are characteristics of any great technology.

These systems will also introduce a standardized level of software and hardware security because they will rely on network technologies employed in non-gaming, high-technology sectors—some of which operate under more regulatory scrutiny than the gaming industry. At a time when many regulators in the gaming industry are faced with the prospect of deregulation due to regional competition as well as other factors, these technologies will create opportunities for regulators to better achieve regulatory objectives without increasing the operational burden to gaming developers. This is because new components, upgrades, and patches are simpler to implement, certify, verify, and deploy in a networked gaming architecture.

While video lottery regulators are largely familiar with some form of networked gaming and Tribal Gaming Regulatory Authorities (TGRA) have experience with networked Class II systems, it has been interesting to observe the pace at which these technologies have been implemented in traditional casino markets. Various challenges encountered during the early stages of this technology have clearly stunted its progress. The primary barriers have been a perceived lack of interoperability among suppliers' networked gaming offerings, a lack of a viable software licensing model and, most importantly, a lack of effectiveness in finding an acceptable cost–benefit solution capable of motivating gaming operators to replace their current offerings. There are also unique operational and business challenges introduced by the proprietary state of the technology. How would a property effectively administer an array of such systems? How could an individual supplier recover its research and development costs should its networked gaming offering not be modular enough to accommodate anything less than a full-scale installation of that particular supplier's system?

As TGRA's can attest, the sheer variety of proprietary implementations in the Class II gaming market can increase the complexity of managing multiple Class II systems, as each system is independently engineered and presents its own unique interfaces, reports, and the like. Similar interoperability challenges occurred during the original adoption of Ticket-In/Ticket-Out (TITO) technology as well as other system-dependent functions. It was not until standardized protocol implementations were uniformly embraced that these features really took root and flourished.

The industry has made numerous attempts over the years to combat these interoperability challenges. One of the most promising innovations involves the creation of a communication protocol layer, which is intended to be implemented by system providers for operations running multiple vendors' systems to enable very different systems to communicate in a consistent format to a central server. This aptly named, System-to-System (S2S) protocol offers at least some hope for operators and regulators faced with working with multiple vendors' systems.

As with most technology acquisitions, cost is also a primary factor. A networked gaming system requires high-bandwidth to realize its full potential. High bandwidth in this case translates into the need for a broadband network, which is not a ubiquitous commodity in most casinos. The cost of this infrastructure is substantial, so the benefits of networked gaming systems must be clearly demonstrated. As a result, adoption of this technology has been slowed. Nevertheless, the technology is gradually taking root, both in the United States and abroad, particularly in new ventures where it makes prudent financial sense to invest in advanced infrastructure as the property takes shape.

Consider the experience of one major casino management company. A typical property managed by this company without networked gaming would use approximately 40–60 network switches. However, one of its newer properties, which opened more recently and was wired to operate networked gaming, utilizes approximately 500 network switches on-site, including 400 switches just for the casino floor and its approximately 2,400 networked gaming-enabled devices. The casino uses gigabit Ethernet (GbE) to each gaming device. Each bank of six games has a dedicated network switch, and each switch has a fiber connection to two closet network switches. The closet switches connect to core network routers and ancillary switches in the casino's data center. The data center has dual connections to a 10 GbE private dark fiber ring, which interconnects the other dozen casinos operated by this firm.

Deploying a network this large presented several challenges. The sheer number of switches in this one property was more than the operator had ever dealt with. Further, an operating goal for the operation's IT organization was to have just one full-time person on-site at the casino to manage the network.

Additionally, when relying on a network for core gaming functions, requirements for network up-time are much higher than they would be in a non-networked casino environment. The most standard functions—like ensuring the network is fully operational while trying to make sure all the network components are at the same software-revision level—are all tremendous challenges. Additionally, as more devices and features are deployed on a network, the system inevitably requires more bandwidth, so it is critical for operators to stay ahead of that curve and re-provision the network ahead of this growth.

The above is just a sample of the changes brought about by a transition to a networked gaming environment. While this example focuses on some of the operational challenges of such an implementation, it also demonstrates the intrinsic complexity for regulators adapting to the technical characteristics of the systems they must regulate.

FUTURE GAMING SECURITY

A primary concern with any networked gaming system is security. One effective example of these concerns is demonstrated in a 2007 National Indian Gaming Commission (NIGC) advisory to tribal gaming commissions regarding networked gaming technologies.[9] The NIGC advisory was the result of a special review by an independent computer technology company that examined a sampling of currently installed and operated Class II networked gaming systems and provided the following observations:

- **Open and Uncontrolled Network Connections**. Due to the network configuration of many systems, the gaming operation is not able to monitor the activity of any particular vendor. A vendor may have independent, uncontrolled network connections directly to the gaming machines. This type of system setup could allow a vendor to make modifications to the system without the gaming operation's knowledge or approval.

- **Lack of Sufficient Auditing Mechanisms**. Many gaming operations do not have the ability to review, audit, and approve reports provided by a vendor. Many current network configurations allow a vendor to potentially change and otherwise manipulate the data in each server without the knowledge or consent of the gaming operations. Some gaming operations do not have the ability to access server data at all.

- **Network Availability**. It is our observation that many gaming networks are not adequately secured from unauthorized access. Many systems have several points of connectivity that may not be monitored and could potentially cause a network disruption. Procedures ought to be implemented to secure the network against unauthorized access that may result in system failures and lost data.

- **Lack of Security Incident Response Plans and Procedures**. In many gaming operations there is no security policy or contingency plan in place to respond to unauthorized access, incident detection, and data or system recovery. Such a plan should provide a security response to secure the network and damage containment.

Based on the security consultant's observations, the NIGC recommended the following to TGRAs:

---

[9] Tim Harper, Server-Based Gaming Network Review and Security Measures Advisory, Mar. 21, 2007, http://www.nigc.gov/Media/Press_Releases/Server_Based_Games_Advisory.aspx.

- Implement policies and procedures to secure access to servers and communication equipment for server-based games.
- Ensure that employees who are custodians of gaming devices, including employees that have access to cash and accounting records within such devices, are subject to background investigations and licensing requirements.
- License gaming machine vendors and technicians, as required by applicable regulations, to ensure that persons associated with these companies are properly vetted before being allowed into the gaming operation.
- Devise a security, contingency, continuity, disaster, or incident response plan that addresses IT and server-based gaming operations.
- Implement an Intrusion Detection System (IDS) for the IT system to provide notification in the event of an attack, loss of network availability, or unauthorized access to the system.
- Utilize servers with operating systems that have discretionary access controls and firewalls that are in place and operational. Further, a Virtual Private Network (VPN) Concentrator can provide a security layer against unauthorized access to the server when properly configured and maintained.
- Require gaming machine vendors to provide a current list of their employees assigned to service each gaming venue. The gaming machine vendor employees should provide proper identification prior to being allowed access to gaming machines on the casino floor, back-of-house areas, and secured areas where gaming machine servers are located. A network vulnerability and penetration assessment test should be performed periodically to determine the effectiveness of the procedures and protections that are in place.[10]

Again, this example effectively portrays the operational challenges for regulators and operators controlling and regulating networked gaming systems. It also speaks to integrity risks faced by jurisdictions' gaming operations should operators and regulators fail to prepare for the unique challenges presented by this technology.

CLOSING

Many current regulatory control processes in the gaming industry are rooted in very traditional security practices, which are no doubt secure but have seemingly failed to evolve at an appropriate pace. The sheer variation of requirements, tools and, methods needed to effectively regulate gaming technology has created a cumbersome process that saps valuable resources from gaming regulatory agencies. Industry trade associations, public and private testing labs, and other industry stakeholders have all collaborated on industry efforts aimed at harmonizing these processes. However, as net-

---

[10] *Id.*

worked technologies continue to advance, it is more important than ever that a process be developed that meets or exceeds current security standards and leverages the attributes of these networks to gain much needed efficiencies in current technology regulation.

It is important to stress that while this chapter focuses heavily on the technical aspects of current and future regulatory processes, these processes are augmented by regulatory agencies on an ongoing basis through comprehensive audit and reconciliation processes. The totality of these processes has allowed the industry to maintain peak levels of operational integrity in a highly regulated climate. Nevertheless, the inefficiencies of current technology controls and processes have inadvertently introduced an imbalance in the resource commitments from regulatory agencies in their execution of these processes. However, every jurisdiction adopts different processes to the control technology. As one would expect, some agencies more heavily weight the significance of administrative audits in lieu of ongoing technology control, while other agencies may fundamentally operate under the premise that ongoing technology control is an essential component of gaming operation integrity. This chapter aims only to describe the requirements and processes in place today and those that may be available in the future. It is not intended to suggest which requirements and processes may be appropriate for a particular agency.

As gaming technology evolves, we will likely observe technological progress in ways that increase security while making the process nearly transparent to gaming operations. This will likely take a form similar to that of a trusted certificate authority or derivative, where the regulator or its designated technical authority issues a unique digital certificate or marker for gaming software components and only those components will ever be able to operate within the gaming systems. While this is a simplistic description of a complex authentication model, it is a model that is in use in other highly regulated markets and seemingly fits with the technology-dependence profile and regulated nature of the gaming industry.

Regulators should welcome the technological challenges ahead. While there will certainly be apprehension in transitioning from known, traditional requirements and methods to advanced network authentication schemes, the inherent security policies coupled with the amount of data collected by these systems will allow regulatory agencies to perform more focused regulation with efficiencies never before thought possible.

12

Auditing and Accounting
of Casino Revenues

Peter J. Kulick

INTRODUCTION

Accounting and audit requirements have been identified as one of the key components of a comprehensive gaming law.[1] Developing effective audit and accounting requirements should begin with an understanding of the underlying public policies of gaming laws.[2] Several policy goals explain the comprehensive laws and the multitude of regulations that govern the operation of the casino gaming industry. The regulation of casino gaming in the United States historically targeted curtailing participation of organized crime. Accordingly, accounting and audit regulations initially were developed to facilitate two purposes: to prevent unlicensed individuals from sharing in the profits of a licensed gaming operation; and to assure that the government received the proper tax revenue.[3] Rules were also implemented to protect players by ensuring that games were fair for the casino patron instead of being rigged to allow owners to always win.[4]

---

[1] *See* Cory Aronovitz, *The Regulation of Commercial Gaming*, 5 CHAP. L. REV. 181, 189 (2002) (citing Cabot *infra* n.3). Aronovitz identifies five "key provisions" of a comprehensive gaming law: "licensing, operational controls, enforcement, tax, and accounting and audit." *Id.* As discussed further in this chapter, the operational controls—normally referred to as internal control systems—are the procedures used by casinos for, among other matters, recording transactions and demonstrating compliance with gaming laws and regulations. Thus, operational controls can be viewed as a subset of the accounting and audit requirements.

[2] See Chapter 2 for an extensive exploration of the public policy and goals relating to the regulation of casino gambling.

[3] *See* ANTHONY N. CABOT, CASINO GAMBLING: POLICY, ECONOMICS, AND REGULATION 395 (1996).

[4] *See id.*

As casino gaming evolved into a significant global economic market,[5] the purpose of and information derived from accounting and audit regulations has similarly expanded. Regulations governing audit and accounting procedures now assist in maintaining the integrity of casino operations and ensure the continuing financial viability of casinos.[6] Accounting and audit requirements are often effectuated through the adoption of minimum internal control standards (MICS) by regulatory bodies.[7] MICS establish the minimal scope and detail that casino internal control procedures must embrace. Internal controls are accounting and audit concepts.[8] Particular internal control standards (ICS) as applied to a casino business can define the procedures for operating a casino game, accounting for winnings and losses, and reporting the financial results from gambling operations over a defined period of time.[9] As discussed in this chapter, ICS have a significant impact on how casino staff responsibilities are assigned, how revenue is recorded, and how the games are conducted.

The scope of audit and accounting regulations for the regulation of the commercial casino gambling industry can be influenced by multiple and differing policy goals. At the macro level, policy goals and the regulatory attitudes can—and will—affect the latitude of audit and accounting rules. To that end, a practical starting point is the specific policy goals intended to be directly achieved through implementing audit and accounting rules. Chapter 2 offers a comprehensive discussion of public policy and policy goals applicable to the regulation of land-based casino gambling. The discussion of public policy goals in this chapter is intended to supplement Chapter 2, but with a singular focus on the public policy reasons for imposing audit and accounting requirements within the body of gaming laws and regulations.

After identifying policy goals aimed primarily at audit and accounting rules, this chapter discusses the theory and history of casino auditing and accounting requirements.[10] This chapter then presents a more detailed dis-

---

[5] *See* AMERICAN GAMING ASSOCIATION, *State of the State: The AGA Survey of Casino Entertainment* (2013) for comprehensive information concerning the economic impact of the commercial gaming industry in the United States.

[6] *See, e.g.,* John Mills, *Financial Viability: Defining a Minimum Casino Bankroll*, CASINO ENTERPRISE MGMT., Oct. 31, 2007. *See also* Aronovitz *supra* note 1 at 198. Accounting and audit procedures contained in gaming laws and regulations have been described as "procedures . . . necessary to control and protect the revenues generated from gaming activities." *Id.*

[7] *See, e.g.,* 25 C.F.R. § 542 (MICS for Indian Tribal Casino Gaming Operations); NEV. REV. STAT. § 463.157 (2013); NEV. GAMING REG. 6.090; NEV. GAMING REG. 6.100; and NEV. GAMING REG. 6.105.

[8] *See, e.g.,* Martin Lipton et al., *Audit Committee Guide & Best Practices*, ALI-ABA COURSE OF STUDY MATERIALS: ELEVENTH ANNUAL CORPORATE GOVERNANCE INSTITUTE 19 (2004).

[9] *See, e.g.,* MICH. ADMIN. CODE R. 432.1903; NEV. GAMING REG. 6.090(d).

[10] Understanding the theory and history of particular auditing and accounting requirements is useful to understand why a regulatory requirement has been imposed. For example, it is useful to inquire how a rule furthers an identified policy goal. The inquiry is not just an academic exercise. Understanding the theory and history behind auditing require-

cussion of ICS and MICS, as well as other mechanisms used in the field of casino gaming audit and accounting regulations to carry-out policy goals.

Public Policy Goals of Casino Audit and Accounting Regulations

When examining policy goals within the context of a regulated industry such as casino gaming, it is often helpful to view the role of public policy and how policy decisions are implemented in a hierarchical manner. At the top tier are public policies. In a democracy, the electorate may directly identify a policy goal, as with the adoption of a ballot initiative.[11] More often, however, the electorate delegates the public policy development process to legislative bodies. The legislative bodies, in turn, adopt policies in the form of laws.

At the second tier, laws are implemented by regulatory agencies. The regulations add flesh to the policies by providing interpretative guidance.[12] Administrative agencies are charged with the task of interpreting and enforcing the policies embraced in the laws and enforcing regulations promulgated under the governing law.

Finally, at the bottom tier are actual operating systems adopted by a regulated business which are designed to comply with legal and regulatory requirements.

Identifying Policy Goals for Casino Gaming Audit and Accounting Requirements

At the core of casino auditing and accounting rules is the policy goal to protect the legitimate flow of funds. Well-designed regulations should focus on the purpose for imposing financial-related regulatory burdens. Poorly designed regulatory practices ultimately end up requiring processes to be undertaken or the disclosure of information and materials, which

---

ments also can reveal the limitations of audits and accounting procedures.

[11] Michigan and Ohio are two recent examples of the electorate selecting a public policy in favor of authorizing commercial casino gambling. The electorate of both states approved ballot initiatives allowing commercial casino gambling.

[12] Administrative law has developed into its own field of the law. *See, e.g.,* Ronald M. Levin, *The Administrative Law Legacy of Kenneth Culp Davis,* 42 San Diego L. Rev. 315 (2005). Issues commonly encountered in the field of administrative law include the binding nature of a rule to the level of deference afforded the rules promulgated by an administrative agency. *See, e.g.,* Matthew C. Stephenson, *Mixed Signals: Reconsidering the Political Economy of Judicial Deference to Administrative Agencies,* 56 Admin. L. Rev. 657, 658–660 (2004). Persons subject to regulations will frequently challenge the validity of a rule. A regulatory challenge is often premised on an argument that the rule exceeds authority granted to the administrative agency under an enabling law. *See id.* A comprehensive discussion of administrative law is well-beyond the scope of this chapter. Regulators must still recognize the legal limitations of the scope of rules when promulgating regulations. *See id.*

provide little, if any, meaningful information. Worse yet, poorly designed regulations often do not operate efficiently to achieve the underlying policy goals embraced by the governing laws.[13]

In addition to protecting the flow of funds, audit and accounting regulations may embrace related policy goals.[14] Regulations addressing casino gambling audits and accounting procedures can be subdivided into at least five public policy domains: (1) ensuring the government receives the proper tax revenue; (2) preventing unlicensed persons from sharing in the profits of gaming operations; (3) protecting against fraud; (4) protecting the integrity of the casino games; and (5) protecting the financial viability of casino enterprises.[15] Further examination of these five policy goals is appropriate to gain a better understanding of the concern the rules intend to protect against.

Ensuring the government receives the proper tax revenue

The main thrust of audit and accounting regulations is to ensure the government actually receives the appropriate tax revenue.[16] In the United States, tax laws are based on self-assessment; that is, tax laws depend on voluntary compliance whereby taxpayers determine their own tax liability and are responsible for timely reporting and paying of the tax liability.[17] A hallmark of self-assessment tax systems is a requirement that taxpayers not only file reports (the reporting obligation) but that they also must maintain adequate records to substantiate the positions taken on such reports (the

---

[13] The impact of regulations on market efficiency is highly important. Imposing regulatory burdens that are onerous can lead to market inefficiencies. Inefficiencies that are significant enough can lead to market failures.

[14] See CABOT, *supra* note 3, at 395. Accounting and audit regulations have traditionally been directed at ensuring the government receives its proper share of tax revenue and prohibiting unlicensed individuals from sharing in profits.

[15] Protecting the financial health of a casino furthers the government's own interests, namely protecting tax revenue. See Mills, *supra* note 6. Furthermore, the 2008–2012 global economic recession demystified the conventional wisdom that casino businesses are immune to economic downturns. At the height of the 2008–2012 recession, gaming revenue plummeted significantly in several markets, forcing some casino operators into bankruptcy proceedings. See Robert W. Stocker II & Peter J. Kulick, *Chapter 11 Cases Involving Gambling Casinos, in* COLLIER GUIDE TO CHAPTER 11: KEY TOPICS AND SELECTED INDUSTRIES, ¶ 25.01 (Alan N. Resnick & Henry J. Sommer eds., 2010).

[16] See id. See also Michael A. Santaniello, *Casino Gambling: the Elements of Effective Control*, 6 SETON HALL LEGIS. J. 23, 25 (1982) (noting that "[t]he reported gross profit or loss of the casino, with its accompanying tax consequences, is dependent upon the continued integrity" of the control mechanisms to ensure that cash and casino chips reach the counting process.).

[17] See, e.g., I.R.C. §§ 6001 and 6011. While the characterization of the United States tax system as voluntary may suggest that taxes are paid only out of altruistic motivation, the legal requirement imposed by United States tax laws is not at all altruistic. Rather, the qualitative "voluntary" aspect of the United States tax system means that taxpayers determine tax liability as opposed to the government computing tax liability.

records obligation).[18] Thus, requiring casino licensees to maintain financial records is not unique to gaming laws. Accordingly, gaming regulations are designed to satisfy the policy goal of ensuring that the proper amount of tax is both reported and paid by including record-keeping obligations.[19]

The unique aspect of the casino gaming industry compared to other business sectors is the nature of how revenue is generated. Gaming conducted in land-based casinos occurs at a fast pace with several transactions occurring either simultaneously or in rapid-fire succession. Thus, with many types of casino games, it is neither efficient nor practical to record each transaction.[20] The reality of how casino games are conducted has resulted in regulations adopting the use of atypical means to account for the financial results of a particular casino game. The accounting method gaming regulations and casinos have adopted requires the use of an aggregate accounting method.[21] To ensure that the use of an aggregate accounting method produces accurate results, special rules have been developed to establish the procedures to record the results of each wagering transaction as accurately as is feasible, along with the corresponding revenue and tax liability.[22]

Protecting against unlicensed individuals sharing in profits

The protection of the public integrity of the gaming industry has long been an underlying public policy goal justifying the extensive regulation of the casino gambling industry.[23] Measures to detect the participation of

---

[18] See, e.g., I.R.C. § 6001; U.S. Treas. Reg. § 1.6001-1. United States Treasury Regulations generally obligate "any person required to file a return of information with respect to income, shall keep such permanent books of account or records, including inventories, as are sufficient to establish the amount of gross income, deduction, credits, or other matters required to be shown by such person in return of such tax or information." U.S. Treas. Reg. § 1.6001-1(a).

[19] The Nevada accounting regulations are illustrative of gaming regulations that impose record keeping obligations. See NEV. GAMING REG. 6.040. Nevada Regulation 6.040 provides that "[e]ach [casino] licensee, in such manner as the chairman may approve or require, shall keep accurate, complete, legible, and permanent records of all transactions pertaining to revenue that is taxable or subject to fees under chapter 463 of 464 of [the Nevada Revised Statutes]."

[20] See Santaniello, supra note 16, at 25 (noting "[t]he reported gross profit or loss of the casino, with its accompanying tax consequences, is dependent upon the continued integrity" of the control mechanisms to ensure that cash and casino chips reach the counting process.). Numerous opportunities for inaccuracies both intentional and unintentional— exist, which can occur in the process of collecting and recording profits from gambling activities. See id. As an example, inadequate controls that allow a dealer to pocket chips can result in underreporting of revenue and the corresponding tax.

[21] See id. at 24.

[22] See id. at 24. "Due to the impracticality of recording each gaming transaction, a casino must rely on aggregate amounts of cash, checks, and gaming chips to determine its gross profits or loss." Id. For further discussion of the control procedures used by casinos to ensure income and loss are properly reported, see generally Santaniello, supra note 16.

[23] See Robert W. Stocker II & Peter J. Kulick, Gambling with Bankruptcy: Navigating a Ca-

unsavory or unsuitable persons, directly or indirectly, in a casino gaming business further the policy goal of protecting the public integrity of the gaming industry.[24] Audit and accounting regulations can help further this policy goal by offering the opportunity to trace revenue earned and revenue distributed. For example, accounting and audit requirements can be used to detect an unsavory person "skimming" money from a casino's gaming revenue.

Protecting against fraud

Embedded in the policy goal of protecting the government's receipt of the proper tax revenue is a policy to prevent fraud. Fraud is any theft from a casino. Fraud can be committed by casino owners or by third parties who steal from the casino.

Ensuring the financial health of the casino industry

Casino gaming is no longer limited to two states on opposite coasts of the United States. Commercial and/or Indian casinos operate in 20 different states in the United States, as well as in several Canadian provinces.[25] Not only has the prevalence of gaming increased in North America, but the industry has also grown exponentially in Asia and other parts of the world. The increased number of casinos has increased the competition for consumers' gambling dollars and has increased the risk of financial failure for casinos.[26] As a result, a new policy has evolved within the purview of accounting and audit regulations: protecting the financial health of casino businesses.[27] Consequently, casino accounting and audit regulations have added mechanisms to monitor the financial health of and provide early warning for potentially troubled operators.[28]

Accounting, audit, and other financial-related gaming regulations often serve a policy purpose to protect the financial health of casino operations. The policy justification for adopting regulations to ensure a financially healthy casino gaming industry is to protect government interests in receiving tax revenue.[29] To advance this policy goal, gaming regulations can include devices which allow regulators to monitor the financial health of casinos and to allow for early detection of financial impairment.[30] Gaming

---

sino *Through Chapter 11 Bankruptcy Proceedings*, 57 DRAKE L. REV. 361, 369 (2009).

[24] *Id.*

[25] *See* AM. GAMING ASS'N, STATE OF THE STATES: THE AGA SURVEY OF CASINO ENTERTAINMENT (2013). Thirty-nine states have some form of legalized gambling, whether consisting of commercial casinos, Indian casinos, racinos, card rooms, or electronic gaming devices.

[26] *See* Stocker & Kulick, *supra* note 15..

[27] *See* Mills, *supra* note 6.

[28] *See id.*

[29] *See id.*

[30] *See id.*

regulations have used different tools to evaluate the solvency of casinos.[31] "Three common financial tools include (1) minimum bankroll requirements, (2) financial liquidity, and (3) financial solvency."[32]

Protecting the integrity of casino games

The governmental interest in adopting accounting and audit regulations is to protect its share of the revenue from casino gaming operations. The government's revenue share is tax revenue. Gambling largely involves transactions in cash or cash equivalents. Thus, incentives may exist for individuals to compromise the integrity of a gambling game in order to profit individually. A classic example includes a dealer pocketing chips or colluding with patrons to cheat. Therefore, a policy goal often embraced by accounting and audit rules is to ensure that procedures are implemented by casinos to protect the integrity of casino games. These procedures are often included within the scope of MICS.

Internal controls, whether in the form of MICS or ICS, developed to satisfy audit and accounting requirements can also be used to detect irregularities in the conduct of casino games. For example, surveillance controls, which may be included within a casino's ICS, can detect uncommon or unusual moves in the play of a game, which in turn may indicate the integrity of the game has been compromised.[33] Thus, accounting and audit rules may advance the policy goal to protect the integrity of casino games.

Summary

Protecting a regulated casino's legitimate flow of funds is the fundamental public policy goal for implementing audit and accounting regulations. As outlined above, the protection of the flow of funds can be verified through five subsidiary policy goals: ensuring that the government receives the proper tax revenue; preventing unlicensed persons from receiving profits; detecting and preventing fraud; protecting the integrity of casino games; and preserving the financial integrity of casino operators.

Ancillary public policy goals are advanced through audit and accounting regulations. In this context, the accounting and audit rules may be used by a jurisdiction to manipulate the regulated business's behavior. For example, MICS could be adopted that mandate casinos implement extensive problem gambling controls. Care must be taken to avoid interest group capture when using accounting and audit regulations to promote ancillary policy goals.[34]

---

[31] *See id.*

[32] *Id.*

[33] *See* Jessica D. Gabel, *CSI Las Vegas: Privacy, Policing and Profiteering in Casino Structured Intelligence*, 3 UNLV GAMING L.J. 39, 40–42 (2012).

[34] "The concept of interest group capture is rooted in the public choice theory." Peter J. Kulick, *Rolling the Dice: Determining Public Use in Order to Effectuate a "Public-Private Taking" - A Proposal to Redefine "Public Use,"* 2000 L. REV. M.S.U.-D.C.L. 639, 671 (2000).

Policy goals identified by a jurisdiction impact the scope of audit and accounting regulations. Fundamentally, the policy rational for imposing audit and accounting rules within the body of gaming regulations is to protect the legitimate flow of funds within the regulated casino gambling market. As discussed above, the policy goal of protecting the legitimate flow of funds can be subdivided into five categories.

A Summary Overview of Regulatory Mechanisms Used to Implement Policy Goals Underlying Casino Accounting and Audit Regulations

Regulations can serve as a means to effectuate the general policy goals embodied in enabling laws. Regulations can interpret the laws and offer guidance with respect to fulfilling the statutory, or code-based, obligations of the persons subject to the laws. The casino gaming regulatory field has historically relied upon multiple tools to effectuate the policy goal of protecting the legitimate flow of money from casino operations.

Mechanisms embodied in audit and accounting regulations to further the policy of protecting the legitimate flow of funds include:

Active governmental participation in the accounting process;[35]

1. Development of minimum internal control standards (or MICS);[36]
2. Imposition of financial and operational recordkeeping requirements;[37]
3. Reporting requirements;[38]

Public choice theory relies on economic laws to explain individual actions and incentives to take action within a governmental system. *See id.* "Interest group capture predicts that individuals, or groups of individuals, will utilize the political process in order to extract economic benefits." *Id.* Public choice theory assumes that all individuals will act to advance their own self-interest. *See id.* Interest group capture predicts that individuals will become involved in the political process in order to obtain economic benefits at a lower cost than what would be available in the private market. *See id.* Thus, a by-product of interest group capture is that individuals will engage in rent-seeking behavior. *See id.* This rent-seeking behavior leads to government mandated wealth transfers to the politically powerful special interest groups. *See id.* at 671–72.

[35] *See* CABOT, *supra* note 3, at 396–97. Governmental involvement in the accounting process raises both efficiency and practical concerns. Specifically, from an efficiency perspective, it is important to address the appropriate level of governmental intrusiveness during the accounting process. For example, regulations could mandate the presence of onsite regulatory personnel to supervise accounting functions. The reliance on active governmental participation in the accounting process, consequently, can raise an economic efficiency concern. *Id.*

[36] *Id.* at 396.

[37] *Id.* As discussed further below, recordkeeping requirements present the question concerning the appropriate scope of records an operator must maintain. Scope consists of the type, content, and period that records must be maintained.

[38] *Id.* From a financial perspective, the primary reporting obligation is ordinarily a requirement to file tax returns periodically. Reporting requirements can also have significant overlap with other regulatory requirements. For instance, reporting requirements can fur-

4. Independent audits;[39] and
5. Government conducted audits.[40]

Ultimately, several factors influence the particular tools implemented to further accounting, audit, and recordkeeping goals.

THEORY AND HISTORY OF CASINO ACCOUNTING AND AUDIT REGULATIONS

Understanding the theory and history of a particular regulatory requirement serves several useful purposes. Understanding history can offer insight with respect to the harm a regulation seeks to prevent. History and theory also teach why certain information is sought and how the information can fulfill particular policy goals.

Initially, more fundamental questions should be raised: what is "accounting," and what purpose does accounting serve? The concept of accounting invokes the method a business uses to record its earnings and expenses. Accounting helps identify what items are treated as income and expenses. Accounting also answers a timing question by determining the point in time that expenses and income will be recognized.[41]

What is an "audit?" An audit is a compliance check to assess the fairness of financial statements to ensure that financial results are accurately reflected in all material respects.[42] The term "audit" has expanded in the regulatory field to include "certification" audits. A certification audit consists of the auditor certifying that a business has complied with certain established requirements, which may include nonfinancial regulatory standards.[43]

A History of the Methods of Casino Accounting

Accounting entails recording transactions in order to determine fi-

---

ther anti-money laundering protections, suitability and licensing requirements, integrity/fairness of the games, player protections/problem gambling, and age and location verification.

[39] Id.

[40] Id.

[41] "Timing" concepts present a multitude of questions and may even introduce tax planning options. Implicit in any timing question is the period over which income and expenses are measured. From an overall financial results perspective, the period is typically an annual period. For other purposes, the measuring period could be shorter, such as quarterly or even daily. Timing introduces tax planning because there are time-value-of-money benefits to defer the recognition of income and advance the recognition of expenses. The complexity of income tax laws is often due to the imposition of rules to force the matching of income and expense recognition for income tax purposes with actual economic incidence.

[42] See David F. Birke, Comment: The Toothless Watchdog: Corporate Fraud and the Independent Audit - How Can the Public's Confidence Be Restored?, 58 U. MIAMI L. REV. 891, 896 (2003).

[43] See Amy Shapiro, Who Pays the Auditor Calls the Tune?: Auditing Regulation and Clients' Incentives, 35 SETON HALL L. REV. 1029, 1036 (2004).

nancial results. The process, as a result, necessarily involves identifying transactions and the associated costs and receipts. To assure casino gaming transactions are properly and accurately recorded, the accounting process relies on the use of internal control procedures.

The history of aggregate accounting in the casino industry

Accepted accounting practices require the identification of revenue and expenses in order to arrive at the financial results of a business.[44] Supporting data must be examined to determine the results of each transaction. For most businesses, accounting consists of a review of receipts and other records to trace the inflow of money (revenue received) and the outflow of money (expenses paid). Internal controls are used to provide confidence that transactions are accurately and properly recorded.[45]

The accounting method used by a business is a critical but generally ignored element of accounting. In the United States, "generally accepted accounting principles" (GAAP) is often the standard demanded by laws and the financial markets. Outside the United States, most businesses are required to use International Financial Reporting Standards (IFRS).[46]

The demand to use GAAP or IFRS is often made without an understanding of what imposing that standard really means.[47] GAAP is an identifiable standard, but it is also a complex system that permits the use of different approaches to account for the same or similar transactions.[48] Thus,

---

[44] *See, e.g.,* CABOT, *supra* note 3, at 396.

[45] *See* LIPTON, *supra* note 8, at 19. The use of internal control standards in the casino industry has evolved into special meaning vis-à-vis regulatory-mandated operations within the gaming industry. MICS are regulatory standards that establish exactly what the name means: the minimum procedures that a casino licensee must employ to record each gaming transaction. ICS are the control procedures actually adopted by a casino licensee to record gaming transactions. As discussed further below, the scope of MICS and ICS ordinarily provide more detail and address significantly more subject matters than merely recording an individual gaming transaction.

A simple analogy can illustrate the procedures that result from MICS and ICS. MICS and ICS can be viewed as a flight of stairs leading to a penthouse suite. Each stair represents but one step in the process that must be taken to arrive at an accurate and complete view of the casino operations. The penthouse suite is the full picture of casino operations for the applicable period. While ICS have derived special meaning within the casino gaming industry, ICS have a much broader accounting application. ICS sets forth procedures that businesses implement to ensure transactions are accurately reported. Businesses universally rely on ICS. In the public company context, internal control policies are an important element of the accounting and audit process. They also assure compliance with the Sarbanes Oxley Act of 2002, 15 U.S.C. § 7201 et seq. *See id.* Sarbanes Oxley, among other US federal laws, obligates publicly-traded companies to adopt internal control policies. *See* 15 U.S.C. § 78(m).

[46] In North America, both Canada and Mexico have either committed to using or have incorporated the use of IFRS in the accounting standards for publicly-traded companies. Most European nations require publicly-traded companies to use IFRS.

[47] *See* Shapiro, *supra* note 43, at 1051–52.

[48] *Id.*

simply requiring the use of GAAP or IFRS may not provide any assurance that the accounting records of a casino will offer meaningful information to the readers of the financial statements.

The casino gaming business industry has not historically used accounting practices that are used by other businesses.[49] The typical business transaction that occurs at a casino is much different than business transactions in other industry segments. Placing a wager at craps differs substantially from purchasing groceries at a grocery store. Consequently, a different accounting process has developed within the casino gaming market.

"Casinos are unique because millions of dollars continually change hands among thousands of people on the casino floor without a complete transactional record being made of how much money is exchanged, how many people are involved, or who those individuals are."[50] Recording every transaction would cause gambling activity to come to a standstill.[51] As a result, ordinary accounting practices are impractical for use in accounting for casino gambling transactions.[52] A specialized accounting system, known as aggregate accounting, has developed for the casino gaming industry.

At a high level, aggregate accounting can be simple to understand. Conceptually, aggregate accounting operates in the following manner: revenue results are measured over a specified period of time. The win or loss of a particular gambling game is measured by comparing the beginning chip inventory, the amount of cash or credit received, and the chip inventory remaining at the end of the specified period.[53]

While aggregate accounting is conceptually simple, in practice, it can be difficult to implement. The difficulty with aggregate accounting lies in having proper and effective internal controls.[54] Effective controls offer a higher level of confidence that casino gaming transactions are properly recorded and the financial results of gambling games are accurate. The protocols casinos rely on to restock chips at table games or electronic gaming devices (EGD) are illustrative of the importance of having effective internal controls:

- chips must be delivered to tables or EGDs (known as "fills");
- money is deposited by gamblers at table games or EGDs (known as "drops"); and
- the "drops" are collected by the casino staff.[55]

Inadequate internal control procedures at each step of this process can result in inaccuracies in determining the financial results of a particular

---

[49] See CABOT, supra note 3, at 396.

[50] Santaniello, supra note16, at 23.

[51] Id.

[52] Id. at 24.

[53] Id.

[54] See Richard A. Meyer, Accounting for the Winnings - Auditing Gambling Casinos, 12 CONN. L. REV. 809, 811 (1979).

[55] Id. at 811–812.

casino game.[56] Any inaccuracy is amplified as financial results are mea-sured across the entire casino gambling operations.

Overview of internal controls used by casino businesses

Internal control policies are used (i) to ensure financial records are ac-curate and (ii) as a safeguard to protect against material misstatements, omissions, and fraud.[57] Internal control policies are a fundamental aspect of financial accounting and auditing.[58] As auditing has increasingly relied on the use of sampling to review entries in the books and records of a business, greater emphasis has been placed on the adequacy of internal controls.[59]

What are the general contours of internal control policies? They consist of (1) procedures which address the maintenance of business records in reasonably sufficient detail to accurately reflect transactions and disposi-tions of company assets; (2) policies that provide reasonable assurances transactions are recorded in a manner that allows financial statements to be prepared in accordance with the accounting system of the business; (3) procedures to ensure receipts and expenditures are made only in accor-dance with management authorization; and (4) policies that provide rea-sonable assurances to either prevent or allow for timely detection of unau-thorized transactions involving company assets that could have a material effect on financial statements.[60]

The unique nature of the conduct of casino gambling games requires the use of "special procedures to ensure that [the casinos'] financial re-cords properly reflect the actual results of gaming transaction."[61] As with any other business, internal controls in the gaming industry "act as checks on the handling of financial operations."[62] The benefits derived from using internal control systems "assist[s] both the state and federal governments in their efforts to control gambling operations, protect the betting public, and collect taxes and fees from the casinos."[63]

Internal control procedures adopted for use in casino gaming focus on three areas: documentation controls, physical/access controls, and per-

---

[56] *See* Santaniello, *supra* note 16, at 23. The importance of internal controls for aggregate accounting can be revealed by an illustration. Recall that aggregate accounting measures the beginning and ending values over a defined period of time for a particular casino game. If a dealer pockets chips during the measurement period, absent adequate internal controls aggregate accounting may not detect the dealer theft. Thus, internal controls are important to prevent irregularities and ensure an accurate measure of income/loss.

[57] *See* Peter Ferola, *Internal Controls in the Aftermath of Sarbanes-Oxley: One Size Doesn't Fit All*, 48 S. Tex. L. Rev. 87, 89 (2006).

[58] Lipton, *supra* note 8, at 19; *see also* Ferola, *supra* note 57, at 89.

[59] *See* Ferola, *supra* note 57, at 89.

[60] Lipton, *supra* note 8, at 19.

[61] Meyer, *supra* note 54, at 812.

[62] *Id.*

[63] *Id.* at 813.

sonnel controls.[64] Casino internal control policies include provisions to provide for the "separation of functions, and extradepartmental [sic] reviews of transactions."[65] Separation of functions is important due to the fast-paced environment of gaming transactions.[66]

Modern Casino Accounting Practices

The US Financial Accounting Standards Board ("FASB") and the International Accounting Standards Board ("IASB") have each issued industry-specific guidance for the accounting of gaming transactions by casinos.[67] The FASB and IASB guidance largely addresses timing questions for the recognition of income for financial statement purposes under GAAP and IFRS.[68]

FASB Topic 924 provides guidance with respect to the treatment of revenue recognition specifically within the gaming industry. Among the matters addressed in FASB Topic 924 are the presentation of financial statements for casino-hotel operations,[69] determining liabilities of casinos arising from gaming operations,[70] and revenue recognition.[71] FASB Topic 924 incorporates the US Securities Exchange Commission (SEC) position with respect to the separate statement of each revenue-producing activity of integrated casino, hotel, and restaurant operations.[72] The treatment of gaming-related liabilities—such as outstanding gaming chips or a jackpot or other payout payable to casino patrons—can vary under FASB Topic 924.[73] Periodic adjustments may be necessary to address changes in liabilities.[74] The casino "win"—which is the revenue earned by the casino—may be required to be recognized immediately or deferred over a period of play.[75]

---

[64] See CABOT, *supra* note 3, at 399–401.

[65] Meyer, supra note 54, at 812.

[66] See *Id.* Separation of functions is important because casino gaming transpires in a fast-paced environment, which can include literally dozens of separate gaming transactions in the course of each incidence of play. For example, depending on the number of seats at a blackjack table (typically five-to-seven), a single game of blackjack could consist of over a dozen isolated wagers, not to mention players exchanging cash for chips or "coloring-up" chips to greater dollar denominations. All of this takes place within a matter of minutes. As a result, the internal control procedures used in a casino gaming environment have been designed to "guarantee that cash, checks, and gaming chips will be properly handled during the gaming day and that they will reach the counting process." Santaniello, *supra* note 16, at 25.

[67] See FASB Topic 924 Entertainment – Casinos; IASB Gaming Transactions (Agenda Paper II(i)) (May 2007).

[68] See *Id.*

[69] See FASB Topic 924-10-599 SEC Materials.

[70] See FASB Topic 924-405 Liabilities.

[71] See FASB Topic 924-605 Revenue Recognition.

[72] See FASB Topic 924-10-599.

[73] See FASB Topic 924-405.

[74] See *id.*

[75] See FASB Topic 924-605.

The IASB has concluded that wagering transactions should be treated as financial instruments for purposes of preparing financial statements under IFRS.[76] Generally, under the IASB interpretation, bets are to be recognized in an entity's balance sheet at fair value with gains or losses taken to the income statement.[77] The IASB staff further noted that in many casino gaming transactions, the acceptance and settling of wagers occurs over a short period of time.[78] As a result, even without treating the wagers as financial instruments, the same financial result should be achieved.[79] Net winnings are accounted for as revenues upon settling of the wager.[80] According to the IASB interpretation, if the acceptance and settlement occurs on the same day, the profit result will be the same as it would be if the wagering transaction were accounted for as a financial instrument.[81]

Casino Audits

Audits can be used for multiple purposes. From an internal business perspective, an audit is a helpful business practice because the audit can serve as a check on the activities of the business.[82] Externally, financial markets depend on audits to assess the value and creditworthiness of a business. Audits can also assist in validating compliance with regulatory requirements through the use of certification audits.

The United States Supreme Court has characterized the role of the auditor as that of a "public watchdog" whose audits assess the fairness of financial statements.[83] While auditors may be hesitant to accept the role of the public watchdog anointed to them by the Supreme Court, the public relies on audit reports as an independent assessment of the fairness of financial statements.[84] The scope of an audit has expanded over time, and an audit is not limited to merely being a tool to assess the fairness of financial statements.[85] The concept of an "audit" is "now used in a variety of contexts to refer to new or more intense account-giving and verification requests."[86] This is especially the case for publicly-traded companies, where audits are required to comply with Sarbanes-Oxley or other applicable laws.

The potential value of an audit is quickly lost without an appreciation for the purpose of imposing an audit requirement and the role of an auditor. To that end, regulators and the rules they write must have a solid

---

[76] *See* IASB Gaming Transactions (Agenda Paper II(i)) (May 2007).
[77] *See id.*
[78] *See id.*
[79] *See id.*
[80] *See id.*
[81] *See id.*
[82] *See* Birke, *supra* note 42, at 894–95.
[83] *See United States v. Arthur Young & Co.*, 465 U.S. 805, 818 (1984).
[84] *See* Birke, *supra* note 42, at 894–95.
[85] *See* Sasha Courville *et al.*, *Auditing in Regulatory Perspective*, 25 L. & Pol'y 179 (2003).
[86] *Id.*

comprehension of (1) the role an auditor is capable of serving, (2) the purpose of the audit is intended to serve, and (3) the content that should be included in the audit report.

The role of an auditor

The traditional role of the auditor is to serve as a detective for the owner of a company.[87] "The standard task of what is now called internal auditing is to inform owners of the activities of their agents and employees."[88] Over the past century, auditors have assumed a secondary role: certifying information to be disclosed to third parties.[89] An auditor serves as a gatekeeper for the third-party user when performing a certification function.[90] In the United States, federal law, notably Sarbanes-Oxley, has further expanded the role of the auditor.

Purpose of the audit

The audit's objective depends on what role an auditor is engaged to undertake. The scope and content of an audit can change depending upon whether an auditor is serving in the traditional detective function or functioning as the certifier for third-party use.

In the traditional "detective" function, the auditor reviews financial statements to express an opinion concerning the fairness of the financial statements' presentation.[91] Additionally, the auditor will express an opinion with respect to whether the financial statements properly disclose, in a material fashion, the financial position and results of the business.[92]

The purpose of a certification audit is to examine the financial records of the business with an eye to whether the financial records meet defined standards, such as accounting or regulatory-imposed standards.[93] "Accounting standards are vital to certification auditing because the third-party information user needs some way to evaluate the information received."[94] Thus,

---

[87] *See* Shapiro, *supra* note 43, at 1034 (2004). Shapiro provides a detailed overview of the traditional role of the auditor.

[88] *Id.*

[89] *Id.* at 1036.

[90] *Id.*

[91] *See id.*

[92] *Id.* at 896 (quoting AICPA Professional Standards: Statements on Auditing Standards No. 1, AU § 110.01 (American Inst. of Certified Pub. Accountants 2001)).

[93] *Id.* at 1037.

[94] *Id* at 1050. Laws and regulations in the United States often express the applicable accounting standard as requiring financial records to be prepared in accordance with GAAP. *Id.* at 1051 n.90 (citations omitted). While designating an accounting standard in a law or rule can be construed as adding legal clarity, the designation of GAAP alone may actually produce ambiguous results. The problem with GAAP is that it "is not only complex, but provides numerous ways to account for even common items such as inventory and depreciation as well as exotic ones such as derivatives." *Id.* at 1052. Accordingly, without understanding the accounting system imposed by a law or rule, a certification audit may prove

"the audit is seen as a particularly important tool of regulation, account-ability, and governance."[95]

Audit content

The content of an audit is driven by the purpose of the audit and the accounting system employed by the audit subject. At a minimum, an audit will set forth notes that explain significant financial transactions and the accounting of the significant transactions. A certification audit is likely to include a summary of internal controls and a certification with respect to whether the internal controls satisfy a defined standard.[96] For example, in the casino gaming field, a certification audit is likely to include a summary of the casino operator's internal control standards and a certification that the internal controls do or do not satisfy the minimal requirements im-posed by the applicable gaming regulations.[97]

Auditing casino operations

The auditor of a casino will ordinarily perform at least two functions. First, the auditor is responsible for expressing a formal opinion with regard to whether the financial results of the casino are properly report-ed.[98] Second, applicable gaming laws may impose additional certification requirements.[99] For example, many jurisdictions require casino licensees to obtain an independent audit that assesses the appropriateness of the casi-no's internal control procedures.[100]

Within the regulated casino gambling market, an audit is important not only for providing confidence that casinos are accurately recording gaming revenue (for example, by fulfilling the traditional detective role of an audit), but also by providing a certification function. Specifically, a certification audit presents an independent review and opinion on a casino's compli-ance with financial-related gaming regulations. Internal controls operate as the backbone of casinos through the establishment of procedures for, among other matters, recording gaming transactions, document control,

---

to be of little value to regulators.

[95] Courville, *supra* note 85, at 179.

[96] *Id.*

[97] *See, e.g.,* Mich. Comp. Laws Ann. § 432.214 (requiring quarterly audits of the financial conditions of casino licensees); Mich. Admin. Code R. 432.11201–432.11209 (2000); Nev. Rev. Stat. § 463.157; *see also* Meyer, *supra* note 54, at 817.

[98] *See* Meyer, *supra* note 54, at 810 ("[audits] are essential parts of the proper reporting of income or loss by gambling casinos."). Beyond ensuring that income or loss is reported, the tasks of the auditor also include studying and evaluating the casino's ICS. The evalua-tion of ICS can be tied to the process of ensuring that the audit is performed in adherence with professional standards. In the United States, auditors typically conduct audits in ac-cordance with Generally Accepted Auditing Standards (GAAS).

[99] *See id.* at 817.

[100] *See* Mich. Comp. Laws § 432.214.

and access control. Casino accounting procedures and audit requirements are intertwined within the regulatory regime that governs the financial elements of casino operations.

REGULATORY TOOLS USED TO FURTHER CASINO AUDIT AND ACCOUNTING REGULATIONS

Government regulation of the casino gaming market represents government intervention into an economic market. Government intervention can affect economic efficiency and runs the risk of causing market failures.[101] The economic costs imposed on the regulated business to comply with the burdens imposed by a regulatory model must continually be assessed during the design, implementation, and on-going business operation phases. At the outset, good policy development practices should analyze regulatory obligations imposed on the regulated business in order to avoid market inefficiencies.

Regulations can adopt various mechanisms to implement audit and accounting policy goals within the casino gaming regulatory environment. Policy analyses principles measure the economic costs of complying with regulations.[102] Cost–benefit analysis can be especially useful to determine the market costs imposed by regulations and the impact of a given regulatory regime on market efficiency.[103] Cost–benefit analysis involves identifying both the costs and benefits of a prospective regulation.[104] Quantifying the costs and benefits of a regulatory standard is complicated and, in some instances, can be controversial.[105] In addition to engaging in a cost–benefit analysis, an assessment of the technological feasibility of regulatory requirements can be beneficial to mitigate against imposing standards that are incapable of being met.[106]

---

[101] *See* TEVFIK F. NAS, COST-BENEFIT ANALYSIS: THEORY AND APPLICATIONS 11 (1996). Economic efficiency is the goal for allocating goods in a market. *See, e.g.,* STEVEN E. RHOADS, THE ECONOMIST'S VIEW OF THE WORLD: GOVERNMENT, MARKETS, & PUBLIC POLICY 63 (1994). *Pareto* optimality dictates that markets reach a state of efficiency "where no one person can be made better off without simultaneously making at least one person worse off." *Id.* Government intervention can threaten the ability of a market to achieve *Pareto* optimality and impose welfare costs (or dead-weight losses) on markets. *See* Rhoads at 64.

[102] *Id.* at 64.

[103] *See* Nas, *supra* note 101, at 11.

[104] *Id.* The actual application of cost–benefit analysis is simple in theory. Consider the following illustration. Suppose that a regulation is implemented requiring a jurisdiction to implement online monitoring of all interactive games, with the costs of the system being directly passed to the regulated Internet gaming operators. If the costs to operators are $200 per year, while operations can only be expected to generate $100 per year, little incentive exists to actually engage in commercial activity. In the example, the costs of the regulation destroyed any potential economic benefit.

[105] Notably, identifying benefits of a regulatory requirement may be difficult to ascertain and to assign a value derived from the regulatory obligation.

[106] *See* EUGENE MARTIN CHRISTIANSEN, CENTRAL SYSTEMS FOR MACHINE GAMING: A GOOD POLICY? (2003). The Christiansen study outlines a classic example of regulatory

While regulatory models have historically relied on a combination of six mechanisms, mandatory MICS is the mechanism that has gained the most attention within the regulated casino gaming field. Accordingly, casino accounting and audit regulations will be intertwined with the ICS adopted by casinos. Several jurisdictions—including the federal government with respect to Indian casinos—have adopted mandatory MICS.[107] The other five mechanisms often can be used to check the adequacies of ICS, including compliance with MICS. These mechanisms can also be used as efficient redundancies to further the policy goal of protecting governmental interests in receiving the proper tax revenue.

Casino gaming regulations traditionally relied on six mechanisms to fulfill casino audit and accounting regulatory standards: government participation in the accounting process, government-conducted audits of gaming operations, imposing independent audit requirements, adoption of mandatory MICS, identifying recordkeeping obligations, and imposing reporting obligations on casino businesses. The six mechanisms overlap and, collectively, can result in significant redundancies. Determining the proper mix of methods to achieve casino accounting and audit policy goals often is a best practice to develop on efficient casino regulatory environment.

Government Participation

Government involvement in casino accounting and audit functions takes the form of direct governmental participation in casino gaming operations.[108] Direct participation in casino operations may consist of government presence and supervision of the count process.[109] Government presence could include having regulatory staff present to observe the periodic counts from casino gambling operations. Government participation may also include direct supervision of any monetary and financial transactions.[110]

A case study of government participation: feasibility of direct governmental monitoring and control of EGDs

Modern technological advances offer regulators the opportunity to monitor electronic game devices (EGDs) in real time. The efficiency of using a central monitoring system to monitor all EGDs operating in a jurisdiction can be analyzed based on actual experience in Louisiana. Louisi-

---

requirements creating inefficient redundancies.

[107] *See, e.g.,* 25 C.F.R. § 542 (minimum internal control standards for gaming operations on Indian lands); Nev. Rev. Stat. § 463.157 (2013); Mich. Admin. Code R. 432.1901–432.1907 (Michigan gaming rules regarding ICS); *see also* Meyer, *supra* note 54, at 815.

[108] Cabot, *supra* note 3, at 396.

[109] *See id.*

[110] *See id.*

ana experimented with direct government participation through the use of a central monitoring system for EGDs.[111] The Louisiana experiment offers a case study to assess the efficiency of direct governmental monitoring of EGDs. A review of Louisiana's implementation of a central monitoring system permits an assessment of the benefits, if any, that can be derived from a central monitoring system. The purpose of implementing the central monitoring system was to allow gaming regulators to monitor remotely play at EGDs and corresponding monetary transactions. Eugene Martin Christiansen assessed the central monitoring system in a 2003 study.[112]

Louisiana permits both commercial gaming and video lottery terminals (VLT). Commercial gaming is conducted at land-based and riverboat casinos. Louisiana authorized truck stops, establishments selling alcohol, racetracks, and off-track betting facilities to operate VLT machines. The Louisiana central monitoring system was intended to be a "State-operated central monitoring and control system providing regulators with control over individual slot-machines, including the ability to shut down malfunctioning machines, in addition to audit and financial monitoring for individual machines and for slot gaming as a whole in real time."[113]

The Christiansen study concluded Louisiana's direct participation in casino operations via an EGD central monitoring system did not produce any additional regulatory benefits.[114] In fact, the study observed that the central monitoring system "is a weak *monitoring* system . . . and essentially duplicates the financial audit controls provided to licensed operators by casino computer monitoring systems designed for this purpose."[115] Thus, the costs paled in comparison to the benefits derived from the use of a central monitoring system.

Several salient points can be elicited from Christiansen's study with respect to the use of direct government participation to carry out casino audit and accounting regulations: (1) casino operators and state regulators share a common interest to ensure that casinos accurately report financial results and to protect the integrity of casino gaming operations; (2) challenges can arise with regard to the capabilities of technology, which can add significant costs and even compromise the strength of regulatory tools; and (3) redundancy does not automatically assure that additional benefits can be derived and may, in fact, have no tangible benefit in furthering casino audit and accounting policy objectives.[116] Furthermore, the sheer volume of EGDs and the number of casino properties operating in a jurisdiction may severely tax regulatory staff resources.[117] As a result, such systems can

---

[111] *See* Christiansen, *supra* note 78, at 5–7.
[112] *Id.*
[113] *Id.* at 7.
[114] *Id.*
[115] *Id.* (emphasis in original).
[116] *Id.* at 5–8.
[117] For example, as of 2013 there were 263 casinos were operating in Nevada. Assuming that each casino averaged 1,000 EGDs, regulators would need to monitor the operations of

reduce the ability of regulatory staff to perform other functions, which may be more effective in advancing policy goals.

Summary of the role of government participation

Direct government participation in casino gaming operations can take various forms. Historically, gaming regulations have either required or made permissive government monitoring of the count process. Other forms of direct government participation may include real-time monitoring of EGDs.

Direct participation can have diminishing returns as its scope is broadened. The Christiansen study illustrates the diminishing returns resulting from overly broad direct governmental participation, and it concluded the additional benefits of using a central monitoring system to monitor all EGDs in a jurisdiction were minimal and duplicated existing accounting and audit reports that the EGDs produced for the operators.[118] Moreover, the Louisiana central monitoring system was expensive to develop, and the ongoing maintenance costs were also substantial.[119]

The Christensen study reveals that the costs of direct government participation by remotely monitoring games and monetary transactions are substantial and outweigh any policy benefits. Just as troubling from a policy perspective is that the regulatory tool created a redundancy when evidence did not support that the other casino audit and accounting regulatory mechanisms were ineffective.[120]

Ultimately, direct governmental involvement in the operational aspects of casinos may have costs that outweigh any benefits. The Christensen study illustrates this point. Accordingly, government participation must be carefully analyzed to assess whether such regulatory approaches are efficient regulatory tools.

Government Audits

A "government audit" in the classic sense often invokes the tax audit by government revenue agencies intending to ensure a taxpayer has paid the legally-required tax. Audits can be used to fulfill other regulatory oversight, accountability, and corporate governance standards.[121] Accordingly, a threshold question relating to requiring governmental audits should be

---

263,000 EGDs.

[118] *Id.*

[119] *Id.*

[120] A more efficient approach to protect government's EGD revenue could be to allow regulators access to software and the data recording of each gaming transaction of an EGD. Access to data would allow regulators to conduct sampling to determine whether casinos are properly reporting the results of the gaming transactions occurring at the EGDs.

[121] *See* Courville, *supra* note 59, at 179.

raised with respect to the intended purpose to be accomplished through a government-conducted audit.[122]

Government audits have been justified as an enforcement mechanism to ensure compliance with required MICS. Audits also track money flow to ensure unlicensed individuals do not financially share in revenues, revenue is reported properly, and all applicable fees and taxes are paid.[123] Government audits can be an effective incentive for casinos to adopt robust self-compliance procedures.[124] Particularly, government audits can be an effective regulatory tool where regulations grant regulators the reasonable discretion to perform a casino audit.[125]

In contrast, a casino regulatory system that requires regulators to periodically perform government audits of each casino licensee may not be efficient. For example, if casinos are required to obtain comprehensive independent audits, an efficiency issue is raised if the government will also perform its own audit. The government audit may merely duplicate the independent audit without adding any additional benefit.[126] Therefore, the flexibility to conduct discretionary and random audits can be a useful regulatory tool.

---

[122] CABOT, *supra* note 3, at 397–98.

[123] *Id.*

[124] *Id.* at 398.

[125] *Id.* From a tax compliance perspective, the reasonable discretion for the government to perform an audit can be an important mechanism to ensure that revenue is properly reported and the correct tax is paid on income. This is particularly the case for North American jurisdictions which often depend upon voluntary compliance models (e.g., self-reporting of income and self-payment of tax, as opposed to mandatory withholding at the source of payments).

[126] The independent audit is designed to be an independent, unbiased check of the fairness of financial statements and certification of compliance with regulatory requirements. *See* Mark Allan Warden, Note, *Securities Regulation: Private Auditor Independence for Non-Audit Services - An Evolving Standard*, 55 OKLA. L. REV. 513 (2002). In other words, an independent audit is not a casino licensee presenting its most optimistic and favorable explanation of its financial results. *See id.* Rather, the independence of the audit is intended to enable third parties to rely on the audit's fairness in all material respects of the matters subject to the audit. *See* Birke, *supra* note 42, at 896. Accordingly, mandating that all casinos will be subject to an annual government audit would likely not add any additional benefit than is already received through the independent audit. Furthermore, casinos may be able to obtain an independent audit in a more cost effective manner than the costs that would be passed through as a result of a government-conducted audit. Thus, the ability to conduct discretionary and random audits within reason to verify information or, to conduct further investigations if red flags are raised, can be a useful regulatory tool. *See* CABOT, *supra* note 3, at 397–98. Discretionary and random audits can serve as an incentive to ensure compliance. *See id.* That is, the threat of the government audit can serve to strike enough fear in the licensee to ensure the licensee will use best efforts to remain in material compliance with regulatory requirements. Similarly, a reasonably discretionary audit can be helpful for regulators to conduct further investigation when suspected problems arise, whether with respect to the integrity of games or financial viability.

Independent Audits

Independent audits are an efficient method to ensure compliance with accounting, audit, and recordkeeping requirements for Internet gaming businesses.[127] Many gaming regulatory models impose an independent audit requirement.[128] Jurisdictions that impose an independent audit requirement ordinarily require casino licensees to submit a complete audit report, as well as any management reports.[129]

Internal Controls Procedures and the Role of Mandatory MICS

As discussed above, ICS are not simply a creation of gaming regulations.[130] ICS are paramount for ensuring accurate financial accounting of the operations of any business. The ICS identify the procedures that personnel of a business must utilize to carry out transactions and record the results of the transactions.[131] Not only do "[ICS] prevent improprieties and promote the integrity of the transactions and the records of results," they also provide detailed procedures for the conduct of casino gaming operations.[132]

Gaming regulations usually include mandatory MICS.[133] MICS generally "safeguard casino assets, ensure the reliability of financial records, and guarantee that all transactions are authorized by casino management."[134] Internal control procedures within the gaming industry cover three categories: (1) documentation controls; (2) access/physical controls; and (3) personnel controls.[135]

Documentation controls center on the types of records a casino operator must maintain in connection with preparing financial statements and demonstrating compliance with gaming laws and rules.[136] For example, Nevada gaming regulations applicable to a "Group I Licensee"[137] require

---

[127] Publicly-traded casino operators listed on US exchanges will already be subject to an obligation to obtain an independent audit under US federal laws. LIPTON, *supra* note 8, at 19.

[128] *See* NEV. GAMING REG. 6.080.

[129] *See id.*

[130] ICS receive considerable attention because the ICS include daily operational procedures.

[131] *See e.g.,* NEVADA GAMING CONTROL BOARD, MINIMUM INTERNAL CONTROL STANDARDS, GROUP I LICENSEES.

[132] Meyer, *supra* note 54, at 812; *see also* Alderney ICS, *supra* note 7.

[133] *See* NEV. REV. STAT. § 463.157; *see also* Meyer, *supra* note 54, at 815–816.

[134] Meyer, *supra* note 54, at 815.

[135] *See* CABOT, *supra* note 3, at 399–401; Meyer, *supra* note 54, at 815; *See also* NEV. GAMING REG. 6.090; 6.100; and 6.105.

[136] *See, e.g.,* NEV. GAMING REG. 6.090; 6.100; and 6.105.

[137] According to the October 24, 2013 revisions, a "Group I licensee" is defined by the Nevada gaming regulations to mean "a non-restricted licensee having gross revenue at or above certain amounts ascertained by the board for a fiscal year." NEV. GAMING REG. 6.010(5). Group I licensees are the large casino operators in Nevada.

certain casino operators to adopt ICS "designed to reasonably ensure that . . . (b) financial records are accurate and reliable; [and] . . . (d) transactions are recorded adequately to permit proper reporting of gaming revenue and of fees and taxes, and to maintain accountability for assets."[138] Documentation requirements may include a requirement to maintain records detailing software and hardware updates to EGDs.[139]

Access/physical controls are procedures that identify which casino personnel are permitted access to the casino operator's business records and assets.[140] For instance, the ICS for Nevada's regulated casinos must include procedures ensuring access to assets is only available in accordance with management authorization.[141]

Personnel controls are procedures that establish an organizational structure for the approval of transactions.[142] Typically, personnel controls rely on the division of duties and responsibilities.[143] Personnel control also can include the use of checks and balances to ensure that no single department or person within a casino gaming operator organization has unfettered control.[144]

---

[138] NEV. GAMING REG. 6.090.

[139] *See, e.g.,* NEVADA GAMING CONTROL BOARD, MINIMUM INTERNAL CONTROL STANDARDS, SLOTS NO. 94. Slots MICS 94 provides:

> 9.4 Records must be maintained documenting the above procedures [relating to duplicating erasable programmable read-only memory ("EPROM") chips in slot machines]. The records must include the following information:
>
> a. Date.
>
> b. Number of slot machine in which a duplicated EPROM is placed. Additionally, indicate the number of the slot machine of the source EPROM when duplicated from an EPROM of another slot machine, or else indicate that the secured master program was used for duplicating.
>
> c. Manufacturer name.
>
> d. Program number.
>
> e. Personnel involved.
>
> f. Reason for duplication.
>
> g. Disposition of any permanently removed EPROM.
>
> h. GLB Lab approval number.

[140] *See* NEV. GAMING REG. 6.090(1)(e). In the context of land-based gaming, access/physical controls have included the use of physical safeguards such as surveillance cameras and restricting the personnel that have access to slot-machine drops or other gaming equipment. *See* CABOT, *supra* note 3, at 399. For further discussion of access/physical controls used in the land-based gaming industry, *see generally* CABOT, *supra* note 3, at 399–400.

[141] *See* NEV. GAMING REG. 6.090(1)(e).

[142] *See, e.g.,* NEV. GAMING REG. 6.090.

[143] *See* Santaniello, *supra* note 16, at 32 (discussing division of responsibilities in the context of land-based gaming operations); *See also* NEV. GAMING REG. 6.090(2).

[144] *See, e.g.,* NEV. GAMING REG. 6.090.

MICS ordinarily included a requirement that casino operators obtain independent certification audits.[145] Accounting control systems typically include both general accounting procedures and audit and recordkeeping procedures.

Once ICS are adopted, casino operators must actually operate in accordance with the ICS. Failure of a casino operator to comply with its ICS can itself amount to a violation of gaming laws and regulations.[146] Gaming regulators have imposed significant fines on operators arising from failures to adhere with ICS.[147]

Recordkeeping Obligations

Recordkeeping obligations serve as an important tool to fulfill accounting and audit policy goals. Retaining records allows gaming regulatory staff to review and confirm the accuracy of reports submitted by casino operators. Gaming regulations typically impose an obligation on casinos to maintain complete records.[148] Regulations often require casinos to maintain the records for a defined period of time.[149]

Reporting Requirements

Gaming regulations implement reporting obligations as a method for fulfilling accounting and audit goals. The reporting obligation represents the culmination of the policy goal of protecting the government's interest in receiving the proper tax revenue. The reports will state the casino's financial results and amount of tax due. Reporting obligations also typically require the submission of independent audit reports.

Regulatory Tools to Protect Financial Health

The conventional wisdom that casino businesses are recession-proof

---

[145] *See, e.g.*, Nev. Gaming Reg. 6.080, 25 CFR § 3542.3(F) (providing that Indian Tribal gaming operators shall engage an independent certified public accountant to verify that tribal gaming operations are conducted in compliance with MICS).

[146] *See* Mich. Admin. Code R. 432.1907. The Michigan gaming regulations are illustrative. Rule 907 succinctly states that the failure to comply with the casino's ICS subjects the casino to disciplinary action. Specifically, Rule 907 provides

> (1) Casino licensees and casino license applicants must comply with all internal control procedures that have been approved in writing by the board or its designee.

> (2) If a casino licensee or casino license applicant fails to comply with any provision of its approved internal control procedures, the board may initiate a disciplinary action.

[147] *See* Craig Greene, *Are Internal Controls Really that Important?*, http://www.mcgovern-greene.com/new/BlogArticles/2014_blogs/NGCB_fraud.html.

[148] *See* Nev. Gaming Reg. 6.060.

[149] *See id.* Nev. Gaming Reg. 6.060 requires casino licensees to maintain all records "within Nevada for at least 5 years after they are made."

was debunked during the Great Recession of 2008–2012.[150] The casino gaming industry has also become much more competitive with an exponential number of venues competing for entertainment dollars. Consequently, accounting and audit regulations have begun to incorporate tools to identify potential signs of casino operators' financial difficulty.

Regulators have used at least three tools to monitor the financial solvency of casinos:[151] imposing minimum bankroll standards, financial liquidity requirements, and solvency standards.[152] Bankroll requirements require casino operators to maintain a prescribed level of cash or cash equivalents to protect against defaulting on paying winnings to casino patrons.[153] Nevada gaming regulations authorize regulators to develop a minimum bankroll formula.[154] New Jersey similarly imposes a bankroll requirement.

Other jurisdictions have imposed liquidity requirements on casino operators. Liquidity requirements ordinarily include typical financial covenants found in lending transactions. For instance, regulators may impose a debt and service ratio or require casino operators to maintain a minimum number of days' cash on hand to insure continued operations.

CONCLUSION

Casino operations involve significant monetary transactions. Wagering transactions transpire in a fast-paced environment. Governments draw substantial revenue from the taxes imposed on casino gaming transactions. The cash transactions at casinos have long piqued the interest of the unsavory. Governments have an interest in protecting the tax revenues that flow from casino gaming operations. Not surprisingly, it is against this backdrop that the casino gaming industry has become a highly-regulated business sector. The significant money involved in the casino gaming industry has led to the development of robust accounting and audit regulations.

An understanding of casino gaming regulatory history is beneficial to comprehending the financial regulations which are imposed on casino businesses. Further, identifying the public policy goal of imposing accounting and audit regulations allows one to assess the viability of particular regulatory requirements and the tools that regulators have used to effectuate the identified policy. While a particular jurisdiction may identify multiple policy goals for imposing accounting and audit regulations on casino businesses, the overriding policy goal is to protect governmental interests. Governmental interests can typically fall within the confines of five categories: assuring that the government receives the appropriate tax revenue; preventing the unsavory from sharing in the profits derived from

---

[150] *See* Stocker & Kulick, *supra* note 15.
[151] *See* Mills, *supra* note 6.
[152] *See id.*
[153] *See* NEV. GAMING REG. 6.150(5).
[154] *See* NEV. GAMING REG. 6.150(1).

casino gaming; protecting against fraud; protecting the integrity of casino games; and guarding the financial health of casino businesses.

The mechanisms jurisdictions have relied on to live up to their enumerated policy goals are many. The regulatory tools have consisted of direct government participation in gaming operations, government conducted audits, independent audits, imposing recordkeeping and reporting obligations, and adopting liquidity requirements. The efficacy of any particular regulatory tool must be weighed carefully. Onerous regulatory requirements may overburden the efficiency of the casino markets and regulations may produce inefficiencies that can ultimately lead to market failures. In the end, policymakers and regulators should choose specific regulatory tools only after carefully weighing the jurisdiction's policy goals and efficiency considerations.

13

A Normative Analysis Of Gambling Tax Policy[1]

Kahlil S. Philander

INTRODUCTION

Gambling is among a small group of sectors that is subject to tax policies which are different from the rest of the economy. Unlike most other industries, casinos, lotteries, horse racing, remote gaming, and nearly all other forms of gambling tend to be subject to tax policies that are at rates over and above those of typical businesses. These tax policies are also often applied inconsistently from jurisdiction to jurisdiction.[2] This study provides a normative analysis of gambling tax policy, using economic theory and empirical gambling studies to describe how government taxes levied on the gambling industry should be structured to maximize economic welfare. In particular, this study provides guidelines for the tax policies that maximize economic benefit in the local economy.

Positive analysis is also provided to highlight actual policies used in the gambling industry. This perspective is necessary to fully understand the normative suggestions, since policy decisions by politicians and bureaucrats are often made with objectives other than to maximize economic welfare. In particular, Smith and Walker and Jackson have suggested that the reason for the observed tax levels is that gambling taxes have been set in order to capture economic rents, rather than to internalize negative externalities or to maximize economic welfare.[3] Similarly, Chen and Chie

---

[1] This chapter appeared in 17 UNLV GAMING RES. AND REV. J. 17 (2013) and is reproduced here with permission of the Editor of the journal with gratitude.

[2] EUGENE CHRISTIANSEN, THE AM. GAMING ASS'N, THE IMPACTS OF GAMING TAXATION IN THE UNITED STATES (2005); Kevin Duncan et al., *Lottery tax rates vary greatly by state*, TAX FOUNDATION (2012).

[3] JULIE SMITH, GAMBLING TAXATION IN AUSTRALIA (1998), www.tai.org.au/ documents/ dp_fulltext/DP16.pdf; Douglas M. Walker and John D. Jackson, *Do U.S. Gambling Industries Cannibalize Each Other?* 36 PUB. FIN. REV. 308 (2008).

found that average lottery tax rates were quite close to the public revenue maximizing estimates that they produced.[4] Not all authors agree on the motivation for tax policy, and indeed some cite multiple objectives. Adam Rose and Associates and Meich both suggest that tax rates reflect a joint objective to raise public funds and to punish an activity characterized as sinful.[5]

This article is separated into distinct areas of tax theory, some of whose policy recommendations may be in conflict with others. The overall findings are summarized in the conclusion, which provides a conceptual overview for how the policy suggestions may interact.

First and Second-Best Taxation

First-best taxation is characterized by what is known as a non-distortive tax, such as lump-sum taxation[6] – effectively, it is a transfer of wealth to the government that does not affect marginal decision making and therefore does not distort what would have been the competitive equilibrium in the absence of a tax.[7] For example, if all residents are forced to pay the government a previously unknown and one-time fee, that would cause minimal distortions, since it would not affect marginal decisions of production. The choice of which products to consume to provide the greatest return remains the same for all members of the economy. We would observe no changes in consumption throughout the economy.

A tax on a specific product is distortive. A commodity tax generally makes its product more costly to consumers and producers (the specific incidence depends on market elasticities), and although it may not cause all consumers to change their consumption, it will cause the marginal consumers to change their consumption pattern. This distorts the economic decisions that would be made in an efficient and tax-free economy, and therefore lowers the economy from its maximum possible output.

In the supply controlled gambling industry, where the number of casino licenses or gambling stations are typically limited by a government quota, a gambling tax that is sufficiently small may actually be non-distortive. An initial deadweight loss is created by government restricting the supply of gambling in the market, and a license fee or revenue tax that is smaller than the economic rents will simply redirect operator profit to the govern-

---

[4] Shu-Heng Chen & Bin-Tzong Chie, *Lottery Markets Design, Micro-Structure, and Macro-Behavior: An ACE Approach*, 67 J. Econ. Behav. & Org. 463 (2008).

[5] Adam Rose & Associates, The regional economic impacts of casino gambling: Assessment of the literature and establishment of a research agenda (1998), http://govinfo.library.unt.edu/ngisc/reports/ecoimprpt.pdf; Bret F. Meich, *The Power to Destroy: The Psychology of Gaming Taxation*, 12 Gaming L. Rev. and Econ. 458 (2008).

[6] N. Gregory Mankiw et al., *Optimal Taxation in Theory and Practice*, 23 J. Econ. Persp. 147 (2009).

[7] The oddly phrased "first-best taxation" is written as such since it is a corollary to "second-best taxation" without lump-sum transfers.

Figure 13.1

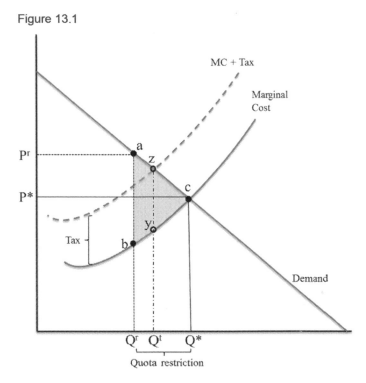

ment, without further changing the level of consumption in the market. Of course, even though the tax may be non-distortive if it is sufficiently small, the market restrictions caused by the gambling license quotas is distortive.

As shown in Figure 1, if the maximum number of licenses in the market is restricted to Q^r from the competitive equilibrium of Q^*, then the restricted market price will be P^r. Unless a specific tax on the license is so large that it discourages entry into the market, the tax on the casino license will not cause any distortions since it will not affect marginal production. That result holds because the intersection of the demand curve and the supply + tax curve at z is characterized by a quantity (Q^t) that is greater than the market restricted quota (Q^r). In an otherwise competitive market, such a tax would cause distortions that lead to a reduction in output from Q^* to Q^t, and a deadweight loss equal to z-y-c. However, in the already constrained market, the addition of a moderately sized tax will not change the market price, the quantity produced, or the deadweight loss (a-b-c).

However, if a gross gaming revenue (GGR) tax is employed, the result is different. The issue with using an ad valorem GGR tax in a market with quotas is that a firm with monopoly power will already be setting their supply at a level below the competitive equilibrium (the monopoly price/quantity). The addition of an ad valorem tax will then cause the operator's per unit costs to increase, causing further distortions, rather than serving

Figure 13.2

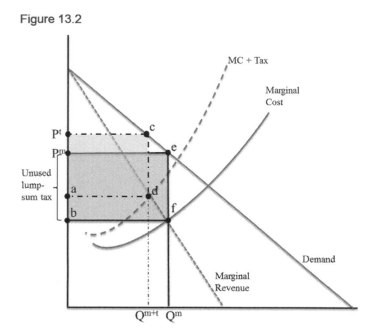

as a pseudo lump-sum tax that transfers the monopoly rents to the government. This effect is illustrated in Figure 2, where the GGR tax increases the operator's cost of production and causes output to fall from Q^m to Q^{m+t}. A lump-sum tax would have generated tax revenue equal to P^m-e-b-f, but the GGR tax reduced output and reduced the tax revenue to Pt-c-a-d.

Philander expands this gambling monopoly model to a market with two consumer types, price sensitive recreational gamblers and price insensitive problem gamblers.[8] He shows that in a market where supply is restricted to a single local monopolist, consumers will generally prefer specific taxation while the monopolist would prefer ad valorem taxation. Under specific taxation, a revenue maximizing government will tend to employ a lump-sum tax on the producer that is equal to his entire monopoly profits – effectively transferring all rents from the producer, whereas under an ad valorem tax, the monopolist will still retain some economic rents due to the imperfect tax mechanism. With a lump-sum tax, consumers obtain a higher provision of government funded public goods than under ad valorem taxes, and also incur the same level of consumption as under no taxation. Under an ad valorem tax, recreational gamblers are noted to have their (no taxation) consumption levels distorted more than problem gamblers, because of the fact that problem gamblers are the least sensitive to price. Recreational gamblers consumption levels are therefore disproportionately reduced relative to problem gamblers, leaving a higher share

---

[8] Kahlil S. Philander, *Specific or Ad Valorem? A Theory of Casino Taxation*, 20 Tourism Econ. 107 (2014).

of problem gamblers in the market to fund the tax. This inequity of incidence provides another reason to use license based taxes, rather than taxes on gross gaming revenue.

In the absence of an ability to use lump-sum taxes, the optimal commodity tax structure is provided by Ramsey.[9] Ramsey finds that commodity taxes should be based on the relative sensitivity of demand to changes in price (demand elasticity) and on the effect that consumption of the commodity has on demand in other markets. That is, goods whose demand will respond least to a change in price should be taxed at a higher rate, since there will be fewer distortions in consumption, and where correlations exist among the demand for goods, the optimal policy becomes more complicated. The effect of commodity taxes on a given good must be balanced against the change in demand (and therefore commodity tax revenue) of other complimentary/substitutionary goods. For example, since casino gambling is strongly tied to the lodging and hospitality industries[10], a high tax on casino revenue may adversely affect tax revenue generated from hotels.

Given the results of Ramsey,[11] the theoretically correct tax policy in gambling is two-fold. First, since many gambling industries are situated well within the elastic portion of the demand curve, they may not be good candidates for further increases in tax rates. In a survey of over two-dozen studies, Forrest found the average value of gambling elasticities to be -1.57.[12] Of course, this may partially be a function of already high taxes and monopolistic conditions in many markets. In any case, lotteries have generally been noted to be a more inelastic form of gambling[13], and therefore the generally higher comparative tax rates for that form of gambling may be warranted.[14]

Due to the second aspect of Ramsey tax design, normative policy is complicated by various gambling industries ties to one another[15] and their

[9] Frank Ramsey, *A Contribution to the Theory of Taxation*, 37 Econ. J. 47 (1927).

[10] *See, e.g.,* George G. Fenich & Kathryn Hashimoto, *Perceptions of Cannibalization: What is the Real Effect of Casinos on Restaurants?*, 8 Gaming L. Rev. 247 (2004); Kathryn Hashimoto & George G. French, *Does Casino Development Destroy Local Food and Beverage Operations?: Development of Casinos in Mississippi*, 7 Gaming L. Rev. 101 (2003).

[11] Ramsey, *supra* note 9.

[12] David Forrest, Competition, the Price of Gambling and the Social Cost of Gambling (2010), http://www.egba.eu/pdf/Forrest_final_economic_review.pdf.

[13] Swiss Institute of Comparative Law, Study of Gambling Services in the Internal Market of the European Union (2006).

[14] Am. Gaming Ass'n, State of the States: The AGA Survey of Casino Entertainment (2011), http://www.americangaming.org/sites/default/files/uploads/docs/sos/aga-sos-2011.pdf; Peter T. Calcagno et al., *Determinants of the Probability and Timing of Commercial Casino Legalization in the United States*, 142 Pub. Choice, 69 (2010); *State Implicit Lottery Tax Revenue Per Capita, Fiscal Year 2010*, Tax Foundation (2012), http://taxfoundation.org/article/state-implicit-lottery-tax-revenue-capita-fiscal-year-2010.

[15] Douglas M. Walker, The Economics of Casino Gambling (2007).

ties to the overall tourism industry.[16] For example, a lower casino gambling tax relative to the lottery tax may be supported by casinos' complementary effects on other taxable industries (such as tourism and hospitality). A high tax on casinos will reduce tax revenue collected from those other local industries, and this may be particularly noticeable for integrated-resort casinos that serve as greater tourism attractions. However, casinos have been noted to be a substitute to lottery gambling.[17] The lower casino tax to complement the tourism industry (and tourism based taxes) must therefore be balanced against the increased substitutionary effects on the more heavily taxed lottery industry. Similar arguments would apply to other forms of gambling based on their demand and cross-elasticities, and any comprehensive policy should make use of careful empirical modeling to balance these effects.

EXTERNALITY BASED TAXES

In the presence of externalities (a cost or benefit that is incurred by a third party of a transaction), optimal commodity tax design is no longer described by the Ramsey conditions.[18] In particular, if consumption of a particular commodity leads to a negative externality, Pigou and Baumol suggest that those goods should be taxed at a higher rate.[19] This "pigovian" tax should be equal in size to the negative externality caused by consumption. The purpose of this tax is to force the private market to "internalize" the social cost of the activity. If the benefit from producing the good is greater than both the cost of production and the cost of the pigovian tax, then it remains economically efficient for continued production.[20]

Since many social costs can be attributed to different forms of gambling, such as those noted by Walker, Collins and Lapsley, and Eadington,[21]

---

[16] INTEGRATED RESORT CASINOS: IMPLICATIONS FOR ECONOMIC GROWTH AND SOCIAL IMPACTS (William R. Eadington & Meighan R. Doyle eds., 2009)

[17] Stephen Fink and Jonathon Rork, *The Importance of Self-Selection in Casino Cannibalization of State Lotteries*, 8 ECON. BULL. 1 (2003); Walker, *supra* note 3.

[18] Ramsey, *supra* note 9.

[19] ARTHUR PIGOU, THE ECONOMICS OF WELFARE (1920); William J. Baumol, *On Taxation and the Control of Externalities*, 62 AM. ECON. REV., 307 (1972).

[20] In some cases, a tax greater than that described by Baumol may be appropriate. Tullock and Sandmo suggest that higher taxes may be desirable if those sin taxes are able to offset distortive taxes elsewhere in the economy, such as income taxes that reduce the incentive to work. Gordon Tullock, *Excess Benefit*, 3 WATER RESOURCES RES. 643-644 (1967); Agnar Sandmo, *Optimal Taxation in the Presence of Externalities*, 77 SWEDISH J. ECON. 86-98 (1975). This phenomenon has been described in the environmental economics literature as a double dividend since the tax both reduces the harmful externality and offsets distortions elsewhere. *See* David Pearce, *The Role of Carbon Taxes in Adjusting to Global Warming*, 101 ECON. J. 938 (1991) The double dividend is frequently cited as a reason to implement pollution based taxes, but can be challenging to effectively implement.

[21] Douglas M. Walker, *Problems in Quantifying the Social Costs and Benefits of Gambling*, 66 AM. J. ECON. & SOC. 609 (2007); David Collins & Helen Lapsley, *The Social Costs and Benefits of Gambling: An Introduction to the Economic Issues*, 9 J. GAMBLING STUD. 123

higher taxes in the gambling sector could be normatively valid if they are commensurate with the increase in external social costs. This does not mean that they are equal the direct costs of a consumer with problem gambling issues, since gamblers would not be a "third party" in the transaction and can conceivably have control over their own costs.[22] Rather, accounting of the externalities could include items such as the need for increased law enforcement or the psychic costs borne by the friends and family of problem gamblers.

Since that measure of externalities is effectively a function of the level of problem gambling, this tax theory implies that higher relative tax rates should be applied to those forms of gambling that have more problem gamblers, such as video lottery terminals or pokies.[23] It also suggests that incentives could be designed for the gambling industry, where the tax rate becomes a function of the problem gambling prevalence rate. Firms would then be able to make rational decisions around investments in responsible gambling programs.

Empirically, gambling taxes do not appear to follow any sort of pigovian objective. Chapman et al. found that the most socially harmful forms of gambling were not taxed at a higher rate in Australia.[24] Taxes on pokies were fairly low, while the tax rate on less socially harmful lotteries was comparatively much higher. Similar comparative tax levels are illustrated in the U.S. by Clotfelter.[25] An important distinction to make with the casino gaming industry, as compared to most other "sin" goods or industries with negative externalities, is that casinos are often designed to be an export good to other jurisdictions. As stated by Eadington:

> Historically, casinos have often been introduced to capture economic benefits from "exporting" casino gaming to customers from regions where the activity is prohibited. Jurisdictions that legalized casinos were often re-

(2003); William R. Eadington, *The Legalization of Casinos: Policy Objectives, Regulatory Alternatives, and Cost/Benefit Considerations*, 34 J. Travel Res. 3 (1996); William R. Eadington, *Measuring Costs from Permitted Gaming: Concepts and Categories in Evaluating Gambling's Consequences*, 19 J. Gambling Stud. 185 (2003). However, the validity of many of the costs are in dispute.

[22] Jonathon Guryan & Melissa S. Kearney, *Is Lottery Gambling Addictive?*, 2 Am. Econ. J.: Econ. Pol'y 90 (2010); Sridhar Narayanan & Puneet Manchanda, *An Empirical Analysis of Individual Level Casino Gambling Behavior*, 10 Quantitative Marketing & Econ. 27 (2012).

[23] Max Wenden Abbott & Rachel Ann Volberg, Statistics New Zealand, Taking the Pulse on Gambling and Problem Gambling in New Zealand: A Report on Phase One of the 1999 National Prevalence Survey (2000); *Australia's Gambling Industries*, Austl. Gov't Productivity Commission (1999), http://www.pc.gov.au/projects/inquiry/gambling/docs/finalreport; Jamie Wieve et al., Can. Cen. On Substance Abuse Responsible Gambling Council, Measuring Gambling and Problem Gambling in Ontario (2001).

[24] R. Chapman et al., Ctr. for Int'l Econ. (Sydney, Austl.), A Framework for National Competition Policy Reviews of Gaming Legislation (1997).

[25] Charles T. Clotfelter, *Gambling Taxes, in* Theory and Practice of Excise Taxation: Smoking, Drinking, Gambling, and Driving (Sijbren Cnossen ed., 2005).

source poor, or under economic duress. One or both of these factors apply to Monaco (1863), Nevada (1931), Macau (in the early 20th century), the Caribbean (1960s), and Atlantic City (1976).[26]

When a large portion of economic activity is in the form of exports, the home state is able to capture the economic rents from foreign visitors, while exporting many of the negative externalities when the visitors return home. This lowers the appropriate pigovian tax of the home state, since much of the externalities are no longer borne by the local economy. Destination resorts and other gambling facilities established near foreign populations should therefore be taxed less than facilities that primarily draw from domestic patrons.

TAX INCIDENCE

Incidence is not a heavily discussed issue in tax theory, but public debates often tend to focus on the degree to which taxes generated by gambling are "regressive" – that is, whether low income residents tend to produce more gambling tax revenue as a share of income relative to high income residents. Much academic gambling research has also focused on this issue, finding that lotteries tend to be quite regressive[27], with casino gambling somewhat less so, but still regressive.[28] Part of this difference may be explained by the limited opportunity for higher income players to engage in high denomination play in lotteries. A single lottery ticket purchase is the same price for a low income gambler as it is for a high income gambler. In a casino, higher income gamblers can wager on high denomination slots while lower income gamblers can wager on "penny slots". Lotteries are also considered to be more likely to be "aspirational gambling." That is, gambling with the aspiration of reaching higher levels of wealth rather than as an entertainment-oriented activity. It would therefore be more likely to appeal to lower income gamblers than already high income gamblers. Eadington summarizes this perspective:

> Lotteries which have low intrinsic entertainment value but very large prizes relative to the cost of participation are the ideal wealth motive gambles.

---

[26] Eadington (1999), *supra* note 21, at 186-87.

[27] *See, e.g.* Kevin S. Daberkow & Wei Lin, *Constructing a Model of Lottery Tax Incidence Measurement: Revisiting the Illinois Lottery Tax for Education*, 37 J. EDUC. FIN. 267 (2012); Linda S. Ghent & Alan P. Grant, *The Demand for Lottery Products and Their Distributional Consequences*, 63 NAT'L TAX J. 253 (2010); Levi Perez & Brad Humphreys, The 'Who and Why' of Lottery: Empirical Highlights from the Seminal Economic Literature, J. ECON. SURV. (2012).

[28] Mary O. Borg et al., *The Incidence of Taxes on Casino Gambling: Exploiting the Tired and Poor*, 50 Am. J. Econ. & Soc., 323 (1991); William C. Rivenbark & Bradley B. Rounsaville, *The Incidence of Casino Gaming Taxes in Mississippi: Setting the Stage*, 20 PUB. ADMIN. QUARTERLY 129 (1996); Andrew C. Worthington, *Implicit Finance in Gambling Expenditures: Australian Evidence on Socioeconomic and Demographic Tax Incidence*, 29 PUB. FIN. REV. 326 (2001).

Fixed odds games with even money pay-offs, on the other hand, are more likely to attract entertainment motivated players than wealth seekers.[29]

The idea of tax regressivity often draws more attention from the public debates than from tax theorists because distributional effects are often ignored in the debates. A complete tax regressivity discussion should highlight the net effect of the tax, after public income is redistributed through government spending. For example, a regressive tax may actually have a net-progressive effect if the revenue is redistributed to low-income groups. For example, a lottery tax could be used to lower income tax rates for persons with low incomes or it could be used to fund public goods that are disproportionately used by lower income residents, such as the public school system.

INTER-JURISDICTIONAL COMPETITION

If a policy maker is able to effectively restrict competition from outside jurisdictions, then the normative analysis outlined above should serve as a useful guide for policymaking. However, if there is a presence (or threat) of competition from surrounding jurisdictions, then the appropriate tax policy may change. Consider for example two casinos, each located on separate sides of the same border and each conforming to different government policies.[30] If casino A is subject to a higher tax rate than casino B, then it will be at a distinct disadvantage due to its higher operating costs. The reduction in profitability could be manifested through high prices (lower return to player), or a reduction in the quality of the product (e.g. fewer amenities, less capital investments, fewer rewards, etc.), but all will lead to lower output and profitability. While casino A may still be able to generate a positive return if the market is under-supplied (and thus producing some economic rents), a less restricted market would ultimately lead to the collapse of the gambling market in state A, since any operator would prefer to provide its product under state B's lower cost regime.

This model may explain the lack of sites that are actually located within the United Kingdom – where applicable taxes include a 15% GGR tax[31], and the large agglomeration of Internet gambling sites that serve UK residents from offshore tax havens. Similarly, the external competition qualification can explain the interest of so many firms in the U.S.

---

[29] William R. Eadington, *Economic Perceptions of Gambling Behavior*, 3 J. GAMBLING STUD. 264 (1988).

[30] This model is closely related to the linear city model describing the location of similar firms given consumers' preferences and travel costs. C. d'Aspremont et al., *On Hotelling's "Stability in Competition,"* 47 ECONOMETRICA 1145 (1979); Harold Hotelling, *Stability in Competition*, 39 ECON. J. 41 (1929).

[31] Betsi Beem & John Mikler, *National Regulations for a Borderless Industry: US Versus UK Approaches to Online Gambling*, 30 POL'Y & SOC'Y, 161 (2011); Brad R. Humphreys & Levi Perez, *Participation in Internet Gambling Markets: An International Comparison of Online Gamblers' Profiles*, 11 J. INTERNET COM. 24 (2012).

online gambling market, despite the expectation of higher tax rates than in offshore tax havens. The Unlawful Internet Gambling Enforcement Act and the events of Black Friday have demonstrated the ability of the U.S. government to effectively restrict participation from unlicensed offshore operators (Rose, 2009, 2011).[32] The U.S. has created effective barriers via difficult financial transaction mechanisms and higher account deposit loss risk. Even if future onshore operators will have to pass-through higher domestic tax rates, these barriers may be effective deterrents to competition from foreign sites.

CONCLUSION

This study provided a normative analysis of gambling tax policy using economic theory. Several key considerations for stakeholders of the industry were identified in order to maximize economic welfare. First, lump-sum taxation is generally preferred over ad valorem taxation, since it leads to fewer distortions in the economy from the competitive equilibrium. In this sense, the use of limited license fees to generate public revenue could be preferable to taxes on gross gaming revenue. This allows operators to profitably serve marginal consumers, since the tax has no effect on production incentives. This design could also yield a distributional benefit. A shift to license based taxes may lower the share of gambling revenue generated by problem gamblers.

Where gross gambling revenue taxes are used to generate public revenue, they should be inversely related to their elasticity. That is, products whose demand is sensitive to prices changes should be taxed less, and products whose demand is less sensitive should be taxed more. Taxes on gambling activities should also be lower if they have complementary effects on other industries, and higher if they have substitutionary effects. This implies, for example, that casino taxes should be lower if they can serve as an attraction to the wider tourism and hospitality industries.

Not all ad valorem taxes are noted to be inefficient. A pigovian tax that is equal in size to the negative externalities caused by gambling is found to improve economic welfare. That is, by forcing the market to internalize the harm caused by the industry – typically called the social costs of gambling – both producers and consumers will be forced to pay the full costs of consumption, including those costs borne on the rest of society. Due to the perceived relationship between problem gamblers and external social costs, gambling industries that tend to have higher rates of problem gambling should be taxed at a higher relative rate. However, many casinos are designed to draw patrons from foreign jurisdictions, and therefore would warrant lower pigovian tax rates since the externalities are not incurred by the local economy.

---

[32] I. Nelson Rose, *New UIGEA Regs Put Benefits and Burdens on States*, 13 GAMING L. REV. & ECON. 1 (2009); I. Nelson Rose, *Poker's Black Friday*, 15 GAMING L. REV. & ECON. 327 (2011).

While empirical studies have repeatedly shown gambling to have a regressive tax incidence, analysis and discussions of tax incidence should not be made without full consideration of the net tax effects. Market structure and the distributional choices with the tax revenue can turn a regressive tax into a progressive tax. Of course, the effectiveness of earmarking revenue from gambling sources must also be considered.

Finally, appropriate tax policy decisions should not be made in a domestic vacuum. The presence of foreign suppliers can cause the domestic market to collapse if there are significant tax advantages to locating in the foreign jurisdiction. However, if the overall market has supply limits and/or the home state is able to establish effective barriers to competition, then a difference in tax rates may be sustainable.

14

Crimes and Advantage Play

Anthony Cabot, Robert Hannum, & Darren Heyman

THE NATURE OF CRIMES

Criminal justice and regulatory systems use similar methods to achieve their respective goals, but they have distinct goals. Both involve attempts by the government to control the behavior of those within its jurisdiction. Criminal law, however, punishes persons for activities that society views as morally wrong, such as murder, theft, or assault. As one author noted:

> The essence of punishment for moral delinquency lies in the criminal conviction itself. One may lose more money on the stock market than in a court-room; a prisoner of war camp may well provide a harsher environment than a state prison; death on the field of battle has the same physical characteristics as death by sentence of law. It is the expression of the community's hatred, fear, or contempt for the convict which alone characterizes physical hardship as punishment.[1]

Regulation involves implementing controls over activity. Violating these controls is often not immoral or publically condemnable. These controls attempt to achieve other policy goals. For example, a gaming regulation may require that only authorized persons have access to the room where the casino counts the money from the gaming tables. This limits the opportunity for owners or employees to skim or steal money. The casino may violate this regulation by letting an unauthorized person observe the count, perhaps a child of one of the authorized counters. Even if no money is stolen and intentions may have been honorable, this activity is a regulatory violation, and the regulators may discipline the licensee.

The first major reason governments may decide that certain casino-related activities involving theft or fraud should be criminal violations because they entail maybe morally reprehensible conduct deserving condemnation, i.e., the social stigma of being a criminal and imprisonment. Theft

---

[1] George K. Gardner, *Bailey v. Richardson and the Constitution of the United States*, 33 B.U.L. REV. 176, 193 (1953).

is theft regardless of whether the victim is a bank, a grocery store, or a casino.

A government may also criminalize violations because it would not otherwise have jurisdiction over the perpetrator. A regulatory agency could pass regulations that govern the conduct of casino operators and discipline those operators that fail to comply with them. In many places, however, the regulatory authority may not have independent authority to regulate the conduct of third parties, such as players, or to impose civil penalties on their conduct. Therefore, the government may pass criminal statutes that govern the conduct of non-licensees, such as the aforementioned players, and provide a basis for enforcement by a branch or division of government separate from the casino regulators.

A third reason that government may decide to criminalize certain activities is because of the sensitivity of the activity. More broadly, as noted in Chapter 7, government protection goals include ensuring casinos pay all taxes on casino revenues. Money lost to cheaters can reduce the casinos' taxable revenues.

Criminal sanctions may have other, more specific, goals. For example, a government may decide that the damage to a casino industry may be significant if the public perceives the casinos as being used to launder illegal drug money. Often, the casinos may be unknowing participants in the money laundering scheme, such as, if a person buys chips at a table with cash and later redeems the chips at the casino cage, without intending to gamble. To prevent money laundering, the government may require the casino to track and report or prohibit certain cash transactions. Because of the importance of the matter, a government may also deem these violations criminal. The government may hope that harsher sanctions will provide a greater deterrent to violations.

Like other activities that involve cash, legal casinos and their players are attractive targets for both sophisticated players and criminals. Some of this activity is relatively easy to define as a crime, such as stealing chips off the table from another player or the dealer's tray. Cheating acts involving theft are the easiest to understand procedurally; it is also easier to understand why these acts are characterized as criminal acts. Theft is the taking of another person's property without that person's permission or consent, intending to deprive the rightful owner. Fraud is a type of theft involving intentional deception. A necessary element in all forms of cheating is intent. Uniformly, courts have required scienter, or fraudulent intent, as an element of cheating.[2]

Much of this chapter involves the relationship between the casino and

---

[2] Under Nevada law, "cheat" means to alter the elements of chance, method of selection, or criteria which determine (a) the result of the game; (b) the amount or frequency of payment in a game; or (c) the value of a wagering instrument approved by the State Gaming Control Board for use in connection with a cashless wagering system. NEV. REV. STAT. § 465.015 (2013).

its players and focuses on the contractual relationship formed between the two. Casino-style gambling[3] involves a contract, which is a promise or set of promises, between the casino and the player.[4] The law provides punishment for the breach of any such promises.[5] In casino play, the casino promises to pay the player a predetermined sum if certain conditions are met. The player agrees to place the wager at risk if those certain conditions are met. Take slot machine play as an example. After the player deposits the correct number of coins or tokens and activates the device by pushing the play button or pulling the handle, the major condition to payment of a jackpot is that the reels must come to rest with a winning combination aligned on the payline.

Most gambling contracts, however, have two unusual aspects. First, the major condition to the contractual obligations of the casino and the player is determined in whole or in part on the outcome of chance, typically a "random" event.[6] Again, using the slot machine example, placement of the symbols on the payline in modern electronic slot machines is determined by a random number generator within the computer that runs the slot machine.[7] A random number generator is merely an algorithm, or a computer program with a well-defined set of instructions, finite in number, that produces numbers that

---

[3] Gambling involves any activity in which a person places a bet or wager. Generally, a bet or wager occurs when a person risks something of value on the outcome of an uncertain event (1) in which the bettor does not exercise any control; or (2) which is determined predominately by chance. *See, e.g.,* Midwestern Enterprises, Inc. v. Stenehjen, 625 N.W.2d 234, 237 (N.D. 2001). Courts often oversimplify this definition by concluding that gambling is any activity that involves a prize, consideration, and chance. Compare N.D. CENT. CODE 12.1-28-01(1) and Midwestern Enterprises, Inc. v. Stenehjen, 625 N. W. 2d 234, 237 (N.D. 2001). Under this simplified definition, the activity is not gambling without all three elements. Chance is a difficult element to define. By its dictionary definition, chance means "An apparent absence of cause." WEBSTER'S NEW TWENTIETH CENTURY DICTIONARY 301 (2d ed. 1979). The difficulty, however, comes in determining when chance predominates a particular activity. To assess whether an activity meets this element, one needs to envision a continuum with pure skill on one end and pure chance on the other. The prevailing rule in the United States is that the element of chance is met if chance predominates, even if the activity requires some skill. *See e.g.,* State v. Hahn, 553 N.W.2d 292, 293 (Wis. Ct. App. 1996). Some games, like a traditional slot machine, meet this requirement since they contain pure chance. Other games, like chess, that contain no chance are not gambling. Between these are many games that contain both chance and skill, such as blackjack (probably gambling) and backgammon (probably not gambling). Yet, once one enters this gray area, he or she is at risk because a court ruling could be upheld regardless of the trial court's decision. In these cases, a court would have to decide whether skill or chance predominates a particular activity. In the only case involving backgammon, however, a New Jersey court held that it was illegal gambling. Boardwalk Regency Corp. v. Attorney Gen. of N.J., 457 A.2d 847, 852 (N.J. Super. Ct. Law Div. 1982). In that case, the court did not apply the majority predominance test, but based its decision on the fact that backgammon contained some chance. To further complicate the analysis, courts in different states can apply the same test to the same activity with conflicting results.

[4] *See infra notes* 116-156 and accompanying text.

[5] *See infra notes* 116-156 and accompanying text.

[6] *See infra notes* 149-153 and accompanying text.

[7] ANTHONY CABOT, CASINO GAMING POLICY, ECONOMICS AND REGULATION (1996).

appear to be random.[8] Each number generated may correspond to a group of symbols on a reel-type machine. Some of these groups are combinations that result in the player winning and others result in the player losing.[9]

In other games, the random events that determine winning and losing combinations are decidedly less technical. In craps, the random event is the roll of two dice; in baccarat and blackjack, it is the shuffle of a standard deck of playing cards; and in roulette, it is the spin of a wheel and the toss of the roulette ball.[10]

A second unusual aspect of a gambling contract is that the economic outcome of the gambling contract, which is based on a random event, will—almost without exception—favor the casino over time.[11] This is because an advantage is built into every house-banked casino game.[12] This is typically accomplished by the casino paying less than "true odds" on every bet. In roulette, the true odds of winning a bet on a single number is 37:1 because 38 possible numbers have an equal probability of coming up. The casino, however, only pays 35:1. Therefore, the casino retains a 5.26 percent advantage over the player.[13] This also can be expressed as the casino having a 5.26 percent positive expectation over the player, or the player having a 5.26 percent negative expectation.

Probability is at the foundation of the gaming business.[14] Every wager in a casino is designed and calibrated according to the laws of chance to exact a certain percentage of the players' money.[15] This is how the casino makes money.[16] In the short run, a player may win or lose, but in the long run the total of all players' losses will exceed the total of all players' wins.[17] Mathematicians call this the law of large numbers.[18]

---

[8] *Id.*

[9] Nigel Turner & Roger Horbay, *How do slot machines and other electronic gambling machines actually work?*, J. GAMBLING ISSUES (July 2004), http://www.camh.net/egambling/issue11/jgi_11_turner_horbay.html.

[10] *See* EDWARD THORP, THE MATHEMATICS OF GAMBLING 11, 30, 43–64 (1984); *See generally*, ROBERT C. HANNUM & ANTHONY N. CABOT, PRACTICAL CASINO MATH (2nd ed. 2005).

[11] HANNUM & CABOT, *supra* note 10, at 13. Exceptions can be found for which the house advantage in a game is not positive, but these are rare. A few video poker machines, for example, return greater than 100 percent to the player if perfect strategy is used. Although advantage play and/or cheating methods theoretically can be used to increase the positive player advantage with such games, this chapter will ignore these anomalies and focus on house-banked games with a positive house advantage.

[12] *Id.*

[13] This assumes a double-zero wheel and except for the five-number bet, in which the house advantage is 7.89 percent.

[14] HANNUM & CABOT, *supra* note 10, at 1.

[15] *See, e.g.*, OLAF VANCURA, SMART CASINO GAMBLING: HOW TO WIN MORE AND LOSE LESS 31 (1996).

[16] One popular author put it this way: "A casino is a mathematics palace set up to separate players from their money." NICHOLAS PILEGGI, CASINO (1995).

[17] HANNUM & CABOT, *supra* note 10, at 12–28.

[18] Vancura, *supra* note 15 at 31. More precisely, the law of large numbers states that in in-

Often, disagreements arise between the casino and the player as to whether the casino has to pay winnings. For example, a player may assert that they played the requisite credits on a slot machine and claimed a jackpot because the requisite combination of symbols appeared on the pay line. The casino may disagree that the proper number of credits were played or that the requisite symbols appeared on the pay line. This is typically a civil dispute that could be handled by the regulatory agency or the courts. More difficult to categorize are instances when the casino or player attempt to change the probabilities that govern the games. These instances are often referred to as advantage play, which is a broad term to describe a situation in which a player, through some method of legal or illegal play, can acquire an advantage over the casino in a gambling contract.[19] In other words, advantage play occurs when the player overcomes the mathematical advantage built into every house-banked casino game. A popular method of advantage play is card counting in blackjack. Advantage play is more than a hypothetical issue. Some experts believe that advantage players make up as much as 3 percent of all moneys wagered in commercial casinos.[20]

This chapter is divided into two sections. The first section describes casino activities that involve theft or fraudulent activity that should be considered crimes and enforcement challenges. The second section covers advantage play, which of the various types of advantage play should be categorized as crimes, and whether casinos should have the power to take countermeasures to prevent such play.

SPECIFIC VERSUS BROAD CRIMINAL STATUTES

Almost every successful challenge to the criminal laws that prohibit cheating at licensed games is based on the legal defense that the law, as written, was too vague. A statute is too vague if it did not place the defendant on fair notice his behavior was criminally actionable. The requirement that criminal statutes define offenses with extreme particularity is unrealistic.[21] Yet, an overly broad statute will fall to a vagueness challenge. If criminal statutes define each crime with extreme particularity, one of two things may happen: (1) the number of such statutes would be voluminous to cover all possible crimes; or (2) if a crime is not precluded by statute, a person in violation could not be punished. Therefore, a balance between specificity and broadness is beneficial with more weight towards specificity.

---

dependent repeated trials of the same experiment, the actual proportion of occurrences of an event eventually approaches its theoretical probability. Thus, if the house advantage is positive, the proportion of money wagered that is won by the house will, in the long run, be a positive amount. HANNUM & CABOT, *supra* note 10, at 12–28.

[19] DUSTIN MARKS, CHEATING AT BLACKJACK AND ADVANTAGE PLAY 101 (1994).

[20] Rod Smith, *Advantage Gambling: Official Request 'Guidance,'* LAS VEGAS REV. J., July 10, 2003, http://www.reviewjournal.com/lvrj_home/2003/Jul-10-Thu-2003/business/21692188.html.

[21] Grayned v. City of Rockford, 408 U.S. 104 (1972).

The due process clauses of the Fifth and Fourteenth Amendments require definiteness.[22] Definition is critically important in criminal law due to the underlying premise, flowing from due process, that the public must be placed on notice as to what conduct is criminal.[23] The public only has fair notice of a criminal offense if the law proscribing such conduct does so with sufficient clarity that an individual of ordinary intelligence would not have to guess at its meaning.[24] To place an individual on fair notice, this higher degree of specificity is necessary.

Criminal statutes pertaining to gaming illustrate the need for specificity.[25] When slot machines were mechanical, a player could hit some slot machines' handles hard enough to break a counter pin in the devices, called "popping." Once broken, the handle could be manipulated to stop the reels to reflect winning combinations on the pay line and increase the probabilities of a win to 100 percent. The Nevada Supreme Court ruled that "popping" the handle was not illegal. The court reasoned that the criminal statute referred to the mechanical alteration of a slot machine and that handle popping did not mechanically alter the slot machines.[26] The Nevada legislature rectified this situation by adopting a more specific statute that made handle popping illegal.

Gaming Crimes can roughly be separated into three categories. The first category is theft by owners. Owners may steal from players by rigging the games to ensure that the player loses more than the amount predetermined by the mathematical probability of a fair game. Another well-known owner crime is skimming, in which the ownership/management takes money from the drop, before it is counted, to reduce potential tax liability. Skimming is known as tax evasion in other industries.

The second category of gaming crimes is employee theft. Employees may steal from both their employers and casino players. In most thefts the casino is the victim, but when the casino suffers, so does the government. Stealing reduces profits from the casino's bottom line, and deprives the government of its taxes. Ways that employees can steal from a casino are numerous. A simple theft may involve a count room employee taking some money from a drop box. Other thefts often are more elaborate. One race and sports book kept unclaimed winning tickets in a locked box. An employee, who had access to the box, reviewed the tickets and found those with large payouts. He then had a friend pose as a tourist claiming to have "lost" his portion of the winning ticket. The book verified the ticket in the unclaimed ticket box, and paid the "tourist." Many schemes exist by which employees can steal from a casino. Employees also steal from casino play-

---

[22] Wayne R. LaFave & Austin W. Scott, Jr., Substantive Criminal Law, § 1.2(b), at 10.

[23] *Id.*

[24] United States v. Harris, 347 U.S. 612, 617 (1954).

[25] Lyon v. State, 105 Nev. 317 (1989).

[26] *Id.*

ers. For example, an employee can palm a chip from the player's stack and hide it on his person until the end of his shift or pass it to a co-conspirator who is at the table.

The third category of casino crimes is theft by third parties against a casino or its players. Again, these thefts can range from the simple to the extremely complex. A simple theft is taking chips belonging to another player when that player is not looking. Other schemes can be more complex. An example of an elaborate theft involved a group that acquired false identifications. The group's leader visited a casino under the pretext of being a player betting high limits. On the first visit, the casino executives assumed the person was a legitimate player, and by the end of his trip invited him to return to the casino and offered him a line of credit. The leader took the established credit and further earned the trust of the casino executives by drawing against his line of credit and promptly paying his losses. After convincing the casino executives of his credit-worthiness, he asked whether, if he brought several friends on a junket, would the casino establish large lines of credit for each player. The leader vouched for the creditworthiness of the group and agreed to guarantee their losses. The casino agreed. The group came and played at the casino. They drew against their credit lines, but did not lose all the money they had withdrawn. They left owing much more than the leader had previously lost and repaid. When payment on this credit line was not made, the casino began collection efforts. To the casino's dismay, all the information provided by the group was false. The casino was bilked. None of the group members was ever caught.

CRIMES BY OWNERS
Skimming

Governments often tax casinos based on gross revenues, i.e., all amounts received as winnings less all amounts paid out as losses. Simply by under-reporting or removing winnings before they can be counted, dishonest owners can reduce or altogether avoid paying "gross revenue" taxes (and income tax). This is "skimming."

Skimming can occur in many ways. Most obviously, employees may take cash from table drop boxes or gaming devices before it is counted. Some governments have online monitoring systems for gaming devices that count money as the players play, then calculate taxes based on the number of coins played less the number of coins paid out plus the hand-paid jackpots. This avoids basing gross revenue on the owner's coin count. Other jurisdictions do not trust the owner to conduct the count or even open a gaming device without a government inspector present to observe.

Policing the cash count from table games is even more difficult. Unlike gaming devices, tables do not have meters that count the number of dollars placed in the drop box. Some operators may not put all money collected into the drop box. Using credit also makes it more difficult to properly track gross revenues. A common 1950s "skim" method was executed by allowing bettors to play on "rim" credit. Here, the player would ask for credit and receive chips. The credit would be registered only by a plastic button or marker placed by the dealer on the rim or edge of the table without any written documentation. After the player accumulated a large debt, the owner could ask the player to come to his office where the debt would be settled in cash, often for less than the face value of the rim credit. The owner would return to the table and simply remove the marker. The skim was completed without any paper trail.

Another method of skimming is to exaggerate losses. This is simpler in jurisdictions that allow credit. Suppose an owner grants credit to a co-conspirator for $100,000, which the co-conspirator takes in chips. Rather than gambling, the co-conspirator exchanges the chips for cash, and gives the cash to the owner. The casino has paid out $100,000 in cash and holds a check or marker for $100,000. If the casino never collects the check or marker, it never receives cash in the win column, but it has recorded a $100,000 loss.

Skimming is a serious crime, particularly in those jurisdictions where government protection goals (such as ensuring the government receives all correct tax revenues due, as discussed in Chapter 2) are emphasized. Yet, even under other policy models, skimming is theft of government funds and should be treated accordingly. Moreover, if an operator is willing to steal from the government, he is likely to steal from players. Therefore, most jurisdictions have laws that explicitly prohibit skimming and provide for serious regulatory, civil, and criminal punishments.

The following Louisiana statute illustrates a statutory prohibition against skimming:

LA Rev Stat § 27:98

§98. Skimming of gaming proceeds

a. The crime of skimming of gaming proceeds is the intentional excluding or the taking of any action in an attempt to exclude any thing or its value from the deposit, counting, collection, or computation of:

   1) Gross revenues from gaming operations or activities.

   2) Net gaming proceeds.

   3) Amounts due the state pursuant to the provisions of this Chapter.

b. Whoever commits the crime of skimming of gaming proceeds when the amount skimmed, or to be skimmed, is less than one thousand dollars may be imprisoned, with or without hard labor, for not more than five years or may be fined not more than five thousand dollars, or both.

c. Whoever commits the crime of skimming of gaming proceeds when the amount skimmed, or to be skimmed, is one thousand dollars or more shall be imprisoned at hard labor for not less than one year and not more than twenty years or may be fined not more than ten thousand dollars or the amount skimmed or to be skimmed, whichever is greater, or both.

d. The crime of skimming of gaming proceeds, for purposes of venue, may be considered to have been committed either in the parish of East Baton Rouge or in the parish or parishes within whose boundary or territorial jurisdiction the riverboat was located at the time the offense was committed.[27]

Cheating Players

Without proper regulation, casino operators can easily cheat players. Some illegal casinos are called "bust out" houses because their sole goal is to dishonestly separate the player from their money. Gaming devices are the easiest for the casino operator to modify (or gaff). In modern machines, this is as simple as altering the software to decrease the players' chances to win beyond what is represented to the player or permitted by regulation.

Table games, however, also can be rigged. Fifty years ago, common buyers of loaded dice in the United States were the illegal casinos, operating from Steubenville, Ohio, to Galveston, Texas. The mathematically fair 1.414 percent house advantage for craps was not sufficient to generate enough money to bribe the sheriff, the judge, the politicians, and still make a reasonably high profit for the casino. Hence, some illegal casinos resorted to using "loaded" dice. These casinos, however, faced a dilemma. They wanted to use loaded dice, but they didn't want players to do likewise. So, they demanded the exacting standards of the dice manufacturers to protect themselves from cheats. These standards included distinctive logos, serial numbers, and sealed containers. So, the illegal operators convinced certain dice makers to make two almost identical sets of dice with the same serial numbers. The major difference, however, was that the dice in the second set were loaded to cheat the players. The loaded dice would see the felts (i.e., be used for play) at the appropriate times to "cool" a table. Besides loaded dice, casinos can use other types of altered dice to cheat the player.

Casino operators also can cheat at blackjack. A simple method is to remove some high cards from a multi-card shoe. This improves the casino's theoretical advantage over the players.[28] Another method is for the dealer to peek at the top card of the deck or to use a marked deck to learn if that card would cause him or a player to bust (i.e., exceed a 21 count). If it would, the dealer would deal "seconds," a technique where it appears that the dealer is dealing the top card, but actually is dealing another card of his choice. By this method, the dealer can decide when he wants to avoid busting or when to cause the player to bust. Many other ways exist for unscrupulous operators

---

[27] Acts 1991, No. 753, §1, eff. July 18, 1991. Redesignated from R.S. 4:557 by Acts 1996, 1st Ex. Sess., No. 7, §3, eff. May 1, 1996, http://law.justia.com/codes/louisiana/2012/rs/title27/rs27-98.

[28] Because a player receives a three-to-two payout (or six-to-five) on a natural blackjack, which requires an Ace and a card with a value of 10, by removing Aces and Tens the players' advantage is decreased.

to illegally increase the house advantage to their own favor. Dealers can stack the deck in favor of the house by picking up discards in a deliberate order and engaging in a non-random shuffle. Dealers also can switch their hole card by slight-of-hand to achieve a better hand. All these maneuvers significantly increase the house advantage in the long run.

Roulette tables can be gaffed with magnets that cause a steel-core ball to fall in predetermined segments of the wheel. By looking at the various bets on the table, the operator can chose that segment of the wheel that has the lowest potential for the player's winning.

Another cheat is by either dealers or gaming devices short-paying players on winning hands or plays. A dealer at a table can rearrange the player's bet on a table by removing a chip during the process of paying him causing the original bet and the payoff to be decreased. Similarly on a gaming device, instead of paying 100 coins on a slot jackpot, a machine could be set to pay only 98 coins.

Cheating by owners is a serious game-related crime, regardless of the policy model employed by the government. Under gambler protection goals, this type of cheating exploits the person the system is designed to protect. Under government protection goals, the essence of the public's trust in the integrity of the industry is threatened by a single incident of casino cheating. Therefore, sanctions for cheating by owners should be severe enough to act as an effective deterrent.

CRIMES BY EMPLOYEES
Theft from Owners
Table games

Cheaters can easily cheat a casino game when the dealer is working with an accomplice posing as a player. This is "dumping off" the game. Four common methods are the "push and pay," "flashing," "peeking," and "stacking." In the "push and pay," the dealer simply pays the player or pushes, even when the player has lost the hand in blackjack. The dealer also can overpay on the accomplice's winning hands. Success of this technique depends on the sophistication of the table game equipment, the level of surveillance, and the skill of the employees that watch the game.

Flashing occurs when the dealer intentionally exposes either his "hole card" or the top card of the deck to the player-accomplice. The player then can use this information to guide his play. In some schemes, he can use the information to guide his own play and in others to cause the dealer to bust more often than usual. The latter can allow other accomplices at the table, who are betting higher amounts, a greater opportunity to win. Peeking is similar to flashing, except that the dealer is the person that sees the top card, then signals his accomplice, who plays accordingly.

Stacking is a method whereby the dealer appears to properly shuffle the deck, but purposefully does not randomly mix the cards. Instead, cards picked up from the previous hand are segregated and left in the same order as before, even after the final "shuffle." The dealer then deals the arranged cards to allow the player-accomplice to win the hand(s).

Employees can also steal directly from the casino. Dealers can use devices such as specially-designed cups or their hands to remove chips from the table and hide them on their person. After completing their shifts, they can pass these chips to others for redemption or use for barter.

Gaming devices

Employees can steal from gaming devices in many ways. Access to the interior of gaming devices should be restricted to authorized personnel because once inside, theft of cash or tickets can occur from the drop box.[29]

Theft from Players

Casino employees may have opportunities to steal from casino players without the knowledge of their employer. The most common method is to steal chips off the table and conceal them somewhere on the employee's person. After his or her shift ends, the employee may pass the chips to a co-conspirator who cashes them in at the cage. The simplest way for a dealer to steal from the players is to palm chips from the player's stack and drop them into hidden pockets in his clothing.

Theft by casino employees from owners or players is a serious crime. At a minimum, it should be treated as severely as theft by a person under general criminal laws. Under player protection goals, theft from players may be treated more severely than simple theft in other contexts. Under government protection goals, theft from the casino decreases tax revenues to the state and theft from players jeopardizes public trust in the integrity of the industry. Both circumstances justify greater penalties for gaming-related theft than non-gaming-related theft.

CRIMES BY PLAYERS

The most common third-party theft is cheating by players. Cheating is any attempt by a player to take the element of chance out of gambling. The most common methods of cheating are (1) altering or determining the outcome of the game by manipulating or modifying the equipment or the game, (2) learning the outcome of the game before placing a bet, or increasing or decreasing a bet after learning the outcome, (3) placing a bet without paying consideration, (4) claiming a winning wager without having made a wager, and (5) stealing from the game. An example of a general statutory prohibition against cheating is as follows:

---

[29] Modern technology hopes to solve this and other problems with accountability in a cash environment. For example, one company offers a hopper device that can account for coins and tokens in the hopper.

NRS 465.083 Cheating. It is unlawful for any person, whether the person is an owner or employee of or a player in an establishment, to cheat at any gambling game.[30]

Cheating by theft or fraud usually involves one of three major distinct situations.[31] The first type criminalizes a player's attempt to overcome the major condition of all gaming contracts, the random event. This may involve altering the selection of outcome by eliminating or altering the random component of the event that determines the outcome of the contract. Some colorful methods may include using loaded dice in a craps game or marking cards in blackjack. Here is an example of a specific statutory prohibition:

Article 225 - NY Penal Law
§ 225.90 Manipulation of gaming outcomes at an authorized gaming establishment.
A person is guilty of manipulation of gaming outcomes at an authorized gaming establishment when he or she . . .
4. Alters or misrepresents the outcome of a game or other event on which bets or wagers have been made after the outcome is made sure but before it is revealed to players.
    Possession of altered, marked or tampered with dice, cards, or gaming equipment or devices at an authorized gambling establishment is presumptive evidence of possession thereof with knowledge of its character or contents and intention to use such *altered, marked or tampered with dice, cards*, or gaming equipment or devices in violation of this section. (*emphasis added*)
Manipulation of gaming outcomes at an authorized gaming establishment is a class A misdemeanor provided, however, that if the person has previously been convicted of this crime within the past five years this crime shall be a class E felony.[32]

A person also may attempt to alter or misrepresent the outcome of a game or event after the outcome is determined, but before the casino reveals it to the players wagering on the game.[33] Suppose two people are playing blackjack. One person has a Six showing and a Queen as his hole card. The other person has a King showing and a Five as a hole card. If these players are playing honestly, their card totals would be 16 and 15, respectively. To improve their positions, if they surreptitiously exchanged hole cards, their card totals would be 20 and 11, respectively. The latter combinations are substantially more likely to beat the dealer's hand.[34]

---

[30] (Added to NRS by 1967, 1282; A 1969, 408; 1977, 325; 1979, 1478; 1981, 1294.).
[31] While cheating in the context of non-gaming activities is theoretically no different than cheating at casino games, most casino states have adopted special statutes to cover casino crimes. *See e.g.*, Nev. Rev. Stat. ch. 465. While many reasons may exist for creating special statutes, the myriad methods of cheating can explain the need for specific legislation to address each methodically.
[32] N.Y. Penal Law § 225.90 (2014), http://ypdcrime.com/penal.law/article225.htm#p225.55.
[33] Nev. Rev. Stat. § 465.070(1) (2013).
[34] For example, the Nevada Supreme Court held that blackjack players who switch or

Besides substituting or switching single cards, a cheater can use sleight of hand to switch out the entire deck of cards being used in the game with a prearranged deck of cards.[35] This type of cheat, known as a cooler, usually requires the aid of at least one casino employee.[36] Writing specific statutes designed to prohibit persons from switching or changing cards dealt may assist in prosecution of such cheats.[37]

Another unlawful activity relating to cards is "card crimping," which entails deforming a card often by bending the corners to make the point value of the card readable to the crimper from the back and the face of the card.[38]

To aid in enforcement, a statute may make it illegal for a person to intentionally mark or crimp the cards used for playing a card game.[39] With this law, regulators can arrest a person who intentionally marks or crimps cards without having to prove that the person did so intending to cheat.

This specific statutory prohibition can be seen in Nevada Revised Statute §465.085(2):

> Unlawful manufacture, sale, distribution, marking, altering or modification of equipment and devices associated with gaming; unlawful instruction.
>
> 1. It is unlawful to manufacture, sell or distribute any cards, chips, dice, game or device which is intended to be used to violate any provision of this chapter.
>
> 2. It is unlawful to mark, alter or otherwise modify any associated equipment or gaming device, as defined in chapter 463 of NRS, in a manner that:
>   a) Affects the result of a wager by determining win or loss; or
>   b) Alters the normal criteria of random selection, which affects the operation of a game or which determines the outcome of a game.
>
> 3. It is unlawful for any person to instruct another in cheating or in the use of any device for that purpose, with the knowledge or intent that the information or use so conveyed may be employed to violate any provision of this chapter.[40]

Shining, also a form of cheating, is a method of learning the dealer's hole card using any reflective device. This could include a metallic cigarette

---

change cards dealt in any manner to use and play different cards than those dealt to them, or who offer cards back to the dealer for payoff either as a winning hand or because the dealer "broke," violate the law. Moore v. State, 692 P.2d 1278–79 (Nev. 1984).

[35] MARKS, *supra* note 19, at 166–181.

[36] *Id.*

[37] Moore, *supra* note 34.

[38] *See, e.g.,* NEV. REV. STAT. § 465.083 (2013). ("It is unlawful for any person, whether he is an owner or employee of, or a player in, an establishment to cheat at any gambling game.") *See, also,* NEV. REV. STAT. § 465.015 (2013); Sheriff of Washoe County v. Martin, 99 Nev. 336, 662 P.2d 634 (1983).

[39] *See, e.g.,* NEV. REV. STAT. § 465.083 (2013).

[40] (Added to NRS by 1967, 1283; A 1975, 697; 1977, 386; 1979, 1478; 1981, 1294; 1989, 972.). The statutory language was retrieved from: http://www.leg.state.nv.us/NRS/NRS-465.html.

lighter, a facet on a ring, a polished fingernail, or a small mirror. As alluded to above, in blackjack, if a player knows the dealer's hole card, that player has an advantage over the casino by having additional information useful in determining whether to double a bet, surrender a hand, or whether to hit or stand.

Blackjack is not the only game in which cheaters can alter the outcome. Dice cheats working in teams have been such good illusionists that the thrower appears to toss both dice, but, in actuality, only throws one. A co-conspirator at the other end of the table places the second die on the felt and thereby manipulates the result.

Other methods of cheating at dice include dice scooters and sliders. Cheaters using these methods can manipulate the outcome by the method in which they throw the dice. As previously discussed, cheats can also alter the outcome of a game by shaving or loading the dice to increase the probability of certain numbers appearing.

In *Skipper v. State of Nevada*, 879 P.2d 732 (1994), the Nevada Supreme Court found that Nevada Revised Statute § 465.085 was a sufficiently specific statutory prohibition against altering the outcome and included dice sliding.

Another form of cheating by players is to acquire "knowledge, not available to all players, of the outcome of the game or any event that affects the outcome of the game."[41] This form of cheating includes card marking and crimping. A card marker can alter the backs of cards and figure out the value of the dealer's hole card in blackjack.[42] Knowledge of the dealer's hole card assures the player an advantage over the casino.[43] These cheaters are so skillful that a novice can be told that a deck contains a marked card, but he cannot identify the markings though the card cheat can read the marking with ease. Commonly, marks are applied with infrared nail polish, which require special glasses that make the mark apparent only to the cheat.

To cover as many of these variations as possible, laws may prohibit a player from placing, increasing, or decreasing a bet, or deciding his course of play after acquiring otherwise-unavailable knowledge of the outcome of the game or any event that affects the outcome.[44] A skilled cheat can increase or decrease his bet after the game ends. A cheat with a losing hand in blackjack, for example, can "pinch the bet" by palming one chip in the stack wagered. If the cheat adds a chip after learning he has a winning hand, he "pressed" or "past-posted" the bet.[45]

An example of a specific statutory prohibition of this type of cheat is as follows:

---

[41] Nev. Rev. Stat. § 465.070(2) (2005).

[42] Bill Zender, How to Detect Casino Cheating at Blackjack (1999) (discussing cheating at blackjack from another perspective—how a casino can cheat the player).

[43] Marks, *supra* note 19, at 38.

[44] *See, e.g.*, Nev. Rev. Stat. § 465.070(2) (2013).

[45] Both pressing and past-posting are illegal in Nevada. *See* Nev. Rev. Stat. § 465.070 (2013).

Cal. Pen. Code § 337u

337u. It is unlawful for any person to commit any of the following acts ...
(b) To place, increase, or decrease a wager or to determine the course of
play after acquiring knowledge, not available to all players, of the outcome
of the gambling game or any event that affects the outcome of the gambling
game or which is the subject of the wager or to aid anyone in acquiring that
knowledge for the purpose of placing, increasing, or decreasing a wager
or determining the course of play contingent upon that event or outcome.

Neither the public nor the courts have a problem understanding these
basic forms of cheating. As one court noted, "The attributes of the game—
its established physical characteristics and basic rules—determine the
probabilities of the game's various possible outcomes. Changing these attributes to affect the probabilities is a criminal act."[46]

Placing a Bet Without Paying Consideration

Cheaters may steal from casinos by playing gaming devices or a table
game without paying. In one reported case,[47] an individual played a quarter
gaming device at the Thunderbird Hotel. The coin he used had a mono-fila-
ment string attached that made it possible to play the same machine several
times while using only one coin. This type of cheat is known as a "stringer."
The colorful name applies to cheats who attach strings to coins, and use
the same coin to repeatedly play the machine. This cheat has become less
popular as coin-operated machines slowly disappear from gambling floors
and are replaced by notes, cards, and tickets.

Before most slot machines operated by ticket or paper currency only,
sluggers were a persistent problem. Slugs are counterfeit tokens used to play
gaming devices. In Nevada alone, over eight tons of slugs pass through gaming
devices each year. Sluggers have given way in most jurisdictions to persons
who attempt to either trick the bill acceptor to issuing credits when either no
currency is inserted or for amounts greater than the currency inserted.

Laws can be enacted that make it illegal for a person to use unapproved
or counterfeit tokens.[48] Government can assist regulators in prosecuting
these types of cheaters by also making it illegal for a person to have any
paraphernalia for manufacturing, testing, or concealing counterfeit tokens
or devices to trick bill acceptors.[49]

Slot Machine Wagering Vouchers, Ticket In/Ticket Out (TITO)

As slot machines become more technologically sophisticated, so too
has the manner in which they receive and pay out money. Instead of paying

---

[46] Sheriff of Washoe County v. Martin, 662 P. 2d 634, 638 (Nev. 1983).
[47] Smith v. Nevada, 482 P.2d 302 (Nev. 1971).
[48] *See, e.g.*, Nev. Rev. Stat. § 465.080(2) (2013).
[49] *See, e.g.*, Nev. Rev. Stat. § 465.080(5) (2013).

out cumbersome, heavy coins or needing sophisticated hardware to store and differentiate currency notes, many slot machines now print out a wagering voucher with the value of the payout on it. This simplifies the process rather considerably and also directs all cash payouts to the cage or to a payout machine on the casino floor.

These tickets, like any type of debit instrument such as cash, casino chips or cheques, are subject to counterfeiting and/or theft. As such, there are specific statutes that govern these ticket in/ticket out (TITO) printouts, and regulate against the possession, use, or production of these counterfeit tickets, such as Nevada Revised Statute § 465.080, which states[50]

> Possession, use, sale or manufacture of counterfeit, unapproved or unlawful instruments or items; possession of certain unlawful devices or paraphernalia for manufacturing slugs.
> 1.   It is unlawful for any licensee, employee or other person, not a duly authorized employee of a licensee acting in furtherance of his or her employment within an establishment, to possess, use, sell or manufacture counterfeit chips, counterfeit debit instruments or other counterfeit wagering instruments in a gambling game, associated equipment or a cashless wagering system.

Whether claiming TITO tickets found on casino floors or still attached to the slot machines is criminal is determined by the abandoned property laws of the state. Many states outright criminalize the appropriation of lost property, such as California, when there are ways to find the rightful owner.[51] Even those states that abide more by the "finders keepers" attitude toward lost property make exceptions for casino chips, cheques, tokens, and slot machine wagering vouchers.[52]

Unauthorized Keys or Devices to Extract Money

Many illegal activities relate to gaming devices.[53] Forged keys and devices, known as "spoons," are used to open gaming devices to relieve them of their tokens. In one reported Nevada case, a person inserted a key in one of

---

[50] *See also* N.M. STAT. § 60-2E-51 (2013).

[51] Cal. Pen. Code §485 states

> One who finds lost property under circumstances which give him knowledge of or means of inquiry as to the true owner, and who appropriates such property to his own use, or to the use of another person not entitled thereto, without first making reasonable and just efforts to find the owner and to restore the property to him, is guilty of theft.

[52] NEV. REV. STAT. § 457 (2013), amending NEV. REV. STAT. § 120A.135, http://www.leg. state.nv.us/Statutes/76th2011/Stats201123.html#Stats201123page2835.

[53] The new solid-state gaming devices are controlled by microprocessors and have sophisticated coin acceptors featuring comparators and optics. These technical advances can prevent virtually every form of cheating by cherry squeezing, using slugs, and stringing. But these new machines have cultivated, high-tech cheats that manipulate the computer program with custom chips. They have also used electronic devices, such as stun guns, to disrupt the programs in attempts to have the machines drop the coins in their hoppers.

two locks on the gaming device.[54] Another person inserted the second key necessary to access the money stored in the machine. Casino security officials detained the pair, and police charged them under the general cheating statute.[55] The defendants argued that the term "cheating device," as listed in the statute,[56] was unconstitutional because it was vague. Rejecting this argument, the Nevada Supreme Court stated that any physical object used for an unintended purpose and to cheat, deceive, or defraud, is a cheating device. When the defendants put the forged keys into the gaming device and opened the door, those keys became cheating devices.

Because of the theft risk through forged keys, government may wish to make it illegal for an unauthorized person to have or to use any key or device to affect the outcome of the game or to open the gaming machine to extract money.

Theft from Owners by Using Gaffed Equipment

In some table games, cheaters can introduce their own paraphernalia to add to or replace the casino's gaming supplies. These can include playing cards, tiles, or dice. The last is the most prevalent because its physical properties can be altered to allow cheaters to defraud the casino.

Dice cheats may attempt to introduce altered dice into the game. One method of doing this is to have the shooter, i.e., the person throwing the dice, toss them so one die leaves the table. Another person working in concert with the shooter will then replace the die that landed on the casino floor with a loaded die. Another method is to use close-up illusions that involve hiding the altered die within the palm (using the thumb), inside clothing, or somewhere else. The cheat then switches the house die with the altered die at the proper moment. A good cheat can continually exchange the dice throughout his play.

Casino dice are usually either 3/4-inch or 5/8-inch perfect squares. Most dice have a standard of variance of about 1/100,000 of an inch, meaning each die is just about a perfect square, give or take the width of a hair. Casinos demand such exacting standards because of physics. Suppose you have a pyramid and were to cut off its top. The remaining shape is a trapezoid. Now suppose you rolled the trapezoid. Intuitively, you would suspect that the trapezoid would land more often on its largest surface area, that is, bottom down. Misshaped dice, called flats, are really trapezoids although it is not as pronounced as the cut pyramid. A "flat" die can have one side as little as 1/10,000 of an inch larger than the other sides, and still be effective for cheating.

Casinos do not want flat dice in their games. Casinos make money on the slight advantage built into their games. A player betting the pass line

---

[54] Laney v. State, 86 Nev. 173, 466 P.2d 666 (Nev. 1970).
[55] *See, e.g.*, NEV. REV. STAT. § 465.080(3) (2013).
[56] *See, e.g.*, NEV. REV. STAT. § 465.083(5) (2013).

faces a mere 1.414 percent disadvantage. A misshapen die from the man-ufacturer will alter the house advantage. It may be in favor of the house or the player. But, in either case, it is something the casino wants to avoid, so they insist on perfect dice.

If a flat die is found on the table, it probably did not come from the manufacturer. The likely source is a cheat who uses flats that favor numbers that give them a slight advantage over the casino. "Crossroaders," which is how casino cheats are often referred, also may try to introduce other types of altered dice into the game.

Perhaps the most well-known cheating method is using loaded dice. Like using flats, the purpose of loaded dice is not to guarantee a win, but to shift the favorable odds from the house to the player. Loading casino dice is difficult. Most casino dice are clear, so a cheat cannot drill one side of a die and fill it with a heavy substance without it being obvious. Instead, the cheat must remove the white resin used to fill the holes of the die and bury a heavy metal in its center. Then the cheat refills the hole and carefully polishes the surface. The weighted side or sides then result in the number, or numbers, opposite it/them to appear more frequently.

"Tops" are another form of altered dice. Instead of having six numbers, like most ordinary casino dice, they have only three. These dice result in the player having an advantage over the house on certain bets depending on the numbers left on the dice. Having only fours, fives, and sixes on the dice gives an advantage to the players on field bets and also means that a seven cannot be rolled, so the players cannot "crap out."

One method the casino uses to reduce the exposure to altered dice is to use five matched dice and to frequently change out the dice. Each time the shooter changes in a game, the stickman collects the dice and mixes them with the three other dice in the set. The five dice are then offered to the next shooter, who chooses two of the five. The theory here is that if one altered die is introduced, the chance of it appearing on the next change of dice is only 40 percent. By changing the dice frequently, bad dice have a short shelf life. A typical casino changes dice on each table once every eight hours.

To assist enforcement, statutes may prohibit using altered gaming equipment and the possession of altered equipment intended for use in a licensed game.

Other Methods of Stealing from Owners
Credit scams

Credit scams are also a common way of cheating a casino. Casinos grant literally billions of dollars in credit each year. While there are elaborate regulations governing the issuance of credit, creative thieves often work within the guidelines of those regulations to cheat the casino.

Laws can prohibit a person from negotiating a bank check knowing the checking account to which it is drawn has insufficient funds. Laws also can make it illegal to obtain credit under false pretenses.

Computers

Many jurisdictions have struggled with whether using a computer to predict outcomes of games should be a crime. Players that use computers to analyze play strategy can greatly increase their probability of success. Sometimes, the player can achieve a statistical advantage over the casino. Jurisdictions vary on the legality of using of computers to analyze strategy in casino games. The policy underlying their prohibition is premised on two arguments. First, computers can analyze strategy in games such as blackjack. Here their purpose is not to remove the randomness from the game, but to allow the player to play in such a manner as to maximize the potential to win. In other circumstances, however, persons may use computers to assist in cheating. Because the casino and regulatory agents cannot learn the intended use of the computer, the only effective method of preventing cheating prohibits using computers for any reason.

Second, the nature of gaming is such that parties to the gaming transaction should not have an unfair advantage over one another. Just as it is unfair for the casino to use computers in blackjack to decide when to shuffle the deck, it would be unfair for the player to use computers to obtain an advantage over the casino. This is appropriate even if the casino is not a participant in the gaming transaction, such as in poker. In this situation, the player using a computer can acquire an advantage over the other players. If the casinos cannot use a computer to determine when to shuffle, the government can decide that allowing players to use computers would present an unfair advantage to the player.

If a jurisdiction prohibits using computers, it must adopt laws that define the offense. Only one legal case discusses applying such laws. This Nevada case involved a person playing blackjack. While playing, a surveillance camera operator noticed he moved his toes often during the game. His toe movements corresponded to the appearance of certain cards.

After casino security officials confronted him, the player, a computer expert, admitted he had hidden a microcomputer in his shoe. To pull off his "computer shoe" scam, the player cut his socks to allow his bare toes to input data into the computer. Velcro held the switches in his shoes. Wires extended up his legs to a battery pack in his left rear pocket.

He strapped the main portion of his computer to his left calf, and the computer sent vibratory signals to a special receiver located inside his athletic supporter. The signal told him whether to hit, stand, double down, or split. The computer calculated his advantage or disadvantage with the casino, and advised him of the remaining cards in the deck.

The police arrested the player and charged him with having and using a device at a casino to keep track of cards played.[57] He was charged under a statute that provided that a person may not use or possess with intent to use, any device to help in (1) projecting the outcome of the game; (2) keeping track of the cards played; (3) analyzing the probability of the occurrence of an event relating to the game; or (4) analyzing betting or playing strategy.[58]

The player argued that the statute was vague on what type of conduct it prohibits. The court restated the standard for evaluating vagueness: whether a person of ordinary intelligence has a reasonable opportunity to know what conduct is prohibited.

The court found the law was not vague as applied to the player because a hidden computer is precisely the type of conduct envisioned by the law. In finding no person of ordinary intelligence could believe otherwise, the court stated that whatever else the term "device"[59] meant, it included computers.[60]

If a jurisdiction prohibits using computers or devices, it may consider exceptions, allowing baccarat and roulette players to make written lists and refer to cards played at baccarat or the numbers chosen at roulette, games for which tracking past outcomes cannot give a player an edge.[61] Using scratch paper and pens to record such events is a traditional method of playing such games and does not affect the outcome as there is no decision-making that will affect the outcome of the event.

Theft from Other Players
Claiming another player's winnings or
taking another player's wager

Observing a craps game is a bewildering experience for the uninitiated. One quickly wonders how it is possible to keep track of the bets. Sometimes even the players forget a bet they have on the table. This allows a cheat to claim the winnings of other players that lose track of their bets.

Claiming another person's winnings is not unique to craps. As discussed earlier, there have been occurrences where persons working in conspiracy with sports book employees have made fraudulent claims on unclaimed winning tickets.

Besides claiming another person's winnings, a thief can steal the other players' wagers or chips. Sometimes, the thief may use a "clip cup" to take the chips. A common ploy is for an "intoxicated" or "interested" bystander

---

[57] *See, e.g.*, NEV. REV. STAT. § 465.075 (2013).
[58] *Id.*
[59] Listed in NEV. REV. STAT. § 465.075 (2013).
[60] Sheriff, Clark Cnty., Nev. v. Anderson, 746 P.2d 643, 644 (Nev. 1987), abrogated by City of Las Vegas v. Eighth Jud. Dist. Ct. ex rel. Cnty. of Clark, 59 P.3d 477, 480 (Nev. 2002).
[61] *See, e.g.*, NEV. GAMING REG. 5.150(1).

to drop a pack of cigarettes over a player's chips. The back of the pack has an adhesive that sticks to a chip. When the player retrieves his cigarettes, he also retrieves the chip.

To assist in enforcement, a specific law can be created to prohibit a person from claiming or collecting, or attempting to claim or collect, money from a game intending to defraud.[62]

ADVANTAGE PLAY

Several reported cases address the legal aspects of advantage play, i.e., when a player through some method of play acquires an advantage over the casino in a gambling contract. These cases, however, have resulted in inconsistent decisions on important controversies such as casinos' rights to exclude advantage players and the legality of advantage play. Court cases have not produced an analytical basis for consideration of advantage play's legal aspects.

The remainder of this chapter will discuss advantage play in light of different legal and ethical considerations. It focuses on the relationships between the government, the advantage player, and the casino in three respects. First, should the advantage player receive any protection from the government to allow him to apply his skills without interference or exclusion by the casinos? Should the advantage player have the right to access the casino, as opposed to the casino's right to exclude the advantage player?

Second, how should contract law be interpreted when dealing with disputes between casinos and players involving advantage play. Here, the primary decision is whether courts will or will not require the casino to pay questionable winnings to an advantage player.

Third, should the government criminalize certain forms of advantage play?

Not all advantage play shares similar elements, but all advantage play can be placed in one of five categories based on the following factors:
- Is the advantage play consistent with the defined rules of the game?
- Does the advantage player attempt to take advantage of known errors by the casino?
- Does the advantage player attempt to acquire and use information not readily available to all players that would provide an advantage in determining or predicting what was intended to be a random event?
- Does the advantage player use information readily available to all players, as opposed to attempting to acquire information not readily available to all players, that would provide an advantage in determining or predicting what was intended to be a random event?
- Does the advantage player attempt to alter the random event that serves as the basis for the game result?

---

[62] *See, e.g.,* Nev. Rev. Stat. § 465.070(3) (2013).

In light of these factors, the first category of advantage play is when the player uses superior skill to analyze game data available to all players, and both the players and casinos contemplate using such data as part of the contractual relationship. This data is typically covered by the basic rules of the game. This type of advantage play applies only to casino games involving some skill. This includes blackjack and video poker.[63]

One court noted this type of advantage play involves a "highly skilled player who analyzes the statistical probabilities associated with [a casino game] and, based on those probabilities, develops playing strategies which may afford him an advantage over the casino."[64] The best and most prevalent example in this category is the card counter in blackjack who has acquired skill in analyzing the cards played and can then determine when he acquires a theoretical advantage over the casino.[65] In blackjack, the basic rules provide that the player shall initially receive two cards and, based on the value of those cards, decide whether to hit, stand or take other actions.[66] Therefore, the game rules anticipate that the player will use the data.

The second category of advantage play is when the player uses superior skill in analyzing the data available to all players, but such data are not part of the basic rules of the game, but can impact outcome. An example of this is shuffle tracking (discussed in more detail later), where the player predicts the order of the cards in the deck based on the location of the cards in the discard rack and how the dealer shuffled the deck. All the factors necessary to conduct shuffle tracking are available to all players, but the shuffle tracker is attempting to defeat the random event that defines the game. The basic contract between the player and the casino contemplates that the shuffle will be random. Therefore, a player who tracks the shuffle is gaining an advantage outside the basic rules of the game.

The third category of advantage play is when the player takes advantage of the casino's mistakes. This could include errors made by the casino in posting its terms and conditions or by taking advantage of malfunctioning gaming devices that either pay too much or too often. An example of this would be a person that trolls the casino floor at a grand opening seeking slot machines that are mislabeled as to the amount of the jackpot where the error favors the player.

The fourth category of advantage play is where the player acquires knowledge, not typically or readily available to other players, that pro-

---

[63] Progressive slot machines are the exception. The play of these machines involves no skill. Because the progressive meter and the potential payout change, however, so does the player expectation. The skill involved in progressive slots is calculating the player expectation and frequency of the payout.

[64] Bartolo v. Boardwalk Regency Hotel Casino, Inc., 449 A. 2d 1339 (1982).

[65] Although the overall house advantage in a typical blackjack game is positive, the advantage shifts back and forth between player and house as cards are removed from play. Simply put, card counting systems identify those hands on which the player has the advantage; in these situations, the card counter then increases the bet size.

[66] Jim Kilby & Jim Fox, Casino Operations Management 139 (1998).

vides an advantage in determining or predicting what was intended to be a random event. An example would be a blackjack player that is able to learn the dealer's hole card before having to decide how to play his hand.[67] This category of advantage play also is outside the defined rules of play.

The fifth category of advantage play is where the player alters the random event to his favor. Some examples are understood as cheating such as using loaded dice or marking cards. An example of a more nuanced situation would be where the player tries to manipulate the throw of the dice at the craps table so they result in a combination that favors the bets placed by the player. Whether this category of advantage play is cheating has been the subject of inconsistent court decisions.[68]

Category One: Using Superior Skill in Analyzing Factors within the Game Rules That Are Available To All Players
Card counting

Advantage play is often associated with card counting in blackjack. A card counter is a person who counts the value of cards played to figure out when the remaining cards in the deck are favorable to the player (such as when it contains more tens and aces than usual), at which point he increases his wager.

Card counters track the value of the cards because as current cards are removed from the deck, the player's chances of winning the remaining hands played from that deck can increase or decrease depending on the cards previously played. This can be measured by adjusting the expectation that the player has of winning future hands. The following table[69] shows the change in a player's expectation from basic strategy by removing one card of each value from a single deck.

Changes in player expectation in the table below reveal that removing low cards from the deck will increase the player's expectation while removing high cards will reduce the player's expectation. When a preponderance of low cards has been played and the remaining deck is rich in high cards, subsequent hands will favor the player. Conversely, if a preponderance of

Figure 14.1

Effects of Removal of Individual Cards (Change in player's expectation)									
2	3	4	5	6	7	8	9	T	A
.38%	.44%	.55%	.69%	.46%	.28%	.00%	−.18%	−.51%	−.61%

high cards has been played, subsequent hands will favor the dealer. These observations establish card counting strategies.[70]

---

[67] MARKS, *supra* note 19, at 113.
[68] See notes 96-101, *infra*, and accompanying text.
[69] HANNUM & CABOT, *supra* note 10.
[70] Dr. Edward Thorp published *Beat the Dealer* in 1962 which explains how blackjack

A player keeping track of the cards played can recognize when the remaining deck is rich in high cards and can then take advantage of the increase in player expectation at these times by increasing the bet size and/or altering playing decisions. When the remaining deck contains proportionally more small cards, the counter will lower his bet. With proper use of such a strategy, a player can achieve a positive overall expectation (i.e., the casino advantage will be negative).

Several reasons exist why a deck rich in high cards favors the player, including the following:

- Naturals (also known as "blackjacks") are more prevalent.[71]

---

could be beaten by the player using a memory-based system. All subsequently devised systems build off this seminar by keeping track of high and low cards to identify favorable and unfavorable situations. The player then adjusts bet size and strategy decisions accordingly. The systems differ in the point values assigned to particular cards, whether a side count is kept for certain cards (Aces, for example), adjustments for number of decks, and associated strategy.

One such system is Harvey Dubner's Hi-Lo (or Plus/Minus) count, first proposed in 1963 and later refined by Julian Braun, who used computers to determine the correct playing and betting strategies for the system This Hi-Lo count system appeared in the second edition of Edward Thorp's *Beat the Dealer* in 1966. In the Hi-Lo count, small cards (Two, Three, Four, Five, and Six) are assigned a value of +1, Tens and Aces are assigned a value of −1, and Sevens, Eights, and Nines are assigned 0. As cards are revealed through play, the player assigns the appropriate value to each and keeps a running total, called the running count, of the values of the exposed cards. The player divides the running count by the number of decks remaining in the shoe to get the true count. This is done by "eyeball" estimating the number of decks remaining, a skill at which proficient card counters are quite good. The player then uses a true count to make decisions about when to deviate from basic strategy, when to raise and lower the bet, and when to take insurance. When the count is high, the remaining deck is rich in high cards—favorable to the player—and the bet is raised. When the count is low, a preponderance of small cards left exists and the player lowers his bet. A card-counter does not need to memorize each specific exposed card—tracking the sum of the values of these cards is all that is needed. A player can accomplish this by pairing high (−1 value) and low (+1 value) cards, which cancel to zero, and then total the excess cards.

The Hi-Lo count is a level-1, balanced, single-parameter system. The level of a system refers to the highest absolute point value assigned to any single card. The system is balanced because the sum of the card values for the entire deck is equal to zero. A multi-parameter system is one in which an additional side count is required, such as for Aces. Since no such separate side count is required in the Hi-Lo count, it is a single-parameter system. Despite its simplicity, the Hi-Lo is an effective system advocated by numerous experts. Stanford Wong espouses the Hi-Lo system in his classic book, *Professional Blackjack*, and Bill Zender recommends the Hi-Lo for multiple deck games in his excellent book, *Card Counting for the Casino Executive*. For single-deck games, Zender suggests the Hi-Opt I, another level-1, balanced system that differs from the Hi-Lo in assigning a point value of zero to Aces and Twos. Hi-Opt I can be attributed to Charles Einstein, who proposed a count system in 1968 that was later refined by Julian Braun, an anonymous Mr. G., Lance Humble, and Carl Cooper. A detailed treatment of the Hi-Opt I can be found in Humble and Cooper's *The World's Greatest Blackjack Book*.

[71] Although both dealer and player will get more naturals when the deck is rich in Tens and Aces, the player is paid a three-to-two, or six-to-five, premium (while the dealer is not). The dealer must hit stiff totals (hard 12–16), and is more likely to bust if there is a

- The dealer is more likely to bust when hitting stiffs.[72]
- Player double downs are more effective.[73]
- Player splits are more effective.
- Insurance can be effective.[74]

The edge gained by a card-counter depends on several factors, including the number of decks in play, the penetration (how far into the pack, or shoe, the cards are dealt before reshuffling), the rules of the game, the bet spread, and the system used. A skilled counter will typically have a 0.5–1.5 percent advantage over the house.[75] More decks and shallow penetration (not dealing far into the pack before reshuffling) decrease the counter's advantage.

Video slot players

Video poker in casinos is a game of mixed skill and chance. In a typical video poker game, the player randomly draws five cards from a deck of 52 cards and has the option of keeping or discarding all of those cards.[76] For each card discarded, the player will randomly draw an additional card from the cards remaining in the original 52-card deck. The combination of cards remaining in the player's hand is compared to a pay chart. If the player has any of the required combinations, he is paid according to the pay chart. The skill element involved in video poker is determining which cards to hold or discard.

Some casinos offer video poker machines that when played at optimum skill pay back more on average than they would collect. The casinos rely on players not playing at optimum skill to insure a profit.[77] Despite this, some players can play at optimum skill and have an advantage albeit slight (about 0.5 percent) over the casino.

---

preponderance of Tens remaining, whereas the player can choose not to hit these stiff hands.

[72] HANNUM & CABOT, *supra* note 10.

[73] Player double downs and splits are more effective since the player is often looking for a high hit card in these situations (and also because in many of these situations the dealer's upcard is weak, leading to more dealer busts).

[74] HANNUM & CABOT, *supra* note 10. More Tens than usual also means that insurance can be a positive expectation wager for the player. Standard expected value calculations show that insurance is advantageous if more than one-third of the remaining cards are Tens. This is because the payoff on the insurance bet is two-to-one. The expected value calculation when exactly one-third of the remaining cards are Tens is $EV = (+2)(1/3) + (-1)(2/3) = 0$.

[75] Martin Millman, in *A Statistical Analysis of Casino Blackjack*, AM. MATHEMATICAL MONTHLY, (1983), estimated that with four decks the counter could gain 1.35 percent and with six decks 0.91 percent.

[76] DWIGHT & LOUISE CREVELT, VIDEO POKER MANIA 25 (1991).

[77] Becky Yerak, *Greektown Bans 30 winners: Skilled Video Poker Players Proved Unprofitable for Casino*, DETROIT NEWS, Nov. 25, 2002, http://www.detnews.com/2002/business/0211/25/a01-19565.htm.

Progressive Slots

Progressive slots are slot machines in which one or more payouts increase by a set amount for each coin or credit played that does not result in the player winning that payout.[78] While slot machines are games of pure chance, on accession a progressive jackpot slot machine may provide the player with a positive expectation or advantage. Knowing when a machine with a progressive jackpot provides a positive expectation involves skill. Suppose a progressive slot machine has a top payout of $100 and five cents of every dollar bet increases the progressive jackpot. If the player plays the machine for one dollar and does not win, the progressive jackpot will increase to $100.05. The progressive jackpot will increase in this way until it is won; it will then be reset to its original starting point. If the progressive jackpot increases to a certain point without being won, then the theoretical payout results in a positive player advantage.

This slight statistical advantage is what attracts the professional slot teams. These are organized and financed teams of professional slot players that attempt to exploit those progressive slots that have a positive player expectation. Only certain progressive slot machines will meet the slot team's criteria. First, the number of slot machines that are linked to the progressive jackpot must be manageable. The team must monopolize all the linked slot machines to avoid the risk that a non-member will win the jackpot. Second, the slot team must know certain fundamental aspects of the machine including its house advantage and frequency of payout for all reel combinations. Third, the statistical frequency of hitting the progressive jackpot must follow the slot team's bankroll. No slot team has an unlimited bankroll. Based on probabilities, the team must have enough cash on hand to play all the linked machines with the progressive jackpot until one team member hits the progressive jackpot. The slot team can use the Poisson probability distribution to determine the probability of hitting the jackpot over the course of a specified number of plays. The Poisson distribution (named after the 19th century French mathematician Simeon Poisson) is commonly used to calculate the probability of rare events. As applied to gaming devices, the probability of X jackpot hits in n plays can be computed using the following formula:

Figure 14.2

$$P(X) = \frac{e^{-\mu}\mu^X}{X!}$$

where μ is the average number of jackpot hits over the course of the n plays (or the number of cycles in the n plays), and e is the mathematical constant approximately equal to 2.71828. The value of μ will depend on the game and the number of plays, and can be computed by dividing the number of plays in question by the number of plays in a cycle. To illustrate, consider a 3-reel, 96-stop-per-reel slot machine with a cycle of 884,736 plays (96 x 96 x 96) and one jackpot combination. This machine will average one jackpot for every 884,736 plays. The probability the jackpot will

---

[78] *See generally* David Sklansky, Getting the Best of It (1997).

not be hit over the course of one cycle ($\mu=1$) is

Figure 14.3

$$P(0) = \frac{e^{-1} \times 1^0}{0!} = 0.3679$$

This implies that 63.21 percent (subtracting $P(0)$ from one) of the time there will be at least one jackpot over the course of a cycle.[79] The probability of no jackpot over the course of any other fixed number of plays can be obtained by replacing the value of μ with the appropriate average as described above.[80] The following table shows the probability of no jackpot being hit on this example machine for a variety of numbers of plays.

The probabilities in the table below refer to the behavior of an individual slot machine for which the probability of hitting the jackpot on a single play is a little better than one in a million ($1/884{,}736 = 0.00000113$). Over the course of one million plays on this machine, the probability of hitting the jackpot is 67.7 percent, with this probability increasing as the number of plays increases. If several machines are considered, the probability that at least one hits the jackpot during the course of a fixed number of plays will be greater than the probability that one specific machine will hit during this same number of plays.[81] For example, the probability that at least one machine in a carousel of ten of these same type will hit the jackpot during one million plays on each is (assuming independence) 0.99998766.[82]

---

[79] This probability of hitting the jackpot at least once (or not at all) over the course of one cycle is the same for any single-jackpot machine.

[80] If reasonable estimates are available for the average number of plays per hour for a given machine, calculating these probabilities over a given time is possible. Suppose, for example, an 884,736-cycle slot machine had not yielded a jackpot in three years. Constant play might produce about 400 decisions per hour, so assuming the machine was played about 50 percent of the time an average of 200 decisions per hour is reasonable. This activity level translates into a little over five million plays for a three-year period. The Poisson formula shows the probability of no jackpot over this many plays to be 0.00263, or about 1 in 380. If the machine was played constantly at 400 plays per hour for three years, there's only a 1 in 145,000 chance of no jackpot during this time. At an average of 100 plays per hour it would be surprising but possible to see no jackpot in three years: the probability is 0.051 (about 1 in 20).

[81] Put another way, for a given device the probability of an extreme outcome, such as no jackpot for a long period of time or several in a short period, is quite small. With many machines on the casino floor, however, there's a good chance that at least one of them will exhibit extreme behavior. To see why, consider the example machine in the table above in which the probability of observing no jackpot over the course of three million plays of this machine is 0.03368. For a collection of 100 of these machines, the probability they all produce at least one jackpot when each is played three million times is $(1-0.03368)100 = 0.0325$, and so the probability at least one of these yields no jackpot over three-million plays is 0.9675, or 96.75 percent. With a collection of 200 such machines, this probability rises to 99.9 percent, and with 300 devices, this probability is 99.997 percent. Even though there is a small probability that an individual device will exhibit a certain extreme behavior, when a large enough collection is considered, there is a good chance this behavior will appear in at least one of the collection.

[82] Assuming independence, one million plays on each of ten machines is equivalent (prob-

Figure 14.4

Probability of No Jackpot: 884,736-play Cycle Slot Machine			
Number of Plays	Avg. Number of Jackpots (μ)	Probability of Hitting Jackpot	Probability of No Jackpot
1 million	1.130	67.7057%	32.2943%
2 million	2.261	89.5708%	10.4292%
3 million	3.391	96.6320%	3.3680%
4 million	4.521	98.9123%	1.0877%
5 million	5.651	99.6487%	0.3513%
6 million	6.782	99.8866%	0.1134%
7 million	7.912	99.9634%	0.0366%
8 million	9.042	99.9882%	0.0118%
9 million	10.173	99.9962%	0.0038%
10 million	11.303	99.9988%	0.0012%

The previous table shows a progressive slot machine that has a cycle of 884,736 and a probability of a little better than one in one million of hitting the progressive jackpot on any play. If the probability of hitting the progressive jackpot is one in ten million (as might be the case on a different machine), the slot team would need an astronomical bankroll to have reasonable assurances it would hit the jackpot before running out of money. Therefore, slot teams avoid the "mega" jackpot progressive that have very infrequent hits or winners. To minimize their potential exposure, they concentrate on progressive carousels that feature lower jackpots with a higher frequency of payouts. The team can calculate its risks by determining the size of its bankroll, on average how many pays that the bankroll will finance given the machine's pay-outs on the various reel combinations and the probability of hitting the progressive within this number of plays.

Category Two: Using Superior Skill in Analyzing Factors outside the Game Rules That Are Available to All Players
Shuffle tracking

Many commercial gambling games rely on proper randomization to ensure fairness and maintain the desired house advantage or players' win/loss rates. Gaming regulators acknowledge the importance of randomization in gaming devices such as video poker, slot machines, and shuffle machines by requiring they meet minimum confidence levels on standard

---

abilistically) to ten million plays on one machine.

statistical tests. A primary regulatory concern is that the device selects the cards or symbols within acceptable levels of randomness.[83]

In card games, the random aspect of the game is the shuffle of the cards by the casino. This is done either by a mechanical shuffler or by hand. Regulatory authorities usually review and approve mechanical shufflers to assure that the outcome of every shuffle will appear random. Non-machine card shuffles are not typically subject to such regulatory scrutiny. A non-random shuffling process may alter the odds of a game, if players can use a predictable pattern inherent in the shuffle process as an advantage play.[84]

Shuffle tracking may allow a player to follow segments of cards through a shuffle to know roughly when these segments will appear during ensuing rounds of play. If such tracking can be employed in a situation when slugs of favorable or unfavorable cards have been identified in the pre-shuffle pack (for example, in blackjack where multi-deck shoe games are common), a player could then utilize knowledge of the slug locations during the play of the next shoe by adjusting strategy and bet sizes accordingly. Such shuffle-tracking techniques are not possible if the shuffle is random.[85]

This "shuffle tracking" method of exploiting non-random shuffles to identify clumps of favorable or unfavorable cards in the post-shuffle deck has been refined to advantage play techniques such as ace prediction, ace tracking, sequence tracking, and key carding.[86]

Category Three: Taking Advantage of the Casino's Mistakes
Mistakes in posting its terms and conditions or
taking advantage of malfunctioning machines

Some advantage players create the advantage by intentionally exploiting mistakes by the casino, its employees, or malfunctioning gaming devices. A good example is the advantage player or team of players that are

---

[83] HANNUM & CABOT, *supra* note 10, at 388.

[84] The theory of card shuffling has been studied by numerous authors using mathematical models. *See e.g.*, David Aldous & Persi Diaconis, *Shuffling Cards and Stopping Times*, 93 AM. MATHEMATICAL MONTHLY (1986) 333–348; Dave Bayer & Persi Diaconis, *Trailing the Dovetail Shuffle to Its Lair*, 2 ANNALS APPLIED PROBABILITY 294–313 (1992); J.R. Donner & V.R.R. Uppulini, *A Markov Chain Structure for Riffle Shuffling*, 18 SIAM J. APPLIED MATHEMATICS 191–209 (1970); PETER A. GRIFFIN, THE THEORY OF BLACKJACK (1996).

[85] Evidence of non-random shuffling as it relates to gambling games can be found in Edward Thorp, *Nonrandom Shuffling with Applications to the Game of Faro*, 68 J. AM. STAT. ASS'N 844 (1973); David Emanuel & Kenneth Sutrick, *Nonrandom Shuffling Strategies in Blackjack*, 17 COMM. IN STAT. 2954 (1988); John M. Gwynn & Arnold Snyder, *Man vs. Computer: Does Casino Blackjack Differ from Computer-Simulated Blackjack?* 8 BLACKJACK F. 6 (1988); STANFORD WONG, PROFESSIONAL BLACKJACK (1994).

[86] For an excellent discussion of shuffle-tracking techniques, particularly ace tracking, and the effects of non-random shuffling on the game of blackjack, *see e.g.*, DAVID McDOW-ELL, BLACKJACK ACE PREDICTION: THE ART OF ADVANCED LOCATION STRATEGIES FOR THE CASINO GAME OF TWENTY-ONE (2004); Arnold SNYDER, THE BLACKJACK SHUFFLE TRACKER'S COOKBOOK (2003).

present on opening nights of any new casino. They understand errors are most likely to occur when a casino is in the midst of training employees and deploying several hundred or thousand new gaming devices. In an unreported case, a newspaper described the exploits of one such player that began on the opening night of a casino:

> He noticed a bank of slot machines where the payouts for the $100 machines and the $1 machines had been mistakenly reversed. Over the course of several hours, he won $27,000 in cash and comps by collecting $100 machine payouts from $1 machines.[87]

Other advantage players attempt to find slot machines that are overpaying, or in other words, have defective software or hardware that results in their receiving greater than the number of coins to which they would otherwise be entitled.[88]

Category Four: Acquiring Knowledge Not Available to Other Players that Provides an Advantage in Determining or Predicting what was Intended to Be a Random Event
Hole-carding

Hole-carding is a technique used primarily in blackjack to learn the value of the dealer's hole card before the player must decide how to play his or her hand.[89] The theoretical advantage derived from hole-carding is far more substantial than that of card counting.[90]

Most hole-carding is done intentionally. One surveillance expert described a typical team that took advantage of a weak dealer.[91] In that case, the team comprised two people. One person was in the "third base side," meaning the seat nearest to the dealer's right hand, and the other was in the first spot, nearest the dealer's left hand. The expert noted:

> Not only was the third base player slouching in his seat, his signals to the other player were simple. The hole-carder on the third-base side of the game had a stock of green ($25 chips) and red ($5 chips). To signal stand, he touched the red (stand/stop), to signal hit, he touched the green (hit/go) and for insurance he tapped the green stack with a chip pinched between his fingers to represent an 'I' (insurance). The dealer later was proven to be a weak dealer and not in the group. . . [92]

With the player sitting on the third base side, slouching, he was right

---

[87] Rod Smith, *Civil Liberties: Disadvantaged: Casinos, Police Officials Often Intimidate Legal Gamblers, Lawyers Say*, Las Vegas Rev. J., July 6, 2003.

[88] *See* William Petroski, *Gamblers Suspected of Cheating Iowa Slots*, Des Moines Register, June 15, 2004, http://desmoinesregister.com/apps/pbcs.dll/article?AID=/20040615/NEWS01/406150340/1001/NEWS&lead=1.

[89] Marks, *supra* note 19 at 113.

[90] *Id.*

[91] Douglas Florence, *Advantage Play: Blackjack*, Global Gaming Bus., July 2004, at 18.

[92] *Id.*

"74 percent of the time at reading the hole card."[93] If a person knows the dealer's hole card, the player has an advantage over the casino through having additional information to figure out whether to double his bet, surrender a hand (thus, only losing half a bet), or hit or stand.[94] The impact that hole-carding has on the house advantage will vary depending on the advantage player's propensity to correctly identify the hole card and to what advantage he uses the information. If the player knows the dealer's hole card every time and played every hand to maximum advantage, it would result in a 10 percent advantage over the house.[95] The typical advantage player, however, would not play to maximum advantage because, for example, hitting a 19 against the dealer's 20 would be too suspicious and draw inquiry.

"Shining" is hole-carding where the player learns the dealer's hole card by using any reflective device. This could include a metallic cigarette lighter, a facet on a ring, a polished fingernail, or a small mirror.

Category Five: Altering the Random Event to the Player's Favor

While the differences between cheating and permitted play may appear simple, various courts have struggled with the distinction particularly when dealing with certain forms of categories two, three, four, and five advantage play. In each case, the ultimate question becomes how far a player can exploit a casino's errors, omissions, or other vulnerabilities before such activity should be a crime. Category five advantage play appears to meet all the elements of casino cheating; however it has still created conflicting court decisions.

Dice sliding

In craps, players are given the opportunity to "toss" two dice that will result in totals from two to 12, although these numbers come up with different frequencies.[96] This "toss" is the random event upon which the gaming contracts between the casino and the players at that table will be decided. In dice sliding, the skilled player slides one or both dice across the table rather than tossing them and allowing them to roll.[97] Thus, a predetermined "roll" may be chosen and the outcome of the game manipulated by the slider.

---

[93] *Id.*

[94] To cover these possibilities, statutes often state that a person may not place, increase, or decrease a bet or decide course of play after acquiring knowledge, not available to all players, of the outcome of the game or any event that affects the outcome of the game. *See* Nev. Rev. Stat. § 465.070(2) (2013).

[95] Stanford Wong, Basic Blackjack (1992).

[96] Andrew Brisman, American Mensa Guide to Casino Gambling 124 (1999).

[97] Marks, *supra* note 19, at 198.

In *Skipper v. State*,[98] a dice slider challenged his cheating conviction on the same ground as that raised by the handle popping slot players in earlier cases. Claiming the criminal statutes[99] were unconstitutionally vague,[100] Skipper argued that the statutes failed to alert the average dice player that dice sliding constituted criminal conduct.

The Nevada Supreme Court rejected the argument finding that the rules of craps require a roll of the dice (the random event that is the basis of the contract). As the dice do not roll when they are slid, dice sliding violated the rules of the game and, as such, the statute provided adequate notice to the average player that sliding violates the anti-cheating statutes.

Again, the basis of the crime of dice sliding is that the person *intentionally* slides the dice to impact the random element of the game. If a player improperly throws the dice so they slide instead of being rolled, the condition of a random event would not be met and the dice would be thrown again. The thrower, however, has committed no crime.

Dice sliding should be contrasted with dice setting. The latter is a process by which the shooter or thrower in a dice game exerts some control over the numbers the dice show after they have been tossed.[101] The concept is that the casino issues rules allowing the throwers to arrange the dice in their hands before throwing them. By controlling (and standardizing) the motion of the throw, dice setters claim to be able alter the random selection of results to favor certain dice combinations that will give them an advantage over the casino.

Both dice setting and dice sliding players are, if they are effective, intentionally altering the random element (odds) of the game. Dice setting differs from dice sliding because the dice setter is working within the prescribed rules of play to influence the roll. The casino prescribed the rule with the belief that regardless of the method the advantage player employs, it will not impact the random-aspect of the throw. In other words, the casino considers dice setting to be more based on superstition than science.

Current Casino Responses to Advantage Play

Because casinos are commercial enterprises, effective advantage players negatively impact net revenues. Some casinos take no measures to deal with most advantage players, such as card counters, reasoning the harm caused does not justify the cost or consequences of taking affirmative action against the advantage players. Other casinos, however, undertake affirmative steps against advantage players where legally available, including criminal arrest, civil exclusion, or changing the rules of play. Criminal

---

[98] Skipper v. State, 879 P.2d 732, 734 (Nev. 1994).

[99] Nev. Rev. Stat. § 465.070(7), 465.083.

[100] In *Lyons v. State*, 775 P.2d 219 (1989), the defendant challenged a Nevada statute that defined cheating to include "alter[ing] the selection of criteria which determine: (a) The result of a game; or (b) The amount or frequency of payment in a game. . . ."

[101] For craps and dice setting information, see http://www.dicesetter.com.

arrest both removes the advantage player from the casino and serves as a deterrent to other advantage players. As discussed later, this is a limited option that is available only where the type of advantage play employed is illegal.

While some forms of advantage play such as card counting are "not considered cheating, nor is it illegal,"[102] some casinos routinely exclude suspected advantage players from gaming. These casinos may exclude advantage players at their discretion.[103] For example, no Nevada statute requires casinos to admit suspected card counters.[104]

Allowing a casino to bar advantage players and others has a common law origin. "At common law, proprietors of privately-owned places of entertainment and amusement were not obligated to serve the general public."[105]

In many states, the major gambling establishments were racetracks. Cases involving exclusion of players from racetracks have provided substantial support for this common law principle.[106]

Casinos also may counter some forms of advantage play by changing the rules of the play of the game. These countermeasures are often statistically designed to reduce or eliminate the player advantage.

For example, any advantage created through card counting is negated when the deck is shuffled. Possible casino countermeasures against card counting include (1) preferential or at-will shuffling,[107] (2) using multiple decks,[108] (3) changing maximum bet size or restricting the bet size to the table minimum for new players to the game,[109] (4) having shills occupy all other seats at table, (5) limiting players to a single wager,[110] (6) prohibiting players from joining game in midshoe,[111] (7) short cut (placing cut card

---

[102] Uston v. Hilton Hotels Corp., 448 F. Supp. 116, 118 (1978).

[103] *Id.* at 119 (holding exclusion did not violate federal civil rights laws).

[104] *Id.*

[105] Perry Z. Binder, Note, *Arbitrary Exclusions of "Undesirable" Racetrack and Casino Patrons: The Courts Illusory Perception of Common Law Public/Private Distinctions*, 32 BUFF. L. REV. 699 (1982).

[106] *See, e.g.*, Phillips v. Graham, 427 N.E.2d 550 (Ill. 1981); James v. Churchill Downs, Inc., 620 S.W.2d 323 (Ky. Ct. App. 1981); Tropical Park, Inc. v. Jock, 374 So.2d 639 (Fla. Dist. Ct. App. 1979); Nation v. Apache Greyhound Park, Inc., 579 P.2d 580 (Az. Ct. App. 1978); Presti v. N.Y. Racing Assn, Inc., 363 N.Y.S.2d 24 (1975); Watkins v. Oaklawn Jockey Club, 86 F. Supp 1006 (W.D. Ark. 1949), aff'd, 183 F. 2d 440 (8th N.Y. App. Div. Cir. 1950).

[107] *See* BILL ZENDER, *CARD COUNTING FOR THE CASINO* EXECUTIVE (1990) (providing further details on casino countermeasures).

[108] Urbino is a website hosted by longtime casino executive Andrew MacDonald. URBINO www.urbino.net/v1/pages/ar3_4.htm.

[109] *Id.*

[110] New Jersey Casino Commission Regulation 19:47-2.14 specifically authorizes this countermeasure. It provides

"A player may only wager on one box at a Blackjack table unless the casino licensee, in its discretion, permits the player to wager on additional boxes."

[111] New Jersey Casino Commission Regulation 19:47 2.5(a) provides

Immediately prior to commencement of play, after any round of

further from back),[112] and (8) using an automatic shuffler or a continuous shuffling shoe.[113] "The shuffle-at-will occurs when the dealer is instructed to reshuffle prior to the cut-card manner because the casino card counting team has determined that the shoe is player-favorable and card-counters are suspected to be playing at a given table."[114]

Technology also has evolved that could allow casinos to achieve advantages over the advantage player. One example is using "smart" gaming tables. These tables can use a variety of technologies to track wagers made, cards dealt, and payouts. A smart table (or shoe) can track every card dealt out of a shoe in blackjack. This table potentially could be used by a casino to call for a reshuffle anytime the deck favors the advantage player.

Likewise, strategies are available for slot teams that play progressive slot machines with a positive player expectation. One strategy is for the casino to retain the discretion to limit players to playing only one machine at a time. Thus, when a slot team tries to monopolize a carousel, they will need more team members and incur greater expense in doing so.

Another strategy is to reduce the increment with which each play of the slot machine will increase the progressive jackpot. If five cents of every dollar normally funds the progressive, this can be reduced to one cent.[115] This substantially increases the risk to the slot team organizer because he will not receive as much of his money back by hitting the jackpot. Therefore, the jackpot at the point the slot team becomes involved must be higher before positive player expectation justifies risking the team bankroll.

How Law and Regulation Should Address Advantage Play

In dealing with advantage players, the government should consider all policy options in establishing the legal relationships between the casino, the

---

> play as may be determined by the casino licensee and after each
> shoe of cards is dealt, the dealer shall shuffle the cards so that
> they are randomly intermixed.

[112] Some casinos may use two cut cards: the first at about 50 percent penetration and the second at about 85 percent. If the casino suspects that a card counter is playing, it will initiate the shuffle at the first cut card. URBINO, Counter Measures, www.urbino.net/v1/pages/ar3_4.htm.

[113] Florence, *supra* note 91, at 18.

[114] Doug Grant, Inc. v. Greate Bay Casino Corp., 3 F. Supp. 2d 518, 525 (D. N.J. 1998). New Jersey Casino Commission Regulations specifically permit shuffling at will. New Jersey Casino Commission Regulation 19:47 2.3 provides

> After the cards have been shuffled . . . , a casino licensee may, in
> its discretion, prohibit any person, whether seated at the gam-
> ing table or not, who does not make a wager on a given round
> of play from placing a wager on the next round of play and any
> subsequent round of play at that gaming table unless the casino
> licensee chooses to permit the player to begin wagering or until a
> reshuffle of the cards has occurred.

[115] Of course, the casino cannot misrepresent what portion of each pull goes toward the progressive jackpot.

advantage player, and the state. The major issue is whether the casino should be able to bar an advantage player from either being in the casino establishment or from playing a game. The highest protection that the government could confer on the advantage player is to acknowledge the player's right to engage in the particular form of advantage play and prohibit the casino from interfering with such rights. This would place the advantage player in the same position as other protected classes (e.g., race, creed) or would establish advantage play in the same category as other protected activities (freedom of speech or assembly) for which the state has established either constitutional or statutory rights. We will refer to these as "protected rights."

Besides protected rights, the government must define the contractual rights between the advantage player and the state. In other words, should the casino and the advantage player have a dispute over a gaming contract, principally whether the casino can be required to pay alleged winnings to the advantage player, the law must define the contractual rights between the advantage player and the casino. We will refer to these as "contractual rights."

Category one: using superior skill in analyzing factors within the game rules that are available to all players

Category one advantage players are the most deserving of legal protection of any advantage players. After all, they are using their skills to play a game offered by a casino consistent with the accepted rules and with no attempt to alter the random events that define the contest. Players in this category are not attempting to alter the random event that defines the game result nor are they attempting to exploit known mistakes by the casino.

With that being conceded, if a category one advantage player is not entitled to a right to play the casino game of his or her choice, then no other advantage player should have the same right. For several reasons, advantage players, like any other players, should have no legal rights to play the game of their choosing under constitutional, contractual, or public policy considerations.

Contracts between advantage players that use superior skills and casinos should be enforced provided that the contract was not fraudulently induced

Within the confines of a gaming contract, the casino promises to pay the player if certain terms and conditions of the contract are met. Any player that meets such terms and conditions, absent special recognized circumstances, should be entitled to the benefits of the bargain. In the case of a gaming contract, the player should be paid. A relevant exception to this rule is contracts that are fraudulently induced. The elements of fraudulent inducement are (1) material misrepresentation made by a party and known to be false; (2) intending to cause inducement/reliance; (3) actual inducement causing another party to enter an agreement; (4) justifiable reliance on the misrepresentation; and (5) resulting damages proximately caused by the reliance.[116]

In advantage play, fraudulent inducement occurs when the player intentionally misrepresents his identity to hide his skill level and, therefore, induces the casino to enter into a gaming contract. For a casino to avoid a contract based on fraudulent inducement, it must meet and prove all the elements of the fraudulent inducement by clear and convincing evidence. Practical obstacles facing the casino are that the person made a material misrepresentation and that the casino relied on it in allowing the person to play.

Rarely do casinos require that a person provide positive identification before allowing them to play in a casino. Where a casino requires identification, it is most likely required for a reason unrelated to ascertaining whether the person is an advantage player. For example, the casino may need to ascertain the person's age because minors are prohibited from gambling or to file cash transaction reports mandated by anti-money laundering laws.[117] Where the casino requests identification from the player for some reason other than assessing whether he or she is an advantage player, false identification by the player would not be detrimentally relied on to allow the player to play any game.

For example, in *Chen v. Nevada State Gaming Control Board*,[118] a card counter entered a Nevada casino and exchanged about $30,000 in cash for casino chips. The casino requested identification and the player produced a fictitious passport. The player won about $85,000 and attempted to cash the chips. The casino refused after again requesting identification and then realizing it was false. The Nevada Supreme Court reviewed this as a fraudulent misrepresentation claim. Although not stated, the case was a fraud in the inducement of a contractual relationship. The court held in favor of the player because there was no evidence that the casino "detrimentally relied on [the player's] false passport when it allowed him to play blackjack."[119] This was a supportable proposition as federal and state law requires the casino to obtain identification when accepting more than $10,000 in cash for playing chips. The second basis for ruling for the player, however, is debatable. The court held that the player's "skill in playing blackjack, rather than his misrepresentations of identity, was the proximate cause of his winnings."[120]

---

[116] *See, e.g.*, Bortz v. Noon, 729 A. 2d 555, 560 (Pa. 1999); *see also* Blumenstock v. Gibson, 811 A.2d 1029, 1034 (Pa. Super. Ct. 2002); Sumitomo Bank of California v. Taurus Developers, Inc., 185 Cal. App. 3d 211, 222 (Cal. Dist. App. 1986); Suffield Dev. Assocs. Ltd. P'ship v. Nat'l Loan Investors, L.P., 802 A.2d 44, 51 (Conn. 2002).

[117] Andrew N.S. Glazer, *Technology thwarts sneaky gamblers*, Detroit Free Press, Nov. 3, 2000, http://www.freep.com/news/casinos/game3_20001103.htm.

[118] Chen v. Nev. State Gaming Control Bd., 994 P.2d. 1151 (Nev. 2000).

[119] *Id.* at 1152.

[120] *Id.*

Countermeasures can be made part of the explicit terms of the gaming contract

Casinos may have the right to incorporate countermeasures to advantage play provided the countermeasures are made part of the express terms of the contract with the player. Any person to a contract has the ability to define those terms under which he or she is willing to enter a contract. Except for some limited overriding policy concerns unique to gambling contracts, the casino should be able to set the terms on which it is willing to accept a wager. Inherent in those terms is the ability to incorporate countermeasures that reduce or eliminate the advantage sought by advantage players. These countermeasures, however, should be express terms, particularly where the countermeasures are contrary to the traditional methods of playing the games.

Casinos, however, may be prohibited from using countermeasures such as preferential shuffling based on using superior skill in analyzing the game factors that are not available to players. Under contract law, this would be permitted provided that the right of the casino to use preferential shuffling was made a part of the contract between the player and the casino. While casinos should generally be permitted to set the terms and conditions of the gaming contracts they are willing to accept, the overriding principle of gaming regulation is whether the games offered are fair and honest. Based on established rules of table game play, players have all the information available to them to determine the house advantage in a game. To allow the casino to use superior technology or skill to determine when to implement countermeasures may, in some circumstances, be a rare exception where public policy through implementing gaming regulations should override contract law. One such circumstance is where a casino may implement smart tables that could track by computer the cards played in blackjack and calculate when the deck favors the player. Based on this information, the casino could then initiate a preferential shuffle.

Allowing a casino to use superior technology, particularly where the player is prohibited from using a computer to assist in his play can raise fundamental issues regarding the honesty and fairness of the games themselves sufficient to justify regulatory intervention. The games offered in casinos do not necessarily have static odds. For example, in blackjack, the player's expectation of winning will change as certain cards are played in the shoe. But, a casino using computers to track the odds and initiate a shuffle can control the odds. This would apply equally where the casino trains dealers to card count and instructs the dealers to initiate the shuffle when the deck favors the player.

Using such technology to identify advantage players alone may fall outside such regulatory concerns. For example, if the casino uses a fixed cut card and authorizes preferential shuffling, using such technologies to thwart the efforts of a card counter does not impact the fundamental odds of the game itself.

Advantage play that involves using superior skill should not be illegal

Advantage play that involves using superior skill to analyze the game factors that are available to all players should never be illegal. Where gambling involves some skill, such as the games of poker and blackjack, exercising that skill is part of the parties' basic contractual understanding. If one party believes that the other has too significant an advantage based on skill or the basic house advantage, that person has the option not to enter the contract with the other party. Once the parties enter a contract, however, the participants' exercise of skill consistent with the rules of the game is expected and proper and should never be unethical or unlawful.

Category two: using superior skill in analyzing factors outside the game rules that are available to all players
Contractual enforcement

The covenant of good faith and fair dealing implied in all contracts requires that neither party to a contract do anything that will injure the right of the other party to receive the benefits of their agreement. Category two advantage play tests the extent to which this covenant applies to a gaming transaction because it involves information intentionally exposed and available to all players. When a player using this information attempts to predict the result of what otherwise should be a random event that determines the outcome of the contract, can it be a violation to use one's cognitive ability to process information that (1) the casino intentionally provides, (2) can be used relevant to randomizing procedures that the casino intentionally employs, and (3) does not involve taking advantage of any mistakes by the dealers of the game? While an argument can be made that using this information would defeat the right of the casino to receive the benefit of their bargain, the casino impacts such rights by choosing the procedural methods of play.

For card games, however, using computers to process the data from the discards and the shuffling procedures presents a much different case. Casinos should not be expected to assume that shuffling procedures that cannot be simple cognitive abilities must be protected from the manipulation of sophisticated computer technologies. Here, the covenant should apply. This situation provides support for the general prohibition against the use on the casino floor of computers to analyze data to predict probabilities.

Computers can provide a player with a tool that often exceed that player's own cognitive ability to analyze probabilities in a game. As a result, some states, like Nevada, have criminalized computers in the casino. The Nevada statute provides that, except as permitted by the Nevada Gaming Commission, a person may not use, or possess with intent to use, any device to help in

- projecting the outcome of the game;
- keeping track of the cards played;
- analyzing the probability of the occurrence of an event relating to the game; or
- analyzing betting or playing strategy.[121]

Legality

While shuffle tracking without the aid of a computer may involve the intent to defeat the random event that determines in part the outcome of the event, how do you define a crime with specificity based on the ability of one's mind to process readily-available information? Can it be illegal to use your mind to process readily-available information?

Moreover, what is the actus reus that establishes the offense? Unlike typical forms of casino cheating, no overt act separates legal from illegal acts. No overt manipulation of the gaming apparatus occurs, whether it be the marking of cards or the sliding of dice. Moreover, the player does not use devices or physical positioning to learn information, such as the dealer's hole card, that is not otherwise available to all players.

Category three: taking advantage of the casino's mistakes
Contractual enforcement

Some advantage players go to casinos looking for errors and then obtain jackpots or awards based on these mistakes. Little difference exists between these advantage players and persons who go to the grocery store and purchase a gallon of milk knowing that the store accidentally mislabeled it for a fraction of its actual cost. If discovered, the person buying the milk could not take advantage of the grocery store's mistake; the customer would have to pay the full price. Just as a grocery store could defend upon a unilateral mistake, the defense would similarly apply to a casino hit by the advantage player.

---

[121] Nev. Rev. Stat. § 465.075 (2013). A player argued that the statute was vague on what type of conduct it prohibits. Childs v. Nevada, 864 P.2d 277, 278 (Nev. 1993). The Nevada Supreme Court restated the standard for evaluating vagueness. The test is whether a person of ordinary intelligence has a reasonable opportunity to know what conduct is prohibited. The court found that the statute was not vague as applied to the player because the use of a hidden computer is precisely the type of conduct envisioned by the statute. In finding that no person of ordinary intelligence could believe otherwise, the court stated that whatever else the term "device" (listed in Nev. Rev. Stat. § 465.075 (2013)) meant, it included computers. The statute allows the Nevada Gaming Commission to permit the use of certain devices. The Commission passed a regulation allowing baccarat and roulette players to make and refer to cards played at baccarat, or the numbers chosen at roulette. Nev. Gaming Reg. 5.150(1). Additionally, the Board Chairman may approve the use of other devices upon written request of a casino. Id. at 5150(2).

Simple ethical considerations, however, that would apply in everyday life seem to take on a different life in the casino environment. Can one seriously argue it is ethically acceptable to take advantage of a patently mispriced product at a grocery store?[122] How about keeping an overpayment on an insurance claim or an ATM withdrawal?[123]

Yet, even courts seem to have difficulty finding unethical simple unethical behavior when practiced against a casino. The distinction, however, is probably based more on the perceived notion of the casino as the exploiter.[124] Therefore, taking advantage of the exploiter is not socially reprehensible.

This notion is misplaced. The house advantage maintained by the casino is necessary to assure the economic viability of the casino, but it is regulated by the government to assure it is fair to the player.[125] This does not differ from the mark-up that a grocer may charge on a gallon of milk. The house advantage reflects the price that a player pays for the opportunity to play the game.[126] If the player believes the casino is being unfair and charging too much, the player is no more compelled to play at the casino than he is to buy a gallon of milk he believes is overpriced.

In the gaming context, cases involving an advantage player who knowingly or intentionally takes advantage of a casino's error should trigger the unilateral mistake defense. A casino offers games to its players, and the games are regulated to be conducted fairly and honestly under certain rules and regulations, odds, and payout guidelines.[127] When the casino player places a wager on a game or puts money into a gaming device, both the player and the casino enter into a contract on the basic assumption that the player will be rewarded if a winning result from the game or machine operated accordingly is achieved.[128]

Advantage play in which the player takes advantage of the casino's mistakes in posting the term of the amount of the jackpot payout should not be enforced if the casino can prove that the player knew of the mistake, and the difference between the posted payout and the intended payout would

---

[122] RANDY COHEN, THE GOOD, THE BAD AND THE DIFFERENCE: HOW TO TELL RIGHT FROM WRONG IN EVERYDAY SITUATIONS (2002).

[123] *See, e.g.,* http://www.ethicschat.com/cgi-bin/Read_Answer.pl?133|30.

[124] *See, e.g.,* James C. Dobson, PhD., *Gambling Has Permeated Every Corner of Society and is Inflicting Great Harm on Families, Individuals and, Especially, on Children,* HOTEL ONLINE SPECIAL REPORT, at http://www.hotel-online.com/Neo/News/PressReleases1999_1st/Mar99_GamblingDobbs.html.

[125] Doug Grant, Inc., 3 F. Supp.2d at 527.

[126] CABOT, *supra* note 7, at 419–424.

[127] HANNUM & CABOT, *supra* note 10, at 207–216.

[128] For example, if a customer puts a quarter in a slot machine that lists three 7s on the payline as a winning combination, once the quarter is inserted into the machine, both the casino and the player agree that the player will be paid if the machine hits three 7s. However, if the three 7s appear below the payline, the casino player could not claim a jackpot because the displayed casino rules require the three 7s to be on the payline and the customer had accepted those terms when he or she put the quarter into the slot machine.

be unconscionable. This would not differ from allowing one person to knowingly take advantage of the other person's mistake in any other contractual context. If the other party knows of or should have known of the mistake, the contract may not be enforceable, even if the enlightened party, in this case the advantage player, did not cause the mistake.

As demonstrated, a casino should be able to assert the defense of unilateral mistake in cases of advantage play. "A unilateral mistake occurs when one party recognizes the true effect of an agreement while the other party does not."[129] The Restatement (Second) of Contracts sets out the basic rules for when a unilateral mistake by one party makes a contract voidable.[130] It provides

> Where a mistake of one party at the time a contract was made as to a basic assumption on which he made the contract has a material effect on the agreed exchange of performances that is adverse to him, the contract is voidable by him if he does not bear the risk of the mistake under the rule stated in 154, and
> a) the effect of the mistake is such that enforcement of the contract would be unconscionable, or
> b) the other party had reason to know of the mistake or his fault caused the mistake.[131]

Therefore the casino must satisfy four requirements before it could avoid the contract based on a unilateral mistake.

Payouts are a basic assumption of the contract

A casino's mistake with a game or gaming device is premised on a basic assumption on which the casino made the contract. The purpose of a gaming contract is for one party to win a defined amount of money and the other party to lose a defined amount of money with the stakes and payouts being defined by the agreed terms of the contract and the result being determined in whole or part by a random event.

Mistaken payouts that result in a player's advantage are material

The types of mistakes typically sought by the advantage player are materially adverse to the casino's performance on the agreed exchange of money with an advantage player that is determined in whole or part by a random event. As one court noted "[a] significant error in the price term of a contract constitutes a mistake regarding a basic assumption upon which the contract is made, and such a mistake ordinarily has a material effect adverse to the mistaken party."[132] In the casino environment, the price term

---

[129] General Tire, Inc. v. Mehlfeldt, 691 N.E.2d 1132, 1136 (Ohio Ct. App. 1997).

[130] *See* Aviation Sales, Inc., v. Select Mobile Homes, 548 N.E.2d 307, 310–311 (Ohio Ct. App. 1988); Nematollahi v. United States, 38 Fed. Cl. 224, 234 (1997).

[131] RESTATEMENT (SECOND) OF CONTRACTS.

[132] Donovan v. RRL Corp., 27 P.3d 702, 716–717 (Cal. 2001) (stating that an error amounting to 32 percent in sales price of an automobile is material).

is determined in part on the amount of the payout.[133] Courts frequently define a material mistake as one which results in an unconscionable contract, or one in "which no man in his senses, not under delusion, would make . . . and which no fair and honest man would accept."[134] This may be restated in economic terms. If the party making the mistake is in the business of making a profit, an unconscionable mistake would be one that results in a loss as opposed to a diminished profit.[135] This goes to the heart of what the advantage player is attempting to accomplish by taking advantage of the casino's mistake, i.e., to find those situations where the casino will sustain a loss to the advantage of the advantage player.

A casino rarely would bear the risk of mistake for advantage play

The Second Restatement addresses this issue of who "bears the risk," in section 154, which provides that a party bears the risk of mistake when
   a)   the risk is allocated to him by agreement of the parties, or
   b)   he is aware, at the time the contract is made, that he has only limited knowledge with respect to the facts to which the mistake relates but treats his limited knowledge as sufficient, or
   c)   the risk is allocated to him by the court on the ground that it is reasonable in the circumstances to do so.[136]

In advantage play, the parties' agreement does not allocate the risk. No agreement term, implied or express, provides that the casino bears the burden of mistakes in posting jackpots. Likewise, mistakes where the casino acts with limited knowledge as to the facts would be rare, but it could occur. These would, however, be predicated on the casino being made aware of the agreement terms including the amount of the payout but assuming the contract obligations without adequate investigation of the consequences. For example, if a player proposed to the casino that he would play 100 hands of baccarat at the casino for $10,000 per hand if the casino agreed to waive the commission on banker bets, the modification of this term alone would change the odds of the game from a slight house advantage to a slight player advantage if the player only bet the banker hand.[137] If the casino accepted the condition without investigating the math associated with accepting the challenge, then the potential exists that a court may conclude that the casino treated its limited knowledge as sufficient to enter the contract. This situation is inapposite to the typical advantage play situation where jackpot amounts are mistakenly posted based

---

[133] Other factors in the pricing of the casino wager include the amount of the wager, the odds of obtaining a winning payout, and the skill level of the player in those games where skill plays a factor.

[134] *See, e.g.,* Alaska Int'l Constr., Inc. v. Earth Movers of Fairbanks, Inc., 697 P.2d 626, 629–31 (Alaska 1985).

[135] Smith v. Mitsubishi Metro Credit of America, Inc., 721 A.2d 1187, (Conn. 1998) (quotations omitted).

[136] RESTATEMENT (SECOND) OF CONTRACTS.

[137] Brisman, *supra* note 96, at 146.

on the equivalent of clerical errors in placing the wrong signs on a gaming device.

The final situation where the casino may bear the risk of mistake is where risk is allocated to the casino because it is reasonable under the circumstances to do so. A casino is typically the unsympathetic party to the contract. For example, in another context, the Nevada Supreme Court reasoned that "card players may exploit a dealer's unintended revelation of his cards" (hole carding) because they are doing nothing more than taking advantage of what the casino gives them.[138] The risk of mistakes should fall on the casino.

While some courts have refused to rescind contracts when the mistake resulted from the affected party's negligence or lack of due care,[139] the prevailing standard is that risk should be allocated to the casino only if the mistake resulted from negligence of a legal duty, not from ordinary negligence.[140] The Restatement imposes liability on the party making the mistake if it fails "to act in good faith and in accordance with reasonable standards of fair dealing."[141]

By seeking out casino mistakes, advantage players have reason to know of the mistake

The advantage player operates by seeking and discovering the mistakes of casinos and obtaining greater winnings. Accordingly, the advantage player has "reason to know of the [casino's] mistake" and exploits it to his or her benefit.

The Restatement uses the language "reason to know" to communicate that the actor "has a duty to another" and "he would not be acting adequately in the protection of his own interests were he not acting with reference to the facts which he has reason to know."[142]

Both activities involve actions that relieve the casino from having to pay the wager. In many situations it may be difficult, however, for the casino to prove that the advantage player knew or had reason to know of the mistake because the burden of proving a unilateral mistake is on the casino seeking rescission and must be proven by clear and convincing evidence.[143] Therefore, the casino must prove, typically by circumstantial evidence, the player entered the casino intending to find a game or device containing a mistake in posting a payout. Where the advantage players work in teams and the

---

[138] Lyons, 775 P.2d at 222.

[139] *See* Fleming Companies, Inc. v. Thriftway Medford Lakes, Inc., 913 F. Supp. 837, 843–844 (D. N.J. 1995). Even in this context, however, the mistake must be more than simply clerical. To be excusable, the mistake must result from clerical, mechanical, or technical errors. *See* Nationwide Mut. Ins. Co. v. Voland, 653 A.2d 484, 489 n.9 (Md. Ct. Spec. App. 1995).

[140] Donovan, 27 P.3d at 717.

[141] RESTATEMENT (SECOND) OF CONTRACTS 157.

[142] RESTATEMENT (SECOND) OF CONTRACTS § 153 cmt.e (1979); *see* Ostman v. St. John's Episcopal Hosp., 918 F. Supp. 635, 646 (E.D. N.Y. 1996).

[143] Jensen v. Miller, 280 Or. 225, 228–229, 570 P2d 375 (1977).

team involves persons with no prior advantage play history, meeting this burden of proof may be difficult.

<u>Legality</u>

Taking advantage of a casino's mistakes in posting payouts could constitute the criminal offense of larceny.

It has long been recognized, however, that when the transferor acts under a unilateral mistake of fact, his delivery of a chattel may be ineffective to transfer title or his right of possession. If the transferee, knowing of the transferor's mistake, receives the goods intending to appropriate them, his receipt and removal of them is a trespass and his offense is larceny."[144]

Larceny requires intent to steal casino property. This stealing deprives the owner of the permanent possession of his property.[145]

Larceny by mistake more typically occurs through clerical mistakes in payment amounts on checks,[146] but it has also been found in other contexts where the party took economic advantage of mistakes. In one case, a bank mistakenly gave unlimited overdraft protection to the defendant who in turn issued 213 checks for almost $850,000. This resulted in a conviction for theft, although one dissenting Justice noted that the bank's "negligence, and not defendant's criminality, was culpable."[147]

The notion that the advantage player may take advantage of whatever the casino gives him is, likewise, devoid of support in the criminal context. As one court noted:

---

[144] United States v. Rogers, 289 F.2d 433, 438 (4th Cir. 1961) ("[It] appears to have become settled in England that . . . if the recipient knows at the time he is receiving more than his due and intends to convert it to his own use, he is guilty of larceny.").

[145] *See, e.g.,* Model Penal Code § 223.0(1). Larceny by mistake is often codified by state statute. For example, New Jersey law provides

> A person who comes into control of property of another that he knows to have been lost, mislaid, or delivered under a mistake as to the nature or amount of the property or the identity of the recipient is guilty of theft if, knowing the identity of the owner and with purpose to deprive said owner thereof, he converts the property to his own use.

N.J. STAT. ANN. § 2C:20-6. Likewise, Pennsylvania law provides:

> A person who comes into control of property of another that he knows to have been lost, mislaid, or delivered under a mistake as to the nature or amount of the property or the identity of the recipient is guilty of theft if, with intent to deprive the owner thereof, he fails to take reasonable measures to restore the property to a person entitled to have it.

18 PA. CONS. STAT. ANN. § 3924.

[146] State v. Hector, 402 A.2d 595, 596–597 (R.I. 1978) (noting defendant was guilty of criminal larceny by accepting $8,051.69 after a bank clerk made the mistake and misread a check for $851.69).

[147] State v. Langford, 483 So.2d 979, (La. 1986) (Watson, J., dissenting).

It might be argued that he got the property rightfully, not having practiced any fraud or trickery in order to obtain it, but . . . the deed of this man amounted to fraud, and he should not escape punishment on the tenuous ground that because the excess payment was made without positive action on his part and while he stood silent he was not guilty of larceny."[148]

Category four: acquiring knowledge not available to other players that provides an advantage in determining or predicting what was intended to be a random event
Contractual enforcement

All contracts include an implied covenant of good faith and fair dealing.[149] This covenant should be considered whenever an advantage player decides he or she will deliberately attempt to acquire knowledge not typically or readily available to other players that provides an advantage in determining or predicting what was intended to be a random event. After all, the basic foundation of the contract itself is that the winner and loser will be determined by a random event. In this case, the player is attempting to gain additional information in advance, in whole or part, about the likely outcome of the random event. The covenant requires that neither party to a contract do anything that will injure the right of the other party to receive the benefits of their agreement.

The probability of winning or losing at certain table games is predefined, and that information is readily available to anyone who wants to know.[150] On one hand, cheating would violate the covenant. For example, it does not take a skilled mathematician to determine that the probability of rolling a seven in craps is one-in-six. Therefore, if either party to the gaming contract tried to change these odds through advantage play (i.e., the player using loaded dice or engaging in "dice sliding."), that party would injure the other party's right to receive the agreement benefits. Likewise, acquiring knowledge not typically or readily available to other players that provides an advantage in determining or predicting what was intended to be a random event has the same practical and mathematical effect. Both involve the player using deliberate methods to alter the outcome of the contract by either altering the random event or learning information upon which the result is based to gain an advantage over the casino. Thus, by attempting to change the odds or learn the results of a random event occurring or not occurring, advantage play would violate the implied covenant of good faith and fair dealing.

---

[148] Sapp v. State, 26 So.2d 646, (1946) (en banc) (defendant accepted $4,328.37 when cashing a check for $36.00).

[149] 17A C.J.S. *Contracts* §346.

[150] A quick search at Amazon.com for gambling books revealed thousands of books on the subject; most of these books offer to explain the odds of the game.

<u>Legality</u>

As scienter or fraudulent intent is an element of cheating,[151] should the law criminalize activity where the player acts on information exposed where he or she did not enter the casino with intent to fraudulently obtain and act on this information? The latter occurs when a typical player sitting at the table learns of the value of the dealer's hole card because the dealer makes an error in exposing the card.

Hole-carding professionals and teams differ from the player who, without fraudulent intent, learns the dealer's hole card because of "a dealer's unintended revelation of his cards."[152] Here, cheaters play the game intending to learn the dealer's hole card to acquire an advantage and undertake some act to either learn hole cards where the dealer is properly protecting the hole card or use techniques that accentuate poor dealing. Note this quote from an interview with a hole-carder:

> Another cute ruse, I used a few times in the '80s, is posing as a wheelchair-ridden muscular-dystrophy victim during the week of the Jerry Lewis telethon. I'd roll up to the table, eyes level with the felt. Using spasmodic movements and twisted posture I announce in a strained voice that I was the 1964 Jerry Lewis Muscular Dystrophy "poster boy." Of course the primary reason for the act was to have my eyes level with the felt to be able to see the dealer's hole card flashing with each round.[153]

Therefore, attempting to acquire knowledge not typically or readily available to other players that provides an advantage in determining or predicting what was intended to be a random event should be illegal and unenforceable if the player uses any artificial or deliberate means to gain the advantage such as mirrors or spotters.

An argument can be made that a typical player that learns the dealer's hole card because of a dealer's error is no less of a thief than a person who cashes a $100 check and knowingly keeps the extra $900 when the bank clerk mistakes it for a $1000 check. In theory, the player that uses such information forms a fraudulent intent when he or she uses the information to gain the advantage created by the mistake. Moreover, using a person's mistake to that person's or his or her employer's disadvantage is unethical. So what is a player supposed to do when he happens to notice the dealer's hole card when it is inadvertently exposed to him? Some might let the dealer know that he or she accidentally exposed the hole card. Others will likely say nothing and treat it much like getting a few extra cents as change from a small purchase.

Category five: altering the random event to the player's favor
<u>Contractual enforcement and legality</u>

Advantage play where the player alters the random event to the player's favor should always be illegal and unenforceable.

---

[151] Martin, 662 P.2d at 638.
[152] *Id.*
[153] The Zengrifter Interview, *at* http://www.cardcounter.com/.

This argument follows the basic premise of contract law as it applies to casino games. In the typical casino game, both the player and the casino base the ultimate win–loss decision on the random event. Where skill is involved, the contract allows the player to exercise his skills consistent with the terms and conditions of the contract. A person engaged in handle popping fraudulently attempts to alter the basic premise of the contract, i.e., to remove the random element upon which the outcome of the contract is based.

In another Nevada handle popping case, the dissent noted

> slot machines are designed . . . to be played in a manner in which the reels are allowed to spin freely and then be stopped by a timing device in *random* fashion. When a player intentionally interferes with this randomness, such a player is clearly manipulating the machine 'in a manner contrary to the designed and normal operational purpose' of a slot machine.[154]

The dissent properly concluded that "[a]nyone who plays a game of chance, a game based on random selection, who *knows* that he cannot lose, and cannot, in fact, lose, can probably be safely called a cheater."[155]

Attempting to reconcile the *Skipper* case, which held that dice sliding is illegal, with these earlier handle popping cases is not possible. Using the same logic, the court would have to conclude that the rules of slot play do not require that the symbols on the payline of the slot machine have to randomly appear but can be manipulated by one of the parties. Fortunately, the handle popping decisions became moot, not by subsequent legislation, but by technological advancements that made handle popping impossible on the newer generations of slot machines.

The correct legal proposition is "[w]hen a person . . . intentionally impedes or destroys [a game's] randomness, that person is cheating."[156]

RESPONSIBILITY FOR CRIMINAL ENFORCEMENT

Police agencies are usually responsible for enforcing criminal laws in their jurisdictions. Often, this involves concurrent jurisdiction between two or more different police agencies. Jurisdiction to enforce the criminal laws in a US city may be shared between the city police, a county sheriff, state police, and some federal agencies, such as the Federal Bureau of Investigation or the Secret Service. In this instance, certain police agencies may have the authority only to enforce certain types of criminal statutes. For example, the FBI may have jurisdiction only if a federal statute is violated.

An issue arises as to the extent to which agents of a gaming regulatory agency should have authority to enforce criminal gaming statutes. The options range from no authority to exclusive authority. Two major issues in determining whether to grant police powers to a regulatory agency are

---

[154] Childs, 864 P.2d at 280 (Springer, J., dissenting).
[155] *Id.* at 281 (Springer, J., dissenting).
[156] *Id.*

experience and training. Most police officers have extensive training in handling the investigation and arrest of criminal suspects. The rules that govern their conduct substantially differ from those that govern regulatory investigations. In the United States, criminal suspects have certain rights, such as protection against unlawful search and seizure or entitlement to *Miranda* warnings. These rules do not apply to civil gaming regulation enforcement. Often, as a condition of obtaining a license, certain casino operators agree to allow the gaming regulators immediate and free access to any part of the casino or its records. Therefore, a gaming regulator may have limited experience handling a criminal investigation and assuring compliance with all constitutional requirements. Unlike a civil regulatory investigation where cooperation from the casino is assured, criminal suspects may become unruly or violent. Gaming regulators may not have significant experience in arresting a hostile suspect.

Gaming agents, however, may bring knowledge and experience to criminal investigations that a traditional police force may not have. This may be appropriate where the police force is small and does not have officers dedicated to gaming crimes. Gaming agents may be better trained and have greater experience detecting cheating or other gaming shams. They also may have better sources of intelligence information of criminal suspects that prey on casinos or their players or of the cheating operations they employ.

A compromise between granting no authority and exclusive authority is to give limited concurrent authority to gaming regulators. This authority can be limited to enforcing the criminal gaming laws and to making arrests for other crimes that occur in their presence within the casino environment (such as the simple theft of chips). Concurrent jurisdiction allows gaming regulators to work with traditional police agencies. This allows each to bring their respective strengths to the investigation and arrest of criminal suspects.

AIDS TO ASSIST IN CRIMINAL ENFORCEMENT
Detaining People Suspected of Cheating

Cheating and theft are a tremendous problem for casino operators. Like other businesses, casinos may face a dilemma apprehending persons suspected of cheating. As noted in the leading legal text on torts, a business proprietor

> who has good reason to believe that he has caught a customer in the act of stealing, of defrauding him of goods, or of sneaking out without paying for goods or services, is placed in a difficult position. He must permit the suspected wrongdoer to walk out, and probably say good-bye to both goods and payment, or run the risk that he will be liable for heavy damages in any detention.[157]

---

[157] PROSSER AND KEETON ON TORTS 141 (5th ed. 1984).

Some states have given business owners limited privilege from liability if they detain persons suspected of theft for a short time to investigate whether the person stole property or services.[158] But, at best, this privilege is limited to brief on-the-spot inquiries.

To provide protection from civil lawsuits, a jurisdiction can provide more extensive statutory protection. While a jurisdiction could give absolute immunity, or in other words, bar all lawsuits against the casino, most statutes that exist give only limited protection. For example, a casino that suspects a person of cheating may have the right to detain and question the individual.[159] If common law limitations are honored, the casino and its employees may be immune from criminal and civil liability for false arrest, false imprisonment, slander, or unlawful detention. In such cases, courts have imposed liability only where the casino did not follow the statute.[160]

---

[158] *Id.*

[159] Under NEV. REV. STAT. § 465.101, a gaming licensee or his agents have the right to take any individual suspected of cheating into custody, detain him in the establishment, and question him.

[160] Jacobson v. State, 89 Nev. 197, 510 P.2d 856 (Nev. 1973); Hazelwood v. Harrah's, 109 Nev. 1005, 862 P.2d 1189 (1993).

15

Licensing

Anthony Cabot

INTRODUCTION

Licensing is the process by which government decides who it will allow to enter or associate with the casino industry. This chapter recommends an approach for government licensure of the casino industry. Unlike other areas of regulation, no best licensing practices exist. Each government must consider the optimum licensing structure to employ in light of its unique circumstances, such as its public policy, funding and resources, industry resources, and market size. All of these factors can influence a government's regulatory structure and licensing.

A model approach, in contrast to best practices, provides a framework for the government to craft and implement a licensing system that meets government's goals and is within government resources. To begin, one must understand the government's interest in licensing industry parties. As covered in Chapter 2, this requires the government to identify public policies and policy goals. Adding to the discussion in Chapter 5, this chapter discusses the economics of licensing. Governments must understand the costs of imposing licensing and the non-licensing alternatives for achieving policy goals. Before a government can decide who must obtain a license, it must appreciate the range of parties involved in casino gaming, the responsibilities of those parties, and how each could impact achieving government's policy goals. After that, government must identify the level of scrutiny for licensing those involved in the industry and set standards and criteria for evaluating license applications.

NATURE OF LICENSING

Licensing is a tool to exclude persons from an industry, occupation or profession before their actions compromise public goals. It is not unique to casino gaming. Governments often impose licensing requirements on various professions to protect the public. Lawyers, doctors, contractors, and even beauticians go through licensing scrutiny before they can offer their services.[1] Gaming licensing is a form of occupational licensing that has been growing in influence in the United States. Only about 10 percent of the US workforce in 1970 had to obtain licenses, but this number grew to nearly 30 percent by 2008.[2]

LICENSING AND PUBLIC POLICY

Under both government and player protection goals, as explained in detail in Chapter 2, government has an interest in assuring the games are honest and players are paid. The genesis of these goals is different. With government protection goals, the honesty of the games is important because the public may not gamble if think they are being cheated. A player protection approach is concerned with players being paid fairly and properly and not being cheated by either the games or the casinos. If one operator cheats, the public may believe or fear the entire industry is dishonest. Related to these goals, licensing attempts to predict whether, if permitted to operate a casino or manufacture a gaming device, a person would likely cheat players or fail to have enough funds to pay winnings or return deposits.

Government protection goals require a licensing inquiry that focuses on both direct and indirect concerns. Persons that can directly harm government interests are those who skim funds without paying taxes or are so incompetent that the government will lose tax revenues through poor management or employee or patron theft. In some jurisdictions, licensing can be based on political considerations. To allow or maintain a controversial legal gambling industry, politicians appoint regulators with an edict to create a strict regulatory regime necessary maintain popular support for the industry among voters, legislators, or national government. In this context, certain individuals can do indirect harm to this interest if their mere presence taints the industry such that legislators may consider making gaming illegal or existing and prospective patrons may be dissuaded from coming to the casinos.

Under a player protection policy approach, focus shifts from economic considerations to the social goal of protecting the gambler. The suitability review of applicants for an operator's license may not be limited to dis-

---

[1] *In re* Application of Cason, 294 S.E.2d 520, 523 (Ga. 1982) (*citing* Penobscot Bar v. Kimball, 64 Me. 140, 146 (Me. 1875)). ("The function of the Fitness Board is to prevent those not demonstrating the requisite moral character and fitness from being allowed to become lawyers. This is for the protection of the public, because by admitting a person to the practice of law, the bar holds that person out to the public as worthy of patronage and confidence.")

[2] Morris M. Kleiner & Alan B. Krueger. NATIONAL BUREAU OF ECONOMIC RESEARCH, THE PREVALENCE AND EFFECTS OF OCCUPATIONAL LICENSING, 48(4) BRITISH J. INDUS. REL. 676–687 (2010).

honesty; it may require applicants have sufficient competency to detect and prevent schemes designed to cheat players, whether by employees or by third parties. In this context, licensing seeks to protect the public by requiring licensing of persons with responsibilities that if not performed competently could compromise the honesty or fairness of the games. This might include casino owners, managers, dealers, and game manufacturers. If the goals are expanded to assuring player funds are protected, the scope of the licensing review may include assessing the financial strength and accounting competency of the operator.

LICENSING AND ECONOMICS

Regulation would be fairly simple if jurisdictions designed licensing systems without concern for the cost to the government, those regulated, and the regulated market. However, this is an unrealistic ideal. An overly burdensome licensing scheme can impact the government's goals, the financial viability of the industry, and even those who the regulations should protect.[3] Much of this is attributable to how licensing can impact market economics.

Gaming licensing is not a costless process supplying unbiased, capable gatekeepers (the regulators) who monitor the gaming industry to keep out dishonest operators and employees.[4] In many jurisdictions, costs for processing a single application are in the millions of US dollars, in both application fees paid to the government and costs related to preparing and navigating the process. In Massachusetts, seven companies seeking a gaming license had to pay initial license fees of US$400,000 each[5] with the totals for some applicants exceeding $1.5 million.[6] Further, many argue that the regulators are not unbiased, nor are they necessarily capable.[7]

Any licensing cost requirement will create some level of entry barrier. Cost, is only one of the barriers created by licensing. Others can result from uncertainty of approval, time, opportunity costs, or risk to reputation. First, licensing can add uncertainty and risk, especially when regulators regularly deny licenses to applicants. All things being equal, a company will

---

[3] The section on Licensing Fundamentals, *infra*, provides examples of jurisdictions' many approaches to licensing schemes and the challenges these schemes face.

[4] *See* Kleiner & Krueger, *supra* note 2.

[5] Bridget Murphy & Bob Salsberg, *7 firms pony up $400,000 Mass. casino license fee*, Assoc. Press, June 14, 2013, http://www.boston.com/news/local/connecticut/2013/01/14/firms-pony-mass-casino-license-fee/V8ycZihflznGcx6Ln8Z7FL/story.html.

[6] Steve LeBlanc, *Wynn Resorts suitable to open Mass. Casino*, Assoc. Press, Dec. 16, 2013, http://www.lasvegassun.com/news/2013/dec/16/panel-wynn-resorts-suitable-open-casino/.

[7] Economist Milton Friedman was a critic of such assumptions and argued the regulated, rather than public interest, influenced the gatekeepers. Thus, consistent with capture theory, the actions in maintaining such licensing and resulting barriers to entry created monopoly rents for the regulated and higher costs to consumers. *See generally* Milton Friedman, Capitalism and Freedom (1962).

devote its resources to a market where it can more likely obtain a license. Second, companies that want to enter a market do so based on current market economics, and the length of the licensing investigation may preclude or deter applications. If licensing takes substantial time, the company must forecast the economics for when it *might* obtain its license. This adds risk to the decision to enter the market.

Moreover, the time and effort required for the licensing process are an opportunity cost; efforts that otherwise could be directed at creating markets or expanding existing markets instead must be directed at the licensing process. For example, the Pechanga Gaming Commission takes about two-to-three months to investigate an applicant and issue a manufacturer's license. This expeditious handling of license applications allows the prospective licensees to plan deployment and marketing strategies. Such planning is very difficult when licensing might take a year or more.

A third is the burden licensing places on the applicant's resources. This includes the efforts of officers, directors, and staff needed to complete applications and successfully navigate the licensing process. Finally, the licensing process may cause social stigma and embarrassment to a potential entrant as investigators delve into every aspect of the entrant's life. This may discourage some companies, especially diversified companies, when embarrassing disclosures in the licensing process might not be disqualifiers for a license but could negatively impact its brand and other businesses.

Sometimes, licensing barriers are explicit and insurmountable—e.g., when only one or few licenses are awarded under a government grant (Malaysia) or Request for Proposals (Australia) or where minimum investment requirements limit the number of competitors (Nevada). Not all licensing barriers, however, are explicit. In Singapore, while the number of casino licenses is capped, the government does not impose a limit on the number of game manufacturers. Still, if Singapore has significantly higher costs and time related to licensing manufacturers and stricter standards than Macau, fewer manufacturers may apply for licensure in Singapore. This could be a competitive disadvantage to Singapore as fewer manufacturers may result in less variety of games than in Macau.

Why should government care about these barriers? Various studies exist on the effect that occupational licensing has on consumer cost. A 2009 study determined that general occupational licensing resulted in a 15 percent wage premium because of barriers to entry and higher unmeasured human capital.[8]

---

[8] MORRIS M. KLEINER & ALAN B. KRUEGER, NATIONAL BUREAU OF ECONOMIC RESEARCH, ANALYZING THE EXTENT AND INFLUENCE OF OCCUPATIONAL LICENSING ON THE LABOR MARKET, J. OF LAB. ECON., U. OF CHICAGO PRESS, VOL. 31(S1), S173-S202. For example, a 1978 study showed that states that did not have licensing reciprocity for dentists had 12–15 percent higher dental prices. Casino companies would face less expense and barriers to entering a market if a jurisdiction would recognize its license from another jurisdiction without undertaking a separate investigation. There are problems with reciprocity. First, one jurisdiction may conduct a different level of review

Higher consumer prices are only one result of licensing. Others include lower supply of licensed qualified workers[9] and decreased mobility of desired products and workers between jurisdictions.[10] If a government wants to increase employment through the legalization of casinos, licensing barriers can prevent startup or thinly capitalized companies from entering the market. Silicon Valley in Northern California, a world center for high-tech companies, would not likely exist if California had imposed high licensing barriers on start-up companies without substantial innovation capital.

Governments must balance the costs of imposing entry barriers against the benefits they hope to achieve. Under government protection goals, if licensing is too lenient, the industry may suffer if a scandal develops that harms the industry's reputation or results in legislation prohibiting legal gambling. Government protection goals also may include ensuring licensees can compete against other regional or world markets. Licensing costs and barriers to entry may impact a jurisdiction's competitiveness.[11] Likewise, a player protection approach may seek to ensure that players get the fairest price when they play with a licensed casino. If licensing results in oligopoly or monopoly pricing, the resulting games are less fair to the players. The most efficient regulation accomplishes key policy goals with the least impact on other government goals particularly maintaining free markets, where applicable.

LICENSING VERSUS OTHER TOOLS

Licensing and enforcement often seek the same policy goals. Licensing relies on the regulator's ability to predict the applicant's future behavior, while enforcement concentrates on verifying the licensee's activities through oversight. If cheating is difficult to police through enforcement, licensing provides governments with a tool to prevent persons with a propensity to cheat or compromise other policy goals from operating licensed

---

for a type of license. With reciprocity, persons may attempt to first obtain a license in the jurisdiction with the easiest licensing process. Likewise, different jurisdictions may use different criteria or standards to assess applications. For example, a jurisdiction with a monopoly structure may decide to only accept an application where no licensing issues exist, while under a competitive model, the regulators may be less selective A 1986 study found that restrictions on optometry practices raised prices by 5–13 percent. Deborah Hass-Wilson, *The Effect of Commercial Practice Restrictions: The Case of Optometry*, 29 J. L. & ECON. 165 (1986). This is likely amplified in the gaming space because licensing most often goes well down the supply chain. Not only must the operator obtain a license, but so must certain employees, suppliers and vendors. These increase prices for labor, supplies, and services.

[9] *Haas-Wilson, supra* note 8.

[10] *See, e.g.,* Leila J. Pratt, *Occupational Licensing and Interstate Mobility*, 15 BUS. ECON, 78, 78–80 (1980).

[11] Some casino markets may have economics where the cost of licensing is simply passed on to the players in the form of higher prices with little impact because of the regional monopoly and lack of competition created by limited licenses.

casinos. In some jurisdictions, regulators attempt to shift the emphasis to enforcement. This may be practical in limited markets with only a few casinos where government can afford to more closely regulate casino operations. Government officials may monitor all critical casino functions. Separate government surveillance facilities may allow government officials to covertly observe operations. Online monitoring of gaming devices also may provide protection.

Regulatory systems can emphasize licensing or enforcement or balance the two. Where reasonably efficient, proactive standards and enforcement can provide a more certain, measureable result. Licensing attempts to predict behavior, while standards and enforcement control behavior. This relationship can be seen using the protection of player funds as an example. The licensing process tries to predict whether a future licensee is likely to divert player funds for other purposes. Conversely, a proactive standard might require licensees to segregate player funds under the control of a trusted third party allowing the regulator to control the funds. Reasonable standards and enforcement will not create the same level of barrier to entry as licensing.

This type of participatory regulatory oversight, however, may be too expensive in competitive environments where the costs would impact the competitiveness of the industry against regional competition. A government must assess where to devote its finite resources. Licensing and enforcement functions compete for limited budgets.

With evolving technological advances in the casino environment, certification may be a preferred alternative to licensing. As one commentator notes:

> Government certification schemes also provide consumer protection. As with licensure, certification conveys a valuable quality signal to consumers, but certification is more flexible than licensure because it preserves free entry; only use of a title is restricted.[12]

Expensive licensing can accomplish an unexpected goal—a potential deterrent to bad behavior that could cause loss of the right to conduct gambling in a jurisdiction or impact the ability to obtain licenses in another jurisdiction, either of which would significantly impact a company's finances.

LICENSING CHALLENGES

Only occasionally does an applicant have such a sordid history or poor reputation that its mere association with the industry contravenes policy goals. Although an investigation can expose hidden ownership, a free Internet search will usually expose issues that could create image problems affecting the broader industry. Instead, licensing is principally a prophy-

---

[12] DAVID S. YOUNG, THE RULE OF EXPERTS: OCCUPATIONAL LICENSING IN AMERICA 18 (1987).

lactic exercise used to exclude "unfit" persons before they enter the gaming industry and to inform those qualified persons of the standards expected of them. Licensing is an attempt to predict the behavior of the applicant with the objective that only those who do not pose a reasonable threat to achieving public goals withstand licensing scrutiny.[13]

Pre-licensing inquiry is flawed when its purpose is to predict the future behavior of an individual.[14] Attempting to predict behavior assumes that people have fundamental character traits that govern their conduct. The validity of this assumption is questionable.[15] According to critics, character assessments have little predictive value because conduct is contextual, and "the situational nature of moral conduct makes predictions of behavior uncertain under any circumstances."[16] Noted one commentator, "a half century of behavioral research underscores the variability and contextual nature of moral behavior: A single incident or small number of acts committed in dissimilar social settings affords no basis for reliable generalizations."[17]

Social scientists, however, can predict behavior in groups. For example, they can use statistics to predict some recovering alcoholics will relapse, but that prediction cannot be reliably extended to an individual alcoholic.[18] One study showed "disciplinary action among practicing physicians by medical boards was strongly associated with unprofessional behavior in medical school."[19] Regulators may decide that past actions put persons into high-risk categories such that those persons should not be licensed even if regulators cannot predict if a given applicant will cause problems.

How well does this work in practice? Studies of whether occupational licensing furthers the quality of services offered are mixed.[20] No studies have considered whether licensing in the casino industry has any discernible impact on the honesty of games offered to the public or what the costs

---

[13] Licensing has a design failure where regulators test applicants against criteria unrelated to achieving public policy.

[14] Banks McDowell, *The Usefulness of "Good Moral Character,"* 33 WASHBURN L .J 323, 327 (1992) (*See also In re* Mostman, 765 P.2d 448, 454, (Cal. 1989); *In Re* Bowen, 84 Nev. 681, 684, 447 P.2d 658, 660 (1968)). Deborah L. Rhode, *Moral Character as a Professional Credential,* 94 YALE L .J. 491, 512 (1985).

[15] Rhode, *supra* note 14, at 556.

[16] *Id.* at 559.

[17] *Id.* at 560.

[18] *Id.*

[19] Maxine A. Papadakis et al., *Disciplinary Action by Medical Boards and Prior Behavior in Medical School,* 353 New Eng. J. Med., 2673, 2673 (2005).

[20] Morris M. Kleiner & Robert T. Kudrle, *Does Regulation affect Economic Outcomes? The Case of Dentistry,* 43 J.L. & ECON. 548 (2000) (finding that tougher state-level restrictions and pass rates for dentists resulted in 15 percent higher hourly wage rates with no measurable increase in quality); David Barker, *Ethics and Lobbying: The Case of Real Estate Brokerage,* 80 J. Bus. ETHICS 23 (2007) (finding occupation licensing for real estate brokers resulted in a raise in broker income without improving the quality of service).

versus benefits of licensing versus other regulatory tools are in assuring the honesty of games or achieving other policy goals.

Despite this criticism, all established governments that allow casinos impose licensing requirements.

LICENSING FUNDAMENTALS

Differences between licensing systems are based on five major factors: criteria, standards of the licensing process, level of review, breadth, and depth.

Criteria are what the government considers in granting licenses. This can include moral character, honesty, connection to criminal elements, financial ability, and business experience. Some places have specialized criteria based on public policy. Under its player protection goals, for example, Great Britain required prospective applicants to prove that the area for a proposed casino has an unsatisfied, unstimulated demand for casino gambling. This criterion stemmed from Great Britain's broader policy goal that casinos not stimulate demand for gaming opportunities.

Standards refer to how rigidly regulators apply criteria. Under the same set of facts, an applicant may obtain a license in one jurisdiction, but not in another because of differing standards of conduct in the two jurisdictions. The minimum attributes of qualified applicants varies based upon the standards used.

Level of review refers to the intensity of the investigative process. A low-level review might include simple criminal background checks. A high-level review may entail that the regulatory agency train special agents to conduct a complete, independent review of the applicant including both background and finances.

Breadth means the extent to which a government requires persons or entities associated with the gaming industry to obtain a license. For example, does a company that provides electronic shoes for table games have to obtain a license?

Depth of licensing means the extent to which a government requires persons within a licensable entity to undergo an investigation. This could require certain officers, directors, shareholders, and employees associated with an entity applying for a gaming license to file individual disclosures and undergo a background investigation.

Criteria

Regulators consider many criteria when assessing a gaming license application. Criteria can be fixed or discretionary. Fixed criteria are quantifiable ones an applicant either meets or does not. Fixed criteria can include whether a person has been convicted of a felony (South Dakota)[21] or

---

[21] S.D. CODIFIED LAWS § 42-7B-33(3) (through 2011).

Figure 15.1

Examples of Fixed Criteria	
Jurisdiction	**Type of Fixed Criteria**
Bulgaria	The person has no criminal record[23]
Mississippi	The person has not been convicted of any crime involving gambling, prostitution, or sale of alcohol to a minor
Portugal	60% of company must be owned by Portuguese citizens[24]
Peru	A 3-,4-, or 5-star hotel[25]
Nevada	Hotel with more than 200 rooms, a bar for 30 people, and a 24-hour restaurant
France	A contract with a municipal government for a building in a community that has thermal waters (spas) or is seaside

whether an applicant has been convicted of any crime involving gambling, prostitution, or sale of alcohol to a minor (Mississippi).[22]

Discretionary criteria are minimum qualifications not subject to quantification, but are based on the discretion of the gaming regulators. For example, Great Britain requires a showing an applicant is likely to act consistently with the licensing objectives.[23] Great Britain's requirement follows the most common discretionary criteria, which involve good character, associations, management capabilities, and financial abilities.

Figure 15.2

Examples Of Discretionary Criteria	
Jurisdiction	**Type of Discretionary Criteria**
Nevada	The person must be of good character, honest, and have integrity.
Puerto Rico	The person must have organizational and financial ability to conduct casino operations.
Germany	The applicant must be reliable and competent.[27]
Queensland	The applicant has, or can obtain, the services of persons with experience in managing and operating a casino.
Great Britain	The person is likely to comply with the gaming controls.

Good character or good moral character

Gaming statutes and regulations often require regulators to consider "good moral character" as a factor in screening applicants for professional and other vocational licenses involving a high degree of public trust. In Indiana, for example, gaming commissioners examine applicants' "good moral character."[24] Besides privileged licenses such as gaming, good moral character is a common criterion for professional licensure in fields such as accounting, law, or medicine. Despite its frequent use, the term has limited practical utility because it is difficult to define and apply. The major problem with using "good moral character" as a criterion is the inherent subjectivity involved when judging another's character.[25]

Judicial attempts in the United States to give concrete standards to the term "good moral character" are unhelpful. One case that attempted to define the term is *Konigsberg v. State Bar of California*.[26] There, the state

---

[22] Miss. Code Ann. § 75-76-67(3) (West 2013).

[23] UK Gambling Act 2005, c. 19 Part 5 Section 70§ 70(2)(b).

[24] Ind. Gaming Comm'n, Occupational License, http://www.in.gov/igc/2344.htm.

[25] Rhode, *supra* note 14, at 529 (1985).

[26] Konigsberg v. State Bar of Cal., 353 U.S. 252 (1957). Other courts have struggled with

bar association denied an applicant's admission because of "questionable moral character" based on certain of the applicant's political statements.[27] The court, discussing the definition of "good moral character" stated that:

> The term, by itself, is unusually ambiguous. It can be defined in an almost unlimited number of ways for any definition will necessarily reflect the attitudes, experiences, and prejudices of the definer. Such a vague qualification, which is easily adapted to fit personal views and predilections, can be a dangerous instrument for arbitrary and discriminatory denial. . . .[28]

Ultimately, what is good or bad depends on the individual perceptions of the person making the judgment. What is good or bad to a Southern Baptist minister in contrast to a Bronx numbers operator will differ greatly. The former might find any applicant for a gaming license to be of bad character because of his choice of profession.[29] Contextually, the concepts vary based on the political, social, religious, and psychological orientation of the regulator.

Other courts' struggles with "good moral character" usually result in defining the phrase with more vague, subjective phrases. The North Carolina Supreme Court defined "good moral character" as

> [S]omething more than an absence of bad character. . . . It means that he must have conducted himself as a man of upright character ordinarily would, should, or does. Such character expresses itself not in negatives, nor in following the line of least resistance, but quite often in the will to do the unpleasant thing if it is right, and the resolve not to do the pleasant thing if it is wrong.[30]

---

the same ambiguities. The Arizona Supreme Court, ten years after *Konigsberg*, conceded that "the concept of good moral character escapes definition in the abstract" and held that each case must be judged on its own merits in an *ad hoc* determination. Application of Klahr, 102 Ariz. 529, 531, 433 P.2d 977, 979 (Ariz. 1967). The conclusion that the individual has good moral character and, therefore, is fit, is a subjective opinion only reached by comparing the individual to one's personal concept of what is moral or immoral.

[27] *Id.* at 258–59.

[28] *Id.* at 262–63.

[29] So might the United States Citizenship and Immigration Services, which considers, in its definition of "good moral character" in determining suitability for US citizenship, whether you earn your principal income from illegal gambling. Emmanuel Tipon, *In the US, Who is a Person of 'Good Moral Character?'*, GMA NEWS ONLINE, May 1, 2013, http://www.gmanetwork.com/news/story/306290/pinoyabroad/ofwguide/immigration-guide-in-the-us-who-is-a-person-of-good-moral-character.

[30] *In re* Farmer, 191 N.C. 235, 131 S.E. 661, 663 (N.C. 1926). An Arizona Court, in attempting to determine bad moral character, adopted a test that inquires "whether that behavior truly portrays an inherent and fixed quality of character of an unsavory, dishonest, debased, and corrupt nature." Klahr, 102 Ariz. at 979 (citing *In re* Monaghan, 126 Vt. 53, 60, 222 A.2d 665, 671 (1966)). Conduct evidencing "bad moral character" (in a lawyer admissions context) has been described as "[c]onduct evidencing dishonesty, disrespect for law, disregard for financial obligations, or psychological instability." Rhode, *supra* note 14, at 532. Conduct most damaging to one's character has been described as conduct evidencing "moral turpitude," another standard open to varying interpretations. Rhode, *supra* note 14, at 531. Moral turpitude is an act or behavior which gravely violates moral

The United States Supreme Court simply restated the overall standard.[31] In *Schware v. Board of Bar Examiners of State of New Mexico*, an applicant for bar admission was rejected for questionable moral character because of his membership in the Communist Party.[32] The Court reversed, stating that:

> [A] state can require high standards of qualification, such as good moral character or proficiency in its law, before it admits an applicant to the Bar, but any qualification *must have a rational connection* with the applicant's fitness or capacity to practice law.[33] (Emphasis added.)

The Court found Communist Party membership alone was not rationally related to one's ability to practice law and ordered the applicant's admission.[34] Applying this criterion in a context other than the practice of law, any "good moral character" requirement would have to be logically connected to a policy goal, such as the qualities and abilities needed to engage in that occupation. The United States Supreme Court, interpreting California decisions on bar admissions, stated that the definition of "good moral character," as a practical matter, is where the absence of proven bad acts fails to raise substantial doubts about the applicant's honesty, fairness, and respect for the rights of others and for the laws of the state and nation.[35] In this context, courts determine relevancy by deciding the good attributes for licensing in the profession being considered. Holding good character, then, equates to having those attributes. Several other states have adopted this definition.[36]

Another problem with using "good character" as a criterion is attempting to define an individual as good or bad. The concept of character necessitates a review of all the person's traits. Character, by definition, is "the pattern of behavior or personality found in an individual."[37]

As one commentator noted:

> One problem of sorting people into two categories -- those of good moral character and those who are not -- is that most people range across the dividing line. Many, if not most, people are usually of good moral character, but not always; are frequently honest, but once in a while untrustworthy; are often loyal, but sometimes unfaithful; will be generally competent, but

---

sentiment or accepted moral standards of the community. It is present in some criminal offenses, but not all. BLACK's LAW DICTIONARY 1009 (6th ed. 1990). Thus "moral turpitude" is similar in definition to "good moral character" and carries the same definitional inadequacies. According to one commentator, "[f]or purposes of Bar discipline, the 'moral turpitude' criteria does nothing to refine the inquiry, but merely removes it one step from its announced concern--fitness for legal practice." Rhode, *supra* note 14, at 532.

[31] Schware v. Bd. of Bar Exam'rs of State of N.M., 353 U.S. 232 (1957).

[32] *Id.* at 238.

[33] *Id.* at 239 (emphasis added).

[34] *Id.* at 246–47.

[35] Konigsberg, 353 U.S. at 263.

[36] *See, e.g., In re* Florida Bd. of Bar Exam'rs, 373 So. 2d 890 (Fla. 1979); Reese v. Bd. of Comm'rs of Alabama State Bar, 379 So. 2d 564 (Ala. 1980); BLACK's LAW DICTIONARY 693 (6th ed. 1990).

[37] WEBSTER's NEW WORLD DICTIONARY 125 (Second Concise Edition (1976)).

occasionally careless; and so on. They range along a continuum, usually acting above minimum standards, but at times falling below.[38]

Defining "good" behavior based on a single event in a person's life may or may not be justified depending on the event. If the person sold confidential government information to enemies of this country, that lone event would probably meet most people's criteria of "bad" character. But, what about other single events? Take a license applicant arrested for a single instance of child abuse who agreed to counseling and had the charges dismissed. Regulators may vary on whether they view this as a disqualifying incident. A definitional difficulty arises because reasonable people can differ about what conduct would raise substantial doubts about one's moral character.[39]

Finally, when regulators use "good character" as a criterion, little credence is usually given to "good" acts as they instead concentrate on trying to prove bad character. Thus, a person has "good moral character" if there are no demonstrable instances where the individual showed "bad moral character." Defining a positive ("good moral character") through the absence of a negative ("bad moral character") is unhelpful, unless there are standards provided to determine when the negative exists.

While "good moral character" is a common criterion for licensure, it is an inherently vague bench-mark that functions as a total grant of discretion to regulators. While courts have tried to narrow the definition of "good moral character," they have been largely unsuccessful. Courts are not the ideal venue for establishing a more concrete definition because it is preferable to have a workable standard in the first instance.

Integrity, honesty, and truthfulness

Integrity, honesty, and truthfulness are three concepts that licensing statutes use as criteria to assess an applicant's suitability. In New Jersey, the commission will grant a license only if the company is under the control of persons of integrity.[40] Under New Jersey law, besides character, the Casino Control Commission reviews applicants' honesty and integrity by considering personal, professional, and business associations, history of criminal convictions, history of civil litigation, credit history, bankruptcies, and personal and professional references.[41]

While related, these concepts of integrity, honesty, and truthfulness have different meanings. Truthfulness means to tell the truth and is only one component of honesty. One can be truthful, but dishonest. It is dishonest to use certain truths and not disclose other truths to create a false

---

[38] McDowell, *supra* note 14, at 323.
[39] Rhode *supra* note 14, at 530.
[40] N. J. Stat. Ann. § 5:12-85 (West 2011).
[41] N. J. Stat. Ann. § 5:12-89 (West 2011).

impression.[42] A person arrested by state police can truthfully state he has not been arrested by city police. If, however, he responded to a question about his criminal record by stating "I have never been arrested by the city police," the statement would be truthful but dishonest. Regulators want full disclosure by applicants and licensees who both tell the truth and convey accurate impressions. Therefore, "honesty" as a criterion is preferable to truthfulness.

That said, how useful is "honesty" as a criterion? Shakespeare wrote in Hamlet, "Ay sir, to be honest, as this world goes, is to be one man picked out of ten thousand."[43] Thomas Fuller conveyed a similar thought: "He that resolves to deal with none but honest men must leave off dealing."[44] Both men's sentiments convey that no matter how committed to honesty a person may be, few people can claim complete honesty in all their dealings.[45] Moreover, lies can be altruistic rather than self-serving by supporting or not wanting to offend another person.[46]

When applying the "honesty" criterion, regulators must rely on a materiality standard in a business context. Two general rules emerge. First, the honesty criterion usually should be considered in a business, as opposed to a personal, context. This is justified because the purpose of licensing is to predict the conduct of an applicant in a business relationship as a gaming licensee. Second, honesty in business conduct becomes more relevant with the importance of the transaction. It may be of minor materiality that an applicant, to cut short a telemarketing call, lied by telling the salesman he recently bought the product being offered. The materiality increases dramatically if the applicant misrepresents the value of inventory to convince a lender to loan money to his business. The crime of perjury, for example, requires that the false statement "must be in some point material to the question in dispute; for if it only be in some trifling collateral circumstance, to which no regard is paid," it is not punishable."[47]

While conceptually a person with "integrity" generally exhibits "honest" behavior, honesty is nothing more than a component of integrity. "The word 'integrity' . . . means soundness of moral principal and character, as shown by one's dealing with others in the making and performance of contracts. . . ."[48] As one commentator noted:

---

[42] Wiggins v. Texas, 778 S.W.2d 877, 889 (Tex. App. 1989).

[43] WILLIAM SHAKESPEARE, HAMLET act 2, sc.2.

[44] Thomas FULLER, GNOMOLOGIA: ADAGIES AND PROVERBS; WISE SENTENCES AND WITTY SAYINGS, ANCIENT AND MODERN, FOREIGN AND BRITISH 93 (1ST ED. 1732), HTTP://BOOKS.GOOGLE.COM/BOOKS?ID=3Y8JAAAAQAAJ&PG=PP1#V=ONEPAGE&Q&F=FALSE

[45] Bella M. DePaulo, & Deborah A. Kashy, *EverydayLlies in Close and Casual Relationships*, 74(1) J. PERSONALITY & SOC. PSYCHOL. 63 (1998).

[46] *Id.*

[47] United States v. Wells, 519 U.S. 482 (1997) (quoting Sir William Blackstone, COMMENTARIES ON THE LAWS OF ENGLAND Vol. 4, 137 (1769), and citing 1 W. Hawkins, Pleas of the Crown, ch. 27, § 8, p. 433 (Curwood ed. 1824)).

[48] *In re* Bauquier's Estate, 88 Cal. 302, 307, 26 P. 178 aff'd, 88 Cal. 302, 26 P. 532 (Cal. 1891).

At a minimum, persons of integrity are individuals whose practices are consistent with their principles, even in the face of strong countervailing pressures. Yet the term also implies something more than steadfastness. Fanatics may be loyal to their values, but we do not praise them for integrity. What earns our praise is a willingness to adhere to values that reflect some reasoned deliberation, based on logical assessment of relevant evidence and competing views. Some theorists would add a requirement that the values themselves must satisfy certain minimum demands of consistency, generalizability, and respect for others.[49]

Integrity is a complex concept that involves commitments to prioritized, personal moral principles. As another commentator noted, "Integrity does not consist of molding and adapting one's principles to whatever behaviors we and those around us find convenient. Integrity means to take the high road, the road of conforming our behavior to our principles."[50] These principals can include honesty, family, friendship, religion, honor, country, or fairness. Integrity means upholding these commitments for the right reasons in the face of temptation.[51] Persons prioritize these commitments such that it is acceptable to violate some commitments to honor others. For example, most people believe lying (dishonesty) is acceptable to protect another from harm or injustice. For regulators to test a person's integrity, they would have to understand the person's personal priorities and decide whether the person is consistently true to these commitments and their priority. This is an impossible task in a neutral setting, but becomes even more problematic because the regulators' sense of personal priorities might differ from the applicant's.

Integrity might even contravene regulatory policy due to the priority of the applicant's commitments. Suppose an applicant, highly values personal friendship has been friends since childhood with a person of a notorious reputation. The regulators demand that licensees not associate with such persons; however, the applicant's personal integrity places his commitment to friendship above the dictates of regulation. The applicant, to maintain his integrity, would continue to maintain his friendship even though it is likely to make him unsuitable to hold a gaming license. Therefore, regulators must be adept at defining which commitments are most important to good regulation, and at testing the person's behavior against those commitments.

Integrity, honesty, and truthfulness all suffer from some degree of difficulty in application. Honesty, however, is an important policy goal in both the player and government protection contexts, but government protection goals place greater emphasis on complying with law. That said, honesty is the easiest of the three criteria for regulators to measure and judge in

---

[49] Deborah L. Rhode, *If Integrity Is the Answer, What Is the Question?*, 72 FORDHAM L. REV. 333, 335–36 (2003).

[50] David Luban. *Integrity: Its Causes and Cures*, 72 FORDHAM L. REV. 279, 289 (2003).

[51] Lynn McFall, *Integrity*, 98 Ethics 5, 9 (UNIV. OF CHICAGO PRESS, OCTOBER 1987).

Figure 15.3

Materiality of Noncompliance	
Less Material	**More Material**
Does not involve dishonesty	Involves dishonesty
Civil violation	Criminal violation
Misdemeanor	Felony
Negligence	Intentional
Many years ago	Recent
Isolated	Repetitive
Accepted responsibility	Denied responsibility
Took corrective action	Took no affirmative action
Minor compared to size of business	Major compared to size of business

a meaningful way, provided the inquiry is limited to material, business-related behaviors.

Compliance with law

An applicant's compliance with all pertinent laws is material in granting a gaming license. One function of the licensing process is to predict whether, if granted a license, the applicant will comply with all gaming laws and regulations. Strict compliance with these laws and regulations is necessary for achieving the policy goals underlying them. Nothing is more predictive of future compliance with business laws and regulations than a review of past compliance in the same context.

Some jurisdictions' laws and regulations have fixed criteria for determining suitability based on legal compliance. A felony conviction or an offense involving gambling may be a disqualifying factor and pose an insurmountable hurdle for convicted applicants.[52] Other jurisdictions follow flexible standards. There, regulators must make a qualitative decision based on a totality of factors as to whether the applicant is suitable. In these jurisdictions, as with the "honesty" criterion, some instances of noncompliance may be less material than others.

Material violation of laws is a useful licensing criterion because past compliance is a strong indicator of future compliance. Compliance is much more than whether the applicant has violated the law, but whether it has institutional controls for assuring compliance with all domestic and foreign laws particularly where the applicant may have or do business with other casinos.

Noncompliance with laws in one's personal affairs is a more difficult proposition because many laws are not enforced. For example, should a married applicant be denied a license because he had an affair that violated a state law prohibiting adultery? This violation is less material to a prediction of his conduct as a licensee than if he violated laws dealing with wire fraud. An intentional violation of a law against tax evasion is a valid consideration because it reflects on the person's honesty. Violating an adultery law is a more problematic predictor of behavior as a gaming licensee because of personal privacy issues, and the offender may conduct his business in an honest and honorable manner.

---

[52] *See, e.g.,* Mo. Rev. Stat. § 313.810 (2010).

Still, regulators may have some concern anytime an applicant knowingly violates a law because of greed, power, notoriety, and the like because it shows that some things will motivate him to commit illegal actions. These actions, however, should be viewed in relation to the severity of the crime and its predictive value as to one's conduct as a licensee.

Manner of doing business

Different people have distinct manners of doing business. While some people are reconciliatory and successfully resolve most disputes without litigation, others are more adversarial and regularly litigate disputes. The adversarial type may create disputes to delay payment and seek favorable settlement by threat of suit. In dealing with regulators, the reconciliatory type is cooperative and agrees on appropriate behavior while the adversarial type challenges regulators' authority and ties up resources in court challenges.

Reconciliatory types make more obedient gaming licensees. They are more willing to conform their behavior to the expectations of the regulators. By not challenging the regulatory authority through litigation, costs are reduced.

Adversarial types, however, may provide an important check on regulators. If no licensee challenges regulatory actions that might exceed the regulator's authority or that might contravene legislative policy, public policy goals might be frustrated, and the legislature and the chief executive may be none the wiser. Citizens in most societies have the right to seek judicial redress of grievances. Prejudicing an applicant for exercising legal rights might appear unjust and may contravene governmental policy goals.

Adversarial types, however, abuse the system when they use litigation to silence critics, avoid paying debts, or extort settlements. Regulators must understand court processes and be able to distinguish frivolous litigation and patterns of abuse. Where an applicant abuses the legal system, regulators may justifiably consider this in assessing suitability for a license.

Criminal history and prior convictions

Most jurisdictions that regulate casinos investigate the applicants' criminal history, background, or records. Given that regulators necessarily must focus on past actions, especially past criminal actions, to predict future behavior, what type of history should disqualify someone from obtaining a license? A jurisdiction may take two approaches.

First, the jurisdiction may use a fixed-criteria system where anyone convicted of a felony, a crime involving gambling, or a crime involving "moral turpitude" is ineligible for a gaming license.

The second approach considers a criminal conviction as evidence of the person's unsuitability but maintains flexibility to consider other evidence to decide suitability. Under this view, a criminal conviction often creates a presumption of unsuitability and shifts the burden to the applicant to rebut that presumption by showing rehabilitation.[53] Still, no definitive tests exist to decide whether a person with a history of criminal activities can earn a gaming license. Regulators may consider several facts in assessing whether to deny an application based on prior criminal activities. These include the following:

- The nature of the crime; criminal activities such as thievery or embezzlement are very significant;
- Seriousness of the crime or the person's involvement;
- Mitigating or extenuating circumstances;
- Temporal proximity of the criminal activity;
- Age at time of the criminal activity;
- A pattern or high frequency of criminal activity;
- The applicant's honesty and forthrightness in revealing the past criminal activity to gaming investigators; and
- Relevancy of the crime to policy goals related to casino gaming.

Some past crimes committed by an applicant may have no relation to casino gambling policy goals. For example, a person convicted of child molestation 15 years ago is probably unfit to be licensed to operate a child care center, but it does not follow that the same person is not suitable to operate a gaming operation. No rational connection exists between the two; that a person was convicted of child molestation provides a poor basis for predicting a person's capability of operating an honest casino.

Predicting future behavior using an applicant's criminal history may be an imperfect assessment, but may provide the strongest predictive evidence available to regulators. Both approaches described above have their costs and benefits. A fixed criteria approach is an easy standard to implement, but it may not be an effective predictive tool, especially when the applicant's criminal history and license obligations do not correlate. A nuanced discretionary approach, on the other hand, can address some shortcomings of the fixed criteria test by looking to the circumstances surrounding an applicant's criminal history and the applicant's subsequent conduct, but this approach can be costly and overly subjective.

Sometimes, an applicant may never have been convicted of a crime but still have a history of suspected criminal activity or arrests. Gaming authorities may deny licenses to persons never convicted of a crime but who failed to show a lack of involvement in criminal activities.

---

[53] Maureen M. Carr, *The Effect of Prior Criminal Conduct on the Admission to Practice Law: The Move to More Flexible Admission Standards*, 8 GEO. J. LEGAL ETHICS, 367, 383 (1995). The Georgia Supreme Court stated this rebuttal must be by clear and convincing evidence. *In re* Cason, 294 S.E.2d at 522. The Court stated that for lawyer fitness purposes, the applicant must reestablish his or her reputation by showing a return to a "useful and constructive place in society." This cannot be evidenced by merely paying a fine or serving time, but must be evidenced by affirmative action, such as community service, occupation, or religion. This "test," allows licensing committees considerable leeway in determining eligibility based upon their own subjective attitudes.

Associations with unsuitable persons

If gaming licensees associate with notorious or unsuitable persons, the public may believe those persons have an interest in or influence over the gaming operations. A person's willingness to associate with disreputable people may also call into question his own judgment or propensity toward crime. The problem with the concept of association is definitional. As one court noted, "the word 'associate' is not of uniform meaning but is, rather, vague in its connotation."[54] Do incidental or involuntary contacts with known criminals constitute association? What if the applicant did not know of the other person's unsuitability?

Some courts define association as more than incidental contact with unsuitable persons. In interpreting a regulation prohibiting police officers from "associating" with criminals, one court held that the term means more than "incidental contacts" between police officers and known criminals.[55] The issue in another case was whether a parolee violated his parole by "associating" with undesirable persons.[56] There the court defined association as "to join often, in a close relationship as a partner, fellow worker, colleague, friend, companion, or ally."[57]

The New Jersey Supreme Court held unknowing associations are not a basis for a finding of unsuitability by gaming regulators.[58] The Court stated, however, that after an applicant knows of the unsuitability of an association, failing to dissociate is a knowing association. There, the New Jersey Casino Control Commission decided that the founder of a casino company was unsuitable in part because of a recurring and enduring relationship with an individual who allegedly had ties to organized crime. The applicant sought judicial review. In upholding the agency decision, the Court noted it was "not critical of a proposition denouncing guilt adjudication predicated solely on unknowing or otherwise innocent association and is sensitive to the difficulties defending against such a premise."[59]

While difficult to define, the concept of unsuitable "associations," should focus on the following:

- Nature and intensity of the relationship. Facts considered include (1) type of relationship, i.e., business or friendship; (2) knowledge of the second person's unsuitability; (3) whether the relationship was voluntary; (4) frequency or involvement of the relationship; and (5) the applicant's attitude after becoming aware of the gaming

---

[54] Weir v. United States, 92 F.2d 634, 638 (7th Cir. 1937), *cert. denied*, 302 U.S. 761, 58 S. Ct. 368 (1937).

[55] Sponick v. City of Detroit Police Dept., 49 Mich. App. 162, 211 N.W.2d 674 (Mich. Ct. App. 1973).

[56] State v. Morales, 137 Ariz. 67, 668 P.2d 910 (Ariz. Ct. App. 1983).

[57] *Id.* at 68.

[58] *In re* Boardwalk Regency Casino License Application, 180 N.J.Super. 324, 434 A.2d 1111 (N.J. 1982).

[59] *Id.* at 340.

authorities' concern with the relationship;
- The influence or control over the applicant by the other person;
- The nature of the concern about the other person and how that concern poses a threat to the public interest; and
- The number of questionable relationships.

An inquiry based on these factors is more likely to avoid the injustices of a simple "guilt by association" approach while preserving regulators' ability to exclude persons truly unsuitable due to their associations.

Conduct during the investigation

Gaming laws require applicants to make full and true disclosure of all information requested on the forms or by the regulatory agents.[60] The applicant's conduct during the investigation may become relevant to his suitability for many reasons. If the applicant attempts to hide or mischaracterize a past transgression, regulators may question the applicant's current credibility. If the applicant is not cooperative, the regulators may question whether the applicant will adopt a similar attitude toward compliance after licensing. If the applicant keeps disorganized and incomplete financial and personal records, regulators may question the applicant's ability to account properly for taxes.

Competency/management abilities

Operating a casino takes special knowledge and skills. Regulators may have concerns that otherwise honest persons might frustrate governmental goals if the operators lack the capacity to properly manage operations. Incompetence can be just as destructive to a jurisdiction's policy goals as malfeasance. Poor managers may not recognize when dishonest dealers cheat or steal from the player. This may frustrate a primary governmental goal by failing to ensure that games are honest. Similarly, professional cheaters and dishonest employees can more easily steal from poorly managed gaming operations. This may frustrate governmental goals of collecting taxes on all revenues derived from gaming operations. Therefore, some jurisdictions, like Alberta, Canada, require applicants to have the appropriate services, skills, and technical knowledge to provide services.[61]

Regulators may scrutinize managerial competence proportionate to the complexity of the organization and gaming operation. If the gaming operation is small and has only state-monitored gaming devices, the requisite level of management skill is minimal and can be acquired. Some casinos,

---

[60] *See, e.g.,* Nev. Rev. Stat. § 463.339 (2011).

[61] *See* Michael D. Lipton & Kevin Weber, *Alberta, in* International Casino Law & Regulation Vol. 1: North America § 1.05, at 10 (William Thompson ed., 2008) (stating that a gaming commission may need a devoted software architect to decide if an operator is technically competent to manage computer security, cashless systems, central casino control systems, computerized audit and analysis systems, and multi-casino systems).

however, have thousands of gaming devices, hundreds of table games, a sports pool, a race book, and other gaming opportunities. Skills needed to manage a facility of this nature are far more imposing, and testing for adequate management skills varies depending on the complexity of the applicant's organization and the gaming operation. The former addresses the nature of the applicant. If it is a large diverse public company, regulators rarely expect the chairperson of the board of directors to have operational experience. Here, the emphasis is on the management structure established for the gaming operations. Regulators often require applicants to provide organizational charts designating the persons in each position, their responsibilities, and lines of authority. These are then tested against standards of depth, i.e., is there enough management coverage? Are all key management areas covered? Are responsibilities properly segregated? Does the person have adequate knowledge and experience?

With lower-level employees, government can use occupational certification to address competence and reduce skill deficiencies. This could be beneficial when the skills required to perform a job are easily identifiable, can be quantified and framed in a license requirement, and can be tested.[62]

Financial capabilities

A government may have varying degrees of concern with the financial capability of a casino license applicant to succeed. In a monopoly or small oligopoly situation, the government may have a strong interest in assuring the prospective casino operator is properly financed, particularly where the government is committing resources to the project through infrastructure or community development funds, hiring additional city personnel, or buying new city equipment. A government may have legitimate concerns that, after committing monetary and other resources, the casino may never open or will close shortly after opening because its owners did not have sufficient financial resources. This concern may become even more acute when the government borrows money to make the infrastructure improvements and is relying on gaming taxes to pay it back. Here, the casino's financial failure may bankrupt or severely strain the government.

Governments may also have a concern as to the financial stability of the casino when it is meant to serve as an icon for tourism. In this environment, where one or two casinos in a resort area are meant to provide a spectacular amenity to promote tourism, casino closure may spoil that tourism. Not only would the closing eliminate the amenity, but if the casino is well known, it may signal to the tourist market that the location is declining as a destination.

---

[62] Frontier Economics, Dept. for Educ. & Skills, An Economic Review and Analysis of the Implications of Occupational Licensing (2003), http://webarchive.nationalarchives.gov.uk/20130401151715/https://www.education.gov.uk/publications/eOrderingDownload/RR467.pdf.

In a competitive economy, the government may have fewer concerns about a new gaming operation's economic viability particularly where adequate assurances are in place to protect player's funds and/or government tax revenues. Market forces often are the best judge of what is viable. If this is done by the government, in the licensing context, the market may lose a potential competitor that could succeed by introducing innovations or creating new markets. The government, however, may have some legitimate concerns. For example, will the operator go to some unsuitable source to get money if times get tough or will it try to create profits by cheating players? Monitoring of the operator and requiring submission of periodic reports, however, can address these concerns.

Similarly, government should not impose absolute restrictions on new casinos to prevent overbuilding. Suppose a mega-resort opens in a market. This resort creates greater competition for players. Initially, this may lower profits to existing casinos that lose patrons to the new resort. The market will be strong enough to support or grow to accommodate the expansion, or the weakest casino will fail. In either case, the market is better off. In the latter case, the quality of the remaining properties is better than before the expansion. With this better stock, this casino market may maintain an edge in competition with casinos and other recreation products elsewhere. Therefore, while the financial ability of an applicant is of some concern to regulators, it may not be necessary to make it a licensing criterion with corresponding barriers to entry in competitive markets where market forces and regulatory oversight provide sufficient protection.

Burden and Standards of Proof

In licensing matters, the burden of proof is usually on the applicant. This should require the applicant to provide affirmative evidence of its suitability that exceeds the minimum licensing standards. This would seem logical because the applicant has the most direct access to the information regulators use to decide suitability. If the applicant cannot produce this evidence, then it probably does not exist. The idea that the applicant "proves" his suitability is misleading. In practice, the applicant merely provides the requested information and documentation. Absent regulators discovering bad acts that raise doubts about the applicant's suitability, the application will be approved. Still the notion of the applicant carrying the burden has meaning because the applicant must provide evidence of good acts or that cast bad acts in the best light and carries the burden to persuade the regulators of his suitability based on all the evidence whether offered by the applicant or discovered by the regulators.

Given discretion to either grant or deny a license, regulators must assess the evidence uncovered in an application against some standard. This can be predefined or left to regulators' intuition. Suppose a person was convicted of theft 20 years ago, and a licensing criterion is honesty. Theft involves dishonesty. Therefore, the theft evidenced the person's lack of honesty. If regulators are compelled to deny a license when any evidence exists to suggest that the applicant does not qualify, the person would be denied. Suppose, further, that the person has led an exemplary life since a conviction for taking the cement bear mascot from a motel's lawn as a college prank. Under a lesser standard, he would probably obtain a license.

Generally, decisions are not made by stacking evidence on opposite sides of the scale and choosing the side with the most substantial evidence. Rather, even when the final decision is left to the discretion of regulators, the decision-makers must "weigh" the evidence to measure it against some standard. Perhaps the most commonly recognized standards are "beyond a reasonable doubt" and "a preponderance of evidence." The former emanates from the standard used in criminal trials; the evidence supporting a verdict should eliminate any reasonable doubt that a contrary conclusion could be reached.

The latter standard, "a preponderance of the evidence," is the common standard for a civil trial. This "scale of justice" test requires the decision-maker to look at the evidence and choose which of different conclusions is more likely to be true.

Another standard is "clear and convincing evidence." This standard calls for the party with the burden of proof to provide "clear and convincing evidence" to support the requested decision. This standard places greater responsibility on the burdened party than a preponderance of the evidence standard, but less than the standard beyond a reasonable doubt.

An even higher burden than "beyond a reasonable doubt" would be to prove a matter "beyond any doubt." If an applicant for a gaming license must prove his suitability "beyond any doubt," he has a substantial burden. If the investigation revealed any evidence that raised any doubt as to his suitability, then the agency would have to deny the application. Suppose the applicant was convicted of shoplifting while a college student but had no other criminal transgressions. This instance alone might create doubt as to his suitability but may not rise to the level of reasonable doubt.

The highest burden is when the applicant must prove that no evidence exists showing he is unsuitable to hold a license. This is an unrealistic standard because virtually every person has some incidents in their lifetime that would provide negative evidence. Usually, however, such incidents are minor and should not disqualify the person from holding a license.

Standards of proof should vary depending on the state's public policy. Under both player and government protection goals, the government has a strong interest in ensuring that unsuitable persons are not involved in the gaming industry. The level to which this standard rises depends on the intensity of the government's policy. If the government insists on and enforces a "clear and convincing" standard, it will have a high-efficiency rate, i.e., it will likely keep out nearly all criminal elements. It also will create a barrier to entry. As the government increases the level of the standard of proof, criminal elements will be less likely to infiltrate the gaming industry, but the barriers to entry will become more insurmountable.

Although rarely codified in statute or regulation, variable standards may apply in a single jurisdiction. Variations may occur in relation to reward or based on the type of approval sought. The former involves applying different standards to applications based on the potential benefits that the jurisdiction can derive from approving the application. This type of analysis is more likely encountered in jurisdictions pursing government protection goals, where the government's economic interest is the major reason for the regulatory system.

Examples are more readily available when reviewing a jurisdiction's evolution or demise. In the 1940s, Nevada licensed many persons considered to be notorious criminal figures, including Benjamin "Bugsy" Siegel. The standards imposed then were far less stringent than today. The change in standards, which are definable from the 1940s to the present, can be correlated to the economic status of the Nevada casino industry. When Siegel proposed the Flamingo Hilton in the late 1940s, Nevada did not have a single major hotel. The prospects for development without Siegel's money were distant. Few mainstream entrepreneurs expressed any interest in an industry considered immoral and corrupt by many. Therefore, those who licensed Siegel accepted the substantial risk of negative publicity and the possibility of federal intervention for the potential reward of development, employment, and tourism expansion.

As Nevada's industry grew, the potential reward of licensing notorious or questionable applicants diminished. Other investors without problem backgrounds became a source of investment. Less desirable applicants and licensees eventually became a deterrent to encouraging legitimate investment and a threat to the casino industry. The late 1950s and early 1960s saw a substantial increase in the risks associated with licensing notorious or questionable applicants. With a thriving industry, coupled with a growing legitimacy acquired after Howard Hughes and others bought casinos, the potential reward from licensing less desirable applicants diminished. The licensing standard became more stringent.

Regulators also may apply a variable standard based on a risk/reward analysis even to contemporaneous applicants. This can happen when an industry is in demise. To attract fresh investment, a jurisdiction that had strict standards of proof may relax them to attract new investors. Likewise, an applicant who provides potential to improve the general economy of a jurisdiction through development and employment offers greater reward. Therefore, regulators may be more willing to assume a greater risk that an applicant will not meet minimum standards where the applicant offers the possibility of substantial reward. This analysis is never defined by statute or regulation, and rarely would a regulator admit it is the basis for a licensing decision. Despite having a logical basis, the belief that applicants for similar licenses might be given unequal evaluation seems contrary to the belief that economic standing should not be the basis for different legal consideration.

Levels of Review

Levels of licensing review in regulatory systems consist of tiers, which categorize groups of individuals or entities associated with the gaming industry. Each tier is then subject to a different level of licensing scrutiny. For example, regulators may extend the breadth of licensing to both owners and gaming employees. The level of review, however, might be different. Owners may undergo a thorough investigation that requires the regulators to spend months vetting virtually all aspects of the owner's life, while the review of gaming employees may simply be a check of their police records. These checks take on several forms depending on the jurisdiction. In British Columbia, licensing authorities review personal background information, financial information, participation in legal activities, and criminal records, to determine whether the owner can be licensed.[63] In contrast, Nevada requires gaming employees like a dealer to obtain a work card after undergoing a police database and other nominal review. From an economic perspective, these tiers can be seen as corresponding barriers; high scrutiny is a substantial barrier to entry, and low scrutiny is a minor barrier.

Placing a group into a tier requires consideration of four factors, the first of which is the relationship between the group under consideration and public policy goals. If the principal governmental policy is to assure the honesty of the game, the obvious persons who must obtain licenses are the game operators. Therefore, owners who can influence operations by position of authority and have much to gain by cheating patrons pose the highest risk and often undergo the most demanding review. Likewise, if government's policy attempts to prevent casino profits from going to criminals who may use them to fund criminal operations, then the span of the most stringent investigation might reach persons sharing in profits from the games. Another example is where a government goal is to ensure that criminals have no involvement of any nature with the industry. This may mandate that suppliers of non-gaming goods and services undergo the highest regulatory scrutiny.

A second consideration is the need to maintain a level of regulatory control over a group. This may vary between jurisdictions. Suppose organized crime in a jurisdiction has strong influence over labor unions and the construction trade. This may justify moving labor unions and construction contractors into a higher tier that gives regulators greater ability to scrutinize their involvement with the casino industry. If the nature of legal gaming within the jurisdiction will not produce large revenues, at-

---

[63] Michael D. Lipton, *British Columbia, in* INTERNATIONAL CASINO LAW & REGULATION VOL. 1: NORTH AMERICA § 3.09, at 15 (William Thompson ed., 2008).

tracting criminals is less likely and less scrutiny may be justified.

A third consideration is capability and budget. Placing all groups into a mandatory licensing tier with full investigations requires substantial government commitment of trained personnel to conduct investigations, even if there is only a single casino in the jurisdiction. Therefore, as a necessity, a government may place groups into the tiers on a priority basis. For example, the top-tier priority may be owners and operators, followed by persons sharing in profits, distributors, manufacturers, and key employees. The government may assign different levels of licensing scrutiny to each tier considering the budget and capacity of its investigative division. Sometimes, it may only fully investigate owners and operators. In others, it may fully investigate everyone, including key employees.

A fourth consideration is the economic impact of requiring licenses of certain groups. As discussed later in this chapter, requiring licensure may discourage persons from applying because they are unwilling to devote the time, pay the cost, or suffer the embarrassment of the licensing process.

Sometimes, decisions on whether to require certain groups to undergo licensing are based on other considerations. Suppose the legislature decides that the gaming industry must realize revenues quickly to help a dire economic crisis. It may require regulators to forego licensing some groups to meet this goal. Alternatively, it may be politically or legally difficult to subject a group to licensing.

Full licensing

The most expensive and intrusive investigation is a full licensing investigation. Full licensing entails a comprehensive independent review of the applicant's financial history and personal background. Full investigations are expensive because government investigators review primary source materials. For example, rather than relying on an acquittal to determine innocence, government investigators may reinvestigate the incident. They will seek to learn if other evidence, perhaps any that was not admissible in the criminal proceeding, might suggest guilt. In a financial context, investigators may not rely on tax returns but instead analyze cash-flow by reviewing actual deposits and withdrawals to figure out both net worth and source of funds. These investigations are expensive and time consuming.

Often, regulatory agencies have the same investigative procedures for a full investigation regardless of the person or entity seeking a license. This approach is inefficient. If a person is applying to be the casino's Chief Technical Officer, her financial wherewithal is far less important than the owners', but her experience and competence in maintaining and securing critical technology is more important. Full licensing means a complete review is conducted of all aspects of the applicant's involvement in the casino, not a cookie cutter investigation.

Partial licensing

Partial investigation involves reviewing only limited areas on each application. Instead of a field background investigation,[64] regulators may conduct only a computer review of federal, state, and local police data banks. If the review reveals no arrests, convictions, or investigations of the applicant, the regulators may issue a license. Partial investigations provide less protection to the government. A partial investigation usually consists of a criminal history check, reviewing responses from the applicant's references, and sometimes a personal interview.[65] Partial investigations have two disadvantages. They may not provide enough information or personal contact with the applicant to provide a basis for accurate prediction of future conduct; and a cursory investigation with insufficient information verification often yields questionable information.[66] Nevertheless, a partial investigation provides some benefits. Most notably, it may inhibit persons with extensive criminal histories from obtaining employment in the casino. Regulators also may obtain useful derogatory information about applicants from third parties that may lead to denial of the application despite the absence of a negative criminal record. Partial investigation can also include review of necessary certification, such as training, or even some level of proficiency testing.

Limited licenses are commonly issued to gaming employees. In such cases, the extent of the partial investigation can be tiered, with key employees being subjected to higher review than lower-level employees. Similarly, the licenses issued can place specific restrictions on the applicant's employment activities or employment category. For example, New Jersey issues different licenses to key gaming employees, regular gaming employees, and non-gaming employees.[67] To differentiate types of licenses, jurisdictions may use different terminology, such as a work "permit" or "card" for licensing gaming and non-gaming employees.

Transactional and temporary approvals

Transactional and temporary approvals address problems created when the cost of licensing poses an absolute or significant barrier to potential suppliers. A jurisdiction that has only one or a few casinos may have problems in attracting casino suppliers if they must undergo a full licensing investigation to sell a small amount of goods. This may prevent the goods from being available or available at a price that not only includes the cost of licensing but also the reduction in competition created. For example,

---

[64] See Chapter 16 regarding field investigations where agents spend considerable time outside the offices gathering information on applicants.

[65] Rhode, *supra* note 14, at 512.

[66] *Id.*

[67] *See generally,* Nicholas Casiello, Jr., *New Jersey, in* INTERNATIONAL CASINO LAW 121 (Anthony Cabot et al., eds., 3d ed. 1999).

gaming device manufacturers may attempt to be the first manufacturer to obtain a license in a small market. If a manufacturer succeeds, it can grab a significant market share of the total potential market. The considerations for other manufacturers to seek a license now differ because the total potential sales in that jurisdiction are less. If other manufacturers decide not to enter the market, the sole licensed manufacturer has monopoly power and may charge corresponding prices.

A transactional approval allows the applicant to enter a specific transaction, such as supplying a fixed number of gaming devices to a casino. Before granting a transactional approval, regulators may require some background information and full disclosure of the transaction that is the subject of the approval.

A temporary approval allows the supplier to make unlimited sales in a jurisdiction for a limited time. Temporary approvals can create a competitive market before the regulatory agency can process the applications of competing suppliers. By granting several temporary licenses, regulators can assure a competitive market at its inception. Even in established markets, regulators can use temporary approvals to rectify market imperfections quickly. This allows introduction of competing products pending the completion of a full investigation.

Preliminary Approvals

A preliminary approval differs from a temporary approval in that the former does not allow the applicant to engage in the licensed activity but suggests he likely will be approved, absent changed circumstances. Suppose an applicant wishes to invest $800 million in a new casino but has never been licensed. A preliminary approval gives it some assurances the proposed location and design of the new casino are suitable before committing its capital. Because incidents may occur between the preliminary and final approvals, regulators may reserve discretion to change the preliminary approval if new facts show the applicant is unsuitable.

Final Approvals

A final approval can have different levels of permanency. One common application limits the license to a fixed period, such as three years. At the end of this period, the license expires. Therefore, before the end of the period, the licensee must reapply for a new gaming license if it wishes to continue operations. This method has various advantages. First, it provides regulators an opportunity to periodically investigate and review their licensees to ensure they are meeting the minimum regulatory standards. Second, it may deter licensees from committing acts that fall below these minimum standards because the periodic investigation is likely to expose these transgressions. Third, regulators may not have to accord full due-process rights to a licensee seeking a new license but would have to afford such rights if it attempted to revoke a license.

Requiring periodic relicensing has various disadvantages. First, it is expensive. Investigations of applicants, particularly large corporations, can be costly for both regulators and applicants. Licensees attempt to pass these extra costs on to the patrons as higher costs. Second, investigations consume both agency and licensee time and effort and divert their efforts from other business. Where the licensee is conscientious, it may be a poor use of agency and licensee time. Third, it introduces more risk to the business opportunity. All other things being equal, a company looking to invest in a casino may choose a jurisdiction where a license can be revoked only by a disciplinary action as opposed to expiring on specified dates. Fourth, financial markets may be less willing to lend funds to a company whose license expires before the loan is due because without a license, the company may not be able to pay the loan.

A jurisdiction can use both temporary and permanent approvals. One method mandates that all first-time licenses are temporary and expire after a (probationary) time, but that the second license is a permanent license. Another method allows the regulators to decide whether a license will be temporary or permanent.

Breadth of Licensing

The casino gaming ecosphere has many participants. Besides the owner and operator of the casino, others—such as employees, contractors, and suppliers of many types of gaming and non-gaming equipment, goods and services—may have integral roles in creating and operating a casino. Breadth means the extent to which a government requires these categories of persons or entities to obtain a license.

Breadth of licensing prevents unsuitable persons from attempting to influence or profit from operations through control of labor, goods, or services critical to the casino.[68] Suppose a casino operator has a valid license but an unsuitable associate wants a hidden interest in the operation. Licensing may prevent the associate from directly sharing in the net profits. The associate's challenge is to obtain the profits without attracting the attention of the gaming regulators. Methods to siphon profits from the casino include selling goods or services to the casino at prices far beyond market price, charging exorbitant "finder's" fees for arranging financing for the casino, and skimming.

Breadth of licensing also can relate to how government achieves other goals, such as preventing persons from being cheated. An operator's honesty does not guaranty that individual gaming devices will not cheat the patron. If government views hidden interests, cheating, or other matters

---

[68] Lester B. Snyder, *Regulation of Legalized Gambling, An Inside View*, 12 CONN. L. REV. 665, 714 (1980).

as potentially detrimental to its public policy, then some level of licensing beyond the operator must be carried out.

The following is a description of the various groups involved in the gaming industry and their regulatory sensitivity.

Owners

Owners hold the rights to conduct the casino business. Owners may operate or hire a manager to run the casino for them. While owners who are not operators may not have direct contact with the gaming tables or equipment or with customers, they may have the rights to gaming profits and the ability to hire and fire the manager.

Owners can pose high risks to player protection goals. The owner can have direct influence over the honesty and fairness of the gaming operations and control over player funds. The owner bears financial responsibility and can implement all the systems and procedures to ensure that players are protected from third party cheating, privacy violations, and data theft. Owners also have primary responsibility for implementing compliance systems and programs designed to address problem gambling and other regulatory requirements.

Owners also can pose a high risk to government protection goals. A government must consider not only the potential influence that an owner has over an operation, but also public perception of unsuitable owners. The owner is typically the most visible person to the public.

Therefore, under both government protection or player protection goals, owners typically are given highest priority.

Operators

Operators have the right to conduct gaming at a casino. They pose a high risk to most government goals. Operators deal directly with the patron, control the play of the game, and have responsibility for accounting. Under the player protection goals, the government is protecting the patron from the operator. Most controls under these goals seek to restrain the activities of the operator. The operator is seen as the potential exploiter, who, given the opportunity, would stimulate demand for gaming and encourage irresponsible play.

The operator's risk profile is equally important in the government protection goals. Industry reputation and public trust are most injured if an operator is revealed as having cheated patrons or is associated with criminals.

Landlords

Landlords own or lease the land or buildings housing the casino but contractually transfer the rights to another party to occupy and operate the casino. A casino can have more than one landlord. For example, one person can own the land, and another can own the buildings. In this situation, the building owner can have a long-term land lease, and then lease the building and sublease the land to a casino owner. In a true lease arrangement, the landlord has no substantial influence over the casino owner/operator. It is the equivalent of a mall owner who leases a store to a retailer.

Casino owners who have the right to conduct the business can compensate landlords in different ways, all of which may be commercially reasonable. The most common is fixed payment rents. Under this scenario, the landlord receives a fixed amount for each period during the lease. As an alternative, the landlord may receive a percentage of the gross or net revenues generated by the business. Landlords also can set a fixed minimum rent plus a percentage of the net or gross revenue.

Despite its common commercial use, percentage rents may pose regulatory concerns. If landlords receiving a percentage of gaming revenues are not regulated, then unsuitable and unlicensed persons may obtain casino profits through percentage lease payments. Under government protection goals, the image of a member of organized crime receiving either a fixed rent or a percentage of gaming revenue may be undesirable, even if it is through a lease payment.

In competitive markets with many casinos, attempting to license all landlords may have undesirable economic consequences. As large institutional investors look to find opportunities, they may be attracted to the casino industry, not to own or operate casinos but to make the part of the sizable investment needed to construct the integrated resorts. A preferred method of investment is to own the asset and lease it to another party to own and operate the casino business. Requiring licensure of these investors may raise the cost of capital and lower the prospective investments into the integrated resorts. It may also deter such firms from making investments in deteriorating markets where they seek inexpensive assets for turnaround strategies.

Requiring licensing of landlords in government created monopoly or oligopoly markets based on Requests for Proposals for integrated resorts rarely creates an issue as to either use of regulator resources or disrupting a competitive market. It is the substantial equivalent of the government doing due diligence on its new business partner. The regulators may need to conduct only one or a few more licensing investigations. Requiring licensure of landlords is more prevalent in these environments despite the investigations often focusing on matters not germane to a successful public-private venture.

In competitive economies, regulators may implement controls that reduce the risk of problems with landlords while not requiring mandatory licensing. These include requiring regulatory review of all lease arrangements to ensure they are commercially reasonable. This requires reporting lease changes and periodic auditing of payments to landlords. Fixed rent payments pose less of a problem because it is more difficult for the landlord to structure these payments to obtain a predictable percentage of the casino's revenue.

A second solution is to require a lower level of licensing for landlords that provides some review but is not as substantial a barrier as the full licensing review imposed on owner/operators.

Another compromise to mandatory licensing is discretionary licensing of landlords. Here the government may require that landlords register with regulators or that casino licensees provide reports on ownership, lease terms, or changes to them. Regulators can then review the reports and decide if they want to require any landlord to apply and obtain a license. A problem with this system occurs when an unsuitable person buys the property on which a casino is located and refuses to apply for licensing after being requested or refuses to divest after being found unsuitable. A simple solution is to require the casino to close, but this may be unfair to an innocent casino operator.

Persons entitled to profits

Some vendors (or others) may bargain for their goods or services to be paid for as a percentage of the other party's profits. This can include providing equipment, patent or other intellectual property rights, financing, management, or marketing services. Persons can obtain profits either narrowly from a game, more broadly from the casino revenues, or even more broadly from the general resort operating revenue that includes gaming, hotel, restaurants, and other revenue centers. This is a sensitive area for gaming regulators because ownership interest can be disguised as a vendor's participatory interest in the gaming operation. The potential for abuse has led some states, like Nevada, to require anyone sharing in a percentage of gaming revenues to obtain a license. This rule has the advantage of certainty and ease of application.

Still, the majority of profit participation agreements in the casino space are likely to be legitimate, consistent with existing general industry practices, and arm's length. A good example of parties that might be entitled to share revenue is the junket representative who drives traffic to the casino. The fairest way to compensate a junket representative is on the value of the players they bring to the casino. The value of the player can be calculated based on the player's profitability to the casino considering all factors, and compensation should be a percentage of the profits from that player. If this is prohibited, then the casino must engage in permitted but convoluted payment schemes that attempt to reflect the actual value of the services performed without violating the prohibitions against sharing in revenues.

Governments that tend toward government protection goals are sensitive that allowing persons of unsavory reputation to share in revenues can damage the industry's reputation. Government protection goals and policies would counsel greater attention to the suitability of any parties sharing in profits.

Jurisdictions that tend toward the player protection goals are more concerned with the ability of profit sharers to influence operations based on their relationship. As detailed in the section on the level of review, regulators may decide to tier this group into smaller sub-groups for license review. One distinction could be based on the total revenue paid to a person. Are substantial regulatory concerns invoked if a junket representative is paid a nominal, monthly fee of a few thousand dollars based on a revenue share for recommending and referring players to a casino? Having different levels of licensing, or sometimes no licensing at all, based on cumulative annual payments to vendors and suppliers is common in the gaming industry.

Another possible distinction is based on the entitlement. A person that licenses a game patent and receives a percentage of the net revenues of that game may not have to undergo licensing, but a private person that finances the casino and receives 20 percent of net profits may have to obtain a license. This is because a person who receives a small percentage of the revenue for licensing a game patent is unlikely to have any significant influence over the casino's operation. Exempting such parties from licensing may allow for the creation and promotion of new game content based on the game's real value to the casino. A government may implement tiers and relaxed standards based on other considerations such as for persons sharing in overall revenues of public casino companies or of individual casinos where the party sharing in the revenues is a finance company, and the transaction is typical of financing in broader contexts.

Both government and player protection goals would prescribe policies for licensing at least some parties that share in the profits of the casino. Notably, however, jurisdictions may consider a lower level (or no) licensing (1) when junket or marketing affiliates (who receive a small percentage of revenue for directing players to the casino) or game patent holders (who receive a portion of revenues their games generate) are involved; or (2) in contexts like financing where revenue sharing is practiced.

Lenders/creditors

Lenders/Creditors are common parties to most business agreements. A casino may have many types of creditors. Lenders of money usually are the largest. Other creditors can include suppliers of gaming and non-gaming equipment; financial institutions and others who provide furniture, fixtures, and equipment leases; and vendors that sell on credit. The government may be a creditor if it is owed taxes. Another type of "lender" is a person who buys a debt security, such as a debenture. A debenture is a bond issued by the casino company to evidence the debt owed. Debentures entitle the holder to certain rights, including the payment of interest. Some debentures or bonds are convertible into stock. In other words, a debenture holder can change his status from a debt holder to an equity investor.

While licensing every lender/creditor would ensure that people can neither hide ownership interests in casino operations nor exert undue control over operations, such regulation could be very costly to implement and enforce.

Four considerations surround the regulatory scrutiny accorded creditors. First, creditors who lend money or provide financing expect a return on their money commensurate with the costs and risks involved in the transaction. Second, the initial cost of capital may decrease if the lender shares in revenues. Third, as the amount lent or financed increases, so does the creditor's vested interest in the success of, and potential influence over, the business. Fourth, unsuitable persons may use the cover of lender or creditor not as a method to lend moneys to a gaming operation at market interest rates but as a guise to participate in revenues from the gaming operations without obtaining necessary licensing. Regulations must balance the first two considerations against the latter two in light of public policy.

Full licensing helps ensure that loans are not used to hide ownership in gaming operations and that a party having potential influence over a casino is suitable. Requiring all creditors to obtain a license, however, raises costs and creates barriers that will deter many legitimate lenders. This policy may cause higher interest costs to gaming operators since competition between lenders will be diminished, and lenders will pass investigation costs to borrowers. Likewise, vendors of equipment and goods may not be willing to provide goods on credit if licensing regulations require them to bear the expense of licensing. Such a regime would place the gaming operators in the position of having to either have cash available for purchases or seek loans from a few approved lenders at interest rates potentially higher than the broader market.

Short of full licensing for all creditors, regulators can exempt certain creditors from licensing scrutiny. One possible exemption focuses on the difference between commercial and noncommercial creditors. Three major types of regulated commercial creditors are (1) banks or savings and loan associations, (2) insurance companies, and (3) pension or retirement funds. Exempting commercial creditors from licensing is based on the idea that other government agencies regulate these lenders. These institutions would not likely violate controls prohibiting their involvement in gaming operations because such violations could jeopardize their other licenses. Because they lend money as a business, they spread their risk over many loans. Therefore, these institutions are less likely to feel compelled to influence gaming operations to protect their investment. Finally, the initial structuring of a loan with a commercial creditor is unlikely to be a scam under which the lender is actually an equity participant.

A second possible exemption is based on the extent and context of credit provided. This exemption recognizes that many transactions by noncommercial creditors are done in the ordinary course of business. This may include transactions with suppliers who ship their product, bill the gaming operator, and expect payment within a certain time. Requiring the operator to prepay all suppliers or pay on delivery would burden operators. Therefore, a standard can be set that exempts creditors from obtaining licensing when the credit extended is below a set dollar threshold. Only creditors owed more than a certain amount may have to register with the regulators, and those over a higher amount must obtain a license.

A third possible exemption may be for transactions not secured by gaming assets, such as gaming receipts and gaming stock. This would recognize that lenders with different types of security interests pose different risks. These creditors with a security interest in gaming assets have more a substantial remedy against the gaming operator for failure to pay its debt. A secured creditor of a financially distressed gaming operator can exercise much more control over gaming operations than an unsecured creditor or a secured creditor in non-gaming assets such as vehicles or hotel furnishings. This can also be addressed by requiring registration of secured interests in gaming assets and giving the interests greater scrutiny.

Instead of granting broad exemptions, regulators may require the gaming operator to report all credit transactions. After reviewing the reports, the regulators would then have the discretion to require the creditor to apply and undergo licensing. This allows the regulators to maintain control over the transaction with only minimal interference in financial markets. The mere possibility of having to obtain a license might cause some lenders to refuse to serve the gaming industry, but this possibility will not be as significant an obstacle as mandatory licenses. Regulators can allay many potential lender concerns by judiciously exercising discretion only when serious concerns arise. Another option is to require approval of secured transactions but not necessarily a licensing investigation of the creditor. A third option is to require prior approval for the secured creditor to foreclose on a security interest in gaming equipment, gaming receipts, or stock.

Governments may be best served by taking a balanced approach to licensing lenders and other creditors. While full licensing would prevent hidden ownership interests and protect operators from the undue influence of unsuitable persons, such a licensing regime could cause higher costs for obtaining credit and a dearth in competition among creditors. Several types of creditors could be exempted from licensing requirements without undercutting governmental policy goals. Some jurisdictions may find that an ad hoc review of credit transactions insulates the casino industry from unsuitable or hidden interests.

Suppliers and vendors
Gaming device manufacturers

A state's interest in licensing gaming device manufacturers can increase as technology advances. Gaming devices evolved from simple devices. Early reel-type slot machines did little more than accept and store coins or tokens, mechanically start and randomly stop reels, and make payment on winning combinations. Today, gaming devices are complex, microprocessor-based devices that count wagers and payouts, analyze play, secure wagers and data, provide system maintenance, and market the device.[69] As described in Chapter 11, regulating these devices is complicated and goes beyond the capacity of many regulatory agencies to understand or test.

Complicating matters, multiple suppliers of both hardware and software may contribute to the gaming equipment that ultimately reaches the casino floor. Many non-licensed independent contractors may have touched the code before it is installed in a gaming device. Software evolves, and code is rarely derived from the ground up. With software increasingly being coded by independent contractors in various remote locations, governments cannot guarantee the code has only been handled or vetted by trusted resources. A licensed manufacturer may use independent contractors based around the world to write portions of the software code that may be integrated into a slot machine or gaming system.

The process on how these independent contractors work has been described as follows:

> A typical model involves independent contractors submitting a proposal to the manufacturer in accordance with written development agreements. Once a project is approved, the independent contractor typically is granted access to a web-based interface platform (commonly referred to as a game development kit) designed and controlled by the licensed manufacturer. The game development kit provides documentation and technical support through which the independent contractor designs source code files. These source code files may include paytables, reel maps, and evaluation functions. Game kits can also facilitate development by allowing prototype games to post simulated win and loss events to an operating system program of the manufacturer in a test environment. Other uses of contractors include hiring specialized engineering firms which employ dozens of programmers to perform massive rewrites and revisions of code for operating systems, games, and slot accounting systems.

Another contractor issue can arise when an individual presents a prototype running on an "off-the-shelf" or homegrown system on a personal computer. If the licensed manufacturer chooses to manufacture the game, the manufacturer will take the game and recode it for use on its own platform. When an independent contractor completes a project, it submits the

---

[69] *See generally*, Leslie E. Cummings & Kathleen Brewer, *An Evolutionary View of the Critical Functions of Slot Machine Technology*, 1 Gaming Res. & Rev. J. 67–68 (1995).

source code files to the manufacturer's engineering department. If accepted, the game source code files become the manufacturer's property subject to the manufacturer's exclusive control, in exchange for payment specified within the agreement. The manufacturer's engineering department will then review the game source code submitted by the independent contractor. Once vetted, the licensed manufacturer compiles and creates a single game computer program, combining game source code, as well as the sound and art files provided by employees or other independent contractors. The result of this compilation process is a game program that operates on a gaming device using the manufacturer's proprietary operating system and ready for regulatory approval.[70]

Because the honesty of the gaming devices is important under both player and government protection goals, the manufacturers of gaming devices are typically given the highest priority for licensing. More problematic is determining which (if any) independent contractors for either hardware or software should have to obtain a license.

An issue is whether these independent contractors can produce flaws or embed bad code that compromises the honesty or fairness of the games. If a manufacturer should have to obtain a license, at what point should those providing software or hardware have to do the same? At what point is a manufacturer merely assembling hardware and software components in contrast to manufacturing? The extent to which a jurisdiction requires independent contractors to be licensed may depend on how confident the government is in its ability, either internally or through outside laboratories, to establish and enforce quality and security protocols and to test the software and functionality of gaming devices to ensure they meet policy goals related to fairness, honesty (randomness) and reliability.[71]

A common approach is not to require suppliers to obtain a license, but to place the responsibility for the final product on the manufacturer and/or the testing procedures to ensure an honest product reaches the casino floor. This requires the manufacturer to undertake due diligence on the supplier and have the technical capacity and quality and security protocols to review and integrate all the hardware and software to ensure the final product meets all standards, including honesty. In essence, this delegates responsibilities to the manufacturer to assume responsibility over design, assembly, and operation of the gaming device. Complete delegation, however, raises the concerns that a licensed manufacturer will act undetected

---

[70] Dan R. Reaser, *Regulation of Gaming Device Software Development: Nevada's Paradigm Shift on Independent Contractors* 2 UNLV GAMING L.J. 1 (2011).

[71] *Id.* Technology has two edges. The positive aspect is that governments and licensees can use it as a tool through certification, oversight, and reporting to bring greater transparency to every gaming transaction. An important issue is whether the given jurisdiction has the expertise and assets to use technology to its advantage. A potentially problematic trend is for regulators to cede authority to regulate gaming technology to independent laboratories. In these jurisdictions, regulators may not have the fundamental ability to determine whether a gaming device or equipment is functioning properly or honestly.

in its own interest instead of serving public goals or will become a surrogate for unlicensed manufacturers who manufacture most, if not all, of the gaming device.[72]

Another approach is to identify what independent contractors can do without having to obtain a license. This requires that the hardware and software components of a gaming device be segregated and licensing be required if the independent contractor provides sensitive components. For example, regulations can require licensing of any independent contractors that provide control programs, including any software, source language, or executable code that affects the result of a wager by determining win or loss (such as the random number generation process or mapping of random numbers to game elements displayed as part of game outcome).[73]

Manufacturers of gaming and associated equipment

Unlike the high technology of the modern gaming devices, some gaming equipment is still mechanical, such as roulette tables and the big wheels. These types of devices decide whether the patron wins or loses. Their operation can be altered to cheat the patron or casino. Therefore, the equipment commands some regulatory attention. The most conservative approach requires both the manufacturer and the equipment to be licensed. The effect of this approach is that some games may not be offered. Suppose a monopoly casino has a need for two roulette tables, but the regulators require their manufacturer to obtain a license. No manufacturer will pay the cost of licensing to earn a profit on two tables. Because the equipment can be easily inspected and tested, however, many jurisdictions do not require these types of equipment manufacturers to obtain a license. This assures that the casinos have suppliers of equipment.

Casinos also use what is commonly called "associated equipment." This is any equipment used in connection with gaming. The most sensitive associated equipment from a regulatory perspective is that which is necessary for gameplay. This includes dice, playing cards, and pai gow tiles. All of this equipment can be altered to allow an unscrupulous person to either cheat the casino or the patron. Neither has been problematic in the recent past, however, because it requires a broad conspiracy. To cheat a player using altered equipment, both the casino and the manufacturer must participate. The manufacturer must make the cheating equipment, and the casino must use it. This is unlikely in a regulated environment where the casinos are licensed and monitored and the equipment subject to inspection.

The next level of equipment is that which has no other use, except in casino gaming. Any computer equipment that links to a modern gaming device may pose concerns because of the possibility it can alter the play of the gaming device. For example, a progressive meter may be designed to alter the play of the device to "create" a jackpot when the meter hits a

---

[72] Id.
[73] Id.

certain dollar amount. If the person that created the rogue program can arrange for an associate to be playing the device at a specified time, he can profit from the jackpot.

Common Forms of Electronic Associated Equipment[74]

Nevada implemented a licensing requirement for manufacturers of cashless wagering systems in 1996. These systems facilitate wagering through computers that allow players to wager without using chips, tokens, or United States legal tender. A common and also proprietary methodol-

Figure 15.4

Automatic Shufflers (Mechanical and with an RNG)	Ball Drawing Devices - Automated Reader
Ball Drawing Devices - Manual	Bill Validator (Used in a Gaming Device or Associated Equipment)
Bingo Systems	Bingo Systems with Electronic Bingo Cards
Bingo Systems - In-House Progressive Payoff Schedules	Bingo Inter Casino Linked Systems
Cage and Credit Systems	Cage and Credit Systems
Coin Counters (Interfaced with a Gaming System or Associated Equipment)	On-line Slot Metering Systems and
Cashless Wagering Systems	Computerized Keno Systems
Currency Counters (Interfaced with a Gaming System or Associated Equipment)	On-line Slot Metering Systems,
Cashless Wagering Systems and Table Games	Keno Display Board
Progressive Controllers	Progressive Sign Controllers
Race, Sports and Pari-Mutuel Systems	Remote Access Equipment
Slot Monitoring Systems	Slot Player Tracking Systems
Soft Count Systems	Electronic Shoes

ogy is called Ticket In Ticket Out (TITO) where players insert currency into a bill acceptor on a gaming device and establish credits on the device. The credits increase or decrease depending on play. At the conclusion of play, a player with credits receives a ticket printed at the device indicating the credits. The ticket can be redeemed for cash at a redemption kiosk or cashier station or inserted into another gaming device for continued play. Other cashless wagering systems are available based on the concept that a central computer administers, monitors, accounts, and retains the wagers between the casino and players. Some new jurisdictions, like Ohio, are mandating casinos use cashless wagering.[75]

Nevada regulators at the time justified this licensing requirement as follows:

> Because of the importance of cashless wagering systems in determining the accuracy of gross revenue calculations, it was apparent to the Board that the regulatory system needed the authority to hold manufacturers and distributors of these systems to the same standards as other gaming licensees. Additionally, it was necessary to establish and enforce minimum standards and controls on these systems to prevent the systems from illegally tampering. Enactment of AB 626 gave state regulators the necessary tools to

---

[74] Nevada Gaming Control Board, Associated Equipment Matrix (2010), http://gaming. nv.gov/modules/showdocument.aspx?documentid=2772.
[75] OHIO REV. CODE ANN. § 3772.22 (West 2010).

investigate and license manufacturers and distributors of these systems and to require such systems to meet minimum internal control requirements.[76]

The least sensitive associated equipment is of the type that has other applications, such as stools and surveillance equipment.

A tiered-licensing structure may require licensing or registration of the manufacturers and distributors of the most sensitive associated equipment and require no licensing or registration of the least sensitive. It may also require inspection, testing, and approval of certain types of equipment.

Suppliers of gaming devices or associated equipment

Unlike a manufacturer, suppliers do not build gaming devices or equipment but act as middlemen, buying the devices or equipment from manufacturers or others and selling them to casinos. The devices can be new or old.

Regulators justify requiring suppliers of gaming devices and equipment to undergo some level of licensing scrutiny on various grounds. First, if a single person or a group acting together control the supply of gaming devices or equipment, that person or group can exert significant control over the operator. Second, the supplier also may have temporary custody and control over the gaming devices or equipment. This may allow for alterations to the game's operation that might allow the supplier to cheat the machines or the casino to cheat the patron. Third, suppliers have control over the destination of gaming devices. A concern is that legal gaming devices do not end in the hands of illegal gaming operators elsewhere. Assuring supplier integrity decreases the flow of devices to these illegal operations. This not only prevents the risk of scandal, but it makes it more difficult and expensive for the illegal operator to conduct business. This may affect a government that wishes to decrease competition to its legal casinos from nearby illegal casinos.

A government may treat suppliers of equipment differently for licensing purposes. Gaming devices are the most sensitive. Suppliers of gaming devices may have to obtain a license. On the other hand, the suppliers of blackjack or craps tables, which can do nothing to affect game play, may not have to obtain a license. This allows regulators to focus their efforts and resources on areas of greater regulatory sensitivity and not disrupt the economics in other areas. A criticism of New Jersey's system is the failure to distinguish between types of suppliers and the requirement that the makers of blackjack tables obtain a license. According to one study, "This non-selective system is both illogical on its face and an impediment to the industry in obtaining a wider range of suppliers of non-gaming goods for use on the floor of a casino."[77]

---

[76] William A. Bible, *1993: A Good Year For Gaming*, 1 GAMING RES. & REV. J. 1 (1994).

[77] POLICY MANAGEMENT AND COMMUNICATIONS, INC., CROSS ROADS: CASINO REGULATION IN NEW JERSEY: THE CASE FOR REFORM 35 (June 1994).

Suploiers of non-casino goods and services

Casinos, like other businesses, purchase a variety of non-casino goods and services. They can include mundane things such as uniforms, beds, televisions, cleaning supplies, and food products. They also can include major goods, such as liquor or food, or services, such as constructing a new casino or running the hotel, restaurants, or other non-gaming portions of a complex.

Three major regulatory concerns exist regarding the suppliers of non-casino goods or services. The first concern arises when a person or defined group controls the entire source of the supply and, therefore, can use its influence to charge the casinos extraordinary fees, acquire a hidden percentage of the revenues or exert influence over operations.

This concern has an historical basis. Benjamin "Bugsy" Siegel was a member of the New York crime organization, "Murder, Inc." He was, by anyone's definition, a person unsuitable to hold a gaming license. In the 1930s and 1940s, a major activity of Murder, Inc., was monopoly control over the wire services. For a race book to operate, it needs information from the track on post positions, starting times, track odds, order of finish, and track pay-outs. Siegel realized that if he could control the information, he could extract high fees from legal and illegal bookmakers that relied on the information for their livelihood. Creating a monopoly was not a significant problem. Following World War II, a new war of sorts broke out, known as the "great wire-service war." People died, including the owner of the largest wire service. After the bleeding stopped, only a few wire services remained. Siegel and his associates controlled all of them. This situation created problems for the race books, which Siegel forced to pay monopolistic prices for the track information. Although Siegel did not employ economists to help him set prices, he used roughly set fees at the highest rate possible without putting the books out of business. The books had no choice: either they paid or Siegel refused to supply the information. He could also discriminate against certain race books by charging different rates. Through his monopoly, Siegel secured partial ownership of some casinos instead of collecting the exorbitant prices.

A second regulatory concern arises when supplying non-casino goods or services is used as a front for ownership by unsuitable persons. A person might use a "clean" applicant as a front to apply for and obtain the casino license but operate the casino under the guise of being the hotel operator.

Similarly, a non-licensed person with a hidden interest in the casino could use his position as a supplier to extract casino profits. If the person has a 10 percent interest in a casino which earns $100,000 in net profits, that person, if licensed, would be entitled to $10,000. If the unlicensed person supplies meat to the casino with a fair market value of $30,000, he may extract his casino profits by charging $40,000 to the casino.

Practical impossibilities exist to license all suppliers. Only suppliers who receive a major amount of revenue from the casinos will consider undergoing licensing scrutiny, not because of unsuitability, but because of the cost. Therefore, the casinos could not buy small amounts of supplies, replacement parts, or hire technicians to repair things such as copy machines. In many areas, those who undergo licensing would have a monopoly and could charge monopolistic prices to the casinos. Therefore, requiring all suppliers to obtain a license is impractical. A common solution is to either retain discretion to license suppliers or to require review only in certain areas or above certain amounts.

A third regulatory concern arises when supplying equipment or systems that directly tie to casino revenues, game honesty, or player data protections. Besides surveillance systems, other systems commonly found in casino resorts include back-office casino accounting that provides information such as audit trails, slot and live-game summary reports, main-cage consolidation, staff planning, and security access/video surveillance. Slot machine management systems detail individual machine events, tilt alerts and management, transaction searches, auto cash box and hopper counts, bar code printing and management, cash-desk management, and machine performance analysis reports. Player-tracking systems include patron loyalty programs, player extracts and analysis, group and promotion tracking, and single player cards. Table games management systems provide float management for vault input/output control, live-game monitoring using chip readers, bill readers and peripheral devices, cash-desk management, and table management. Casino marketing systems provide customer relationship marketing tools for promotional mailing, target audience segmentation, point-of-sale customer kiosks, players' club tracking and management, entrance-flow analysis, player-tracking, and promotional display animation. Hospitality management systems automate hotel functions such as guest bookings/details, reservations, point of sale, telephone, accounts receivable, sales and marketing, banquets, food and beverage costing, materials management, maintenance management and quality management. They may interface with property management systems such as central reservation systems and revenue or yield management systems, front and back office accounting, point of sale, door-locking, pay-tv, energy management and payment card authorization.

Persons doing business on the casino premises

Casinos often have many persons who are not employees working on the casino premises. These can include persons who rent space, such as shopkeepers, travel agents, and hair stylists, or those who pay the casino owner for the right to sell goods or services directly to patrons, such as roaming cigarette salespeople, photographers, florists, or valet parkers.[78]

---

[78] A state law allowing regulators to require persons doing business on the premises of a casino to submit to licensing has withstood constitutional challenge from the owner of

Unsuitable persons in this category may benefit from having a presence in the casino for three primary reasons. First, if the person has a hidden interest in the casino, having a business on the casino premises explains being at the casino while he protects his interests in the casino.

Second, some casino concessions may be very lucrative, particularly, if the concession fees are artificially low. Suppose an unsuitable person shares in casino profits. Profits taken directly from the casino would cause detection, so he must derive profits from other sources. The sales of cigarettes to patrons may be lucrative. In a competitive market, the casino would sell this concession to the highest bidder. If the casino owner, however, wishes to allow an unsuitable person to reap extraordinary profits, he might sell the concession at below market price. The unsuitable person could then retain profits that would otherwise flow to the casino.

Third, even in a competitive environment, unsuitable persons may be attracted to businesses that operate on casino premises. This may be for legitimate reasons, such as knowing the concession business and profiting from it. On the other hand, such persons may use the opportunity to promote unlawful businesses, such as loan-sharking, prostitution, or drug sales. Under both government protection and player protection goals, regulators have a strong interest in assuring persons doing business on the casino premises are not engaged in illegal activity that would prey on the patrons. Under government protection goals, regulators have additional concerns that the industry may be damaged by the potential public reaction to the casino's association with an unsuitable person.

A jurisdiction may require all persons who do business on casino premises to obtain a license. This, however, can directly affect the profitability of the casinos. With a licensing requirement, fewer vendors will bid for concessions. This probably will cause lower concession fees. Vendors will figure the costs of licensing in their bids and probably bid even lower. In an extreme case, no vendors may bid on concessions with marginal or small profit potential.

An alternative to mandatory licensing gives the regulators the discretion to require these persons to obtain a license. The latter does not disturb the competitive markets for concessions, but provides the regulators the ability to control this area.

---

two shops in Nevada casino-hotels. In that case, state regulators ordered the shop owner to apply for suitability to have an association with a casino. Rather than go through a regulatory hearing, the shop owner filed a state court action seeking to invalidate the law. State v. Glusman, 98 Nev. 412, 651 P.2d 639 (1982). The Nevada Supreme Court ultimately held the law to be constitutional. The Court reasoned that the restrictions have a legitimate purpose to control potential threats to the continued viability of gaming. The Court felt that the law did not infringe upon constitutional rights of association because it concerns business associations, not political or social associations. The Court concluded that a "person or entity voluntarily situated and doing business within such proximity of a gaming establishment cannot override legitimate governmental control mechanisms . . . [because] to do so would substantially frustrate the State's capacity to regulate the gaming industry." *Glusman*, 651 P.2d at 648.

Gaming schools

Gaming schools provide instruction to persons wishing to learn how to deal casino games or to repair gaming devices. Gaming schools rarely pose substantial regulatory concerns. In some places, however, they may justify closer scrutiny. This would be the rare circumstance where a gaming school operator can assert influence over, or gain profits from, casinos because he or a small group controls the availability of casino employees. This, however, is extremely difficult in most casino industries because the casinos could set up in-house training if the availability of trained employees became scarce.

Regulators also may have an interest in ensuring gaming schools properly train their students so students can protect the game from third-party cheats and will follow all procedures needed to protect the casino assets. Still, casinos have the same interest. If a school is providing inadequate instruction, casinos are unlikely to continue to hire their graduates.

Finally, regulators may be concerned with whether the public's trust in the industry's integrity would be impaired if the media revealed that a gaming school operator was a felon or had connections to organized crime. Because gaming schools are not directly associated with the casinos, however, this type of adverse publicity is less damaging than if the person owned, operated, or had a business in a casino. Requiring registration and allowing discretionary licensing may deter unsuitable persons from establishing gaming schools.

Labor organizations

Labor unions can pose substantial regulatory concerns. Two primary factors determine the level of concern. The first factor is the strength of the labor unions in the casino industry. Where many casino employees are union members, the union may exert substantial influence over the casino by threats of labor disruption. The second factor is the involvement of criminals in the labor union. If the union has a long history of criminal influence, the risk exists that criminals will attempt to use the union to extort or profit from the casino.[79]

---

[79] In the United States, regulators have special considerations in even attempting to subject unions to licensing scrutiny. Normally, the federal government has exclusive regulatory control over labor unions. Federal labor organization regulation is primarily found in three major federal statutes: The Labor Management Relations Act of 1947, § 29 U.S.C. §141 et seq. (1947); The Labor-Management Reporting and Disclosure Act of 1959, §29 U.S.C. §401 et seq. (1959); and The Employee Retirement Income Security Act of 1974, 29 U.S.C. §1001 et seq. (1974). Federal law establishes criteria for disqualification of union officials, including membership in a communist organization and conviction of certain crimes. As a rule of constitutional law, when Congress comprehensively regulates an area, federal law preempts state regulation. *See* Rice v. Santa Fe Elevator Corp. 331 U.S. 218 (1947). The question arises whether federal law preempts state regulation of gaming-related labor unions. The United States Supreme Court addressed, and partially answered,

Recommendation

As detailed above, the breadth of licensing is highly contextual. Apart from owners and operators, who should be given the highest licensure priority, the need for licensing depends greatly on the extent to which a party

---

this question in 1984. New Jersey has a statutory scheme to regulate labor unions involved in the casino industry. N.J. STAT. ANN. § 5:12 et seq. Under it, regulators can require key labor union officials to meet certain qualifications. The law allows regulation of labor unions that represent employees working in both gambling activities and related service industries. The law also includes enforcement procedures. In 1981, the New Jersey statutory scheme came under challenge when regulators recommended that hearings be held on whether a union complied with the regulation. The union sued in State District Court in New Jersey for injunctive and declaratory relief. It argued that federal law preempted the New Jersey law. The union also argued that the New Jersey law violated the First, Fifth, and Fourteenth Amendments to the United States Constitution. Hotel & Restaurant Employees & Bartenders Int'l Union Local 54 v. Danzinger, 536 F. Supp. 317 (D.N.J. 1982). After the District Court decided the law was constitutional, the union appealed to the United States Supreme Court. Brown v. Hotel & Restaurant Employees & Bartenders Int'l Union Local 54, 468 U.S. 491 (1984). The Supreme Court was faced with determining whether the National Labor Relations Act precluded New Jersey from mandating certain qualifications for labor union officials. In a four to three decision (with two judges abstaining), the Court held that the Federal Act "does not preclude . . . imposition of qualification standards on casino industry union officials. . . ." *Id.* at 510. In reaching this decision, the Court did not decide whether the sanctions imposed by the New Jersey Act were permissible. The Court remanded the case to the lower court to decide whether a ban on collecting dues as an enforcement procedure would seriously conflict with the union's statutory function as a bargaining representative. Before the Court, on remand, could decide whether the enforcement procedures were constitutional, the regulators changed their stance and rendered the issue moot. On the remaining issues, the District Court held that the New Jersey Act did not violate the union's First Amendment right to act for its members, and that the "qualification provisions" were not unconstitutionally vague or overbroad. Hotel & Restaurant Employees & Bartenders Int'l Union Local 54 v. Read, 641 F. Supp. 757 (D.N.J. 1986). Taking these decisions together, it is still not clear whether the enforcement procedures would be upheld. Still, the courts probably will allow states to enforce some regulations on gaming-related labor unions. Three months after the US Supreme Court's decisions on the preemption issue, Congress enacted amendments to the Labor-Management Reporting and Disclosure Act of 1959 (LRMDA). *See* § 28 U.S.C. § 524a. The amendments provide that states can enact and enforce a comprehensive statutory scheme to eliminate the threat of pervasive racketeering activity. These statutes, however, must apply equally to employers, employees, and collective-bargaining representatives. The statutory scheme must govern service in any position in a local labor organization which acts or seeks to act in that state as a collective bargaining representative . . ." in the industry subject to the comprehensive statutory scheme. Based, in part, upon this amendment to the LRMDA, an international union challenged a Nevada regulation that required the union to submit a list of certain union officials to the regulators. The union argued that federal law preempted this provision. A federal court dismissed the challenge. Upon appeal, the United States Ninth Circuit Court of Appeals held that, rather than preempting state regulation, the amendment to the LMRDA was a congressional affirmation of the United States Supreme Court's four-judge decision on preemption. *See* Brown v. Hotel & Restaurant Employees & Bartenders Int'l Union Local 54 [1984]. The appellate court held that the regulation was not preempted by federal law. Hotel Employees v. Nevada Gaming Comm'n, 984 F.2d 1507 (9th Cir. 1993).

can influence factors like the honesty and fairness of games and the public's perception of the gaming industry. This can be a multi-step process.

Step one – identify the ecosphere

Governments should identify all persons that have any relationship with the integrated resort.

Step two – identify the regulatory sensitivity of each group within the ecosphere.

The regulatory sensitivity of each group may and often will differ between jurisdictions based on culture, circumstances, competitive versus limited competition markets, integration of technology, emphasis on enforcement and testing, adequacy of compliance programs and other factors.

Step three – determine if regulatory risks can be more efficiently addressed or mitigated by enforcement, compliance procedures, or testing

Once all the players in the ecosphere are identified and grouped, policymakers can then determine if they can reduce the regulatory sensitivity of any group through oversight, compliance, technical requirements, and regulatory enforcement and sufficiently protect against risks.

Step four – understand the costs of licensing both to the government and the regulated

The government's costs associated with licensing are both monetary and human-resources-associated. The costs to the industry are the impact of the barriers to entry including cost and impact on innovation.

Step five – place the different groups into the requisite level of review

The government then must prioritize the groups and, according to its limited resources, assign the requisite level of review to each group.

Figure 15.5

An Example of Licensing: Types of Positions and Level of Regulatory Review		
Tier	Group	Level of Review
1	Operators. Owners. Persons entitled to profits. Suppliers of gaming devices.	Full licensing scrutiny, including independent investigation.
2	Manufacturers of gaming devices. Key casino personnel.	Licensing required. Routine review of intelligence files and police checks.
3	Manufacturers of associated equipment. Other casino personnel, junket representatives, landlords, lenders, labor organizations, gaming schools.	Registration with the gaming authorities is required. A routine police and intelligence review may be done. Gaming authorities retain rights to require licensing of any of those entities.
4	Suppliers of non-casino goods and services. Non-gaming employees. Persons doing business on the premises of a casino.	No registration required. Gaming authorities retain right to require licensing.
5	All others who do business with or on the premises of the casino.	No registration. Gaming authorities may ban a person from entering casinos and prohibit casinos from dealing with that person.

Depth of Licensing

When a government requires an entity to acquire a license to engage in gaming-related activities, the entity that must apply for and obtain a license often is not an individual. The owners of most major casinos are publicly traded corporations. Depth of licensing refers to which persons associated with the applicant-entity must apply and obtain a license.

Regardless of the type of approval sought, it is first necessary to determine which parties associated with the applicant must be licensed. Jurisdictions around the world have varying requirements as to who within or associated with an applicant must be licensed. Decisions on who must be licensed are based mostly on the relationship between the party required to be licensed and the applicant-gaming operation. Determining the depth of who must be licensed requires an analysis of the involvement of parties in the management and operations of the casino.

Individuals

When a casino operator or gaming manufacturer is an individual, called a "sole proprietor," requiring that person to submit the application and undergo an investigation is obvious. If casino licenses were issued only to individuals, the licensing process would be simple. Individual ownership is the least complex business form. To license an individual, authorities need only to investigate that person, not an entire business entity. As a business form, however, individual ownership is often the least desirable. The individual owner is subject to losing personal assets if the business fails and is personally liable in a lawsuit for damages. Besides, individual ownership may create problems in obtaining the financing or investment to expand or to meet cash demands. Because a sole proprietorship is usually the least desirable business form, few choose it as a business structure. Most operators or other business entities associated with the gaming industry, such as manufacturers and suppliers, are corporations or partnerships.

Corporations

Most owners, operators, suppliers, and vendors for casino gaming are a business entity, usually a corporation. A corporation is an artificial person or legal entity that the government authorizes to conduct business. The principal benefits of a corporation are the limited liability of equity owners (known as shareholders), transferability of interest, and continuity of existence.

Corporate structures differ among countries but usually involve officers, directors, shareholders, and employees. Shareholders are persons or entities that hold equity, as represented by shares, in a company. Shares entitle the holders to control the corporation by voting for the board of directors. In the discretion of the board of directors, shareholders are entitled to earnings through current or accumulated dividends and to pro-rata distribution of assets upon liquidation.[80] Shareholders typically elect directors who manage the corporation through officers. Officers are corporate agents and have management responsibilities that the board of directors delegates to them. Typical officers are the president (or Chief Executive Officer); a Chief Operating Officer; the treasurer, who is the chief financial officer; and the secretary, who is the ministerial officer. Corporations also may have one or more vice presidents and assistant officers.

Directors must use their best judgment when deciding and executing corporate policy. These include (1) selecting officers and setting officer salary and compensation, (2) making major policy decisions, and (3) deciding material financial matters, including dividends and financing. Directors often are described as inside or outside directors. An "inside" director is a board member who is an employee, officer, or significant shareholder in the company. An "outside" director is not an employee, significant shareholder, or otherwise charged with operational responsibilities. An "outside" director is independent of management and is often selected for their general business or specific industry knowledge or experience. Outside directors are often viewed as having objective and informed opinions regarding the company's decisions, health, and operations and bring diverse experience to the company's decision-making processes.

All forms of business entities that a license applicant may use include the concept of equity ownership. In a corporation, which is the most common form of business entity, shareholders hold the equity ownership.

A corporation can be public or private. A publicly-traded company is a listed corporation[81] whose stock is traded on a public market and is typically regulated by a government entity such as a securities commission.[82] An attractive feature of being a publicly-traded corporation is the ability to raise capital through a public offering.[83] Most often, a public offering occurs when the company, after registration with the securities commis-

---

[80] H. HENN & J. ALEXANDER, CORPORATION LAWS, HORN BOOK SERIES, § 396 (3rd ed. 1983).

[81] Before a company's stock can be traded on an exchange, through NASDAQ, or over-the-counter, the corporation must register its stock with the Securities and Exchange Commission (SEC), and meet the criteria of the SEC or NASDAQ to list its stock.

[82] The three major US markets are local and national stock exchanges, an authorized quotation system (such as NASDAQ), or between broker-dealers (called over-the-counter). In the United States, the major national exchanges are The New York and American Stock Exchanges. An example of a local exchange is the Pacific Stock Exchange. NASDAQ means the National Association of Securities Dealers Automated Quotations. The NASDAQ System is authorized by Federal law but is an association regulated by private industry. NASDAQ has a Board of Directors that sets rules and policies. Shares in private companies are exchanged between persons or through private placements that meet federal or state securities laws.

[83] In the United States, a "public offering" encompasses the sale of securities subject to the registration requirements of Section 5 of the Securities Act of 1933.

sion,[84] sells either stock or debt instruments to the public through brokers. Public company stock is attractive to investors because it is normally liquid. If a person buys the stock, he can usually sell it immediately in the public market.

Corporations may have executive committees with duties and responsibilities segregated from the corporate officers to provide a system of checks and balances. Typical executive committees include executive compensation, surveillance, and internal audit. A director of surveillance may report to an executive committee instead of the president or vice president of security. Similarly, the director of internal audit may report to an executive committee instead of the vice president of finance.

Depth of licensing for a corporation concerns which officers, directors, and shareholders must undergo licensing scrutiny. Similar considerations are needed for other business formations, such as general and limited partnerships, trusts, joint ventures, limited liability companies, and joint stock associations

Public companies

Benefits aside, allowing publicly-traded corporations to own and operate casinos or to manufacture gaming devices poses regulatory issues. As a practical matter, a publicly-traded corporation cannot be licensed if all its shareholders must apply because thousands of shares may trade daily in the public market. Therefore, if a jurisdiction wants to encourage publicly-traded corporations to invest in its gaming industry, it must allow licensing without each shareholder having to be registered or obtain a license.

Waiving licensing requirements for some shareholders, however, allows unsuitable persons the ability to buy shares and have an ownership interest in the gaming companies. This may not pose substantial problems if the person owns a few shares out of millions, but it can create regulatory issues if the person owns a significant percentage of the stock. Government protection goals addressing public perception of the honesty of the industry can be compromised if the media exposes that a notorious criminal has major holdings in a publicly-traded gaming company.

Regulatory problems may occur where the person's holdings allow him to exert influence or control over the corporation. Jurisdictions that want publicly traded corporations must balance these regulatory concerns with market realities. They can do so by setting thresholds at which shareholders in publicly traded corporations must apply for and obtain a gaming license. In the United States, these levels are commonly set at 5 percent, 10 per-

---

[84] In the United States, the role of the SEC is to evaluate the adequacy and accuracy of information in the registration statement and prospectus distributed to prospective investors. Securities brokers can only offer the stock for sale to their clients if the company receives SEC approval of their registration statement and prospectus.

cent, or 15 percent.[85] These levels are often tied to government reporting or filing requirements triggered when a shareholder acquires a beneficial interest greater than a certain amount. In the United States, for example, persons who acquire more than 5 percent of the outstanding shares of any class of voting securities of registered public companies must file reports with the Securities and Exchange Commission.[86] The reports contain basic personal background disclosures and holdings and investment intentions (active versus passive). Many jurisdictions have registration or licensing requirements that mirror these federal disclosures. As an example, a license application may ask the corporate applicant to name and provide a curriculum vitae of every shareholder that holds more than 5 percent of the company.[87]

Regulations can only partially deal with the problem of stock being held in street names. At the request of regulators, a registered publicly-traded corporation must help figure out who holds the beneficial ownership of such stock. A jurisdiction, however, must accept that some unsuitable persons may hold and profit from casinos undetected if they hold less than 5 percent of the corporation's stock. Government must accept the risk that if the company has a large market capitalization, e.g., $1 billion or more, the undesirable person's investment can be several million dollars.

---

[85] ANTHONY N. CABOT, CASINO GAMING: POLICY, ECONOMICS, AND REGULATION 275 (2001).

[86] This report is usually SEC Schedule 13D or 13G. A 10 percent rule also has a foundation in federal securities law. Under Section 16(a) of the Securities and Exchange Act of 1934, beneficial owners of more than 10 percent of a class of equity securities registered under Section 12 of the Act must disclose their holdings, and any changes to them, in a filing with the SEC. A purpose of this requirement is because 10 percent or greater holders are deemed "insiders" whose transactions can be followed by the media and public. These individuals may be subject to short-swing profit recovery under Section 16(d) of the Act.

[87] Attempting to require persons owning less than 5 percent is unworkable because the identity of these shareholders is difficult to discover. Because the stock can be held in street names (held by brokers in their accounts for clients), the identities of those owning less than 5 percent of the equity securities of a company will rarely come to the attention of the gaming authorities. The only practical way that regulators may acquire knowledge of beneficial ownership of voting securities of registered publicly-traded corporations is through SEC reporting requirements. An advantage of tying gaming approvals to SEC reporting is that the SEC rules on who must report are well established and supported by legal precedent. For example, in Mississippi, each person acquiring beneficial ownership of more than 5 percent of any class of voting securities that requires reporting of the acquisition to the SEC also must file a copy of that report with the gaming authorities within ten days after filing it with the SEC. Each registered, publicly-traded corporation must furnish the regulators with a list of its shareholders of record annually, or more frequently, as such lists are prepared.

Different Jurisdictions and Level of Licensing Review

Singapore	Shareholders owning less than 12% of the casino company.[88]
Louisiana	Shareholders owning 5% or less of a public corporation (land-based and river boat casinos).[89]
Mississippi	Shareholders owning 10% or less of any class of voting securities of a public corporation.[90]
Nevada	Shareholders owning 10% or less of the voting securities of a public corporation.[91] Institutional investors owning 25% or less of the voting securities of a public corporation.[92]
New Jersey	Shareholders owning less than 5% and institutional investors owning less than 25% of a public corporation.[93]
South Dakota	Shareholders of public or private corporations owning less than 5%.[94]

Tying licensure to a percentage ownership in a public company can present some anomalies. For example, a 10 percent shareholder in a public company with a market capitalization of $10 million may have to obtain a license but a 4 percent shareholder of a company with a $20 billion market capitalization does not even though the latter's value is 800 times more valuable. As a result, many jurisdictions will retain the right to require any shareholder to apply regardless of their percentage ownership. Rarely, however, does a jurisdiction make qualitative decisions based solely based on the value of the investment.

Still, if a concern exists that a shareholder (under either the five- or ten-percent-rule) can influence corporate decisions, a jurisdiction can adopt exceptions to the exemptions from licensing. These exceptions might target activity inconsistent with the notion of the shareholder as a passive investor, such as sitting on the board of directors, causing a change in the majority of the board, or causing a change in the charter, bylaws, management, policies or operations of the publicly-traded corporation or its casino subsidiary.

Institutional investors, such as banks, insurance companies, retirement or pension funds, hedge funds, investment advisors, and mutual funds

---

[88] Singapore Casino Control Act (33A) § 66 (2012).

[89] La. Rev. Stat. Ann. § 27:28(H) (2006).

[90] Miss. Code Ann. § 75-76-263(3) (West 2013).

[91] Nev. Rev. Stat. § 463.643 (2011).

[92] Nev. Gaming Reg.16.430(1). The regulation requires an institutional investor to apply for a waiver to hold more than 10 percent and up to 25 percent. It is possible to qualify for a waiver while owning more than 25 percent, provided that the additional ownership was acquired through debt restructuring. For purposes of the Nevada gaming regulations, a "debt restructuring" is defined to mean (a) any proceeding under the United States Bankruptcy Code; or (b) any out of court reorganization of a person that is insolvent or generally unable to pay its debts as they become due. Nev. Gaming Reg.16.010(8).

[93] N.J. Admin. Code § 5:12-85.1 (West 1977) (current as of March 17, 2014).

[94] S.D. Admin. R. 20:18:06:09 (2014).

pool large sums of money typically from smaller investors and invest this money into different industry sectors. When the gaming industry offers attractive returns, institutional investors can provide the extraordinary sums needed to finance even multibillion dollar integrated resorts. Therefore, in many jurisdictions their involvement is critical to the creation of the industry. Institutional investment would be more challenging if, as an example, a single investor was capped at 5 percent. Some places, such as Nevada and New Jersey, allow institutional investors to hold over 10 percent.[95] In Nevada, regulators set a maximum limit (25–29 percent) that an institutional investor subject to obtaining a waiver may hold in either a public or private company without obtaining a license.[96] In both Nevada and New Jersey, the institutional investor must show it is holding the stock for investment only.[97]

Some jurisdictions do not distinguish between private and public companies and set levels for shareholder licensing based solely on percentage of ownership. Portugal requires the suitability of everyone who owns more than 10 percent of outstanding shares,[98] while South Africa

---

[95] NEV. GAMING REG. § 16.430(1) (for public companies) NEV. GAMING REG. § 15.430(1) (for private companies); N.J. STAT. ANN. § 5:12-85.1(g) (West 1977) (current as of March 17, 2014). NEV. GAMING REG.16.430 provides:

> An institutional investor that becomes or intends to become subject to NRS 463.643(4) as a result of its beneficial ownership of voting securities of a publicly traded corporation registered with the commission may apply to the commission for a waiver of the requirements of NRS 463.643(4) with respect to the beneficial ownership of the voting securities of such publicly traded corporation if such institutional investor holds the securities for investment purposes only; provided, however, that an institutional investor shall not be eligible to receive or hold a waiver if the institutional investor beneficially owns, directly or indirectly, except as otherwise provided in subsection 2, more than 25 percent of the voting securities and if any of the voting securities were acquired other than through a debt restructuring. Voting securities acquired before a debt restructuring and retained after a debt restructuring or as a result of an exchange, exercise or conversion, after a debt restructuring, of any securities issued to the institutional investor through a debt restructuring, shall be deemed to have been acquired through a debt restructuring. A waiver granted under this section shall be effective only as long as the institutional investor's direct or indirect beneficial ownership interest in such voting securities meets the limitations set forth above, and should the institutional investor's interest exceed such limitations at any time, it shall be subject to NRS 463.643(4).

[96] NEV. GAMING REG. § 16.430(1) (for public companies); NEV. GAMING REG. § 15.430(1) (for private companies).

[97] NEV. GAMING REG. § 16.430(1, 3) (for public companies); NEV. GAMING REG. § 15.430(2) (for private companies); N.J. Stat. Ann. § 5:12-85.1(g) (West 1977) (current as of March 17, 2014).

[98] Jan Rodrigo, *Portugal, in* INTERNATIONAL CASINO LAW & REGULATION VOL. 2: EUROPE § 4.05, at 7 (William Thompson ed., 2008).

sets the bar at 5 percent.[99] The historical experience of some jurisdictions that grant exemptions only to public companies has provided little reason to distinguish between public and private companies. These jurisdictions licensed gaming before the advent of public gaming companies. They made general exceptions to the requirement that all shareholders be licensed to allow public companies to enter the industry. This limited relaxation of regulatory oversight was deemed an acceptable tradeoff for the benefits brought by public company investment. The requirements were not relaxed for private companies. Even Nevada, however, has since relaxed requirements that all shareholders of private companies must obtain a license.

Therefore, typically, the need for licensing shareholders is linked to the extent of that shareholder's investment. Institutional investors may avoid licensure where individuals may not. Another important regulatory consideration is whether a company is public or private since requiring all public shareholders to carry a license is a practical impossibility.

Holding companies

A distinction exists between a corporation holding the gaming license and a holding company, i.e., a company that owns the stock of a gaming licensee. A holding company is a company that owns the stock of a gaming licensee and is owned by a publicly-traded corporation. Holding companies usually pose no licensing issues because their officers and directors are also officers and directors of either the parent or the subsidiary. Therefore, these persons are subject to licensing in those other positions. Because there may be rare cases where officers and directors are different, laws may impose the same licensing requirements on holding companies as their parent publicly-traded corporations or their subsidiary corporation.

Partnerships

A general partnership is a business association of two or more persons carrying on business as co-owners for profit.[100] Recognized by common law, statutes in most places now codify the relationship of partners. Under a general partnership, all partners have equal rights in the management and conduct of the partnership business. Unlike shareholders in a company, partners in a general partnership are subject to unlimited liability to partnership claimants even to the extent of the partner's individual assets.[101] When any partner ceases to be a partner, there is a technical dissolution of the partnership.

Because the general partnership form has more disadvantages than

---

[99] Marita Carnelley, *South Africa, in* INTERNATIONAL CASINO LAW & REGULATION VOL. 3: THE REST OF THE WORLD § 16.05, at 11 (William Thompson ed., 2008).

[100] *See, e.g.,* NEV. REV. STAT. §87.060(1) (West 2006).

[101] *See, e.g.,* NEV. REV. STAT. §87.150 (West 2006).

advantages in regulated gaming operations, its use is rare. Limited partnerships are fairly common and have substantial advantages. A limited partnership has at least one general partner and at least one limited partner. The general partner has full authority and control over the partnership's business and affairs. The limited partners are passive investors. The limited partner is much like a corporate shareholder in that the person maintains protection from personal liability. Unlike the shareholder, the limited partner must take no part in the control or management of the business.[102] Limited partnerships have organizational restrictions similar to those of corporations. There is no double taxation of the partnership and its partners because the US tax code does not consider the partnership a taxable entity.[103] Limited partners share in the profits, but they do not share in losses beyond their capital contributions. They have limited personal exposure and limited assessments.[104] A limited partnership presents less of a regulatory problem than a corporation, even a public corporation, because limited partners cannot legally exert influence over the partnership's activities.

Allowing privately-held limited partnerships with reduced licensing requirements is less valuable to a jurisdiction than publicly-traded corporations. The latter overwhelmingly are better capitalized and have greater access to financing. These qualities are more conducive to building or expanding a large gaming industry. Most limited partnerships have 20–50 limited partners, compared to hundreds or thousands of shareholders in a public company.

Balancing these considerations, some jurisdictions treat limited partnerships similar to publicly-traded corporations by exempting limited partnerships holding less than a threshold amount. Others have no exemption for limited partners. Still others grant limited waivers after requiring the limited partners to apply and undergo a lower level review.

Other business forms
Limited liability company

A limited liability company combines the tax benefits of a partnership with the limited liability benefits of a corporation for its owners ("members") and "managers." Unlike a limited partnership, all members of a limited liability company can participate in the management of the company and retain limited liability.[105] Because of this, exempting from licensure those limited liability companies holding less than a threshold amount poses slightly more regulatory concern than exempting limited

---

[102] Grynberg v. B.B.L. Associates, 436 F. Supp. 564 (D. Colo.1977).
[103] 26 U.S.C. § 701 (1954).
[104] Garbo v. Hilleary Franchise Systems, Inc., 4790 S.W.2d 491 (Mo. App. 1972).
[105] *See, e.g.*, NEV. REV. STAT. §§ 86.291 & .371 (West 2006).

partners. A limited liability company provides no greater opportunity to capital markets or capital than limited partnerships. Therefore, no regulatory reasons exist for providing greater exemptions to a limited liability company than a limited partnership for licensing purposes. However, the slight difference that allows the member of the limited liability company to participate in management may not be enough to justify denying it the same exemptions.

Trusts

Trusts are common vehicles when a person wants to give another the benefits of an asset, such as stock, but does not want to give the rights to sell or dispose of the asset. For example, parents may wish to provide income for their children derived from the parents' stock, but they do not want to allow the children to sell the stock. Parents may place the stock in trust and allow the children to receive dividends and other benefits, but have another person control the assets as, frequently, trusts are used to minimize individual taxes and to avoid probate.

A common type of trust is a family trust. Often, upon advice of tax and estate counsel, persons with interests in casinos form trusts so their interests can pass to their spouses or children without having to pass through probate. Three categories of persons are typically involved in a trust: settlors, fiduciaries, and beneficiaries. A settlor is the person who creates the trust, and contributes an interest in a licensed gaming establishment to the trust. The fiduciary, as the administrator, trustee, escrow agent, or depository, carries out the written desires of the settlor according to the trust. The fiduciary may be a bank, a lawyer, or any other person. The beneficiaries are those persons who benefit from the trust.

A settlor creates a trust instrument providing instructions for handling of the assets. The settlor may decide his children will not receive title to the trust's assets until they reach 25 years of age, but the fiduciary can distribute the profits from the trust's assets to the beneficiaries before that age to fund their education. Trust terms are limitless.

Whether the settlor must obtain a license may depend on whether the trust is revocable or irrevocable. The settlor in a revocable trust can regain title to the trust's assets by revoking the trust and, therefore, regulators should consider the settlor as the owner of the interest. In an irrevocable trust, where the settlor lacks the power to regain an interest or title to the trust's assets, the settlor may have no controls over the trust. Therefore, in theory, a person can be denied a license, but the person's irrevocable family trust can still obtain approval to hold an interest in a casino operation. Regulators, however, face two issues in this instance. First, this arrangement should be carefully scrutinized to assure it is not a subterfuge for an unsuitable person to hold a casino interest. Second, regulators may consider the effect that such approvals may have on public perception of the gaming industry. This may differ greatly based on the notoriety of the settlor. If the settlor is an unknown person whose unsuitability relates to an obscure felony conviction, then the fear of adverse publicity may be minimal. The situation, however, is different if the settlor is a notorious, recently-convicted head of a crime family.

The fiduciary of a trust is technically the person that controls the trust and, thus, is the most sensitive from a regulatory perspective. Sometimes a fiduciary is appointed as the result of the unexpected death of a licensed owner. Therefore, provisions may be allowed for temporary approval of a fiduciary. Likewise, if the appointed fiduciary is a bona fide financial institution, regulators may want to consider some waiver of licensing requirements.[106]

Trust beneficiaries are those persons that receive the benefits of the trust's principal and growth. Beneficiaries usually have less control over the trust than shareholders have over a corporation. Most shareholders have voting rights that allow them to vote against the directors of the corporation if they disagree with how the corporation is being managed. Beneficiaries have no such rights. Like shareholders or other beneficial owners, regulatory sensitivity regarding beneficiaries concerns both the potential influence that a beneficiary may have over the operator and the public's perception of unsuitable persons benefiting from casino profits.

A recurring issue with beneficiaries is how to treat children that are the beneficiaries of their parents' family trust. If a jurisdiction requires licensing of beneficiaries, how does it license a five-year-old? This can be addressed in different ways. One solution exempts beneficiaries from licensing until they reach a certain age, such as 21-yearsold. This allows the minor to retain the benefits of the trust while he is a minor but not beyond that without being licensed. At age 21, a beneficiary may have sufficient life history to allow regulators to decide the beneficiary's suitability. Another solution gives transactional approval to beneficiaries, and allows regulators to require full investigation. As a beneficiary grows up, if he makes choices inconsistent with regulatory policy, such as joining a criminal gang, regulators can require him to undergo a full investigation and decide whether he should be licensed.

Officers/key employees

Gaming executives oversee gaming operations. One gaming executive critical to gaming operations and the well-being of the casino company is the **Chief Executive Officer** (CEO). The CEO is the highest ranking executive in a company; as such, the CEO has overall responsibilities for the operation of the casino-resort, including the hotel and all related operations. The CEO develops and implements high-level strategies, makes major corporate decisions, and interfaces with the board of directors.

---

[106] *See, e.g.,* NEV. REV. STAT. § 463.175 (West 2006).

Figure 15.7

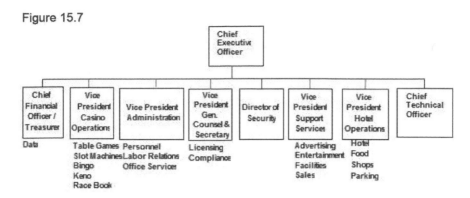

The **Chief Financial Officer** (CFO) is the senior manager responsible for overseeing the financial activities of the casino resort. The CFO's duties include financial planning and monitoring cash flow. Divisions directly reporting to the CFO include accounting, cage, credit, collections, and purchasing. The CFO analyzes the company's financial strengths and weaknesses and suggests plans for improvement. The CFO is responsible for ensuring that gaming taxes are reported and paid and that the company's financial reports are accurate.

Responsibility for casino operations usually falls on the **Chief Operating Officer** (COO) or **Vice President of Casino Operations** in larger casinos and the casino manager in smaller casinos. Larger casinos also may have a casino manager that works for the Vice President of Casino Operations. This management official supervises all casino operations. She may chair the credit committee for establishing high limit credit applications and is involved in credit write off decisions. She assists in department forecasts (e.g., table games, slots), budgeting, and capital improvement decisions. She also makes policy and procedure decisions.

The **General Counsel** or **Chief Legal Officer** (CLO) oversees the casino resorts' legal matters and may have responsibility for corporate and gaming compliance. The CLO advises the company's other officers and board members on legal and regulatory issues, oversees litigation and regulatory matters handled by outside law firms, and is often the main interface with gaming regulators.

The **Chief Technical Officer** (CTO) focuses on the technology issues within the casino environment. A CTO can have different roles depending on the size of the casino operation and the emphasis placed on the position by the board of directors and the CEO. Small casinos may not have a CTO but instead rely on third-party contractors to supply and maintain segregated systems. In larger casinos, the CTO can be the infrastructure manager and external facing technologist who identifies, exploits, and integrates new technologies, leverages these technologies across the profit centers of an integrated resort, helps drive business strategies, enhances client rela-

Figure 15.8

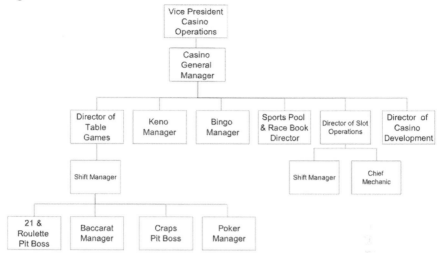

tions, drives revenues, and reduces costs through technology.[107] The CTO also can have prominence in a casino organization as the visionary on the future of the casino design.

Regardless of whether they are defined by job title, function, or compensation, "C" level corporate officers performing essential functions are likely to be subject to licensing in most jurisdictions. Increasingly, CTOs and CLOs (or compliance officers) are being required to undergo full licensing. CTOs are being targeted because of the increasing sophistication and reliance on technology in the casino environment. Unless other management has a technology background, CTOs have increasing influence and responsibility for the most regulatory-sensitive activities including assuring the honesty of the games, protecting player funds and data, and assuring proper reporting of income and taxes. Likewise, as CLOs and compliance officers more often are required to be a regulatory bellwether for corporate decisions, they are more likely to be required to file licensing applications.

Other management-level employees like the Vice President of Administration (or Human Resources) and Vice President of Hotel Operations have limited regulatory sensitivity.

Casino personnel

Some casino positions are of greater regulatory sensitivity than others. Compared to a chip runner, a casino manager has more opportunity to steal from the casino, be involved in a skim, or participate in cheating pa-

---

[107] Tom Berray & Raj Sampath, *The Role of the CTO: Models for Success*, http://www.brixtonspa.com/Career/The_Role_of_the_CTO_4Models.pdf.

trons. Consequently, a casino manager should be subject to more regulatory review than a chip runner.

Beyond generalizations, however, no universal rules can exist as to which casino positions have greater regulatory sensitivity and what the regulatory requirements should be for each position. A jurisdiction's regulatory system and technological advances help shape the regulatory sensitivity of particular casino positions. Where the government mandates an on-line monitoring system for all gaming devices, the regulatory sensitivity of hard count room personnel may decrease. This may occur when the government requires a government employee be present during the count or has its own surveillance camera in the count room. Similarly, whether the government should require a casino employee to obtain a license after a full investigation, a restricted license after a cursory investigation, or no license, depends on many factors. Where a new jurisdiction is legalizing casinos and has a limited regulatory budget, it may require full licensing only of the casino owners and top executives. Requiring more persons to undergo licensing may dilute regulators' ability to conduct a comprehensive investigation of all applicants. Here, the decision may be to assure the suitability of those persons holding the most sensitive positions at the risk that some unsuitable persons may obtain positions of less sensitivity.

A hypothetical licensing tiering of casino employees[108]

Where a casino has both a vice president of casino operations and a casino manager, the casino divides their responsibilities, with the vice president having overall responsibilities. The casino manager may direct all phases of casino operations, including table games, slots, counter games, marketing, junkets, and sales representatives absent the vice president of casino operations. The casino manager often supervises all activity that occurs in the casino. Areas under his control usually include table games, gaming devices, cage operations, keno operations, and casino marketing. Typically, the casino manager can hire and fire all casino employees and is integral in the decision to grant credit. He may assist in department forecasts (e.g., table games), budgeting, and capital improvement decisions. The casino manager reviews daily slot operations, analysis of statistical data, and department budgets. He is often responsible for compliance with all federal, state, and local regulations and controls and the enforcement of rules, policies, and procedures. The vice president of casino operations and the general manger hold positions of high regulatory sensitivity.

Table game employees

The table game areas of a casino have many levels of employees from the table game manager to shills. The regulatory sensitivity of these em-

---

[108] Job descriptions and reporting lines, however, may differ between jurisdictions and between casinos in some markets.

ployees ranges from high to low. To segregate the level of licensing scrutiny accorded these different positions, a jurisdiction can categorize them individually or as a group, such as requiring "key" employees, i.e., those with greater responsibility, to undergo a higher level of review than regular employees. The following table game employees are roughly ranked according to regulatory sensitivity.

Larger casinos may have a **table game manager**. Besides recommending game types and mix, he has direct responsibility for all table game activity, including employee supervision, hiring, and discipline.

Under the table manager or casino manager are **shift managers or bosses**. Shift managers oversee the table games and associated personnel for a shift (usually eight hours). Frequently, they may approve credit and extensions, and complimentaries. They are responsible for game protection, complying with rules and regulations and assuring the security of cards and dice. Shift managers approve staffing levels and discipline employees. They also interact with gaming authorities on matters related to fraud and patron complaints. The service shift manager may function as the Casino Manager in his or her absence.

Responsibility for performance and protection of games in the assigned area known as a pit falls on the **pit managers or bosses**. They assure security of cards and dice in their assigned area. They handle disciplinary problems with staff. Pit bosses set table minimums and supervise ratings and table inventories. Pit bosses often can give some complimentaries to patrons.

Supervisors (or **floorpersons**) also are responsible for performance and protection of games in an assigned area. In a pit, they supervise a group of tables and report to the pit boss. Their responsibility is to correct errors and enforce rules, policies, and procedures within that area. Supervisors track and verify table inventories, fills, and credits. They also track and verify patron wins and losses and initiate cash transaction reports. Supervisors handle credit, reservation, and complimentary requests of patrons. They attempt to settle disputes with and claims of patrons.

Boxpersons are common to craps. They are responsible for performance and protection of the game. They correct errors and enforce rules, policies, and procedures on assigned games. Boxpersons track and verify table inventories, fills, and credits. They also relay patron requests for credit to floorpersons. They assure that the pace and conduct of an assigned game meets casino standards.

Dealers operate assigned games according to casino rules, policies, and procedures. Each dealer is responsible for performance and protection of his or her game. Dealers make cash and chip change for patrons. They verify and sign all fills, credits, and marker credit disbursements. Dealers assure underage persons are not gambling. They monitor and report any unusual or illegal activity.

Pit clerks work the podium in the pit and record transactions, such as rim credit, patron's credit limits and draws, marker transactions, and currency reports. Pit clerks also communicate with the casino cage regarding table fills and credits.

Shills are casino employees who pose as patrons to either provide enough players to conduct a game (such as poker) or to give others the perception of casino activity. Casinos may use shills to start games that have no patrons and expect shills to leave when patrons join the game.

Gaming devices

A **slot manager** directs all phases of slot operations except the count. These responsibilities include staffing and maintenance of operating documents. They also help in slot department forecasts, budgeting, and capital improvement decisions. They make recommendations on machine floor configuration, type and mixes. Responsibility for compliance with all federal, state, and local regulations and controls typically falls on a slot manager. They recommend and then enforce all rules, policies, and procedures. A slot manager issues and controls jackpot payout documents. They review daily slot operations, analysis of statistical data, and department budgets.

Shift managers supervise all aspects of the slot department operations absent the slot manager. They help in slot department forecasts, budgeting, and capital improvement decisions. They are involved in customer relations. A shift manager may verify large jackpots and review daily slot operations, analysis of statistical data, and department budgets for their assigned shift. They are responsible for compliance with all federal, state, and local regulations and controls on their assigned shifts. They recommend and enforce rules, policies, and procedures.

A casino may have many types of slot attendants and hosts. The most common are **slot floorpersons**. They often have assigned areas in the casino over which they have responsibility. They are expected to quickly respond to any disruption in play, such as a patron winning a jackpot that must be hand-paid or a gaming device needing service. Typical slot malfunctions include problems with currency or credits, short payouts, and tilts. Usually, the floorperson can fix the problem and place the device back in play. Where he cannot, he contacts mechanics for service. When a patron hits a jackpot that must be paid by hand, the floorperson is usually the first to respond; he informs the patron of the situation and may have to alert surveillance and his superiors depending on the size of the jackpot. The floorperson may complete the jackpot forms, including tax forms, and obtain and deliver checks or cash for the unpaid jackpot.

Catering to slot patrons may be the responsibility of the slot floorpersons, slot hosts, or both. **Slot hosts** promote slot business in the casino by providing personal attention to slot patrons. Slot hosts identify patrons playing to certain levels, introduce themselves, offer certain complimentaries, and encourage the patron to join the casino's slot club. The level of complimentaries may correspond to the level of play, such as food, beverage, and show tickets. They can usually extend complimentaries to a certain limit. Certain slot hosts may be assigned to the slot club. They enroll slot players in the casino's slot club and cater to the slot club members.

Technicians

Unlike low level slot hosts and cashiers, a group of gaming device employees that have a moderately high level of regulatory sensitivity are slot mechanics. This sensitivity arises from their access to the interior of gaming devices. Without adequate controls, this provides opportunity to alter the play of the device or to remove coins or tokens.

A **lead mechanic** supervises slot mechanics' repair and maintenance of machines. He may be a signatory for hopper fills, jackpots, credits, and fills. He monitors play for illegal activity and verifies proper machine function on large jackpots.

Under him are **slot mechanics** who repair and maintain the machines. A casino may have two types of mechanics: one that repairs and services the reel-type slot machines and another that specializes in video machines. A slot mechanic may be a signatory for jackpots and credits.

Poker

The **poker manager** directs all phases of the poker room operations, including staffing and overseeing game integrity. He hires, fires, and disciplines employees, and prepares employee performance evaluations. The poker manager helps in poker department forecasts, budgeting, and capital improvement decisions. He is responsible for compliance with all federal, state, and local regulations and controls. He recommends and enforces rules, policies, and procedures. He reviews daily poker operations, analysis of statistical data, and department budgets. He also has the ability to give complimentaries.

A **poker shift supervisor** manages and directs all phases of poker room operations absent a poker manager. He protects the game and assures compliance with rules and regulations. He is responsible for the security of the cards. He interacts with gaming authorities on matters related to fraud and patron complaints. A poker shift supervisor also staffs the poker room and makes recommendations for hiring and firing. He may approve some complimentaries.

Assistant supervisors in the poker room protect the game and assure compliance with rules and regulations. They are responsible for the security of cards. They work with patrons and employees regarding procedures. Rules interpretation is an important part of the assistant supervisor's job. When questions arise, they must make decisions consistent with established policies. Assistant supervisors recommend the hiring and firing of employees and make the daily dealers' lineup. They also organize and start games and assist with keeping department daily logs. They have some complimentary privileges.

Brushpersons keep accurate patron lists on all games in progress. When a seat becomes available, they notify the information center. They then seat the patron. Brushpersons prepare tables for the start of games. They bring setups to tables. Among brushpersons' other jobs are answering questions concerning rules, regulations, and procedures, running chips for patrons and orders, and verifying table fills.

Dealers operate assigned games according to established dealing procedures. They are responsible for game protection. They also watch chips for patrons who temporarily leave the game. Dealers make up decks when a game breaks and help keep the poker room neat and clean. They must comply with all established rules, regulations, and procedures.

Desk clerks are the communication link for the poker room. They answer the telephone and page patrons waiting to play. They also take messages or route calls for patrons and management. Desk clerks may also answer questions about the games and procedures, make setups, and help keep the poker room neat and clean.

Like their counterparts on the casino floor, **chip runners** in the poker room run chips to table games. They also run chips for patrons. Chip runners may also help brushpersons, notifying the information center when a seat becomes available, cleaning the poker room, and making setups as necessary and when time permits.

Keno

A **Keno Manager** directs all phases of the keno operations, including staff, game integrity, and customer relationships. He assists in keno department forecasts, budgeting, and capital improvement decisions. He is responsible for compliance with all federal, state, and local regulations and controls. Among his other responsibilities are recommending and enforcing rules, policies, and procedures. He reviews daily keno operations, analysis of statistical data, and department budgets. He can also hire, fire, suspend, and review employees.

A **Keno Shift Supervisor** manages and directs all phases of keno operations absent the Keno Manager. He verifies winning tickets and money payouts and opens and closes games.

2nd/3rd Persons supervise keno writers and runners and control the game's pace. They initiate games, drop balls from the last game, and call the draw. They oversee writers and runners to assure all bets are timely.

Keno writers complete and record outside ticket numbers selected by patrons. They accept wagers, and make change. They help patrons figure out winners and pay off winning tickets up to a predetermined limit. They may call games, if needed.

Keno runners circulate through their assigned area in the casino to pick up patron tickets. They supply cards and crayons in their assigned area. They collect wagers and tickets from patrons and deliver them to keno writers for transcription. They then return the tickets to patrons after the tickets are entered by the writers. Keno runners help patrons determine winners. They can make payouts up to a set amount. They can also make change for patrons.

Casino marketing

A **casino marketing director** coordinates the marketing and sales activities between the casino marketing department, hotel sales, and room reservations to maintain optimal balance between hotel occupancy and potential casino revenue per room. He works with the casino manager to develop a general marketing strategy for the casino and is responsible for its implementation. He develops and maintains customer databases. He oversees, evaluates, and approves player clubs, branch offices, junkets, special events and promotions, bus programs, and invited guest activities. He supervises the casino hosts and junket representatives and ensures they comply with all gaming laws and regulations.

There are many levels of **casino hosts**. Sometimes, hosts merely walk the casino floor to spot unknown high stakes players, greet them, and offer complimentary services. More typically, casino hosts attract premium patrons and ensure that they stay at the casino. Casino hosts might arrange room, food, beverages, show tickets, transportation, and other matters for premium players. They usually can extend complimentaries to a certain limit. They help the patron establish credit and may extend credit to a certain limit. They may call and visit patrons and host parties in other cities. They help collect debts from patrons.

Independent agents, also called "**junket representatives**," work on a commission to bring patrons to the casino. If a casino uses salaried sales staff for the same task, these employees are called "casino hosts" if they work at the casino or "branch managers" if they work in another city. Most often, independent agents and casinos bring premium patrons who spend considerably more on gambling than the average patron.

Unlike mass marketing efforts, such as billboards, radio, newspaper, and television advertising, establishing a premium patron market requires personal contact with the patron. Premium patrons are not day visitors to many casinos who bet only a little at each casino. They commit to gambling large sums at a casino for certain complimentary items, such as travel, room, food, beverages, and entertainment. Because of this larger commitment, these patrons invest more time and require more information to decide which casino they want to patronize. Independent agents, casino hosts, and branch managers are often the vehicle for conferring this information.

Many casinos prefer using independent agents over casino hosts or branch managers because the latter are employees paid even if they generate no revenues. They also incur additional expenses, such as health benefits and the cost of providing offices and staff. Independent agents receive no commissions unless they produce premium patrons.

Independent agents can earn commissions in many ways. One common method of calculating commissions is as a percentage of the premium patron's losses. Another common method bases commissions on the premium patron's theoretical loss. A commission based on theoretical loss compensates the independent agent for bringing in qualified patrons, despite whether the patron wins or loses. This calculation includes the patron's average bet, the number of hours played, and the type of game played. With these statistics, the casino can figure what the patron should theoretically lose based on his play. In actuality, the patron may win or lose more or less than this amount.

Using independent agents and branch offices poses certain regulatory issues. A problem with independent agents is they operate outside the jurisdiction. Regulators, therefore, have greater difficulty policing their activities. If violations occur, regulators often have no means of enforcing the regulations except by prohibiting the casino from conducting further business with the agent.

Under the player protection goals, using independent agents to promote casino activities is prohibited as it stimulates demand for casino gaming. Therefore, this group would not exist in a licensing tier schematic.

Under the government protection goals, using independent agents poses certain concerns. Unlike casino employees, independent agents act independently of the casino. This creates less accountability to corporate codes of ethics and internal controls. Independent agents also often operate beyond regulators' jurisdiction. Independent agents often are subject to more licensing scrutiny than a typical casino employee but less than a casino operator.

Internal marketing employees pose fewer problems than junket representatives and other third parties because they are subject to corporate codes of ethics and internal controls. Because they are employees, operators have greater interest and control over their actions. Casino licensee oversight (with the threat of prospective disciplinary action) will likely ensure marketing employees do not contravene a government's casino regulations and policies; thus licensing is largely unnecessary.

Finance/accounting

The accounting departments of casinos are arranged differently among properties. Often, supervisory responsibilities are broken down by functional areas such as Casino Accounting, Hospitality Accounting, Financial Reporting, and General Accounting. In each organization the job titles may be unique.

The finance department of a gaming operation is led by the Chief Financial Officer (CFO). A gaming operation controller oversees the accounting department. Together, the finance and accounting departments maintain the gaming operation's financial records, prepare licenses and tax forms, and balance the gaming operation's books.

Figure 15.9

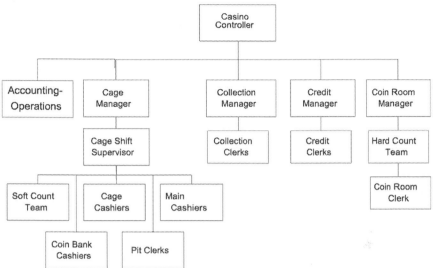

Although the two departments seem to have access to much of the gaming operation's financial records and bank accounts, the access is limited. Employees of the two departments can view the financial information, but generally they cannot alter the data. Internal policies prevent the employees from transferring the gaming operation's funds into other accounts. The departments are not deeply associated with actual gaming activities. Because their duties are primarily post-gaming (e.g., journaling entries, reporting results), their regulatory sensitivity is lower than the casino personnel, with the exception of the most senior accounting officials.

A **casino controller** manages and directs all financial activities within the casino property. He reconciles all the accounting transactions in the casino and enforces all internal controls, administrative controls, and audit functions. He reviews and approves the general ledger. The casino controller sets policies and practices to protect property assets; comply with federal, state, and local regulations; and meet cost-control objectives. He is responsible for the control of all revenues and disbursements, internal controls, and audits. The casino controller also prepares management reports and reports to regulatory and tax agencies.

An **assistant controller (operations controller)** is responsible for the operation of the property's accounting under the direction of the controller. He manages and directs all phases of the accounting department absent the controller. He reviews all accounting functions with the controller and suggests rules, policies, and procedures.

He develops the operating budget for the property and produces financial reports to inform management of the performance of the departments.

An assistant controller also responds to inquiries from management and regulatory agencies.

Accounting/reporting supervisors (often called chief accountants) direct, supervise, and maintain all financial general records. They prepare all journal entries and compile information from the general ledger into a monthly financial statement. They prepare federal, state, county, and city licenses and tax forms. They supervise the reconciliation of bank accounts, audit financial data, and balance the property's books.

Senior accountants often install and maintain accounting procedures. They design or modify accounting systems to provide exacting records of assets, liabilities, and financial transactions. They prepare accounting procedures manuals and the procedures for training accounting personnel. They also monitor and survey department operations to determine if accounting methods are adequate and up-to-date.

Internal audit

Internal audit departments often have a director and one or more internal auditors and audit clerks. The **director** supervises the activities of the internal audit department. He decides the adequacy of internal controls including the adequacy and proper application of all accounting, financial, and operating controls. The director also coordinates the internal audit with the external audit by independent public accountants.

The director reviews the accounting systems and records of vendors and subcontractors to decide if they are correct and comply with negotiated agreements. He sets rules, policies, and procedures affecting financial reporting to assure they comply with all federal, state, and local law. He also monitors consistency of organizational objectives, industry trends, business conditions, and government legislation.

Internal auditors analyze and verify the gaming operation's transactions to ensure they meet established regulatory and internal guidelines. Internal auditors, led by the director, determine if the gaming departments are following accounting rules, custodial policies, and control procedures. While internal auditors are focused on the workings of gaming departments, audit clerks audit the revenue generating areas. They determine if departments are correctly following accounting, custodial, or control rules, policies, and procedures. Audit clerks verify the accuracy of revenue and expenditure figures, correct discrepancies, audit account balances, and prepare reports about daily operations. The internal audit department seeks to verify information post-event and so is not directly involved in actual gaming operations. As with the financing and accounting departments described above, the audit department's post-gaming role greatly mitigates the need for licensing. They evaluate the adequacy and effectiveness of management controls. They also prepare reports of the results of the audit examinations, report audit findings, and suggest corrections of unsatisfactory performances and cost reductions. Internal auditors may conduct special reviews for management. They may recommend methods for obtaining, analyzing, and evaluating data.

Audit clerks perform accounting functions to audit the revenue generating areas. They verify accuracy of figures, calculations, and postings of business transactions, and they correct discrepancies. They review profit and loss reports for accuracy and may help with the auditing of registers. Audit clerks prepare daily operating statements and management and tax reports. They observe drops and procedures in the hard count room and input meter readings into the computer; they may also help the count teams.

Cage operations

The **cage manager** is responsible for all cage operations. He often can hire and fire cage workers. He helps develop cage procedures and carries out those procedures, cash reporting laws, and casino's internal controls. The cage manager also ensures proper recording and maintenance of all cash transactions, credit instruments, returned checks, deposits, payments, staff sheets, balancing reports, staff sheets, and daily cash and inventory summaries.

Large casinos often have separate **credit and collection managers**, while the same person may do both jobs in smaller casinos. The credit manager assures that a casino grants credit only if that credit is properly authorized by all respective casino executives. Before the casino grants credit, the credit manager may obtain and verify credit information from the patron and conduct an independent evaluation of the patron's credit-worthiness. The collection manager attempts to collect all unpaid casino receivables. He maintains all uncollected credit instruments that the cage released. He recommends collection procedures and directs the course of the collection efforts. He may recommend the initiation of lawsuits to collect unpaid debts or the writing off of particular debts.

The **cage shift manager** is responsible for cage operations during his shift. The shift manager supervises all cage cashiers to assure they properly execute all transactions during the shift. The cage shift manager may have to sign and verify certain transactions including fills and credits, cash summaries, count sheets, cage inventory count sheets, and check cashing over a certain amount.

Cage cashiers service patrons at the casino cage. This involves buying and selling chips and tokens, but also may include check cashing, completion of credit applications, and accepting deposits and payments. They also interface with security or chip runners to prepare fills and accept credit from table games. The cashier also works with slot personnel in documenting and paying jackpots. Cage cashiers post entries to staff sheets. The cage cashier may control the keys to sensitive areas of the casino, such as the hard and soft count room, and document their use. Often other parts of a resort complex will deposit their receipts with the cage cashier.

Chip runners deliver chips and cash between the gaming tables and the casino cage. They verify and document the amounts transferred at both the table and the cage.

Security

Security officers maintain order in the casino and protect casino employees, patrons, and physical assets. They observe casino activity to detect illegal activities and to ensure minors are not gambling. Security plays several important roles in internal control procedures including the secure transportation of chips and drop boxes, card and dice transfers, access and key controls to restricted areas, fills and credits, and large jackpots. In some small casinos, they may act as chip runners. Casinos with large security forces often organize them similarly to police organizations, with a chief and various other levels of authority.

Surveillance

Surveillance uses a system of video cameras that can be in virtually every place on the casino resort property to transmit an audio and video signal to a specific surveillance room. There, specially-trained employees can review video either in real time or via recorded footage to detect crimes or improper activities, concentrating on high stakes gambling and sensitive areas such as cage and count. Surveillance plays an important role in internal control procedures by converting observing controlled casino transactions such as fills, jackpot payouts, count rooms, and cage transactions. Surveillance can have access to player data to help profile particular players and third party databases of known or suspected cheats and criminals. Some surveillance systems incorporate other software like non-obvious relationship awareness (NORA) software to determine relationships between, for example, a player and a dealer to signal possible collusion, biometric face recognition to identify known or suspected cheats, OCR software to record license plates of persons visiting the resort, and integration with other systems such as card readers on shoes.[109]

A **director of surveillance** manages and directs all phases of the surveillance operations, including staffing, scheduling, games, asset and guest protection and compliance with internal controls. He sets policies and procedures to prevent loss of assets due to theft and to ensure that all gaming activity conforms to established guidelines. He is also responsible for the policies and procedures for monitoring compliance with state, local, and casino administration, or other regulatory agencies. He evaluates gaming procedures and suggests improvements when vulnerabilities are detected. He communicates with the gaming regulators and provides regulatory and police agencies with video footage and records and provides courtroom

---

[109] Michael Kaplan, *How Vegas Security Drives Surveillance Tech Everywhere*, POPULAR MECHANICS, Jan. 1, 2010, http://www.popularmechanics.com/technology/how-to/computer-security/4341499.

testimony. He also assists in surveillance department forecasts, budgeting, and capital improvement decisions.

Surveillance shift managers are responsible for the proper operation of an assigned shift. They train and update surveillance operators. A shift manager will manage and direct all phases of the surveillance department absent the director.

Surveillance operators observe procedure and conduct at the table games, slots, cashier's cage, slot booths, and coin redemption windows. They make audio and/or video tapes of the count rooms. They detect illegal activities in all areas of the facility. They test and check all equipment to ensure proper working order. They coordinate the storage and rotation of tapes. They are familiar with photos of undesirable persons and cheating techniques.

Governments must understand their own resources and the limitations of testing strategies even when performed by independent testing facilities.

Figure 15.10

An Example of Employee License Tiering	
Independent Agents	Must undergo a full investigation and obtain a license before beginning work.
Casino Manager Controller (Vice President - Financial Operations) Vice President - Casino Operations	Must obtain a work card or undergo other check that is less than full licensure before beginning work, and file an application for licensure. Investigation has high priority.
Assistant Controller (Operations Controller) Director of Surveillance Cage Manager Poker Manager Shift Manager Slot Manager Table Games Manager	Same as second tier (above), but investigation priority is medium unless facts dictate otherwise.
Credit and Collection Manager Casino Hosts Keno Manager Pit Bosses	Same as second tier (above), but licensing priority is low unless facts dictate otherwise.
Boxpersons and Brushpersons Cashiers Dealers Floor Persons Internal Audit Keno Supervisor/Shift Manager Keno 2nd/3rd Person & Writers Pit Clerks Poker Assistant Supervisors Security Guards Poker Shift Supervisor Slot Attendants and Hosts Slot Mechanics & Supervisors Surveillance Operator & Shift Manager	Is only required to obtain a work permit, but regulators have the discretion to require the person to undergo full licensing.
Chip Runners Desk Clerks Keno Runners Shills	Does not have to obtain a work card, but regulators should have the discretion to order the casino to terminate the person's employment or relationship.
Marketing Director	Is not subject to regulatory scrutiny.

While controls over the software can be implemented to ensure the computer code is fully functional and that no avenues exist for programmers to insert malicious code that would change probabilities or transfer funds to incorrect accounts, these things cannot be accomplished with absolute guarantees. The assurance depends on many factors including the stringency of the standards, the quality of the manufacturers' internal testing and controls, the competence and capability of the testing agency, and the degree and sophistication of the government's industry-wide oversight. Once the software is implemented into the operations, except for follow up releases and bug fixes, software engineers are not involved; the technical operations personnel take over the role of managing the software.

Non-gaming employees

A casino, even if it has no amenities such as a hotel or restaurant, may have many non-gaming employees. They can include maintenance personnel, such as janitors, carpenters, valet parkers, and cocktail servers. These persons have varied responsibilities, but rarely do they affect sensitive areas of the casino. Except computer service employees, non-casino employees are of the lowest regulatory priority. Effective implementation of internal control systems should adequately protect casino assets from potential theft by non-casino employees.

Notable exceptions are computer information service employees. Regulators may wish to treat computer service employees, particularly those with access to software, at a higher level of regulatory priority, perhaps as they would gaming employees. As gaming operations become more computer-based, the staff dedicated to the maintenance of these systems increases. A gaming operation can have many sensitive computer systems, including player tracking systems, slot tracking systems, debit card systems, marker issuance and collection systems, bingo and keno systems, accounting systems, and sports and horse race totalizers.[110] Such employees have greater opportunity to manipulate game outcomes or player/operator accounts.

Except for certain computer service employees, non-gaming operation employees are of the lowest regulatory priority. Effective implementation of internal control systems should adequately protect gaming operator assets from potential theft by non-gaming employees. Regulators, however, may wish to make computer service employees, especially those with access to software, a higher regulatory priority.

---

[110] A totalizer is a computer used in pari-mutuel horse race wagering to register and divide the total of all wagers made after the race track has subtracted its commission among all the persons having placed a wager on a winning horse or combination of horses.

16

Investigation of Industry Participants

Rick Lopes, Anthony Cabot, & Brian Callaghan

"It is a capital mistake to theorize before one has data."
Sir Arthur Conan Doyle

INTRODUCTION

In most jurisdictions that offer regulated gaming, working in the industry is a privilege. That said, obtaining a gaming license to do so is difficult. Most who apply for a license in the gaming industry are surprised to learn the standards by which they are measured. For example, California's Gambling Control Act addresses an applicant's qualifications:

No gambling license shall be issued unless, based on all of the information and documentation submitted; the Commission is satisfied the applicant is a person:

    a. of good character, honesty, and integrity.

    b. whose prior activities, criminal record, reputation, habits, and associations do not pose a threat to the public interest of this state, or to the effective regulation and control of controlled gambling, or create or enhance the dangers of unsuitable, unfair, or illegal practices, methods, and activities in the conduct of controlled gambling or in the carrying on of the business and financial arrangements incidental thereto.

    c. that is in all other respects qualified to be licensed as provided in this chapter.[1]

These stringent qualifications are not unique to California but are standard across most jurisdictions that offer regulated gaming.[2] So whether you want to own a casino, manufacture gaming equipment or work in the gaming industry, trying your luck, so to speak, to obtain licensure with a problematic background probably will not work.

---

[1] CAL. BUS. & PROF. § 19857.
[2] *See* 41 NEV. REV, STAT. § 463.170 (2013); N.J STAT. ANN. § 5:12-86.

Predictably, when applying for a gaming license, all applicants are subject to some level of suitability investigation. In many jurisdictions, this investigation is the most important piece of the regulatory process. Based on the information revealed during the investigation, a decision will be made whether an applicant is suitable to work in the gaming industry.

Much depends upon the outcome of a licensing decision. If you are applying as a sole applicant, your livelihood is at stake. If you are a large, multi-national firm, a gaming license denial in one jurisdiction can negatively impact your company's brand around the globe. A poor decision based on inadequate or misinformation is not fair to the applicant, the gaming industry, or the legislative bodies that have entrusted regulators with the responsibility of regulating the industry. Therefore, the suitability investigation process must be concise, thorough, accurate, unbiased, and equitable.

This chapter offers an overview of this investigative process. Various approaches are available to regulators in this process, and the following is an effort to help establish the general topics and parameters of those inquiries. For investors, manufacturers, or corporations wishing to enter the gaming space, this chapter will provide some insight as to what to expect during the investigative process. For regulators, the information outlined throughout this chapter can be used to develop an approach that conforms to your respective jurisdiction's policies and procedures, and where applicable, any state, federal, or local laws and ordinances.

While this chapter discusses investigative techniques with a bias toward US investigations, the same techniques are available worldwide. For example, if the investigated company is listed on the Tokyo stock exchange, background investigators can seek information from the Securities and Exchange Surveillance Commission (証券取引等監視委員会), which falls under the authority of the Financial Services Agency instead of the US Securities and Exchange Commission.[3]

GOALS OF THE INVESTIGATION

The goal of any licensing investigation is to provide regulators with sufficient and truthful information on which to base decisions consistent with public policies, goals, and licensing criteria. For example, if the public policy is to protect the public, a policy goal may be that the games offered in the casino are fair and honest. The legislature or regulators may determine that certain applicants such as those with criminal records involv-

---

[3] When conducting investigations on foreign companies or individuals, however, regulatory investigators should take caution that they clear their foreign investigatory activities with that country's proper authorities. Investigators also need to have a working plan that addresses how and which documentation must be translated and who can provide the assistance to navigate differing government structures, law enforcement agencies, accounting rules, privacy laws, and other matters unique to each foreign jurisdiction.

ing dishonesty may pose a threat to that policy goal. They may further adopt criteria to test whether the applicant is acceptable. Consistent with this objective, criteria related to criminal acts can be fixed (e.g., felons are not eligible) or discretionary (e.g., criminal arrests and convictions will be considered but are not dispositive). Investigations differ greatly depending on whether the jurisdiction has fixed or discretionary criteria.

Fixed Criteria Investigations

Evaluations of fixed criteria are those in which an investigator must evaluate specific facts to determine the suitability of an applicant for a gaming license. Typical fixed criteria inquiries in many jurisdictions include

- Criminal Convictions. Investigators conduct local, national, and/or international background checks and research court documents to determine whether the applicant has been convicted of a felony or a misdemeanor crime of moral turpitude within a period of time.
- Adequate Financing. Investigators review bank accounts, loan and credit arrangements, and other sources of funds to ensure they are legitimate, committed, and without unreasonable conditions.
- Minimum Capital Investment. Investigators review and monitor the applicant's proposed investment to ensure it meets the minimum criterion.
- Equity Participation by Local Residents. When governments require residents have an ownership interest in local casinos, to ensure compliance investigators must review ownership. Though legal restraints may limit such a review to the letter of the law, when an investigator has the discretion to evaluate whether the applicant meets the spirit of the law, he or she should review ownership for evidence that the applicant is evading the policy goals or intent behind the ownership requirement. For example, ownership of a worthless class of stock may contravene the intent behind the requirement because local citizens do not receive the financial benefits of ownership. Other methods of evading policy goals may include structures that drain the operating company of excess cash before making dividend distributions. Therefore, investigators should review the applicant's corporate documents carefully to ensure the local owners receive what is required by law. Investigators should also review salaries, consulting agreements, and other contracts to ensure the amounts paid are commercially reasonable and not disguised methods to distribute profits.
- Facility Requirements. When the government compels an applicant to utilize facilities that meet certain minimum requirements, investigators should inspect the premises to ensure compliance. This often entails room counts, casino or card room measurements, and other similar physical inspections.

- Local Ordinances. State law may require that the gaming establishments adhere to local ordinances. Examples of such ordinances include the number of gaming tables allowed in a city or county, hours of operation, location, and signage. Investigators therefore must also inspect the applicant's premises to ensure compliance with any local ordinances.

Fixed criteria investigations tend to be linear. An applicant either has or does not have a felony record. The facilities either meet or do not meet minimum requirements. The project either has or does not have the minimum capital and reserve requirements. Investigative agents can often use predefined checklists to manage the investigation and rarely have to deviate into uncharted areas.

Discretionary Criteria Investigations

The method by which investigators gather facts to evaluate discretionary criteria is challenging. Often, discretionary criteria provide little or no guidance to investigators. Typical discretionary criteria in many jurisdictions include an evaluation of an applicant's character, honesty or integrity. To investigate an applicant's character, honesty, or integrity, virtually every detail of the applicant's life may provide insight. No boundaries exist for this type of investigation. Every allegation of good or bad acts, whether such acts amount to criminal violations or not, reflects on how that applicant may act as a licensee. Facts may be found in obscure places. For example, identifying who the applicant has associated with, how he or she handled disclosures to a prospective buyer of his or her house, and whether he or she revealed all income to the federal government may be relevant. The possibilities are endless.

WHO SHOULD CONDUCT THE INVESTIGATION?

When deciding who should conduct the investigation, policy makers should be guided by the principles that the licensing investigators must be competent, accurate, neutral, and efficient. Competency means the investigator has the skill set to conduct the investigation to obtain the results needed by the regulators to assess the applicant's suitability to hold a gaming license in light of the state policy goals toward casino gaming. Neutrality is important because the goal is to present accurate, unbiased information about the applicant to the regulatory agencies making the ultimate licensing decision. The ideal licensing investigator also is efficient. He or she should spend only as much time or money as necessary to obtain the information needed to evidence the applicant's suitability. Gaming investigations are characteristically expensive and often needlessly so. Unfortunately, a government that is willing to spend only $500 of its own funds to do a pre-employment check for a teacher (who we entrust with our children) or a police officer (who we entrust with the power to use deadly force) may have no issue with requiring a manufacturer to spend $60,000 to license its Chief Financial Officer who has already been found suitable in other jurisdictions. These costs can be substantially reduced by using licensing investigators dedicated to efficiency.

A licensing investigator, however, should not sacrifice accuracy for efficiency. Adverse licensing decisions are increasingly being challenged by applicants in courts of law, subject to peer review and criticism, and played out in the court of public opinion. Therefore, regardless of the investigative model applied, regulatory bodies need to be prepared to defend their final determination and the evidence on which it is based both in court and to the public. This is where objectivity must be asserted and proven. The best proof is comprehensive, well-documented investigative files, which includes both financial and background files.

Finally, because challenges to adverse licensing decisions are increasing, regulatory agencies must consider implementing systems of checks and balances to ensure that the investigators present findings fairly, accurately, and efficiently.

When determining who should conduct the licensing investigation, governments have three main options: (a) existing local, state, or federal law enforcement agencies; (b) special investigators hired and trained for the task; or (c) third-party contractors. In making this choice, an initial consideration is whether the government believes existing law enforcement investigators have adequate training and can maintain neutrality. For example, tracing an applicant's funds to their primary source may require knowledge of accounting and banking. Existing investigators may not have the forensic accounting skills for this kind of work.

Some governments require their investigators to be sworn law enforcement officers with powers of arrest, and some use civilian or non-sworn personnel for such assignments. Sworn law enforcement officers have an advantage in that they often can access intelligence records and other law enforcement files based on cooperative agreements. If the investigator is not a sworn law enforcement officer, he or she may have to compel the applicant to secure the information or undertake requests under state or national freedom-of-information acts. This may lead to extra investigative time or leave an area of inquiry or concern unresolved.

A gaming regulatory agency that uses law enforcement officers to conduct investigations may experience problems. Law enforcement officers typically deal with criminals, and their perspective toward witnesses and the target of the investigation may be focused on trying to deduce evidence of guilt. As a result, transferring good criminal investigators into what is a primarily business environment can be difficult as most applicants are not criminals but legitimate business persons that seek to invest in a community. Law enforcement officers must transcend the mindset that the applicant is the perpetrator of a crime and the purpose of the investigation is to prove guilt. Instead, the investigation should be a neutral fact-finding mission consistent with state policy goals. If the investigator is biased, the system fails. Most stories can be told two ways. For example, was an applicant's failure to report the gain from the sale of a stock tax evasion or an oversight? An investigator who favors the applicant might conclude that the amount of the gain was small and the applicant properly reported all other gains from other accounts. An investigator who dislikes the applicant may insinuate the omission was intentional because the sale was close to the end of the tax year, and the brokerage house sent him notice of the gain just before he filed his taxes. A neutral report will say both and will better empower the determining body to make an informed decision.

A finding-of-suitability investigation is distinct from a criminal investigation because the investigator has fewer constraints. Laws may define the primary goals of licensing, but the fact-finding method to learn whether the applicant meets the licensing criterion is often not addressed. For example, if a law requires an applicant to be a person with good character, honesty, and integrity, how does an investigator learn facts necessary to making such a determination? They could be found virtually anywhere, from the applicant's high school records and accessible court documents to statements made by prior business partners and former spouse(s). This open-ended investigation differs from typical criminal investigations wherein the investigator is searching for evidence of certain activity, such as a criminal act, or determining the cause of an accident.

Because of the functional differences between criminal and licensing investigations, a person with a criminal investigation background may not initially possess all the skills necessary to conduct a successful suitability investigation that might involve forensic accounting, open-ended background investigation, and knowledge of the casino industry.[4] Unlike a criminal investigation, a gaming-suitability investigation attempts to gather all credible information, both positive and derogatory, about an applicant to determine if the applicant meets the criteria for a gaming license. Licensing investigators can gather information from sources who will never testify in court, and whose credibility the applicant's counsel cannot challenge. Not only is this foreign to criminal investigations, it places great reliance on the integrity and fairness of the investigator.

With proper training, control, indoctrination in licensing investigations, and education on the policy goals of regulated gaming, however, former criminal investigators can excel at gaming-licensing investigations.

---

[4] The goals of a finding-of-suitability investigation and a pre-employment background investigation, however, are similar. Both determine if an applicant meets the qualifications to work in a specific industry, not if someone should be incarcerated for their behavior, actions, or lack thereof. Investigators experienced in conducting pre-employment background investigations may find this transition easier.

The second option is to hire and train special gaming investigators. This typically involves maintaining two types of investigators: financial investigators and background investigators. Financial investigators usually have accounting or finance degrees, and background investigators usually have investigative or law enforcement experience. The advantage to this method is the agency maintains qualified investigators that report solely to the regulatory agency, which is responsible for quality controls, ethical standards, and efficiency. While this system, properly implemented, is preferred method, it is also expensive, particularly for smaller jurisdictions where workflow is less predictable. Moreover, jurisdictions new to gaming will have separate start-up time and costs.

When using either law enforcement officers or special gaming investigators, a need exists in some jurisdictions to professionalize the gaming investigations. One solution is to grant professional designation to investigators who meet a minimum education level, meet the minimum years of experience, and pass a competency test. It should test knowledge of background/legal, general business/finance, and gaming. The latter may include the review of all facets of a hotel/casino, such as rack rates, casino rates, comps, drops, hard count, soft count, surveillance, slots, table games, race and sports books, and other operational issues. With the professional designation, a standardized system between jurisdictions could evolve. Uniform practices may include peer review that may ensure honesty and reduce political influence.

A trend among some emerging and smaller jurisdictions is to use third-party contractors to conduct licensing investigations. These for-profit companies are usually skilled at conducting investigations as they often employ investigators with substantial gaming experience. The question remains, however, whether these contractors and their employees are neutral and efficient. For obvious reasons, caution is justified when the third-party contractor works for both governments and private companies because potential conflicts can arise. Suppose the third-party contractor is hired to investigate an applicant for a casino license in a state. Suppose further that the third-party contractor does private work, such as due-diligence reports on vendors, for that applicant's primary competitor. The applicant investigation may be tainted by the appearance of a conflict. Second, are third-party contractors efficient? A third-party contractor may have no motivation to conclude an investigation efficiently. Often, as profit seekers, private companies have exactly the opposite motivation and will increase costs by dragging out investigations.

Some hybrid methods are available. For example, a government may use existing police agencies to do background investigations and special investigators to do financial investigations. In some foreign investigations, the regulatory agency may use a combination of its own investigators and third-party contractors. This may be useful where internal gaming investigators work with a third party contractor such as an accounting firm in a foreign jurisdiction to assist with interpreting, understanding, and converting financial reports and documents.

PAYING FOR THE INVESTIGATION

No ideal method for funding a licensing investigation exists. All methods have advantages and disadvantages. Three principal methods are (1) pay-as-you-go applicant-funded investigations; (2) fixed-fee investigations; and (3) government-funded investigations.

Pay-As-You-Go

The most common financing method is applicant-funded, pay-as-you-go investigations. During an applicant-funded investigation, the applicant reimburses the regulatory agency for the costs of the investigation, including paying for the regulators' and investigators' time at an established hourly fee. In these pay-as-you-go systems, regulators pass the costs associated with processing the application directly to the applicant. If the system is working properly, regulators bill the applicant in direct proportion to the complexity of the investigation. A justification for the pay-as-you go system is that it requires applicants to pay for their own investigation, and it places the financial burden on the party requesting the benefit of a privileged license. Under this system, larger corporate organizations and applicants with complex backgrounds or business dealings pay higher investigative costs. For example, a person wishing to open a small casino with 12 gaming tables will pay significantly less than a multinational publicly traded company with offices worldwide.

One problem with pay-as-you-go systems, however, is that given an open ticket, who assures the cost of the investigation is reasonable? Without budgetary restraints, the agency may use its investigative powers to maximize its growth or to ensure full-employment of its staff. Moreover, the agency may have little motivation to police investigator spending when costs do not come out of the agency's budget but are billed directly to the applicant. Likewise, when third-party contractors are used, their motivation is to maximize their profit. When this occurs, applicants are paying not only for the cost of the investigation but also for the contractor's profit. This lack of policing can result in additional abuses with economic consequences. For example, an investigator may take an "investi-cation," which is an unnecessary trip to an exotic location where an applicant once resided. Often, the applicant will never learn if an investigator has abused his prerogative. The summary of expenses, if the regulators provide one, may only generically describe time and expenses spent. Unlike a legislature that may question an agency's expenditures, an applicant is unlikely to question the spending of an agency responsible for issuing its license.

Another downfall of pay-as-you-go systems is their tendency to reduce the number of prospective applicants. Because predicting what it will cost to obtain licensure is difficult, pay-as-you-go systems infuse uncertainty into the licensing process. A company considering entering a gaming market will undoubtedly compare probable costs against potential profits when deciding whether to apply for a license. If government predetermines or fixes the cost, the applicant can easily assess whether the cost justifies the potential reward. With no fixed costs, a company can only guess at the exposure.

To reduce some uncertainty and abuses, governments adopting pay-as-you-go systems should be businesslike in their approach. Applicants should be told the estimated investigation cost early in the process and how long it is expected to take. Regulators can make these predictions by reviewing an application as soon as it is received and deciding what the investigation's scope. With this knowledge, companies can make informed decisions about whether obtaining a license is the best use of their or their shareholders' money. Regulators also can prevent abuses by establishing checks and balances. A team approach that uses a supervisor to review the investigators' methods and findings often accomplishes this. The supervisor should review the time and cost of the investigation, a detailed report regarding the scope of the investigator's work and timeline, and his or her final report. In larger regulatory agencies, a person above the supervisor may periodically review the conduct and cost of the investigation to provide a second check. Travel and expense guidelines(including travel methods) should also be set. These guidelines can include prohibiting first-class air travel prescribing maximum per diem charges for room and food. All travel and extraordinary expenses should be subject to explicit supervisory approval, the level of which depends on the type of expenditure involved.

Licensing expenses can also be checked by involving another agency or branch of government, which serves as a watchdog. For example, the applicant may directly reimburse the government for investigation costs, paying directly into a general fund overseen by the legislature or budget office. Rather than draw from this fund, the agency must periodically request and justify paying for its investigations from the legislature or the budget office. When that occurs, the legislature or budget office may choose to review the general efficiency of the agency. This may not prevent all instances of abuse, but it provides some level of legislative overview of expenses. Systems of this kind also incentivize regulators to more closely monitor investigators' activities in order that they keep within the confines of the legislative budget.

Fixed Fee Systems

Another common method of funding investigations is to require a standard fee for all applicants. This funding method is based on the regulator's estimate or actual average cost of an investigation. For example, a supplier's application fee may be fixed at $2,500. This method is more common for lower levels of licensing such as a registration for a junket representative or a work card for a gaming employee.

A fixed-fee system brings certainty to the licensing process. A potential applicant can determine if it is worth entering the gaming industry in a particular jurisdiction and can adequately budget for the investigation. Casino workers can easily determine whether a move from one jurisdiction to another makes financial sense.

Inequities, however, still exist in fixed-fee systems. If an applicant with a clean and simple background seeks a license to operate a small casino or card room, it seems unfair to charge that applicant the same amount as a large corporation that might have many regulatory issues and may want to open a larger gaming establishment. Using graduated fee schedules that base costs on the number of individual applicants may overcome some of these inequities.

Another concern with the fixed-fee method is that the money the regulatory agency has in its investigative fund may influence the investigation. If a surplus exists, the regulators may conduct excessive investigations to justify the fee structure or an increase to it. On the other hand, if a deficiency in the fund exists, regulators may not conduct as thorough an investigation.

Government-Financed Systems

A regulatory agency may be required to finance investigations out of a legislative budget. This shifts the monetary burden from the applicants to the government. This eliminates a barrier to potential entrants who fear the high or unknown cost of licensing. The budget process by which the agency obtains funding to conduct investigations also may involve closer legislative scrutiny because the funds are obtained from the government's general fund.

This method may be unappealing because it requires the use of tax proceeds to fund investigations. In many jurisdictions, the only practical way to raise these funds is to earmark them from gaming tax revenues. This shifts the financial burden of investigations to existing licensees. Without these expenses, governments could presumably impose lower taxes on the industry, which in turn, might lead to lower prices for patrons and increased competitiveness of the gaming industry.

A government-financed system might be more appealing when applied only to specific groups in particular jurisdictions. For example, some governments may need to encourage suppliers of certain goods or services to supply their gaming industry. When a monopoly market has a single casino with only a few hundred gaming devices, it does not make sense for manufacturers to bear the expense of an investigation on a pay-as-you-go system to serve such a small market. Therefore, by choosing a government-financed system and agreeing to bear the cost, the government can ensure its casinos and card rooms have an adequate supply and diversity of gaming equipment at competitive rates.

Government-financed systems are also often employed when regulators are prohibited from assessing the applicant for the cost of the investigation. Nevada, for example, retains the right to investigate persons that have businesses on the casino premises, such as jewelry and dress store owners, but its courts have held it cannot charge these businesses for the investigation.[5]

PRELIMINARY MATTERS
Permitting Applicants to be Represented by Counsel

Applicants frequently retain gaming attorneys to assist them with obtaining a privileged gaming license. The applicant may have varying motives for retaining an attorney. Some applicants believe that the process can be influenced by an attorney with political connections. An immense problem in many jurisdictions where gaming is now legal is the concept of "juice"—that an applicant will be given preferential or special consideration unrelated to the merits of his or her application by hiring a consultant, attorney, or accountant who has close ties with the governor. Regulators should be most appalled by claims that an applicant has "juice." The "juice" concept implies corruption because for juice to work, regulators must violate their duties or responsibilities to the state. Methods to inhibit corruption are set forth in Chapter 7.

Experienced gaming lawyers can provide legitimate positive impacts on the investigation, however. These impacts may include ensuring applicants understand the application questions and respond to them appropriately. Gaming attorneys might also assist an applicant by ensuring that information requests from investigators are logged and fulfilled in a timely manner. In rare cases, the attorney can intervene with the investigator's supervisor if the investigator exceeds boundaries like providing confidential information to competitors, invades the personal rights of non-applicants, harboring an irrational prejudice against the applicant, or otherwise conducts an unfair investigation. Another valuable skill an attorney can bring to the application process is problem-solving. This could be as simple as figuring out ways to obtain information in foreign countries, under sealed record, or in third-parties' possession. On the other hand, attorney involvement could be as complex as a major restructuring of a multibillion dollar development to meet all regulatory objectives without compromising the financial objectives of the lenders, equity holders, and others.

---

[5] *See State v. Glusman*, 98 Nev. 412, 651 P.2d 639 (1982) (holding investigations of non-gaming operations on casino property are legal, but requiring the government to pay the costs of these investigations as it was "not within the scope or purpose of gaming control infinitive to selectively impose on non-gamers the financial burden of gaming enforcement.").

These positive impacts do not preclude some gaming attorneys from being obstructionists. Frequently, gaming attorneys' adversarial attitudes frustrate investigator's goals. In these instances, applications might be better handled by the individual applicant.

Privacy and Confidentiality of Personal/Proprietary Information

As noted throughout this chapter, individuals and companies applying for licensure must disclose intimate personal details, financial data, and proprietary information to regulators. The expectation that these disclosures and corresponding documents will remain confidential is realistic. Unfortunately, the regulatory landscape does not support that expectation.

The right to privacy differs both in importance and concept between societies, but is becoming increasingly accepted. Even the United Nations, in its Universal Declaration of Human Rights, states, "No one shall be subjected to arbitrary interference with his privacy, family, home or correspondence, nor to attacks upon his honor and reputation. Everyone has the right to the protection of the law against such interference or attacks."[6] Privacy is often considered a societal cornerstone as it promotes freedom of conscience, diversity in thought, and democratic participation, including the freedoms of speech and association.

Others see privacy as necessary for the attainment of human autonomy and dignity. Professor Ruth Gavison noted that "privacy is central to the attainment of individual goals under every theory of the individual that has ever captured man's imagination."[7] This was aptly described as it relates to the medical profession:

> Humans, unlike animals, formulate aims and beliefs, reason about them, make choices on their basis, and attempt to plan for the future. This means that respect for autonomy—for the attributes which define humanity—goes hand in hand with human dignity. Autonomy encompasses not just the right to self-determination about our bodies and how they are treated, but also to information about ourselves, our lifestyles, and our health. The right to control who knows the things about us which we regard as private is integral to our sense of self and sense of identity.[8]

Still others see privacy as contextual and necessary to maintain a free society. This was framed by Professor Gavison who said, "Privacy is needed to enable the individual to deliberate and establish his opinions. If public reaction seems likely to be unfavorable, privacy may permit an individual to express his judgments to a group of like-minded people. After a period of germination, such individuals may be more willing to declare their un-

---

[6] Universal Declaration of Human Rights, G.A. Res. 217A, at 73-74, U.N. GAOR, 3d Sess., 1st plen. Mtg., U.N. Doc. A/810 (Dec. 12, 1948).

[7] Ruth Gavison, *Privacy and the Limits of Law*, 89 Yale L.J. 421, 445 (1979).

[8] J. O'Brien & C. Chantler, Confidentiality and the Duties of Care, 29 J. Med. Ethics 1, 36–40 (2003).

popular views in public."[9]

With increased technology use and governments' ability to access information electronically, privacy is been popular topic. Still, it has been of concern for a long time. In 1890, Sam Warren and Louis Brandeis wrote in the Harvard Law Review:

> The intensity and complexity of life, attendant upon advancing civilization, have rendered necessary some retreat from the world, and man, under the refining influence of culture, has become more sensitive to publicity, so that solitude and privacy have become more essential to the individual; but modern enterprise and invention have, through invasions upon his privacy, subjected him to mental pain and distress, far greater than could be inflicted by mere bodily injury.[10]

Professor Daniel Solove conceptualized four categories of privacy concerns:

- information collection, including surveillance, and interrogation;
- information processing, including aggregation, identification (connecting information to individual), insecurity (glitches, security lapses, abuses, and illicit uses of personal information), secondary use (uses of information beyond those purposes for which it is collected), and exclusion of information (failure to provide individuals with notice and input about their records);
- dissemination, including breach of confidentiality (betrayal of trust), disclosure (public disclosure of private facts), exposure (exposing to others of certain physical and emotional attributes such as grief, suffering, trauma, injury, nudity, or sex), increased accessibility (making available information easier to access), blackmail, appropriation (use of one's identity or personality for the purposes and goals of another), distortion (being inaccurately exposed to the public); and
- invasion including intrusion (invasions or incursions into one's life) and decisional interference (government interference in decisions such as abortion).[11]

Gaming investigations can involve all of these privacy concerns. Gaming investigators first collect massive amounts of information and frequently question the applicant about personal and potentially embarrassing facts. The process often involves incursion into one's life at a very personal level such as political affiliations or family matters such as illegitimate children. Agents may covertly observe the applicant's business. The information collected must be protected from disclosure to third parties. Few would argue that personal information like social security numbers and credit card account numbers should be made readily available to the

---

[9] Gavison, *supra* note 7, *at* 450 (1979).

[10] Samuel D. Warren & Louis D. Brandeis, *The Right to Privacy*, 4 HARVARD L. REV. 193, 196 (1890).

[11] Daniel J. Solove, *A Taxonomy of Privacy*, 254 U. PA. L. REV. 477, 489 (2006).

public. In every respect, gaming investigations strike to the heart of most persons' basic privacy concerns.

Few would argue that the right to privacy should be absolute. For example, the United Nations proclamation provides protection only against arbitrary invasions of privacy. The right to privacy is continually balanced with other public goals, whether they are increased data collection, relaxed wiretaps to respond to terrorism,[12] or the public's legitimate right to know certain information about their government officials. In most situations where the right to privacy is breached, the law will set limits on how and when the government can intrude into people's private lives. For example, some limits include the rules of law and procedures police must follow when searching a person's home for criminal evidence.

Privacy expectations are lower when a person seeks a gaming license than when a person is being investigated in a criminal context. Although license applicants should expect that gaming investigators will pursue information that might otherwise be confidential, they typically do not completely abandon their expectation of privacy when applying for a license. Just because a gaming investigator can use a technique that is legal, it does not mean the technique is acceptable or should be a common practice. In an extreme case, waterboarding may be a permitted form of interrogation in some jurisdictions, but it is questionable as a means of conducting a gaming applicant interview.

Jurisdictions can do four things to protect an applicant's expectation of privacy. First, investigators should follow the law when conducting a license investigation. In addition to following the law in their own jurisdiction, investigators should also abide by any applicable laws where the investigation takes place and where data is derived. This requires investigators to familiarize themselves with the laws of foreign jurisdictions before traveling there. Some jurisdictions have statutory limits on information collection, processing, and distribution. Under the Australian Federal Privacy Act, for example, a third party cannot disclose information for a purpose other than that for which they were provided the information.[13] This may restrict a gaming investigator from passing on information obtained during an investigation to another law enforcement agency.

Second, a jurisdiction should establish policies regarding the confidentiality of information provided by gaming applicants and obtained by investigators. Perhaps the jurisdiction that most stringently protects confidentiality is Nevada. By statute, all information and data prepared or obtained by regulators or investigators relative to a license application, a finding-of-suitability investigation, or any approval is confidential and absolutely privileged. It may only be revealed in whole or in part when

---

[12]Stefanie Olsen and Evan Hansen, Terrorist threat shifts priorities in online rights debate, Cnet News.com, September 17, 2001.

[13] BAKER HOSTETLER, 2014 INTERNATIONAL COMPENDIUM OF DATA PRIVACY LAWS, WWW. DATAPRIVACYMONITOR.COM.

administering gaming regulations or after the regulators' specific authorization and waiver of privilege. Regulators, however, may reveal such information and data to an authorized agent of any agency of the United States government, any state or any political subdivision of a state, or the government of any foreign country.

After Nevada, no true assurances exist in the United States that personal or proprietary information obtained during a license investigation can or will remain confidential. A review of a several jurisdictions revealed that medical and library records are better protected than information and data associated with gaming license applications. For example, in jurisdictions such as Massachusetts and Ohio, on license applications, applicants must designate what information should be kept confidential and provide justifications for the requested confidentiality. Unfortunately, however, should a jurisdiction wrongly disclose personal or proprietary information, that jurisdiction is typically excused by arguing that it was part of the application process. With this indemnity, jurisdictions may not closely monitor how and why they disclose data and information. In a worst-case scenario, in some jurisdictions, an applicant may find their personal information splashed across the front page of the local newspaper. In summary, disclosure is the most extreme cost of doing business due to lack of confidentiality guarantees.

Third, the privacy and confidentiality policies of the regulatory body should be communicated to the applicant. Under federal trade laws, online sites must have clear and prominent terms in their privacy policies that consumers will likely find material in deciding to participate in the service or order the product being advertised.[14] Following this same reasoning, in gaming investigations, an agency should provide an applicant with an acknowledgement that information furnished may be given to other law enforcement agencies or that his or her financial information may be given to tax authorities. Though doing so may discourage some potential applicants from even applying for a license, it could be beneficial to the regulatory agency. The applicants dissuaded from applying by these disclosures are most likely those that would ultimately be denied a license. Therefore, the agency does not have to waste valuable resources on these fruitless investigations.

Fourth, the regulatory agency should have internal policies for when investigators want to go beyond standard investigative techniques. This could include, for example, seizing and downloading private emails on a home computer. In an attempt to establish institutional responsibility, Professor William Beaney promoted standards to sensitize administrative agencies to undesirable consequences of their actions. He suggested before deciding upon a course of action encroaching upon a person's privacy, a jurisdiction should ensure:

---

[14] Susan E. Gindin, Nobody Reads Your Privacy Policy or Online Contract: Lessons Learned and Questions Raised by the FTC's Action Against Sears, 1 Nw. J. Tech. & Intell. Prop. 8 (2009).

(a) that the means selected are necessary and appropriate; (b) that there is no equally suitable means of attaining the objective that avoids an adverse effect on privacy values; (c) that where the confidentiality of data is required by law, adequate safeguards will be observed to maintain confidentiality in fact; and (d) that the agency provides some form of internal review of decisions that involve privacy issues.[15]

BEFORE THE INVESTIGATION
The Application Forms

In some respects, a suitability investigation is easier than a criminal investigation because the gaming applicant must cooperate by providing information and files. Because of this, requiring the applicant to complete well-drafted forms can provide investigators with a wealth of useful information they can use to build a framework on which to conduct the investigation. An applicant begins the licensing process by providing personal and professional information to the regulatory agency that is conducting the investigation. This is typically accomplished by the applicant filing out various forms provided by the investigative agency. Regulators should design forms that elicit information about the applicant's antecedents, criminal record, business activities and associates, and financial affairs for the years preceding the filing.[16] Applications should be crafted depending on the level and the criteria for licensing a particular applicant group. For example, no need exists for a card dealer who is obtaining a work permit, or even the Chief Technology Officer of a major public company, to complete extensive financial disclosures. Likewise, a Chief Executive Officer may not need the background or training to competently deal blackjack.

Multijurisdictional forms are becoming more popular. The obvious advantage to these forms is cost and efficiency for companies that operate in multiple jurisdictions. These companies can store each individual's information in a database and use it to complete most of the forms. The problem with these forms is that they tend to be over-inclusive. Regardless of the person's position or the jurisdiction's criteria for licensing, the forms are the same. This is usually an acceptable trade off, but it requires the investigating jurisdiction to use judgment in determining the materiality of the information on the multijurisdictional forms. Standardized forms should not mandate standardized investigations for all applicants.

Among the more typical forms are

- An application form that asks for the identity of the applicant and

---

[15] William Beaney, *The Right to Privacy and American Law*, 31 LAW & CONTEMP. PROBS. 253, 270 (1966).

[16] *See, e.g.,* INT'L ASS'N OF GAMING REGULATORS, http://iagr.org/multi-jurisdictional-form/ (providing an example of a Multi-Jurisdictional Personal History Form and a Multi-Jurisdictional Business Form).

the type of license or approval sought. There may be separate forms for individuals, private corporations, public companies, holding companies, and partnerships.

- A personal financial form that often covers the amount and source of investment in the gaming establishment, tax information, salary information, and a detailed statement of assets and liabilities.
- A personal history form, which is described in Figure 16.1 on the following page. This form also may request nongaming business and financial interests and character references.

An applicant should take great care completing all forms. Investigators will rely on the information provided through this initial process to develop an investigative plan. An applicant should expect every detail on these forms will be verified, analyzed, and thoroughly investigated.

Apart from these basic forms, regulators can request many releases, waivers, and other relinquishments of rights or privileges. The most important waiver is that which obtains the applicant's consent not to sue the gaming regulators or their investigators for anything related to the gaming application or the investigative process. A separate release form often contains this provision. This form protects the government and regulators from civil liability. Suppose an investigator shares negative or false information with the applicant's banker. If the banker subsequently cancels a loan with the applicant, the applicant could not successfully sue the investigator or regulators because of the signed release.

Typical application forms also include releases that allow third persons to share information with investigators without fearing a lawsuit being brought against them by the applicant for libel, slander, or any other reason. These releases also may allow third parties to provide information they could not otherwise legally provide.

Finally, the applicant may sign release forms that allow investigators to obtain privileged or confidential information from other parties, such as banks and businesses. These forms enable a person to provide information to the investigator, which would otherwise be protected by a legal privilege. For example, accountants may refuse to give a client's information to investigators, citing an accountant-client privilege. To get around this, the form might state that the applicant authorizes the person to whom the form is given to cooperate with the investigators by providing information and documents, that the applicant waives any legal privileges, such as the accountant-client or attorney-client privilege, and releases the person giving the information from any liability.

Whether the release should apply to the applicant's gaming attorney is a difficult question. Effective assistance of counsel is jeopardized if the applicant's attorney must share confidential documents and conversations about the investigation with investigators. If investigators are reviewing a lawsuit, questioning the lawyer who represented the applicant about that lawsuit may be appropriate. However, interrogating the applicant's attorney

Figure 16.1

Areas Covered	Types of information that may be requested
Identifiers	Full name; maiden name; date of birth; federal identification number; mailing, home, and business addresses; home, mobile, and business telephone numbers; physical characteristics; photograph; fingerprints
Citizenship	Countries of citizenship, place of birth, country of birth, passport numbers, country of passport issue, place issued, date issued, expiration date
Residence	Current and past residence(s) including dates and address(es); ownership or rental status; name, address, and telephone number of landlord or mortgage/bond holder, if known
Marital	Current and past marriages, dates and places of marriage(s), identifiers of and employment information for current and past spouses
Family	Identifiers and occupations of parents, parents-in-law, former parents-in-law, legal guardians, children, and siblings (same may be requested for spouse(s))
Military Service	Branch, service serial number, highest rank held, period(s) of active service, date and type of discharge or separation, any military court martial or charges
Education	Names and addresses of schools, dates of attendance, degrees, if applicable,
Corporate or trust positions	Dates, title of office or position held, name and address of government agency/organization (same may be requested for spouse(s))
Government positions	Dates, title of office or position held, name and address of government agency/organization (same may be requested for spouse(s))
Employment	Dates, position, duties, employer identifiers, supervisor identifiers, compensation, disciplinary actions, reason for leaving
Privileged Licenses	Applied for or held, dates, name and address of licensing agency, denials, revocations, disciplinary actions
Motor vehicle operator licenses	Jurisdiction, date last issued, license number, type of license, jurisdiction issuing license, expiration date of license
Business Ownership	Identifiers on business, status, percentage ownership, identifiers on other owners
Criminal History	Detained, arrested, questioned or charged for any crime; nature of charge; date, place, and location where incident occurred; law enforcement agency or court involved; disposition; any criminal indictment; information or complaint where no arrest was made or where named as an unindicted party or unindicted co-conspirator; information where subject of any government investigation; interviews by law enforcement; whether provided testimony, given a polygraph, subpoenaed to appear, given immunity from prosecution, pardoned, or given deferred prosecution

Litigation history - personal or as an officer, director, or equity holder	Date filed, name and address of court, docket/case number, other parties to suit, nature of suit, disposition, disposition date, garnishments, protective or restraining orders.
Governmental liens/debts	Nature of lien/debt, when filed, where filed, current status
Bankruptcy, insolvency, receiverships, government administration - business or personal	Date filed, docket/case number, name and address of court, name and address of filing party, name and address of trustee

about what the applicant may have said in preparing for an investigation interview is inappropriate.

Some jurisdictions require the applicant to provide sworn statements attesting to the accuracy of the information in both personal history and financial forms. This may include an affidavit wherein the applicant attests that he or she is the sole owner of the interest for which he or she is seeking a license, and no undisclosed party has any present or future interest in the license. Affidavits also may require sworn statements that all information provided to the regulators is true, complete, and not misleading. This form is also likely to request that the applicant keep the regulators consistently advised of any changes in the information provided in the application.

Other required forms typically include fingerprinting and credit reports. Fingerprint checks are used to verify the applicant's identity and to obtain criminal records. These checks may be sent to central processing agencies, such as the Federal Bureau of Investigation in the United States, to learn if the applicant has a criminal history. Credit reports can be used to verify addresses, determine if an applicant is current in meeting financial obligations, or has filed for bankruptcy.[17]

As noted in Chapter 15, an applicant's conduct during the investigation can be an important criterion that regulators assess in determining whether to grant a license. The burden of proving suitability starts with the initial application. Applicants should submit complete and accurate application forms and provide all requested supporting documentation. Incomplete or inaccurate applications can show a lack of appreciation for the regulatory process, incompetence, or lack of preparation.

Whether the applicant is a company or an individual, regulators may reasonably expect applicants conduct due diligence reviews prior to submitting their application forms. Failing to conduct a due diligence review is akin to playing Russian roulette in the gaming industry. For example, with Internet gaming coming to the forefront, normally cautious and es-

---

[17] The Federal Trade Commission (FTC) is the nation's consumer protection agency. The FTC enforces the Fair Credit Report Act (FCRA) which is the law that protects the privacy and accuracy of the information in credit reports. The FCRA spells out the rights of applicants and the responsibilities of employers.

tablished gaming companies may be associated with employees or suppliers who are likely to create licensing issues for them. In the name of due diligence, applicants should therefore conduct their own finding of suitability tests on employees or associates similar to those the jurisdiction or regulatory agency will perform. They should conduct background reviews on individual applicants, and when practicable, have the applicants scrutinized by independent compliance committees. Even today, publicly-traded companies and privately-held gaming companies file repeatedly rejected faulty applications. The costs associated with these rejections can likely be prevented if companies conduct their own due diligence on applicants before filing the application.

Jurisdictions are correct to reject incomplete or poorly crafted application forms. Every regulatory agency has limited budgetary and human resources. Trying to build an investigative plan around a faulty application is difficult. It not only delays the investigation, it increases costs. If a jurisdiction requires and expects that applications will be complete and accurate when filed, any delays in licensure and pending business operations will be the applicant's fault.

Investigators should inform applicants in writing that when completing the forms they should compile and maintain up-to-date supporting documents. This may include a list of available and current documents the investigators will need during the investigation. For example, once a tax return is filed or new financial statements are produced, copies should be added to the applicant's record database.

Before the Opening Interview

Investigations should be preplanned and logical. A supervising investigator or manager should review the application and assign it to a qualified staff member based on the complexity of the application. An investigative team can have as few as one investigator or as many as a dozen. The size of the team depends on the regulators' capabilities, the complexity of the investigation, time requirements, and other considerations. Unfortunately, some regulatory agencies have a small staff and limited resources. These agencies can only place one or two investigators on an investigation despite the anticipated complexity of an application.

Where an agency has the human resource capabilities, it might consider a team approach to complex investigations. The supervising investigator is usually an experienced investigator who has direct responsibility for the daily activities of the investigators involved in the investigation. The supervising investigator provides guidance to investigators and formulates the investigative strategy. The team may also consist of financial investigators who hold degrees in accounting. Financial investigators scrutinize the applicant's financial status, past business activities, business probity, and the financial status of the proposed gaming operation. Other team members might include background investigators tasked with investigating the applicant's background, general reputation, and personal and business associates.

The team might begin the investigation by asking the applicant to appear at an opening interview. If an investigator is prepared, however, he will already have completed some preliminary tasks. Before the initial interview, the investigator or team should meet with a supervisor to discuss the entire application, noting any conflicts in the application and proposing a plan for processing it. Investigators should then review the application and access easily available information, such as anything contained in the agency's files. A primary responsibility before the opening interview is to reconcile the information in the application. For example, investigators review whether the past addresses provided by the applicant reconcile with the applicant's list of previous employers. Another pre-opening interview step is to uncover any unexplained gaps in the applicant's records. Any area of concern in the application is a proper subject during the opening interview. At this stage, investigators should attempt to ensure that all the information they are working with is accurate and complete.

A delicate balance exists between having a standardized investigative format and encouraging the background and financial agents' discretion to pursue a direction to which evidence or suspicions may lead. The standardized format's value is that it ensures agents are covering all the areas of inquiry expected by the regulators so that when the report is ultimately generated, it is comprehensive. The danger with standardized procedures, however, is that they can become a checklist that rigidly restrains what the agents cover. When this occurs, any information outside of the standard areas of inquiry may not be investigated. On the other hand, too much discretion can lead to the agents pursuing irrelevant or unproductive inquiries. This is where the role of the supervisor in each investigation is critical. The supervisor should make sure that all the expected avenues of inquiry are covered according to standard written or historical protocol, but just as importantly, the supervisor should make sure that investigators are pursuing additional areas of inquiry that merit further scrutiny.

The Opening Interview

An opening interview is the first opportunity for the applicant to meet with the investigators who will be handling the investigation. It gives investigators an opportunity to explain procedures and demystify the investigative process. The investigators should review the initial application forms line by line with the applicant to ensure that no unintentional omissions, mistakes, or typographical errors exist.

The opening interview may provide a second opportunity for the applicant to reveal previously undisclosed matters before the failure to disclose is held against him or her. If investigators uncover a major issue during the investigation the applicant failed to reveal both in the application and upon direct questioning in the opening interview, it may affect whether they are ultimately granted a license. During the opening interview, investigators may also make requests for initial documents.

Initial Document Requests

The applicant investigation usually begins with the request for basic financial documents. Some of these documents are requested merely to confirm the person's identity and to collect identifiers to conduct the background investigation. Initial information requested for the background investigation typically includes the following:

Figure 16.2

Applicant's birth certificate.
Government identification card
Naturalization or alien registration papers
Social security card
Current and previous passports
The applicant's last will and testament
Any trust agreements, trust tax returns, and a list and valuation of assets held by the trusts, to which the applicant is a party
Any current employment and/or stock option agreement(s)
Any federal, state, county, or city licenses held by the applicant individually or as a representative of a business
Any litigation and arbitration involvement for the applicant as an individual, member of a partnership, member/manager of a limited liability company, or shareholder, director, or officer of a corporation whether the applicant was a plaintiff/defendant or defendant/respondent. Documentation may include the following: <ul><li>Original complaint</li><li>Amended complaint(s)</li><li>Cross complaint(s)</li><li>Disposition, summary judgment, settlement agreement</li><li>Written narrative describing the circumstances that led to the lawsuit or</li><li>arbitration</li></ul>

Most initial documentation requests, however, concern the applicant's finances. This documentation is necessary to conduct a cash flow analysis and to verify the applicant's net worth. These requests may include the following:

Figure 16.3

Federal income tax returns	Savings passbooks, bank statements, canceled checks, deposit slips, and check registers
Escrow documents for the purchase and sale of real estate	All other documents and supporting records to substantiate or verify sources of income

The initial or supplemental document request may also include the following:

Figure 16.4

Records of certificates of deposit	Records of any cashier's checks purchased
Notes and loans receivable	Notes and loans payable
Financial statements	Accountant's work papers
Brokerage accounts	Contingent liabilities (i.e., guarantees)
List of all business investments	Appraisals of real estate holdings

Business records requested may include the following:

Figure 16.5

General ledgers	Cash receipts and disbursement journals
Minute books	Stock certificate books
Canceled checks and bank statements	Accounts payable ledgers
Accounts receivable ledgers	Payroll records
State revenue reports	Financial statements
Loan agreements	Notes and loans payable, including original date, amount of loan, present balance, and names of lenders
Notes and loans receivable	Partnership agreements
Savings accounts, passbooks, and deposit records	Copies of federal and state income tax returns
Copies of federal and state income tax audit adjustments	Accountant's work papers
Names and addresses of all partners and co-shareholders of closely-held corporations	Escrow papers for the purchase and sale of real estate

Investigators use these basic documents to begin their investigation. Initial review of these documents may evoke questions requiring the investigator to make further document requests. Investigators also may request to review personal items, such as diaries, day calendars, phone lists, Christmas card lists, and personal correspondence. Investigators may also need to inspect documents and items in safety deposit boxes and safes.

A potentially controversial issue is the extent to which investigators may review and copy data from smart phones and home computers. Technology is readily available to investigators to copy phone contacts, text messages, emails or even entire computer hard drives. Though this has occurred in several cases before, it is a tactic only usually employed when investigators have some reason to believe that information on an applicant's telephone or computer is particularly relevant to the investigation. In any case, the regulatory agency should establish a policy regarding the availability of data on cell phones and computers. When doing so, the regulatory agency should carefully evaluate applicable privacy laws and consider the practical implications of invading a space where the public and the applicant have a heightened expectation of privacy. Most applicants understand their business records are fair game for the regulators but are more sensitive toward dairies, personal text messages, and private personal photographs that may reside on home computers or cell phones.

THE BACKGROUND INVESTIGATION

Background investigators usually have broad powers particularly in discretionary background investigations. They can inspect premises, demand access to examine and photocopy records, and interview witnesses. They may also review civil lawsuits and criminal charges filed against the applicant. No set rules should exist about how far back in the applicant's past the investigators may search. Although the focus may be on the last 10 years, if pertinent, investigators should be able to review a transgression that occurred 20 years ago.

The two primary purposes of fieldwork are to verify the information provided by the applicant and to uncover information the applicant may not have revealed. Because of the nature of fieldwork, an applicant may not have much contact with the background investigators. Investigators are often working with other law enforcement agencies and conducting extensive interviews to evaluate the character of the applicant. Most investigators prefer personal contact with persons providing information over telephone calls or email correspondence. This allows the investigator to ask questions that may result in more complete answers and lead them towards other areas of inquiry. It also allows the investigator to assess the credibility of the person they are interviewing.

A full discretionary background investigation starts with verification of the information contained in the application and goes beyond a mere check of the applicant's police record. The investigation identifies the applicant's known business and personal associates and their methods of doing business. Investigators review civil court records to examine the nature of all civil litigation involving the applicant and to ensure that the applicant has fully revealed their litigation history.

Background investigations of applicants can be local, national, or international. Each requires special consideration. However, local and national investigations are less problematic because procedures are familiar and cooperation across jurisdictions is more likely. Regardless, investigations should involve standard checks of court and regulatory agency files. Schools and universities are contacted to verify an applicant's educational background. Military information is verified with the applicant's respective branch. When assessing military records, investigators will pay close attention to any disciplinary history or other derogatory information. Marital information is reviewed with special attention given to divorces. This is important because divorces often are acrimonious, and the files may allege wrongdoing. Often, former spouses are sources of information relevant to the investigation.

Criminal Background

A criminal background investigation begins with a criminal history check of the applicant. This is done by having the applicant submit fingerprints to determine if the applicant has been arrested or convicted of committing a crime. This is just the beginning of the process. A complete criminal background investigation includes contacting local, state, federal, and other policing agencies.

Local law enforcement agencies such as police and sheriffs' departments maintain information that may be of use to the gaming investigator. Agencies maintain crime reports, incident reports, accident reports, traffic citation information, field interview cards, and intelligence files. Asking a local agency to query their records management system for calls from the applicant's home or business may also be of value as law enforcement agencies do not write a report each time they respond to a call for service. If the incident can be handled on the scene, and documentation does not seem warranted, a report will most likely not be prepared. However, the local records management system should have information relative to who called, the date and time the call was made, a summary of the incident, the individuals involved, and a disposition.

A local law enforcement check should be conducted in each jurisdiction where the applicant has lived, regularly frequents, and has previously worked.

State law enforcement agencies also provide useful information to the gaming investigator. In the United States, state law enforcement agencies may assist local agencies in complex investigations, traffic enforcement, crime lab services, or should an investigation cross jurisdictional boundaries. Like local law enforcement agencies, state agencies maintain crime reports, incident reports, accident reports, traffic citation information, field interview cards, and intelligence files. However, state law enforcement agencies maintain records management systems separate from local agency systems so a query of both systems should be conducted.[18]

---

[18] The Association of State Criminal Investigative Agencies maintains a list of member

Federal law enforcement agencies maintain even more records. US government agencies that may have criminal background information on an applicant include the Federal Bureau of Investigation; Drug Enforcement Administration; Immigration and Enforcement; Bureau of Alcohol, Tobacco, Firearms, and Explosives; Department of Homeland Security; Department of the Treasury; the Postal Service; and the Internal Revenue Service.[19] Each agency creates distinct reports and maintains separate records management systems and databases.

Besides law enforcement agencies, local, state, and federal task forces might maintain records and information that could be useful to a gaming investigator. Although multi-jurisdictional task forces may be comprised of representatives from local, state, and federal law enforcement agencies, such task forces are usually dedicated to a limited function like narcotic or gang enforcement. They also might have been formed to investigate a specific crime or criminal organization. Regardless, these task forces maintain their own records, which can include crime reports, incident reports, intelligence files, and general investigative files.

Private security companies may also provide useful information to gaming license investigators. With budget reductions at the local level, many communities employ private security companies to provide policing services in their communities. This is especially true in large, gated communities. Besides providing uniformed patrol, some security companies are now issuing parking and traffic citations, conducting investigations, photographing and collecting evidence, and responding to calls for service. These companies often maintain good records, and in some cases their records management system is superior to that of local law enforcement agencies.

Irrespective of where they find evidence of an applicant's criminal history, background investigators should review all criminal charges no matter their disposition. Just because criminal charges against an applicant were dismissed, it does not mean a crime was not committed. A key witness may have refused to testify, and as a result, the prosecution may have dismissed the action because it knew it could not win the case without the testimony.

Unlike criminal courts, regulatory agencies are not burdened by stiff rules regarding what can be considered at trial. For example, in criminal trials, the prosecution cannot introduce most evidence that is referred to as "hearsay." Hearsay is typically any statement given by a person other than the one presently testifying before the court. For example, a sworn statement by a person unavailable to testify may not be considered by the court. A regulatory agency, however, may consider such a statement when assessing an applicant's request for a privileged gaming license. This is so because in licensing situations, the goal is not to decide the guilt or inno-

---

agencies, and the list is quite comprehensive. The list can be viewed at www.ascia.org.

[19] USA.GOV, *A-Z Index of U.S. Government Agencies*, http://www.usa.gov/directory/federal/ (providing a comprehensive list of federal agencies).

cence of the applicant but to assess whether the applicant poses a threat to the integrity of the industry.

Whether the prosecutor dropped the charges against the applicant, or even if the applicant was acquitted, should not be conclusive in a licensing investigation. Standards for granting gaming licenses and standards for proving criminal guilt are different. An incident may not justify a criminal conviction, but it may justify a finding of unsuitability in a gaming license investigation. In a criminal action, the prosecutor must prove his case beyond a reasonable doubt. Therefore, if some reasonable doubt exists, then the person should be acquitted. In a gaming investigation, much less is required. If substantial evidence exists that an applicant committed a serious crime, such as extortion for example, regulators may be justified in denying the applicant a gaming license.

Further, the applicant's failure to disclose a criminal arrest raises credibility issues. Apart from traffic violations, encounters with police involving criminal offenses usually are not forgotten. Applicants may, however, confuse charges. For example, a person may not remember whether he or she was charged with disorderly conduct or public drunkenness when in college. Confusion over the charge is more common than failing to reveal the incident, and it typically does not rise to the same level of concern unless there is evidence the applicant attempted to mislead the regulators.

When the inquiry leads to the applicant's potential ongoing criminal activities, regulatory agents must be careful not to inadvertently prejudice or compromise an ongoing criminal investigation. In those cases, they should coordinate their investigation with other criminal enforcement agencies that have jurisdiction over the matter.[20] Though it does not happen often, gaming investigations have uncovered instances of child pornography, illegal gambling, tax evasion, and other crimes committed by applicants.

Background checks do not end with the applicant. They may extend to the applicant's family, friends, business partners, and associates. These inquiries are necessary to determine whether the applicant is merely a front for persons who would not qualify for a license on their own. These inquiries also reveal if the applicant knowingly associates with persons of notorious backgrounds or uses poor judgment by entering into business arrangements with unsavory individuals or criminals.

Use of Confidential Sources

Transparency in the methods by which agencies grant gaming licenses is important for public confidence. Transparency, however, has different dimensions. On one hand, a lack of transparency may suggest to the public that regulators are biased towards particular applicants due to political or

---

[20] Pat Leen & Tom Nelson, *Regulatory Investigations Made Simple*, CASINO ENTERPRISE MGMT., Apr. 30, 2009, http://www.casinoenterprisemanagement.com/articles/may-2009/regulatory-investigations-made-simple.

other corrupting influences. Open hearings and public access to the information upon which licensing decisions are made promotes the perception that the investigation is a truth-seeking function that permits regulators to make informed decisions consistent with policy goals. Sometimes, however, regulators may want to consider probative evidence where disclosure may be detrimental or prohibited.

One such circumstance occurs when information comes from a source that wishes to remain confidential. As one professor noted about informants in criminal cases, "the use of informants can be seen as a relaxation of public, rule-bound decision-making in the most practical sense."[21] Where the intelligence obtained from the informant is not disclosed to the applicant, the process itself appears both unfair and tainted because the applicant cannot present countervailing evidence or impugn the credibility of the informant. Regulators may exasperate the appearance of unfairness by attempting to justify a denial based on other information in the record that may not seem appropriate to the public.

The use of confidential information in the licensing investigation should be approached with caution and within sound policies. Investigators should always treat the informant in a professional manner. The investigator's goal is not to deny the applicant a gaming license but to discover the truth. When confronted with a confidential informant, the investigator must assess the credibility of the informant and the materiality of the intelligence. Then, the investigator must determine whether significant cause exists not to disclose both the informant and the information to the applicant. When dealing with a confidential informant, the investigator should maintain proper interviewing techniques to draw out as many details as possible and to best assess the probative value of the information provided.

In assessing the informant's credibility, investigators should do a background check on the informant. Information provided by informants with unreliable backgrounds or extensive criminal histories should be weighed accordingly.

The investigator also should attempt to corroborate the information provided by the informant. Uncorroborated or partially corroborated evidence has limited value. Another significant reason to corroborate information provided by an informant is that it can lead to a source other than the informant who can be disclosed to the applicant. If this occurs, the applicant can then address the informant's allegation on the merits.

The investigator also needs to assess why the informant will not allow the intelligence to be disclosed. This is particularly important where the applicant has signed releases as part of the applications. Legitimate reasons may include fear of physical retaliation, disclosure of the informant's own personal information, or possible malicious lawsuits by a particularly affluent or powerful applicant. Suspect reasons include wanting to hurt the

---

[21] Alexandra Natapoff, *Snitching: The Institutional and Communal Consequences*, 73 U. Cin. L. Rev. 645, 649 (2004).

person competitively or seeking revenge. Without valid and substantiated reasons, the probity of a confidential informant's information is marginal.

Finally, investigators should independently determine the reliability of any confidential source or information. Therefore, besides reporting the allegation itself, investigators should prepare a detailed investigative report that sets out the informant's background, potential motives, whether the intelligence was corroborated or refuted in whole or in part, and any other relevant information.

Regulatory Agencies

Regulatory agencies may have helpful information about applicants. A regulatory agency is typically an independent government body formed to set standards in a specific private sector or field of activity. This government body may be a board, commission, committee, department, or agency. Gaming investigators should start with other gaming agencies where the applicant has been licensed or may have previously sought licensure. Tribal gaming agencies should not be overlooked during this process.[22]

Besides gaming regulatory agencies, many professions, occupations, and even hobbies have a governing body controlling their activities. If an interest requires a license or certification, then a regulatory agency will likely be involved. Regulatory agencies maintain files, which may include application for licensure or certification, training records, and reports.

Civil Litigation

Records of court proceedings often provide information that proves relevant to a background or financial investigation. Basic to most investigations is a record search for litigation involving the applicant or his business in the jurisdictions where the applicant has lived or worked. These lawsuits may allege unscrupulous business practices and reveal the identity of persons who have had unsatisfactory business experiences with the applicant.

Domestic suits, such as divorces or child custody disputes, may also provide relevant information. A pleading in a custody case may attack the competency of the applicant based on illegal activities, such as drug use. In a divorce, pleadings may allege hidden assets, sources of income, or other information inconsistent with the application or the applicant's tax return, or which are related to criminal activities.

Court records may be found in many places all within the same jurisdiction. In a typical US city, there may be small claims courts, family courts, local courts, probate courts, and federal courts. Each of these courts may have separate clerks and filing systems. Clerks maintain indexes of the

---

[22] NAT'L INDIAN GAMING COMM'N, *List and Location of Tribal Gaming Operations*, http://www.nigc.gov/Reading_Room/List_and_Location_of_Tribal_Gaming_Operations.aspx (maintaining a list and location of tribal gaming operations).

names of parties to lawsuits. Some courts keep these records on computer and others keep them by hand. Therefore, search time for court records varies from a few minutes to a few days. Once the search is completed, the clerk must retrieve the court files, which can be stored on paper, micro-fiche, or computer media.

Once retrieved, the pleadings usually contain a brief, succinct description of the court action. This provides a good background of the case, but it is typically void of evidence to support the allegations. The best source of evidence is a trial transcript or transcripts of other evidentiary hearings. Most court cases, however, are decided by motion, dismissed, settled or abandoned before they reach trial. Therefore, investigators must look elsewhere in the filings for useful evidence. Filed motions are a good source because these are often supported by written affidavits and documents. Investigators also should look for depositions (i.e., oral questioning of persons under oath), answers to interrogatories (i.e., written answers to written questions), and requests for production of documents. While these may not be in the court files, they can be requested from the applicant or another party to the lawsuit.

Evidence of disposition is important. Cases end for many reasons. Sometimes the person seeking relief abandons the case. He or she may realize that the case will be lost or that the defendant does not have the money to pay even if they win. The case also may become too expensive or time consuming.

Other cases may settle. This may be documented as a court-approved settlement agreement or through voluntary dismissal of the case. If no settlement is in the court files, the investigators may obtain it from the applicant. Settlement terms may suggest the validity of the allegations. For example, if the person sued pays a substantial portion of the amount requested, it may show that the allegations have some merit.

Without evidence that the lawsuit was decided against the applicant, however, investigators should give little credence to unsubstantiated allegations in pleadings. Nothing prevents persons from filing spurious lawsuits, and it is truly a common occurrence. The investigator should look beyond the complaint, find out if any credible evidence supports the allegations, and then decide whether such evidence bears on the applicant's suitability.

An applicant's failure to list all civil court proceedings on his or her application should be kept in context. An application may contain a broad request to disclose all litigation involving a company where the applicant was an officer, director, or shareholder. If the applicant was an officer of a large company, he probably would not know of all lawsuits involving the company and may inadvertently fail to disclose some routine corporate litigation. This omission is not probative of the applicant's qualifications. The significance is much different, however, if the applicant failed to reveal a lawsuit involving fraud in which he was personally named and lost.

Beyond the nature or omission of civil lawsuits, a review of litigation may reveal that an applicant has a habit of abusing the civil court system to gain economic advantages. Investigators may find that the applicant is using the judicial system to avoid or compromise legitimate debts. This may be evidenced by the existence of a number of lawsuits wherein an applicant sues his or her creditors and uses the claim to obtain a reduction of amounts he or she owes. Other evidence might include the settlement of suits brought against the applicant for less than face value of what was owed. Most creditors will accept less than face value of claims to avoid the expense of litigation.

Public Information

Investigators may obtain useful information on an applicant from sources that are generally available to the public. With the aid of popular search engines, the investigator can locate extensive archives of news stories, public records, and corporate information. Governments and regulatory agencies can also pay for products and services provided by companies who specialize in collecting and analyzing public information. For a fee, investigators can have instant access to a database of public records. With a paid subscription and access to the Internet, an investigator can access case judgments, public records, real property deeds and mortgages, social security numbers, federal tax identification numbers, voter registration, motor vehicle registration, marriage and divorce records, professional licenses, and liens. The subscription cost is minimal considering all the information one can obtain while sitting at a computer. As with all information, an investigator will need to verify the accuracy of these records.

Investigators can obtain public information from other government agencies such as

- The Secretary of State - Records from the Secretary of State can verify certain aspects of the recorded structure, purpose, and representatives of a business. Filing documents may include other helpful information on the business structure.
- United States Securities and Exchange Commission (SEC) - SEC filings for publicly-traded companies can provide valuable information about a company, such as its organization and management structure, litigation, major shareholders and financial information, and sales and acquisitions.
- Public Access to Court Electronic Records (PACER) - PACER is an electronic public database that allows the user to obtain case and docket information from Federal Appellate, District, and Bankruptcy Courts.

Investigators can access public information maintained by nongovernment agencies such as Dun & Bradstreet. This public database contains information on various aspects of a business operation including legal and trade names, physical and mailing addresses, geographical descriptions, and product and industry descriptors.

Social Media

Social networking websites may contain information relevant to the suitability investigation. Useful information may include a list of the applicant's contacts, posts, photos and videos, travel destinations, and other information the applicant shared with others. The five most popular social networking sites based on website traffic are Facebook, Twitter, LinkedIn, Google Plus, and Pinterest.[23]

Other Areas - Employment

Verification of employment history is important for many reasons. First, it establishes the person's experience in an industry. For example, if the applicant says he left a job as vice president of casino operations, this might be only the last position held. He could have had experience in accounting, surveillance or other areas with that employer before his promotion to vice president. Likewise, he may have only been a vice president for a short time. Verifying employment may explain the time spent in each position and the responsibilities of that position.

Verification is also a useful vehicle to explore the applicant's honesty. Here the investigators should go beyond the disclosed reasons for changing employment and decide if other causes exist. Often in many industries, the stated reason for termination is not the actual reason. On paper, the reason may be a reduction or change in staffing, when the employer really terminated the person because of suspected theft. Employers who suspect an employee is stealing may not use that reason to fire the employee because they fear they may get sued for doing so. If another legitimate reason is available to fire the person, they may seize the opportunity to use that excuse. An investigator should take advantage of the applicant's release of all liability to convince the employer to detail the facts leading to the applicant's firing or resignation.

References

Whether investigators can learn any relevant information by checking an applicant's references is a matter of some dispute. On one hand, why would an applicant list a person as a reference if that person will provide negative information to the investigators? Some investigators, however, have cited instances where this has occurred. Regardless, requiring the applicant to provide references of long-term associations may give the investigator the opportunity to verify some information on the application with the references.

---

[23] EBizMBA, *The Top 15 Most Popular Social Networking Sites*, http://www.ebizmba.com/articles/social-networking-websites.

This might include, for example, asking a former college classmate about a disciplinary action or a former business associate about a lawsuit.

THE FINANCIAL INVESTIGATION

An applicant is likely to have more contact with financial investigators than with the background investigators because the production of financial documentation plays a major part in the investigation. Financial investigators use financial documents for many reasons. If the applicant provides part or all the financing for the gaming establishment, these records reveal the adequacy of the applicant's resources and the suitability of his or her sources. Financial records often reveal the identities of and economic arrangements with the applicant's associates. Financial investigators also scrutinize sources of income and records of payments through these documents.

Tasks that financial investigators can perform during their investigation include (1) analyzing the source of funds; (2) tracing primary holdings to their original sources; (3) verifying personal income information to confirm current holdings are consistent with income reported to the tax authorities; (4) preparing a cash-flow analysis; and (5) verifying the applicant's net worth. An applicant should be required to identify the source of bank deposits or the nature of payments reflected on canceled checks.

A source-of-funds analysis traces where the applicant receives income and the source of funds from which assets are purchased. The regulatory goal is to ensure that the applicant is not a front for unsuitable individuals who are financing the acquisition of a casino. It also provides insight into the applicant's business and associations.

Depending on the complexity of the financial investigation, the investigator may need to use a Certified Public Accountant who specializes in forensic accounting or an investigative auditor with a background in gaming investigations. Forensic accounting integrates accounting, auditing, and investigative skills. In complex financial investigations, an investigator can literally get lost in the myriad documents submitted by an applicant. This is especially true in investigations where the applicant is a large, multinational firm adhering to different accounting standards around the globe. The key here is to employ the services of a trained, seasoned specialist who can identify substance over form. An experienced specialist can summarize transactions, trace assets, perform regression or sensitivity analysis, utilize computerized applications such as spread sheets, and utilize charts and graphics to explain the analysis.

Bank Records

Bank records are the most common vehicle for establishing the source of funds, provided all accounts are revealed. Bank statements are the typical beginning point because they contain both deposits and withdrawals. Deposits often reveal sources of income. All deposits are reviewed to learn if they are ordinary, such as biweekly salary deposits, or extraordinary, such as the one-time sale of an automobile. Large deposits should be verified by reviewing source documents. Particular attention should be made to sizeable cash deposits. While good reasons may exist for an applicant to deposit cash into an account, it is also the easiest method by which criminal activity may be hidden because it has no trail. Whether an applicant made an extraordinary deposit in cash can be determined by reviewing a teller's cash sheets.

Standard bank records investigators may review include (1) signature cards showing who is authorized to use the bank account; (2) monthly statements showing all activity on the account, including deposits, withdrawals, and checks paid; (3) canceled checks; and (4) deposit tickets that show a breakdown of checks, cash deposited, and identification of checks. The applicant may have other documentation that will greatly help in the investigation, such as check registers, copies of all checks deposited, and canceled checks.

Many persons use check record programs on their home computers, such as Quicken, which can generate several helpful reports. Computer programs can generate net worth reports that investigators should use to compare with the application. A better source, however, is a review of a bank's loan files. Most loans require the applicant to make some level of disclosure of assets to qualify for the loan.

Other Financial Records

Bank accounts are the usual place into which funds can be deposited, but they are not the only place. Other possible depositories include brokerage accounts and savings and loans associations. An investigator should review all accounts before conducting a cash-flow analysis or reconciling income to expenses.

Other financial records investigators should consider include the following:

Figure 16.6

Airline and travel records	Bonding company records
Credit card and credit agency records	Insurance company records
Public utility company records	Telephone company records
Internet carrier records	Money orders
Bank records	Laundry and dry cleaning records
Abstract and title company records	

Tax Returns

Regulators' principal concern in some jurisdictions is to protect state tax revenues. Applicants who intentionally fail to pay taxes, such as federal or state income tax, may be unqualified to hold a gaming license. A primary method for investigating whether a person pays federal income tax in full is to compare cash flow with reported income. This requires the investigator to identify all banks and other accounts that the applicant has used for personal transactions throughout the year. They can derive this information from the application by tracing the flow of funds, conducting credit checks, reviewing correspondence, and locating bank checks. Once all accounts are identified, the investigator should then total all deposits and deduct transactions that do not involve taxable income (e.g., sale of a car for less than the purchase price, transfers between accounts, the principal amount on repayment of loans). If a substantial difference remains, the investigator should consider confronting the applicant for an explanation of the difference. Beyond serving as an indication of character, tax returns can provide information on the applicant's sources of income, verify his or her businesses, and provide information about his or her associations.

THE CORPORATE INVESTIGATION

Most applicants for a casino or card room operator's license or a manufacturer's and distributor's license are corporations or other business entities rather than individuals. A corporation is a legal entity separate from the people that make up the corporation (i.e., its shareholders, officers, and directors). However, regulators should investigate a corporation from both the perspective that it has independence from its shareholders, officers, and directors, and that it reflects its shareholders, officers, and directors.

From the corporate perspective, investigators should review

- Funds - Does the corporation have funding from suitable sources? This includes a review and verification of the nature of the capitalization (e.g., capital investments or loans).
- Compliance - Does the corporation have adequate personnel, structure, and supervision to reasonably assure compliance with all laws and regulations? What is the corporation's history of compliance with federal and state laws and other business, professional, or legal standards?
- History - What is the corporation's history of honest and fair business dealings? What is the corporation's history of proper and timely tax payments? Are the company's business practices consistent with the standards of honesty, integrity, and good character expected of members of the gaming industry?
- Ownership - Is reported ownership consistent with actual ownership?

Typical items that a corporate applicant should provide to investigators include the following:

Figure 16.7

General and limited partnership agreements of partnerships
Articles of incorporation of corporations
A list of all partners, shareholders, officers, directors, members, and managers, and the percentage of ownership, social security numbers and dates of birth for all parties—plus, stock or membership certificates, if applicable
Board-of-directors minutes from inception to present
Identification of the members and functions of all committees to the board of directors
A list and description of active and inactive subsidiaries
A list and description of all joint venture partnerships (including ownership interest in each)
The most recent stockholders' list
All applications and related files for all jurisdictions where the company has a gaming license or has an application pending for a gaming license
An update on the status of all equity investments
All SEC filings with exhibits
All correspondence between the company and the SEC from inception to present, including comments regarding the initial registration
All correspondence between the company and the NASD from inception to present, including the application for listing on NASDAQ
An organizational chart including a list and description of job functions of all key employees
Audited financial statements
A list and description of gaming related subsidiaries
A list and description of material litigation from inception to present, both pending and settled
All correspondence between the company and any stock exchange from inception to present
All correspondence between the company and its independent auditors from inception to present
Industry research reports prepared on the company
Any business and strategic plans

Source of Funds

A corporation is a separate entity in financial terms. Shareholders generally are not liable for corporate debts, nor are they obligated to fund the corporation with the exception of paying for their stock interest. Thus, an investigation into a corporate applicant requires investigators to learn the amount and sources of the corporation's capitalization.

Tracing the source of funds is as important for a corporate applicant as it is for an individual applicant. It requires the same level of cash-flow analysis and the use of similar procedures to verify each source and use of funds. The nature of funding public corporations may allow investigators to shift the focus of the financial investigation almost entirely from the individual officers, directors, and shareholders to the corporation itself. It is irrelevant whether an outside director is a multimillionaire or makes a mere $65,000 a year as a business consultant when the corporation does not rely on capital infusions.[24] In closely-held, shareholder-funded corporations however, the review should focus on both the finances of the company and its owners.

Compliance with Laws

A corporate investigation should look at the corporation's compliance with regulations and laws. Often, failure to comply with the law is not a result of the individual actions of directors and officers but is a result of failure in corporate structure. For example, inexperienced bookkeeping may lead to records that are inadequate to properly complete tax returns, or it might lead to missed or late filings. Lack of proper controls may lead to criminal or regulatory violations by employees. These are as much corporate failures as they are failures of individual employees, officers, and directors.

Corporate History

Investigations into public companies can provide a wealth of information about the corporate background. Most jurisdictions require companies to provide detailed registration statements that include audited financial statements. These statements provide information that the investigators can verify for accuracy, truthfulness, and full disclosure.

The federal Securities and Exchange Commission (SEC) is the recipient of complaints from shareholders or others regarding corporate activities. Often, the SEC may have conducted investigations into corporate or "insider" activities.

Corporate Ownership

Many jurisdictions have different rules governing the licensing of shareholders in public and private corporations. A jurisdiction may require that all shareholders of a private corporation obtain a gaming license. In comparison, it may require that only those owning a certain percentage

---

[24] Review of the financial records of these individuals may be useful in other respects, particularly in identifying the applicant's associations, whether he engages in illegal activities, or whether he pays all taxes. This review, however, is different from a source and suitability-of-funds analysis.

of a public company obtain a license. An economic reason exists for this distinction. If all shareholders of a public company had to obtain a license, very few, if any, public companies would apply for licensure in that jurisdiction. Without these companies, investment in the jurisdiction would decrease.

Once a corporation is identified as publicly-held, investigators should review whether it complies with the criteria that define a public company. This requires gaming investigators to investigate the company's registration with the appropriate governmental agencies on state and federal levels.

When collaborating with these agencies, investigators should verify that the company is properly registered in compliance with all securities laws. If the company is registered in a foreign country, the investigation may involve a review of that country's securities laws and regulations. This review may reveal the registration criteria in that jurisdiction are similar to those criteria in the gaming investigator's jurisdiction. Investigators should also ensure that the securities regulation is adequate in the foreign jurisdiction.

GAMING ESTABLISHMENT INVESTIGATION
Initial Documentation

Like other licensing investigations, the gaming establishment investigation begins with the applicant's submission of documentation, such as:

- A Proposed Internal Control System
- First-Year Cash Flow Projections
- A Statement of Pre-Opening Cash
- A Pro-Forma Balance Sheet
- A Proposed Surveillance System
- Calculation and Proof of Minimum Bankroll

These documents relate to the three basic functions of the gaming establishment investigation, which include feasibility, applicant competence, and adequate procedures and equipment.

Feasibility

In many jurisdictions, the financial health of corporate applicants is important. This is particularly important where the government issues only a limited number of operator licenses because the number of critical suppliers is limited by law or by natural market forces. In either case, if the applicant's financial health fails, it could have significant—even devastating—impacts on the jurisdiction and its policy goals.

A feasibility review of a proposed casino or card room attempts to address three questions. First, does the applicant have adequate funding to buy or build and operate the business? Second, is the funding committed pending the application's approval? Third, does the casino company or its parent have the financial strength to successfully operate the casino? These questions are relevant when a government has a strong economic interest in ensuring the success of a gaming venture. Sometimes, it may have committed substantial public funds for infrastructure improvements needed to accommodate a casino. In other instances, a government may rely on tax revenues from casinos to fund basic services. When these situations occur, regulators should assess the adequacy of the casino venture's financing and its likelihood of success. The latter may include assessing the quality and experience of the proposed management team.

Another less critical reason for undertaking this analysis is to decide if the casino or card room may be under-financed or poorly operated. These businesses may fall into financial trouble and then turn to unacceptable methods to save their investments. At an extreme, they may seek additional funding from unsuitable sources for a hidden interest in the casino or change the odds of the games by cheating patrons. Regulators should monitor these casinos more closely.

To assess the adequacy of funding to support ongoing operations, regulators often look at various ratios to determine the financial health of a company. This may include reviewing the business plan, available reserve requirements, revenue and expense projections, cash flow analyses, and a variety of ratios such as cash ratio, current ratio, capitalization ratio, debt to asset ratio, debt to equity ratio, interest coverage ratio and operating cash flow ratio.

Professor John Mills describes the purposes of feasibility reviews as follows:

> The first concern is whether the gaming property has the capability to meet day-to-day cash requirements for customer payouts. Casinos should have enough cash or cash equivalents on hand to pay off all gaming bets for the day. . . .
>
> Financial liquidity reflects a company's ability to generate enough cash to pay its current and maturing obligations. Financial liquidity evaluates all the segments of the property, including the casino, hotel and other non-gaming operations. The concerns are whether the property is generating enough revenues or has enough assets (cash or cash equivalents) to meet ongoing operating expenses that are essential to the maintenance of continuous and stable casino operations. This includes the ability to pay all local, state and federal taxes, including the tax on gross revenues when due. A series of liquidity ratios and analysis of trends of these ratios provide the foundation for the evaluation of this element of financial viability.
>
> While current operating activities are important, to remain in existence properties must be able to meet all future obligations. The final part of evaluating financial viability is to look at the long-term prospects of casino properties. The concern is whether the property is generating enough cash to not only run current operations, but also to meet future commitments such as loans, bond payments, guarantees and capital improvements. A combination of ratios and trend analysis is used to evaluate this element of financial viability.[25]

[25] John R. Mills, *An Introduction to the Financial Viability of Casinos*, Casino Enterprise

Apart from assuring funding adequacy to guarantee the feasibility of the casino, regulators may wish to protect the rights of casino patrons by ensuring the payment of winnings. This may prevent harm to the casino industry's reputation as a whole. This type of review can involve the payment of both current and future winnings. In the former, review assures that the casino has adequate cash on hand to immediately pay all winnings. In the latter case, investigators should ensure that patrons who win jackpots that are to be paid over time will receive their winnings regardless of whether the casino remains in operation.

Competence of Applicant

An applicant should possess the skills, either personally or through key employees, to properly operate a casino or card room. This helps ensure that the gaming business will be operated according to the law and in compliance with internal controls. Competent management also helps reduce the risk of cheating or theft by employees and third parties. It also contributes to the economic success of the business. To complete this review, regulators may require organizational charts, employment contracts, job duties, and résumés of all key employees.

The type of the proposed casino operation should be kept in mind when reviewing the competence of the applicant. A large casino requires many skilled employees including casino managers, accountants, and security and surveillance personnel. A much lower level of sophistication may be needed to competently manage a small card room.

Adequate Procedures and Equipment

A proposed casino or card room operation should have adequate procedures in place and the equipment necessary to protect the business's assets and the patrons from theft or cheating. Regulators may review these procedures and equipment as part of the investigative process. This may include reviewing and approving the physical layout of the casino or card room in order to ensure it can be properly controlled, as well as reviewing the surveillance system, staffing, and internal controls.

INTERIM INTERVIEWS

Depending on the jurisdiction, an applicant may have an extensive interview with the investigator, or the applicant may never meet the investigator. Often, because of the applicant's position at the casino, applicable policy goals, and other factors such as prior licenses in other jurisdictions, an investigation may not require interviews. An interview for the sake of

MGMT., Sept. 30, 2007, http://www.casinoenterprisemanagement.com/articles/october-2007/introduction-financial-viability-casinos.

doing an interview is unlikely to accomplish much, but it will cost the applicant and the government time and money. Where, however, credibility or detailed explanations are required, scheduling an interview can be valuable.

Although investigators may request to interview the applicant during the investigation, an interim interview may occur for a variety of reasons. Most often, the applicant is asked to explain a business transaction or a similar event that the investigators do not understand. However, the investigators may also use the interim interview to confront the applicant with information the investigators deem damaging or incriminating.

When investigators find problems, an interim interview gives the applicant an opportunity to address the issues in a timely manner. Difficulties can occur any time during the investigation, but are often not disclosed to the applicant until after investigators have invested significant time and money. Addressing these difficulties in an interim interview can prevent this.

If the applicant and investigators cannot resolve the problem in an interim interview, the damage to the overall application should be assessed and communicated to the applicant. In some instances, resolving difficulties—whether they be background- or financially-related—may require certain individuals separate themselves from a company so that the company can move forward in the investigative process.

THE CLOSING CONFERENCE

Near the end of the investigation, investigators may conduct a final interview or closing conference with the applicant. At this interview, the investigators will likely question the applicant about any unresolved areas of the investigation and discuss the results of the investigation. By this time, questions should be few.

THE INVESTIGATIVE REPORT

At the end of an investigation, investigators will prepare a written report for the decision maker. This report usually contains the results of the investigation and sets forth areas of concern. The report may contain a summary of the investigation, synopses of interviews, the applicant's criminal history, summaries of court and police records, and financial analyses.

INFORMING THE APPLICANT OF CONCERNS

Whether the licensing process is fact-finding or adversarial, investigators may gather information that should not be made available to the applicant. The primary reason for this is that the investigators want to protect their information sources. Often, the reports contain information from other police agencies or from confidential informants who would not have provided such information if it was to be revealed publicly. This may place the applicant at an extreme disadvantage in the application process. Refuting evidence or the credibility of the party providing the evidence is difficult if the applicant does not know what the evidence is or who provided it.

Because a gaming license is a privilege not a right, the principal argument for not providing investigative reports to applicants is that it is more important to ensure the availability of incriminating evidence via a confidentiality pledge than it is to provide the applicant with a fair hearing. Often, the agency can mitigate the perception of unfairness by providing the applicant with portions of the report and a summary of any areas of concern.

VALUE OF HEARINGS/INTERVIEWS

Some jurisdictions will grant or deny a license application without a hearing or interview. This can present problems when regulators need to make decisions that revolve around the credibility of the applicant's version of the story. Hearings and interviews are also helpful in weighing whether the applicant has been truthful—something that is often a criteria for licensing. One professor maintains that hearings and interviews are important to ensure

- Consistency of the applicant's testimony with what is agreed or clearly shown by other evidence to have occurred. This frequently occurs where discrepancies emerge between police reports and the applicant's description of his arrest;
- Internal consistency of the applicant's evidence;
- Consistency with the applicant's past statements, actions or depositions; and
- An accurate sense of the applicant's demeanor.[26]

Evaluating an applicant's demeanor or credibility requires regulators to be able to determine whether a person is being truthful. Regulators should heed advice from experts as to how to make these determinations, and they should also seek specific training in order to better judge applicants. An applicant who is intimidated by a public hearing or who is in fear of simply not being believed may appear to be lying when in fact he or she is telling the truth. Likewise, a well-rehearsed applicant or a natural liar may appear to be telling the truth when in fact he or she is lying.

Some studies suggest that people and police, at best, are 60 percent accurate in distinguishing lies from truth. According to Professor Hazel Glenn at the University College London, however, there are certain methods that can help humans detect lies.[27] Some of these methods are impractical in

---

[26] RICHARD EGGLESTON, EVIDENCE, PROOF AND PROBABILITY 155 (1st ed., Weidenfeld and Nicolson 1978).

[27] Hazel Genn, *Assessing Credibility*, TRIBUNALS 11, no. 1 2-5 (2004), http://www.judiciary. gov.uk/Resources/JCO/Documents/Tribunals/17%20Assessing%20credibility%20-%20

the hearing setting. For example, delving in key areas in a situation where the applicant has not had the opportunity to anticipate the questions.[28] In a gaming setting, these situations often arise during the investigation when the investigators confront the applicant regarding evidence they have uncovered as opposed to the hearing on the application.

Therefore, experienced investigators should do as complete an investigation as possible on a particular topic before confronting the applicant. This way, they have a full array of questions the applicant will not anticipate. Investigators, where possible, should also seek to record interviews with applicants so regulators can review them at a later date. Transcripts of the interviews are obviously less helpful. Other methods of eliciting the truth from applicants include the following:

- Emphasizing that severe punishment for perjury is available. This should be a feature of the overall regulatory structure;
- Instructing the regulator to maintain an open mind and to avoid preconceived notions and making conclusions before fully exploring an issue;
- Instructing the regulator to not only allow but encourage the applicant (not his attorney) to provide a full explanation;
- Choosing an investigator who speaks the same language as the applicant and has a similar background; and
- Encouraging a courteous, collegial approach to hearings and interviews so that the applicant will not fear being misbelieved and will hesitate to lie due to potential feelings of guilt.[29]

To best accomplish this result, regulators and investigators should undergo training and understand the difficulties associated with identifying lies from the truth.

Genn.pdf.
[28] *Id.*
[29] *Id.*

17

Exclusions

Keith Miller

INTRODUCTION

When one speaks of "exclusions" in the context of casino regulation, there are several possible applications. All exclusionary situations in this chapter concern a patron who for some reason or another is denied the opportunity to gamble at a casino.

First, some people who want to gamble are *required* to be excluded by the licensed facility. Known cheaters, crime figures, and other unsavory persons fall into this category. Laws and regulations in states like Nevada and New Jersey provide for "exclusion lists."

Second, licensed facilities such as casinos can exclude a person from their premises when they believe the person is cheating or attempting to cheat. There are many forms of cheating, including dice sliding and altering chip values. Cheating and the laws that criminalize it are discussed in Chapter 14.

Third, and most controversial, is the exclusion of a patron for a reason that is sometimes difficult to ascertain. Facility staff may claim the person's presence is inimical to the facility's interests. But it may also just be that the facility says they simply do not want the gambler's "action." Why would this be? Is the person winning too much? Yet is it sporting to exclude a person who is a winning bettor rather than a losing one? When facilities exclude a patron in this situation, one may ask whether there is a statutory or common law right to exclude a person from a gambling operation.

This type of exclusion is often a reaction to a player using "advantage play" in an effort to increase his chances of winning. The most notorious form of advantage play is "card counting," a tactic used by some blackjack players to gain a statistical edge over the house. Chapter 14 addresses the many types of advantage play and the differences between types that amount to cheating and those that do not. This chapter focuses on the power to exclude advantage players even when their conduct does not constitute cheating.

A fourth exclusion type is "self-exclusion." Sometimes gamblers recognize they have a problem controlling their gambling. In an attempt to remedy their problem, they sign a document telling the casino they should not be permitted to return and that they may be removed if they do. Many states permit this in an effort to address gambling addiction. Admirable as this policy may be, it is not without controversy.

Related to self-exclusions is problem gambling. Even if gambling is a form of entertainment a person chooses to spend his money on, there is no question that a person who cannot control his gambling can bring ruinous consequences upon himself and others. There are certainly ways of treating this addiction, but are there ways to reduce the chance it will occur? Chapter 10 examines the issue of problem gambling in detail. This includes self-exclusion programs, gambling establishments' responsibility to recognize "problem" gamblers and take steps to protect them, and the casino's potential liability if it does not. The present chapter, consequently, makes only incidental references to the self-exclusion process.

MANDATORY EXCLUSIONS

Mandatory exclusion (i.e., excluding people as required by law) is the exclusionary form most fundamental to the regulation of gambling. Known cheaters, crime figures, and other unsavory persons may encounter mandatory exclusions resulting from laws and regulations in a number of states concerning "exclusion lists."

The Templates: Nevada and New Jersey

Because of its lengthy gambling regulation history, Nevada's mandatory exclusion process is an instructive template for examining this exclusion process. In Nevada, the Gaming Commission is authorized to enact a regulation providing "for the establishment of a list of persons who are to be excluded or ejected from any licensed gaming establishment."[1] The list can include those "whose presence in the establishment is determined by the [Gaming Control] Board and the Commission to pose a threat to the interests of this state or to licensed gaming."[2] The statutory criteria that inform regulators' decisions predictably involve felony convictions and state gaming laws violations.[3] But a person may also earn his way onto the list by having a "notorious or unsavory reputation which would adversely affect public confidence and trust that the gaming industry is free from criminal or corruptive elements."[4] According to Nevada law, the presence of any of the specified factors is sufficient for exclusion.[5] However, the grounds for

---

[1] Nev. Rev. Stat. § 463.151(2) (2013).
[2] *Id.*
[3] *Id.* § 463.151(3)(a).
[4] *Id.* § 463.151(3)(c).
[5] Nev. Gaming Reg. 28.010(2). Other criteria supporting exclusion are crimes of moral

placing someone on the list cannot be discriminatory in such a way that would violate the Fourteenth Amendment.[6]

Several justifications for placing someone on the list have been challenged in court and upheld, including (1) the existence of a recording of the excluded person instructing confederates about how to skim revenues from casinos followed by a conviction for doing so,[7] and (2) a prior conviction for "attempting to fix the outcome of a college basketball game in North Carolina" in combination with a previous exclusion from race tracks in Florida.[8]

A person placed on an exclusion list must be served and notified.[9] Within 30 days of service (or 60 days of notice by publication), the person can demand a hearing before the Gaming Commission to show cause why he or she should not be on the list.[10] The hearing must be scheduled within 30 days after it is demanded.[11] The hearing's results are recorded by an order in the Commission's minutes, which is judicially reviewable.[12] In part because of these provisions, the exclusion list framework has been held not to violate due process.[13] Courts have also rejected the claim that an exclusion list is a First Amendment violation, holding that its regulatory purpose does not criminalize one's freedom of association.[14] Likewise, courts have rejected arguments that exclusion lists constitute a bill of attainder or are overbroad.[15]

Licensees can be fined or have their licenses limited, conditioned, or revoked if they knowingly allow an excluded person in their establishment and fail to eject that person.[16] The regulation contains a procedure the licensee must follow "[w]henever an excluded person enters or attempts to enter or is upon the premises."[17] The licensee must immediately notify

---

turpitude, failing to disclose an interest in a gaming establishment for which the person must obtain a license, and willfully evading taxes or fees. NEV. REV. STAT. § 463.151(3) (a)–(b) (2013).

[6] NEV. REV. STAT. § 463.151(4) (2013).

[7] *See* Thomas v. Bible, 694 F. Supp. 750, 754–55, 769 (D. Nev. 1988).

[8] *See* State v. Rosenthal, 819 P.2d 1296, 1298–99, 1301 (Nev. 1991).

[9] NEV. REV. STAT. § 463.152 (2013); *see also* NEV. GAMING REG. 28.060 (providing a more detailed process for notifying candidates, including a sample notice form).

[10] NEV. REV. STAT. § 463.153(1) (2013).

[11] *Id.* § 463.153(2).

[12] *Id.* § 463.153(3)(b). A person may seek judicial review of the commission's order placing them on the list even if they do not request a hearing within the allotted time frame. *Id.* § 463.153(1).

[13] Bible, 694 F. Supp. at 761

[14] *See* Spilotro v. State *ex rel.* Nev. Gaming Comm'n, 661 P.2d 467, 469–70 (Nev. 1983).

[15] *Id.* at 470–71. *But see generally* Michael W. Bowers & A. Costandina Titus, *Nevada's Black Book: The Constitutionality of Exclusion Lists in Casino Gaming Regulation*, 9 WHITTIER L. REV. 313, 330 (1987) (arguing—pre-*Thomas* and pre-*Rosenthal*—that exclusion lists "punish a person on the basis of status or reputation, deny him equal protection of the laws and violate his rights of free association, movement, and speech").

[16] NEV. REV. STAT. § 463.154.

[17] NEV. GAMING REG. 28.090(2).

the board of gaming control, request that the excluded person leave, and notify law enforcement if the person does not comply with the request.[18] The person on the list is punished for entering gaming establishments; they are guilty of a gross misdemeanor.[19] It is conceivable that someone on the list could violate the statute without the licensee also violating the statute; if the person enters the establishment and the licensee, upon knowledge that the person has entered, immediately ejects him, the licensee commits no statutory violation.

The statute authorizes the Gaming Commission to enact an administrative regulation establishing an exclusion list, and the Commission has capitalized on that authority. The regulation incorporates the statutory authorization, but goes further, providing specific criteria by which the Commission can find evidence of a person's notorious or unsavory reputation.[20] It also provides that the list is open to public inspection and specifies the information and data that must be included on the list.[21]

To get off the list, a person may "petition the Commission in writing."[22] If the Commission entertains the petition, it then holds a hearing.[23] The Commission can rely upon the record of evidence and testimony it used to initially place the person on the exclusion list when it considers whether the person should be removed.[24] However, the petitioner bears the burden of proof.[25] So far, no person has successfully carried this burden; "death has been the only way a patron's name has been removed."[26]

Another jurisdiction with an extensive gaming regulation history, New Jersey, has a similar process. One "whose presence in a licensed casino . . . would be inimical to the interest of the State of New Jersey or licensed gaming therein," as demonstrated by a list of offenses, can likewise be placed on the exclusion list.[27] Unlike Nevada, the New Jersey statute *directs* the Division of Gaming Enforcement to develop regulations defining standards for an exclusion list.[28] Additionally, the statute—as opposed to the regulation—provides that the Division may impose sanctions upon a

---

[18] *Id.*

[19] Nev. Rev. Stat. § 463.155; *see also* Morris v. State, No. 58646, 2012 WL 1305946, at *1 (Nev. Apr. 12, 2012) (affirming a defendant's conviction for "entry of a gaming establishment by an excluded person").

[20] Nev. Gaming Reg. 28.010(3)–(4).

[21] Nev. Gaming Reg. 28.040(1)–(2). One way of ensuring the list is open to public inspection is making it available online. The Nevada "rogue's gallery"—another name for the Excluded Person List—can be viewed at http://gaming.nv.gov/index.aspx?page=72.

[22] Nev. Gaming Reg. 28.080(1).

[23] Nev. Gaming Reg. 28.080(2).

[24] Nev. Gaming Reg. 28.080(3).

[25] *Id.*

[26] Nicole Laudwig, Note, *Gaming Regulatory Systems: How Emerging Jurisdictions Can Use the Three Major Players as a Guide in Creating a Tailored System for Themselves,* 3 UNLV Gaming L.J. 277, 283 (2012).

[27] N.J. Stat. Ann. § 5:12-71(d).

[28] *Id.* § 5:12-71(a).

casino for a failure to exclude, and that the Division's list of criteria is not necessarily exhaustive.[29] Lastly, the procedure for notifying excluded persons is set out in the statute as opposed to the regulation.[30]

When the Division determines a person should be placed on the list, it notifies that person, who can then challenge his or her placement by requesting a hearing within 20 days.[31] Once placed on the list, persons can petition to be removed after either five or ten years, depending upon the reason they were placed on the list in the first place.[32] When a person is initially placed on the list, the Division bears the burden of proving that the person satisfies criteria for exclusion, but when petitioning for removal, the person must show cause why he should be removed.[33]

Other States

While the mandatory exclusion process may have originated in the gaming bastions of Nevada and New Jersey, exclusion lists exist in a number of other jurisdictions in the United States. In most respects, there is considerable similarity among the processes for establishment and administration of exclusion lists. Mississippi's statute, for example, copies the Nevada statute nearly verbatim.[34] The exception is that an excluded person who enters a casino is guilty only of a misdemeanor rather than a gross misdemeanor.[35] Also like Nevada, the list is available online.[36]

Other states with exclusion lists and their notable characteristics are as follows:

Illinois

Exclusions may be temporary, but temporary exclusions must last at least six and can only be imposed for criteria "relating to conduct."[37] All other exclusions are permanent.[38] A person on the excluded list can petition for removal one year after they are placed on it or one year after any other hearing on a petition for removal.[39]

---

[29] *Id.* § 5:12-71(c)–(d).
[30] *Id.* § 5:12-71(e)–(h).
[31] N.J. Admin. Code § 13:69G-1.5(b).
[32] *Id.* § 13:69G-1.8(a)–(b).
[33] *Id.* § 13:69B-2.8(b).
[34] *See* Miss. Code Ann. § 75-76-35. The Gaming Commission regulation imposes on licensees a duty to exclude people on the list (Miss. Admin. Code 13-4:1.1) and also provides that someone's presence on another state's list is grounds for exclusion in Mississippi. Miss. Admin. Code 13-4:1.3(d). A person on the list may petition to be removed. Miss. Admin. Code 13-4:1.5.
[35] Miss. Code Ann. § 75-76-43.
[36] *Exclusion List*, Miss. Gaming Comm'n, http://www.msgamingcommission.com/index.php/exclusion_list.
[37] Ill. Admin. Code tit. 86, § 3000.730(c).
[38] *Id.*
[39] *Id.* tit. 86, § 3000.740(a).

Licensees have a duty to exclude people on the list, but the regulations do not contain specific penalties for licensee noncompliance.[40] Instead, licensees may face discipline under the general disciplinary authority of the board, for "[f]ailing to comply with or make provision for compliance with the Act [or] these rules."[41]

Indiana

Administrative regulations mandate the exclusion or eviction list and provide criteria for placement on the list.[42] Criteria include cheating, theft, disorderly conduct, or any other lawful reason.[43] The Indiana Gaming Commission's 2013 First Quarter Business Meeting—held in March 2013—contains additional discussion about the exclusion list and provides examples of the conduct that lands a person on the exclusion list. Between November 2012 and March 2013, 24 new individuals were placed on the list.[44] The reasons for placement on the list were as follows:

1. Posting or pinching bets: six individuals.[45] This constitutes cheating under Indiana's statutory definition[46] and is an express criterion for placement on the eviction list.[47]
2. Taking illegal possession of chips or currency in excess of $500, or making fraudulent cash withdrawals at a casino: 13 individuals.[48]
3. Robbing other casino patrons: one individual.[49]
4. Initiating or participating in a scheme for one person to claim a jackpot so that another would avoid having the jackpot confiscated for delinquent child support: four individuals (in two schemes).[50]

This brought the total number of people on the list to 381.[51] Further, the meeting also affirmed administrative judgments against excluded persons who had violated their exclusion orders by entering gaming establishments.[52] These orders did not impose additional penalties but simply sought forfeiture of the amounts the excluded persons possessed when apprehended—including a jackpot one of them had won.[53]

---

[40] *Id.* tit. 86, § 3000.701.
[41] *Id.* tit. 86, § 3000.110(a)(1).
[42] 68 IND. ADMIN. CODE 6-2-1.
[43] *Id.* 6-2-1(a)(3).
[44] IND. GAMING COMM'N, FIRST QUARTER 2013 BUSINESS MEETING 6–7 (2013), http://www.in.gov/igc/files/2013.03.21-tra.pdf.
[45] *Id.* at 7.
[46] *See* IND. CODE § 4-33-2-4 (defining "cheat").
[47] 68 IND. ADMIN. CODE 6-2-1(a)(3)(A).
[48] IND. GAMING COMM'N, *supra* note 44, at 7.
[49] *Id.*
[50] *Id.*
[51] *Id.*
[52] *Id.* at 15–19.
[53] *Id.* at 16, 18.

Michigan

Statutory authorization comes from a broad grant of power to the Gaming Control Board, permitting the Board to promulgate rules as necessary to, among other things, promote the "safety, security, and integrity of casino gaming."[54] There is also a statute governing a "disassociated persons list," but the language of this statute and court decisions interpreting it indicate that "disassociated" governs only *voluntary* exclusions.[55] The administrative regulations also provide for mandatory exclusions based on the standard criteria set out above.[56] Temporary exclusions are permitted, but these must be at least six months, and as with Illinois, can only be imposed for exclusions related to conduct.[57] Licensees are tasked with a duty to exclude, but no specific sanctions for failure to exclude are stated.[58]

Missouri

A notable requirement is that licensees must notify newly excluded persons by certified mail that they are no longer welcome[59]—in addition to the typical step of the commission mailing notice of exclusion.[60] In one case, a person convicted of a felony for operating an illegal gambling business appealed the denial of his petition to be removed from the list, arguing the commission lacked authority to promulgate the regulations forming the basis for his exclusion.[61] The regulation was found "valid as a proper exercise of the commission's authority granted by [statute]."[62]

Ohio

By statute, the state Casino Control Commission is directed to establish a mandatory exclusion list.[63] The statute provides criteria to consider when determining whether to place someone on the list and sets out a procedure for notifying excluded persons that they have been excluded.[64] So far, the

---

[54] MICH. COMP. LAWS § 432.204(17)(d)(ii).

[55] *Id.* § 432.225; *see also* Ormanian v. Mich. Gaming Control Bd., No. 254225, 2005 WL 1684565, at *1 (Mich. Ct. App. July 19, 2005) (describing this statutory section as "essentially a list of people who have voluntarily identified themselves as problem gamblers and have requested to be placed on this list"); Rush v. MGM Grand Detroit, LLC, No. 248861, 2005 WL 356307, at *2 n.1 (Mich. Ct. App. Feb. 15, 2005) (citing this statutory section as a method by which individuals can "seek relief from permissive policies by voluntarily excluding themselves from gambling facilities").

[56] MICH. ADMIN. CODE R. 432.1603.

[57] *Id.* R. 432.1604(5).

[58] *Id.* R. 432.1601.

[59] Mo. CODE REGS. ANN. tit. 11, § 45-15.020(1).

[60] *Id.* tit. 11, § 45-15.040(1).

[61] Termini v. Mo. Gaming Comm'n, 921 S.W.2d 159, 160–61 (Mo. Ct. App. 1996).

[62] *Id.* at 162.

[63] OHIO REV. CODE ANN. § 3772.031(A).

[64] *Id.* § 3772.031(B)–(D).

list contains four names, the date each person was placed on the list, and the reason they were involuntarily excluded.[65]

The Commission's regulations provide additional criteria for exclusion,[66] direct licensees to create internal controls to ensure compliance with the exclusion list, and require them to train employees regarding the exclusion list.[67] Licensees are subject to discipline for failing to do this and for failing to eject someone on the exclusion list.[68] Sanctions for failure to comply or failure to exclude can be related to the license itself—such as revocation or suspension—or can be a fine or civil penalty.[69] Neither the authorizing statutes nor the regulations provide a procedure for removing a person from the list.

Perhaps the threat of sanctions leads casinos to be especially vigilant in monitoring their premises. For example, in March 2013, security at the Horseshoe Casino in Cincinnati approached a woman twice because her name matched a name on their exclusion list—although the woman had never been to that casino before.[70] The woman was ultimately allowed to gamble, because even though her name matched the list, her other information—namely, her birthdate and state of residence—did not.[71] The excluded person was actually from California and coincidentally shared the same name.[72] The Horseshoe's treatment of this situation illustrates the "better safe than sorry" mindset.

Pennsylvania

A statute requires the board to establish an exclusion list.[73] The Pennsylvania Gaming Control Board has established regulations with very detailed criteria for exclusion.[74] The central feature of the regulations is a finding that someone is inimical to the interests of gaming in the state. Someone may be inimical to the interest of gaming in the state if attributes of their character and background

1. Are incompatible with maintaining public confidence in gaming;
2. May reasonably be expected to impair public perception of and confidence in gaming;

---

[65] OHIO CASINO CONTROL COMM'N, INVOLUNTARY EXCLUSION LIST (2013), http://casino-control.ohio.gov/Portals/0/Involuntary%20Exclusion%20List%20Posting%2012172013.pdf; *see also Ohio's Involuntary Exclusion List*, OHIO CASINO CONTROL COMM'N, http://casinocontrol.ohio.gov/Legal/InvoluntaryExclusion.aspx.

[66] OHIO ADMIN. CODE § 3772-23-03.

[67] *Id.* § 3772-23-06(A), (D)–(E).

[68] *Id.* § 3772-22-01(A).

[69] *Id.* § 3772-22-01(B).

[70] *Local Woman Kicked Out of Horseshoe Casino Twice Over the Weekend*, WCPO, Mar. 12, 2013, http://www.wcpo.com/news/local-news/local-woman-wrongfully-kicked-out-of-horseshoe-casino.

[71] *See id.*

[72] *See id.*

[73] 4 PA. CONS. STAT. § 1514(a).

[74] *See* 58 PA. CODE § 511a.3.

3. Create or enhance the risk of unsuitable, unfair, or illegal practices in gaming.[75]

A person placed on the list can demand a hearing upon receiving notice[76] and can petition for removal from the list—although one cannot do so until five years have passed since placement on the list.[77]

EXCLUSION OF CHEATERS

Casinos are perhaps most justified in excluding patrons who cheat or attempt to cheat because permitting them to gamble would damage the integrity of gaming operations. In some states, these patrons are statutorily barred for life.[78] Additionally, courts have recognized casinos' authority to exclude and permanently ban cheaters or suspected cheaters from their premises,[79] and there is little consternation over statutory or administrative provisions allowing them to do exactly that.[80] For example, a man caught cheating at a Pennsylvania casino in 2010 expressed surprise about the resulting criminal charges, because he assumed "he would simply be asked to leave the casino."[81] Similarly, in Australia, a person implicated in a cheating scheme "was booted out of an opulent villa . . . in the dead of night after the scam was uncovered" and "was hit with a withdrawal of licence notice,

---

[75] *Id.* § 511a.3(b).

[76] *Id.* § 511a.6(b).

[77] *Id.* § 511a.9(a).

[78] *See, e.g.,* 230 Ill. Comp. Stat. 10/18(d)(4); Ind. Code §§ 4-33-10-2, 4-33-10-4; Iowa Code § 99F.15(4)(d) (2013); Mich. Comp. Laws § 432.218(2)(f); Mo. Rev. Stat. § 313.830(4)(4).

[79] *See* Arabo v. Greektown Casino, LLC, No. 12-11003, 2013 WL 572315, at *1–2 (E.D. Mich. Feb. 13, 2013) (granting summary judgment for the casino on various claims brought by a patron who "remains banned from the casino" after he lost blackjack bets yet refused to surrender the chips); Brown v. Harrah's N. Kansas City, L.L.C., 226 S.W.3d 145, 145 (Mo. 2007) ("In March 2000, Harrah's accused Dr. Brown of cheating in its casino and banned him from its property."); State v. Taylor, 31 A.3d 872, 874 (Conn. App. Ct. 2011) (affirming a cheating conviction when the defendant orchestrated "a conspiracy to cheat at craps by placing late bets" after he had already been "banned from Foxwoods [Casino's] premises for alleged gambling improprieties"—perhaps the very same improprieties for which he was later convicted); *see also* Husain v. Casino Control Comm'n, 265 F. App'x 130, 134 (3d Cir. 2008) (finding that a patron who had been accused of cheating had "no constitutionally protected property interest in the opportunity to gamble").

[80] *See, e.g.,* 68 Ind. Admin. Code 6-2-1(a)(3)(A); *see also* N.J. Stat. § 5:12-71(a)(1)–(2) (permitting exclusion of "career or professional offenders," or persons "[w]ho have been convicted of a criminal offense under the laws of any state"). Cheating at any gambling game is, of course, a criminal offense. *See, e.g.,* Cal. Penal Code § 337x; Conn. Gen. Stat. § 53a-127d; Iowa Code § 99F.15(4)(d); Mich. Comp. Laws § 432.218(2)(f); Miss. Code Ann. § 75-76-307; Mo. Rev. Stat. § 313.830(4)(4); Nev. Rev. Stat § 465.083; Ohio Rev. Code Ann. § 2915.05; Or. Rev. Stat. § 167.167; Va. Code Ann. § 18.2-327; Wash. Rev. Code §§ 9.46.196–.1962.

[81] *See Man Admits He Cheated at Hollywood Casino Blackjack Table,* ABC 27 WHTM, July 28, 2010, http://www.abc27.com/story/12887808/man-admits-he-cheated-at-holly-wood-casino-blackjack-table.

prohibiting him from entering the . . . complex [in the future]."[82] In fact, because it is nearly axiomatic that a casino can exclude cheaters, the critical focus is the question of what conduct *constitutes* cheating. This issue is addressed in Chapter 14. The process of excluding and ejecting a cheating patron is not free of potential problems. These problems are the same as those involving the exclusion of advantage players, like card counters, which is considered below.

DISCRETIONARY EXCLUSIONS
Introduction

If the authority to exclude patrons was limited to those who were known or suspected cheaters or others who pose a threat to the integrity of gaming, the issue would be rather unremarkable. However, one of the most controversial practices engaged in by gambling establishments is that of excluding patrons for some reason other than their actual or suspected criminal activity. The controversy often arises from the fact the exclusion is based on the patron winning more money than the casino wants to lose. This prompts the fundamental question: may a gambling establishment exclude a person for no reason other than it simply does not want that person's action?

Exclusions at the Track

When a casino excludes a person in these situations, it often bases its authority to do so on the common law right of land owners and proprietors of privately-owned places of entertainment and amusement not being obligated to serve the general public. One area where this has arisen is at pari-mutuel facilities. In many states, the major gambling establishments are race tracks. Cases involving exclusion of patrons from race tracks have provided substantial support for the common law principle allowing exclusion,[83] and the application of this common law concept has been addressed in numerous cases. For example, in *Brooks v. Chicago Downs Association*, the plaintiffs were "self-proclaimed expert handicappers."[84] The defendant,

---

[82] Mark Buttler, *Crown Casino Hi-Tech Scam Nets $32 Million*, HERALD SUN, Mar. 14, 2013, http://www.heraldsun.com.au/news/law-order/crown-casino-hi-tech-scam-nets-32-million/story-fnat79vb-1226597666337.

[83] *See, e.g.*, Rodic v. Thistledown Racing Club, Inc., 615 F.2d 736, 740 (6th Cir. 1980) (finding that Ohio law and administrative rules did not create a "right of admission . . . [or] mandate that the track admit all would-be spectators"); Watkins v. Oaklawn Jockey Club, 86 F. Supp 1006, 1016 (W.D. Ark. 1949), *aff'd*, 183 F.2d 440 (8th Cir. 1950); Nation v. Apache Greyhound Park, Inc., 579 P.2d 580, 582 (Ariz. Ct. App. 1978); Tropical Park, Inc. v. Jock, 374 So. 2d 639, 639 (Fla. Dist. Ct. App. 1979); James v. Churchill Downs, Inc., 620 S.W.2d 323, 324 (Ky. Ct. App. 1981); Silbert v. Ramsey, 482 A.2d 147, 153 (Md. 1984); Tamelleo v. N.H. Jockey Club, Inc., 163 A.2d 10, 12 (N.H. 1960); Madden v. Queens Cnty. Jockey Club, Inc., 72 N.E.2d 697, 698 (N.Y. 1947).

[84] Brooks v. Chi. Downs Ass'n, 791 F.2d 512, 513 (7th Cir. 1986).

a race track, was a privately-licensed corporation, which conducted har-ness racing in Illinois.[85] Defendant denied plaintiffs entry to all harness events at its race track for no reason other than the plaintiffs' skills in hand-icapping horses.[86]

The race track argued "that it should be able to exclude a patron absent any cause at all, as long as it" did not violate civil rights statutes prohibiting discrimination "on the basis of race, color, creed, national origin, or sex."[87] The trial court agreed, and granted the race track's motion to dismiss.[88] The Seventh Circuit Court of Appeals affirmed.[89] It acknowledged that while the case law states "that a proprietor has the absolute right to exclude, the facts of the case show that just cause existed to exclude the patron."[90] The court concluded:

> [P]roprietors of amusement facilities, whose very survival depends on bringing the public into their place of amusement, are reasonable people who usually do not exclude their customers unless they have a reason to do so. What the proprietor of a race track does not want to have to do is prove a just reason. He doesn't want to be liable to [a patron] solely because he mistakenly believed he was a mobster. The proprietor wants to be able to keep someone off his private property even if they only look like a mobster. As long as the proprietor is not excluding the mobster look-a-like because of his national origin (or because of race, color, creed, or sex), then the common law, and the law of Illinois, allows him to do just that.[91]

With remarkably few exceptions,[92] courts have upheld the right of pa-ri-mutuel authorities to exclude bettors from the racing facilities. Some-times this is based on statutory or administrative authority;[93] frequently,

---

[85] *Id.*

[86] *See id.*

[87] *Id.* at 514.

[88] *Id.*

[89] *Id.* at 519.

[90] *Id.* at 516.

[91] *Id.* at 517; *see also* Nation v. Apache Greyhound Park, Inc., 579 P.2d 580, 582 (Ariz. Ct. App. 1978) ("We are not persuaded that the common law rule of exclusion should be changed. The policy upon which it is based is still convincing. The race track proprietor must be able to control admission to its facilities without risk of a lawsuit and the necessity of proving that every person excluded would actually engage in some unlawful activity.").

[92] *See* Narragansett Racing Ass'n v. Mazzaro, 357 A.2d 442, 442 (R.I. 1976) (holding that a statute abrogated the track's common law right to exclude and required the racetrack to determine, before excluding a patron, that the person is undesirable and that their pres-ence would interfere with the proper conduct of races). The *Mazzaro* holding has since been superseded by a statute restoring the common law rule. R.I. GEN. LAWS § 41-3-17; *see* Bennett Liebman, *The Supreme Court and Exclusions by Racetracks*, 17 VILL. SPORTS & ENT. L.J. 421, 465 (2010).

[93] *See, e.g.*, 230 ILL. COMP. STAT. 5/9(e); N.H. REV. STAT. § 284:39; OR. REV. STAT. § 462.080(4); IOWA ADMIN. CODE R. 491-5.4(5)(d); 810 KY. ADMIN. REGS. 1:026(23); MD. CODE REGS. 09.10.01.45(V), (Y) (giving stewards power to exclude both licensed and un-licensed individuals); N.D. ADMIN. CODE 69.5-01-02-06.

however, the common law right to exclude is recognized.[94] In either case, arguments by bettors that they cannot be excluded without cause to suspect they are detrimental to the integrity of gaming have been overwhelmingly unsuccessful.

Advantage Play Exclusions

The issue of discretionary exclusions has arisen most controversially in the context of casinos excluding advantage players. The classic advantage player is one who is "counting cards" in blackjack. Chapter 14 provides detailed coverage of the issue of "advantage play" and the practice of counting cards. However, for this chapter's purposes, several points need emphasis.

First, as the discussion in Chapter 14 indicates, under some circumstances, a blackjack player may gain a statistical advantage over the house by keeping track of the cards that have been played and adjusting his bet accordingly.[95]

Second, counting cards is not cheating and has not been found to be cheating by any court in the United States.[96] For example, Nevada's rele-

---

[94] On the issue of common law exclusion, the seminal decision is *Marrone v. Washington Jockey Club*, in which Justice Holmes applied the English common law rule established in *Wood v. Leadbitter* and concluded a track could exclude patrons. Marrone v. Wash. Jockey Club, 227 U.S. 633, 635 (1913) (citing Wood v. Leadbitter, 153 Eng. Rep. 351 (Ex. 1845)). More recent cases continue to recognize this principle. *See, e.g.*, Tropical Park, Inc. v. Jock, 374 So. 2d 639, 640 (Fla. Dist. Ct. App. 1979) (holding that statutes did not preempt a racetrack operator's absolute common law right to exclude patrons); James v. Churchill Downs, Inc., 620 S.W.2d 323, 325 (Ky. Ct. App. 1981); *see also* John J. Kropp et al., *Exclusion of Patrons and Horsemen From Racetracks: A Legal, Practical and Constitutional Dilemma*, 74 Ky. L.J. 739, 742–63 (1986) (taking a comprehensive look at the historical development of both the common law and statutory rights of exclusion—and the challenges thereto).

[95] The practice of "card counting" is often misunderstood. It does not require the player to have a "photographic memory" of all cards that have been played. The most common card counting method involves a player grouping the cards dealt into three categories: cards with a value between 2 and 6 are each given one point; cards with a value between 7 and 9 are awarded zero points; and for each 10, face card, and ace, one point is deducted. As the deck of cards is dealt, the player keeps a running count of the cards' value. If, toward the end of the deck of cards being dealt, the "count" is a significant positive number such as +12, the player knows that there are many more high value cards remaining to be played. This is regarded as favorable to the player. Accordingly, the player will increase his bet substantially. *See, e.g.*, Robert C. Hannum & Anthony N. Cabot, Practical Casino Math 139–41 (2d ed. 2005); Nathaniel Tilton, The Blackjack Life 29–30 (2012). The dramatic increase in the wagered amount is what draws casinos' attention—and often ire. In other words, the casino does not object to card counting per se, only to the large increase in the size of the player's bet. As noted, advantage play is discussed more fully in Chapter 14. Perhaps the most famous description of card counting and the lore associated with it is Ben Mezrich, Bringing Down the House (2002).

[96] *See* Anthony Cabot & Robert Hannum, *Advantage Play and Commercial Casinos*, 74 Miss. L.J. 681, 709–10 (2005); *see also* Hoagburg v. Harrah's Marina Hotel Casino, 585 F. Supp. 1167, 1170 (D.N.J. 1984) ("Card counting is not a crime."); Uston v. Hilton Hotels Corp., 448 F. Supp. 116, 118 n.1 (D. Nev. 1978) ("[Card counting] is not considered cheat-

vant gaming statute defines cheating as "alter[ing] the elements of chance, method of selection or criteria which determine the result of a game or the amount or frequency of payment in a game."[97] As the Nevada Supreme Court has stated, the card counter "does not alter any of the basic features of the game. He merely uses his mental skills to take advantage of the same information that is available to all players."[98] Similarly, the New Jersey Supreme Court has indicated that card counting is not cheating.[99]

Third, despite the fact that no court has found card counting to be cheating, and no state regulations prohibit it, many casinos do not want to allow blackjack players to engage in this practice.[100] The question, then, is whether casinos have authority to exclude these non-cheating patrons. Is the exclusion of the player a violation of any common law, statutory, or constitutional protection? What are the potential liabilities that can attend the ejection of a card counter? Finally, are there circumstances in which exclusions of counters are inadvisable, though not legally proscribed?

Majority view

Perhaps because card counting is not considered to be cheating, the exclusion of card counters is not explicitly approved in any state by statute or regulation. Rather, the ability to exclude derives from common law and is therefore developed through court decisions. The origin of judicial consideration of this issue can be traced to 1978.[101] Kenneth Uston was an advantage blackjack player asked to leave the Flamingo Hilton casino premises, escorted to the door of the casino, and read the Nevada trespass statute, which effectively barred him from the casino premises.[102] He brought a

---

ing, nor is it illegal."); Donovan v. Grand Victoria Casino & Resort, L.P., 934 N.E.2d 1111, 1114 (Ind. 2010) ("[A]lthough the [administrative] rules contain numerous provisions prohibiting certain conduct by patrons playing the game of blackjack, the mental exercise of counting cards is not expressly prohibited.").

[97] Nev. Rev. Stat. § 465.015(1)(a)–(b). The statute also defines cheating to include altering the value of a wagering instrument or the value of a wagering credit. Id. § 465.015(1)(c)–(d).

[98] Sheriff of Washoe Cnty. v. Martin, 662 P.2d 634, 638 (Nev. 1983).

[99] Uston v. Resorts Int'l Hotel, Inc., 445 A.2d 370, 373 (N.J. 1982) ("There is no indication that [the card counter] has violated any [Casino] Commission rule on the playing of blackjack.").

[100] See, e.g., Doug Grant, Inc. v. Greate Bay Casino Corp., 232 F.3d 173, 179 (3d Cir. 2000) ("The casinos . . . prefer to decrease the card-counters' opportunity to bet high on a player-favorable shoe."); Donovan, 934 N.E.2d at 1112 (reciting facts indicating that a casino banned a card counter only from playing blackjack, while still allowing him to play other games at the casino); see also Bill Zender, Detecting Card Counters: Knowing and Using a Detection Shortcut, Casino Enterprise Mgmt., May 2013, http://www.casinoenterprise-management.com/articles/may-2013/detecting-card-counters-knowing-and-using-detection-shortcut (advising casinos about how to detect card counters and cautioning them about being overzealous).

[101] See Uston v. Hilton Hotels Corp., 448 F. Supp. 116 (D. Nev. 1978).

[102] Id. at 118.

number of claims against the casino, some based on federal law and some premised on state law protections.[103]

Uston's federal law claims all asserted that the casino's exclusion of him from its premises violated his rights under the Fourteenth Amendment's Due Process and Equal Protection Clauses.[104] The focus of these claims is under 42 U.S.C. § 1983, which essentially provides a cause of action when a person's constitutional rights are denied under color of state law.[105] Because the defendants were the casino and private individuals, Uston had to connect their actions to some provision of state law. He contended that state action inhered in the gaming industry itself because it is so extensively regulated by state law and state administrative bodies.[106] The state had refused to prohibit the exclusion of card counters, and Uston asserted this constituted action by the state that deprived him of his Fourteenth Amendment constitutional protections.[107]

The court declined to accept this formulation of state action. It ruled that despite the admittedly significant state involvement in the regulation of gaming, and the inaction of state legislators or regulators to prohibit the exclusion of counters, the "state action" necessary for a constitutional claim was not present.[108] State regulation of an industry alone does not constitute state action.[109] Rather, the state must be substantially and directly involved in promoting the activity being challenged.[110] As the court stated:

> [T]here has been no demonstration that the State of Nevada, either through its regulation and/or licensing of the gaming industry, has to any significant degree promoted or participated in the exclusion of persons suspected by gaming establishments to be card counters.[111]

Uston also argued that casinos could only exclude those persons who were named on the state list of "undesirable persons."[112] Because Uston was not on that list, he contended, the state "thereby undertook the affirmative duty to compel the admittance of all persons."[113] But the omission of the state to act and prohibit the exclusion of card counters was not akin to approval of the practice, the court held and did not constitute constitutionally required state action.[114]

Uston had also raised a number of state law claims: assault, false impris-

---

[103] *Id.*

[104] *Id.*

[105] *See* 42 U.S.C. § 1983 (2012). State law can mean "any statute, ordinance, regulation, custom, or usage, of any State or Territory or the District of Columbia." *Id.*

[106] *Uston*, 448 F. Supp. at 118.

[107] *Id.*

[108] *Id.* at 120.

[109] *Id.* at 118.

[110] *Id.*

[111] *Id.* at 119

[112] *Id.* For more on mandatory exclusion lists, see *supra*, Part II Mandatory Exclusions.

[113] *Uston*, 448 F. Supp. at 119.

[114] *Id.*

onment, intentional infliction of emotional harm, and a violation of the state's public accommodations law.[115] But the jurisdictional basis for these claims in federal court was the existence of complete diversity of citizenship between the parties.[116] Unfortunately, Uston was a California resident and Hilton Hotels, the defendant which owned the casino involved—the Flamingo in Las Vegas—had its principal place of business in California. Consequently, the federal district court ruled that it did not have jurisdiction over the subject matter of the case.[117]

The court's ruling on the state action question is unquestionably in line with the United States Supreme Court's analysis of this issue over the years.[118] The mere fact of state regulation of an industry or activity, even when it is comprehensive and detailed, does not constitute state action. Only when there is a finding of direct involvement in the specific activity involved will courts reach the conclusion that state action, in the constitutional sense, is present. For example, in the context of card counters, if the state affirmatively promulgated a regulation addressing the exclusion of card counters, the requisite state action would likely be found.[119]

As has been noted, the *Uston* case reflects the majority view that permits casinos as private entities to exclude anyone they want, for any reason, as long as that reason does not violate civil rights laws.[120] This is true even in the absence of statutory or administrative authority to support exclusion. Apart from the state action claim, card counters have frequently argued that because gaming is so extensively regulated, the absence of any

---

[115] *Id.* at 120.

[116] *Id.*

[117] *Id.* at 120–21.

[118] *See, e.g.,* Am. Mfrs. Mut. Ins. Co. v. Sullivan, 526 U.S. 40, 52 (1999) (holding that a private insurer's "decision to invoke utilization review" is not state action even though the state regulates insurers extensively); Blum v. Yaretsky, 457 U.S. 991, 1009–10 (1982) (holding that regulation of nursing homes did not mean individual decisions to discharge or transfer patients constituted state action); Rendell-Baker v. Kohn, 457 U.S. 830, 841 (1982) (holding extensive regulation of schools did not transform a charter school's personnel decisions into state action); Jackson v. Metro. Edison Co., 419 U.S. 345, 358–59 (1974) (holding that a private utility's termination of service to a customer was not state action even though the utility was heavily regulated and possessed a state license); Moose Lodge No. 107 v. Irvis, 407 U.S. 163, 175–177 (1972) (holding that detailed regulation by the liquor control board did not transform the racially discriminatory admission policy of a private club into state action).

[119] *See Uston*, 448 F. Supp. at 118 ("Something more, more in the nature of a substantial and direct state involvement in promoting the challenged activity, must be demonstrated in order to establish state action."); *see also* Pub. Utils. Comm'n v. Pollak, 343 U.S. 451, 462 (1952) (holding that regulation plus the regulatory agency's investigation and approval of a challenged practice constituted state action); Am. Comm'ns Ass'n v. Douds, 339 U.S. 382, 401 (1950) ("[W]hen authority derives in part from Government's thumb on the scales, the exercise of that power by private persons becomes closely akin . . . to its exercise by Government itself.").

[120] *See Uston*, 448 F. Supp. at 120; *see also* Donovan v. Grand Victoria Casino & Resort, L.P., 934 N.E.2d 1111, 1115–16 (Ind. 2010) (canvassing "the overwhelming weight of authority emanating from gaming jurisdictions" in agreement).

authority to exclude them indicates lack of authority on the part of casinos to do so.[121] In other words, state regulation has occupied the field, and pre-empted casinos from adding to the regulation by excluding card counters. At least one court has rejected this claim, however, and other courts have rejected similar claims in the pari-mutuel context.[122]

Minority view

New Jersey's treatment of the issue has followed a somewhat different path, however. In a 1982 case featuring the same Ken Uston from the Nevada case, the New Jersey Supreme Court accepted the argument that the comprehensive nature of gaming regulation precluded casinos from excluding card counters.[123] Allowing such exclusion by casinos would undermine the Casino Control Commission (CCC)'s authority, the court held, and would "subvert the important policy of ensuring the credibility and integrity of the regulatory process and of casino operations."[124] But what about the CCC's authority? Could the CCC abrogate the common law right of access of card counters by permitting their exclusion? The court declined to answer this question.[125] Instead, the court gave the CCC 90 days to adopt regulations that permitted "countermeasures."[126]

The topic of countermeasures is addressed in detail in Chapter 14. Briefly stated, countermeasures are casino actions impairing a player's ability to count cards in a manner that gives the player a statistical advantage. Countermeasures can include frequent shuffling of the cards, setting lower bet limits, using multiple decks of cards, and using a "perpetual" shuffling device, among other things.[127] In New Jersey, the CCC promulgated regulations that permitted casinos to employ countermeasures.[128] In 2000, the

---

[121] The most recent iteration of this argument is in a Sixth Circuit case, Arabo v. Greektown Casino, LLC. No. 13-1636 (6th Cir. Jan. 15, 2014) (rejecting the player's constitutional claims).

[122] *See Donovan*, 934 N.E.2d at 1115–16; *cf.* Ziskis v. Kowalski, 726 F. Supp. 902, 908–09 (D. Conn. 1989) (collecting cases); Bresnik v. Beulah Park L.P., 617 N.E.2d 1096, 1097 (Ohio 1993).

[123] Uston v. Resorts Int'l Hotel, Inc., 445 A.2d 370, 372 (N.J. 1982).

[124] *Id.* at 373 (quoting N.J. STAT. ANN. § 5:12-1(b)(6)) (internal quotation marks omitted).

[125] *Id.* at 375.

[126] *See id.* at 376.

[127] *See* John M. Norwood, *Gambling in the Twenty-First Century: Judicial Resolution of Current Issues*, 74 MISS. L.J. 779, 802 (2005) (providing a few examples of countermeasures); *see also* Bill Zender, *Card Counting Costs the Casino Industry Millions Each Year (But It's Not the Person Sitting at the Table Doing It)*, CASINO ENTER. MGMT., Mar. 2013, http://www.casinoenterprisemanagement.com/articles/march-2013/card-counting-costs-casino-industry-millions-each-year-it%E2%80%99s-not-person-sitting-t (describing frequently-used countermeasures and explaining why using them might actually reduce casino revenue).

[128] *See* Doug Grant, Inc. v. Greate Bay Casino Corp., 232 F.3d 173, 181–83 (3d Cir. 2000) (describing the CCC countermeasure regulations, which were enacted after the New Jersey *Uston* case).

Third Circuit Court of Appeals upheld the validity of these actions against attack under RICO and other state and federal statutory provisions.[129]

Other arguments & issues

Those challenging casino exclusion have also invoked negligence, contract, and consumer protection arguments, with little success. In one case, the plaintiff attempted to place a blackjack bet but was informed by casino personnel he was not allowed to play blackjack, though he could play other games at the casino.[130] The patron argued that when the casino advertised and offered the game of blackjack, it created an offer that the patron was empowered to accept, and when he was prevented from playing blackjack because he was a card counter, the casino breached its contractual duty.[131] The court ruled that the advertisements were not specific enough that they could be reasonably construed as offers.[132] Rather, they constituted invitations to make an offer and to patronize the casino.[133] Similarly, a consumer protection statute which protects purchasers of goods or services from "unlawful merchandising" was not applicable because, among other reasons, plaintiff's attempt to place a bet did not constitute a "purchase" as required by the statute.[134] Finally, the patron claimed that the casino was negligent in not informing him that card counters were excluded, and that this amounted to negligent misrepresentation or fraudulent misrepresentation.[135] However, the court held that there was no business transaction between the player and casino that would support the misrepresentation claim. While the casino had "superior knowledge" of its practice excluding counters, it did not have a duty to disclose this practice beforehand.[136]

In light of court decisions that card counters either have no common law right of participation and therefore can be excluded, or that they cannot be excluded but can have countermeasures used against them, it is clear that casinos have been overwhelmingly successful in their battle to combat card counters.[137] Nevertheless, the issue has several wrinkles that courts have

---

[129] *Id.* at 187 ("[A]ppellants' allegations that the casinos . . . ha[ve] committed predicate RICO acts are completely insubstantial and border on the frivolous.").

[130] Ziglin v. Players MH, L.P., 36 S.W.3d 786, 788 (Mo. Ct. App. 2001).

[131] *Id.*

[132] *Id.* at 790.

[133] *See id.* at 789–90.

[134] *Id.* at 790.

[135] *Id.* at 790–91.

[136] *Id.*

[137] *See* Bill Zender, *Confirming a Suspected Player is Counting Cards: Fact or Educated Guess?*, CASINO ENTER. MGMT., June 2013, http://www.casinoenterprisemanagement.com/articles/june-2013/confirming-suspected-player-counting-cards-fact-or-educated-guess ("During a recent . . . seminar, I asked participants, who represented various casino operations throughout the West and Midwest, if any of their properties had 'backed' a customer off blackjack for card counting during the past calendar year. Practically all the hands went up.").

addressed. Several of these issues warrant discussion, as they can affect to some extent the nature of the casino's right to exclude.

One set of problems involves advertising or promotion claims. What if a player who has been excluded from a casino later receives invitations and advertisements from the casino? Can the player assume these offers rescind the previous exclusion? In one case, the Ninth Circuit Court of Appeals suggested that in light of the player's repeated exclusions from the casino, the player could not reasonably have thought the trespass warnings had been rescinded.[138] Nevertheless, the court did note that the marketing and security departments of a casino may act at cross purposes, with the latter not notifying the former of persons who had been excluded.[139] Although this lack of coordination did not help the plaintiff in that case, it seems advisable for the two departments of the casino to share information to ward off such claims.[140]

In another case, a California resident sued Nevada casinos alleging their advertising was misleading because it welcomed all players to gamble in Nevada, and it did not specify that card counters were unwelcome.[141] The court reiterated casinos' right to "exclude suspected card counters at their discretion."[142] It further denied the plaintiff's deceptive advertising claims because as a card counter he possessed "natural aptitude and super reasoning" and therefore was not an ordinary consumer likely to be confused by the ads.[143]

Some card counters have been able to evade detection at the casino by using false identification or even a physical disguise. In one case, a player used a fake passport when exchanging approximately $44,000 in cash for

---

[138] Tsao v. Desert Palace, Inc., 698 F.3d 1128, 1145 (9th Cir. 2012) ("Tsao is a professional gambler, and, having been kicked out of the casino at least five times under a variety of aliases, was well aware that she was most likely not welcome at the Caesars Palace blackjack tables.").

[139] *See id.* at 1144.

[140] *See* Luck v. Mount Airy No. 1, LLC, 901 F. Supp. 2d 547, 551–52, 565 (M.D. Pa. 2012) (permitting a suit for false imprisonment against casino security personnel to proceed when the banned individuals were detained after returning to the casino not knowing they had been banned despite the casino's ability to use marketing information for notification purposes). However, a few recent cases have duplicated *Tsao*'s result, finding no rescission despite an excluded patron's claim that marketing materials and other events either expressly or impliedly rescinded a trespass ban that had been imposed. *See* Pittman v. Boyd Biloxi, LLC, No. 1:12CV64HSO-RHW, 2013 WL 3283961, at *1–2 (S.D. Miss. June 28, 2013) (granting summary judgment to the casino defendant on various claims arising out of an incident that occurred after the marketing department expressly lifted a patron's ban yet did not remove the patron's name from the security department's exclusion list); Blackford v. Prairie Meadows Racetrack & Casino, Inc., 778 N.W.2d 184, 191 (Iowa 2010) (denying a patron's request for a jury instruction on implied consent when, after he had been banned for striking and breaking a slot machine, he still successfully joined the casino slot club, obtained a slot club card, and gambled at the facility numerous times).

[141] Franceschi v. Harrah's Entm't, Inc., No. 2:10-cv-00205-RLH-RJJ, 2011 WL 9305, at *1 (D. Nev. Jan. 3, 2011).

[142] *Id.* at *5.

[143] *Id.* at *6.

chips.[144] He won another $40,000 before casino personnel identified him as a card counter and terminated his play.[145] A state gaming control agent was summoned, determined the player's true identity, and had the casino issue the player a receipt for the $84,000.[146] A subsequent investigation by the Gaming Control Board determined that no crime had been committed.[147] Nevertheless, the casino returned only the original amount exchanged for chips and retained the player's winnings.[148] This action was upheld by the Board on the basis the player had committed a fraud on the casino.[149]

While noting the deference given to Board decisions, the Nevada Supreme Court reversed the decision.[150] The casino's request for identification was not in an effort to identify card counters. Rather, it was for regulatory compliance purposes.[151] The casino did not have its employees cross-check the patron's identity with other sources that might identify card counters.[152] Therefore, this defeated the casino's claim that it detrimentally relied on the fake passport when it allowed him to play blackjack.[153] Also, the court held, it was the player's skill and not the misrepresentation of identity that produced the winnings.[154] For these reasons, the Board's decision that the player had committed fraud on the casino was contrary to law.[155]

Even when casinos have the right to exclude a patron whom they believe is counting cards, the removal process is fraught with peril. That is, the process and details of expulsion can lead to a wide variety of tort claims. Some of these claims implicate state law enforcement authorities and state or federal constitutional claims. Several cases illustrate this problem.

In *Grosch v. Tunica County*, the casino suspected the plaintiff of being a card counter and asked a county deputy to evict him.[156] The deputy claimed that he approached the patron and asked him for identification and that the patron became unruly and loud, thereby committing the misdemeanor of disorderly conduct.[157] The patron maintained that he was not unruly and that he told the deputy he would provide identification so long as the

---

[144] Chen v. Nev. State Gaming Control Bd., 994 P.2d 1151, 1152 (Nev. 2000).
[145] *Id.*
[146] *Id.*
[147] *Id.*
[148] *Id.*
[149] *See id.*
[150] *Id.* at 1152–53.
[151] *Id.* at 1152.
[152] *Id.*
[153] *Id.*
[154] *Id.*
[155] *Id.*; *see also* M & R Inv. Co. v. Mandarino, 748 P.2d 488, 489–90 (Nev. 1987). In *Mandarino*, a card counter was wearing an "obvious disguise," and when he tried to cash in his chips and was asked for ID, he bolted. *Mandarino*, 748 P.2d at 489–90. Although the casino prevailed on a number of tort claims, its confiscation of his chips supported an action for conversion. *Id.* at 494.
[156] Grosch v. Tunica Cnty., No. 2:06CV204-P-A, 2009 WL 161856, at *3 (N.D. Miss. Jan. 22, 2009).
[157] *Id.*

deputy did not give the identification document to the casino.[158] In reviewing the jury's verdict in favor of the patron on his § 1983 action against the casino, the court cited previous authority to the effect that "a private defendant can only be subject to § 1983 liability if the arresting officer failed to conduct an independent investigation."[159] The court held the jury's verdict reflected its finding the officer did not conduct an independent investigation, and this finding was supported by the evidence.[160]

Several other claims the patron advanced were also accepted by the jury and affirmed by the court. For example, the evidence supported a conclusion that the casino "intentionally procured the unlawful detention" of the patron, and this justified the claim of false arrest and false imprisonment.[161] Similarly, the patron's malicious prosecution claim was supported by the evidence. The casino had the burden of proving that the disorderly conduct charge against the patron was due to "prosecutorial leniency" and the jury was justified in concluding that the casino had not met this burden.[162] There was similar factual support for the abuse of process claim,[163] and a finding that the casino's refusal to return the patron's chips to him constituted a conversion.[164]

Certainly the most prominent feature of the court's decision was that it upheld the jury's award of $600,500 in punitive damages.[165] Substantial evidence existed, the court ruled, to support a finding that the casino "intentionally or recklessly violated the plaintiff's constitutional rights against unreasonable searches and seizures in order to obtain the plaintiff's property to which the casino was not legally entitled."[166] As for the state law claims, the jury had ample grounds to find that the casino "acted with actual malice and/or gross negligence evidencing a willful, wanton or reckless disregard for the safety of the plaintiff with respect to the state-law claims of false imprisonment, false arrest, malicious prosecution, abuse of process, trespass to chattels, and conversion."[167] This conclusion was consistent with Mississippi statutory law on the award of punitive damages.[168]

The *Grosch* case illustrates what can happen when a licensed entity enlists the assistance of law enforcement in ejecting or detaining a patron. It

---

[158] *Id.*
[159] *Id.* at *2.
[160] *Id.* at *3.
[161] *Id.* at *4.
[162] *Id.* at *5.
[163] *Id.*
[164] *Id.* at *6.
[165] *Id.* at *7.
[166] *Id.*
[167] *Id.* at *8.
[168] *Id.* The Mississippi Code provides that punitive damages are unavailable "if the claimant does not prove by clear and convincing evidence that the defendant against whom punitive damages are sought acted with actual malice, gross negligence which evidences a willful, wanton or reckless disregard for the safety of others, or committed actual fraud." Miss. Code Ann. § 11-1-65.

sends a clear message that a casino needs to establish and maintain scrupulous processes when exercising its right to exclude patrons. The right to exclude without a need to show cause is of little value if the casino exercises its right in a way that exposes it to liability. However, the *Grosch* decision is one of the few cases where a casino has been held liable in this setting. Claims based on alleged tortious conduct by the casino in dealing with card counters or enforcing its right to exclude are, as noted, rarely successful.[169]

It may be that card counter exclusion is overblown.[170] There is no guarantee that a person who engages in the blackjack card counting form of advantage play will win. Much of the popular culture treatment of card counting ignores the fact that the small statistical edge card counting may give to a player does not necessarily produce a bonanza of winnings.[171] If this is the case, casinos might be advised not to overreact to a player engaging in this activity. As indicated above, while casinos—and other gambling facilities—have been successful in retaining the right to exclude, there are potential liabilities. There is also the "bad press" generated by a narrative that the only persons casinos will allow to gamble are those who lose money and that gamblers who win will not be allowed to play. Though daring, what about a strategy where a casino marketed itself as welcoming card counters?[172] That is, might there be a marketing niche for some casinos to advertise they *welcomed* card counters, believing that the action they would receive from bad counters would more than offset what is paid

---

[169] *See, e.g.*, Hoagburg v. Harrah's Marina Hotel Casino, 585 F. Supp. 1167 (D.N.J. 1984). While the *Uston* case was pending in the New Jersey appellate courts, Hoagburg was ejected for card counting and brought defamation and First Amendment claims. *Id.* at 1170–71. The court held exclusion was not a violation of free speech rights, nor was it defamatory. *Id.* at 1170, 1174. It also held that *Uston* would not be given retroactive effect because it was not in force at the time of Hoagburg's ejection. *Id.* at 1176–77. For another example of an unsuccessful tort claim brought by a card counter, see Lamelza v. Bally's Park Place, Inc., 580 F. Supp. 445 (E.D. Pa. 1984). Lamelza alleged that when a dealer indicated he was a card counter and called him "scum," this was defamatory. *See id.* at 446. However, Lamelza failed to make out the elements of a defamation claim, and because the conduct was not outrageous, he could not recover punitive damages either. *Id.* at 447. Further, although he was identified as a card counter, he was still allowed to play, with casinos simply taking countermeasures against the advantage counting cards provides. *See id.* at 446.

[170] *See, e.g.*, Bill Zender, *A Rare Breed: The Truth About Card Counters*, CASINO ENTERPRISE MGMT., June 2007, http://www.casinoenterprisemanagement.com/articles/june-2007/rare-breed-truth-about-card-counters ("[C]asinos, in general, perceive card counting as more of a threat than it actually is. . . . [T]he number of unnecessary Blackjack exclusions may be quite high—in excess of 50 percent.").

[171] *See id.* (providing a chart demonstrating that even professional card counters cannot expect to win much unless they risk large bets).

[172] *See* Jeff Murphy, *Card Counters: They Aren't So Bad After All*, CASINO ENTERPRISE MGMT., Aug. 31, 2009, http://www.casinoenterprisemanagement.com/web-exclusives/card-counters-they-aren%E2%80%99t-so-bad-after-all ("[T]he casino industry made card counting a problematic issue rather than a positive marketing opportunity. . . . Rules should not be in place to ward off potential counters from today's blackjack tables, as the percentage of true professional caliber card counters are few.").

out to the successful counter?[173] Is there a market solution to this issue? Some sports books have marketed themselves in this way, announcing to the world that they are willing to accept very large wagers.[174]

It is entirely understandable that casinos under siege from a team of coordinated card counters will not passively wait for the statistical edge gained by counting to kick in.[175] In this setting, the broad right of exclusion, exercised reasonably, is useful.[176] In combating the "retail" card counter, however, casinos may be well-advised to use their judgment in balancing their legal and business interests.

EXCLUSION ISSUES IN SELECT ASIAN JURISDICTIONS

Some Asian jurisdictions provide various types of exclusions. The following is a representative sampling of how this is addressed.

Macau

Exclusions seem to be mostly voluntary at this point. However, there is a program for "third-party" exclusions, which occur when a gambler's relative (i.e., spouse, parent, child, sibling) applies to have the gambler excluded. These exclusions last for no longer than two years, but the excluded person can apply to have the exclusion revoked.[177] Exclusion applications are decided within five days, and failure to comply with exclusion is "a crime of disobedience."[178]

Macau investigated a mandatory exclusion program for problem gamblers in 2011, but based on the lack of information about such a program

---

[173] *See id.* ("It's time to stop the madness and let card counters into our casinos with open arms. . . . Card counters provide the stimulus toward creating more play simply by demonstrating some success and sharing it with others."); *see also* Bill Zender, *Table Game Management for the Small Casino, Part 2*, CASINO ENTER. MGMT., Nov. 2013, http://www.casinoenterprisemanagement.com/articles/november-2013/table-game-management-small-casino-part-2 ("[T]o operate a successful table games pit, the small casino operator needs to forget that card counting in blackjack, or the threat of card counting, even exists.").

[174] *See* Liz Benston, *Will Las Vegas Sports Books Adopt More Bettor-Friendly British Wagering Style?*, L.V. SUN, Apr. 27, 2011, http://www.lasvegassun.com/news/2011/apr/27/will-sports-books-take-british-betting-style ("Cantor [Gaming] welcomes large wagers and professional gamblers . . . . [and] could significantly increase the market for big-time sports betting.").

[175] Murphy, *supra* note 172 ("If an advanced team infiltrates a gaming pit to consummate a potentially large advantage it is completely within a casino's best interest to take intelligent action.").

[176] *See id.* ("For the few players that actually possess card counting skills of the highest level, a respectful business conversation, an agreement of understanding and a hand shake will most often ward off the potential problems. . . . Both sides can part respectfully, with no harm, no foul for either the player or the casino.").

[177] *Self-Exclusion and Third-Party Exclusion Applications*, GAMING INSPECTION & COORDINATION BUREAU MACAU, http://www.dicj.gov.mo/web/en/responsible/isolation/isolation.html#1.

[178] *Id.*

since then, it appears the measure did not pass.[179]

New blackjack rules went into effect March 30, 2009.[180] These rules are promulgated by the Secretary for Economy and Finance, who derives authority to make gaming rules from Law No. 16/2001, art. 3, ¶ 5.[181] Law No. 16/2001 is referred to as the "Legal Framework for the Operations of Casino Games of Fortune" and was passed by the Legislative Assembly of Macau.[182] Under the 2009 blackjack rules, gaming tables must include an automatic shuffler.[183] Cards can be reshuffled at any point, and are always placed back into the continuous automatic shuffler after each hand.[184] This effectively prevents the advantage play tactic of card counting in blackjack.

Singapore

Generally, Singapore codifies a right of exclusion for casino operators.[185] Singapore law also has detailed provisions for exclusions of various types. For example, it provides for self-exclusion and family exclusion. Family exclusion is identical to the exclusion available in Macau to parents, children, spouses, or siblings of gamblers.[186] "Third-party exclusion" has a different meaning in Singapore, however. It refers to an automatic exclusion for people who are undischarged bankrupts or who are receiving government aid.[187] As of August 2012, there were nearly 40,000 individuals on the third-party exclusion list in Singapore.[188]

There is also an exclusion category called visit limits. In this category, a person is not barred from visiting casinos, but the number of times they may do so per month is limited. There can be self-imposed visit limits, family visit limits (imposed through application by a family member), and

---

[179] See Alexandra Lages, *Gov't Considers Ban on Problem Gamblers*, MACAU DAILY TIMES, Apr. 11, 2011, http://www.macaudailytimes.com.mo/macau/31148-Govt-considers-ban-problem-gamblers.html.

[180] Dispatch of the Secretary for Economy & Finance no. 57/2009 (March 30, 2009), http://www.dicj.gov.mo/web/pt/rules/BlackJackOU21Alt02.html. These rules are also discussed at http://www.777.com/blackjack/automatic-shufflers-for-macau-blackjack.

[181] *See id.*

[182] *Macau Gaming History*, GAMING INSPECTION & COORDINATION BUREAU MACAU, http://www.dicj.gov.mo/web/en/history.

[183] Dispatch no. 57/2009, *supra* note 180, art. 1, ¶ 4.

[184] *Id.* art. 2, ¶ 2(2), (4).

[185] Casino Control Act (Chapter 33A), § 115 ("[A] person enters and remains on any casino premises only by the licence of the casino operator."). The Casino Control Act is accessible through the Singapore Attorney General's website at http://statutes.agc.gov.sg/aol/home.w3p.

[186] *See Casino Exclusion Measures*, NAT'L COUNCIL ON PROBLEM GAMBLING, http://www.ncpg.org.sg/draw-the-line/casino-exclusion-measures.html.

[187] *Id.*

[188] NAT'L COUNCIL ON PROBLEM GAMBLING, ANNUAL REPORT 2011/12, at 12 (2012), http://www.ncpg.org.sg/pdf/Requestor_NCPG%20Annual%20Report%202011%20-%202012.pdf.

third-party visit limits. Like third-party exclusions, visit limits are imposed automatically on "casino patron[s] who [are] deemed to be financially vulnerable." They can be contested, but final decision lies with the National Council on Problem Gambling.[189]

Additionally, patrons may be excluded under written exclusion orders from the casino, the Casino Regulatory Authority of Singapore (CRAS), or the police.[190] Once issued, an exclusion remains in force unless it lapses (which only occurs with oral exclusions), is revoked by the person/licensee/entity who imposed it, or is revoked by the Minister on appeal.[191]

Excluded patrons and licensees are both liable if the excluded person is allowed to gamble. The excluded person is subject to a criminal offense, and the casino is subject to disciplinary action.[192] The excluded person also forfeits any winnings.[193] The Casino Control Act contains a procedure to follow for removing excluded persons from the premises.[194]

In November 2013, the CRAS fined both Singapore casinos for failing to remove excluded persons. Between May 1 and December 31, 2012, the Marina Bay Sands permitted 16 excluded persons to enter or remain on the premises. During that same period, Resorts World at Sentosa permitted five excluded persons to enter or remain on the premises. Marina Bay was fined $235,000, and Resorts World was fined $70,000.[195]

Philippines

Many casinos in the Philippines are both operated and regulated by a state entity, the Philippine Amusement and Gaming Corporation (PAGCOR).[196] This regulation is controversial, and recent legislative sessions have seen some momentum toward privatization or separation of the entity's operational and regulatory functions,[197] although no such proposal has passed yet. In the meantime, PAGCOR lobbying led to an exemption for casinos from new anti-money laundering laws enacted in 2013.[198]

---

[189] *Casino Visit Limit Measures*, Nat'l Council on Problem Gambling, http://www. ncpg.org.sg/draw-the-line/visit-limit-measures.html.
[190] Casino Control Act (Chapter 33A), §§ 120–122.
[191] *Id.* § 123(1).
[192] *Id.* §§ 125–126.
[193] *Id.* § 128.
[194] *Id.* § 127.
[195] *See Enforcement Actions*, Casino Regulatory Auth., http://app.cra.gov.sg/public/ www/content.aspx?sid=137.
[196] Philippine Amusement & Gaming Corp., http://www.pagcor.ph.
[197] *See, e.g.*, An Act Creating the Philippine Amusement and Gaming Commission, Providing Funds Therefor and for Other Purposes, H. Bill No. 3398, 15th Cong., 1st Reg. Sess. (Philippines 2010), http://www.congress.gov.ph/download/basic_15/HB03398.pdf.
[198] *See Casinos Get a Pass in Philippines Laundering Law*, Wall St. J., Feb. 6, 2013, http:// blogs.wsj.com/corruption-currents/2013/02/06/casinos-get-a-pass-in-philippines-laundering-law.

According to the PAGCOR website's frequently-asked-questions page, there is a "standing policy that intemperate gamblers can be banned from entry and playing in its casinos if their immediate family so desires."[199] Family members can request bans for their relatives; they must write a letter to PAGCOR and include "proof of affiliation to the person involved."[200] Otherwise, PAGCOR has discretion to exclude players.[201] The presidential decree establishing PAGCOR lists a few categories of people who are and who are not allowed to play.[202] Filipino residents are only allowed to play if they have a certified amount of gross income.[203] Members of the military are not permitted to play.[204]

With the recent influx of foreign investment and creation of a new "Entertainment City" in Manila,[205] rules for exclusion may be in a fluid state.

South Korea

South Korea has a National Gambling Control Commission that controls and supervises the industry.[206] There is also a National Gambling Control Commission Act, which was enacted January 26, 2007.[207] One notable aspect of Korean casino regulation is that apart from one casino located in a rural mountain town, Korean residents are automatically excluded from Korean casinos.[208] There is ongoing debate about whether this is a useful social policy.[209]

---

[199] *Frequently Asked Questions*, PHILIPPINE AMUSEMENT & GAMING CORP., http://www.pagcor.ph/casino-filipino-branches.php.

[200] *Id.*

[201] *See id.* ("People of legal age (21 years and above), regardless of sex and nationality, are allowed entry . . . *provided they have no ban or entry suspension order* issued by PAGCOR.").

[202] Presidential Decree No. 1869 (July 11, 1983), tit. IV, § 14(3)–(4), http://www.pagcor.ph/transparency-seal-presidential-decree-1869.php.

[203] *Id.* § 14(3)(b).

[204] *Id.* § 14(4)(b).

[205] *See* Kate O'Keeffe, *Philippines Makes Play as a Gambling Mecca*, WALL ST. J., Apr. 19, 2012, at B10.

[206] *Functions of NGCC*, NAT'L GAMBLING CONTROL COMM'N, http://www.ngcc.go.kr/eng/start.html.

[207] *See Composition of NGCC*, NAT'L GAMBLING CONTROL COMM'N, http://www.ngcc.go.kr/eng/ngcc02.html.

[208] *See Why Most S Korean Casinos Are Open to Everyone Except Koreans*, ABS-CBN NEWS, http://www.abs-cbnnews.com/business/01/28/13/why-south-koreas-casinos-are-open-everyone-except-koreans.

[209] *See Should Casinos Allow Koreans?*, KOREA HERALD, AUG. 1, 2011, http://www.koreaherald.com/view.php?ud=20110801000817.

About the Contributors

Anthony Cabot

Anthony Cabot is on the executive committee and was former chair of the gaming law practice at Lewis Roca Rothgerber LLP with offices in Las Vegas, Reno, Phoenix, Tucson, Albuquerque, Denver, Colorado Springs, and Silicon Valley. He has practiced in the field of gaming law for over 30 years. He is a past president of the International Masters of Gaming Law, past president of the Nevada Gaming Attorneys Association and past general counsel to the International Association of Gaming Attorneys. He also serves as an adjunct professor at the William S. Boyd School of Law and is a faculty advisor to the *UNLV Gaming Law Journal*.

Cabot is a prolific author on gambling law. He is the founding editor of *The Internet Gambling Report XI* (2009). He has co-authored *Casino Credit and Collections* (2003), *Practical Casino Math* (2d ed. 2005), *International Casino Law* (3d ed. January 1999) and *Federal Gambling Law* (1999), and *Regulating Internet Gaming: Challenges and Opportunities* (2013).

Brian Callaghan

Brian Callaghan has been involved in the gaming industry for over 30 years. He first became introduced to the casino industry as a financial investigator with the Nevada Gaming Control Board and he has since served as a consultant and executive to the pari-mutuel industry, multi-national gaming equipment and system companies and Tribal gaming enterprises. Callaghan is currently the executive director of the Snoqualmie Gaming Commission which regulates the liquor and gaming activities at the Snoqualmie Casino in Snoqualmie, WA. Callaghan holds a BS in Business Administration from Arizona State University and an MBA from Regis University.

Eugene Martin Christiansen

Eugene Christiansen is the founder of Christiansen Capital Advisors, LLC, which provides advisory services to companies, investors, investment banks and other financial institutions, governments, legislatures, regulatory agencies and law firms concerned with casino gaming and other forms of commercial gambling. Christiansen served on the advisory board of the Institute for the Study of Gambling and Commercial Gaming founded by William R. Eadington at the University of Nevada, Reno. He is a graduate of the University of California at Berkeley.

Toni Cowan

Toni Cowan's expertise is in state gaming compliance, Internet gaming, and federal Indian gaming compliance. Her experience stems from her many years of public service as a senior attorney at the New Jersey Casino Control Commission, and the Nevada Attorney General's Office, Division of Gaming, and as staff attorney at the National Indian Gaming Commission.

In Nevada, she represented the State Gaming Control Board and the Nevada Gaming Commission prosecuting all licensing, and civil regulatory matters involving the Nevada casino industry. She personally prosecuted high dollar regulatory assessments and auditing deficiencies as well as issues of commercial free speech before the Nevada Gaming Commission.

Cowan has authored several published articles on gaming-related topics. Her 2003 article on cross-border gaming, *The Global Gaming Village*, has been frequently cited, most notably by the World Trade Organization in its 2005 panel decision concerning the dispute between the United States and Antigua and Barbuda on the cross-border supply of gambling and betting services.

She has a BA from the Pennsylvania State University, an MA from New York University, and a JD from Villanova University School of Law.

Gary Ehrlich

Gary Ehrlich is a principal and vice president of Catania Gaming Consultants, and a founding partner in the law firm of Catania & Ehrlich. He has provided legal analysis and advice on all aspects of casino and online gaming both to governmental entities and private sector clients. For more than 25 years, Ehrlich was with the New Jersey Division of Gaming Enforcement, ending his tenure as deputy director. He has authored numerous published articles on gaming-related topics, presented expert testimony in court as well as before legislative bodies, and spoken at many gaming conferences. Ehrlich holds an LLM from New York University School of Law, a JD from Seton Hall University School of Law, and a BS from Seton Hall University. He is admitted to the New York and New Jersey bars, as well as that of the United States Supreme Court.

Robert Hannum

Bob Hannum, PhD, is professor of Risk Analysis & Gaming at the University of Denver, specializing in gaming mathematics and the theory of gambling. He is co-author of *Practical Casino Math* and has published numerous articles on gaming math and the interface of mathematics and gaming law. His consulting includes work with casinos, regulatory agencies, law firms, and game developers. He has given seminars for casino personnel nationally and internationally, and has served as an expert witness in both criminal and civil cases involving gaming mathematics.

Darren Heyman

Darren Heyman, JD, MBA (Cantab.) has been on the operations side of the international gaming industry for over 20 years. He has helped run both online and brick and mortar casinos in four different countries across the globe. He is currently the managing partner of Panacea Consulting Group, LLC, a managerial consulting company with a focus on international gaming and company formations, as well as the Heyman Law Group, LLC, a law firm concentrating on immigration and visa law for those in the U.S. gaming industry or academia. He received his JD from Northwestern University School of Law, and his MBA from the Judge Business School at the University of Cambridge. He is currently working on his PhD in Hospitality Administration at the University of Nevada, Las Vegas, concentrating in international gaming.

Peter Kulick

Peter Kulick is a tax and gaming attorney and a member of Dickinson Wright, PLLC, which has an international gaming law practice with offices in Michigan, Nashville, Washington, D.C., Toronto and an affiliated office in Macau. He is a prolific author on gaming law with articles published in leading publications such as *Casino Lawyer, Casino Enterprise Management, ABA Gaming Law Gazette, Gaming Law Review*, and various other gaming industry publications and frequent panelist at national gaming law and tax law conferences.

Richard J. Lopes

Richard Lopes was appointed by Governor Brown to the Gambling Control Commission on January 2, 2013. Chairman Lopes has been a peace officer in the State of California for nearly 28 years. Lopes began his career in 1986 as a deputy sheriff for the Tulare County Sheriff's Office where he worked uniformed patrol, jail operations, and narcotic investigations. In 1989, Lopes was hired by the Laguna Beach Police Department where he worked uniformed patrol, narcotic investigations, and general investigations. Lopes was also the department's tactical instructor and use of force expert. In 1996, Lopes was hired by the California Department of Justice (DOJ), Division of Law Enforcement (DLE) where he worked a variety of investigative assignments throughout the State. Lopes served as the department's lead tactical instructor and taught several courses at DOJ's Special Agent Academy. At the time of his departure from DOJ, Lopes was the assistant director of DLE. As DLE's second in command, Lopes provided administrative and program direction to the division's bureaus which included the Bureau of Forensic Services, the Bureau of Investigation, the Bureau of Firearms, and the Bureau of Gambling Control. Lopes was also responsible for the day-to-day administration and operation of the Office of the Director. Chairman Lopes holds an AS in Criminal Justice from Irvine Valley College; a BS in Business and Management from the University of Redlands; and an MA in Organizational Leadership from Chapman University. Chairman Lopes is the member with a background in law enforcement.

Stephen Martino

Stephen Martino has served as director of the Maryland Lottery and Gaming Control Agency since 2010. He oversees all operations of the Lottery, the 15th largest in the world based on per capita sales. Under his direction, the agency also regulates the state's commercial casino industry. He developed Maryland's gaming regulatory structure and organized the opening of all of the state's casinos.

From 2005 to 2010, Martino served as executive director of the Kansas Racing and Gaming Commission. He was the chief executive officer of that state's criminal justice agency charged with regulating pari-mutuel race tracks and state-owned casinos. He managed the effort to establish Kansas' gaming regulatory framework, directed the state's casino selection process and led the opening of the first state-owned-and-operated casino in the United States.

Martino has emphasized the importance of responsible gambling awareness and problem gambling treatment and has promoted education and programming about each. He serves as chairman of the responsible gambling committee of the North American Association of State and Provincial Lotteries and of the Maryland Alliance for Responsible Gambling. He holds a BA and a BS from the University of Kansas and a JD from Washburn University School of Law.

Keith C. Miller

Keith Miller is the Ellis and Nelle Levitt Distinguished Professor of Law at Drake University in Des Moines, Iowa. Professor Miller teaches Gaming Law at Drake and has authored many articles and scholarly works on the topic, as well as being co-author (with Anthony Cabot) of *The Law of Gambling and Regulated Gaming*, a law school casebook published by Carolina Academic Press. He is vice president of Educator Affiliates for the International Masters of Gaming Law (IMGL), and is a frequent speaker at IMGL and American Bar Association conferences on Gaming Law. Professor Miller has been a Professeur Invité at the University of Nantes (France) since 1993.

Patrick Moore

Patrick Moore currently serves as Gaming Laboratories International's (GLI) senior director of Tech Compliance. Patrick has worked with GLI since 2002; beginning as a test engineer in GLI's engineering organization. Patrick's formal technical education is based in computer programming, computer networking and Internet technologies. Patrick's primary responsibilities with GLI include conducting gaming technology seminars and speaking engagements for international and domestic gaming regulators, performing ongoing research of new gaming technologies, and providing consultation to global emerging gaming markets and gaming industry stakeholders regarding industry-standard best practices, relating to the technical compliance of electronic gaming devices and systems.

Kevin P. Mullally

Kevin P. Mullally is the vice president of Government Relations and general counsel for Gaming Laboratories International, LLC (GLI). Mullally is GLI's chief legal officer, and is responsible for all risk management policies for the company as well as supervision of all outside attorneys and consultants. In addition, he serves internationally as GLI's primary liaison to elected and appointed officials at the federal, state and local level. As such he regularly interacts with regulatory agencies, key organizations devoted to developing gaming and casino policy as well as senior level executives of gaming equipment manufacturing companies, lotteries, pari-mutuel wagering facilities, social gaming companies and casino operators.

Mullally provides GLI with over 30 years of diversified leadership in law, management, public policy, public relations, economic analysis, and organizational administration. Prior to joining GLI, Mullally was the executive director of the Missouri Gaming Commission. Previously, he served as general counsel and chief of staff to Missouri State Senator Harry Wiggins. Mullally serves on the Board of Directors of the National Center for Responsible Gaming. He is a frequent teacher, author, and speaker on issues relating to administrative and business law topics, public policy development, regulatory issues, and problem gambling.

Kahlil S. Philander

Kahlil Philander, PhD, is a gambling economist with extensive experience in socio-economic impact and policy analysis. Dr. Philander is currently the director of research at the University of Nevada, Las Vegas (UNLV), International Gaming Institute, and an assistant professor at the William F. Harrah College of Hotel Administration. He formerly held the position of senior policy researcher at the Responsible Gambling Council of Canada, Center for the Advancement of Best Practices. Dr. Philander received his doctorate from UNLV, where his dissertation focused on the economic impacts of casino gambling policy.

Ngai Pindell

Ngai Pindell is a professor and associate dean for Academic Affairs at the University of Nevada Las Vegas, William S. Boyd School of Law. Professor Pindell practiced community development law in a nonprofit law firm in Baltimore, Maryland and taught the Community Development Clinic at the University of Baltimore School of Law. Professor Pindell came to the Boyd School of Law in 2000. His research interests include economic development, cities, housing, and gaming law, and he teaches Property, Local Government Law, and Wills, Trusts & Estates. He directs the law school's Gaming Program, is a faculty advisor to the *UNLV Gaming Law Journal*, and co-edited *Regulating Internet Gaming: Challenges and Opportunities* (2013).

Richard Schuetz

Richard Schuetz was appointed commissioner of the California Gambling Control Commission by Governor Edmund G. Brown, Jr. in September 2011. Schuetz has worked as a senior executive in the gaming markets of Las Vegas, Atlantic City, Reno/Tahoe, Laughlin, Minnesota, Mississippi, and Louisiana. Joining the gaming industry in 1972, Schuetz has served in positions ranging from keno writer, to dice dealer, to executive vice president, to president and chief executive officer.

Leonard C. Senia

Leonard C. Senia, B.A., M.P.A., recently retired from his last position as a senior regulatory project officer, Financial Crimes Enforcement Network ("FinCEN"), United States Department of the Treasury. During his 21 year career with the Treasury Department he wrote numerous Federal Government regulations and guidance documents for the casino and card club industries pertaining to FinCEN casino regulatory requirements. Also, he was FinCEN's resident casino expert who provided numerous customized training classes and case support work, upon request, to Federal and State prosecutors, criminal investigators, and civil examiners pertaining to: (a) Bank Secrecy Act casino regulatory requirements, (b) how casinos and card clubs are organized and operate, (c) casino computerized and manual recordkeeping and reporting systems, (d) casinos and card clubs vulnerabilities to money laundering, and (e) Internet gambling. He worked closely with the IRS on civil investigations into the casino gambling industry. Also, he led 23 Treasury/FinCEN investigations of casino gaming industry to evaluate its compliance with anti-money laundering (AML) rules regarding currency transaction and suspicious activity reporting, which all ended in civil monetary penalties being paid. He has spoken regularly at many national & international conferences as a subject matter expert on casino AML programs. In September 2013, the Secretary of the Treasury recognized Senia with the "Albert Gallatin Award" commendation for 20 years of esteemed contributions to the public service. In 2006, the director of the Federal Bureau of Investigations recognized him for "Exceptional Service in the Public Interest." During 2001 and 2002, he was a member of the six-person team that established money services business ("MSB") Federal regulatory program, which received the FinCEN Director's Award as "FinCEN's Top Team."

Since October 2013, he has been consulting, lecturing, training, and writing in areas of AML/financial crimes, computerized casino and card club reporting systems, cage and credit systems, player tracking systems, slot data systems, Internet gaming systems, and Macau VIP rooms. He is a member of the Association of Certified Anti-Money Laundering Specialist ("ACAMS").

Doug Walker

Doug Walker is a professor of economics at the College of Charleston, in Charleston, South Carolina, and owner of Casinonomics Consulting, LLC. He has published more than 40 articles on the economic and social impacts of legalized casino gambling. His publications have appeared in journals such as *Applied Economics*, *Contemporary Economic Policy*, *Growth and Change*, *International Gambling Studies*, *Journal of Gambling Studies*, *Journal of Health Economics*, *Public Choice*, *Public Finance Review*, and *Review of Regional Studies*. In 2013 Springer published Walker's second book, *Casinonomics: The Socioeconomic Impacts of the Casino Industry*. Walker serves as the Economics Editor for *Gaming Law Review and Economics*, and a Regional Assistant Editor for *International Gambling Studies*. Through his consulting firm, Casinonomics Consulting, Walker has served as a consultant for state governments and the casino industry throughout the United States.

Index

Other Books by the UNLV Gaming Press

Regulating Internet Gaming: Challenges and Opportunities

Ngai Pindell and Anthony Cabot, editors

Frontiers in Chance: Gaming Research Across the Disciplines

David G. Schwartz, editor

The UNLV Gaming Press, a collaboration between the University Libraries, the UNLV Harrah Hotel College, and the UNLV William S. Boyd School of Law, was established in 2012 in order to make available the scholarly output of university-sponsored conferences, historic materials that the university holds, and new work that illuminates the legal, economic, social, and historical dimension of gambling and gaming in all of its forms.

For more information:

http://gamingpress.unlv.edu